Academic
Learning
Series

Microsoft®

Windows NT® Server Enterprise Technologies

Microsoft Press

PUBLISHED BY
Microsoft Press
A Division of Microsoft Corporation
One Microsoft Way
Redmond, Washington 98052-6399

Library of Congress Cataloging-in-Publication Data
Microsoft Windows NT Server 4.0 Enterprise Technologies Training /
   Microsoft Corporation.
      p. cm.
   Includes index.
   ISBN 1-57231-710-8
   ISBN 0-7356-0520-3 (Academic Learning Series)
   1. Microsoft Windows NT. 2. Operating systems (Computers)
3. Client/server computing. I. Microsoft Corporation.
QA76.76.063M74515 1998
005.4'4769--dc21
                                 97-43134
                                    CIP

Printed and bound in the United States of America.

6 7 8 9 WCWC 3 2 1 0

Distributed in Canada by Penguin Books Canada Limited.

A CIP catalogue record for this book is available from the British Library.

Microsoft Press books are available through booksellers and distributors worldwide. For further information about international editions, contact your local Microsoft Corporation office or contact Microsoft Press International directly at fax (425) 936-7329. Visit our Web site at mspress.microsoft.com.

Project Manager: Bill Setten
Project Editor: Stuart J. Stuple

Part No. 097-0002128

Contents

About This Book

Welcome to *Microsoft Windows NT Server 4.0 Enterprise Technologies Training*. This book provides the knowledge and skills necessary to work with Windows NT Server 4.0 in an enterprise that consists of a single-domain or multiple domains. It also helps prepare you to meet the certificate requirements to become a Microsoft Certified Professional.

Note For more information on becoming a Microsoft Certified Systems Engineer, see the section titled "The Microsoft Certified Professional Program" later in this chapter.

Each chapter in this book is divided into lessons. Most lessons include hands-on procedures that allow you to practice or demonstrate a particular concept or skill. At the end of each lesson is a summary of key points, and when appropriate, references to additional information on the lesson material or related topics. Each chapter ends with a short summary of all chapter lessons and a set of review questions to test your knowledge of the chapter material.

The "Getting Started" section of this chapter provides important setup instructions that describe the hardware and software requirements to complete the procedures in this course. It also provides information about the networking configuration necessary to complete some of the hands-on procedures. Read through this section thoroughly before you start the lessons. All lessons depend on the completion of the Setup procedures in this chapter.

Intended Audience

This book is intended for experienced Windows NT support professionals who work with or support a Windows NT Server network in an enterprise environment, and for those who are on the Microsoft Certified Systems Engineer Windows NT 4.0 Track.

Prerequisites

- A strong familiarity with Windows NT as covered *in Supporting Microsoft Windows NT 4.0 Core Technologies* and *Administering Microsoft Windows NT 4.0.*

- Microsoft Certified Professional on Windows NT Server or equivalent level of knowledge.

- Experience planning and implementing a Windows NT network.

- Although not required, a familiarity with TCP/IP terminology and concepts is highly recommended, as provided in *Microsoft TCP/IP Training* or later TCP/IP courseware.

Reference Materials

You will find references to Windows NT documentation and Windows NT Help throughout this book. These references point you to more information about the task at hand.

- Microsoft Windows NT Server *Concepts and Planning* explains how to implement and optimize Windows NT Server. It is designed for new and experienced administrators of small networks and advanced users of operating systems. The online version of Microsoft Windows NT Server *Concepts and Planning* is included on the Windows NT Server compact disc.

- The *Microsoft Windows NT Server Resource Kit* (for version 4.0) provides detailed information on implementing Windows NT Server in larger networks.

- The *Microsoft Windows NT Workstation Resource Kit* (for version 4.0) provides detailed information on the Windows NT Workstation operating system, plus topics that are either new for version 4.0 or that reflect issues that Microsoft Technical Support Engineers consider timely and important.

- Windows NT Help, available online when you install Windows NT, provides references and how-to information for all Windows NT tasks.

- Microsoft TechNet is a living database of support articles that apply to Microsoft technology. TechNet is a valuable tool in supporting Microsoft software in any environment. TechNet is available for a monthly subscription. For more information, visit the Microsoft Web site at http://www.microsoft.com.

About The CD-ROMs

This book includes a compact disc labeled *Microsoft Windows NT Server 4.0 Enterprise Technologies Training CD-ROM Course Materials*. This compact disc contains the files and simulations needed to complete the procedures in this book. The Network Monitor should be used with the capture files on the compact disc for the Chapter 6 exercises.

All files required to successfully complete the exercises in Chapter 6 are in a directory named *\labs,* on the course materials disc.

The multimedia presentations supplement some of the key concepts covered in the book. You should view these presentations when suggested, and then use them as a review tool while you work through the material. Also available on the CD-ROM is a complete, searchable HTML version of this book that enables you to quickly locate specific information with only a click of the mouse. For more information about using the online book, see the section "About the Online Book" later in this introduction.

The other CD-ROM contains an 120-day evaluation edition of Microsoft Windows NT Server version 4.0.

Features of This Book

A consistent organization is used for each chapter within the book to help reinforce the presentation of the material.

- Each chapter opens with a "Before You Begin" section, which prepares you for completing the chapter.

- Whenever possible, lessons contain procedures that give you an opportunity to use the skills being presented or explore the part of the application being described. All procedures are identified with a bullet symbol like the one to the left of this paragraph.

- The "Review" section at the end of the chapter allows you to test what you have learned in the lesson.

- The "Questions and Answers" appendix contains all of the book's review questions and corresponding answers.

Notes

Notes appear throughout the lessons.

- Notes marked **Tip** contain explanations of possible results or alternative methods.

- Notes marked **Important** contain information that is essential to completing a task.

- Notes marked **Note** contain supplemental information.

- Notes marked **Caution** contain warnings about possible loss of data.

Conventions

- Hands-on practices that you are to follow are presented in numbered lists of steps (1, 2, and so on). A triangular bullet (➤) indicates the beginning of a practice.

- The word *select* is used for highlighting folders, file names, text boxes, menu bars, and option buttons, and for selecting options in a dialog box.

- The word *click* is used for carrying out a command from a menu or dialog box.

Notational Conventions

- Characters or commands that you type appear in **bold lowercase** type.

- *Italic* in syntax statements indicates placeholders for variable information. *Italic* is also used for book titles.

- Names of files and folders appear with a capital letter at the start of each word, except when you are to type them directly. Unless otherwise indicated, you can use all lowercase letters when you type a file name in a dialog box or at a command prompt.

- File name extensions appear in all lowercase.

- Acronyms appear in all uppercase.

- Monospace type represents code samples, examples of screen text, or entries that you might type at a command prompt or in initialization files.

- Square brackets [ ] are used in syntax statements to enclose optional items. For example, [*filename*] in command syntax indicates that you can choose to type a file name with the command. Type only the information within the brackets, not the brackets themselves.

- Braces { } are used in syntax statements to enclose required items. Type only the information within the braces, not the braces themselves.

Keyboard Conventions

- A plus sign (+) between two key names means that you must press those keys at the same time. For example, "Press ALT+TAB" means that you hold down ALT while you press TAB.

- A comma (,) between two or more key names means that you must press each of the keys consecutively, not together. For example, "Press ALT, F, X" means that you press and release each key in sequence. "Press ALT+W, L" means that you first press ALT and W together, and then release them and press L.

- You can choose menu commands with the keyboard. Press the ALT key to activate the menu bar, and then sequentially press the keys that correspond to the highlighted or underlined letter of the menu name and the command name. For some commands, you can also press a key combination listed in the menu.

- You can select or clear check boxes or option buttons in dialog boxes with the keyboard. Press the ALT key, and then press the key that corresponds to the underlined letter of the option name. Or you can press TAB until the option is highlighted, and then press the spacebar to select or clear the check box or option button.

- You can cancel the display of a dialog box by pressing the ESC key.

Chapter and Appendix Overview

This self-paced training combines text, hands-on procedures, and review questions to give you the knowledge and skills necessary to plan, analyze, optimize, and troubleshoot Windows NT Server in an enterprise environment.

The book is divided into the following chapters and appendix:

- Chapter 1, "Planning Your Windows NT Server Enterprise," provides you with a foundation of knowledge that is useful for all chapters in this book. It includes an overview of Microsoft Windows NT Server version 4.0 in the enterprise and examines four primary planning issues. It examines trusts and domains, essential tools that enable you to balance the administrative needs required to create a manageable environment with the organizational needs necessary to provide services to large numbers of users who may be geographically separated. The chapter also explores the issues of planning reliable and responsive disk systems, selecting appropriate network protocols, and determining server sizing requirements.

- Chapter 2, "Installation and Configuration," reviews the fundamental concepts essential to understanding the Windows NT Server installation process and investigates its roles in the enterprise. The browser service, a central component in Windows NT domain functionality, is covered in detail. Finally, the chapter examines the various enterprise clients that Windows NT Server is capable of supporting and the various caveats associated with each.

- Chapter 3, "Managing Enterprise Resources," discusses managing resources in a multiple domain environment. The chapter lessons provide explanations of how users, groups, policies, and profiles behave among multiple domains, how domains interact with one another, and how domains and domain resources can be managed remotely.

- Chapter 4, "Connectivity," introduces the Windows NT tools available to support publishing and accessing services on the network. This chapter also introduces the tools needed to ease network administration and interoperability with other network services.

- Chapter 5, "Server Monitoring and Optimization," introduces the procedures and guidelines for analyzing and optimizing Windows NT Server performance. It emphasizes the importance of collecting and analyzing server usage data for the purposes of optimizing the current configuration and predicting future requirements.

- Chapter 6, "Network Monitoring and Optimization," analyzes methods of recognizing and avoiding a slow and unreliable Windows NT Server network through network analysis and optimization. The chapter examines the network packets that are used in the communication between various services on a Windows NT network and explains how they are used.

- Chapter 7, "Troubleshooting Tools and Methods," provides strategies for efficiently approaching and solving Windows NT Server problems through the perspective of Windows NT architecture, registry, and the boot process. It identifies troubleshooting resources available for answering questions and finding information, and introduces some troubleshooting tools available with Windows NT and the Windows NT Resource Kit.

- Appendix A, "Answer Key," provides answers to lesson exercises and procedures. Use it to check your answers.

Finding the Best Starting Point for You

This book has been designed to allow you to tailor the course content to meet your training needs. The book's chapters can be completed out of sequence; however, it is important to note that Chapters 3 through 7 require completion of the procedures in Chapter 2, "Installing Windows NT." If you don't have access to a computer, many of the questions in the exercises will still be useful in helping you prepare for the exam. The following table provides the suggested learning paths for specific training needs.

If you	Follow this learning path
Are preparing to take the Microsoft Certified Professional examinations:	Complete all procedures in the book. Read and review the information contained in the Online Book.
Are preparing to design and implement a Windows NT architecture in your enterprise	Complete Chapters 1 through 4.
Need to manage Windows NT Server in the enterprise	Complete Chapters 3 through 6.
Need to support Windows NT Server in the enterprise	Complete Chapters 2 through 4, and Chapter 7.
Need to analyze Windows NT Server resource consumption	Complete Chapters 5 and 6.
Need to analyze Windows NT Server network resource consumption	Compete Chapter 6.
Need to understand Windows NT network traffic	Complete Chapter 6.
Need to optimize Windows NT Server in the enterprise	Compete Chapters 5 and 6.

Where to Find Specific Skills in This Book

The following tables provide a list of the skills measured on certification exam 70-068, Implementing and Supporting Microsoft Windows NT Server 4.0 in the Enterprise. The tables provide the skill, and where in this book you will find the lesson relating to that skill.

Note Exam skills are subject to change without prior notice and at the sole discretion of Microsoft.

Planning

Skill Being Measured	Location in Book		Lesson Title
	Chapter	**Lesson**	
Plan the implementation of a directory services architecture. Considerations include:			
Selecting the appropriate domain model	1	1	Directory Architecture
Supporting a single logon account	1	1	Directory Architecture
Allowing users to access resources in different domains	1	1	Directory Architecture
Plan the disk drive configuration for various requirements. Requirements include choosing a fault-tolerance method.	1	2	Disk Decisions
Choose a protocol for various situations. Protocols include:			
TCP/IP	1	3	Network Protocols
	1	4	NT Server Requirements
TCP/IP with DHCP and WINS	1	3	Network Protocols
	1	4	NT Server Requirements
NWLink IPX/SPX Compatible Transport Protocol	1	3	Ne twork Protocols
	1	4	NT Server Requirements
Data Link Control (DLC)	1	3	Network Protocols
		4	NT Server Requirements
AppleTalk	1	3	Network Protocols
	1	4	NT Server Requirements

Installation and Configuration

Skill Being Measured	Location in Book		Lesson Title
	Chapter	**Lesson**	
Install Windows NT Server to perform various server roles. Server roles include:			
Primary domain controller	1	4	NT Server Requirements
	2	1	Configuring Server Roles
Backup domain controller	1	4	NT Server Requirements
	2	1	Configuring Server Roles
Member server	1	4	NT Server Requirements
	2	1	Configuring Server Roles

(continued)

Installation and Configuration, *continued*

Skill Being Measured	Location in Book		Lesson Title
	Chapter	Lesson	
Configure protocols and protocol bindings. Protocols include:			
TCP/IP	1	3	Network Protocols
	4	4	Configuring Routable Protocols
TCP/IP with DHCP and WINS	4	1	Managing DHCP
	4	2	Managing WINS
NWLink IPX/SPX Compatible Transport Protocol	1	3	Network Protocols
	4	4	Configuring Routable Protocols
DLC	1	3	Network Protocols
AppleTalk	4	4	Configuring Routable Protocols
Configure Windows NT Server core services. Services include:			
Directory Replicator	3	6	Managing Shared Resources
Computer Browser	2	2	Browsing in the Enterprise
Configure hard disks to meet various requirements. Requirements include:			
Providing redundancy	1	2	Disk Decisions
Improving performance	1	2	Disk Decisions
	5	1	Server Analysis and Optimization Basics
Configure printers. Tasks include:			
Adding and configuring a printer	3	6	Managing Shared Resources
Implementing a printer pool	3	6	Managing Shared Resources
Setting print priorities	3	6	Managing Shared Resources
Configure a Windows NT Server computer for various types of client computers. Client computer types include:			
Windows NT Workstation	2	3	Client Connectivity
Windows® 95	2	3	Client Connectivity
Macintosh®	2	3	Client Connectivity

Managing Resources

Skill Being Measured	Location in Book		Lesson Title
	Chapter	Lesson	
Manage user and group accounts. Considerations include:			
Managing Windows NT user accounts	3	1	User and Group Accounts
Managing Windows NT user rights	3	1	User and Group Accounts
Managing Windows NT groups	3	1	User and Group Accounts
Administering account policies	3	1	User and Group Accounts
Auditing changes to the user account database	3	1	User and Group Accounts
Create and manage policies and profiles for various situations. Policies and profiles include:			
Local user profiles	3	2	Profiles and Policies
Roaming user profiles	3	2	Profiles and Policies
System policies	3	2	Profiles and Policies
Administer remote servers from various types of client computers. Client computer types include:	3	7	Remote Management of Servers
Windows 95	3	2	Profiles and Policies
Windows NT Workstation	3	2	Profiles and Policies
Manage disk resources. Tasks include:			
Creating and sharing resources	3	6	Managing Shared Resources
Implementing permissions and security	3	1	User and Group Accounts
	3	6	Managing Shared Resources
Establishing file auditing	3	6	Managing Shared Resources

Connectivity

Skill Being Measured	Location in Book		Lesson Title
	Chapter	Lesson	
Configure Windows NT Server for inter-operability with NetWare servers by using various tools. Tools include:			
Gateway Service for NetWare	4	6	Configuring NT Services for NetWare
Migration Tool for NetWare	4	6	Configuring NT Services for NetWare
Install and configure multiprotocol routing to serve various functions. Functions include:			
Internet router	4	4	Configuring Routable Protocols
BOOTP/DHCP Relay Agent	4	1	Configuring Routable Protocols
IPX router	4	4	Configuring Routable Protocols
Install and configure Internet Information Server.	4	5	Configuring Internet Information Server
	4	5	
Install and configure Internet services. Services include:			
World Wide Web	4	5	Configuring Internet Information Server
DNS	4	3	Managing DNS
Intranet	4	5	Configuring Internet Information Server
Install and configure Remote Access Service (RAS). Configuration options include:			
Configuring RAS communications	4	7	Managing Remote Access Servers
Configuring RAS protocols	4	7	Managing Remote Access Servers
Configuring RAS security	4	7	Managing Remote Access Servers

Monitoring and Optimization

Skill Being Measured	Location in Book		Lesson Title
	Chapter	**Lesson**	
Establish a baseline for measuring system performance. Tasks include creating a database of measurement data.	5	2	Server Analysis and Optimization Basics
	5	1	
Monitor performance of various functions by using Performance Monitor. Functions include:			
Processor	5	1	Server Analysis and Optimization Basics
	5	2	Implementing a Measurement Baseline
	5	3	Performance Analysis, Forecasting, and Record Keeping
	5	4	Analyzing File and Print Server Performance
	5	5	Analyzing Application Server Performance
	5	6	Analyzing Domain Server Performance
Memory	5	1	Server Analysis and Optimization Basics
	5	2	Implementing a Measurement Baseline
	5	3	Performance Analysis, Forecasting, and Record Keeping
	5	4	Analyzing File and Print Server Performance
	5	5	Analyzing Application Server Performance
	5	6	Analyzing Domain Server Performance

(continued)

Monitoring and Optimization, *continued*

Skill Being Measured	Location in Book		Lesson Title
	Chapter	Lesson	
Presenting Data	6	1	Network Analysis and Optimization Basic
	6	2	Analyzing Client Initialization Traffic
	6	3	Analyzing Client to Server Traffic
	6	4	Analyzing Server to Server Traffic
	6	5	Predicting Network Traffic
Filtering Data	6	1	Network Analysis and Optimization Basic
Identifying performance bottlenecks	5	3	Performance Analysis, Forecasting, and Record Keeping
Optimize performance for various results. Results include:			
Controlling network traffic	6	All	
Controlling server load	5	All	

Troubleshooting

Skill Being Measured	Location in Book		Lesson Title
	Chapter	Lesson	
Choose the appropriate course of action to take to resolve installation failures.	7	1	Overview of Troubleshooting in the Enterprise
Choose the appropriate course of action to take to resolve boot failures.	7	4	Examining the boot process
Choose the appropriate course of action to take to resolve configuration errors. Tasks include:			
Backing up and restoring the registry	7	3	Modifying the System through the Registry
Editing the registry	7	3	Modifying the System through the Registry

(continued)

Troubleshooting, *continued*

Skill Being Measured	Location in Book Chapter	Lesson	Lesson Title
Choose the appropriate course of action to take to resolve printer problems.	3	6	Managing Shared Resources
Choose the appropriate course of action to take to resolve RAS problems.	4	7	Managing Remote Access Servers
Choose the appropriate course of action to take to resolve connectivity problems.	7	2	Examining Microsoft Windows NT Architecture
Choose the appropriate course of action to take to resolve resource access and permission problems.	3	1	User and Group Accounts
Choose the appropriate course of action to take to resolve fault-tolerance failures. Fault tolerance methods include:			
Tape Backup	1	2	Disk Decisions
Mirroring	1	2	Disk Decisions
Stripe set with parity	1	2	Disk Decisions
Perform advanced problem resolution. Tasks include:			
Diagnosing and interpreting a blue screen	7	5	Examining Microsoft Windows NT Architecture
Configuring a memory dump	7	5	Examining Microsoft Windows NT Architecture
Using the Event Log service	7	2	Examining Microsoft Windows NT Architecture

Getting Started

This self-paced training book contains hands-on procedures to help you learn about Windows NT Server and Window NT Workstation.

To fully complete all the lessons and the exercises in those lessons, you will need a computer that meets or exceeds the requirements for running Windows NT Server 4.0. In addition, it will be helpful to have your computer connected to a Local Area Network.

Note It is important to understand the implications of installing Windows NT Server on a computer along with the implications of enabling the services on the Windows NT Server. If you plan on installing Windows NT Server on your computer in order to complete the exercises in this book, the current configuration of your computer will be lost.

Hardware Requirements

Windows NT 4.0 computers must have the following minimum configuration:

- Personal computer with a 486/33 or higher Intel-based processor.
- 16 MB of RAM (32 MB of RAM recommended).
- A minimum of 450 MB of available hard disk space.
- Super Video Graphic Adapter (SVGA) display adapter and monitor capable of 256 colors.
- Microsoft mouse or compatible pointing device.
- Network adapter card and related cables.
- One 3.5 inch high-density disk drive.
- CD-ROM drive.
- Sound card and speakers (optional).Software Requirements

Note The computer must have an existing Microsoft operating system such as MS-DOS, Windows 3.x, Windows 95, or Windows NT 3.x.

Software Requirements

The following software is required to complete the procedures in this course. 120-day evaluation copies of each of these products are included on the CD-ROMs in this kit.

- Microsoft Windows NT 4.0 Server

Caution The 120-day Evaluation Editions provided with this training are not the full retail product and are provided only for the purposes of training and evaluation. Microsoft Technical Support does not support these evaluation editions. For additional support information regarding this book and the CD-ROMs (including answers to commonly asked questions about installation and use), visit the Microsoft Press Technical Support web site at http: //mspress.microsoft.com/ mspress/support/. You can also email TKINPUT@MICROSOFT.COM, or send a letter to Microsoft Press, Attn: Microsoft Press Technical Support, One Microsoft Way, Redmond WA 98052-6399.

Setup Instructions

Set up your computer according to the manufacturer's instructions.

Caution If your computers are part of a larger network, you *must* verify with your network administrator that the computer names, domain name, and other information used in setting up Microsoft Windows NT 4.0 Server, as described in Chapter 2, do not conflict with network operations. If they do conflict, ask your network administrator to provide alternative values and use those values throughout all of the exercises in this book.

Windows NT 4.0 Server 120-day Evaluation Edition

Use the following steps to install the Windows NT Server software on your computer.

RISC-Based Computers

To install Windows NT Server on reduced instruction set computing (RISC)-based computers, Windows NT Server Setup must be invoked directly from the compact disc using the Setupldr program. Depending on the computer's firmware version, this may be as simple as clicking **Install Windows NT from CD-ROM** on the firmware's supplementary menu. If the computer does not have this option, click **Run a Program** (or an equivalent command) on the firmware menu, and then enter the path to Setupldr. Setupldr loads and initializes Windows NT Server Setup from the compact disc.

➤ **To Create the Windows NT Server setup disks**

These steps will create three Windows NT Server setup disks that you will then use to install Windows NT Server to your system.

Caution It is possible to run setup directly from the Windows NT Server CD-ROM without first creating the setup disks. However, this could cause your system to become unusable if the Windows NT Server installation process is interrupted. Microsoft Press recommends that you do not run Setup directly from the CD-ROM.

1. Log on to your computer in the usual way. Have three formatted, empty floppy disks available.

2. Insert the Microsoft Windows NT Server Evaluation Edition compact disc into the CD-ROM drive.

   Note A Microsoft Windows NT CD-ROM Autorun window may appear when you insert the compact disc. The setup button in this window will run Setup directly from the Windows NT CD-ROM. Do not click the Setup button in this window. Instead, close this window.

3. Click the Start button, point to Programs, and then click MS-DOS Prompt or Command Prompt, or select MS-DOS from the appropriate program group. Type the command for your operating system:

   MS-DOS, Windows 3.1, Windows for WorkGroups, or Windows 95:

   D:\i386\winnt /ox

   and then press Enter.

   Note If necessary, replace the "D" with the letter of your CD-ROM drive.

   Windows NT:

   D:\i386\winnt32 /ox

   and then press Enter.

   Note If necessary, replace the "D" with the letter of your CD-ROM drive.

4. If the path to your compact disc does not already appear on the Windows NT setup window type:

   D:\i386

   and then press Enter to continue.

   Note If necessary, replace the "D" with the letter of your CD-ROM drive.

5. When prompted, label a blank disk as Windows NT Server Setup Disk #3, insert the disk into drive A, and then press Enter.

6. When prompted, label a blank disk as Windows NT Server Setup Disk #2, insert the disk into drive A, and then press Enter.

7. When prompted, label a blank disk as Windows NT Server Setup Boot Disk, insert the disk into drive A, and then press Enter.

8. Close the Command Prompt, and remove the CD-ROM from the CD-ROM drive.

9. With the Windows NT Server Setup Boot Disk in drive A, restart the computer.

➤ **To install Windows NT 4.0 Server 120-day Evaluation Edition**

1. When prompted, insert the Windows NT Server Setup Disk #2 (from setp 6 above) into drive A, and press Enter.

2. At the Welcome to Setup screen, press Enter to install Windows NT Server.

3. Press Enter and follow the directions on your screen to allow Setup to detect your disk controllers.

4. When prompted, insert the Windows NT Server Setup Disk #3 (from step 5 above) into drive A, and press Enter.

5. If asked if you are upgrading or installing a new version of Windows NT Server, type **n** for new version.

6. Confirm that NT Server has detected your computer's hardware correctly. Press Enter when ready.

7. When prompted, insert the compact disk Windows NT Server CD-ROM into the CD-ROM drive and press Enter.

8. Review the license agreement and press F8 if you agree.

9. Review the hardware and software components list. If necessary, make changes as directed, then press Enter.

10. Select a partition that has enough free disk space to install Windows NT Server.

11. Select "Leave Current File System Intact", and press Enter.

12. When prompted for a location to install Windows NT files, if you are installing the evaluation copy of Windows NT Server on the same computer as another version of Windows NT, type a different name (for example, \NTEval or \120Eval); otherwise, accept \Winnt.

13. Press Escape to stop the exhaustive examination when prompted.

14. When prompted, remove the floppy disk from drive A and the CD-ROM from the CD-ROM drive, then press Enter to restart the computer.

15. Click Next, on the Windows NT Setup Window.

16. Type your name and your organization's name when prompted to do so.

17. When prompted for a CD-key, type **040** followed by **0048126**.

18. In the Per Server For box, type **10** for the maximum number of client access licenses provided with the evaluation copy of Windows NT Server.

19. If you are installing Windows NT Server onto your first computer, type **server1** as the name for your computer. If you are installing Windows NT server on your second computer, type **server2**.

20. If you are installing Windows NT Server on your first computer, click Primary Domain Controller. Click Backup Domain Controller if you are installing on your second computer.

21. Type a password for the default Administrator account. Keep in mind that passwords are case sensitive.

22. If asked about the floating-point workaround, click "Do Not Enable The Floating-Point Workaround."

23. When asked about the Emergency Repair Disk, click "No, Do Not Create An Emergency Repair Disk."

    Note You may want an Emergency Repair Disk for your computer, but it will not be used in the book.

24. Make sure that the default components to install are selected, and then click Next.

25. When asked how this computer should participate on the network, select "Wired To The Network."

26. Click the Install Microsoft Internet Information Server check box to clear it, and then click Next.

27. When asked about the the Network Adapter, click Start Search. If Setup cannot detect the installed network adapter, click Select From List, and select your network adapter.

28. When asked about network protocols, accept TCP/IP Protocol and NWLink IPX/SPX Compatible Transport.

29. Click Next to accept the default Network Services or change the services to match your specific network configuration and then click Next.

30. When asked whether you want to use DHCP, click No.

Caution If your computers are part of a larger network, you must verify with your network administrator that the following computer names, domain name, and IP address information do not conflict with network operations. If they do conflict, ask your network administrator to provide alternative values and use those values throughout all of the practices in this book.

31. Type the following network configuration settings and then click OK.

IP Address	131.107.2.200
Subnet mask	255.255.0.0
Default Gateway	131.107.2.1

32. Accept the default values for your network bindings by clicking Next.

33. Type **domain1** as the name of your domain.

34. Click Finish when prompted.

35. In the Date/Time Properties window, select your time zone and then click Close.

36. In the Display Properties window, set the color palette for 256 colors and the desktop area for 800 x 600 pixels.

37. Restart the computer when prompted to do so.

38. Log on as administrator.

39. In user Manager for Domains, open the Policies menu and click User Rights.

40. In the Rights dialog box, click Log on Locally.

41. Add Domain users and click OK.

42. Click OK.

About The Online Book

The CD-ROM also includes an online version of the book that you can view on-screen as you work through the lessons. It is a powerful, searchable HTML version of the book that enables you to quickly locate specific information, such as a procedure or a definition, with only a click of the mouse.

As part of the installation process, the setup program will automatically install Microsoft Internet Explorer version 4.01 if it is not already installed on your system. Microsoft Internet Explorer 4.01 runs on Microsoft Windows 95 or on Microsoft Windows NT with Service Pack 3. If you are running Windows NT and have not yet installed Service Pack 3, it is located on the Course Materials CD-ROM in the \SP3 folder. You must install Service Pack 3 before attempting to install the online book.

To install the online version of the book, do the following:

1. Insert the CD-ROM labeled "Course Materials" into your CD-ROM drive.
2. On the Windows taskbar, click Start.
3. Select Run from the Start menu.
4. Type **d:\nt4enter\setup** (where d is your CD-ROM drive letter).
5. Click OK.
6. Follow the setup instructions that appear.

The Setup program for the online book installs a desktop icon and a program item identified with the title of the book. If it does not already exist, the Setup program creates a Microsoft Press Titles program group for the program item. To view the online book, you can either select the program item or double-click the desktop icon.

The Microsoft Certified Professional Program

The Microsoft Certified Professional (MCP) program provides the best method to prove your command of current Microsoft products and technologies. Microsoft, an industry leader in certification, is on the forefront of testing methodology. Our exams and corresponding certifications are developed to validate your mastery of critical competencies as you design and develop, or implement and support, solutions with Microsoft products and technologies. Computer professionals who become Microsoft certified are recognized as experts and are sought after industry-wide.

The Microsoft Certified Professional program offers six certifications, based on specific areas of technical expertise:

- *Microsoft Certified Professional (MCP).* Demonstrated in-depth knowledge of at least one Microsoft operating system. Candidates may pass additional Microsoft certification exams to further qualify their skills with Microsoft BackOffice products, development tools, or desktop programs.

- *Microsoft Certified Professional + Internet.* MCPs with a specialty in the Internet are qualified to plan security, install and configure server products, manage server resources, extend servers to run CGI scripts or ISAPI scripts, monitor and analyze performance, and troubleshoot problems.

- *Microsoft Certified Systems Engineer (MCSE).* Qualified to effectively plan, implement, maintain, and support information systems in a wide range of computing environments with Microsoft Windows 95, Microsoft Windows NT, and the Microsoft BackOffice integrated family of server software.

- *Microsoft Certified Systems Engineer + Internet (MCSE+Internet).* MCSEs with an advanced qualification to enhance, deploy and manage sophisticated intranet and Internet solutions that include a browser, proxy server, host servers, database, and messaging and commerce components. In addition, an MCSE+Internet-certified professional is able to manage and analyze Web sites.

- *Microsoft Certified Solution Developer (MCSD).* Qualified to design and develop custom business solutions with Microsoft development tools, technologies, and platforms, including Microsoft Office and Microsoft BackOffice.

- *Microsoft Certified Trainer (MCT).* Instructionally and technically qualified to deliver Microsoft Official Curriculum through a Microsoft Authorized Technical Education Center (ATEC).

Microsoft Certification Benefits

Microsoft certification, one of the most comprehensive certification programs available for assessing and maintaining software-related skills, is a valuable measure of an individual's knowledge and expertise. Microsoft certification is awarded to individuals who have successfully demonstrated their ability to perform specific tasks and implement solutions with Microsoft products. Not only does this provide an objective measure for employers to consider; it also provides guidance for what an individual should know to be proficient. And as with any skills-assessment and benchmarking measure, certification brings a variety of benefits: to the individual, and to employers and organizations.

Microsoft Certification Benefits for Individuals

As a Microsoft Certified Professional, you receive many benefits:

- Industry recognition of your knowledge and proficiency with Microsoft products and technologies.

- Access to technical and product information directly from Microsoft through a secured area of the MCP Web Site.

- Logos to enable you to identify your Microsoft Certified Professional status to colleagues or clients.

- Invitations to Microsoft conferences, technical training sessions, and special events.

- A Microsoft Certified Professional certificate.

- Subscription to Microsoft Certified Professional Magazine (North America only), a career and professional development magazine.

Additional benefits, depending on your certification and geography, include:

- A complimentary one-year subscription to the Microsoft TechNet Technical Information Network, providing valuable information on monthly CD-ROMs.

- A one-year subscription to the Microsoft Beta Evaluation program. This benefit provides you with up to 12 free monthly CD-ROMs containing beta software (English only) for many of Microsoft's newest software products.

Microsoft Certification Benefits for Employers and Organizations

Through certification, computer professionals can maximize the return on investment in Microsoft technology. Research shows that Microsoft certification provides organizations with:

- Excellent return on training and certification investments by providing a standard method of determining training needs and measuring results.

- Increased customer satisfaction and decreased support costs through improved service, increased productivity and greater technical self-sufficiency.

- Reliable benchmark for hiring, promoting and career planning.

- Recognition and rewards for productive employees by validating their expertise.

- Retraining options for existing employees so they can work effectively with new technologies.

- Assurance of quality when outsourcing computer services.

To learn more about how certification can help your company, see the back-grounders, white papers and case studies available on http: www.microsoft.com/train_cert/cert/bus_bene.htm:

- The Microsoft® Certified Professional Program Corporate Backgrounder (mcpback.exe 50K)

- A white paper (mcsdwp.doc 158K) that evaluates the Microsoft Certified Solution Developer certification.

- A white paper (mcsestud.doc 161K) that evaluates the Microsoft Certified Systems Engineer certification.

- Jackson Hole High School Case Study (jhhs.doc 180K)

- Lyondel Case Study (lyondel.doc 21K)

- Stellcom Case Study (stellcom.doc 132K)

Requirements for Becoming a Microsoft Certified Professional

The certification requirements differ for each certification and are specific to the products and job functions addressed by the certification.

To become a Microsoft Certified Professional, you must pass rigorous certification exams that provide a valid and reliable measure of technical proficiency and expertise. These exams are designed to test your expertise and ability to perform a role or task with a product, and are developed with the input of professionals in the industry. Questions in the exams reflect how Microsoft products are used in actual organizations, giving them "real-world" relevance.

Microsoft Certified Product Specialists are required to pass one operating system exam. Candidate may pass additional Microsoft certification exams to further qualify their skills with Microsoft BackOffice products, development tools, or desktop applications.

Microsoft Certified Professional-Specialist: Internet are required to pass the prescribed Microsoft Windows NT Server 4.0, TCP/IP, and Microsoft Internet Information System exam series.

Microsoft Certified Systems Engineers are required to pass a series of core Microsoft Windows operating system and networking exams, and BackOffice technology elective exams.

Microsoft Certified Solution Developers are required to pass two core Microsoft Windows operating system technology exams and two BackOffice technology elective exams.

Microsoft Certified Trainers are required to meet instructional and technical requirements specific to each Microsoft Official Curriculum course they are certified to deliver. In the United States and Canada, call Microsoft at (800) 636-7544 for more information on becoming a Microsoft Certified Trainer. Outside the United States and Canada, contact your local Microsoft subsidiary.

Technical Training for Computer Professionals

Technical training is available in a variety of ways, with instructor-led classes, online instruction, or self-paced training available at thousands of locations worldwide.

Self-paced Training

For motivated learners who are ready for the challenge, self-paced instruction is the most flexible, cost-effective way to increase your knowledge and skills.

A full-line of self-paced print and computer-based training materials are available direct from the source—Microsoft Press. Microsoft Official Curriculum courseware kits from Microsoft Press are designed for advanced computer system professionals are available from Microsoft Press and the Microsoft Developer Division. Self-paced training kits from Microsoft Press feature print-based instructional materials, along with CD-ROM based product software, multimedia presentations, lab exercises, and practice files. The Mastering Series provides in-depth, interactive training on CD-ROM for experienced developers. They're both great ways to prepare for Microsoft Certified Professional (MCP) exams.

Online Training

For a more flexible alternative to instructor-led classes, turn to online instruction. It's as near as the Internet and it's ready whenever you are. Learn at your own pace and on your own schedule in a virtual classroom, often with easy access to an online instructor. Without ever leaving your desk, you can gain the expertise you need. Online instruction covers a variety of Microsoft products and technologies. It includes options ranging from Microsoft Official Curriculum to choices available nowhere else. It's training on demand, with access to learning resources 24 hours a day.

Online training is available through Microsoft Authorized Technical Education Centers.

Authorized Technical Education Centers

Authorized Technical Education Centers (ATECs) are the best source for instructor-led training that can help you prepare to become a Microsoft Certified Professional. The Microsoft ATEC program is a worldwide network of qualified technical training organizations that provide authorized delivery of Microsoft Official Curriculum courses by Microsoft Certified Trainers to computer professionals.

For a listing of ATEC locations in the United States and Canada, call the Microsoft fax service at (800) 727-3351. Outside the United States and Canada, call the fax service at (206) 635-2233.

Technical Support

Every effort has been made to ensure the accuracy of this book and the contents of the companion disc. Microsoft Press provides information about known issues for books through the World Wide Web at the following address:

http://mspress.microsoft.com/support/

If you have comments, questions, or ideas regarding this book or the companion disc, please send them to Microsoft Press using either of the following methods:

E-mail:

TKINPUT@MICROSOFT.COM

Postal Mail:

Microsoft Press
Attn: Microsoft® Windows NT® Server 4.0 Enterprise Technologies
      Training Editor
One Microsoft Way
Redmond, WA 98052-6399

Please note that product support is not offered through the above mail addresses. For further information regarding Microsoft software support options, please connect to http://www.microsoft.com/support/ or call Microsoft Support Network Sales at (800) 936-3500.

Evaluation Edition Software Support

The Evaluation Edition of Microsoft Windows NT Server version 4.0 included with this book is unsupported by both Microsoft and Microsoft Press and should not be used on a primary work computer. For online support information relating to the full version of Microsoft Windows NT Server version 4.0 that might also apply to the Evaluation Edition, you can connect to:

http://support.microsoft.com/

For information about ordering the full version of any Microsoft software, please call Microsoft Sales at (800) 426-9400 or visit www.microsoft.com. Information about any issues relating to the use of this evaluation edition with this training kit are posted to the Support section of the Microsoft Press Web site (http://mspress.microsoft.com/support/).

C H A P T E R   1

Planning the Enterprise with Microsoft Windows NT Server 4.0

About This Chapter

This chapter provides you with a foundation of knowledge that is useful for the rest of the chapters in this book. It includes an overview of Microsoft Windows NT Server version 4.0 in the enterprise and examines four primary planning issues. It examines trusts and domains, essential tools that enable you to balance the administrative requirements for a manageable environment with the organizational requirements for providing services to large numbers of users who may be geographically separated. The chapter also explores the issues of planning reliable and responsive disk systems, selecting appropriate network protocols, and determining server sizing requirements.

Before You Begin

To complete the lessons in this chapter, you must have:

- A strong familiarity with Windows NT as covered in Supporting Microsoft Windows NT 4.0 Core Technologies and Administering Microsoft Windows NT 4.0.

- Microsoft Certified Professional on Windows NT Server or equivalent level of knowledge.

- Experience planning and implementing a Windows NT network.

- Although not required, a familiarity with TCP/IP terminology and concepts is highly recommended, as provided in Microsoft© TCP/IP.

Lesson 1: Directory Architecture

Windows NT Server Directory Services provide a domain model of enterprise computing that can centralize account information and management into a single domain account database while focusing network resource management with the owner/administrator of the resource. This lesson introduces two networks run on Windows NT: the domain model, and the workgroup model. An overview of the four types of domain models is also included.

After this lesson, you will be able to:

- Explain the key differences between a workgroup model and a domain model.
- Describe the advantages of Windows NT Server Directory Services.
- Explain the purpose of trusts.
- Describe the differences between the four types of domain models.

Estimated lesson time: 30 minutes

The Enterprise Environment

Unlike a simple computing environment, which typically contains one or more servers in a single domain and a single location, an enterprise environment can expand to multiple servers in multiple domains and locations.

Networking Models

The main goal of networking is to allow users to share resources. Although there are different ways to structure a network to accomplish this goal, there are two distinct models supported by Windows NT: the workgroup model and the domain model. Implementation depends on your networking needs; however, in all but the smallest organizations, the domain model is the most often used.

Workgroup Model

The workgroup model (also known as the peer-to-peer model) has little or no centralized management. In this model, all resources are made available and administrated by individual members of the workgroup. In other words, all account administration is local to each machine, and each machine maintains its own account database. The workgroup model is appropriate for very small networks where the number of users is quite small, but as the network increases in complexity, the administration becomes more difficult. In addition, it is not necessary to have a Windows NT Server in a workgroup. Users can share resources on workstations with no centralized file, print, or application server.

Domain Model

The domain model (also known as the enterprise model) was developed by Microsoft as a response to the management challenges presented by the growing workgroup. The domain model maintains a centralized database of user and group account information. Resource access is subject to user and group permissions configured for specific resources. Users and groups are members of the domain, and thus appear in the domain's account database. When a resource is accessed, the user information in the domain's account database is compared against the permissions assigned to the resource, and access is permitted or denied. This model provides a high level of security for resource managers. Unlike the workgroup model, the domain model is appropriate for both small and large organizations.

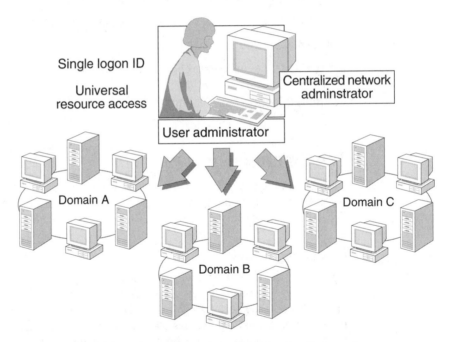

Windows NT Server Directory Services in the Enterprise

Windows NT Server is the central component of Microsoft BackOffice. BackOffice includes Microsoft Internet Information Server, Microsoft SNA Server, Microsoft Systems Management Server, Microsoft Exchange Server, Microsoft Proxy Server, and Microsoft SQL Server. The successful planning and implementation of Windows NT Server is essential to the deployment of BackOffice because all BackOffice applications run as services on the Windows NT Server.

Windows NT Server Directory Services are based upon the configuration and use of Windows NT Server domains. The Windows NT Server domain is the administrative unit of the Windows NT Server Directory Services. Within a domain, an administrator creates a user account for each user. The account includes user information, group memberships, and security policy information.

Through the domain structure, Windows NT Server Directory Services provide several key advantages:

- Support single network logon ID and password to gain access to all shared domain resources.

- Manage resources and accounts from a centralized location.

- Implement services to update network account and security information.

- Maintain user accounts and passwords in diverse environments.

- Incorporate BackOffice Directory Services such as authentication management and single logon access to all BackOffice applications.

Windows NT Server Directory Services offer the solution to these challenges. Windows NT Server Directory Services manage a secure, distributed directory database and provide services for both end users and network administrators. For users, Windows NT Server Directory Services provide authentication services that permit each user to have a single logon ID and password that can be entered from any desktop on a network allowing access to services, applications, and resources located anywhere else on the network. For administrators, Windows NT Server Directory Services provide graphical management and security services. These features simplify the creation and maintenance of user identities and rights for user populations ranging from workgroups to the entire organization.

Single Network Logon

Windows NT Server Directory Services maintain the concept of "one user, one account" allowing users to connect to multiple servers with a single network logon. With "one user, one account," users avoid having multiple accounts that require memorization of multiple passwords. Windows NT Server Directory Services extend this process to all Windows NT Server services and Windows NT Server applications.

Centralized Network Administration

A centralized view of the entire network from any workstation on the network provides the ability to track and manage information on users, groups, and resources in a distributed network. This single point of administration for multiple servers simplifies the management of a Windows NT Server-based network.

A single domain user account and password is all the user needs to access available resources throughout the network. Through Windows NT Server Directory Services, account validation is extended to allow seamless user access to multiple network domains.

Updated Network Account and Security Information

Windows NT Server Directory Services provide the security of Windows NT Server which may not be available to an application outside the directory services environment. For example, SQL Server, running outside of a directory services environment, cannot take advantage of the encrypted password feature of Windows NT Server. Exchange Server will not allow any user who has not been validated by the domain into his or her mailbox. Exchange Server is fully dependent on the Windows NT Server domain security and its implementation.

Because Windows NT Server Directory Services provide single user access to network services and applications across the enterprise, BackOffice application developers can:

- Leave user authentication to the network operating system.

- Avoid writing code with duplicate functionality.

- Provide thorough security in applications.

Maintenance of User Accounts and Passwords in Diverse Environments

Because the Windows NT environment recognizes accounts outside of the domain in which they were created, users can access resources in any domain for which they have appropriate permissions. This is true no matter where on the network the account is located. If the network operating system could not maintain the "one user, one account" concept, duplicate accounts could potentially have conflicting permissions in different domains.

With a Windows NT Server Directory Services single account, a user can log on from any location in a trusting domain environment. As described later in this chapter, when there are multiple domains, one domain can be configured to trust another domain. The trusting domain allows the trusted domain's users access to resources in that trusting domain. For example, a businesswoman whose home domain is in North America logs on while in Europe at a computer that is a member of the European resource domain. In this example, the European domain controller will forward the logon request to the North American domain for validation. Once the businesswoman's home domain validates the account, she can access resources anywhere on the network where she has the appropriate permissions.

The figure on the following page illustrates another example: the logon request is forwarded or "passed-through" the European domain, across the trust, to the North American domain where the account resides and the request can be validated. Validating accounts across domain, a process called "pass-through authentication," makes "one user, one account" possible.

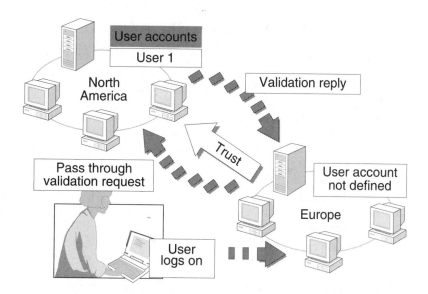

Incorporation of BackOffice Directory Services

BackOffice applications were developed to take advantage of Windows NT Server Directory Services. The BackOffice suite is engineered to use the directory services database to identify users and groups that have access to its product functions and information, such as mail folders, databases, and management functions. As a result, the security subsystem of Windows NT Server is used by BackOffice applications to permit or deny access to the objects or resources that BackOffice applications provide.

Authentication Management

The utilization of the security subsystem by BackOffice allows users and administrators the benefits of single account management. This simplifies user authentication which guarantees the identity of users logging on to the system and control of permissions to access network resources such as files or application data (for example, mail folders). The same single logon account can be used to log on to the network, access a home directory, print to a print server's devices, connect to an Exchange mailbox, manipulate a SQL database, or remotely control another computer through System Management Server (SMS). Users that were validated during the logon process are not required to provide a second logon to access any of the BackOffice applications that require Windows NT authentication. Administrators can avoid the expense and complexity of managing and synchronizing separate user accounts for each application.

Windows NT Server Domain

A domain is a logical grouping of network servers and other computers that share common security and user account information. Within domains, administrators typically create one user account for each user. Users then log on once to the domain, not to the individual servers in the domain.

A domain is simply the administrative unit of Windows NT Server Directory Services. The term domain does not refer to a single location or specific type of network configuration. Computers in a single domain can share physical proximity on a small local area network (LAN) or can be located in different corners of the world, communicating over a wide area network (WAN). WAN connectivity can be provided by using a number of physical connections, including dial-up line connections, Integrated Services Digital Network (ISDN) connections, fiber connections, Ethernet connections, token ring connections, frame relay connections, satellite connections, and leased lines connections.

Although small organizations can store accounts and resources in a single domain, large organizations typically establish multiple domains. With multiple domains, user and machine accounts are usually stored in one domain and resources in another domain or domains.

Domain Controllers

Domain controllers manage all aspects of user-domain interactions. Domain controllers are computers running Windows NT Server that share one directory database to store security and user account information for the entire domain; they comprise a single administrative unit. Domain controllers use the information in the directory database to authenticate users logging on to domain accounts. There are two types of domain controllers: primary domain controllers and backup domain controllers.

Primary Domain Controllers

The primary domain controller (PDC) tracks changes made to domain accounts. When an administrator makes a change to a domain account, the change is recorded in the directory database on the PDC. The PDC is the only domain server that receives these changes directly. A domain can have only one PDC.

Backup Domain Controllers

A backup domain controller (BDC) maintains a copy of the directory database. This copy is synchronized periodically and automatically with the PDC. Typically, BDCs authenticate user logons, but they also can be promoted to function as the PDC. Multiple BDCs can exist in a domain.

You create a domain when you install Windows NT Server on a computer and designate that computer as the PDC. Once the domain is defined by the existence of a PDC, BDCs can be added to the domain to share the load of authenticating network logons. In a small organization, a PDC and a single BDC in one domain might be all that is required.

Directory Database

The directory database stores all security and user account information for a domain. The directory database is also referred to as the Security Accounts Manager (SAM). The master copy of the directory database is stored on the PDC and is replicated to the BDC and synchronized on a regular basis to maintain centralized security. When a user logs on to a domain, Windows NT domain controller validates the user's password against the directory database.

Trust Relationships

Domains can be linked to each other by establishing a trust relationship. A trust relationship is a secure communication link between two domains. With a trust relationship, a domain can accept user accounts created in other domains as valid accounts and allow those accounts to use local resources.

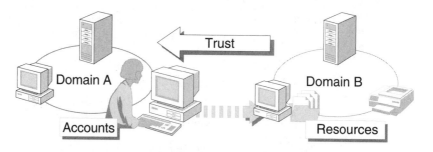

There are two types of trust relationships: one-way trust relationships and two-way trust relationships.

One-Way Trust Relationship

In a one-way trust relationship, one domain trusts users in the other domain to access its resources. More specifically, one domain trusts the domain controllers in the other domain to validate user accounts to access its resources. The available resources are in the trusting domain, and the accounts that are allowed access to the resources are in the trusted domain. However, if user accounts located in the trusting domain need to use resources located in the trusted domain, the situation requires a two-way trust relationship.

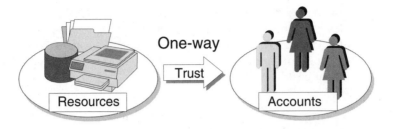

Two-Way Trust Relationship

A two-way trust relationship consists of two one-way trusts in which each domain trusts user accounts in the other domain. Users can log on from computers in either domain to the domain that contains their account. Each domain can have both accounts and resources. Global user accounts and global groups can be used from either domain to grant rights and permissions to resources in either domain. In other words, both domains are trusted domains.

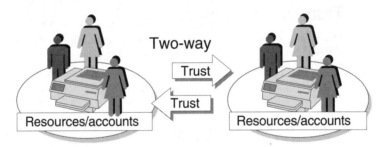

Planning Considerations

Setting up trusts properly requires knowledge and planning. To implement trusts correctly, consider the following guidelines:

- Trust relationships can be established only between Windows NT Server domains.

- Physical location of the domains does not matter.

- Use the fewest number of trusts possible. The fewer the number of trusts, the simpler it is to manage the network.

- Determine the number of one-way trusts. For example, will a single one-way trust between two domains, with one domain used for accounts and the other used for resources, be enough, or will your network require two one-way trusts so each domain can be used for both accounts and resources?

- Where the users are physically or logically located is not important. Pass-through authentication makes a user's physical location irrelevant because it allows him or her to log on from any location on the network.

- Where user accounts reside is important. As long as a user has an account in the trusted domain, the user can log on from anywhere in any domain once appropriate trusts have been established.

Domain Models

There are four types of domain models, each with a specific set of advantages: single domain model, single master domain model, multiple master domain model, and complete trust model. Although an organization's choice of domain topology is determined by an organization's need, the number of users and complexity of the network architecture also affects what topology is chosen.

Single Domain Model

The single domain model is the simplest domain model. The single domain model consists of one PDC with one or more BDCs. The PDC and each BDC can support 2000 user accounts to validate user logons and provide fault tolerance. In most cases, the single domain model is an appropriate choice for organizations that require both centralized management of user accounts and ease of administration. Any member of the Domain Administrators Group can administer all the network servers and domain accounts on the PDC.

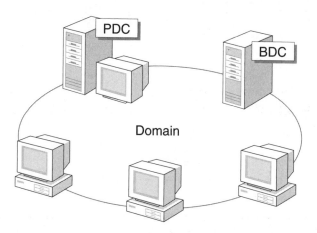

A network can use the single domain model if it has a small enough number of users and groups to ensure good performance (generally up to 26,000). The exact number of users and groups depends on the number of servers in the domain and the hardware of the servers.

The single domain model allows any network administrator to administer any network servers. Splitting a network into domains enables you to create administrators who can administer only some servers, such as those in their own department.

Single Master Domain Model

When the network needs to be split into domains for organizational purposes, but has not exceeded the number of users and groups that can be supported by a single domain, the master domain model is probably the best choice. This model gives both the centralized administration and the organizational benefits of multiple domains. According to the single master domain model, one domain, referred to as the master domain, acts as the central administrative unit for both user and group accounts. The master domain contains all user and group accounts. The other domains contain resources such as printers, application servers, and workstations. The resource domains trust the master domain to authenticate their users, thereby granting users access to resources. If a company has a management information system (MIS) department that manages a LAN, it is logical to have the MIS department administer the master domain since that is where all user and group accounts are located.

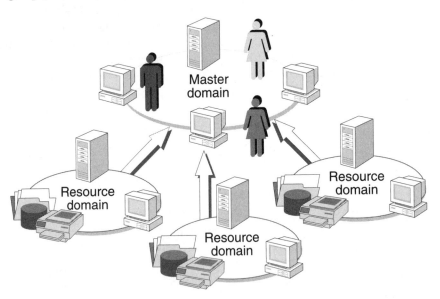

All users log on to accounts in the master domain. Resources, such as printers and file servers, are located in the resource domains. Each resource domain establishes a one-way trust with the master (account) domain, enabling users with accounts in the master domain to use resources in all other domains. The network administrator can manage the entire multiple domain network, including users and resources, from a central location.

The benefit of the single master domain model is its flexibility of administration. For example, in a network requiring four domains for network resources, it might seem obvious to also create user accounts in all four domains. However, by putting all user accounts in a single directory database in a master domain, and then implementing one-way trust relationships between the four resource domains and the master domain, you can consolidate administration of user and computer accounts. You can also administer all resources or delegate these to local administrators. Users will need only one logon name and one password to use resources in any of the four resource domains.

The single master domain model balances the requirements for account security with the need for readily available resources on the network because users are given permission to use resources based on their master domain logon identity.

The single master domain model is appropriate for a situation in which a company has developed a complex assortment of divisions and departments, each wanting its own separate resource management, but still requiring centralized account management

The single master domain model is particularly suited for:

- Organizations with fewer than 40,000 domain accounts.

- Centralized account management.

- Decentralized resource management or local system administration capability. Department domains can have their own administrators who manage the department's resources.

Multiple Master Domain Model

The multiple master domain model is composed of two or more master domains and several resource domains, each of which trust all master domains. Like the single master domain model, each master domain in the multiple master domain model serves as an account domain, with every user and global group account created and maintained on one of the master domains. A company's MIS groups can centrally manage these master domains. Another similarity to the single master domain model is that the other domains on the network are called resource domains; they don't store or manage user accounts but do provide resources such as shared file servers and printers to the network and can store machine accounts.

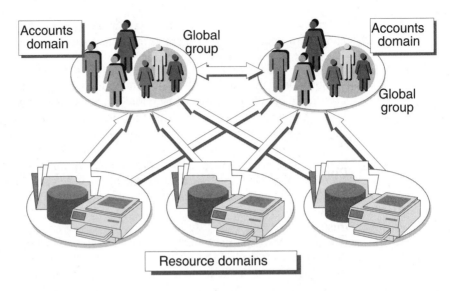

In this model, every master domain is connected to every other master domain by a two-way trust relationship. Each resource domain trusts every master domain with a one-way trust relationship. The resource domains can trust other resource domains but are not required to do so. Because every user account exists in one of the master domains, and since each resource domain trusts every master domain, every user account can be used on any of the master domains and any of the resource domains. Users log on to the domain that contains their account. Each master domain should contain one PDC and at least one BDC.

The multiple master domain model is the best choice for large companies that require multiple administration units spread across the company. With this model, each administrative unit has control of its own accounts. Administrators for each domain can create users and groups and manage those accounts within their own domain.

In a large corporation, for example, employees of Marketing, Sales, Manufacturing, Finance, and other major department may want their own administrators to manage the users and groups in their own departments. A multiple master domain model supports this type of corporate structure.

The multiple master domain model incorporates all the features of a single master domain but also accommodates:

- Organizations of more than 40,000 domain accounts or more than 15,000 users. The multiple master domain model is scaleable to any number of network users.

- Mobile users. Users can log on from anywhere in the network or anywhere in the world.

- Centralized or decentralized administration.

- Organizational needs. Domains can be configured to mirror specific departments or internal company organizations.

- LAN-Wide Area Network (WAN) interactions. BDCs can be distributed between sites to facilitate LAN-WAN interactions.

Complete Trust Model

The complete trust model makes more extensive use of Windows NT Server Directory Services than any other model because the complete trust model uses trusts to implement two-way communication among all the domains in a network. If you want the management of users and resources to be distributed among different departments, rather than centralized, you might want to use the complete trust model. In this model, every domain on the network trusts every other domain, so no single domain exerts control over the other domains. The complete trust model distributes the administration of users, groups, domains, and resources among different departments rather than centralizing it. Unfortunately, the complete trust model is often found in organizations that implement Windows NT Server without a plan or design. Keep in mind that as the number of domains grows, the number of trusts also increases.

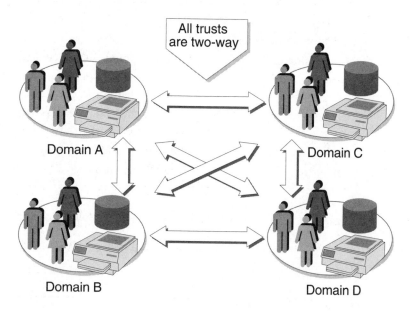

The complete trust domain model can quickly become unmanageable, but can be beneficial because:

- The model can be used by companies with no central MIS group.

- The model is scaleable to work with any number of users.

- Each department has full control over its user accounts and resources.

- Both resources and user accounts are grouped into departmental units.

Designing Your Network Using Directory Services

Miller Textiles is in the process of replacing its older, midrange system with Windows NT-based computers. Most employees gain access to the midrange system through terminal devices. Some users have 486-based computers, and a few users have Pentuim-based computers. These computers are not networked. The company has already purchased the hardware for the migration. The network will be used for basic file and print sharing and will also have one Windows NT server running SQL Server. The majority of users will need access to SQL Server. Desktop applications will be installed on the local computers, but data files will be saved on the servers. You will draft a network design using the criteria in the table below.

Environmental Components	Detail
Users	100
Location or locations	Single office
Administration	Fulltime administrators, centrally located
Servers	Three computers: Pentium/166 with 64-MB RAM, and 4-GB hard disk; one dedicated to SQL Server
Clients	All 486 and Pentium/66 computers, running Windows for Workgroups 3.11 or Windows 95
BackOffice applications	SQL Server, and Messaging
Server usage	Basic file and print

Based on the above information, answer the following questions:

1. Would you recommend a domain model or a workgroup model? Why?

_____

_____

2. How many PDCs are needed? How many BDCs are needed?

_____

_____

3. If two departments within the company want to administer their own user accounts, which domain model would you recommend?

_____

_____

4. How many trusts would be required for the two domain model?

_____

_____

5. If an organization had four domains in a complete trust model, how many trusts would be required?

_____

_____

Choosing a Domain Model

In this exercise, you identify the domain model necessary to meet customer requirements.

Scenario 1

Your company, Fabrikam, Inc., is implementing Windows NT Server across the enterprise. You have five departments: sales, marketing, accounting, development, and headquarters. Each department has between 500 and 1000 users. Several departments have applications specific to the department, but all departments share e-mail and a SQL-Server-based customer database. You want users to have a single logon and to take advantage of your centralized MIS group.

1. What domain model should you implement? Why?

_____

_____

Scenario 2

Your company, West Coast Sales, is a large corporation with 50,000 users across three divisions. Each division has several departments as well as its own MIS team. Each division wants to manage its own accounts with access to company-wide resource domains. Users in one division need access to resources in other divisions. When users move from division to division, MIS should not have to create a new user.

1. What domain model will you implement? Why?

_____

_____

Lesson Summary

The following information summarizes the key points in this lesson:

- The workgroup model has little or no centralized management, provides for limited security, and is appropriate only for networks with very small numbers of users.

- Through domain structure, Windows NT Server Directory Services provide several key advantages including, single network logon ID, centralized account administration, management of network account and security information as well as integration with other BackOffice applications.

- Trusts enable secure links between two domains, so users in one domain can access resources in another domain.

- Windows NT Server's four domain models provide alternatives that enable an organization to accommodate differences in size, geographical dispersion, and security requirements. The four domain models are single domain, single master domain, multiple master domain, and complete trust. A single domain model contains all accounts and resources in one domain. A single master domain model has all user accounts contained in one domain and resources distributed among one or more domains that trust the user domain. A multiple master domain has several domains that contain user accounts where each user account domain trusts every other user account domain, and has one or more resource domains that trust all of the user account domains. A complete trust model has domains that contain both users and resources where every domain trusts every other domain.

For more information on	See
Domains & Trust relationships	AVI on enclosed CDROM.
	<CDROM drive letter>: \videos\main.exe

Lesson 2: Managing Partitions

Managing disk partitions is an important building block for designing a successful Windows NT Server implementation. Choosing the appropriate file system and method to protect your data from hardware failure is discussed in this lesson.

After this lesson, you will be able to:

- Choose the appropriate file system.
- Identify which levels of RAID fault tolerance are supported by Windows NT Server.
- Select the appropriate RAID level option.
- Plan fault tolerant systems.

Estimated lesson time: 15 minutes

Choosing a File System

Choosing the appropriate file system to enable security and performance and to protect your data from hardware failure is an important aspect of designing a successful Windows NT Server implementation. The two main types of file systems are file allocation table (FAT) and NT file system (NTFS).

FAT Partition

The FAT file system originated with Microsoft MS-DOS and now is the simplest file system supported by Windows NT Server.

The major advantages of FAT are:

- FAT requires little overhead on medium-sized devices.
- FAT performs sequential reads and writes more efficiently than other file systems such as NTFS. There are some applications, such as Exchange Server, that experience increased performance when their transaction logs are written to a FAT partition.
- A FAT partition can be accessed when the computer is booted into MS-DOS. For example, if a corrupt Windows NT Server system file is keeping Windows NT from booting, and the Windows NT Directory is on a FAT partition, it may be possible to boot the computer from a floppy disk into MS-DOS and then repair the corrupt file since it is accessible from MS-DOS. This is not the case with NTFS.

The major disadvantages of FAT are:

- Unlike NTFS, there is no file or directory level security.

- The degradation of file system performance occurs on large devices.

NTFS Partition

The NTFS file system includes security features required for file servers and workstations. The NTFS file system supports data access control and ownership privileges that are important for the integrity of critical data. While shared folders on a Windows NT Server computer using FAT can be assigned specific permissions, NTFS files and folders can have permissions assigned whether or not they are shared.

The major advantages of NTFS are:

- Disk volumes can easily exceed 400 MB. This is because performance does not degrade under NTFS as it does under larger FAT volume sizes.

- File and directory level security is required.

- NTFS partitions support different levels of fault tolerance.

When to Use FAT or NTFS

Consider the following recommendations when determining which file system to use for which volume. Use a small FAT primary partition (between 250 and 500 MB, depending on the total disk space and page file size) as the C drive. Use this partition for both your system and boot partition. This will allow access to the FAT partition from MS-DOS. Format the rest of your disk space as NTFS, and use the NTFS volumes for application programs and data so that file and directory level permissions can be applied. You may want to create more than one NTFS volume.

The benefits of this configuration are:

- Recoverability: the NTFS file system has the ability to recover your data.

- Efficiency: FAT is more efficient for smaller volumes; NTFS is more efficient for larger volumes.

- File and Folder Security: NTFS provides file and folder security for your application programs and data.

- Troubleshooting: if you have a startup failure on an x86-based computer, you can start up the computer with a MS-DOS bootable floppy disk to troubleshoot and recover from the problem.

RAID: Improved Performance and Fault Tolerance

Windows NT Server implements disk fault tolerance with Redundant Array of Inexpensive Disks (RAID) technology. RAID allows data being streamed to the disk drives by the Windows NT disk subsystem to be divided up among several physical disks. Individual data files are written to more than one disk in a manner that, depending on the RAID level used, can improve performance or reliability. The RAID implementations discussed here are administered using Windows NT Server Disk Administrator and are software implementations of RAID. Some hardware vendors implement RAID technology completely within the hardware and this implementation is transparent to Windows NT. Some of these hardware implementations support hot swapping of disks so you can replace a failed disk while the computer is still running Windows NT Server.

RAID Levels

As technology evolved, RAID became more complex and efficient. There are six RAID levels (levels 0–5).

RAID Level 0 is really a misnomer. RAID 0 is really not a fault tolerant system because there is no redundancy; RAID 0 is disk striping only. When data is written to a RAID 0 logical device, the data is broken up and distributed to several devices. This makes the write process more efficient because the data is being written to several devices simultaneously, but no parity information is created, and there is no redundancy.

RAID Level 1, also known as mirroring or duplexing, allows all data written to one disk to also be written to another disk. This provides fault tolerance but requires twice the disk space needed to support the system. If a system requires 500 MB of disk space, RAID Level 1 requires 1000 MB because everything is stored twice.

RAID Levels 2–4 are not supported by Windows NT Server and will not be discussed in this book.

RAID Level 5, takes parity information and spreads it across the data disks. This way, if one disk fails, the remaining disks contain parity information necessary to rebuild the disk without interrupting service to the operating system.

RAID Level	Supported by Windows NT Server	Description
Level 0	Yes	Disk striping
Level 1	Yes	Disk mirroring
Level 2	No	Disk striping with error correction code (ECC)

(continued)

continued

RAID Level	Supported by Windows NT Server	Description
Level 3	No	Disk striping with ECC stored as parity
Level 4	No	Disk striping large blocks; parity stored on one drive
Level 5	Yes	Disk striping with parity distributed across multiple drives.

The RAID levels supported by Windows NT are described in the following section.

RAID Level 0: Disk Striping

RAID Level 0, disk striping, divides data into 64-KB blocks and spreads it equally in a fixed rate and order among all disks in an array. The entire configuration of data spread across all the disks in an array is called a stripe set. Disk striping does not provide any fault tolerance because there is not any data redundancy. A minimum of two disks are required to implement a striped set and as many as thirty-two disks can be supported.

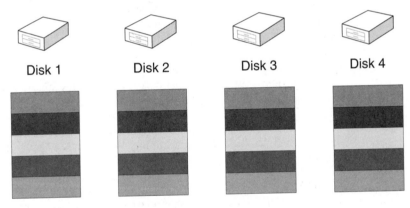

Disk 1   Disk 2   Disk 3   Disk 4

Advantages of disk striping include:

- Allows you to combine several small partitions into one large partition.

- Can improve performance by spreading I/O across multiple disks and controllers.

Disadvantages of disk striping include:

- Does not include any redundant data, therefore there is no fault tolerance.

- If one physical disk in the stripe set fails, the entire stripe set is lost.

RAID Level 1: Disk Mirroring

RAID Level 1, disk mirroring, is the duplication of a partition. The second partition is an exact duplicate of the initial partition. Both partitions are constantly updated and provide a full redundant copy of the partition. A minimum of two disks are required for disk mirroring.

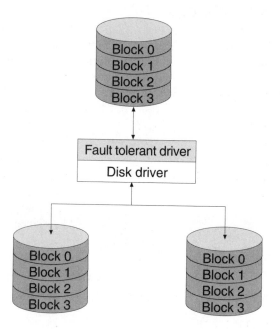

Advantages of disk mirroring include:

- Simple to implement, requiring only two disk drives.
- Fast recovery if a disk fails.

Disadvantages of disk mirroring include:

- Only 50 percent disk utilization, resulting in high cost per MB.
- Less efficient disk write time.

Disk duplexing adds an additional controller for the second drive of a mirrored set. This eliminates the disk controller from being a single point of failure in the mirror set. With duplexing, if a single drive or a controller fails, the existing drive and controller will produce disk services.

Disk duplexing also has the added benefit of increasing performance. Each controller can handle the read/write requests of a single device, rather than having to control several devices.

Advantages of disk duplexing include:

- Protects against controller failures in addition to disk failures.
- Reduces channel traffic and increases performance.

RAID Level 5: Disk Striping with Parity

RAID Level 5, disk striping with parity, writes parity information across all disks in the stripe set. The data and parity information are kept on different disks. In the event of a single drive failure, information on the remaining disks is sufficient to reconstruct the data from the failed disk. A minimum of three disks are required, and as many as thirty-two can be supported.

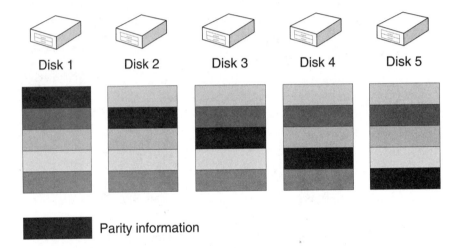

Advantages of disk striping with parity include:

- Best performance for read operations.
- Highest degree of fault tolerance.
- A single disk failure doesn't make the server inoperable.

Disadvantages of disk striping with parity include:

- Write operations require three times the amount of memory because of parity calculations.
- When a disk fails, performance is severely degraded.

Fault Tolerance in the Enterprise

Windows NT Server has fault tolerance features built into the operating system. However, RAID is only one piece of a fault tolerant system. Fault tolerance is the ability of a system to continue functioning when a component on the computer fails. The term fault tolerance is typically used to describe disk subsystems, but it can also apply to other system components or to the system as a whole. Fully fault tolerant computers use redundant disk controllers and uninterruptible power supplies (UPSs) as well as fault tolerant disk subsystems and clustered computers. When planning your enterprise deployment of Windows NT Server, fault tolerance is essential to providing reliable availability of the server.

Choosing a File System

In this exercise, you will make file system decisions based on the following information. You need to configure a new server to act as a simple file server and BDC. You expect to house 3 GB of user data you need to keep secure. The server has one 500-MB and two 2-GB hard disk drives.

1. Which drive would you put the system partition on? Why?

   _____

   _____

2. Would you format the system partition as FAT or NTFS? Why?

   _____

   _____

3. How would you format the remaining partitions?

   _____

   _____

Lesson Summary

The following information summarizes the key points in this lesson:

- Windows NT supports both FAT and NTFS file systems. FAT should be used on drives smaller than 400 MB when security is not a concern. NTFS provides both directory and file level security and should be used on drives larger than 400 MB, as well as when implementing fault-tolerance.

- Windows NT Server supports disk mirroring (RAID Level 1) and disk striping with parity (RAID Level 5).

- Disk striping (RAID Level 0), although not fault tolerant, can be used to increase performance.

Lesson 3: Network Protocols

One of the significant differences between the Windows NT Server operating system and other operating systems is that several networking capabilities are built into Windows NT Server. Understanding the benefits and limitations of each protocol supported by Windows NT Server is required for effective enterprise planning. This lesson will review TCP/IP, NetBEUI, and NWLink (IPX/SPX-compatible) protocols.

After this lesson, you will be able to:

- Identify the benefits of TCP/IP.
- Identify the benefits of NetBEUI.
- Identify the benefits of NWLink (IPX/SPX).
- Analyze DHCP as a TCP/IP administration tool.
- Identify how WINS is used for NetBIOS name resolution.

Estimated lesson time: 20 minutes

Transmission Control Protocol/Internet Protocol (TCP/IP)

Transmission Control Protocol/Internet Protocol (TCP/IP) is an industry-standard suite of protocols designed for intranets and internets. TCP/IP was developed in 1969 by the U.S. Department of Defense Advanced Research Projects Agency as a result of a research sharing experiment called ARPANET. The purpose of TCP/IP was to provide high-speed communication network links. Since 1969, ARPANET has grown into a worldwide community of networks known as the Internet.

The advantages of TCP/IP are:

- Connectivity across multiple operating systems and hardware platforms.
- Interoperability with the internet.
- A routable protocol.
- Dynamic Host Configuration Protocol (DHCP) which provides dynamic Internet Protocol-address assignments.
- Windows Internet Name Service (WINS) which provides a dynamic database of IP address-to-NetBIOS name-resolution mappings.

Every host interface on a TCP/IP network is identified by a unique IP address. This address is used to identify the host on a network; it also specifies routing information in an internetwork. An IP address consists of 32 bits divided into four octets, or fields. An address is usually represented in dotted decimal notation which depicts each octet in its decimal value and separates each octet with a decimal.

131.107.2.200 = 10000011.01101011.00000010.11001000

A logical line is drawn within the 32-bit address that divides it into two parts: the network ID and the host ID. The network ID identifies the physical network. The host ID uniquely identifies a host on a network. When combined, the IP address is used to determine the exact TCP/IP host on a specific network.

If you want to participate on the Internet you must use a unique IP address. These can be obtained by contacting either the Internet Network Information Center (InterNIC) or an Internet Service Provider (ISP). The InterNIC can be contacted by email at info.internic.net, or on its website: http:\\www.internic.org. You can find an ISP in your local telephone directory or by contacting your local computer reseller.

The Internet community has defined multiple address classes to accommodate networks of varying sizes. Windows NT Server supports class A, B, and C networks. The class of address defines the possible number of networks and the number of hosts on a network.

Class	Number of Networks	Number of Hosts per Network	First Octet of Address Range
A	126	16,777,214	1–126
B	16,384	65,534	128–191
C	2,097,152	254	192–223

Subnet Mask

A subnet mask is used to mask a portion of the IP address so that TCP/IP can distinguish the network ID from the host ID. When TCP/IP hosts communicate, the subnet mask is used to determine whether a host is located on a local or a remote network.

A custom subnet mask is often required when you have only one network ID but you have several networks for which you want to assign network IDs. A custom subnet mask will allow you to divide the single network ID into several subnets. For example, if the InterNIC assigns your company one network ID, and you have a WAN consisting of multiple sites, you would define a custom subnet mask for your network ID that is based on the number of subnets and the number of hosts required on each subnet. Custom subnet masks allow you to use the single network ID for all subnets.

Default Gateway

The default gateway is the intermediate network node on the network or subnet that has addresses for the network IDs of other subnets in the network. When a host determines that the destination host is not on its local subnet (using the subnet mask), the host will send the packets to the default gateway. The default gateway can forward the packets to other gateways until the data is eventually delivered to its final destination. TCP/IP hosts can be configured for only one default gateway.

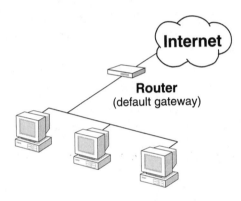

Domain Name System (DNS)

DNS resolves friendly host names to IP addresses. DNS makes it easy for users to access information from servers on the Internet. For example, it's easier to remember the name www.microsoft.com than to remember the IP address for that server.

To use the DNS, workstations must be configured to recognize at least one DNS server's IP address. DNS server addresses can be assigned to a computer in one of two ways:

- Static TCP/IP configuration on the workstation.
- Dynamic assignment by a DHCP server.

Dynamic Host Configuration Protocol (DHCP)

Implementing DHCP eliminates many of the configuration problems associated with manually configuring TCP/IP. DHCP centralizes TCP/IP configurations and manages the allocation of TCP/IP information by automatically assigning an IP address to computers configured to use DHCP.

DHCP leases an IP address to hosts. This alleviates the need for someone to visit each host and assign an IP address. Along with the IP address, DHCP will also assign the subnet mask, default gateway, and IP addresses for WINS servers.

DHCP Relay Agent

The DHCP Relay Agent allows a computer to relay DHCP messages from one local area network (LAN) to another. For example, suppose a network has two LANs (LAN A and LAN B) with a router between them, but there is only one DHCP server on LAN A. In a conventional setup, in order for LAN B clients to get addressing information, a DHCP server would be required on both networks, which would result in higher maintenance and cost. Instead, install a DHCP Relay Agent on any computer in LAN B, and it will relay messages through the router to the DHCP server on LAN A.

Windows Internet Naming Service (WINS)

While DNS resolves host names to IP addresses, WINS resolves NetBIOS names to IP addresses. WINS is a NetBIOS name server. With WINS, the number of NetBIOS name resolution broadcasts on the local subnet are reduced, and remote NetBIOS names on other subnets can be resolved. When WINS clients communicate across subnets, the destination host's IP address is retrieved from the database rather than by using a broadcast.

Routing Information Protocol (RIP)

RIP facilitates the exchange of routing information. A RIP router is a computer or other piece of hardware that broadcasts routing information (such as network addresses) and forwards IP frames on connected networks.

RIP allows a router to exchange routing information with neighboring routers. As a router becomes aware of any change in the internetwork layout (for instance, a downed router), it broadcasts the information to neighboring routers. Routers also send periodic RIP broadcast packets containing all routing information known to the router. These broadcasts keep all internetwork routers synchronized.

Windows NT Server supports RIP for dynamic management of IP routing tables. RIP eliminates the need to establish static IP routing tables. This version of RIP routing does not support RIP over dial-up (switched WAN) links.

If RIP for IP is installed on a computer that has only one network card, the computer will be placed in Silent Mode. In Silent Mode, the computer listens to RIP broadcasts and updates its route table but does not advertise its own routes.

Routing and Remote Access Service (RAS) provide advanced routing and inter-networking capabilities and make Windows NT Server an even more compelling platform for communications. It provides branch offices, departments, and small businesses with routing, remote access, and Virtual Private Network (VPN) capability all in one easy to manage service.

Routing and RAS features include:

- A unified service for routing and remote access that's integrated with the operating system.
- A full set of routing protocols for IP and Internet Packet Exchange (IPX) (including Open Shortest Path First [OSPF] by Bay Networks).
- An easy, intuitive, remotable graphical user interface and command line interface with scripting.
- Application programming interface (API) for third-party routing protocols, user interface, and management.
- Demand-dial routing.
- Point-to-Point Tunneling Protocol (PPTP) server-to-server for secure Virtual Private Networks.
- Remote Authentication Dial-In User Service (RADIUS) client support.

NetBEUI

NetBEUI (NetBIOS Enhanced User Interface) was designed as a small, efficient protocol for use in department-sized LANs of 20–200 computers that do not need to be routed to other subnets. Today, NetBEUI is used almost exclusively on small, non-routed networks.

The Windows NT-based implementation of NetBEUI does the following:

- Uses the Windows NT-based Transport Driver Interface (TDI) which pro-vides an emulator for interpretation of NetBIOS network commands.
- Uses the Windows NT-based Network Device Interface Specification (NDIS) version 3 with improved transport support and a full 32-bit asynchronous interface.
- Removes the NetBIOS session number limit.
- Uses memory dynamically to provide automatic memory tuning.
- Supports dial-up client communications with RAS services.
- Provides connection-oriented and connectionless data transfer services.

NWLink

NWLink is an IPX/Sequenced Packet Exchange (SPX)-compatible protocol for the Windows NT Server network architecture. NWLink is simply a protocol. By itself, NWLink does not allow a computer running Windows NT Server to access files or printers shared on a NetWare server, or to act as a file or print server to a NetWare client. To access files or printers on a NetWare server, a redirector must be used, such as the Gateway Service for NetWare (GSNW) on Windows NT Server.

NWLink is useful if there are NetWare client/server applications running that use sockets or NetBIOS over the IPX/SPX protocol. The client portion can run on a Windows NT Server or Windows NT Workstation system to access the server portion on a NetWare server and vice versa.

Data Link Control (DLC)

Unlike other protocols, DLC is not designed to be a primary protocol for network use between personal computers. DLC provides applications with direct access to the data link layer but is not used by the Windows NT operating system redirector. Since the redirector cannot use DLC, this protocol is not used for normal-session communication between computers running Windows NT Server or Windows NT Workstation.

The DLC protocol is primarily used for two tasks:

- Accessing IBM mainframes, which usually run 3270 applications.
- Printing to Hewlett-Packard printers connected directly to the network.

Network-attached printers, such as the HP III, use the DLC protocol because the received frames are easy to take apart and because DLC functionality can easily be coded into read-only memory (ROM).

DLC needs to be installed only on those network machines that perform these two tasks, such as a print server sending data to a network HP printer. Client computers sending print jobs to the network printer do not need the DLC protocol; only the print server communicating directly with the printer needs the DLC protocol installed.

The registry location for the DLC parameters is:

```
HKEY_LOCAL_MACHINE\System\CurrentControlSet\Services\DLC
```

The registry entry for the DLC driver indicates that it is loaded after the kernel has been started (Start 0x1), and it is dependent on having an NDIS group service available. Its linkage shows that it is bound to the network adapter by the appropriate NDIS device driver.

Configuring TCP/IP Parameters

In this exercise, you answer questions about TCP/IP and its configuration.

1. When the originating TCP/IP host is sending packets to the receiving TCP/IP host, what TCP/IP configuration parameter does it use to determine if the receiving host is on the local subnet or the remote subnet?

   _____

   _____

2. When the originating TCP/IP host determines that the destination TCP/IP host is on a remote subnet, what TCP/IP configuration parameter does the originating host send TCP/IP packets to?

   _____

   _____

3. Other than the TCP/IP address, what other Microsoft TCP/IP parameters are typically sent to the host leasing an address from DHCP?

   _____

   _____

4. What service comes with Windows NT Server to resolve NetBIOS names to IP addresses?

   _____

   _____

5. What service comes with Windows NT Server to resolve host names to IP addresses?

   _____

   _____

6. What protocol is supported by Windows NT Server that facilitates the exchange of routing information between Windows NT Servers and routers?

   _____

   _____

Lesson Summary

The following information summarizes the key points in this lesson:

- TCP/IP is the default protocol for NT Server. DHCP, WINS, and RIP are but a few of the utilities provided with NT Server to make TCP/IP an easily managed protocol.

- NetBEUI is a fast and efficient workgroup protocol that is not routable.

- NWLink is best when used in coexistence with Netware servers and communication with Netware clients.

- DHCP simplifies the distribution and management of TCP/IP addresses in the enterprise.

- WINS resolves NetBIOS names to IP addresses, reducing NetBIOS names query broadcasts, and allowing NetBIOS name resolution across routers.

For more information on	See
TCP/IP	Microsoft TCP/IP Training
NWLink and NetBEUI	Microsoft Windows NT 3.51 Training Plus Version 4.0 Upgrade Training

Lesson 4: Microsoft Windows NT Server Requirements

Defining the server requirements for a Windows NT Server network is a process that requires statistics, measurements, and experience. Because Windows NT is a versatile server, it has many roles in the enterprise. Each of these roles has its own requirements and preferences. This lesson outlines the basic hardware requirements necessary to support a Windows NT Server.

After this lesson, you will be able to:

- Estimate the requirements for a Windows NT Server in the enterprise.

- Estimate the number of domain controllers needed to support an organization.

- Estimate the size of the domain controllers needed to support an organization.

Estimated lesson time: 30 minutes

Minimum Server Requirements

Before you install Windows NT Server, your computer must meet the minimum Windows NT Server hardware requirements. The minimum hardware requirements for Windows NT Server are essential for properly installing the product, but they do not necessarily provide enough resources to implement an efficient server in a production environment. The hardware requirements are outlined in the table below.

Resource	Requirement
Processor	Intel 486/33 or greater, or Digital Alpha AXP class processor
Intel and RISC computer RAM requirement	16-MB RAM
Free disk space	Intel–125 MB RISC–160 MB (200 MB could be necessary if using 32 KB)

When planning the size of your Windows NT Server, four resources crucially impact the performance of a server. These resources include the amount of memory, size and number of processors, amount of available disk space, and the network. The server can require different resources. When sizing a Windows NT Server, ask yourself the following questions: How much memory is necessary?

How many processors are needed to provide a comfortable level of performance? How much disk space will the server require now and in the future? What type of network connectivity will be required to provide adequate client access? Your decision should be based on current user statistics, trends in resource consumption, and plans for future growth.

Hardware Capability List

Along with the recommendation that you exceed the minimum hardware requirements in most production environments, it is also highly recommended that all the server's hardware components are listed on the *Windows NT Hardware Capability List*. This list, managed by Microsoft, certifies that the different components have passed a series of tests running Windows NT Server. Officially, Microsoft supports only Windows NT Server on components running from this list. The *Windows NT Hardware Capability List* can be obtained from most hardware vendors or at http://www.microsoft.com/ntserver.

Processor

The development of Windows NT Server version 4.0 marked the first time a Windows operating system discontinued its support of the Intel 386 processor. Windows NT Server version 4.0 requires the minimum processor to be a 486/33 on the Intel Platform.

The Digital Alpha AXP processor, the MIPS Rx400 class of computer, and the PREP compliant PowerPC are all supported by Windows NT Server.

Required Memory

Windows NT Server will not install with less than 16 MB of memory. Because Window NT Server supports preemptive multitasking, Virtual DOS Machine, Windows on Windows, Server, and Workstation services, a considerable amount of RAM is consumed. A minimum of 16 MB is required; however, more memory is typically needed for a server to reach an acceptable level of performance.

Free Disk Space

When installing Windows NT Server on an Intel-based computer, a minimum of 125 MB of free disk space is required to run setup; however, most production environments will require significantly more disk space.

Network

If a server is to provide services to clients, it is necessary for the server and clients to communicate. Therefore, networking hardware and services are a minimum requirement of Windows NT Server.

Domain Controllers

Domain controllers are responsible for authenticating user logon information and replicating the directory services database. Because these responsibilities use varying amounts of resources, they require planning.

Directory Services Database

All user, group, and computer accounts are stored in the directory services database. Each domain controller stores a copy of the directory services database locally on a hard disk and loads it into memory for quick and efficient access. Therefore, domain controllers must have enough free disk space and memory to house the directory services database.

Domain Account Types

There are two types of domain accounts: user accounts and group accounts. These accounts are discussed below.

User Accounts

Each domain user requires a domain account to access resources in the domain. You should create a plan before implementing user and group accounts that includes naming conventions for users and groups, group associations, profile configuration, password policies, and logon restrictions.

Group Accounts

There are two types of group accounts: local group accounts and global group accounts. Local group accounts are local to the computer or if created on a domain controller, to all of the domain controller computers as they share the same security database. Global group accounts are contained in the directory services database and are part of the domain and can be used in other domains. Global groups can be members of local groups, but local groups cannot be members of global groups.

There are several built-in local and global groups. Because these groups are, by default, part of the domain, use them if they meet your requirements.

Here is a list of the built-in local groups:

- Account Operators
- Administrators
- Backup Operators

- Guests
- Print Operators
- Replicators
- Server Operators
- Users

Here is a list of the built-in global groups:

- Domain Admins
- Domain Guests
- Domain Users

Computer Accounts

As with user and group accounts, both Windows NT Workstation and Windows NT Server require an account in the domain. This account allows the computers to be administered remotely from any Windows NT Server, Windows NT Workstation, or Windows 95 computer running a Server Manager for domains.

Windows NT Server accounts are usually added to the domain during setup, but an existing Windows NT Server computer can be added to the domain later, provided it was initially configured as a member server. In either case, a Domain Administrator account and password is required for a Windows NT Server computer account to be created and the computer to join the domain.

Database Size Calculation

Once you know the type of accounts you will be creating, the next step is to determine the number of account types your domain will require. Finally, you need to calculate the total disk space used by the directory services account database.

The following table outlines the disk space requirements for each type of account in the directory services database.

Account Type	Disk Space Requirement
User Account	1.0 KB
Computer Account	0.5 KB
Global Group Account	0.5 KB + 12 bytes per member
Local Group Account	0.5 KB + 36 bytes per member

To calculate the amount of space used by group accounts, use the following formula:

Bytes Used by Local Groups = (# of Local Groups X 512) + (# of Members* X 36)

Bytes Used by Global Groups = (# of Global Groups X 512) + (# of Members* X 12)

total number of memberships for the group under consideration.

Take into consideration not only the current number of users, computers, and groups your domain must support, but also the number of accounts you plan to support in the future.

The following table shows some projections and the subsequent database size.

	Users	Computers	Groups	Total SAM*
1 Workstation/User	2000	2000	30	3.12 (MB)
2 Workstations/User	5000	10,000	100	10.4
2 Users/Workstation	10,000	5000	150	13.1
1 Workstation/User	25,000	25,000	200	38.3
1 Workstation/User	25,000	26,000	250	40
1 Workstation/User	40,000	10	11	40

Security Accounts Manager

Note The directory services database should not exceed 40 MB. If the domain has a sufficient number of accounts to increase the database to 40 MB, an additional account domain should be created.

Directory Services Application

Domain controllers run a process called Net Logon. The Net Logon process handles authentication requests from workstations by accepting requests. Once the request has been accepted, the logon information is authenticated with what is stored in the directory services database.

To provide redundancy, local network access, and load balancing, it is possible to create multiple domain controllers each with a Net Logon process that can authenticate user logon requests.

Number of Domain Controllers

As the number of users increases, it is advantageous to create multiple domain controllers in order to add efficiency and to provide redundancy to the authentication process. When a domain spans a wide area network (WAN) connection, you need to create a domain controller on each local area network (LAN) to keep users from crossing the WAN connection to be authenticated. This procedure keeps the WAN connection (and all its components) from being a single point of failure and allows users on each LAN to continue to be authenticated if the WAN connection fails. Therefore, the number of domain controllers depends on the number of users in the domain, the need for redundancy, and the need to provide local directory services.

One domain controller is suggested for every 2000 users. However, 3000 users in one domain could require three domain controllers: two domain controllers are needed to handle 3000 user validation requests, and one domain controller is needed for redundancy. If there were only two domain controllers, and one were to go down, a single domain controller would have to service the authentication requests of 3000 users. By adding a third domain controller for redundancy, there is an added level of fault tolerance.

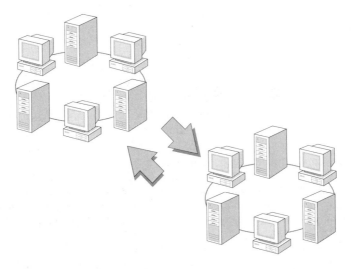

This situation is somewhat different when users are geographically separated. Suppose an organization has 3000 users in a single domain who are geographically separated across five locations (600 users per location) but are connected by a WAN. In this example, 10 domain controllers would be required. Despite only 600 users per location, two domain controllers per location would be required to provide local authentication to users in case one domain controller failed.

When users are not geographically separated, and the number of user accounts dictates the number of domain controllers, the following table can be used as a guideline to determine the number of domain controllers necessary in a single domain.

Number of Users	Number of BDC Servers (no redundancy)
10	1
100	1
500	1
1000	1
2000	1
5000	3
10,000	5
20,000	10
30,000	15

Size of Domain Controllers

The number of user accounts, computer accounts, and group accounts determines the hardware required for the domain controllers. Domain controllers often perform additional tasks that need to be taken into consideration when determining the amount of resources required.

Hardware requirements can also differ depending on the location of a domain controller. A domain controller for 1500 users located in one geographical area needs more resources than a domain controller for 100 users located in several geographical areas.

Because the directory services database is loaded from disk into random access memory (RAM) during the startup of Windows NT Server, it is necessary to have adequate RAM to accommodate the directory services database. Generally, you can calculate the amount of RAM required for an account database as 2.5 times the size of the database. The following table shows some examples of RAM requirements for different database sizes.

Number of Accounts	Directory Services Database Size	Minimum CPU size	Minimum RAM
7500	10 (MB)	486DX/66	32 (MB)
10,000	15	Pentium/133 or RISC	48
15,000	20	Pentium Pro or RISC	64
20,000-30,000	30	Pentium Pro or RISC	96
30,000-40,000	40	Pentium Pro or RISC	128

Comparing Primary and Backup Domain Controllers

Both primary domain controllers (PDCs) and backup domain controllers (BDCs) validate user logon attempts. The PDC controls changes to the directory services database. All changes to the directory services database are made to this copy and replicated to the BDCs. When a PDC, BDC, or remote administrator runs any domain management utility, such as User Manager for Domain, the PDC database is changed. The changes are then replicated down to the BDCs.

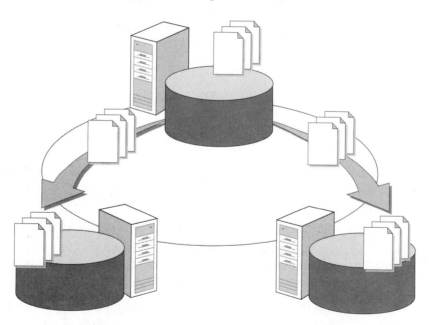

If a PDC fails, it is possible to promote a BDC to the role of PDC. The new PDC's directory services database will then become the master copy of the directory services database, and it will start replicating down to the remaining BDCs.

When the original PDC is repaired and rebooted, it will attempt to reestablish itself as the PDC for that domain. When the original PDC detects the presence of another PDC with the same domain name, the Net Logon service will fail to start. At this point, it is necessary to demote the new PDC back to a BDC, and start the Net Logon service of the original PDC.

Multiple Master Domains

When the number of users in a domain affects the performance of the domain controllers, it is necessary to create multiple master domains. Of the four domain models discussed in Lesson 1, the multiple master domain model is the one recommended for large organizations that have many users and want to centralize user account administration to a limited number of domains.

For example, suppose an organization has the following profile:

- 30,000 users.
- 15,000 users have Windows NT Workstation computers.
- All users have standardized on Pentium/133 with 48-MB RAM.
- The management information system (MIS) department controls all user accounts.

Given this configuration, it can be calculated:

- 30,000 users = 30-MB database consumption (30,000 X 1.0 KB).
- 15,000 computers = 7.5 MB database consumption (15,000 X 0.5 KB).
- Total = 37.5 MB for the directory services database.

Given that the organization's standard server can support a 15 MB database, the company will need at least three master domains.

Calculating the Size of a Directory Services Database

In this exercise, you calculate the size of the directory services database for your organization, Wide World Importers, and the number of master domains required to accommodate users.

Wide World Importers has decided to migrate to Windows NT Server. Design the new directory services structure using the following criteria:

- Corporate MIS wants control of all user accounts.
- 20,000 users will have desktop computers, and approximately 4000 users will have two computers. All computers are running Windows NT Workstation.

- It has been decided that resource control and resource domains will be divided between six organizations in the company.

Wide World Importers has standardized on the following hardware configuration for computers running Windows NT Server:

- A Pentium 133 MHz processor.

- 48 MB of RAM.

- 6 GB of hard disk space.

Based on the above information, answer the following questions:

1. What is the size of the directory database in MB?

2. Based on the hardware used, what is the largest directory database file size?

3. How many master domains should you create?

Location of Controllers

Locating BDCs for each geographical location will provide fast and efficient user logon because the network traffic will travel from the client to the domain controller across the LAN. If the client had to contact a domain controller across the WAN, the time necessary to log on would increase. In addition, there are more possible points of failure when communicating across a WAN than when communicating across a LAN. In large organizations, sometimes only a few clients need to log on to the domain. In this case, it is best to have users log on across the WAN rather than synchronize the directory services database over the WAN. In general, however, the WAN is a single point of failure for users who logon across the WAN.

Directory Services Database Synchronization

When domain controllers are located throughout an organization, they need to be regularly updated with the most recent directory information. This is accomplished by the PDC duplicating its copy of the directory services database to all BDCs in the domain.

The time it takes to synchronize the database will depend on the speed of the network and the size of the database. When synchronization occurs, the PDC announces that a change in the directory services database has taken place. A BDC then calls the PDC and requests the changes.

Designing a Directory Services Structure for Nobell Chem

In this exercise you will evaluate your design for the Nobell Chem Company. Nobell Chem Company is in a single office location and has approximately 100 users. The network will be used for basic file and print sharing and will also have one Windows NT Server running SQL Server. The majority of users will need access to SQL Server. Desktop applications will be installed on the local computers, but data files will be saved on the servers.

The design will take into account:

- Number of users.
- Number of administrative units.
- Number of sites.

Based on the above information, answer the following questions:

1. How many domains will you need to use?

_____

_____

2. How many trusts will need to be configured?

_____

_____

Designing the Directory Services Structure for Miller Textiles

In this exercise, you evaluate your design of the directory services structure for Miller Textiles. Miller Textiles has 10,000 employees who use computers; 8000 are located in four primary sites, the remaining 2000 users work out of the company's 20 branch offices that are located in several major U.S. cities. The company currently has LANs installed in each location, but will be upgrading to Windows NT. Plans are to maintain the four administrative units, but this can change based on your recommendations. Three of the primary sites, which are located in Atlanta, Chicago, and Portland, are separate business units and operate independently. The fourth site is corporate headquarters in Boston. Branch offices have between 25 and 250 users who need access to all four of the primary sites, but users seldom need access to the other branch offices.

The design will take into account:

- Number of users.
- Number of administrative units.
- Number of sites.
- Speed and quality of links connecting sites.
- Available bandwidth on links.
- Expected changes to network.
- Line of business applications.

Additional information you have discovered in your research:

The four primary sites are connected by T1 speed WAN links. All branch offices are connected to the nearest primary site by 56 Kbps lines. Corporate headquarters has decided to centralize all user accounts. Primary sites will continue to maintain their own equipment and the equipment of the branch offices connected to them. For browsing purposes, the four administration groups have decided to implement unique resource domains for branch offices in addition to unique resource domains for the four primary sites. Bandwidth utilization during peak times is currently 60 percent. Network growth for the next 12–18 months is expected to be minimal. In addition to the 20 branch offices, you have discovered that the company has a temporary research location that employs 10 people. The site has one server that connects to Boston by means of dial-on-demand routers. This site is a stand-alone operation requiring connectivity for messaging only and is expected to be closed within six months.

Based on the above information, answer the following questions:

1. How many domains will you need to configure?

   _____

   _____

2. How many master domains will be configured?

   _____

   _____

3. How many resource domains will need to be configured?

   _____

   _____

4. How many PDCs will need to be configured?

_____

_____

5. How many BDCs will need to be configured?

_____

_____

6. To which domain will the branch office sites belong?

_____

_____

7. How many trusts will need to be configured?

_____

_____

Designing the Directory Services Structure for the Terra Firm Company

In this exercise, you evaluate your design of the directory services structure for the Terra Firm Company. Terra Firm employs 60,000 users who located around the world. The corporate headquarters are located in Geneva, Switzerland. North and South American headquarters are located in New York City. The Asia and Australia headquarters are located in Singapore. Each of the regional headquarters will maintain total control of users and equipment within their areas. Users will require access to resources in the other regional headquarters.

The three regional headquarter sites are connected by T1 lines. Each of the three regional headquarters has line of business applications that need to be available to all sites within their areas as well as the other regional headquarters. These line of business applications are all running on Windows NT-based computers that will be configured as servers within the domains.

You will be designing the Windows NT Server Directory Services for the Asia/Australia region. The design for the Asia/Australia region will take into account:

- Logon validation.
- Pass-through authentication.

Additional information you have discovered in your research:

The links between Singapore, Australia, and Malaysia are typically operating at 90 percent capacity. The Asia/Australia region has 10 subsidiaries: Japan, Korea,

China, Taiwan, Thailand, Singapore, Malaysia, Indonesia, Australia, and New Zealand. In addition, Malaysia and Australia have major manufacturing sites to which all regional subsidiaries will need access. Due to import restrictions within some of the subsidiaries, it has been decided to give control of the equipment to each subsidiary and to include a resource domain in each subsidiary. Windows NT Workstation has recently been installed on most of the computers the subsidiaries have purchased. The company has authorized redundant hardware where you can justify it. This region supports 20,000 users: 6,000 are in Singapore; the others are distributed evenly among subsidiaries.

1. How many domains will you need to configure?

_____

_____

2. How many master domains will be configured?

_____

_____

3. How many resource domains will need to be configured?

_____

_____

4. How many PDCs will need to be configured?

_____

_____

5. How many BDCs will need to be configured?

_____

_____

6. To which domain will the branch office sites belong?

_____

_____

7. How many trusts will need to be configured?

_____

_____

Hint: Singapore is considered both headquarters and a subsidiary. Make sure you don't count it twice.

Lesson Summary

The following information summarizes the key points in this lesson:

- Windows NT Server is sized for an organization by evaluating requirements for memory, size and number of processors, disk space, and network connectivity.

- The number of domain controllers needed to support an organization depends on the number of users in the domain, the need for redundancy, and the need to provide local directory services.

- Domain controllers have a minimum memory requirement of 2.5 times the sum of the user accounts (1 KB/user), computer accounts (.5 KB/computer), and group accounts (approximately .5 KB/group) that will exist in the domain.

For more information on	See
Regulating partial synchronization	Windows NT Server 4.0 Network Analysis and Optimization course.
Synchronization parameters	Microsoft Windows NT Resource Kit.
Regini.exe and creating script files for Regini.exe	Resource Kit Tools Help file (Rktools.hlp) of the Microsoft Windows NT Resource Kit.

CHAPTER 2

Installation and Configuration

About This Chapter

This chapter introduces the fundamental concepts essential to understanding the Windows NT Server installation process and investigates the role of NT Server in the enterprise. The browser service, a central component in Windows NT domain functionality, is covered in detail. Finally, the chapter examines the various enterprise clients that Windows NT Server is capable of supporting and the various components associated with each.

Before You Begin

To complete the lessons in this chapter, you must have:

- Completed the setup instructions in "Getting Started" section of "About This Book."
- Familiarity with the installation of Windows NT Server. This topic was covered by the Windows NT Server courseware.
- A firm understanding of the following concepts covered in Chapter 1:
  - Trust and domain architecture.
  - Using administrator tools.
  - Planning reliable and responsive disk systems.
  - Selecting appropriate network protocols.
  - Determining server sizing requirements

Lesson 1: Configuring Server Roles

Windows NT Server can be configured to serve specific roles in the enterprise. Windows NT Server can be configured as a primary domain controller (PDC), backup domain controller (BDC), or a member server configured as a file and print or application server. This lesson discusses the different Windows NT Server 4.0 configurations that are available, and the considerations that you must take into account prior to installing Windows NT software.

After this lesson, you will be able to:

- Identify the three server types.

- Determine necessary server resources for a given function.

- Troubleshoot improperly configured servers.

Estimated lesson time: 20 minutes

PDC

The PDC is the computer that creates the domain. Only one PDC exists per domain. This computer contains the master accounts database for the domain. The PDC also authenticates users and is responsible for synchronizing the database information with the BDCs that belong to its domain. The PDC is also the domain master browser.

The greater the number of accounts, the greater the demand on the PDC. In large organizations you may want to limit the use of the PDC to these functions to improve performance. In order of importance, the resources needed for the PDC are: memory, network subsystem, processor, and disk subsystem.

Memory

Memory is extremely important because the SAM will be loaded into the RAM. This design speeds up the logon process. The recommended minimum RAM is 2.5 times the Security Account Manager (SAM) database size.

Network Subsystem

The network subsystem is nearly as important as the amount of physical RAM. The network interface card (NIC) should be a high performance card capable of handling communications within the network with minimal involvement of the central processing unit (CPU). If the server is connected to multiple network environments, consider multiple NICs to segment the network traffic.

Processor

The processor is one of the most important PDC resources. Pay particular attention to CPU utilization when performing an analysis of a PDC bottleneck. Because the PDC manages the entire domain, it needs the use of a processor more than a traditional member server.

Disk Subsystem

The disk subsystem is the least important resource because the PDC is intended to store only the directory services database and domain policies. Because the account data is loaded into the RAM for authentication, the subsystem does not have to be the fastest and most expensive configuration in your domain.

BDC

The BDC contains a copy of the directory services database which it receives from the PDC. The BDC will keep your domain running in the event the PDC is offline for service or because of failure. The placement of the BDCs in the enterprise environment impacts the time it takes to log on and can minimize the traffic on the wide area network (WAN).

In terms of resources, the BDC requires the same considerations and in the same order of importance as the PDC: memory, network subsystem, processor, and disk subsystem. However, on a BDC, the system overhead is slightly reduced because BDC is not responsible for contacting the PDC when the directory services database is not up-to-date. The BDC responds to the PDC for synchronization only when called by the PDC. It is, however, advantageous to have the BDCs configured with the same level of resources as the PDC in case they have to assume the PDC's responsibility.

Member Server Configured as a File and Print Server

When a server is configured as a file and print server, the resources that have the most significant impact are, in order, memory, processor, and disk subsystem.

Memory

Memory has the greatest potential impact on performance. The more physical RAM that is available, the more Windows NT caches. Any local and network requests for folder and file access will be cached. Installing a server with a minimal amount of memory will yield a small cache, which will decrease the effectiveness of this important performance feature.

Processor

The processor, almost as important to performance as memory, is needed to handle all the I/O requests from the NIC and disk subsystem. Installing bus mastering cards can reduce the Disk I/O load of the processor. These interface cards do much of their own I/O processing and will reduce the number of central processor interrupts, thereby releasing central processor cycles for other tasks. Consider adding additional processors for increased performance. When the server is a print server, the processor will be used extensively for rendering the final spooled data and sending the data to the printing device.

Disk Subsystem

Finally, the disk subsystem should include multiple fast access disk drives and multiple fast disk controllers. Use the RAID 0 (striping with no parity) disk configuration for resources that do not require fault tolerance, and RAID 5 (striping with parity) for disks that do require fault tolerance. Because this server is supplying shared folders (possibly home folders) and network printers, the disk will be heavily accessed for information and spooler functions.

Member Server Configured as an Application Server

Using the member server as an application server shifts resource requirement priorities. In order of importance, these are processor, memory, disk subsystem, and network subsystem.

Processor

The processor is the most significant component. With a true client/server application installed on the server, the processor is needed to handle all I/O requests from the NIC and disk subsystem. This is also true with file and print servers. However, with the application server, the applications run on the server's processor and not on the client that requested the service. This translates to many additional threads competing for processor time. If the processor proves to be a bottleneck, consider, as with the PDC, installing multiple processors. Add additional processors to handle the additional threads.

Memory

System memory is the second most important item on the resource list. The more physical RAM that is available, the more Windows NT caches. Local and network requests for folder and file access are cached. Having ample memory is very important to performance. Once your application server runs out of memory and starts paging to disk, your application performance will drop dramatically.

Disk Subsystem

As with the file and print server, the faster the disk subsystem, the higher the server's performance. On an application server, some sort of data access is usually the focus of the application. Fast access to this data will help provide sufficient application performance.

Network Subsystem

The application server's network subsystem probably won't have the same network session demand as the a file and print server's. This is because most of the client/server sessions are query-type requests, and the data is relatively small. Therefore, while it is still important to monitor the network subsystem for potential bottlenecks, it is usually a lower priority on an application server.

Resource Requirements

In this exercise you will answer some questions about the roles a Windows NT Server plays in the enterprise.

1. What is the minimum amount of RAM recommended for a PDC?
   (Hint: it has to do the size of the SAM.)

   _____

   _____

2. What resource has the greatest impact on a file and print server's system performance?

   _____

   _____

3. What resource has the greatest impact on an application server's system performance?

   _____

   _____

Lesson Summary

The following information summarizes the key points in this lesson:

- Windows NT Server can be configured as a PDC, a BDC, or a member server that can be configured for a file and print or application server environment.

- Each server role (such as the domain controller, file and print server, or an application server) has different resource requirements. The processor, memory subsystem, network subsystem, and disk subsystem can become bottlenecks if system resources are not considered during system configuration.

- The important areas to examine when tuning a server for optimal performance are memory, processor, disk subsystem, and network subsystem.

Lesson 2: Browsing in the Enterprise

Users on a Windows NT network often need to know what domains and computers are accessible from their local computer. Viewing all the available network resources is called browsing. The Windows NT browser service maintains a list (called the browse list) of all available domains and servers. The browse list can be viewed using Windows NT Explorer and is provided by a browser in the local computer's domain. This lesson reviews the basic browser roles and processes. The impact of browser failures and the integration of the browser service in a Transmission Control Protocol/Internet Protocol (TCP/IP) wide area network (WAN) environment is also examined.

After this lesson, you will be able to:

- Identify and configure Windows NT computers to perform various roles in the browser process.
- Explain the role of various categories of browser service traffic.
- Explain the process the browser service uses to overcome browser computer failures.
- Describe the special issues involved with browsing across WANs using TCP/IP.

Estimated lesson time: 45 minutes

Browser Roles

Windows NT assigns browser roles to computers on the network. The computers work together to provide a centralized list of shared resources, eliminating the need for all machines to maintain their own lists. This reduces the central processing unit (CPU) time and the network traffic needed to build and maintain the list. The following table describes the roles Windows NT clients can perform in a Microsoft networking environment.

Browser Role	Description
Domain master browser	Collects and maintains the master list of available network servers, as well as the names of other domains and workgroups.
	Distributes this list to the master browser of each subnet in the Windows NT domain.
	The PDC serves this role.
Master browser	Collects and maintains the list of available network servers in its workgroup or subnet.
	Shares this information with the domain master browser and incorporates information about other workgroups, domains, and subnets received from the master browser into its list of available resources.
	Distributes a complete list of available resources (the browse list) to the backup browsers.
	Only one per workgroup or subnet of a domain.
Backup browser	Receives a copy of the browse list from the master browser.
	Distributes the list to browser clients upon request.
Potential browser	Capable of becoming a backup browser if instructed by the master browser.
	Does not maintain a browse list.
Non-browser	Configured so that it will not become a browser.
	Does not maintain a browse list.

Browser Configuration

When you start a computer running Windows NT Workstation or Windows NT Server, the browser service looks in the registry to determine whether or not a computer will become a browser. This parameter is found under:

\HKEY_LOCAL_MACHINE\System\CurrentControlSet\Services\Browser
\Parameters**MaintainServerList**

Note The term server refers to any computer that can provide resources to the rest of the network. If a computer running Windows NT Workstation can share file or print resources with other computers on the network, it is considered a server in the context of the browser system. The computer does not have to be actively sharing resources to be considered a server.

Use Registry Editor to configure the following entries.

Value Entry	Configures the Computer as Follows
NO	This computer will never participate as a browser. It is a non-browser.
YES	This computer will become a browser. Upon startup, this computer attempts to contact the master browser to get a current browse list. If the master browser cannot be found, the computer will force a browser election. This computer will either be elected master browser or become a backup browser. **Yes** is the default value on a computer running Windows NT Server.
AUTO	This computer, referred to as a potential browser, may or may not become a browser, depending on the number of currently active browsers. The master browser notifies this computer whether or not it will become a backup browser. **Auto** is the default value for computers running Windows NT Workstation.

On any computer with an entry of **Yes** or **Auto** for the **MaintainServerList** parameter, Windows NT Setup configures the browser service to start automatically when the computer starts.

Another parameter in the registry helps to determine which servers become master browsers and backup browsers. The registry path for this parameter is:

\HKEY_LOCAL_MACHINE\System\CurrentControlSet\Services\Browser\
Parameters**IsDomainMaster**

Setting the **IsDomainMaster** parameter entry to **True** or **Yes** on a computer makes that computer a preferred master browser. A preferred master browser has priority over other computers in master browser elections. Whenever a preferred master browser starts, it forces a browser election.

Any computer running Windows NT Workstation or Windows NT Server can be configured as a preferred master browser. When the browser service is started on the preferred master browser computer, the browser service forces an election. Preferred master browsers are given priority in elections, which means that if no other condition prevents it, the preferred master browser will always win the election. This gives an administrator the ability to configure a specific computer as the master browser.

Browser Traffic

The browser service uses registry information and various categories of traffic to manage computer browser role assignments and provide browse lists. This traffic includes browser elections, announcements, and requests.

Browser Elections

A browser election occurs when a Windows NT domain controller system starts, a preferred master browser comes online, or a computer cannot locate a master browser. A computer initiates an election by sending a special datagram called an election datagram. The datagram includes election criteria that all browsers will compare against their own. If the browser has better election criteria than the sender of the election datagram, the browser will issue its own election datagram and enter what is called an election-in-progress state. If the browser does not have better election criteria than the sender of the election datagram, the browser attempts to determine which system is the new master browser.

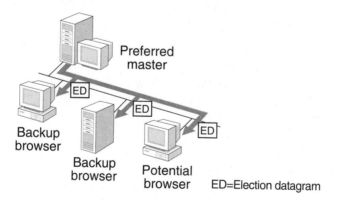

The election criteria for a browser are based on the browser's current role in the domain and its current state using a hierarchy. The following criteria are compared consecutively until one computer's state or value is greater—at which point it wins the election:

Criterion	Advantage To
"Stronger" operating system type	NT Server, then Workstation, then Windows 95, finally Windows for Workgroups.
Greater election version	The greater value: election version is a value that identifies the version of the browser election protocol. (This is not related to the operating system version.)
Is PDC?	Yes
Is WINS system?	Yes
Is preferred master?	Yes
Running as a master browser	Longer period
MaintainServerList setting?	Yes
Running as a backup browser	Longer period
Computer name	Earlier alphabetical name (A before Z)

When a browser receives an election datagram indicating that it wins the election, the browser enters the running election state. While in this state, the browser sends out an election request.

The browser sends up to four election datagrams. If no other browser responds with an election criteria datagram that would win the election, the computer is promoted to master browser. If the browser receives an election datagram indicating that another computer will win the election, and the computer is currently the master browser, the computer will demote itself from master browser and become a backup browser.

Browser Announcements

A browser announcement is another category of browser traffic that serves several purposes. When a network computer running Windows for Workgroups, Windows 95, Windows NT Workstation, or Windows NT Server starts, it sends an announcement to the browser service that it is an available resource. Master browsers receive this announcement and add the new resource to their browse lists. Master browsers then return a list of backup browsers. Additionally, if the new resource's **MaintainServerList** parameter is set to **Auto**, the master browser is responsible for telling the system whether or not to become a backup browser.

When a computer becomes the master browser by winning an election and the browse list is empty, it sends a second type of announcement, a Request-Announcement. This forces all systems to announce. All computers that receive this datagram must answer randomly within 30 seconds.

Announcements are also sent by non-browsers, potential browsers, and backup browsers. These announcements are sent on a periodic basis starting at one minute, then increasing to 2, 4, 8, and finally 12 minutes. From this point on, these announcements are repeated at 12-minute intervals and serve to keep their owners on the master browser's browse list. If the master browser fails to receive an announcement for three periods, it removes the resource from the browse list.

Backup browsers also call the master browser every 15 minutes to obtain updated network-resource browse lists and lists of workgroups and domains. The backup browser caches these lists and returns the browse list to any client that sends out a browse request. If the backup browser cannot find the master browser, it will force an election.

Because it can take up to 15 minutes for a backup browser to request an updated browse list, it is possible that a computer will appear in the browse list for as long as 51 minutes after it is no longer an available resource on the network. The time period consists of 36 minutes, which is three 12-minute announcement cycles plus the 15 minutes for the backup browser to receive an updated list.

Browse Requests

Browse requests are the third major category of browser traffic. Since the purpose of the browser service is to make a list of network resources available to users, requests are a very important element of the process. A client computer must first know which computer to contact to request a copy of the list. To get this information, the client sends a request to the master browser, which it discovered when it last announced itself on the network.

Note If the master browser for the workgroup or domain being queried cannot be found after three attempts, the client will force the election of a new master browser in the domain. The client returns an ERROR_BAD_NETPATH message to the application, indicating that the master browser could not be found.

The master browser receives and processes this request and returns a list of backup browsers active within the workgroup or domain being queried. The client selects the names of three backup browsers from the list and stores these names for future use.

After discovering the backup browsers, the client randomly selects one of the three backup browsers and requests a list of available network resources. This request is sent when **net view** is entered at the command prompt or when the **Map Network Drive** dialog box lists the network resources.

Monitoring Browsers

Browsers within a workgroup or domain can be monitored with two utilities included in the *Microsoft Windows NT Server Resource Kit*. Browmon.exe is a graphical utility that can be used to view browsers—both the master and backups—for selected domains. It lists the browser servers for each protocol in use by computers in the domain. Browstat.exe is a command-line utility that can be used to view the browser servers—both the master and backups—in the specified workgroup or domain. Browstat.exe has some capabilities that Browmon.exe does not have, such as the ability to force an election and the ability to force a master browser to stop so that an election occurs.

Browser Shutdown or Failure

If a backup browser shuts down properly, it sends an announcement to the master browser that it is shutting down. The backup browser does this by sending an announcement that does not include the browser service in the list of running services.

If a master browser shuts down gracefully, it sends a ForceElection datagram so that a new master browser can be chosen.

If a computer does not shut down properly or if it fails for any reason, it must be removed from the browse list. The Browser service handles browser failures.

Non-Browser Failure

When a non-browser fails, it stops announcing itself. The configured announcement period is between 1 and 12 minutes. If the non-browser has not announced itself after three announcement periods, the master browser removes the computer from the browse list. Therefore, it can take up to 51 minutes before all browsers know of a non-browser's failure. This figure includes up to 36 minutes for the master browser to detect the failure, and 15 minutes for all of the backup browsers to retrieve the updated list from the master browser.

Backup-Browser Failure

As with a non-browser failure, when a backup browser fails, it may not be re-moved from the master-browse list for up to 51 minutes. If a browse list cannot be obtained from the missing backup browser, the client selects another backup browser from its cached list of three backups. If all a client's known backup browsers fail, the client attempts to get a new list of backup browsers from the master browser. If the client is unable to contact the master browser, the client forces an election.

Master-Browser Failure

When a master browser fails, a backup browser detects the failure within 15 min-utes and forces an election of a new master browser.

If a client performs its browse request after a master browser fails but before a backup browser detects the failure, the client forces an election. If a master browser fails and there are no backup browsers, browsing in the workgroup or domain will not function correctly.

During the gap between the master browser's failure and the election of a new master browser, the workgroup or domain can disappear from the lists that are visible to computers in other workgroups and domains.

Domain Master-Browser Failure

If the domain master browser fails, the master browser for each network segment provides a browse list, containing only the servers in the local network segment. All servers that are not on the local network segment will eventually be removed from the browse list. Users will still be able to connect to servers on the other network segments if they know the name of the servers.

Because a domain master browser is also a primary domain controller (PDC), an administrator can correct the failure by promoting a backup domain controller (BDC) to PDC. A BDC can perform most PDC network tasks, such as validating logon requests, but does not promote itself to PDC and does not become domain master browser in the event of a PDC failure.

Browsing Across a WAN

When using domains that are split across routers, each TCP/IP network segment functions as an independent browsing entity with its own master browser and backup browsers. Therefore, browser elections occur within each network segment.

Domain master browsers are responsible for spanning the network segments to collect computer-name information, in order to maintain a domain-wide browse list of available resources. The domain master browser and cooperating master browsers on each WAN segment provide browsing of domains that exist across multiple TCP/IP network segments. The domain master browser is the PDC of a domain. The master-browser computers on the subnets can be running Windows NT Server, Windows NT Workstation, Windows for Workgroups version 3.11b, or Windows 95.

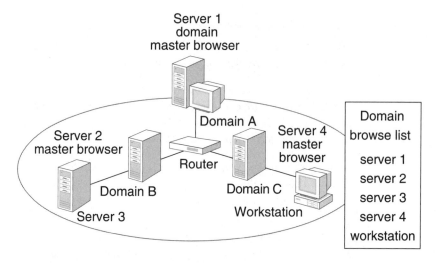

When a domain spans multiple network segments, the master browser for each network segment uses a directed datagram called a MasterBrowserAnnouncement datagram to announce itself to the domain master browser. The MasterBrowser-Announcement datagram notifies the domain master browser that the sending computer is a master browser in the same domain and that the domain master browser needs to obtain a copy of the master browser's browse list. When the domain master browser receives a MasterBrowserAnnouncement datagram, it sends a request to the network segment's master browser, which announced itself in order to collect a list of the network segment's servers.

The domain master browser then merges its own server list with the server list from the master browser that issued the announcement. This process is done every 15 minutes and guarantees that the domain master browser has a complete browse list of all the servers in the domain. When a client issues a browse request to a backup browser, the backup browser returns a list of all the servers in the domain, regardless of the network segment on which they are located.

Workgroups using Windows NT or Windows for Workgroups cannot span multiple network segments. Any workgroup of either kind that does span network segments will function as two separate workgroups with the same name.

Browse Service Across a WAN with TCP/IP

Currently, browser service communication relies almost entirely on broadcasts. In a WAN environment, such as TCP/IP, where domains are separated by routers, special broadcast problems can arise because broadcasts, by default, do not pass through routers. There are two issues to consider.

- How browsers separated by a router perform browser functions.

- How local clients browse remote domains that are not on their local network segment.

The following topics discuss three methods that can be used to set up WAN browsing with TCP/IP. They are presented in order of preference.

The Windows Internet Name Service (WINS)

The WINS resolves NetBIOS names to Internet Protocol (IP) addresses so that datagrams can be sent to the targeted computer. Implementing WINS eliminates the need to configure the LMHOSTS file or to enable User Datagram Protocol (UDP) port 137. Using WINS requires the following configuration.

- WINS is configured on a computer running Windows NT Server 3.5 or later.

- Clients are WINS-enabled.

- WINS clients can be configured with Windows NT 3.5 or later, Windows 95, Windows for Workgroups 3.11b running TCP/IP-32, LAN Manager 2.2c for MS-DOS, or Microsoft Network Client 3.0 for MS-DOS. The latter two are provided on the compact discs for versions 3.5 or later of Windows NT Server.

It is usually recommended that you implement WINS for name resolution and browsing support. As an alternative, it is possible to have full domain browsing by using only LMHOSTS files on all computers, but this limits browsing to the local domain. Non-WINS clients still need the LMHOSTS file to browse a WAN, even if WINS has been implemented in the domain.

Note A client will participate in domain browsing only when that client is using a workgroup name that is equivalent to the domain name (workgroup=domain). In the case of Windows NT computers, the client can also join the domain to gain this functionality, instead of participating in a workgroup.

The LMHOSTS File

NetBIOS name resolution is typically performed through broadcasts, which will resolve names only on the local network segment. To resolve names of computers located on another network segment, the LMHOSTS file (located under \<*winnt_root*>\System32\drivers\etc) must be configured. The LMHOSTS file must contain a NetBIOS name-to-IP address mapping for all computers that are not on the local network segment.

To implement communication between network segments and the domain master browser, the administrator must configure the LMHOSTS file with the NetBIOS names and IP addresses of all browsers. To ensure that the master browser for each network segment can access the domain's PDC, the PDC for each domain must exist in the LMHOSTS file on each master browser and have the #DOM tag.

The LMHOSTS file on each network segment's master browser should contain the following information.

- IP address and NetBIOS name of the domain master browser.

- The domain name, preceded by the tags #PRE and #DOM, as in the following example.

  130.20.7.80 <*Browser_name*> #PRE #DOM:<*domain_name*>

To guarantee that the PDC can request the local browse list from the network segment's master browser, TCP/IP and all other WAN transports must cache the client's IP address.

UDP Port 137 (NetBIOS Name Service Broadcasts)

Not all WANs will have problems browsing. Some routers can be configured to forward specific types of broadcasts and filter out others.

All NetBIOS over TCP/IP (NetBT) broadcasts are sent to the UDP port 137, which is defined as the NetBT Name Service. This usage is defined by Request for Comment (RFC) 1001 and 1002. Routers normally filter out these frames because they are sent to the hardware and subnet broadcast addresses. However, some routers allow all frames sent to this particular UDP port—which is used only by NetBT—to be forwarded. As a result, the browser looks as if it is on one, big, network segment. All domains and computers within the network segments are seen by all computers, including Windows for Workgroups computers.

Browsing the Network

In this exercise you will answer questions on browsing services and the roles Windows client can play on the network.

1. What are the five browser roles a Windows client can perform?

   _____

   _____

2. Is it possible for a Windows for Workgroups client to be the master browser?

   _____

   _____

3. When a Windows NT client starts, and it's configured as the preferred master browser, what will it initiate?

   _____

   _____

4. Who will win an election between a preferred master browser and a PDC?

   _____

   _____

5. How often do backup browsers communicate with the master browser?

   _____

   _____

6. If a computer is turned off abruptly, and not shut down properly, how long will that computer appear in the browser list?

   _____

   _____

7. In a single domain environment that is spread across multiple segments, how many domain master browsers are there? How many master browsers?

   _____

   _____

Lesson Summary

The following information summarizes the key points in this lesson:

- The computer browser service maintains a centralized list of available network resources with a combination of master browsers, backup browsers, and potential browsers. Computer roles are configured with the registry entries **MaintainServerList** and **IsDomainMasterBrowser** located in \HKEY_LOCAL_MACHINE\System\CurrentControlSet\Services\Browser \Parameters\

- Browser traffic includes announcements, which "announce" the presence of servers on the network; elections, which identify master browsers on workgroups, subnetworks, or domains; and requests, wherein clients locate other servers on the network.

- The browser service removes non-browsers and backup browsers from the browse list after they fail to announce themselves for three consecutive announcement periods. A master browser failure will be detected by a backup browser within 15 minutes, at which time the backup browser forces a new election. Failure of a domain master browser will cause the browse lists to remove all resources not within the local network segment. Promotion of a BDC will restore the browse service.

- Currently, browser service communication relies almost entirely on broadcasts which, by default, do not pass through routers. The preferred way to overcome this limitation is to configure a WINS server and establish WINS-enabled clients.

For more information on	See
Browsing in the enterprise	Chapter 3, "Windows NT Browser Service," *NT Server 4.0 Networking Guide*, in the *Microsoft Windows NT Server Resource Kit*

Lesson 3: Client Connectivity

In order to connect to a computer running Windows NT Server, the appropriate client software and transport protocols must be installed and configured on the client computer. In addition, the appropriate licensing for the servers and client computers must be obtained to ensure compliance with the Microsoft licensing legal requirements. This lesson explains how to use the client software included with Windows NT Server and describes the licensing options available for connecting client computers.

After this lesson, you will be able to:

- Identify the clients included with Windows NT Server.

- Explain how to properly configure protocols to communicate with Windows NT Server.

- Describe the client licensing options available with Windows NT Server.

- Use the Network Client Administrator to configure client workstations.

Estimated lesson time: 20 minutes

Windows NT Server Licensing

With the BackOffice licensing model, Windows NT Servers and client computers are licensed separately. You purchase only the licenses required to accommodate your company's networking environment. A server license is required for each server, and a Client Access License (CAL) is required for each client computer that accesses a server. Microsoft offers two licensing modes: Per Server licensing and Per Seat licensing.

Per Server Licensing

In Per Server licensing, CALs are assigned to the server. The number of CALs determines the number of simultaneous connections that can be made to that server.

When you choose the Per Server licensing mode, you must enter the number of CALs purchased for that server. There must be at least as many CALs purchased for the server as the maximum number of client computers that connect simultaneously to the server. For example, if the maximum number of clients that simultaneously connect to the server is 20, then you must have 20 CALs.

The Per Server licensing mode can be the more economical choice when client computers:

- Ordinarily connect to only one occasional-use or special-purpose server.

- Do not all need to connect to the server at the same time.

Per Seat Licensing

In Per Seat licensing, a CAL is purchased for each client computer. With a Per Seat license, a client can access network resources such as file, print, and communications on any computer running Windows NT Server in the network, and can log on to multiple servers simultaneously.

The Per Seat licensing mode can be the more economical choice when client computers:

- Connect to multiple servers simultaneously.

- Use resources on different servers occasionally.

Licensing Administration

Tracking licenses manually on local computers within a small domain or across an entire organization with multiple domains can be time consuming and expensive.

Windows NT 4.0 includes two administrative tools that help reduce these costs and the administrative overhead of license tracking:

- Licensing program in Control Panel.

- License Manager program on the Administrative Tools (Common) menu.

These tools enable you to automatically replicate licensing data from all of the primary domain controllers (PDCs) in the organization to a centralized database on a specified master server, making it easier for you to comply with legal requirements.

Client Connectivity

For a computer to access another computer running Windows NT, you must install and configure client software on that computer. On computers running Windows NT Server, Windows NT Workstation, or Windows 95, the client software is automatically installed during the installation of the operating system. If you need to set up computers that are running some other operating system than Windows NT or Windows 95, Microsoft provides networking client software on the Windows NT Server 4.0 compact disc. The client software provided by Windows NT Server is located in the Clients folder that contains subfolders, including the following software:

- Microsoft Network Client 3.0 for MS-DOS and Windows. Contained in the Msclient folder.

- Microsoft LAN Manager 2.2c Client. Contained in the Lanman folder.

- Microsoft LAN Manager 2.2c Client for OS/2. Contained in the Lanman.os2 folder.

- Windows 95 operating system. Contained in the Win95 folder. Includes all operating system files required to install Windows 95.

Note Windows NT Server 4.0 also supports Windows for Workgroups as a client, but does not include the Windows for Workgroups software. Because the version of Transmission Control Protocol/Internet Protocol (TCP/IP) included with Windows for Workgroups does not support Dynamic Host Configuration Protocol (DHCP) and Windows Internet Name Service (WINS), Windows NT Server does include an add-on product, Microsoft TCP/IP-32 for Windows for Workgroups 3.11, which provides support for DHCP and WINS.

Supported Protocols

The clients supported by Windows NT Server allow connectivity by using a choice of two or more network protocols. The following is a list of network protocols supported by each of the client platforms.

Microsoft Network Client 3.0 supports the following protocols:

- NetBEUI.

- Internetwork Packet Exchange (IPX) Compatible Transport.

- TCP/IP. The TCP/IP protocol included with this client software supports DHCP; it does not support either Domain Name System (DNS) or WINS name resolution.

- Data Link Control (DLC).

LAN Manager 2.2c for MS-DOS supports the following protocols:

- NetBEUI.

- TCP/IP. The TCP/IP protocol included with this client software supports DHCP; it does not support either DNS or WINS name resolution.

- Microsoft DLC.

LAN Manager 2.2c for OS/2 supports the following protocols:

- NetBEUI.

- TCP/IP. The TCP/IP protocol included with this client software does not support either DHCP or WINS.

Windows 95 supports the following protocols:

- NetBEUI.

- IPX Compatible Transport.

- TCP/IP. The TCP/IP protocol included with this client software supports DHCP, WINS, and DNS name resolution.

Note Some network protocols, such as NetBEUI, are not routeable across subnetworks. NetBEUI should not be selected as a network protocol in an enterprise environment consisting of more than one subnetwork, for this reason.

Network Client Administrator

The Network Client Administrator is located in the Administrative Tools (Common) menu on computers running Windows NT Server. The Network Client Administrator is used to:

- Install network client software by creating a network installation startup disk or an installation disk set.

- Share the installation files contained on the Windows NT Server 4.0 compact disc.

- Copy the folders and files contained on the Windows NT Server 4.0 compact disc to a network server and share them. Creating a network share is the recommended method for installing the client software.

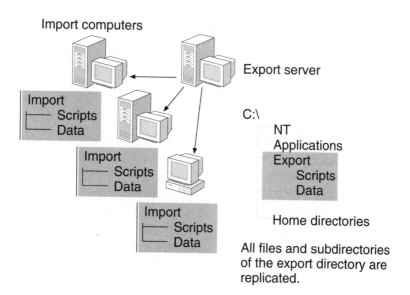

Import computers

Export server

Import
├── Scripts
└── Data

Import
├── Scripts
└── Data

Import
├── Scripts
└── Data

C:\
├── NT
├── Applications
└── Export
    ├── Scripts
    └── Data

Home directories

All files and subdirectories
of the export directory are
replicated.

The following table describes each option in the Network Client Administrator dialog box.

Option	Use This Option To
Make Network Installation Startup Disk	Create an MS-DOS network installation startup disk that can be used to automatically connect to a server and install Windows 95 or Microsoft Network Client 3.0 for MS-DOS and Windows.
Make Installation Disk Set	Create an installation disk set for Microsoft Network Client 3.0 for MS-DOS and Windows, LAN Manager 2.2c for MS-DOS, LAN Manager 2.2c for OS/2, Remote Access v1.1a for MS-DOS, or TCP/IP 32 for Windows for Workgroups 3.11.
Copy Client-Based Network Administration Tools	Install client-based Windows NT administration tools on Windows NT Workstation or Microsoft Windows 95 clients to enable administration from those clients.
View Remoteboot Client Information	View Remoteboot client information. Remoteboot is a Windows NT service that can be used to start MS-DOS, Windows 3.x, and Windows 95-based computers over the network. The Remoteboot service is installed through the Network program in Control Panel.

Services for Macintosh

Windows NT Server includes Services for Macintosh. These services give you the ability to manage a Windows NT network environment that includes computers using an AppleTalk internetwork. Services for Macintosh also enables computers running Windows NT Server 4.0 to provide file and print services for computers using an AppleTalk internetwork. In addition, once Services for Macintosh are enabled, it is possible to connect networks with Macintosh clients to create an AppleTalk internetwork.

Setting up Services for Macintosh requires a computer running Windows NT Server, with 2 MB of disk space available, and an NT file system (NTFS) partition, which is required for Macintosh-accessible volumes. Client computers must have the Macintosh operating system 6.0.7 or later, and AppleShare (the Apple networking software for the Macintosh). This includes most Macintosh computers except for the Macintosh XL and Macintosh 128K models.

Services for Macintosh can be installed during the installation of Windows NT Server, or after installation, using the **Services** tab in the Network program located in Control Panel.

After Services for Macintosh is installed, a **MacFile** menu is added to Server Manager. You use the **MacFile** menu to create Macintosh-accessible volumes.

Client Services for Macintosh

In this procedure, you install Services for Macintosh on Server1.

➤ **To install Services for Macintosh**

1. Start Server1, and then log on as Administrator.

2. Double-click the **Network** icon in Control Panel.

3. Click the **Services** tab, and then click **Add**.

4. Click **Services for Macintosh**, and then click **OK**.

   A Windows NT Setup dialog box appears.

5. Type the path to your NT Server CD, and then click **Continue**.

6. If you do not have an NTFS partition, a **Setup Message** dialog box appears stating that Service for Macintosh requires an NTFS partition, and that you can create one after you install Services for Macintosh. If this message appears, click **OK**.

7. The **Network** dialog box reappears. Notice that Services for Macintosh is now included in the list of Network Services.

8. Click **Close**.

9. A **Microsoft AppleTalk Protocol Properties** dialog box appears. This is where you would indicate the Zone.

10. Click **OK**.

11. A **Network Settings Change** dialog box appears stating that you must shut down and restart your computer, and prompting you to restart your computer now.

12. Click **Yes**.

Lesson Summary

The following information summarizes the key points of this lesson:

- Microsoft offers two licensing modes: Per Server licensing and Per Seat licensing. A server license is required for each server, and a CAL is required for each client computer that accesses a server.

- Windows NT Server 4.0 includes the Network Client 3.0 for MS-DOS and Windows, Microsoft LAN Manager 2.2c Client, the Microsoft LAN Manager 2.2c Client for OS/2, and the Windows 95 operating system client software.

- Client networking software must be configured with the same protocols as the Windows NT Server in order to properly communicate.

- Windows NT Server 4.0 includes the Network Client Administrator, a tool that you can use to install client software.

- Windows NT Server 4.0 includes Services for Macintosh, which allows Microsoft clients and Apple Macintosh clients to share file, print, administrative, and other network resources.

CHAPTER 3

Managing Enterprise Resources

About This Chapter

This chapter discusses managing resources in a multiple domain environment. The chapter lessons provide explanations of how users, groups, policies, and profiles behave among multiple domains, how domains interact with one another, and how domains and domain resources can be managed remotely.

Before You Begin

To complete the lessons in this chapter, you must have:

- An understanding of Windows NT Server Directory Services.
- A familiarity with Windows NT Server administration tools.

Lesson 1: User and Group Accounts

User and group accounts allow users to participate in a domain and to access its resources. Rights and permissions granted to user and group accounts provide the appropriate amount of freedom and restrictions that an organization's various resources require. Managing these accounts involves careful planning, but the procedures for administering the accounts are simple and straightforward. This lesson examines the management of domain user and group accounts.

After this lesson, you will be able to:

- Manage user and group accounts in an enterprise environment.
- Decide when to use global groups.
- Decide when to use local groups.

Estimated lesson time: 20 minutes

User Accounts

Each person who regularly uses the network and participates in a domain must have a user account in a domain on the network. User accounts contain information such as the user's name, password, and various optional entries that determine when and how the user logs on and how his or her desktop settings are stored. From the client, the user will then need to be authenticated by a domain controller to be associated with that user account.

Default User Accounts

The Administrator account and the Guest account are two built-in user accounts created automatically when Windows NT Server is installed.

Built-in Administrator Account

The built-in Administrator account is configured when you first set up a new domain or member server. Use this account before you create any other accounts. The Administrator account is a member of the Administrators local group on a domain controller or member server. The Administrator account can never be deleted, disabled, or removed from the Administrators local group, ensuring that you never lock yourself out of the computer by deleting or disabling all the administrative accounts. This feature sets the Administrator account apart from other members of the Administrators local group.

The built-in Administrator account gives a user automatic rights to perform domain management tasks on a domain controller or member server that resides within that domain or a trusting domain. The password can be changed but it does not expire. After the primary domain controller (PDC) is set up, the built-in Administrator account can be renamed, but it can never be deleted or disabled.

Built-in Guest Account

The built-in Guest account is used by people who do not have a computer or domain account, or an account in any of the domains trusted by the computer's domain. A user whose account is disabled (but not deleted) can also use the Guest account. The Guest account does not require a password and can be used for two types of guest logons: local guest logons and network guest logons. You can configure each domain and computer to allow both types of guest logons, allow only one type of guest logon, or allow neither type. The Guest account is disabled by default when Windows NT Server is installed, but you can enable it again.

As in any user account, you can set rights and permissions for the Guest account. By default, the Guest account is a member of the built-in Guests group, which allows a user to only log on locally to a workstation or member server. Other rights, as well as any permissions, must be granted to the Guests local group by an administrator or an account operator.

Guests have no predefined rights on a domain controller.

A local guest logon takes effect when a user logs on interactively at a computer running Windows NT Workstation or at a member server running Windows NT Server that specifies Guest as the user name in the Logon Information dialog box.

A network guest logon takes effect at a computer that uses the Guest account when a user has logged on interactively to a domain account and tries to connect to the computer that uses the Guest account with:

- A computer running Windows NT Workstation in either a workgroup or a domain.
- A member server.
- A domain controller.
- A LAN Manager 2.x client computer.

A network guest logon is approved only if the Guest account of the destination computer is enabled and has no password set. The guest user then has all rights, permissions, and group memberships on the computer that are granted to the Guest account even though the guest user has not specified Guest as his or her user name.

Group Accounts

Local groups and global groups are two types of groups that can be maintained in a Windows NT Server domain.

Global Groups

A global group contains a number of user accounts from one domain that are grouped together under one group account name. A global group can contain only user accounts from the domain where the global group is created. Once a global group is created, it can be granted permissions and rights in its own domain, on workstations or member servers, or in trusting domains. However, it is best to group domain users in global groups as appropriate. When assigning permissions to a resource, make global groups a member of a local group that has permissions on the resource. This way, you can manage group membership on the global level and not individually at the local level.

Global groups can be added to local groups in the same domain, in domains that trust that domain, to member servers, or computers running Windows NT Workstation in the same or a trusting domain. Global groups contain domain user accounts only.

The "global" in "global groups" indicates that the group is available to receive rights and permissions in multiple (global) domains. A global group can contain only user accounts; it cannot contain local groups or other global groups.

Built-in Global Groups

On a domain's PDCs and backup domain controllers (BDCs), three global groups are built-in: Domain Admins, Domain Users, and Domain Guests. None of these groups can be deleted.

Domain Admins

The Domain Admins global group is initially a member of the Administrators local group for the domain and a member of the Administrators local group for every computer in the domain running Windows NT Workstation or Windows NT Server.

The built-in Administrator user account is a member of the Domain Admins global group. It is also a member of the Administrators local group and cannot be removed.

Because of these memberships, a user logged on as an administrator can administer the domain, the PDCs and BDCs, and all other computers running Windows NT Workstation and Windows NT Server in the domain.

To provide administrative-level abilities to a new account, add the account to the Domain Admins global group. Members of this group can administer the domain, the servers and workstations of the domain, and a trusting domain that has added the Domain Admins global group from this domain to the Administrators local group in the trusting domain.

Domain Users

The Domain Users global group initially contains the domain's built-in Administrator account. By default, all new accounts created thereafter in the domain are added to the Domain Users group, unless you specifically remove them.

The Domain Users global group is, by default, a member of the Users local group for the domain and of the Users local group for every computer in the domain running Windows NT Workstation or member servers running Windows NT Server. Domain Users is the default primary group for each user.

Because of these memberships, users of the domain have basic user access to the computers in the domain running Windows NT Workstation and Windows NT Server as member servers. You can prevent Domain Users from being granted this access on a particular workstation or on a server that is not a domain controller by removing the Domain Users global group from that computer's Users group.

Domain Guests

The Domain Guests global group initially contains the domain's built-in Guest user account. If you add user accounts that are intended to have more limited rights and permissions than typical domain user accounts, you might want to add those accounts to the Domain Guests group and remove them from the Domain Users group.

Local Groups

A local group contains user and global group accounts from one or more domains grouped together under one group account name, specific to the local computer or if on a domain controller, specific to all the domain controllers as they share a security database. Users and global groups from outside the local domain can be added to the local group only if they belong to a trusted domain. Local groups make it possible to quickly assign rights and permissions for the resources on one domain (that is, the local domain) to users and groups from that domain and other domains that trust it.

Local groups also exist on member servers and computers running Windows NT Workstation and can contain user accounts and global groups. Being a member of one of the built-in local groups of a domain gives a user rights and abilities to perform various tasks on the domain controllers in the domain. Similarly, being a member of a built-in local group on a member server or workstation gives the user rights and abilities on that computer.

You can add a user to more than one built-in group. For example, a user in both the Print Operators and Backup Operators groups has all the rights granted to print operators and all the rights granted to backup operators.

However, not all built-in local groups exist on both Windows NT Server domain controllers and on individual Windows NT computers. The following table shows which built-in local groups exist on domain controllers and on individual computers.

Windows NT Server Domain Controllers	Windows NT Member Servers
Administrators	Administrators
Backup Operators	Backup Operators
Server Operators	Power Users
Account Operators	Users
Print Operators	Guests
Users	Replicator
Guests	
Replicator	

By default, every new domain user (global or local) is a member of the Domain Users global group, which is a member of the Users built-in local group. Each new workstation or member server user is a member of the Users built-in local group on the computer.

In general, you will want to add administrator users for a domain to the Domain Admins global group rather than adding them directly to the Administrators local group. By adding users to the Domain Admins global group, users also become administrators on workstations and member servers.

Group Account Strategies and the Enterprise

A local group is a single security entity that can be granted access to many objects in a single location (a domain, a workstation, or member server) rather than having to edit the permissions on all those objects separately. Global groups allow you to group user accounts that might be granted permissions to use objects on multiple domains and workstations.

For example, in a multiple-domain setting, you can think of global groups as a means of adding users to the local groups of trusting domains. To extend users' rights and permissions to resources on other domains, add the users' accounts to a global group in your domain, and then add the global group to a local group in a trusting domain.

Domain global groups can also be used for administrative purposes on computers running Windows NT Workstation or on member servers running Windows NT Servers. For example, the Domain Admins global group is added by default to the Administrators built-in local group on each workstation or member server that joins the existing domain. Membership in the workstation or member server local Administrators group enables the network administrator to manage the computer remotely by creating program groups, installing software, and troubleshooting computer problems.

The following table provides some guidelines in using global and local groups:

Purpose of Group	Use	Comments
Group users of this domain into a single unit for use in other domains or user workstations	Global	The global group can be put into local groups or given permissions and rights directly in other domains.
Need permissions and rights only in one domain	Local	The local group can contain users and global groups from this and other domains.
Need permissions on computers running Windows NT Workstation or on member servers	Global	A domain's global groups can be given permissions on these computers, but a domain's local groups cannot.
Contain other groups	Local	The local group can contain only global groups (and users); however, no group can contain other local groups.
Include users from multiple domains	Local	The local group can be used in only the domain in which it is created. If you need to be able to grant this local group permissions in multiple domains, you will have to manually create the local group in every domain in which you need it.

User Manager for Domains

To create additional user accounts or modify existing accounts, use User Manager for Domains.

When adding a user account, provide a user name of up to 20 characters in length. The user name must be unique to the domain or computer being administered.

As discussed in Chapter 1, create a naming convention and adhere to it. Usually the naming convention is a shortened combination of the first and last names. For example, user Max Benson may have a Windows NT account that is MaxB, MBenson, or MaxBen.

You will also be asked to provide the user's full name. Again, the naming convention will determine whether you begin with the last name (Benson, Max) or the first name (Max Benson). The full name can also affect the sort order because the user account list in the User Manager for Domains window can optionally be sorted by full name instead of user name.

Adding Several Accounts at One Time

User accounts can contain a great deal of information. Entering information for each user can be time-consuming; however, Windows NT Server Directory Services makes creating user accounts easy. One way to create a new account is to copy an existing account and simply change the user name, full name, initial password, and any other information that must be changed. You can also create one or more template accounts. These accounts are not used by real users; they serve only as a template for the real accounts you create. The template account can be disabled to ensure that no one can use it to log on. The copies that you make are enabled by default.

Selecting User Accounts

The user account list in the User Manager for Domains window includes all user accounts of the displayed domain. One or more user accounts can be selected from this list so you can:

- Copy, delete, rename, or modify the properties of a selected user account or create a new group that contains that account.

- Modify or delete multiple user accounts at the same time.

- Modify the properties of a group, delete a group, or create a new group containing the selected accounts.

Copying Existing Accounts

It is often quicker and more convenient to copy an existing user account than to create a new one. By copying an existing user account, you ensure that the group memberships and many other properties are copied to the new account.

When a user account is copied, the description, group memberships, logon hours, logon workstations, and account information are copied exactly.

To have the system automatically enter the account user name into the home directory path, use %USERNAME%.

The user name, full name, and password boxes of the new account are blank and must be entered. The **User Cannot Change Password** and **Password Never Expires** check boxes are copied.

Note When copying an account that is a member of the Administrators local group, the User Cannot Change Password setting is not copied.

Usually, the **User Must Change Password At Next Logon** check box is selected, regardless of its setting in the original account. However, if the **User Cannot Change Password** check box is copied as selected, then the **User Must Change Password at Next Logon** check box is cleared.

The **Account Disabled** check box is always cleared, regardless of the setting in the original user account. You can create a new user account, configure it as needed, disable it, and then use it as a template. You can quickly make numerous copies of a disabled template account.

User Manager for Domains does not copy rights and permissions granted to a user account. However, it is recommended that these be provided only to groups and not granted directly to user accounts. Because the group memberships of the original account are copied to the new user account, the new user account will usually have the same abilities and access to resources as the original account.

Auditing Changes to the User Account Database

Windows NT includes auditing features you can use to collect information about how the server is being used. The Account Management class of audits (User and Group Management) describe high-level changes to the user-accounts database, such as User Created or Group Membership Change. Potentially, a more detailed, object-level audit is also performed. The more detailed audit (File and Object Access) describes both successful and unsuccessful accesses to protected objects.

Creating User Accounts

Answer the following basic questions about the rules associated with user and group accounts.

1. Can local groups belong to global groups? Why or why not?

   _____

   _____

2. Can global groups belong to local groups? Why or why not?

   _____

   _____

3. In a multi-domain environment, what is the most efficient way to minimize the number of groups that users belong to when assigning permissions to resources?

   _____

   _____

4. Is the Guest account enabled by default on Windows NT Server?

   _____

   _____

5. Which group, the local group or the global group, can contain users from multiple domains?

   _____

   _____

Lesson Summary

The following information summarizes the key points in this lesson:

- Only one user account is necessary with a domain implementation in the enterprise. This user account can be granted permissions on resources across the enterprise when domains and trusts are configured correctly.

- Using local and global groups can ease the management of permissions.

- The most efficient way to implement permissions across the enterprise with groups is to add users to global groups as needed, and then assign local groups appropriate permissions to resources. You can then add the appropriate global groups to the local group with the permissions for a given resource.

Lesson 2: Profiles and Policies

User work environments include desktop properties such as screen colors, mouse settings, window size and position, and network and printer connections. Managing user environments in an enterprise setting offers benefits to both network administrators and users. This lesson introduces two Windows NT Server tools to assist in managing user environments: user profiles and system policies.

After this lesson, you will be able to:

- Identify user profile types.
- Choose and implement user profiles types.
- Implement user profiles.
- Define system policies.
- Use System Policy Editor to implement system policies.
- Choose between user profiles and system policies.

Estimated lesson time: 20 minutes

User Profiles

A user profile contains all user-definable settings for the work environment of a computer running Windows NT, including display settings and network connections. All user-specific settings are automatically saved into the Profiles folder within the system root folder.

On computers running Windows NT Workstation or Windows NT Server, user profiles automatically create and maintain the desktop settings for each user's work environment on the local computer. In most cases, a user profile is created for each user when the user logs on to a computer for the first time. If you create a mandatory profile and assign it to a user, a default profile for that user is not created.

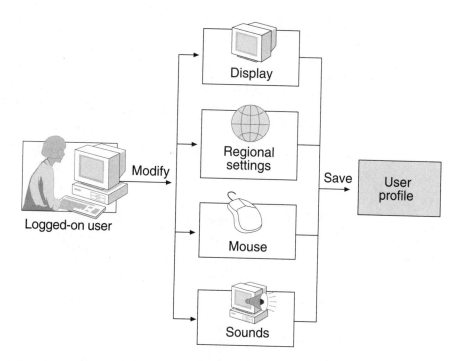

User profiles provide the following advantages to users:

- Workstation desktop settings don't change from logoff to logon.

- Each computer user can have his or her own customized desktop settings.

- Roaming user profiles are stored on a server that will follow the user to any Windows NT computer he or she logs on to.

User profiles provide the following advantages to network administrators:

- Customized user profiles can be created and assigned to users to provide consistent work environments that are appropriate to tasks.

- Common group settings can be specified for all users.

- Mandatory user profiles can be assigned to prevent users from changing desktop settings.

User profiles can be used on computers running Windows 95, but user profiles must be enabled before they are available. User profiles have no effect on computers running MS-DOS, Windows 3.1, UNIX, or OS/2.

Default Profiles

Every user profile begins as a copy of default user, a default user profile stored on each computer running Windows NT Workstation or Windows NT Server. The NTuser.dat file, in the Default User directory, displays configuration settings from the Windows NT Registry. Every user profile also uses the common program groups contained in the All Users folder. The Default User Profile folder, User Profile folders for each user, and All User Profile folders are located in the Profiles folder in the system root (by default C:\Winnt). The Default User folder and individual User Profile folders contain an NTuser.dat file plus a directory of links to desktop items.

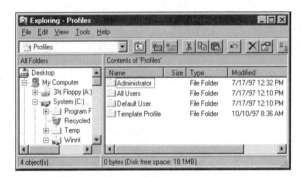

The User Profiles folders contain links to various desktop items as shown in the table below.

User Profile Folder	Contents
Application Data	Application-specific data. For example, a customer dictionary. Application vendors decide what data to store in the User Profile folder.
Desktop	Desktop items, including files and shortcuts.
Favorites	Shortcuts to program items and favorite locations.
NetHood	Shortcuts to Network Neighborhood items.
Personal	Shortcuts to program items.
PrintHood	Shortcuts to Printer folder items
Recent	Shortcuts to the most recently used items.
SendTo	Shortcuts to document items.
Start Menu	Shortcuts to program items.
Templates	Shortcuts to template items.

NTuser.dat File

The NTuser.dat file is the registry portion of the user profile. NTuser.dat is a cached copy of the Windows NT Registry HKEY_CURRENT_USER subtree on the local computer. The registry is a database repository for information about the computer's configuration, including the hardware, installed software, environment settings, and other information. In the registry, the settings that determine the work environment for the user who is currently logged on to the computer are stored in HKEY_CURRENT_USER.

All Users Folder

Although they are not copied to User Profile folders, the settings in the All Users folder are used with User Profile folders to create the user profile.

The Windows NT platform supports two program group types:

- Common program groups are always available on a computer, no matter who is logged on. Only administrators can add, delete, and modify common program groups.

- Personal program groups are private to the user who creates them.

Common program groups are stored in the All Users folder under the Profiles folder. The All Users folder also contains settings for the Desktop and **Start** menu. On computers running Windows NT Workstation or Windows NT Server, only members of the Administrators group can create common program groups.

Server Based Profiles

Roaming user profiles can be implemented in three ways:

- Add a user profile path to each user account to automatically create an empty User Profile folder named for the user in the server location and to allow users to create their own user profiles.

- Add a user profile path to each user account and copy a preconfigured user profile to the user profile path specified in each user account.

- Add a user profile path to each user account, copy a preconfigured user profile to the user profile path specified in each user account, and then rename the NTuser.dat file to NTuser.man in the user profile path specified in each user account. This creates a mandatory user profile.

In User Manager for Domains, you can assign a server location for user profiles. If you enter a user profile path into a user's domain account, a copy of the user's local user profile is saved both locally and in the user profile path location when the user logs off. The next time the user logs on, the user profile in the user profile path location is compared to the copy in the local user profile folder, and the most recent copy of the user profile is opened. The local user profile becomes a roaming user profile by virtue of the centralized domain location. It is available wherever the user logs on, providing the server is available.

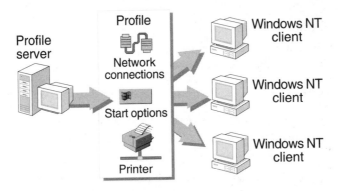

If the server is not available, the local cached copy of the roaming user profile is used. If the user has not logged on to the computer before, a new local user profile is created. In either case, if the centrally stored user profile is not available at logon, it is not updated when the user logs off. If the user profile is not downloaded due to server problems, it is not uploaded when the user logs off. The next time the user logs on, he or she must specify which user profile to use—the newer locally cached copy of the user profile or the older centrally stored copy.

To create a preconfigured roaming user profile, use User Manager for Domains to assign a server location for a user profile, and then use the **User Profile** tab of the System option in Control Panel to copy a preconfigured user profile to the server. The first time the user logs on, instead of getting a copy of the default profile, the user gets a copy of the preconfigured user profile from the server. Thereafter, the user profile functions just like a standard roaming user profile. Each time the user logs off, the user profile is saved locally and is also copied to the server.

A mandatory user profile is simply a preconfigured roaming user profile that the user cannot update. The user can still modify the desktop, but the changes are not saved when the user logs off. The next time the user logs on, the mandatory user profile is downloaded again. User profiles become mandatory when you rename the NTuser.dat file on the server to NTuser.man. This extension makes the user profile read-only. As many users as needed can use the same mandatory user profile.

Adding the User Profile Path to User Accounts

In User Manager for Domains, you can use the **User Environment Profile** dialog box to add the user profile path location. Open the **User Properties** dialog box for a user account, and click the **Profiles** button to add the user profile path.

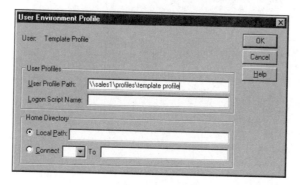

Use a full path in each user account:

*server**share**profilename*

For the *share* value, create a Profiles folder, if one does not already exist, and share the folder with Everyone permissions.

For the *profilename* value, use the user account name.

The user profile path can be on any server; it does not have to be a domain controller. When the user logs on, Windows NT Server checks the user's account to see if there is a user profile path. If the path exists, the user profile is located by the system.

Copying the User Profile to the Server Location

To provide a specific user profile for some users, copy the user profile to the proper location by running Control Panel, choosing System, and then selecting the **User Profiles** tab. This location must match the **User Profile Path** entry for the user's account in User Manager for Domains.

On the **User Profiles** tab in the Control Panel, **System Properties** dialog box, all user profiles that have been created on the computer are listed in the **Profiles Stored on This Computer** box. To copy a specific user profile, click **Copy To**, and then either type the name of the destination folder or browse the network for it.

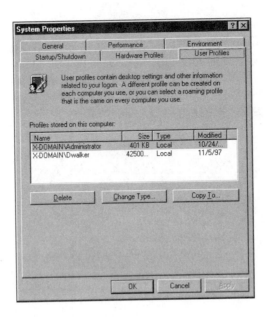

Adding Users and Groups to the Permissions List for a Roaming User Profile

The System option in Control Panel also copies appropriate permissions along with the user profile so users have access to the user profile. However, when you copy a user profile to a location for use by another user or group, you must add the user or group to the permissions list. The **Permitted To Use** box shows the user who has permissions to use the user profile. Click **Change** to add the user or group to the permissions list for the user profile.

Creating Roaming User Profiles

To implement roaming user profiles, you need to complete the following tasks:

- Create a template user profile with the appropriate configuration. You do this by creating a user account, and then configuring the appropriate desktop settings.

- Create and share a folder named Profiles. This will allow users to access the profiles from a remote computer.

- Copy the template user profile to a network server and specify the users who are permitted to use the profile.

- Specify the path to the profile for the user account in the **User Environment Profile** dialog box.

Creating a Template User Profile

In this exercise you will create a template user profile. You will then copy the user profile to the Network server. Finally, you will specify who has permissions to use the profile.

➤ **To create a template user profile**

In this procedure, you create a user account named Template Profile. This user account will be the model for a profile. Once this user account has been created, you can configure the settings.

1. In the **New User** dialog box, create a user account named **Template Profile** with no password. Clear the **User Must Change Password at Next Logon** check box.

2. Log on as **Template Profile**. A local user profile is automatically created for the Template Profile user on the local computer in the *drive:\systemroot*\Profiles folder.

3. Right-click anywhere on the desktop, and then on the shortcut menu, click **Properties**. The **Display Properties** dialog box appears.

4. Click **Appearance**. Notice the current color scheme.

5. In the **Color Schemes** box, select a different color scheme, and then click **OK**. The change will take effect immediately.

6. Log off and log on as the same user. Notice that the screen colors are those saved in the user's profile.

Copying the Profile to a Network Server

You copy a user profile using the System properties in Control Panel. When you click the **User Profiles** tab of the **System Properties** dialog box, the default profiles appear for all users who have previously logged on to the computer.

➤ **To copy the template user profile to a network server**

In this procedure, you copy the Template Profile user profile to the server for User2.

1. Log off and log on as Administrator.

2. In Windows NT Explorer, share the directory \<winntroot>\profiles on the network server with a share name of "Profiles."

3. In User Manager for Domains, create a user account named User2 with no password requirements.

4. Click the **Start** button, point to **Settings**, and then click **Control Panel**.

5. In Control Panel, double-click **System**.

   The **System Properties** dialog box appears.

6. Click the **User Profiles** tab.

Note Notice that a user profile has been created for all users who have previously logged on to the computer, including a user profile named Template Profile.

---

7. Under **Profiles stored on this computer**, click **Template Profile**, and then click **Copy To**.

   The **Copy To** dialog box appears.

8. In the **Copy profile to** box, type *computer_name***profiles\user2** (where *computer_name* is the name of your computer).

Important If you were to make the Template Profile mandatory, in the Copy profile to box, you would type *computer_name*\profiles (do not specify a user name).

➤ **To specify the users who are permitted to use the profile**

1. In the **Copy To** dialog box, under **Permitted to use**, click **Change**.

   The **Choose User** dialog box appears.

2. In the **List Names From** box, make sure the domain where your accounts reside appears, and then click **Show Users**.

3. In the **Names** box, click **User2**, and then click **Add**.

   Domain\User2 appears in the **Add Name** box.

4. Click **OK**.

   Domain\User2 appears as the user permitted to use this profile.

5. Click **OK**.

   A folder named after the user name you specified is created in the Profiles folder with all the desktop settings configured for the Template Profile user account.

6. In Windows NT Explorer, view Profiles\User2. Notice the folders for the desktop settings that are stored in the Template Profile folder and the file Ntuser.dat.

Important If you were to make the Template Profile mandatory, you would rename the Ntuser.dat file to Ntuser.man. If you did not specify a user name, this file would be located in the Profiles folder.

Specifying the Path to the Roaming Profile

After you copy the roaming profile to a network server, specify the path to the profile for a user account in the **User Environment Profile** dialog box in User Manager for Domains.

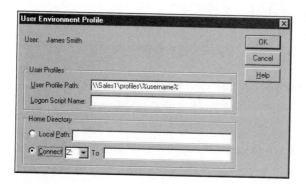

In the **User Profile Path** box, specify the server location of the user profile.

- If the profile is a roaming personal profile, enter the name of the server, the share name to the Profiles folder (in this lesson, the Profiles folder is shared as "Profiles"), and %Username%. If you use %Username%, Windows NT will substitute %Username% with the user account name.

- If the profile is a roaming mandatory profile, enter the name of the server, the share name to the Profiles folder, and the actual profile name. For example: \\Server1\Profiles\Ntuser.man.

If you have many users that require roaming profiles, you can specify the path to the profile for multiple user accounts at one time by doing the following:

1. In the User Manager window, select multiple accounts.

2. On the **User** menu, click **Properties**.

3. In the **User Properties** dialog box, click **Profile**.

➤ **To specify a path to the roaming profile**

1. In the User Manager window, double-click User2.

    The **User Properties** dialog box appears.

2. In the **User Properties** dialog box, click **Profile**.

3. In the **User Profile Path** box, type *computer_name***profiles**
    %username% (where *computer_name* is the name of your computer).

4. Click **OK** twice to apply your changes.

5. Exit User Manager for Domains and log off Windows NT.

➤ **To test the roaming profile**

1. Log off and log on as User2.

Notice that the screen colors are the same as the screen colors set for Template Profile.

➤ **To test the roaming profile from another computer**

If you have access to two computers on the same network, complete this procedure from the second computer.

1. Log on to the second computer as User2.

2. If a dialog box appears which provides profile options, click **Download**.

   Notice that the screen colors are the same as those set on the first computer because the roaming profile for the template user account is downloaded from the server and applied to the computer that the template user logs on to.

3. Log off.

➤ **To determine the type of profile assigned to a user**

1. Log on as an Administrator, and start Control Panel.

2. Double-click System, and then click **User Profiles**.

   Notice that the profile type for User2 is a roaming profile.

3. Exit all programs and log off Windows NT.

Policy Editor

System policies enable you to control the user-definable settings in Windows NT and Windows 95 user profiles as well as system configuration settings. On computers running Windows NT Workstation or Windows NT Server, the contents of the user profile are taken from the user portion of the Windows NT Registry. Another portion of the registry, the local computer portion, contains configuration settings that can be managed, along with user profiles, using System Policy Editor. With this tool, you create a system policy to control user work environments and actions, and to enforce system configuration for all computers running Windows NT Workstation and Windows NT Server.

With system policies, you can control some aspects of user work environments without enforcing the restrictions of a mandatory user profile. You can restrict what users can do from the desktop such as restrict certain options in Control Panel, customize parts of the desktop, or configure network settings.

The desktop settings in user profiles, as well as logon and network access settings, are stored in the computer's registry database. System policy for users overwrites settings in the current user area of the registry, and system policy for computers overwrites the current local machine area of the registry. This allows you to control user actions (user profiles) as well as computer actions for users and groups. In System Policy Editor, you manage the user desktop by changing the **Default User** settings, and you manage the logon and network settings by changing the **Default Computer** settings.

Using System Policy Editor, you create a file called NTConfig.pol that contains settings for users (user profiles) and computers (logons and network access settings). To enable a uniform policy for all network computers running Windows NT Server or Windows NT Workstation, you save this file to the Net logon folder in the system root folder of the primary domain controller (PDC): *PDCservername\Netlogon*.

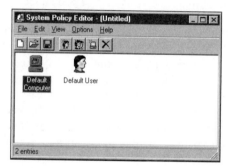

When a user logs on to any network computer running Windows NT, the operating system looks in the Net logon folder in the logon server's system root folder to see if there is an NTConfig.pol file present. If the file is found, the contents of the file are copied to the local computer's registry, and is used to overwrite the current user and local machine portions of the registry.

System Policy Editor entries change local computer registry settings in the following ways:

- Desktop settings for Default User in System Policy Editor modify the HKEY_CURRENT_USER key in the registry, which defines the contents of the user profile that is in effect for the computer.

- Logon and network access settings for Default Computer in System Policy Editor modify the HKEY_LOCAL_MACHINE key in the registry.

When a user logs on to the domain, the contents of the NTConfig.pol file on the server are merged with the NTuser.dat file found in the user profile location for the user logging on. Settings in NTuser.dat that do not match NTConfig.pol settings are overwritten, and thus system policy controls the user profile settings for the entire domain. Settings for Default Computer that are not contained in the user profile are added to the local machine portion of the registry.

Customizing System Policy for Users, Groups, and Computers

If you have special users, groups, or computers that need settings that are different from the default settings, you can change the default settings to accommodate special needs and add users, groups, and computers as appropriate. Users, groups, or computers you add receive separate entries in the NTConfig.pol file that contain the settings that are different from the default system policy settings. When a user or group member who has special policy settings in NTConfig.pol logs on, the system finds NTConfig.pol and also the special settings that apply specifically to the user or group member. Similarly, if a computer is added and special settings entered in System Policy Editor, anyone logging on to that computer receives those computer settings.

Computer policy is applied when the user logs on. Policy is taken from the user's logon domain, not the computer's domain. This can cause problems when users log on to a different domain and not all domains use system policy. For example, suppose employee Amy Jones has a user account in the South domain, and travels to the North site. When she logs on to a computer in the North domain, a logon server in the South domain validates her. If James Smith, who has a user account in the North domain, logs on after Amy logs off, and the North domain doesn't use system policies, the South domain computer profile is not overwritten and remains in effect. You can correct this problem by implementing system policies on all domains, or by using the manual update mode to load a specific policy on affected computers.

Profile Evaluation for Users and Computers

When multiple profiles apply to one user, a user profile for a specific user takes precedence over a user profile for a group that the user is a member of. Similarly, if no specific user profile has been defined for the user, a group profile for a group that includes the user is used, if available, before the Default User profile is used.

If no computer profile is defined for a specific computer, the Default Computer profile is used. If multiple group profiles apply to a user, they are applied in the order specified in the **Group Priority** dialog box.

Using Manual Update Mode

Manual update mode ensures that system policy is always copied from a specific server, regardless of who logs on. When you can change the remote system policy file update mode from automatic to manual, you specify a path other than the Net logon folder on the PDC. To use this feature, you must use System Policy Editor on individual computers to change the update path.

Supporting Windows 95 System Policy

You have learned that system policies allow you to override local registry values for user or computer settings. When a user logs on, system policy settings overwrite the current settings in the user's registry to enable administrators to control individual desktop and registry settings.

For computers running Windows 95, the following rules also apply:

- System policies can be stored only on the domain controllers.

- Group policies, if used, must be enabled on each computer running Windows 95. You can enable group policies when you install Windows 95, using a custom setup script, or use Add/Remove Programs in Control Panel after Windows 95 is installed.

- Windows 95 policy must be saved in a file named Config.pol (not Ntconfig.pol), and stored in the Net logon share of the PDC.

Remember that system policy files created on computers running Windows NT cannot be used on computers running Windows 95, and vice versa. Therefore, when modifying system policy for a computer running Windows 95, you run System Policy Editor on a computer running Windows 95, and you save the policy settings to a file named Config.pol in the Net logon share on the PDC.

Load Balancing

Ordinarily, computers running Windows 95 get policy settings from the PDC only. Load balancing allows computers running Windows 95 to take policies from multiple domain controllers. Therefore, enabling load balancing can prevent network slowdown when many Windows 95 clients try to access the same policy file.

To enable load balancing, use the Windows 95 System Policy Editor to open Config.pol, then double-click the Default Computer icon, open Network\Update \Remote Update Policy, and then check Load-balanced.

System Policy Templates

System policy templates allow you to set system policy for networks using computers running Windows NT Workstation, Windows NT Server, Windows 95, or a combination (user profiles must be enabled on each computer running Windows 95). The templates provide the necessary framework for overwriting the registry keys on the different systems.

When you install System Policy Editor, the following template files are installed automatically:

- WINNT.adm. Provides System Policy Editor settings specific to the Windows NT operating system and registry structure.

- WINDOWS.adm. Provides System Policy Editor settings specific to the Windows 95 operating system and registry structure.

- COMMON.adm. Provides the System Policy Editor settings that are common to both the Windows NT and Windows 95 registry structures, and that are not contained in either WINNT.adm or WINDOWS.adm.

System policy files created on computers running Windows NT Server cannot be used on computers running Windows 95, and system policy files created on Windows 95 cannot be used on computers running Windows NT.

Creating a System Policy

In this exercise you will use the System Policy Editor to create a domain system policy containing a computer policy for Workstation1. You then configure the computer policy to display a logon banner that appears whenever a user logs on to Workstation1 and to prevent the display of the last logged on user name.

Complete these procedures on Server1 logged on as Administrator.

➤ **To create a domain system policy for Workstation1 that displays a logon banner**

1. Start System Policy Editor.

2. On the **File** menu, click **New Policy**.

3. On the **Edit** menu, click **Add Computer**.

4. In the **Add Computer** dialog box, type **Workstation1** and then click **OK**.

5. Double-click the **Workstation1** icon.

    The **Workstation1 Properties** dialog box appears.

6. Expand **Windows NT System**.

7. Expand **Logon**.

8. Click the **Logon Banner** option.

   Notice at the bottom of the screen that a **Settings for Logon banner** dialog box appears. If this box appears dimmed, you have not yet selected this option (there is not a check mark in the check box).

9. In the **Caption** box, type **Attention:**

10. In the **Text** box, type **Unauthorized use of Workstation1 is prohibited.**

11. Click **OK**.

System Policy Editor stores this information in two values (LegalNoticeCaption and LegalNoticeText) in the registry under:

HKEY_LOCAL_MACHINE\SOFTWARE\Microsoft\Windows NT\Current-Version\Winlogon

➤ **To disable the display of the last logged on user name on Workstation1**

1. Double-click the **Workstation1** computer profile icon.

2. Expand **Windows NT System**, and then expand **Logon**.

3. Click the **Do not display last logged on user name** check box.

4. Click **OK**.

➤ **To save the new system policy file in Net logon**

1. On the **File** menu, click **Save**.

2. Save the file in the C:\Winnt\System32\Repl\Import\Scripts folder, and name it Ntconfig.

   System Policy Editor automatically appends the .pol extension.

3. Close **System Policy Editor**.

Implementing User Policies and Profiles

In this exercise you will answer questions pertaining to the implementation and management of user policies and profiles.

1. What is the difference between a local and a roaming profile?

   _____

   _____

2. Describe the purpose of system policy.

_____

_____

3. Who can implement system policy?

_____

_____

4. Name two major functions of System Policy Editor.

_____

_____

5. Name two policies that you might create to secure a computer.

_____

_____

6. If a user logs on to a domain that has system policy, but system policy editor has not been defined for that user, what happens next?

_____

_____

7. Your network has 500 computers running Windows 95 and 400 computers running Windows NT Workstation. The Windows 95 users are complaining that the network is slow when everyone is trying to log on in the morning. What could cause this problem, and how do you resolve it?

_____

_____

Lesson Summary

The following information summarizes the key points in this lesson:

- A local user profile contains all user-definable settings controlling a user's desktop environment on the local computer.

- Roaming user profiles provide users with the same desktop environment from any Windows NT-based computer on a network.

- A roaming mandatory user profile cannot be changed by users. One profile is assigned to many users.

- A roaming personal user profile is updated whenever a user makes a change to his or her desktop configuration. Each user has his or her own personal profile.

- By default, to implement a domain system policy on computers running Windows NT, the policy settings must be stored in a file named Ntconfig.pol in the Net logon share of the PDC.

- By default, to implement a domain system policy on computers running Windows 95, use the Windows 95 System Policy Editor to create system policy on that operating system. These system policy settings must be saved to a file named Config.pol in the Net logon share of the PDC.

- Both Ntconfig.pol and Config.pol must be stored on the PDC in the following folder: *systemroot*\System32\Repl\Import\Scripts. By default this folder is shared as Net logon.

- Replication must be enabled for all domain controllers to receive copies of the Ntconfig.pol and Config.pol files. Remember that load balancing must be enabled on computers running Windows 95 in order for them to access Config.pol on backup domain controllers (BDCs).

- You can specify customized settings for individual users, groups, and computers to meet the needs of your organization.

- System Policy Editor can be used to directly edit portions of the registry.

For more information on	See
Modifying user accounts	User Manager for Domains Help.
Copying user profiles	Control Panel Help.
Using system policy for computers running Windows 95	*Microsoft Windows 95 Resource Kit.*

Lesson 3: Domains as an Organizational Unit

Windows NT Server domains give users the ability to share resources such as user accounts, groups, profiles, policies, and computer accounts. To fully understand domains, it is important to understand how computers running Windows NT, Windows 95, Windows for Workgroups, and MS-DOS participate and interact with domains. This lesson explains how computers running different Microsoft operating systems can interact with domains.

After this lesson, you will be able to:

- Explain the purpose of creating a Windows NT computer account in a domain.
- Describe how to create a Windows NT computer account in a domain.

Estimated lesson time: 20 minutes

Adding Computers to a Domain

Windows NT and other Microsoft operating systems interact with domains in different ways. The following sections explain how different Microsoft operating systems interact with domains.

Windows NT

A computer running Windows NT that participates in a domain has its own account, called a computer account, in the domain's directory services database. A computer account in the domain allows other domain users, and users of other trusted domains, to share resources on the computer.

A computer account is created when the computer is first identified to the domain during network setup. A computer running Windows NT can be added to a domain using the computer's networking properties or by using the Server Manager tool.

Other Microsoft Operating Systems

Although client computers running Windows 95, Windows for Workgroups, and MS-DOS can interact with domains, they do not have computer accounts in the domain's directory services database. The people using these computers can have user accounts stored in the directory services database, however.

Adding a Computer to the Domain

In this exercise you will add an NT Workstation to the domain. In order to successfully complete this exercise, your computer must be on the same network as an NT domain you do not belong to, but in which you have access to an administrator's user name and password.

➤ **To add a computer running Windows NT to a domain using the computer's Networking Properties**

1. Right-click the computer's **Network Neighborhood** icon and select **Properties**.

2. Click the **Change** button on the computer's Identification tab in Networking properties.

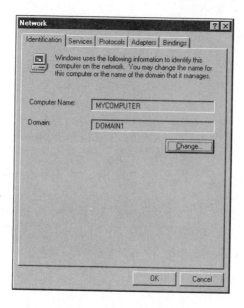

3. Click the **Domain** radio button and specify the domain in which the computer is being added.

4. Specify an existing domain User Name and Password with the ability to add computer accounts to the domain.

5. Click the **OK** button to add the computer to the domain.

Adding a Computer to the Domain Using Server Manager

In this exercise you will add an NT Workstation to the domain using Server Manager for Domains. If you are working stand-alone, you will be able to complete this exercise only to the point of adding a computer to the domain.

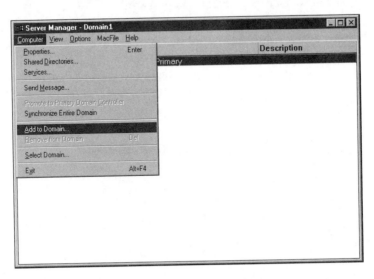

➤ **To add a computer running Windows NT to a domain using the Server Manager tool**

1. On a Windows NT Server, click **Start**, point to Programs, point to Administrative Tools (Common), and then click **Server Manager**.

2. Select **Computer** from the pull-down menu.

3. Select **Add to Domain**.

➤ **To select the appropriate radio button for Windows NT Workstation, Windows NT Server, or Windows NT Backup Domain Controller (BDC)**

1. Enter a name for the computer in the Computer Name field.

2. Select the **Add** button to add the computer to the domain.

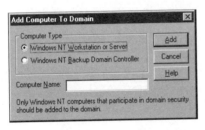

Lesson Summary

The following information summarizes the key points in this lesson:

- Windows NT computer accounts can be created in the domains directory database in order to share computer resources with other domain users.

- A domain user account should be used with computers running Windows 95, Windows for Workgroups, and MS-DOS in order to share domain resources without creating a computer account in the domain.

Lesson 4: Domain Synchronization

Domain synchronization refers to the synchronization of the Windows NT Directory Services database. Directory services database synchronization occurs when a primary domain controller (PDC) copies its directory database to the backup domain controllers (BDCs) within a given domain. The Net Logon Service controls the directory database synchronization process. In planning an NT Directory Services (NTDS) environment, administrators need to understand what domain synchronization is, and how it affects network activity. This lesson explains the process of domain synchronization and prepares network designers to effectively implement domain controllers in order to accommodate synchronization.

After this lesson, you will be able to:

- Understand the synchronization process.

- Calculate synchronization times.

- Accommodate synchronization over slow WAN links.

Estimated lesson time: 30 minutes

The Synchronization Process

When synchronization occurs, the PDC announces that a change in the directory services database has taken place. A BDC then calls the PDC and requests the changes, as shown in the figure below.

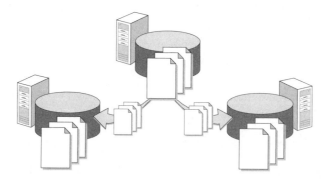

There are two types of changes: full synchronization and partial synchronization. The following table describes differences between the two.

Change	Details
Full synchronization	Full synchronization occurs when the PDC sends its entire directory services database to a BDC. Full synchronization always occurs when bringing a new BDC online. However, full synchronization of the directory services database is not necessary when there is a change in PDC data.
Partial synchronization	Partial synchronization occurs when the PDC sends only the changes in the directory services database that have occurred since the last synchronization. The PDC keeps track of the synchronization level of each BDC which allows the PDC to control the rate of partial synchronization.

The Change Log in Synchronization

The change log controls whether a full or partial synchronization takes place. Each change entry is typically 32 bytes. The default size for the change log is 64 kilobytes (KB), which means it will hold approximately 2000 changes. A version number in the change log will represent each change. When the change log becomes full, it returns to the beginning of the log and overwrites existing version numbers. If the BDC sees the last change it received has been overwritten, the BDC will initiate a full synchronization. The maximum size for the change log is 4 MB. To change this value, you must first add the value as a **REG_DWORD**. The change log is controlled by a registry entry in:

```
HKEY_LOCAL_MACHINE
    \SYSTEM
        \CurrentControlSet
            \Services
                \NetLogon
                    \Parameters
                        ChangeLogSize
```

Regulating Partial Synchronization

The PDC sends a message announcing a change in the directory services database to only those BDCs that need the changes rather than to all BDCs. These messages are sent to a subset of the domain controllers in each pulse. A pulse defines the frequency (in seconds) of account synchronization. This method prevents all BDCs from responding simultaneously, helping to reduce network traffic and insuring that the PDC does not become overloaded by requests for synchronization from the BDCs.

Synchronization Over WAN and RAS Links

Give consideration to the amount of traffic that account synchronization places on a wide area network (WAN) or remote access server (RAS) dial-up line. In particular, the network should avoid full synchronization across WAN links because the slow speed across the link will affect total network performance.

Controlling Aspects of Synchronization

The network administrator can control different aspects of synchronization, and therefore network performance, through several items in the Windows NT Server registry.

Calculating Synchronization Times

An important aspect of network administration is managing the amount of network traffic so that synchronization time remains acceptable. Synchronization time depends upon several factors including:

- Password changes per month.

- Additional changes per month.

- Amount of data to be replicated per month.

Calculating Data to be Synchronized per Month

Use the table below to calculate the amount of data to be synchronized per month.

	Factors	
Password changes per month	Number of user accounts	A
	Password expires in how many calendar days	B
	Divide B by 30	C
	User group changes ....Multiply A by C	D
Additional changes per month	(If number unknown, use 5% of D)	E
	Newer user accounts	F
	Total group changed from Job Aid 1	G
	Newer computer accounts	H
Amount of data to be synchronized per month	(D + E + F + G + H) x 1K	I

Estimating Synchronization Time

When the PDC is separated from BDCs by a WAN or modem link, it is necessary to estimate the amount of data and time needed to replicate directory database changes. Once the amount of data to be synchronized per month has been calculated, it can be used with the job aid table to determine the synchronization time.

Synchronization Over a Slow WAN Link

Windows NT Server 4.0 has a parameter that can be used to increase the performance of replication across slow links. This parameter is called the Replication-Governor. A BDC uses the ReplicationGovernor parameter in the Windows NT Registry to increase the performance of domain synchronization over a slow WAN link. This requires both the BDCs and the PDC to be running Windows NT Server 4.0.

Adjusting the ReplicationGovernor

Adjusting the ReplicationGovernor is important because for each Windows NT Server 4.0 BDC, the ReplicationGovernor parameter defines:

- The size of the data transferred on each call to the PDC.

- The frequency of those calls.

Adjusting the ReplicationGovernor parameter has the following effects:

- It changes the size of the buffer used on each call from the BDC to the PDC, ensuring that a single call does not occupy the WAN link for too long.

- It causes Net Logon to "sleep" between calls. While Net Logon is "sleeping," other applications can use the WAN link.

Adding the ReplicationGovernor Parameter to the Registry

The ReplicationGovernor parameter can be added to the registry of a BDC under the following key:

```
\HKEY_LOCAL_MACHINE
   \SYSTEM
      \CurrentControlSet
         \Services
            \NetLogon
               \Parameters
```

To add this parameter, assign a type of **REG_DWORD** and a value from 0 (zero) to 100 (the default is 100). This value defines a percentage for both the amount of data transferred on each call to the PDC and the frequency of those calls. For example, setting the ReplicationGovernor value to 50 will use a 64-KB buffer rather than the default 128-KB buffer. In addition, the BDC will have an outstanding synchronization call on the network for a maximum of only 50 percent of the time.

Caution Care must be taken in setting this value. If the ReplicationGovernor is set too low, synchronization may never complete. A value of zero will cause Net Logon to never synchronize, and the directory database can become completely out of synchronization. Setting the value below 25 is not recommended.

Configuring ReplicationGovernor in Conjunction with Change Log

If you configure ReplicationGovernor on the BDCs to reduce the amount of data being replicated, this will increase the amount of time required to complete the replication process. This will also increase the number of changes that might be in the change log. Make sure that you have a large enough value for the change log size so that the change log does not wrap or begin to overwrite entries that a BDC may not have had time to receive.

Implementing Different Replication Rates

It is possible to have different replication rates at different times throughout the day. A network administrator can implement this by adjusting the Replication-Governor parameter in the registry and then restarting the Net Logon service from within a batch file that is scheduled by means of the **at** command. Such a batch file could be created using the **Regini.exe** or **Regchg.exe** command from the *Microsoft Windows NT Resource Kit* and would, for example, contain:

```
regini scriptfile
net stop netlogon
net start netlogon
```

The scriptfile would contain the full path in the registry to the Replication-Governor parameter and the new value selected for it.

User Account Database Synchronization Optimizations

Domain user account database synchronization can be optimized in several ways, as summarized below.

1. Changes to the user account database, such as a changed password, are not immediately synchronized. For example, in the case of a password change: when a user changes his or her password, the change is made on the domain's PDC.

2. If the user then logs off and logs back on again, and the logon request is sent to a BDC in the domain, the BDC may not yet have synchronized with the PDC, and therefore the BDC may not yet know of the users new password.

3. If the password is invalid for the user, the BDC will send a request to the PDC to see if the PDC has a different password for the user.

4. When the next user account database synchronization occurs, the BDC will receive the user's new password.

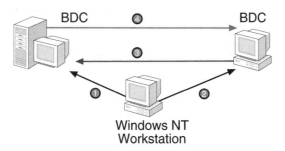

Windows NT Server is designed to support a domain with a hypothetical maximum of up to 2000 domain controllers spread across a WAN with up to 40,000 user accounts. The Net Logon service supports this in the following ways.

The Net Logon service can be paused on a PDC. When paused, the Net Logon service will not be the target of any pass-through authentication requests. These requests will be handled by the other domain controllers.

Even though the Net Logon service is paused, it is still capable of performing user account database synchronization. For example, one can pause the Net Logon service on the PDC of a domain to allow it to spend its time synchronizing the BDCs, rather than synchronizing and handling pass-through authentication requests.

Note What a service can do when paused varies from service to service. In the case of Net Logon, when it is paused, it still performs user account database synchronization, but does not perform logon or pass-through authentication.

BDCs can control the load placed on the WAN, resulting from user account database synchronization, with the ReplicationGovernor registry value. This reduces the bandwidth needed for replication across a WAN, as discussed earlier.

Planning Directory Synchronization

In this exercise you answer some basic questions about the Windows NT Server directory synchronization process.

1. What are the two types of synchronization, and how do they differ?

_____

_____

2. What occurs when entries are written into the change control log that over-write previous entries?

_____

_____

3. How does the PDC keep all the BDCs from responding simultaneously for directory updates?

_____

_____

4. How does the ReplicationGovernor keep BDCs from consuming WAN bandwidth?

_____

_____

5. What impact does changing the ReplicationGovernor have on the change log?

_____

_____

6. How can replication rates be scheduled for different times of the day?

_____

_____

Lesson Summary

The following information summarizes the key points in this lesson:

- Domain synchronization is a complex process that has a considerable impact on network utilization and performance, particularly over slow WAN links.

- To meet specific network needs, network administrators can use tools such as the change log and the ReplicationGovernor to manage and optimize the domain synchronization process.

For more information on	See
Synchronization parameters	*Microsoft Windows NT Resource Kit.*
Regini.exe and creating script files or **Regchg.exe**	Resource Kit Tools Help file (Rktools.hlp) of the *Microsoft Windows NT Resource Kit.*

Lesson 5: Trust Relationships

A trust relationship is a link between domains that allows pass-through authentication in which a trusting domain honors the logon authentications of a trusted domain. With trust relationships, a user who has only one user account in one domain can potentially access the entire network. User accounts and global groups defined in a trusted domain can be given rights and resource permissions in a trusting domain even though those accounts do not exist in the trusting domain's directory database. Implementing Windows NT trust relationships involves planning group strategies and granting permissions across trusts. It also involves accounting for the impact of the Net Logon service and pass-through authentication. This lesson provides an overview of trust relationships and explains how they are used in an enterprise setting.

After this lesson, you will be able to:

- Determine when to implement a one-way or two-way trust relationship, and differentiate between a trusted (accounts) domain and a trusting (resource) domain.

- Use groups to manage large numbers of accounts in a multiple-domain environment.

- Identify the three functions of the Net Logon service.

Estimated lesson time: 45 minutes

In a network environment where users and administrators are widely dispersed, resource sharing needs to be fast and simple, and network administration needs consolidation options. Toward this end, Windows NT Server Directory Services provide:

- Single-logon capability.

- Universal resource access.

- Centralized network administration.

Trust relationships make single-logon capability, universal resource access, and centralized network administration possible.

The figure on the following page illustrates the concept of a trust relationship and and shows that a resource domain trusts an account domain.

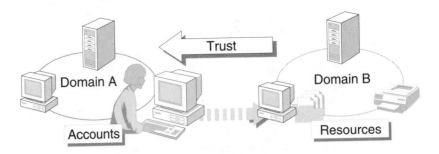

Functions of Trust Relationships

Trust relationships provide a communications channel between two domains. Without trusts, domains are completely separate, as if someone had cut the cable between them. With a trust relationship, one domain accepts user accounts from another domain as valid accounts. This allows users on one domain to be assigned permissions on resources in another domain. This occurs even though the account does not exist in the local domain. For example, if a user has an account in Domain A, but needs to use a resource in Domain B where he or she does not have an account, a trust relationship can be established that allows resource sharing across domains.

Because trusts unite domains, they allow administrators to see the network as one large organization rather than as a collection of local area networks (LANs) that must be managed separately. By combining two domains into a single administrative unit, trust relationships bring centralized administration to the enterprise level.

When trust relationships are properly established, a single account can have access to the entire multiple-domain network and all its resources. A user has to log on and provide a password only once to use any shared resource on the network for which his or her account has been granted permissions.

Types of Trust Relationships

Trust relationships can be set up as one-way or two-way relationships.

One-Way Trust Relationships

In a one-way trust relationship, accounts in one domain can be given permission to access resources in another domain. One-way trust relationships are typically used in networks where user accounts must be centrally managed in one domain, but resources require distributed control. Let's say, for example, that a company is migrating to Windows NT Server and wants centralized control over employee accounts, but also wants each department to control its own servers and workstations. To meet this challenge, the network planner creates a corporate domain for all user accounts. Each department, however, then creates its own domain for its servers and workstations. By establishing a one-way trust relationship between the resource domains and the account domains, the network planner can give users permission to use resources in all departmental domains.

Two-Way Trust Relationships

When the domains are joined by two one-way trusts, it is known as a two-way trust relationship. Accounts and resources are administered in each domain but can be given permission to access resources in the other domain. For example, let's say a company, Trey Research, has two independent business units that want total control over its users, servers, and workstations. Each business unit can create its own domain with user accounts and resources. By establishing a two-way trust relationship between the domains, the users with accounts in each domain can have access to resources in the other domain.

The graphic below illustrates the differences between one-way trust relationships and two-way trust relationships.

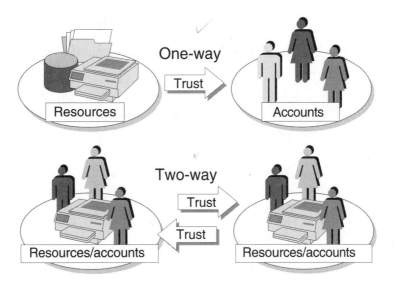

Representing Trusts Between Domains

When diagramming trusts and domains, trusts are always indicated with an arrow. In a one-way trust, the point or head of the arrow points to the trusted domain, where the accounts reside, and away from the trusting domain, which usually contains shared resources.

In a two-way trust relationship, indicated by two arrows pointing in opposite directions, each domain contains accounts that may use resources in the other domain.

Trusting and Trusted Domains

In every trust relationship, one domain is always the trusted domain and the other is the trusting domain.

- Trusted domain: The key to understanding all trusts lies in the phrase "arrows point to people you can trust." The arrows in all trust diagrams point to the domains where accounts are kept. These domains will be known as trusted or account domains.

- Trusting domain: The arrows point away from the trusting domain. Resources are usually located in trusting domains, also known as resource domains.

The concepts of trusted versus trusting can be thought of in terms of users and resources. The domain with the resources trusts users from a remote domain and allows them to use the resources if the proper trust relationship has been established and appropriate permissions have been assigned.

For example, if your neighbor wanted to watch your television while you were on vacation, you would give your neighbor the key to your house so your neighbor could enter your house and use your television while you were gone. You have set up a one-way trust relationship with your neighbor in which you trust your neighbor.

Your neighbor with the key represents an account from the trusted domain. Your house represents the trusting domain with resources in the form of the television. In a diagram of this arrangement, the arrow would point from your house, with its television, to your neighbor.

The figure below illustrates the difference between a trusting and a trusted domain.

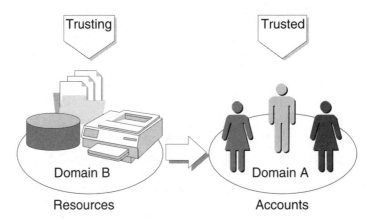

Accounts in Trust Relationships

In an enterprise network without trusts, domains would exist as independent network entities unable to communicate easily with each other. Each domain would have to be managed separately. This would affect not only network traffic and resource access, but also the type of accounts the network can use.

Account Types and Trusts

An environment in which domains are unconnected by trusts would require separate network accounts for each domain. These accounts would be able to use resources only in their own domains. Such accounts, called local accounts, do exist in Windows NT Server. However, in an environment where it is essential to share resources across domains, Windows NT uses another more versatile type of user account called a global account.

Global Accounts

In the Windows NT Server environment, global accounts can cross trusts to use resources in different domains. Therefore, global accounts are essential to the concept of "one user, one account."

Because global accounts are used so extensively in the Windows NT Directory Services environment, it is understood that the word account refers to a global account unless otherwise noted. In fact, global accounts are the default Windows NT account.

The figure below illustrates the differences between global and local Windows NT accounts.

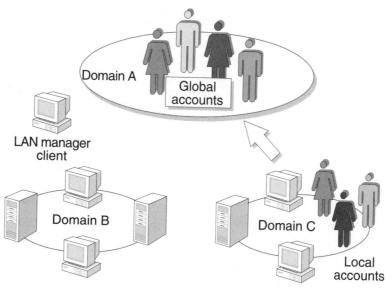

Local Accounts

Local accounts refer to user and group accounts that are local to a particular domain. Users and global groups from outside the local domain can be added to local groups only if they belong to a trusted domain. Local signifies that the group can be granted rights and permissions to use resources in only a single (local) domain. A local group can contain users and global groups, but it cannot contain other local groups.

The Limitations of Local Accounts

The use of local accounts in Windows NT Directory Services is limited because they cannot:

- Support interactive logon processes.
- Cross trusts.

In fact, there are only two uses for local accounts in Windows NT. Use local accounts in the following situations:

- When a user has an account in a domain that does not have a trust relationship with the remote domain in which he or she is accessing resources. A domain that does not have a trust relationship with a remote domain is often referred to as an untrusted domain.
- When a user needs access to resources on a Windows NT Server domain from a network, such as Microsoft LAN Manager, that does not participate in trusts.

Using Built-in Groups to Manage Trusts

The appropriate use of trust relationships and global and local groups can centralize the administration of a multiple domain environment. In such an environment, the primary group strategy is the same as that of a single domain: putting users into global groups and global groups into local groups. However, across trust relationships, the global groups are defined in the trusted domain, and the local groups exist in all domains.

In most cases, built-in groups are the key to efficient network management.

Built-in Local Groups

Windows NT Server comes with several built-in local groups. Built-in local groups are used to give users rights to perform system tasks, such as backing up and restoring files or changing the system time, and also to administer system resources.

Built-in local groups are divided into three categories:

- Administrators: members of this group have full capabilities on a computer.
- Operator-groups: members of these groups have limited administrative capabilities to perform specific tasks.
- Other: members of these groups have capabilities to perform limited tasks.

The figure below explains where built-in local groups reside, either on a Windows NT Member Server (configured as a server) or on a Windows NT Server domain controller, and lists the capabilities the groups have.

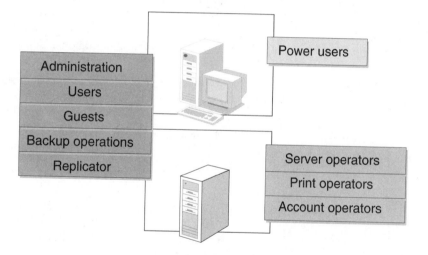

The table on the following page lists the local groups that are built into Windows NT Server domain controllers.

Local Group	Initially Contains	Who Can Modify?	Capabilities
Administrators	Domain Admins (global group) Administrator (user account)	Administrators	Create, delete, and manage user accounts, global groups, and local groups. Share directories and printers, grant resource permissions and rights. Install operating system files and programs.
Users	Domain Users (global group)	Administrators, Account Operators	Perform tasks for which they have been given rights. Access resources to which they have been given permissions.
Guests	Domain Guests (global group)	Administrators, Account Operators	Perform tasks for which they have been given rights. Access resources to which they have been given permissions.
Server Operators	None	Administrators	Share and stop sharing resources. Lock or override the lock of a server. Format the server's disks. Log on at servers. Back up and restore server. Shut down servers.
Print Operators	None	Administrators	Share and stop sharing printers. Manage printers. Log on locally at servers and shut down servers.
Backup Operators	None	Administrators	Back up and restore servers. Log on locally. Shut down the server.
Account Operators	None	Administrators	Create, delete, and modify users, global groups, and local groups. Cannot modify Administrator or any operator groups.
Replicator	None	Administrators, Account Operators Server Operators	Used in conjunction with the Directory Replicator Service.

Built-in Global Groups

The following table summarizes which global groups are built into Windows NT Server domain controllers.

Global Group	Initial Contents	Who Can Modify?	Initially Member of What Local Group?
Domain Admins	Administrator	Administrators	Administrators local group
Domain Users	Administrator	Administrators, Account Operators	Users local group
Domain Guests	Guest	Administrators, Account Operators	Guests local group

Global groups do not have the inherent authority to perform network functions that local groups do. To perform administrative tasks, global groups must be added to a local group; an example would be the addition of the global group Domain Admins to the local group Administrators.

User and Group Account Summary

The following table summarizes the different types of Windows NT accounts and their usage.

Type of Account	Function	Members
Local user—must be specially created	To access resources in a trusted domain from an untrusted domain. To access resources in a Windows NT domain from a network that does not use trusts.	
Global user—the default Windows NT account	To access resources across trusts.	
Local group	To provide users with permission to access a network resource or rights to perform designated system tasks such as backing up or restoring files in the local domain.	Local and Global users from the local domain. Global users and global groups from trusted domains.
Global group	To organize domain user accounts and cross trusts from trusted domains to trusting domains.	Global users from the local domain.

Group Strategies Across Trusts

The strategy for using local and global groups across trusts can be the same re-gardless of the domain model.

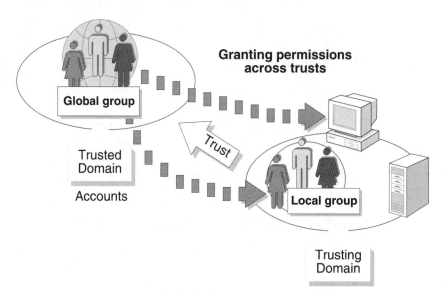

Guidelines for Effective Use of Local and Global Groups

To use both local and global groups effectively as a network management tool, an administrator should follow these guidelines:

1. Determine if there is a local group that can perform the task. If not, create one and give it an applicable name.

2. Assign permissions to the local group, if necessary.

3. Assign the appropriate users to existing or newly created global groups.

4. Assign global groups to the appropriate local groups.

This strategy requires minimal maintenance when your staff changes. All changes are made to global group membership at the domain controller; nothing needs to happen to the local groups or to the permissions and rights assigned to those local groups.

Domain controllers implement this strategy by default. For example:

- When a user account is created, it is automatically made a member of the global group Domain Users.

- Domain Users is a member of the local group Users. Therefore, the newly created user is a member of the local group, Users.

- Then, when a computer running Windows NT Workstation or Windows NT Server joins a domain, the global group, Domain Users, is automatically made a member of the new computer's local group, Users.

This exemplifies the strategy of putting users into global groups, and putting global groups into local groups.

Types of Groups Used in Network Management

The following table outlines which type of group you should use to manage a specific administrative activity.

Administrative Activity	Best Type of Group to Use	Explanation
Group domain users into a single unit for use in other domains.	Global	A global group can be put into local groups, or be given permissions and rights directly in other domains.
Manage permissions and rights on a particular domain.	Local	The local group can contain users and global groups from its own domain or from trusted domains.
Need permissions on a computer running Windows NT Workstation or Windows NT Server in a domain.	Global	Local groups in a domain only work on Windows NT Server domain controllers.
Contain other groups.	Local	Local groups can contain users and global groups.
Include many users from many domains.	Local	A local group can include users and global groups from its own domain and from trusted domains.

Global groups have no built-in user rights. They get their user rights from the local group to which they are assigned. Global groups are available within a domain or across a trust in a trusting domain. For example, members of the Domain Administrators global group do not become administrators unless the Domain Administrators global group is added to the local Administrators group.

Granting Permissions Across Trusts

Once a trust has been established, an administrator can grant permissions across the trust. Permissions can be set at the time a user or a group is added to a domain, or permissions can be modified at a later time.

Note Permissions are added and modified through Windows NT Explorer as described in *Administering Microsoft Windows NT 4.0*.

The Net Logon Service

The Net Logon service governs communication between domains. The Net Logon service is responsible for three functions that affect network performance:

- Logon validation: when a user logs on to a Windows NT Server domain, the Net Logon service validates that user.

- Synchronization of backup domain controllers (BDCs) with primary domain controllers (PDCs): this function keeps the directory services databases synchronized between the PDC and one or more BDCs.

- Pass-through authentication: this occurs when a user account must be validated, but the local computer or domain cannot validate the account. In this case, the user name and password are forwarded to a Windows NT Server domain controller that can validate the user. The user's information is then returned to the requesting computer.

The figure below illustrates the functions of the Net Logon service.

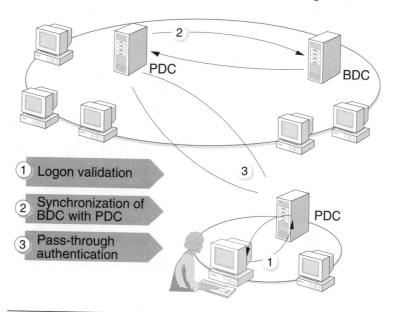

Note Each computer running Windows NT that is participating in the domain must be running the Net Logon service. In addition, each computer must also be running the Workstation and Server services because the Net Logon service is dependent on these services.

Pass-Through Authentication

Pass-through authentication makes it possible for users to log on to the network from computers or domains in which they have no account. With pass-through authentication, a user with an account on one domain can access the entire network—including all domains that trust the user's account domain. Once logged on, the user is known on the network as DomainName\Username, where Domain-Name is the domain that contains the user's account and authenticates the logon request. For example, in a large network consisting of several domains linked by trust relationships, a user can log on at a computer in Domain B and be verified by the user account database in Domain A.

Pass-through authentication can occur during either of the following instances:

- At initial logon when a user is logging on to a trusted domain.
- When connecting to a resource in a trusting domain.

The figure below illustrates the process of pass-through authentication between two domains.

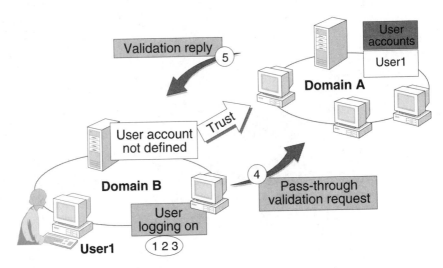

The trusted domain logon process is done in the following sequence:

1. The Windows NT computer starts. When its Net Logon service starts, it locates a Windows NT Server domain controller in its domain (Domain B).

2. User1 attempts to log on at a computer in Domain B with a user account from Domain A by selecting Domain A in the domain entry of the logon dialog box.

3. The Windows NT Server domain controller in Domain B cannot authenticate the request because the request is for a Domain A user account.

4. The authentication request is passed through the trust to a Windows NT Server domain controller in Domain A. This Windows NT Server domain controller checks Domain A's account database for the existence of User1's account and for correct password information.

5. The domain controller in Domain A authenticates User1's request and passes the security ID (SID) and group information about User1 back to the domain controller in Domain B. The domain controller in Domain B then passes the information to User1's Windows NT-based computer and completes the logon process.

Note For more information on viewing the structure of an existing domain, see "Domain Monitor" in the *Windows NT Server Resource Kit.*

Examining Resource Management Scenarios

The following figure depicts six resource management options. Read the following scenarios and answer the questions to see if you can figure out which of the six resource management situations are successful and which are not.

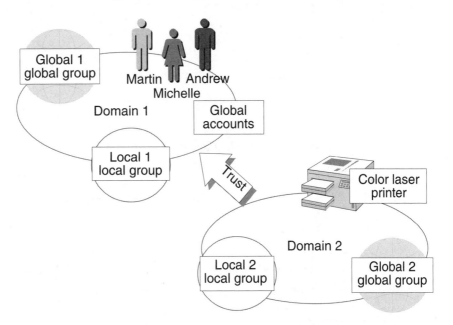

Use the components pictured in the figure above when working on the following scenarios. When you have completed the scenario exercises, you should be able to answer the following questions:

- Which of the following scenarios would be successful?
- Which of the following scenarios would not be successful?
- Why would unsuccessful ones fail?

Scenario 1

Problem

The administrator wants Andrew, Michelle, and Martin to be able to use the color laser printer.

Procedure

The administrator assigned Andrew, Michelle, and Martin to Global 2 and gave Global 2 permissions to use the printer.

Evaluation

Answer the following questions.

1. Did the scenario work?

   _____

   _____

2. If the scenario failed, why did it fail?

   _____

   _____

3. What could the administrator do to make this work?

   _____

   _____

Scenario 2

Problem

The administrator wants Andrew, Michelle, and Martin to be able to use the color laser printer.

Procedure

The administrator assigned Andrew, Michelle, and Martin to Global 1, assigned Global 1 to Global 2, and gave Global 2 permissions to use the printer.

Evaluation

1. Did the scenario work?

   _____

   _____

2. If the scenario failed, why did it fail?

   _____

   _____

3. What could the administrator do to make this work?

   _____

   _____

Scenario 3

Problem

The administrator wants Andrew, Michelle, and Martin to be able to use the color laser printer.

Procedure

The administrator assigned Andrew, Michelle, and Martin to Local 1, assigned Local 1 to Local 2, and gave Local 2 permissions to use the printer.

Evaluation

1. Did the scenario work?

   _____

   _____

2. If the scenario failed, why did it fail?

   _____

   _____

3. What could the administrator do to make this work?

   _____

   _____

Scenario 4

Problem

The administrator wants Andrew, Michelle, and Martin to be able to use the color laser printer.

Procedure

The administrator assigned Andrew, Michelle, and Martin to Global 1, assigned Global 1 to Local 2, and gave Local 2 permissions to use the printer.

Evaluation

1. Did the scenario work?

   _____

   _____

2. If the scenario failed, why did it fail?

   _____

   _____

3. What could the administrator do to make this work?

   _____

   _____

Establishing and Managing Trust Relationships

Trust relationships are primarily for managing accounts. When first setting up a trust relationship, identify which domain is going to be the trusted domain.

There are two keys to establishing one-way and two-way trust relationships:

- One domain must allow another domain access to its user accounts.
- The second domain must confirm that permission has been granted to access the first domain.

Once a trust relationship has been established between domains, permissions can be granted across the trust.

Important   The trust relationship will not be complete until both domains have done their part to establish the trust relationship. The trust can be initiated from either domain.

Trust Relationship Requirements

There are several requirements for establishing a trust between two domains:

- Each domain in the trust requires a unique SID. All user account authentication is based on that account's SID. If there are anomalies in a domain's SID, this will cause problems using trust relationships.

  Note   To verify a domain SID, use the GETSID utility included in the *Windows NT Resource Kit*.

- Only users with administrator accounts have the right to set up either side of a trust relationship.

- The PDCs in each domain in the trust relationship must be free of any sessions between them.

- One computer cannot connect to another computer using two different accounts. When a trust relationship is established, the system account must be used. If another session is already established between the two PDCs, that session will fail.

- Although setting up trust relationships can be done from any domain client using the server tools (User Manager for Domains), communication between the two PDCs is required.

- If the PDCs in each domain do not share a common protocol and cannot connect to each other, the trust relationship will not be established. This common protocol should be set to the highest-level binding for both the server and workstation components on each PDC.

- If the connection between the two PDCs fails, the trust will not be established.

The figure below outlines the requirements for establishing a trust.

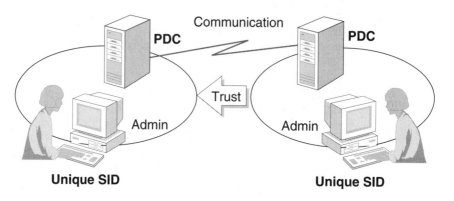

Setting Up a One-Way Trust

Trust relationships are established using User Manager for Domains. To set up a one-way trust relationship, start User Manager for Domains, and then, on the **Policies** menu, click **Trust Relationships**. There are two sections in the Trust Relationships dialog box:

- The Trusted Domains box is completed by the trusting domain. This section specifies "what domain do I trust?" that is, "who is my trusted domain?"

- The Trusting Domain is completed by the trusted domain. It specifies the names of the trusting domains, that is, "who is permitted to trust me?"

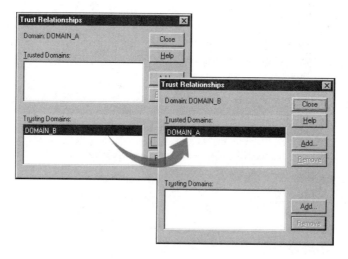

The order in which trusts are established is not critical. However, it is better to establish the trusting domain relationship first, and then establish the trusted domain relationship. This way, the new trust relationship takes effect immediately. If the trusted domain relationship is established before the trusting domain relationship, it can take up to 15 minutes for the trust relationship to take effect.

Below is a recommended sequence that ensures that the administrator from the trusting domain receives a verification of a successfully established trust relationship:

1. The administrator in a trusted (account) domain initiates a trust by adding the name of a trusting (resource) domain in the **Trusting Domains** box.

2. The administrator in the trusting domain completes the trust by adding the name of the trusted (account) domain in the **Trusted Domains** box.

Setting Up a Two-Way Trust

After you set up a one-way trust, you can set up a two-way trust. Setting up two-way trust relationships is very much like setting up one-way trust relationships.

1. Establish a one-way trust.

2. Set up another one-way trust, but reverse the roles of trusted and trusting.

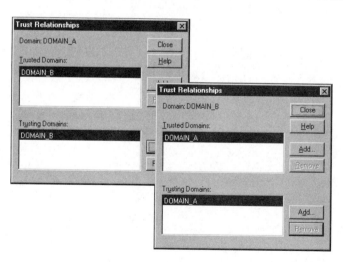

When a two-way trust is established, the same domain name appears in both the **Trusted Domains** and the **Trusting Domain** boxes.

Passwords

The administrator in the trusted (account) domain may provide a password as part of implementing the trust. The administrator in the trusting (resource) domain must enter this password when it is time for the trusting domain to complete the trust. That is the only time the trusting domain administrator needs to enter the password.

This password is another form of security. The trusted domain administrator uses the password to control which domains will be allowed to participate in trust relationships.

Note Turning a computer off will not affect trusts. As long as there is one domain controller running in the trusted domain, the trust will remain in effect. If all domain controllers are off, starting one will reestablish the trust.

Non-Transitive and Broken Trusts

A trust relationship involves only two domains, and therefore a trust relationship is not transitive.

Two types of problems can complicate trust functions in an enterprise system:

- The non-transitive nature of trusts.

- Broken trusts.

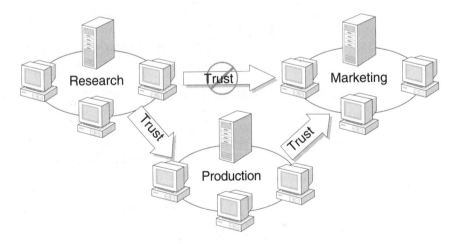

Trusts Are Non-Transitive

Windows NT trust relationships are non-transitive, meaning permissions between two domains cannot be passed through to a third domain. For example, as illustrated above, although the Research domain trusts the Production domain, and the Production domain trusts the Marketing domain, the Research domain does not trust the Marketing domain.

A user with an account in the Marketing domain who attempts to log on while physically located in the Research domain will not be authenticated because pass-through authentication will not occur between Research and Marketing. Marketing and Research have to set up their own trust relationship before pass-through authentication can occur between them.

Broken Trusts

A trust can be successfully implemented, function correctly for a period of time, and then fail. A failed or broken trust is rare, but it can be caused by the following:

- The renaming of one of the domains in the trust.

- A broken physical link (the network cable).

- A faulty or stopped Net Logon service.

Managing Trust Relationships

The most common problems that you will have with trust relationships are listed below.

- Cannot establish a trust relationship.

- Cannot verify the trust relationship.

- The trust is broken.

- Cannot reestablish a broken trust.

- Cannot use trusted accounts.

- Cannot administer another domain.

- Access is denied using trusted accounts.

- Cannot access other domain resources using a local account.

When creating, maintaining, and using trust relationships, there are a number of issues that can inhibit proper use of the trust. The table on the following page contains a list of common trust relationship issues and possible resolutions.

Issue	Possible Resolution
Trust relationship can't be established.	Verify that the PDC in each domain is running. Verify that the PDC in each domain can resolve the other's name, using Windows Internet Naming Service (WINS) or some other name resolution method.
Verifying the trust relationship doesn't work.	The trusted domain must allow the trusting domain before the trusting domain can attempt to establish the trust relationship. Verify that no session exists with the PDC.
Broken trust relationship.	If a trust relationship is broken, trusted accounts will not be available for use anymore. Reestablish the trust relationship.
Reestablishing a broken trust fails.	Verify that the PDC in each domain is running.
Trusted accounts are not useable.	The trust relationship may have been established in the wrong direction. Break the existing relationship, and have the trusted domain allow the trusting domain, and the trusting domain trust the trusted domain.
Cross-domain administration fails.	Verify that the trusted domain's Domain Admins group is added to the local Administrators group.
Access is denied when using trusted accounts.	Check to see if the same account name exists in both domains. In a trust relationship, each account should appear only in one domain, either the trusted domain or the local domain, but not both.
A local account can use resources in a remote domain.	Check if the same account name exists in both domains. In a trust relationship, each account should appear only in one domain, either the trusted domain or the local domain, but not both.

Trust relationships are powerful tools that give network administrators the ability to manage user and group permissions across multiple domains in an enterprise network. The Net Logon service is the key to creating and managing multiple trust relationships. Once trust relationships between domains have been established, pass-through authentication allows users to log on from anywhere on the network and receive the appropriate permissions. Having acquired a sound understanding of these technologies, network designers are further equipped to plan efficient and easily managed Windows NT Enterprise Networks.

Designing NT Networks

In the following exercise you use the knowledge of trust relationships you have gained to adjust the network designs

Scenario 1

The Just Togs company is located in a single office and has approximately 100 users. The network will be used for basic file and print sharing and will also have one Windows NT Server running SQL Server. The majority of users will need access to SQL Server. Desktop applications will be installed on the local computers, but data files will be saved on the servers.

1. How many domains will you need to use?

   _____

   _____

2. How many trusts will need to be configured?

   _____

   _____

Scenario 2

Parnell Aerospace has 10,000 users. Eight thousand are located in four primary sites with the remaining employees located in 20 branch offices in major U.S. cities. The company currently has LANs installed in each location but will be upgrading them with Windows NT Server. Plans are to maintain the four administrative units, but this could change with your recommendations. Three of the four primary sites are separate business units that operate independently of the others. The fourth is the corporate headquarters. Branch offices have between 25 and 250 users needing access to all four of the primary sites but seldom needing access to the other branch offices.

1. How many trusted domains will you need to configure?

   _____

   _____

2. How many resource domains will need to be configured?

   _____

   _____

3. How many trusts will need to be configured?

_____

_____

Scenario 3

Wide World Importers has 60,000 users located around the world. The corporate headquarters are in Geneva, Switzerland. North and South American headquarters are located in New York City. The Australia and Asia headquarters are located in Singapore. Each of the Regional headquarters will maintain total control of users and equipment within their areas. They will require access to resources in the other regional headquarters.

Draft a network design using the following criteria.

Environmental Components	Detail
Users	60,000
Locations	3 primary sites with 60 smaller sites in major cities around the world.
Administration	Full-time administrators at each of the 3 primary sites; some of the smaller sites have part-time administrators.
Number of domain controllers	To be determined.
Clients	386 and 486 computers, running Windows for Workgroups 3.11, Windows 95, or Windows NT Workstation.
Server applications	SQL Server, Microsoft SNA Sever, Microsoft Systems Management Server, and Messaging.

Zurich
Users: 15,000
Sites: 15

New York City
Users: 20,000
Sites: 20

Singapore
Users: 25,000
Sites: 25

1. How many trusted domains will you use?

   _____

   _____

2. How many trusting domains will need to be configured?

   _____

   _____

3. How many trusts will need to be configured?

   _____

   _____

4. Use the space below to sketch your network design.

   _____

   _____

Lesson Summary

The following information summarizes the key points in this lesson:

- Implementing a one-way trust relationship involves using User Manager for Domains to establish a one-way trust relationship with another domain.

- The Net Logon service is responsible for three functions that affect network performance.

  - Logon validation: validation of all users logging on to a Windows NT Server domain.

  - Synchronization of BDCs with PDCs: maintains a current directory database for all domain controllers.

  - Pass-through authentication: the forwarding of validation of user accounts to the appropriate server.

- Use global and local groups to perform administration across a trust relationship involves adding a global group from the trusted domain to the local Administrators group in the trusting domain.

- Implementing a two-way trust relationship involves establishing two one-way trusts with another domain.

Lesson 6: Managing Shared Resources

Windows NT Server allows you to designate resources you want to share with other users. Resources can be files, directories, or printers. This lesson examines the issues involved in sharing files and printers and the management of these resources.

After this lesson, you will be able to:

- Identify the differences between directory, file, and share permissions.
- Compress and decompress NTFS volumes.
- Secure shared directories and files.
- Establish replication of shared directories.

Estimated lesson time: 20 minutes

Sharing a Server Directory

When a directory is shared, authorized users can make network connections to the directory and access its files from their workstations. When a printer is shared, users can print from it over the network.

Once a resource is shared, you can restrict its availability to certain users and grant certain types of permissions. These restrictions, called share permissions, can vary from user to user. Windows NT Server allows you to create the appropriate level of network resource security with a combination of resource sharing and resource permissions.

Directory or File Permissions and Share Permissions

Windows NT Server provides superior performance, reliability, and security for file sharing. Windows NT file system (NTFS) allows you to use permissions to protect individual files. You can apply this protection to local access as well as to access over the network. Share permissions determine who can use shared directories over the network and in what manner.

NTFS File and Directory Permissions

NTFS volumes allow you to set permissions on directories and files, and these permissions apply to users accessing the files from the server. When the NTFS directory is shared, these same file and directory permissions apply to users accessing the shared directory over the network. Therefore, share permissions are not critical to security of NTFS directories.

NTFS volumes also allow you to set file permissions on files and directory permissions on directories, specifying which groups and users have access. Additionally, you can specify what level of access is permitted. NTFS file and directory permissions apply both to users working on the computer where the file is stored and to users accessing the file over the network when the file is in a shared directory.

Share permissions for NTFS volumes work in combination with file and directory permissions. When a directory is shared, share permissions allow users to connect to the share. By default, the permissions for a new share is Everyone/Full Control on an NTFS partition. Using Full Control permission for Everyone on all NTFS shared directories is the easiest way to manage NTFS file security. This way, you have to manage only the file and directory permissions. Share permissions are opened for Everyone to have Full Control.

FAT Share Permissions

Volumes that have the file allocation table (FAT) file system allow you to protect files only at the directory level, over the network, and if the directory is shared. Once a directory is shared, you can protect it by specifying one set of share permissions that applies to the share point, and thus to users who connect to the shared directory over the network. Share permissions are significantly less versatile than the file and directory permissions used for NTFS volumes. File level protection is not available for FAT volumes.

File and Directory Compression on NTFS Partitions

Windows NT allows NTFS volumes to be compressed. Directory and file compression can be useful tools in managing shared resources. Files and directories on NTFS volumes can be configured for compression using Windows NT Explorer or the command line utility compact.

Once configured for compression, Windows NT handles the compression and decompression of files as they are written and read from the disk drive. NTFS disk compression has the following properties:

- You can compress one file or all files in a directory. Compressing a directory ensures that new files created in the directory are automatically compressed. Decompressing a directory ensures that new files created in the directory are created decompressed.

- When you copy a file into a directory or subdirectory within an NTFS volume (or from one NTFS volume to another), the file inherits the compression state of the destination directory.

- When you move a file into a directory or subdirectory within an NTFS volume, the file retains its compression state, regardless of the compression setting of the destination directory.

- When you move a file from one NTFS volume to another, the file inherits the compression state of the destination directory.

- When you compress or decompress a directory, Windows Explorer prompts you to indicate whether to compress or decompress existing subdirectories in the selected directory. Existing subdirectories in compressed or decompressed directories retain their compression state unless you change it.

- You can choose to highlight compressed files and directories in an alternate color by clicking **Options** on the **View** menu.

- Other file operations can be performed during compression and decompression.

How NTFS Permissions Work

Before sharing a directory on an NTFS volume, set individual permissions on the directory and its files and subdirectories. Each permission specifies the access that a group or user can have to the directory or file.

Windows NT Server offers a set of standard permissions for NTFS directories and files. The standard permissions are a combination of specific types of access, called individual permissions. The individual permissions and their abbreviations are:

Read (R)	Write (W)	Execute (X)
Delete (D)	Change Permissions (P)	Take Ownership (O)

Standard permissions and their significance for directories and files are shown in the following tables, along with the individual permissions they represent. In the first column of the first table (for directory permissions), the first set of parentheses following the standard permission indicates the individual permissions for the directory itself. The second set of parentheses indicates the individual permissions that apply to new files subsequently created in the directory.

Standard Permissions for NTFS Directories and Files

File level and directory level access rights are listed in the table below.

Permission	Meaning
Directory:	
No Access (None) (None)	User cannot access the directory in any way, even if the user is a member of a group that has been granted access to the directory.
List (RX) (Not Specified)	User can list only the files and subdirectories in this directory and change to a subdirectory of this directory. User cannot access new files created in this directory.
Read (RX) (RX)	User can read the contents of files in this directory and run applications in the directory.
Add (WX) (Not Specified)	User can add files to the directory but cannot view the contents of the directory.
Add & Read (RWX) (RX)	User can add files to the directory and read current files but cannot change files.
Change (RWXD) (RWXD)	User can read and add files and change the contents of current files.
Full Control (All) (All)	User can read and change files, add new ones, change permissions for the directory and its files, and take ownership of the directory and its files.
File:	
No Access	User cannot access the file in any way, even if the user is a member of a group that has been granted access to the file.
Read (RX)	User can read the contents of the file and run it if it is an application.
Change (RWXD)	User can read, modify, and delete the file.
Full Control (All)	User can read, modify, delete, set permissions for, and take ownership of the file.

When you set a standard permission, the abbreviations for the individual permissions appear beside the standard permission. For example, when you set the standard permission Read on a file, the abbreviation RX appears beside it.

In addition to setting standard permissions, you can set special access permissions. Special access permissions allow you to define a custom set of individual permissions for directories and files.

To Effectively Work with NTFS Security

- Users can use a directory or file only if they have been granted permission to do so or if they belong to a group that has permission to do so.

- Permissions are cumulative, but the No Access permission overrides all others.

- When you create files and subdirectories in a directory, they inherit permissions from the directory.

- The user who creates a file or directory is the owner of that file or directory. The owner can always control access to the file or directory by changing the permissions set on it. Users who are members of the Administrators group can always take ownership of a file or directory.

- File permissions always override directory permissions.

- The easiest way to administer security is by setting permissions for groups rather than individual users.

Taking Ownership of NTFS Files and Directories

Every file and directory on an NTFS volume has an owner. The owner controls how permissions are set on the file or directory and can grant permissions to others.

When a file or directory is created, the person creating the file or directory automatically becomes its owner. It is expected that administrators will create most files on network servers, such as when they install applications on the server. Most files on a server will be owned by administrators (except for data files created by users and files in users' home directories).

Ownership can be transferred in the following two ways:

- The current owner can grant the Take Ownership permission to other users, allowing those users to take ownership at any time.

- An administrator can take ownership of any file on the computer.

Managing Files Shares and Permissions

In this exercise you answer questions about File Share and its permissions.

1. Are share permissions as important on an NTFS share as on a FAT share? Why or why not?

   _____

   _____

2. You can compress only entire directories at a time; you cannot compress individual files.

   True _____

   False _____

3. When you move a file from one NTFS partition to another NTFS partition, the file inherits the file compression state of the destination directory.

   True _____

   False _____

4. When you move a file into a directory within an NTFS volume, the file retains its compression state, regardless of the compression settings of the destination directory.

   True _____

   False _____

5. If a user has Read (RX) permissions and No Access (none) permissions on a file in an NTFS directory, the user will be able to read the file.

   True _____

   False _____

6. File permissions always override directory permissions.

   True _____

   False _____

7. Which user can always take ownership of a file regardless of permissions on that file?

   _____

   _____

Network Print Shares

To share a printer with network computers, select the **Sharing** tab in the printer's Properties sheet, click **Shared**, and then provide a share name.

Although you can create long printer names containing spaces and special characters, some clients do not recognize or handle these names correctly. If you use a mixture of clients on your network, choose printer names that have 31 or fewer characters and do not contain spaces or special characters.

Windows NT computers can connect to a printer using either the printer name or the printer share name. Computers running other operating systems connect to the printer share name. If you are sharing printers with computers running MS-DOS, share names must be no more than eight characters, optionally followed by a period and one to three characters, and should not contain spaces.

Use the **Scheduling** tab of the printer's Properties sheet to change the document scheduling and spooling settings. You can set:

- The range of time the printer is available.

- Document priority.

- Document spooling options.

- Print-queue management options.

The following table shows the specific options in the **Scheduling** tab of the printer's Properties sheet.

Option	Description
Available	Defines when the printer is available.
Priority	Sets up a varied priority print queue based on document priority.
Start printing after last page is spooled	Prevents delays when the print server prints pages faster than clients can provide them.
Start printing immediately	Prints documents as quickly as possible (the default).
Print directly to the printer	Sends documents to the print device without first writing them to the print server's hard disk drive.
Hold mismatched documents	Has the spooler hold documents if they do not match the available form. This allows other documents that do match the form to print until the correct form is loaded.

(continued)

Option	Description
Print spooled documents first	Has the spooler print documents in the order that they finish spooling, rather than in the order that they start spooling. Use this option with Start printing immediately.
Keep documents after they have printed	Allows users to resubmit a document from the print queue instead of from an application.

Print Queues

All direct management of printers and documents takes place through the Printers folder. Some queue management options control the entire print queue; others control a single document.

When managing the queue you can:

- View a list of documents for each installed printer.
- Pause or resume printing.
- Purge documents waiting for a printer.

When managing a document you can:

- Pause or resume printing.
- Restart the document from the beginning.
- Delete a document.
- View, and optionally change, various document settings.

Troubleshooting Printing Problems

When troubleshooting printing problems, the best approach is to change the control of the printing flow to avoid using a particular component; then, if the symptoms change, the component you isolated is involved in the problem. The following section provides a list of tests that are useful in isolating components.

Creating a Printer, Connecting to a Printer

- Create a new printer using a different, more simplistic name.
- Share the existing printer with a different, more simplistic name.
- Quit sharing a printer, then reshare it.

- Delete the printer that is malfunctioning, stop and restart the spooler service, and recreate the printer.

- Try a different client operating system using the same type of connection.

- Try the same client operating system with a different type of connection.

- Try a different client operating system and a different type of connection. (Note: Windows NT can both send and receive jobs over any type of connection.)

- Log on to the client as a different user, preferably a network administrator.

Creating a Print Job

- Create and print a new document containing only a few characters, formatted in one, commonplace font with no graphics or embedded objects.

- Print from the same application running on a different client.

- Try another version of the same application.

- Test with a different application.

- Verify that you have the right printer driver (make and model), configured to match the target print device's configuration (memory, fonts, paper trays, and so on).

- If the device supports multiple languages (such as PCL and PostScript), try a driver for one of the other languages.

Delivering the Job to the Spooler

See the suggestions for "Creating a Printer, Connecting to a Printer," and follow the instructions below:

- Print to a file on the client, and copy that file to the Windows NT print server. Log on at the print server, share the target printer, and from a command prompt, copy the file to the print share. For example:

```
COPY  CLIENT.PRN  \\SERVER\PRINTER
```

If the symptoms change, the problem involves job delivery or modification, and you should follow the instructions in the next section.

Modifying the Job

- Reconfigure the client so that the server-side service assigns a different data type.

- Use a different type of connection (Windows Network, NetWare, LPR, and so on) to force the job to receive a different data type.

- Change the Default Datatype value in Print Manager.

- Print to a file on the client, then send that file to a Windows NT printer that prints to FILE: If the client's and server's output files are identical, the server didn't modify the job.

Delivering the Job to the Destination

- Print to FILE: to verify that the local port monitor finishes processing the entire job.

- Print to the same device using a different type of port (many network-attached print devices support several port types).

- Print to a different device of the same make, model, and configuration.

- Print to a different printer on the same remote print server.

- Print to a different remote print server.

- Print to a print server running a different operating system.

Accessing Network Resources

There are several ways to connect to shared directories. In Windows NT Server, Windows NT Workstation, and Windows 95, you can use the **Find** command on the **Start** menu to connect to any computer or shared directory on the network, or double-click a computer in Network Neighborhood.

To assign a drive letter in My Computer for a particular share, use the **Map Network Drive** command on the **Tools** menu in the Explorer. Type the server name and share name into the **Path** box using the form *servername\sharename*. For **Drive,** you can use the next letter available or select a letter from the drop-down list.

For example, to connect to the shared directory Applications on the server named DEPT35, type the location in the **Path** box as shown below:

In Windows Explorer and My Computer, the mapped drive appears in the window as Applications on 'DEPT35' (J:)

The share appears as a drive on your computer, and the contents of the shared directory can be viewed as if they were on your computer. You can have the connection reestablished each time you log on, or clear the **Reconnect at Logon** check box to automatically disconnect when you log off.

In addition to uniform naming convention (UNC) names such as the names of network servers, domain name system (DNS) names can be used in the **Map Network Drive** dialog box. DNS names use periods to separate each part of the name; for example, \\accounting.trey.com\public.

If you want to connect to a shared directory using a different user account, use the **Connect As** box to type the user name for that account. If the account is in a different domain, type the domain name followed by a backslash and then the user name; for example, **projects\patc**.

Connecting to a Shared Printer

Printer permissions specify the type of access a user or group has to use the printer. The printer permissions are No Access, Print, Manage Documents, and Full Control.

Note If you are the owner of the printer or have Full Control permission, you can set and change printer permissions.

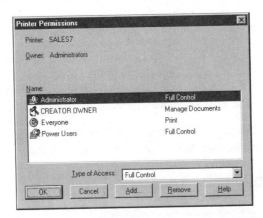

Directory Replication

Keeping shared resources current is a helpful task performed by Windows NT Server Directory Replicator service. If you have a set of files that you want distributed to many users, you can set up and maintain identical directory trees on multiple servers and workstations, and split the load among several computers.

Configure one server to act as an export server. Place the master copies of the files here. Configure the other computers to act as import computers.

Only one copy of each file needs to be maintained, yet every computer that participates has an available, identical copy of that set of files. Each export server maintains a list of computers to which subdirectories are exported, and each import computer maintains a list of computers from which subdirectories are imported.

When you update a file in the directory tree on one server (the export server), the updated file is automatically copied to all the other computers (the import computers). Only servers running Windows NT Server can be export servers; import computers can run either Windows NT Server or Windows NT Workstation.

A file is replicated when it is first added to an exported directory and every time a change is saved to the file on the export server.

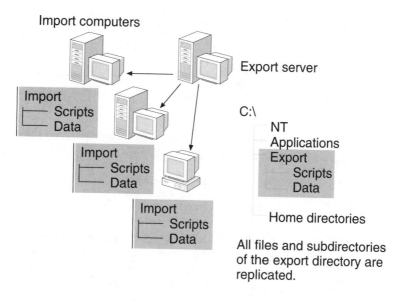

All files and subdirectories of the export directory are replicated.

Replication helps balance loads. If you have many users who need to periodically access the same file, you can replicate the file directory to several computers to prevent any one server from becoming overburdened.

You can even replicate directories between computers in different domains. Export servers can export to domain names, and import computers can import from those domain names. This is a convenient way to set up directory replication for many computers; each export server and import computer needs to specify only a few domain names for export or import, rather than a long list of many computer names.

Export Server

Directory replication is initiated and carried out by the Directory Replicator service. This service operates on each export server and import computer that participates in replication. The service on each computer logs on to the same user account, which you create for this purpose.

You set up an export server and import computers to send and receive updated files. An export directory on the export server contains all the directories and subdirectories of files to be replicated, and when changes are saved to files in these directories, the files automatically replace the existing files on all the import computers.

You can also specify whether to have the export server send changes out as soon as a file has changed or, to prevent exporting partially changed trees, to wait until one export subdirectory has been stable for two minutes before exporting.

In addition, you can lock a particular export or import directory when needed. Changes to the locked directory are not exported or imported until you unlock the directory.

On the export server, you also designate which computers or domains are to receive replicated copies of the directories this server is exporting.

An export server has a default export path:

C:*systemroot*\\SYSTEM32\\repl\\Export

All directories to be replicated are exported as subdirectories in the export path. Subdirectories created in the export path, and files placed in those subdirectories, are automatically exported. Export servers can replicate any number of subdirectories (limited only by available memory) with each exported subdirectory having up to 32 subdirectory levels in its tree.

An import computer has a default import path:

C:*systemroot*\\SYSTEM32\\repl\\Import

Imported subdirectories and their files are automatically placed here. You do not need to create these import subdirectories. They are created automatically when replication occurs.

A network can have multiple export servers. To ensure the integrity of replicated information, the export servers usually do not export duplicate subdirectories. Each master export subdirectory is usually maintained on, and exported by, a single export server. It is possible to set up multiple servers that export the same subdirectory, but the exported files in those multiple master subdirectories might not be identical.

Replication Prerequisites

Before a computer can participate in replication, you must create a special user account. Then for each computer in a domain that will participate in replication, configure its Directory Replicator service to log on using that special account:

- In User Manager for Domains, create a domain user account for the Directory Replicator service to use to log on. Be sure the user account has the **Password Never Expires** option selected, all logon hours allowed, and membership in the domain's Backup Operators group.

- After the user account is created for each computer that will be configured as an export server or an import computer, use Server Manager to configure the Directory Replicator service to start up automatically and to log on under that user account. Be sure the password for that user account is typed correctly.

Any computer running Windows NT Server can be set up as an export server. (A computer running Windows NT Workstation cannot.)

Before you set up an export server, you must perform these tasks on the export server:

- Assign a logon account to the Directory Replicator service of the export server.

- Create the directories to be exported. They must be subdirectories of the replication export path (usually C:*systemroot*\SYSTEM32\REPL\EXPORT).

Use the **Directory Replication** dialog box to set up an export server.

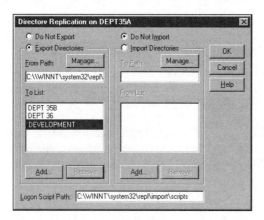

Managing Exported Subdirectories

By clicking **Manage** under **Export Directories** in the **Directory Replication** dialog box, you can manage certain features of subdirectory replication by the export server:

- You can lock a subdirectory to prevent it from being exported to any import computers. For example, if you know a directory will be receiving a series of changes that you do not want partially replicated, you can put one or more locks on the subdirectory in the export path. Until you remove the lock or locks, the subdirectory will not be replicated. The date and time the lock was placed is displayed so that you know how long a lock has been in force.

- When you stabilize a subdirectory, the export server waits two minutes after changes before exporting the subdirectory. The waiting period allows time for subsequent changes to take place so that all intended changes are recorded before being replicated.

- You specify whether the entire subtree (the export subdirectory and all of its subdirectories) or just the first-level subdirectory in the export directory path is exported.

To manage locks, stabilization, and subtree replication for the subdirectories exported from an export computer, click **Manage** under **Export Directories** in the **Directory Replication** dialog box.

By default, replication is configured so that Windows NT Server computers export subdirectories and logon scripts from the directory C:*systemroot*\\SYSTEM32\\REPL\\EXPORT\\SCRIPTS, and import subdirectories and logon scripts to the directory C:*systemroot*\\SYSTEM32\\REPL\\IMPORT\\SCRIPTS. For the primary domain controller (PDC) and each backup domain controller (BDC), the path to imported logon scripts must be entered in the **Logon Script Path** box of the **Directory Replication** dialog box.

Import Server

Both Windows NT Server and Windows NT Workstation computers can be set up as import computers. A computer running Windows NT Server that is configured as an export server can also be configured as an import computer.

Before you set up an import computer, you must assign a logon account to the Directory Replicator service of the import computer.

On the import computer, you do not need to create the imported subdirectories. A subdirectory is automatically created the first time it is imported.

Use the **Directory Replication** dialog box to set up an import computer. The Windows NT Server version of the **Directory Replication** dialog box is slightly different from the Windows NT Workstation version of this dialog box. The Windows NT Workstation version contains only the items related to imported directories.

You can set up a server to replicate a directory tree to itself (from its export directory to its import directory). This replication can provide a local backup of the files, or you can use the import version of these files as another source for users to access, while preserving the export version of the files as a source master.

Managing Locks and Viewing Import Subdirectory Status

You can use locks to prevent imports to subdirectories on an import computer. Import of a locked subdirectory to that import computer is prevented until the lock is removed. Locking a subdirectory on an import computer affects replication to only that computer, not to other import computers.

You can manage locks on subdirectories and also view the status of each subdirectory by clicking **Manage** under **Import Directories** in the **Directory Replication** dialog box.

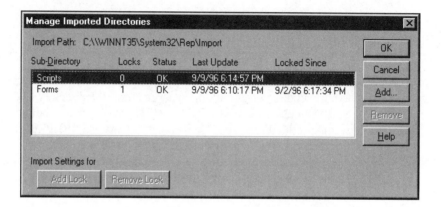

The **Status** column can have one of four entries:

- OK indicates that the subdirectory is receiving regular updates from an export server and that the imported data is identical to that exported.

- No Master indicates that the subdirectory is not receiving updates. The export server might not be running, or a lock might be in effect on the export server.

- No Sync indicates that although the subdirectory has received updates the data is not up-to-date. This could be due to a communications failure, open files on the import computer or export server, the import computer not having access permissions at the export server, or an export server malfunction.

- No entry (blank) indicates that replication never occurred for that subdirectory. Replication might not be properly configured for this import computer, for the export server, or both.

The **Last Update** column shows the date and time of the latest change to the import subdirectory or to any of its subdirectories.

Troubleshooting Replication

Directory replication problems can have a variety of causes. When the Replicator Service generates an error, you view the error in the Event Viewer. The Event Viewer displays information about the **Status** column in the **Manage Import Directories** dialog box and information about messages that appear while you are configuring directory replication servers.

The following sections describe some of the common problems encountered during directory replication.

Access Denied

If the Event Viewer shows "access denied" errors for the Directory Replicator service, be sure the service is configured to log on to a specific account and that the account used by the import computer's Directory Replicator service has permission to read the files on the export computer.

The default permissions for an export directory grant Full Control to the Replicator local group. If Full Control permission is removed from the directory, exported files are copied to the import computers but receive the wrong permissions, and an access denied error is written to the event log. If necessary, click **Permissions** in the export directory's **Sharing** tab to grant Full Control to the Replicator local group for the export directories.

Exporting to Specific Computers

Be sure to specify export servers and import computers in the **To List** and **From List**, respectively, in the **Directory Replication** dialog box. If you do not, exporting will occur to all import computers in the local domain, and importing will occur from all export servers in the local domain.

Lost Permissions on SYSTEM32\REPL\IMPORT

Do not use the Explorer or File Manager to examine permissions on the SYSTEM32\REPL\IMPORT directory. If you do, the special permissions initially set there can be lost. These initial permissions enable directory replication to work, and you do not need to change them.

Replication to a Domain Name Over a Wide Area Network (WAN) Link

Directory replication to a domain name does not always succeed when some or all replication import computers are located across a WAN bridge from an export server. When adding names to the export **To List** on an export server, and when adding names to the import **From List** on an import computer, specify the computer names (instead of, or in addition to, specifying the domain name) for those computers separated by a WAN bridge.

Sharing Printers and Network Resources

In this exercise you answer questions about print shares and network resources.

1. When sharing a printer on the network, computers can connect to the printer using the share name. Windows NT computers can also connect to the printer by using what name?

   _____

   _____

2. If you are going to share printers with MS-DOS computers, how many characters can the share name have?

   _____

   _____

3. When connecting to a network share, what is another method for connecting to the share other than through Network Neighborhood?

   _____

   _____

4. If you are logged on to Windows NT as user1, is it possible to connect to a share as user2?

   Yes ____

   No ____

Lesson Summary

The following information summarizes the key points in this lesson:

- There are permissions on the files and directories of NTFS partitions. In addition, there are permissions associated with directory shares. Share permissions are most useful when applied to shares on FAT partitions that do not have file and directory level permissions.

- NTFS volumes can be configured to compress files that reside on individual directories. This is transparent to the user and economizes disk space.

- Windows NT Server provides replication functionality. You can replicate files between servers.

Lesson 7: Remote Management of Servers

To remotely manage servers, you need to determine what services are running on the servers and what tools are needed to manage them. This lesson introduces the tools available to manage Windows NT Servers from Windows NT Workstation and Windows 95 computers.

After this lesson, you will be able to:

- Describe the Windows NT Server Tools available for Windows NT Workstation and Windows 95 computers.

- Describe how to install Windows NT Server Tools on Windows NT Workstation and Windows 95 computers.

Estimated lesson time: 10 minutes

Windows NT Server Tools

Windows NT Server Tools allow you to use a computer running Windows NT Workstation or Windows 95 to administer Windows NT Servers and the domain. These tools use Remote Procedure Calls (RPCs) to communicate between the workstation and the server they are administering. Through RPCs, administrative tasks normally done at the server can be done at the workstation. Access to the server's systems is given the same level of security as users administering from the service's server.

Windows NT Workstation Tools

The Windows NT Server Tools available for Windows NT Workstation include:

- DHCP (Dynamic Host Configuration Protocol) Manager.
- Policy Editor.
- RAS (Remote Access Service) Administrator.
- Server Manager.
- User Manager for Domains.
- WINS (Windows Internet Naming Service) Manager.

The Windows NT Workstation Tools are available on the Windows NT Server CD in the \\clients\srvtools\winnt folder.

➤ **To install Windows NT Workstation Tools**

1. Confirm that your boot drive has at least 3 MB of free disk space.

2. Create a folder on your hard drive called c:\srvtools.

3. Copy the files from the \\clients\srvtools\winnt\i386 folder into the c:\srvtools folder you created.

4. To add the programs to your Start menu, click **Start**, point to Settings, and then click **Control Panel**.

5. Click **Add**, click **Browse**, double-click the c:\srvtools folder, and point to the program file for the tool to be added.

6. Click **Open,** click **Next**, select the folder to create the shortcut in and click **Next**, give the program a name, and select Finish.

7. Follow the above six steps for each of the Tools.

Windows 95 Tools

The Windows NT Server Tools available for Windows 95 include:

- Event Viewer.
- Server Manager.
- User Manager for Domains.
- Extensions to Windows 95 Explorer.

Extensions to Windows 95 Explorer allow editing of security properties of printers and Windows NT File System (NTFS) file objects and the administration of File and Print Services for NetWare and NetWare-enabled users. The Windows 95 Tools are available on the Windows NT Server CD.

➤ **To install Windows 95 Tools**

1. Confirm that your boot drive has at least 3 MB of free disk space.

2. Click **Start**, point to Settings, and then click **Control Panel**.

3. Double-click **Add/Remove Programs**.

4. Click the **Windows Setup** tab, and then click **Have Disk**.

5. In **Copy Manufacturer's Files From**, enter the \Win95 directory (local, CD-ROM, or network drive) that contains the Client-based Network Administrations Tools files (there must be a Srvtools.inf file in this directory), and then click **OK**.

6. Click **Windows NT Server Tools**, and click **Install**.

7. Windows NT Server Tools are installed in a \Srvtools folder on the computer's boot drive.

8. Manually adjust the AUTOEXEC.BAT file to include C:\Srvtools in the PATH (if drive C is the boot drive).

For example, if you boot from drive C, append the following to the line that starts with PATH

\srvtools

Planning Remote Administration

In this exercise you answer questions about Remote Administration server tools.

1. Where are the Remote Administration server tools located?

_____

_____

2. What protocol is required to run the Remote Administration server tools?

_____

_____

Lesson Summary

The following information summarizes the key points in this lesson:

- Windows NT Server Tools are available for Windows NT Workstation and Windows 95 computers.

- Windows NT Workstation Tools include DHCP Manager, Policy Editor, RAS Administrator, Server Manager, User Manager for Domains, and WINS Manager.

- Windows 95 Tools include Event Viewer, Server Manager, User Manager for Domains, and extensions to Windows 95 Explorer. Extensions to Windows 95 Explorer allows editing of printer's security properties and NTFS file objects, as well as the administration of file and print services for NetWare and NetWare-enabled users.

CHAPTER 4

Connectivity

About This Chapter

Managing network connectivity in Windows NT requires knowledge of how computers running Windows NT access both internal and external network resources. Because the network is a vital component to any server product, this chapter introduces the Windows NT tools available to support publishing and accessing of services on the network. This chapter also introduces the tools needed to ease network administration and interoperability with other network services.

Before You Begin

To complete the lessons in this chapter, you must have:

- Completed the exercises in Chapter 2.

- Read Chapters 1, 2, and 3 or have an understanding of Windows NT Server planning and installation.

- The knowledge and skills covered in Chapter 2, "Installation and Configuration."

- The knowledge and skills covered in Chapter 3, "Managing Enterprise Resources."

Lesson 1: Managing DHCP

Dynamic Host Configuration Protocol (DHCP) is an open industry standard that is designed to reduce the complexity of Transmission Control Protocol/Internet Protocol (TCP/IP) network administration. DHCP specifies methods for simplified and dynamic configuration of computers on TCP/IP networks and reduces the administrative burden of adding, moving, and configuring computers on TCP/IP networks. DHCP is specified by Internet Engineering Task Force (IETF) Requests for Comments (RFCs) 1533, 1534, 1541, and 1542. After a review of implementation of DHCP in a single network, this lesson examines issues related to providing DHCP services in a subnetworked environment typically found in an enterprise. Topics include planning, configuring, maintaining and troubleshooting DHCP services.

After this lesson, you will be able to:

- Identify planning considerations for implementing DHCP in an enterprise.
- Configure DHCP services used in the enterprise.
- Describe steps to take to improve DHCP fault tolerance.
- Troubleshoot DHCP failures.

Estimated lesson time: 30 minutes

Dynamic Host Configuration Protocol (DHCP)

The implementation of the DHCP service requires two types of computers: DHCP Servers and DHCP Clients. DHCP Servers allocate and manage IP configuration parameters necessary for clients to communicate in a TCP/IP environment. Clients are configured to obtain their IP address and related information from a DHCP Server and must be running a Microsoft network client such as Windows NT, Windows 95, Windows for Workgroups 3.11, the Network client 3.0 for MS-DOS, or LAN Manager 2.2c.

At a minimum, DHCP will provide clients with an IP address, subnet mask, and default gateway. Other information that Microsoft DHCP clients can obtain from the DHCP Server include IP addresses for Domain Name System (DNS) and NetBIOS name servers, and the DNS domain name.

How Clients Lease DHCP Addresses

DHCP uses a four-phase process to configure a DHCP client. The following graphic illustrates DHCP Client and Server interaction during system startup.

DHCP client   DHCP servers

IP lease request

IP lease offers

IP lease selection

IP lease
acknowledgment

At bootup, a DHCP client has only limited IP information. As a result, each of these four messages is a broadcast on the network. Within a single subnet, the use of broadcast messages presents no difficulties.

DHCP Server Configuration and DHCP Scopes

A DHCP Server itself cannot use the DHCP service, instead it must be configured with a static IP address, subnet mask, and, optionally, a default gateway. After the DHCP Server service has been installed on a computer running Windows NT Server, it must be configured with a range of addresses that can be assigned, or leased, to DHCP clients. Together with other common configuration parameters, this range, or pool, of addresses is called a DHCP scope. The scope must be defined and activated before DHCP clients can use the DHCP Server for dynamic TCP/IP configuration.

Creating DHCP Scopes

To create a DHCP scope, you use DHCP Manager (installed when the DHCP Server service is added) to enter the following required information:

- Scope name assigned by the administrator when the scope is created.

- Unique subnet mask used to identify the subnet to which an IP address belongs.

- Range of IP addresses (the pool) contained within the scope.

- Time interval (known as lease duration) that specifies how long a DHCP client can use an assigned IP address before it must renew its configuration with the DHCP Server.

It is possible that not all addresses in a range are available for lease, as might be the case if there are static IP addresses in use on non-DHCP clients. DHCP Manager allows addresses, contained within the pool, to be excluded from client lease.

Adjusting the lease duration allows DHCP to be tailored to the network environment. If IP addresses are in short supply, short leases are generally advantageous. The option to provide leases for an unlimited period should be avoided. After a client receives an IP address with an unlimited duration, it no longer needs to dialog with the DHCP Server. This makes it very difficult for the DHCP Server, and consequently the administrator, to withdraw the address from use or to change the client's IP address assignment.

Additional Scope Options

In addition to the required DHCP scope information, you can define individual scope options by using DHCP Manager (Select Scope, Add Reservations and Scope, Active Leases). The following table lists additional scope options:

Option	Description
Deactivate	You can release an IP address if a computer is removed from a network.
Renewal	You can change the renewal period for IP-address leases. By installation default DHCP clients begin the renewal process when 50 percent of the IP address lease time has expired.
Reserve	You can reserve a specific IP address for a DHCP client, such as an Internet Information Server or WINS Server. An IP address can also be reserved if a computer on the network is not DHCP-enabled. Also, for TCP/IP security, computers designated as network firewalls are configured with reserved IP addresses.

DHCP Options

Other options, known as DHCP options, can also be configured on the DHCP Server by using DHCP Manager. In addition to defining the required DHCP Scope configuration parameters, you can use DHCP Server to automatically assign DHCP clients with advanced TCP/IP configuration options, such as the IP address for the Windows Internet Name Service (WINS) Server and the DNS Server. To do this, you select one or more DHCP options when using DHCP Manager.

There are four methods that can be used to set the DHCP options, and these are reviewed in the table below.

Option	Description
Global	Setting a Global DHCP Option will cause the option configured to take affect for all DHCP Scopes defined on the selected DHCP Server.
Scope	Setting a Scope DHCP Option will only set the option for the selected Scope when the DHCP Options Scope menu is selected.
Default	Setting a Default DHCP Option modifies the default value for one of the DHCP Options. By doing this, the default value that appears when setting a Global or Scope DHCP Option will be the default value that the administrator set, rather than the DHCP default set during installation of DHCP.
Client	This method can be used to configure one or more of the DHCP Options for a specific DHCP Client. DHCP Options can only be set for a Client if the DHCP Client has a reserved IP address. The only way to see if a DHCP Option is set for a DHCP Client is to view the Properties of an active client lease (from the Scope Active Leases menu) and then click on the **Options** button.

If a DHCP Option is set at two or more of the available levels, such as being set for both Global and Scope, the following order of precedence is used:

- Client level settings override both Scope and Global level settings.
- Scope level setting override Global level settings.
- If there is no Client or Scope level settings for a DHCP Option, then the Global level settings will take affect.

DHCP Server provides the ability to configure many standard DHCP options as defined by RFC 1541. However, while you can use DHCP Server to set any of the options, Windows-based and Windows NT-based DHCP clients support only a few. The most commonly used are displayed in the table on the following page.

Code	Option Name	Meaning
1	Subnet Mask	Specifies the subnet mask of the client subnet. This option is defined in the DHCP Manager **Create Scope** or **Scope Properties** dialog box. It cannot be set directly in the **DHCP Options** dialog box.
3	Router	Specifies a list of IP addresses for routers on the client's subnet.
6	DNS servers	Specifies a list of IP addresses for DNS name servers available to the client. Multihomed computers can have only one list per computer, not one per adapter card.
15	Domain Name	Specifies the DNS domain name that the client should use for DNS host name resolution.
44	WINS/NBNS servers	Specifies a list of IP addresses for NetBIOS name servers (NBNS).

DHCP Fault Tolerance

Two or more DHCP Servers have no way to coordinate management of IP addresses with each other. Assigning all available IP addresses to a single server would leave your network exposed to failure of this single server. However, you can provide a measure of fault tolerance by installing two DHCP Servers and then splitting the available address pool between them so that each address is available for assignment by only one server.

Providing DHCP Services in the Enterprise

Thus far, DHCP has been examined in a single network environment. However, TCP/IP networks are frequently interconnected by routers that connect network segments (subnets) and pass IP packets between the subnets. As previously noted, the DHCP IP address leasing process uses broadcast messages. Since broadcasts are not generally passed across routers, DHCP uses another feature to provide IP addresses to clients in multiple subnets. RFC 1542 specifies the DHCP/BOOTP relay agent. (DHCP is an extension of the bootstrap protocol [BOOTP], defined earlier in RFC 951.)

DHCP Relay Agent

A relay agent is a program used to pass specific types of IP packets between subnets. A DHCP/BOOTP relay agent is simply hardware or software that passes DHCP/BOOTP messages (packets) from one subnet to another subnet according to the RFC 1542 specification. If the routers that connect the subnet are RFC 1542-compliant routers, the DHCP/BOOTP relay agent can provide IP addresses to clients in multiple subnets. If the router cannot function as a relay agent, each subnet that has DHCP clients requires its own DHCP Server.

Using Multiple Subnets and Configuring Scopes

In a sub-netted network, separate scopes are defined for each subnet. A DHCP Server can manage DHCP scopes for multiple subnets and must lease an IP address from the DHCP scope that corresponds to the DHCP client's subnet.

The best method for implementing DHCP on a network with multiple subnets is to place a DHCP Server on each subnet and connect the subnets via routers that can act as RFC 1542 (BOOTP) relay agents. A router that functions as an RFC 1542 (BOOTP) relay agent does not simply forward the DHCP broadcasts onto the other subnets, but instead modifies the DHCP message to indicate which subnet the broadcast came from. This allows the DHCP Server to determine which of its DHCP scopes to lease an IP address from, if it even has a valid scope for the subnet.

Each of the DHCP Servers should ideally be configured with a large portion of the IP address pool (~75%) for its local subnet and small portion (~25%) of the IP address pool for another subnet.

When a dynamic client computer on the subnet where the BOOTP relay agent resides requests an IP address, the subnet's BOOTP relay agent receives the request. The BOOTP relay agent forwards the request directly to the correct computer running Windows NT Server DHCP service. The computer running Windows NT Server DHCP service returns an IP address directly to the requesting client thus overcoming the limitations of DHCP service's broadcast messages.

The DHCP Database

The DHCP Server service stores the DHCP data, such as active IP address leases, in a database. Under Windows NT Server 4.0, the DHCP Server database uses the performance-enhanced Exchange Server storage engine version 4.0. This format replaces an earlier one used in Windows NT 3.51 and provides an improved database engine that is faster and that compacts automatically to prevent fragmentation and consequent growth of the database.

When you install DHCP Server, the files shown in the following table are automatically created in the *systemroot*\System32\Dhcp directory.

File	Description
Dhcp.mdb	The DHCP Server database file.
Dhcp.tmp	A temporary file used by the DHCP database as a swap file during database index maintenance operations. This file may remain in the *systemroot*\System32\Dhcp directory after a crash.
J50.log and J50#####.log	A log of all database transactions. This file is used by the DHCP database to recover data if necessary.
J50.chk	A checkpoint file.

Important The J50.log file, J50#####.log file, Dhcp.mdb file, and Dhcp.tmp file should not be removed or tampered with in any manner.

The DHCP Server database is a dynamic database that is updated as DHCP clients are assigned, or release, their TCP/IP configuration parameters. The DHCP database and related registry entries are backed up automatically at a specific interval (60 minutes by installation default). This installation default can be changed, within a range of possible values of 5 to 60 minutes, by changing the value of the registry parameter **BackupInterval** in the registry key:

SYSTEM\CurrentControlSet\Services\DHCPServer\Parameters

Backing Up the DHCP Directory and Files

The DHCP service provides a backup of the database and files in the System32\ DHCP\Backup directory. By default, the backup directory is located on the same physical drive as the DHCP database directory. This installation default can be altered by changing the value of the registry parameter **DatabasePath** in the same registry key listed above. Additional fault tolerance can be achieved by selecting a backup location on a second physical disk and by replicating the backup folder to another server.

Restoring the DHCP Database

If a DHCP Server fails for any reason, you can restore the database from a backup copy.

➤ **To restore a DHCP database**

1. Before starting, make a copy of the DHCP Server database files.

2. In the *systemroot*\System32\Dhcp directory, delete the J50.log, J50#####.log, and Dhcp.tmp files.

3. Copy an uncorrupted backup version of the Dhcp.mdb to the *systemroot* \System32\Dhcp directory.

4. Restart the DHCP Server service.

Troubleshooting DHCP

DHCP is a reliable system for managing IP addresses; however, there are a few areas where troubleshooting might be required. Outlined below are some DHCP Server troubleshooting tactics that can be used if problems arise.

Problems Leasing an IP Address

The following error conditions indicate potential problems with the DHCP Server:

- The administrator can't connect to a DHCP Server by using DHCP Manager. The message that appears might be "The RPC server is unavailable."

- DHCP clients cannot renew the leases for their IP addresses. The message that appears on the client computer is "The DHCP client could not renew the IP address lease."

- The DHCP Client service or DHCP Server service might be stopped and cannot be restarted.

The first troubleshooting task is to make sure that the DHCP services are running. To verify that the DHCP services are running, open **Services** in **Control Panel**. "Started" should appear in the Status column for the DHCP Client service and "Started" should appear in the Status column for the DHCP Server service. If the appropriate service is not started, start the service.

Note Use Event Viewer in the Administrative tools to find the possible source of problems with DHCP services.

On a DHCP Client, a popup message may appear indicating either 'The DHCP Client couldn't obtain an IP address' or 'The DHCP Client couldn't renew the IP address lease'. Both these errors indicate that for some reason the DHCP Client system was unable to communicate with a DHCP Server. Both error messages could be a result of a DHCP Server not being available or a network failure between the DHCP Client and DHCP Server.

The error message, 'The DHCP Client couldn't obtain an IP address' can also be generated if the DHCP Servers that received the DHCP Client's request have no more IP addresses available to lease.

Problems Leasing Addresses Across Routers

Another difficulty may arise in multiple sub-netted networks where DHCP messages must transit routers.

Most older routers will not function properly as an RFC 1542 (BOOTP) relay agent with DHCP. The DHCP messages include new fields as well as some fields that are used in a different manner. For instance, the broadcast bit in a DHCP message causes most 'normal,' that is, non RFC 1542 (BOOTP), relay agents that perform any validity checking on BOOTP requests to silently discard the DHCP message. If you are using the router as an RFC 1542 relay agent, verify that the router supports RFC 1541 and RFC 1542.

Configuring Routable Protocols

1. List two disadvantages of using TCP/IP and two advantages of using DHCP.

   _____

   _____

2. From the DHCP Client, how can an administrator find out what IP address the DHCP Client has leased? At a DHCP Server, how can an administrator find out what IP address a DHCP Client has leased?

   _____

   _____

3. What does a DHCP Scope consist of (that is, the four main items that must be configured)?

   _____

   _____

4. When an administrator has configured some additional DHCP Options, what is the order of precedence for the various option types (Global, Scope, and Client)?

   _____

   _____

5. What are the four messages sent between a DHCP Client and a DHCP Server, when the DHCP Client is leasing an IP address?

_____

_____

6. Will all routers that can function as an RFC 1542 (BOOTP) relay agent work properly with DHCP?

_____

_____

Lesson Summary

The following information summarizes the key points in this lesson:

- The DHCP Server service relies on broadcast messages. As a result, in a subnetted network, DHCP services can be provided only if routers are RFC 1541 and RFC 1542 capable or if a DHCP relay agent has been configured on each subnet that has no DHCP Server.

- Only a single DHCP Server can manage any given IP address that is available for lease to DHCP clients. To provide DHCP service fault tolerance with more than one DHCP Server, scopes for each server must contain unique IP addresses.

- DHCP fault tolerance can be improved by locating the DHCP backup directory on a second physical disk and by replicating the backup directory to a non-DHCP Server.

- DHCP failures can be traced to a halted DHCP Server or client services, interrupted network connectivity, and incompatibility of older BOOTP-capable routers.

For more information on	See
Managing DHCP	Chapter 7, "Managing MS DHCP Servers," NT Server 4.0 Networking Guide, in the *Microsoft Windows NT Server Resource Kit*

Lesson 2: Managing WINS

This lesson looks at managing Windows Internet Naming Service (WINS), Microsoft's NetBIOS name server. WINS is a database of NetBIOS names that have been registered by Transmission Control Protocol/Internet Protocol (TCP/IP) hosts on the network with their IP addresses. When a NetBIOS name is to be resolved by a host, WINS can provide the resolution, thus decreasing network broadcasts and providing WINS resolution across subnets.

After this lesson, you will be able to:

- List the drawbacks of the current name resolution methods.

- Describe the benefits of using WINS to resolve names.

- Define the information provided by the WINS Manager utility when managing a WINS server.

- Describe how to configure replication between WINS servers.

- Explain how to force replication of the WINS database.

- Describe what is replicated between the WINS servers each time replication occurs.

- List the four different NetBIOS over TCP/IP name resolution methods.

- List the files that make up the WINS database.

Estimated lesson time: 30 minutes

Windows Internet Naming Service (WINS)

When using TCP/IP to communicate on a network, the friendly computer name is used. The friendly computer name is either a NetBIOS name, such as in a 'net use' command, or a host name, such as in a FTP command. When the friendly name is used, it must be resolved to an IP address. This is necessary because TCP/IP does not know how to establish communication with a computer name, such as \\server1, but does know to communicate with 223.223.223.1. In order to resolve a NetBIOS name to its IP address, TCP/IP can use a variety of methods: broadcasts, a static mapping file (LMHOSTS or HOSTS), a Domain Name System (DNS) server, or a name server (WINS).

WINS Clients

WINS Clients are configured with the IP address of one or more WINS servers. On startup, WINS Clients communicate directly with a WINS server to register their computer name (NetBIOS name) and corresponding IP address. When a WINS Client needs to resolve a computer name to an IP address, such as when a net use \\server\share is performed, the WINS Client sends a request to the WINS server for the IP address for the computer name being used.

WINS Servers

WINS server maintains a database that maps the IP addresses of WINS Clients to their NetBIOS name. Therefore, instead of using broadcasts to resolve a computer name to an IP address when trying to establish a network connection, WINS Clients request the IP address for the desired system from a WINS server which retrieves the IP address from its database.

Why Use WINS

To understand the benefits of using WINS to resolve computer names to IP addresses, it is important to first understand some of the drawbacks of existing name resolution methods.

Drawbacks of Existing Name Resolution Methods

Currently, there are three methods used by TCP/IP to resolve computer names to IP addresses:

- Broadcasts
- LMHOSTS File
- DNS Server

Each of the existing name resolution methods has drawbacks; these are listed below.

Broadcasts

By relying on broadcasts, the NetBIOS name to IP address resolution method results in additional network traffic. The more hosts that are on a given network, the more broadcasts there will be on the network, which can lead to large amounts of additional network traffic. Each time a network connection is attempted, the system that is originating the connection broadcasts up to three times in order to try to resolve the NetBIOS name to an IP address.

When using broadcasts to resolve computer names to IP addresses, broadcasts must be forwarded throughout the network as indicated in the illustration below.

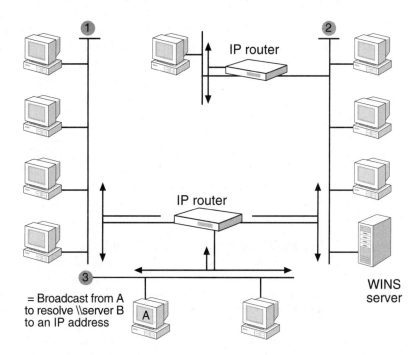

= Broadcast from A
to resolve \\server B
to an IP address

When Workstation A needs to resolve Server B's computer name, such as when a net use \\serverB\share is performed, it broadcasts for Server B. If Server B is on the other side of a router, that does not forward broadcasts, Server A will not be able to resolve the NetBIOS name to an IP address.

LMHOSTS File

The LMHOSTS file contains mappings of computer names to IP addresses. Using the LMHOSTS file from the \<winnt_root>\system32\drivers\etc directory to resolve a computer name to IP address requires the network administrator to maintain the LMHOSTS file. The network administrator must keep track of each workstation's computer name and the IP address that the workstation is using. If a workstation changes computer names or IP addresses, as a DHCP client will do, the network administrator must then update the LMHOSTS file as each workstation must have its own local copy of the LMHOSTS file. Therefore, every time a computer name or IP address changes, the network administrator will need to update the file and then distribute it to each workstation. Therefore, using the LMHOSTS file proves to be too much maintenance in all but the smallest network.

Domain Name System (DNS) Server

DNS is typically used to resolve host names to IP addresses, but it can also be used to resolve NetBIOS names. The WINS client will query a DNS Server for the IP address of a NetBIOS name. The DNS Server will treat this query as a normal host name query and return the IP address of any host name that matches the NetBIOS name. DNS is not a dynamic database, so any changes to the host name or IP address has to be manually changed in DNS.

Benefits of WINS

WINS provides a mapping of computer names to IP addresses through a distributed database. A given network will have one or more WINS servers that WINS Clients can contact when they need to resolve a computer name to an IP address. All of the WINS servers on a given network can be configured to replicate all computer name to IP address mappings in their WINS database. WINS provides the following benefits:

- Reduces broadcast traffic on the network. By using WINS servers, the amount of broadcast traffic on a given network will be greatly reduced. Instead of broadcasting to resolve a computer name to an IP address, the workstation sends a message directly to a WINS server to find out the IP address for a given computer name. This can be done because part of configuring a workstation to use TCP/IP involves supplying the IP address for a primary and secondary WINS server. As will be discussed, the IP addresses for WINS servers can be provided to DHCP Clients by a DHCP Server.

- No need to maintain the LMHOSTS file. Using WINS eliminates the need for network administrators to maintain the LMHOSTS file. As a result, there is less administrative overhead involved in using TCP/IP because administrators no longer need to keep track of which computer name maps to which IP address.

- No need for DNS Servers. Because WINS uses NetBIOS names, and is a dynamic database, it is more flexible than DNS for name resolution.

- Dynamic name registration. WINS makes it easier for administrators to implement DHCP on their networks. If WINS is not used and DHCP is used, the network administrators will have a significant amount of work to keep the LMHOSTS file up to date. Using WINS with DHCP provides the benefits of dynamic IP addressing and name resolution without the need for broadcasts or static files.

- Prevents duplicate computer names. WINS Clients must register their computer names with a WINS server when they start. If the WINS server already has a registration for the requested computer name, the WINS server will reject the WINS Client's registration attempt, thereby preventing duplicate computer names.

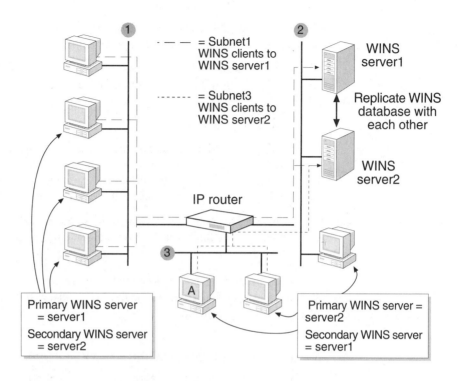

The Contents of the WINS Database

The contents of the WINS database on a given WINS server can be examined and searched for specific entries through the **Show Database** option under the Mappings menu:

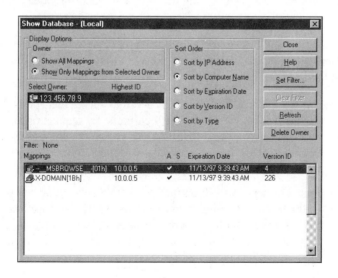

- Mappings. Under the Mappings column the group, internet group, multihomed names, and unique computer names are listed.

- 'A' and 'S'. A check in the 'A' column indicates that the WINS Client is active, and a check in the 'S' column indicates that this is a static mapping.

- Timestamp. The Timestamp column displays the date and time the name was registered or last renewed.

- Version ID. The Version ID is assigned by the WINS server when the name is registered with the WINS server. It is used by the WINS server's Pull partners to request the entries in the WINS database that are newer than the last entry the pull partner received during the last replication.

- Delete Owner. This button will remove the selected WINS server in the **Select Owner** box, including all WINS database entries owned by the selected WINS server.

Note The value in the brackets [ ] after each name registered in the WINS database is always the 16th byte of the name that was registered, as specified by the LAN Manager naming convention.

Replication of the WINS Database (Push and Pull Partners)

All of the WINS servers on a given network can be configured to communicate with each other so that a name registered with one WINS server will eventually be known by all WINS servers. In addition to being aware of all name registrations on the network, all of the WINS servers will also be notified when a name is released. Having all of the WINS servers communicate with each other in this manner is done by configuring the WINS servers to replicate their WINS database entries with each other.

To configure WINS servers to replicate their WINS database entries amongst each other requires each WINS server to be configured as a 'Pull' or 'Push' partner with at least one other WINS server:

- Pull Partners. A Pull partner is a WINS server that 'pulls' WINS database entries (replicas) from its Push partners, by requesting any new WINS database entries (replicas) that the Push partners have. The Pull partner requests the new WINS database entries by requesting entries with a higher version number than the last entry it received during the last replication.

- Push Partners. A Push partner is a WINS server that sends a message to its Pull partners notifying them when its WINS database has changed. When the WINS server's Pull partner(s) respond to the message with a replication request, the WINS server sends a copy ('pushes') of its new WINS database entries (replicas) to its Pull partner(s).

Configuring WINS servers to replicate their WINS database entries with each other extends the benefit of WINS across the entire network.

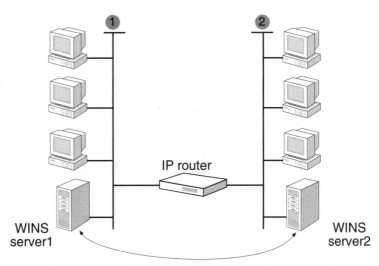

WINS database entries are
replicated between WINS servers

In the illustration above, WINS Clients on subnet 1 register their computer name with WINS server1, and WINS Clients on subnet 2 register their computer name with WINS server2. When WINS Clients on subnet 1 need to resolve a computer name to IP address, they contact WINS server1. Since WINS server1 and WINS server2 replicate their WINS Database entries with each other, WINS server1 can resolve a computer name from subnet 2 to its IP address.

If WINS server1 and WINS server2 did not replicate their WINS database entries with each other, WINS server1 would not be able to resolve a computer name from subnet 2 to its IP address.

The following dialog box, which is available via the **Replication Partners...** option under the Server menu, can be used to add, delete, and configure Push and Pull partners on the selected WINS server. In addition, this dialog box can be used to replicate the WINS Database immediately to all partners or send a push or pull trigger to the selected Push or Pull partner.

- Replication Options. Under Replications Options, the selected WINS server can be configured as a Push and/or Pull partner with the WINS server that WINS Manager is being used to administer.

  The **Configure...** button for Push partners lets the administrator set the update count (number of new WINS database entries) that the WINS server must reach before it will send a push message. The **'Configure...'** button for Pull partners allows the administrator to set the start time and replication interval for the selected partner.

- Send Replication Trigger Now. The 'Push' and 'Pull' buttons permit an administrator to send push or pull messages to only the selected WINS servers, whereas the 'Replicate Now' button will initiate replication with all partners.

- Checking the **Push With Propagation** box will cause the selected WINS servers to obtain any new WINS database entries from the WINS server that sent the message. If the selected WINS servers received any new entries, they will propagate the push message to all their Pull partners. If the selected WINS servers did not receive any new entries, they will not propagate the push message.

WINS Database Replication Considerations

There are three methods by which replication of the WINS database can be started:

1. At system startup and then repeated at an administrator-configured interval, the WINS server can request any new WINS database entries from its Pull Partners.

2. When a WINS server has reached an administrator configured threshold for the number of registrations and changes to the WINS database. When the threshold (the update count setting) is reached, the WINS server will notify all of its Pull partners who will then request the new entries.

3. The administrator can cause replication to occur through WINS Manager.

Note WINS servers only replicate any new entries in their database, the entire WINS database is not replicated each time replication occurs.

Determining whether to configure a WINS server as a Pull partner or Push partner will depend a great deal on the configuration of the network being used. For instance, in the case of a Wide Area Network (WAN), there are going to be special considerations for the speed of the WAN links.

Once it has been determined whether a WINS server will be a Push partner or Pull partner, the push or pull settings will then have to be configured appropriately. For Pull partners the appropriate interval between replication attempts will need to be set based on the network. Typically, WINS servers that are located near each other will replicate more frequently than WINS servers across WAN links. For Push partners, an appropriate update count will have to be determined based on the number of registrations a server handles. Typically, a WINS server that receives hundreds of name registrations every morning when users first logon should not be configured to replicate a small number of registrations.

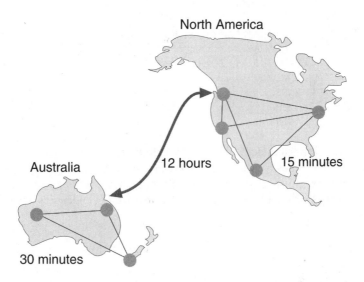

In the above diagram, the network administrators decided to configure the WINS servers as Pull partners. For example, the WINS servers on the North America continent are configured to replicate the new entries in their WINS databases between each other every 15 minutes, whereas the WINS servers in Australia and North America only replicate across the WAN link every 12 hours. This was done because the WAN link between North America and Australia is not as fast as the links between the locations in North America. Therefore, to prevent WINS replication from impacting performance on the WAN between Australia and North America, WINS replication is only performed every 12 hours.

Managing WINS Servers

WINS servers in the enterprise share tasks common to other database applications. Periodically, it is necessary to cleanup, backup, and even restore the database. The following sections look at these processes.

The WINS Services

The WINS server is made up of only one service, the Windows Internet Naming Service. This service can be started and stopped through Control Panel Services.

The configuration settings for the WINS server service are stored in the Registry in two locations:

```
\HKEY_LOCAL_MACHINE
  \SYSTEM
    \CurrentControlSet
      \Services
        \WINS
\HKEY_LOCAL_MACHINE
  \SOFTWARE
    \Microsoft
      \WINS
```

The settings under **...Microsoft\WINS** are the version and install date as well as the NetRules for the WINS server service. WINS depends on Rpcss (remote procedure call service) and NTLMSSP (NT LM security support provider service). WINS will not be able to start until its two dependencies have first been loaded.

Scavenging the WINS Database

Much like any database, the WINS database occasionally needs to be cleaned up, a process referred to in WINS Manager as scavenging.

The WINS server automatically performs scavenging based on the following:

- If a WINS Client does not renew its name registration before the renewal interval expires, its registration will be marked as 'released'.

- Once the extinction interval expires for a 'released' entry, it will be marked as 'extinct' in the WINS database.

- Finally, after the extinction timeout has expired, the 'extinct' entry will be scavenged (removed) from the WINS database.

Using the default times for all of the intervals and timeouts, a name registration that was not removed will remain in the WINS database for about four hours. If any of the intervals or timeouts have been increased, the entry will remain in the database even longer. Therefore, it is possible to use WINS Manager to force the WINS database to be scavenged through the **Initiate Scavenging** option under the Mappings menu.

The WINS Database Files

The size of the WINS database is not directly proportional to the number of active client entries. Over time, as some WINS client entries become obsolete, and are deleted, there remains some unused space.

To recover the unused space, the WINS database is compacted. Under Windows NT Server 4.0, WINS server database compaction occurs as an automatic background process during idle time after a database update.

Because the WINS server database compaction occurs while the database is being used, you do not need to stop the WINS server to compact the database.

Note In most cases there is no need to manually compact the WINS server database under Windows NT Server 4.0.

The following database files are stored in the \%systemroot%\System32\Wins directory.

File	Description
J50.log and J50#####.log	A log of all transactions done with the database. This file is used by WINS to recover data if necessary
J50.chk	A checkpoint file
Wins.mdb	The WINS server database file which contains two tables: ■ IP address-Owner ID mapping table ■ Name-to-IP-address mapping table
Winstmp.mdb	A temporary file that is created by the WINS server service. This file is used by the database as a swap file during index maintenance operations and may remain in the %systemroot% \System32\Wins directory after a crash

Important The J50.log, J50#####.log, Wins.mdb, and Winstmp.mdb files should not be removed or tampered with in any manner.

Backing Up the WINS Database

WINS Manager provides backup tools so you can back up the WINS database. After you specify a backup directory for the database, WINS performs complete database back ups every three hours, by installation default.

For specific instructions on how to back up and restore the WINS database, see the Help topic "Backing Up and Restoring the Database" in WINS Manager Help.

You should also periodically back up the Registry entries for the WINS server.

Restoring the WINS Database

If the WINS server needs to be restored or rebuilt, the following steps can be used.

➤ **To restore the WINS database**

1. Stop the Windows Internet Name Server service, if it is started.

2. Delete any files under the **...\system32\wins** subdirectory and then restore the backed up files.

3. Start the Windows NT Registry Editor, REGEDT32.EXE, and restore the contents of the **...\SYSTEM\CurrentControlSet\Services\WINS** Registry key. This can be done by selecting the **...\SYSTEM\CurrentControlSet\ Services\WINS** key, choosing '**Restore...**' from the Registry menu, and then selecting the file that contains the backup of this key.

4. Start the Windows Internet Name Server service.

Implementing WINS

In this exercise you will answer questions about WINS management.

1. How is WINS used with TCP/IP?

    _____

    _____

2. How does the WINS server learn of the WINS clients' NetBIOS names and IP addresses?

    _____

    _____

3. What are the two major benefits of using WINS on a network?

    _____

    _____

4. What are some of the drawbacks of using broadcasts to resolve NetBIOS names?

    _____

    _____

5. What are some of the drawbacks of using LMHOSTS files to resolve NetBIOS names?

    _____

    _____

6. What tool is used to view the WINS database?

    _____

    _____

7. What are the two relationships that can be configured between WINS servers for replication?

_____

_____

Lesson Summary

The following information summarizes the key points in this lesson:

- Compared to other resolution methods, WINS is the most efficient way to resolve NetBIOS names.

- Using WINS reduces network broadcasts and allows for NetBIOS name resolution across routers.

- The WINS Manager utility allows you to see the content of the WINS database, setup static mappings, and setup replication between WINS servers.

- The four NetBIOS name resolution methods are WINS, broadcasts, LMHOSTS, and DNS.

- Typical management of a WINS server includes the backup and restore of a WINS database.

Lesson 3: Managing DNS

This lesson explains the function of the Domain Name System (DNS) Server service, and how it can be configured to locate resources on an internetwork. In addition, it examines how Windows Internet Naming Service (WINS) is integrated with DNS, allowing computers running Windows NT to access information on the Internet using Internet naming conventions.

After this lesson, you will be able to:

- Describe the purpose of DNS.

- Install and configure the DNS Server service.

- Explain the differences between WINS and DNS.

- Integrate WINS and DNS.

Estimated lesson time: 20 minutes

Domain Name Systems (DNS)

DNS is a distributed database providing a hierarchical naming system for identifying hosts on the Internet. DNS was developed to solve the problems that arose when the number of hosts on the Internet grew dramatically in the early 1980s. DNS computer names consist of two parts: a host name and a domain name, which combine to form the fully qualified domain name (FQDN). For example, research.widgets.com is a FQDN where research is the host name and widgets.com is the domain name.

Note The term domain, when used in the context of DNS, is not related to the term domain used when discussing Windows NT Directory Services. An Internet domain is a unique name that identifies an Internet site. In order to register a domain name, you must contact the Internet Network Information Center (InterNIC).

DNS uses a client/server model, where DNS server (name servers) contain information about a portion of the DNS database (zone) and make this information available to clients (resolvers).

DNS name servers perform name resolution by interpreting network information to find a specific Internet Protocol (IP) address. The name resolution process is outlined on the following page.

1. A resolver (or client) passes a query to its local name server.

2. If the local name server does not have the data requested in the query, it queries other name servers on behalf of the resolver.

3. When the local name server has the address requested, it returns the information to the resolver.

DNS Server Service

The DNS server service is a name resolution service that runs on a Windows NT Server. DNS resolves a FQDN to the IP address that is then used by the internetwork. For example, you can use Internet Explorer to open research.widgets.com, and a DNS server can resolve this friendly name to the correct IP address on the Internet.

Domain Name Space

The DNS database is a tree structure called the domain name space. Each domain is named and can contain subdomains. The domain name identifies the domain's position in the database in relation to its parent domain. A period separates each part of the name for each network node in the DNS domain. For example, the DNS domain name csu.edu, specifies the csu subdomain whose parent is the edu domain; microsoft.com specifies the Microsoft subdomain whose parent is the com domain. The root node of the DNS database is unnamed (null). The root node is referenced in DNS names with a trailing period. For example, in the name: "research.widgets .com." it is the period after com that denotes the DNS root node.

Top-level Domains

The root and top-level domains of the DNS database are managed by the InterNIC. In most of the world, top-level domain names consist of geographical 2-character country codes such as .uk for the United Kingdom. In the United States many top-level domains are organizational 3-character names, for example .com for commercial organizations and .edu for educational organizations.

Fully Qualified Domain Names

With the exception of the root, each node in the DNS database has a name (label) of up to 63 characters. Each subdomain must have a unique name within its parent domain. This ensures name uniqueness throughout the DNS name space. DNS domain names are formed by following the path from the bottom of the DNS tree to the root. The node names are concatenated, and a period (.) separates each part. An optional period that signifies the root can appear at the end of the name. Such names are known as FQDN.

Delegation

Responsibility for managing the DNS name space below the top level is delegated to other organizations by the Internet Network Information Center (InterNIC). These organizations further subdivide the name space and delegate responsibility down the hierarchical tree structure. This decentralized administrative model allows DNS to be autonomously managed at the levels that make the most sense for each organization involved.

Zones

The administrative unit for DNS is the zone. A zone is a subtree of the DNS database that is administered as a single separate entity. It can consist of a single domain or a domain with subdomains. The lower-level subdomains of a zone can also be split into separate zone(s).

WINS and DNS

Although DNS might seem similar to WINS, there are two major differences. The following table summarizes the differences.

DNS	WINS
Resolves Internet names to IP addresses.	Resolves NetBIOS names to IP addresses.
Static database of computer name to IP address mappings. It must be manually updated.	Dynamic database of NetBIOS names and IP addresses. It is dynamically updated.

WINS and DNS have two different charters: WINS to resolve NetBIOS names to IP addresses, and DNS to resolve host names to IP addresses. Each Windows computer running TCP/IP has two names: the NetBIOS name and the host name. The NetBIOS name is the computer name configured during setup. The host name is inherited from the computer name. Typically, the NetBIOS name and the host name are the same, but they don't have to be.

WINS/DNS Integration

In Windows NT 4.0, Microsoft's implementation of DNS is tightly integrated with WINS. This allows non-WINS clients to resolve NetBIOS names by querying a DNS server. Administrators can now remove any static entries for Microsoft-based clients in legacy DNS server zone files in favor of the dynamic WINS/DNS integration. For example, if a non-Microsoft-based client wants to get to a Web page on an HTTP server that is DHCP/WINS enabled, the client can query the DNS server, the DNS server can query WINS, and the name can be resolved and returned to the client.

Prior to the WINS integration, there was no way to reliably resolve the name because of the dynamic IP addressing.

Installing and Configuring DNS

To install the DNS server service on a computer running Windows NT Server, use the Network program in Control Panel. On the **Services** tab, click **Add**, and then click **Microsoft DNS server**. You must restart your computer for the service to start. DNS servers require a static IP address.

All DNS management and configuration is performed through DNS Manager located in the Administrative Tools (Common) group. Its primary function is to configure DNS objects. Each of these objects has a defined set of manageable properties (or attributes). DNS Manager can be used to visually identify any one of these objects, and to view, add, or modify associated properties.

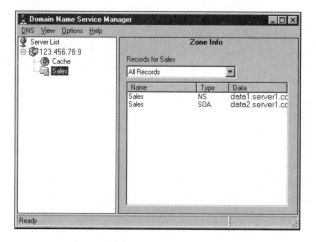

Configuring a DNS Client

Windows NT Server, Windows NT Workstation, Windows 95, and Windows for Workgroups 3.11 with Microsoft TCP/IP-32 installed all include DNS-resolver functionality.

There are two ways to configure a Windows NT client to use the DNS server to resolve host names, either manually or in conjunction with DHCP.

Manually

You can manually configure a DNS client by using the Network program in Control Panel. On the **Protocols** tab, click **TCP/IP Protocol**, and then click **Properties**. In the **Microsoft TCP/IP Properties** dialog box, click the **DNS** tab. You then provide the domain name for the client, and the IP addresses and search order for all DNS servers that you want to use to resolve host names.

In Conjunction with DHCP

When you configure your DHCP Server to work in conjunction with your DNS server, you save the administrative overhead of individually configuring your DHCP clients to also be DNS clients. By using DHCP Manager to add and configure the DHCP option, 006 DNS servers, your DHCP Server can provide the address of a DNS server to be used for Internet name resolution to the DHCP clients.

Installing the Domain Name System Server Service

In this exercise you will install the Microsoft DNS service on your Windows NT Server then test its functionality.

Note This exercise will not work if you do not have a network interface adapter installed on your computer.

➤ **To install the Microsoft DNS service**

In this procedure you will install the Microsoft DNS service.

1. Insert the Microsoft Windows NT Server CD into your computer's CD drive.

2. Right click on the **Network Neighborhood**, then click **Properties**.

   The Network Services dialogue will appear.

3. Click the **Services** tab.

4. Click **Add**.

   A list of available Windows NT Services will open.

5. From the list of available services, choose the **Microsoft DNS server,** then click **OK**.

6. When prompted, enter the path to the Windows NT directory on the CD (D:\i386).

   The Microsoft DNS services will install and files will be copied to the hard drive.

7. When the installation is finished, click the **Protocols** tab.

   The list of installed protocols will appear.

8. Click **TCP/IP Protocol** then click **Properties**.

   The TCP/IP properties will appear.

9. Click the **DNS** tab.

10. In the DNS Service Search Order, Add **131.107.2.200** as the IP address of a DNS server.

11. For the Domain enter **microsoft.com**.

12. Click **OK**.

    The Protocol dialogue will close.

13. Click **Close**.

    The Network dialogue will close.

14. When prompted to restart the computer, choose **Yes**.

    The computer will reboot.

➤ **To create the microsoft.com domain**

In this procedure you will install the Microsoft DNS service.

1. Click **Start, Programs, Administrative Tools,** then **DNS Manager.**

   The DNS manager will open.

2. Click **DNS** then **New Server**.

3. Enter the IP address of your computer, **131.107.2.200**.

   The DNS server will appear under the Server List.

4. Right Click on your DNS server then click on **New Zone**.

   The New Zone dialogue will appear.

5. Click the **Primary** radio button, then click **Next**.

6. For Zone Name enter **microsoft.com** then press **Tab**.

   A Zone File Name will be created.

7. Click **Next**.

8. Click **Finish**.

9. Right Click on the zone **microsoft.com,** then click **New Host.**

10. For the host name enter **server1**.

11. For the IP address enter **131.107.2.200**.

12. Click **Add Host**.

➤ **To test the Microsoft DNS service**

In this procedure you will install the Microsoft DNS service.

1. Open a Command prompt by Clicking **Start, Run** , and entering **CMD.**

2. At the command prompt, type **nslookup server1.microsoft.com**.

3. The IP address for server1.microsoft.com will be resolved.

4. Type **exit** to close the command prompt.

Lesson Summary

The following information summarizes the key points in this lesson:

- The Windows NT DNS server service is a name resolution service that uses a static database that resolves host names to IP addresses.

- All DNS management and configuration is performed through DNS Manager located in the Administrative Tools (Common) group.

- DNS resolves Internet names to IP addresses while WINS resolves NetBIOS names to IP addresses.

- The DNS database is a tree structure called the domain name space.

- The domain name space is broken down into zones for ease of administration.

- Microsoft's implementation of DNS is tightly integrated with WINS. This allows non-WINS clients to resolve NetBIOS names by querying a DNS server.

Lesson 4: Configuring Routable Protocols

Windows NT Server includes support for routing network protocols. These protocols can be configured using the Network program in Control Panel. This lesson discusses the routable network protocols and explains how to configure Windows NT Server to act as a router.

After this lesson, you will be able to:

- Identify the routable network protocols.

- Explain how to configure Windows NT Server to act as a router.

Estimated lesson time: 15 minutes

Network protocols, such as NWLink Internetwork Packet Exchange/Sequenced Packet Exchange (IPX/SPX) Compatible Transport, NetBEUI, and Transmission Control Protocol/Internet Protocol (TCP/IP) provide a mechanism for computers to connect with each other and exchange information over a network. Protocols communicate with network adapter cards by mean of Network Driver Interface Service (NDIS) 4.0-compatible network adapter card drivers. In addition, Windows NT supports multiple protocols, bound to one or more adapters, simultaneously.

Windows NT Server provides support for routing the NWLink IPX/SPX Compatible Transport, TCP/IP, and AppleTalk Network protocols.

NWLink

NWLink IPX/SPX Compatible Transport is the Microsoft 32-bit NDIS 4.0-compliant version of Novell's IPX/SPX protocol. NWLink is most commonly used in network environments where Microsoft clients need to access client/server applications running on Novell NetWare servers, or NetWare clients need to access client/server applications running on computers running Windows NT. NWLink can also be used in small network environments that only use Windows NT and Microsoft clients.

Routing NWLink

Windows NT Server supports Routing Information Protocol (RIP) for NWLink IPX/SPX Compatible Transport. It can be added via the **Services** tab in the Networking properties. Use the **Routing** tab in the **NWLink IPX/SPX Properties** dialog box to enable or disable the RIP. Using RIP routing over IPX, a Windows NT Server can act as an IPX router.

RIP allows a router to exchange information with neighboring routers. A RIP router is a computer or other piece of hardware that broadcasts routing information, such as network addresses. As a router becomes aware of any change in the internetwork layout—for example, a downed router—it broadcasts the information to neighboring routers.

Network Number

Windows NT uses an IPX network number for routing purposes. This number is sometimes referred to as the external network number, and must be unique for each network segment. If you do not know the appropriate network numbers to use, you must obtain them from the NetWare administrator. You then assign a network number to each configured frame type and adapter combination on your computer.

Internal Network Number

Windows NT also uses an internal network number to uniquely identify the computer on the network for internal routing. This internal network number, also known as a virtual network number, is represented by an eight-digit hexadecimal number. By default, the internal network number is (00000000).

Windows NT does not automatically detect the internal network number. In each of the following situations, you need to manually assign a unique non-zero internal network number:

- You have File and Print Services for NetWare (FPNW) installed, and you choose multiple frame types on a single adapter.
- You have bound NWLink to multiple adapters in your computer.
- Your computer is acting as a Windows NT Server for an application that uses the NetWare Service Advertising Protocol (SAP), such as SQL or SNA.

TCP/IP

TCP/IP is a flexible suite of protocols designed for wide area networks (WANs) and adaptable to a wide range of network hardware. TCP/IP can be used to communicate with Windows NT systems, with devices that use other Microsoft networking products, and with non-Microsoft systems, such as UNIX systems.

Routing TCP/IP

Windows NT Server supports RIP for Internet Protocol. It can be added via the **Services** tab in the Networking properties. Use the **Routing** tab in the **Microsoft TCP/IP Properties** dialog box to enable or disable RIP. Using RIP for Internet Protocol, a Windows NT Server can act as an IP router.

Subnet

A subnet is a network in a multiple network environment that uses IP addresses derived from a single network ID. Using subnets, an organization can divide a single large network into multiple physical networks and connect them with routers.

Subnet Mask

A subnet mask is used to block out a portion of the IP address so that TCP/IP can distinguish the network ID from the host ID. When TCP/IP hosts try to communicate, the subnet mask is used to determine whether the destination host is located on a local or a remote network. A sample subnet mask is 255.255.0.0. In order for computers to communicate on a network, they must have the same subnet mask.

Default Gateway

For communication with a host on another network, an IP address should be configured for the default gateway. TCP/IP sends packets that are destined for remote networks to the default gateway if no other route is configured on the local host to the destination network. If a default gateway is not configured, communication may be limited to the local network (subnet). A sample default gateway is 131.107.2.1.

AppleTalk

Windows NT Server includes Services for Macintosh; these services give you the ability to manage a Windows NT network environment that includes computers using an AppleTalk internetwork. AppleTalk is the protocol used by Macintosh clients to communicate on an internetwork.

Routing AppleTalk

Windows NT Server supports AppleTalk routing through Services for Macintosh. It can be added via the **Services** tab in Networking properties. Use the **Routing** tab in Services for Macintosh to enable or disable AppleTalk routing. Using AppleTalk routing allows a Windows NT Server to act as an AppleTalk router.

Enabling RIP

In this exercise you will enable RIP for Internet Protocol.

➤ **To enable RIP for Internet Protocol**

To enable RIP for Internet Protocol, you need to open the TCP/IP protocol properties and enable RIP.

1. Right Click on **Network Neighborhood** and Click on **Properties**.

   The Network dialogue will appear.

2. Click on **Services**, then click on **Add**.

   A list of available Windows NT services will appear.

3. Choose RIP for Internet Protocol and click **OK**.

4. Enter the path to the Windows NT Server CD and click **OK.**

5. RIP for Internet Services will be installed.

6. Click **Close**.

7. When prompted to reboot, click **OK**

Lesson Summary

The following information summarizes the key points in this lesson:

- Windows NT includes support for routing NWLink IPX/SPX Compatible Transport, TCP/IP, and AppleTalk.

- RIP for NWLink, RIP for Internet Protocol, and Services for Macintosh are added, removed, and configured using the Network program in Control Panel.

Lesson 5: Configuring Internet Information Server

This lesson introduces you to the Internet and the intranet and discusses their functions and characteristics. The World Wide Web (WWW), a graphical interface that overlays the Internet to create a virtual network, or Web of information, is also introduced. Finally, the security issues that should be considered when connecting to the Internet, as well as when integrating a local intranet with the Internet, are examined.

After this lesson, you will be able to:

- Discuss IIS and PWS functions and features.
- Install and configure IIS.
- Understand the Internet and intranet security issues.

Estimated lesson time: 15 minutes

The Internet is a network of networks around the world. An intranet exists at a local level, and consists of computers that are connected by means of local area networks (LANs). The following illustration shows both Internet and intranet connectivity.

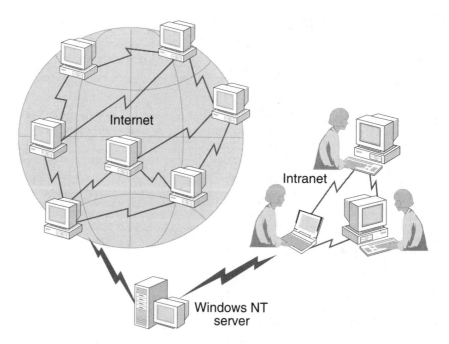

Internet

The Internet is a global network of computers that communicate using common languages and protocols.

The Internet has been evolving since the early 1970s. Early servers on the Internet conformed to original Internet protocols, such as the File Transfer Protocol (FTP) or Virtual Terminal Protocol (VTP, now called Telnet). These protocols generally provide a way to copy files, issue commands, or start programs through a character-based interface.

Internet technology has grown beyond the simple file transfers on character-based FTP or Telnet servers and incorporates graphical interfaces.

A key graphical network service on the Internet is the World Wide Web (WWW, or the Web). The user creates Web pages that are then linked together by means of the Hypertext Transfer Protocol (HTTP). Every Web page, including a Web site's home page, has a unique address called a Uniform Resource Locator (URL). The following shows a sample URL:

http://www.microsoft.com/ntserver/

Web pages are hypertext documents—files that have been formatted by using the Hypertext Markup Language (HTML)—that contain hyperlinks. Hyperlinks have Web addresses embedded in them and are represented as underlined or bordered words and graphics. When you click a hyperlink, you "jump" to the location on the Internet that was specified in the hyperlink.

Web servers automatically provide formatted text, graphics, sounds, and animation to Internet users. In order to connect to Web servers and view the information, you must use a Web browser such as Internet Explorer. Internet Explorer also supports the older standards, such as FTP, so you can use Internet Explorer to access multiple servers and data types.

Intranet

Intranets are networks, internal to a company or organization, that use Internet technology, such as the HTTP servers and Web browser services, to improve an organization's internal communications, information publishing, and application development process. In this book, intranet refers to any Transmission Control Protocol/Internet Protocol (TCP/IP) network using Internet technology that is not connected to the Internet.

Security Considerations
When Connecting to the Internet

It is important to remember that the Internet, like other networks, provides two-way communication. When you are connected to the Internet, other computers can see your computer. By default, Windows NT security protects your computer from casual intrusion. However, while it is very unlikely that your computer will be attacked while you are browsing the Internet, it is still a good idea to configure your computer securely. Before you install and configure TCP/IP and dial-up networking, you should review the security configuration of your computer.

Security Considerations for
Integrating an Intranet Site with the Internet

It is possible to integrate a corporate intranet with the Internet. Both can be supported by the same network system. If your computer is also connected to an in-house network (an intranet), it is especially important to prevent access to your intranet from the Internet.

The following are security issues to keep in mind if you intend to integrate an intranet with the Internet:

- Typically, intranet sites are casual and informal, while Internet sites generally reflect the organization's public image.

- Separate the information that is downloaded to an intranet site from that distributed over the Internet. For example, proprietary documents are often distributed on intranets but would violate trade secrets if they were released to the Internet.

- It is usually not advisable to grant full intranet access to Internet users.

IIS and PWS Networking Components

Windows NT is equipped with several components that support interoperability with the Internet and private intranets. Internet and intranet components supported by Windows NT are the Internet Information Server (IIS) and Peer Web Services (PWS).

IIS and PWS provide computers running Windows NT with the ability to publish resources and services on the Internet and on private intranets. Use IIS and PWS for publishing hypertext Web pages and client/server applications, and for interactive Web applications.

Functions of IIS and PWS

The following illustration shows the roles of IIS and PWS in Internet and intranet communications.

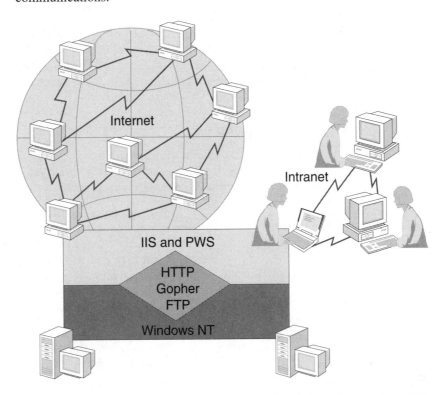

The IIS and PWS are network file and application servers that use HTTP, the Gopher service, and FTP to provide information over the Internet or an intranet.

- HTTP is used to link to and navigate Web hypertext documents and applications.

- The Gopher service is a hierarchical system used to create links to other computers or services, to put these links into custom menus, and to annotate files and directories.

- FTP is used to transfer files between two computers on a TCP/IP network.

Using IIS and PWS, it is possible to publish information or services such as Web pages, interactive applications, and catalogs for customers, and to post and track databases on the Web.

IIS and PWS support the Internet Server Application Programming Interface (ISAPI). ISAPI is used to create interfaces that can be used for client/server applications. For example, ISAPI can be used to create applications that allow clients to access and enter information into a Web page.

IIS and PWS Comparison

Any computer running Windows NT Server can support IIS, and any computer running Windows NT Workstation can support PWS. IIS is designed to support the heavy usage that can occur on the Internet. PWS, on the other hand, is optimized for use as a small scale Web server suitable for exchanging information for a small department or individuals on an intranet.

Features of IIS and PWS

Among the features included with IIS and PWS are file publication, network management, and security. The following table provides an overview of some of the key features that IIS and PWS offer to a computer running Windows NT.

Feature	Use This Feature To
File Publication	Publish existing files from Windows NT and other file servers.
Network Management	Monitor and record network activity and provide clients with access to valuable network resources such as HTML pages, shared files and printers, corporate databases, and legacy systems.
Security	Provide clients with secure access to Internet and intranet resources.
Support for common Internet standards	Enable development of Web applications, using such languages as CGI (Common Gateway Interface) and PERL (Practical Extraction and Report Language).
Microsoft Internet Explorer	Enable clients such as Windows 3.11, Windows for Workgroups, Windows NT, Windows 95, and Macintosh to gain easy access to information on the Web.
Scalability	Enable Internet access to multiple platforms running on standard hardware packages, including single and multiprocessor servers using Intel 486, Pentium, Pentium Pro, Digital Alpha AXP, PowerPC, and MIPS processors.
Support for Microsoft Back-Office applications such as SQL Server and SNA Server	Provide businesses with the ability to deliver commercial solutions on the Web to customers.

Installing IIS

IIS can be installed when Windows NT Server is installed, or at a later time using either the Network program of Control Panel or the Install Internet Information Server icon located on the Windows NT Server desktop.

IIS Installation Requirements

Microsoft IIS has the following requirements for IIS installation:

- A computer running Windows NT Server 4.0 with TCP/IP.

- A CD-ROM drive for the Windows NT Server compact disc or a LAN connection to a server sharing the installation files.

- Adequate disk space for the published information content. It is recommended to use NT file system (NTFS) file and directory permissions to secure all of the disks used with IIS.

- Changes can be made to a current installation of IIS through the Internet Information Server Setup icon located in the Microsoft Internet Server (Common) folder. Before adding or removing components, or reinstalling IIS, disable any previous versions of FTP, Gopher, or other Web service that may be installed on Windows NT Server.

The following illustration shows the components available when installing IIS.

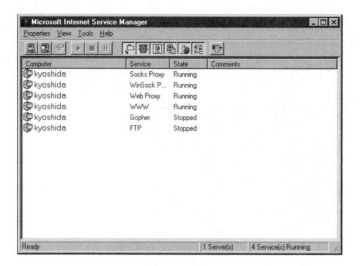

Configuring IIS and PWS

All of the Internet and intranet services can be configured and managed from one central point using a simple interface.

Use the Microsoft Internet Service Manager (ISM) to enhance IIS and PWS configuration and performance. ISM is located in the Microsoft Internet Server Tools (Common) folder on a computer running Windows NT Server, or in the Microsoft Peer Web Services Tools (Common) folder on a computer running Windows NT Workstation. ISM provides a mechanism to configure and monitor all of the Internet services running on any computer running Windows NT in the network.

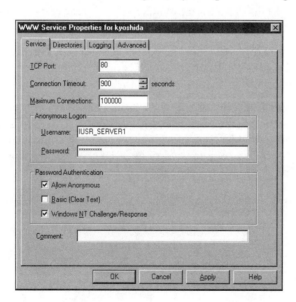

Internet Server Manager List Box

Using ISM, it is possible to manage multiple servers from one computer. ISM's default view is the Report view. Report view lists the computers on the network and the services installed on them. Report view also provides users with a mechanism to perform the following tasks:

- Connect to servers and view server properties.

- Start, stop, or pause a service.

- Select which services should be displayed.

- Configure properties of the services, if necessary.

Properties

In ISM, double-click a computer or service name to display its properties. The following illustration shows the WWW service properties displayed on the Service tab.

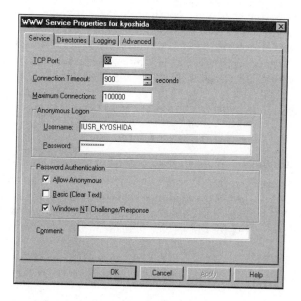

The different services (WWW, Gopher, FTP) have different properties. The properties that can be configured through the **Properties** dialog box include those listed below:

- Service tab. Connections, user logon, and authentication requirements.

- Directories tab. Directories used by each service, default document, and directory browsing.

- Logging tab. Server activity tracking and log file directory.

- Advanced tab. Secured access by IP address and bandwidth. The advanced tab is available only on IIS and not on PWS.

Configuring Services

ISM can also be used to configure the following:

- WWW Service. Set a default document so clients who are browsing can always receive the default document if they do not specify a particular file.

- FTP Service. Enable FTP clients to view files on NTFS partitions in the same format as a traditional UNIX FTP server.

Securing Internet and Intranet Sites

IIS and PWS are built on the Windows NT security model. Windows NT security helps protect Internet and intranet sites by requiring an assigned user account in order to access the site. When configuring these services, you specify whether to allow anonymous access to your site through the Internet Guest Account or another account designated by you, or to require a Windows NT user name and password. You can enable both anonymous connections and client authentication for the WWW and FTP services.

In addition, it is possible to control access to all computer resources by controlling the permissions assigned for each user or group to NTFS files and folders.

Allow Anonymous Access with the Internet Guest Account

On many Internet servers, access is anonymous; that is, the client request does not contain a user name and password. When you allow anonymous connections to your WWW, Gopher, and FTP services, Windows NT uses the user name and password configured for the service to make the anonymous connections.

The Internet Guest account, IUSR_*computername*, is created during the IIS or PWS installation. By default, this account is used when allowing anonymous connections.

Note The Internet Guest account is added to the Guests group. Changes to the Guests group user rights and resource permissions also apply to the Internet Guest account. Review the user rights and resource permissions for the Guests group to ensure that they are appropriate for the Internet Guest account.

If remote access is available only to the Internet Guest account, remote users do not provide a user name and password, and have only the permissions assigned to the Internet Guest account. This prevents unauthorized users from gaining access to sensitive information with fraudulent or illegally-obtained passwords.

Require a User Name and Password

The WWW and FTP services can be configured to require a valid user name and password to access your site's Internet resources. When this option is configured, the client request must contain a user name and password.

There are two types of authentication available when requiring a user name and password: Basic and Windows NT Challenge/Response.

- Basic authentication does not encrypt transmissions between the client and server, so names and passwords are sent in clear text over the networks. Intruders sniffing your transmissions could discover valid user names and passwords.

- Windows NT Challenge/Response authentication, supported by Internet Explorer version 2.0 or later, protects the password, thereby providing for secure logon over the network. In this method, the user account obtained from the client is the one that the user is logged on with at the client computer.

Note The FTP service only supports basic authentication, so your FTP site is more secure if you only allow anonymous connections.

Guidelines for Securing an Internet and Intranet Site

The following are guidelines for creating an account policy for a secure Internet or intranet site:

- Do not allow blank passwords.
- Require a minimum password length.
- Require users to change their passwords frequently.
- Require users to use different passwords each time they are changed.
- Lock out accounts after multiple failed logon attempts.
- Require an administrator to unlock all locked accounts.
- Require users with restricted hours to be automatically disconnected.

Installing IIS

In this exercise you will install IIS, and use the web browser to view an HTML document.

➤ To install IIS

In this procedure you will install the IIS on to your computer.

1. Right Click on **Network Neighborhood** and Click on **Properties**.

   The Network dialogue will appear.

2. Click on **Services**, then click on **Add**.

   A list of available Windows NT services will appear.

3. Choose the **Microsoft Internet Information Server version 2.0** then click **OK**.

4. Enter the path to the Windows NT Server CD and click **OK.**

5. Click **OK** to start the IIS setup.

6. Click **OK** to select the default options.

7. Click **OK** to choose the default installation paths.

8. Click **Yes** to confirm that you want to create those paths.

   Microsoft Internet Information Server v2.0 will be installed.

9. Click **Close**.

10. When prompted to reboot, click **OK**.

➤ To test the Internet Information Server

In this procedure you will test the IIS on your computer.

1. Start the Internet Explorer.

2. Enter your server name, **server1**, in the Open field and press **Enter.**

   The IIS home page on your server should open.

Lesson Summary

The following information summarizes the key points in this lesson:

- The Internet is a network of computers located around the world that communicate with one another through telephone lines; an intranet exists at a local level, and consists of computers that are connected by means of LANs.

- The Internet and intranets communicate using common languages and protocols.

- IIS and PWS provide computers running Windows NT with the ability to publish resources and services on the Internet and on private intranets. Use IIS and PWS for publishing hypertext Web pages and client/server applications, and for interactive Web applications.

- There are security issues that you need to be aware of when you connect an intranet to the Internet. The Internet, like other networks, provides two-way communication. When you are connected to the Internet, other computers can see your computer. By default, Windows NT security protects your computer from casual intrusion. However, while it is very unlikely that your computer will be attacked while you are browsing the Internet, it is still a good idea to configure your computer securely.

For more information on	See
IIS	Product documentation available in the Microsoft Internet Server (Common) folder
PWS	Product documentation available in the Microsoft Peer Web Services (Common) folder

Lesson 6: Configuring NT Services for NetWare

Windows NT Server provides several features and services that permit computers running Windows NT to coexist and interoperate with Novell NetWare servers. Some of these services are included in Windows NT, while others are available as separate products, commonly called add-ons. This lesson describes NetWare connectivity tools and explains how they can be used to integrate Windows NT and NetWare environments.

After this lesson, you will be able to:

- List the features and services that allow computers running Windows NT to interoperate with computers running NetWare.

- Explain the function of GSNW.

- Explain the function of FPNW.

- Describe the Migration Tool for NetWare.

Estimated lesson time: 20 minutes

Windows NT Connectivity with NetWare

In order for computers running Windows NT to access and share resources with computers running NetWare, you must install some additional software on your computers running Windows NT. The type of connectivity you require determines the software that you must install. The software included with Windows NT Server is Gateway Services for NetWare (GSNW) and Migration Tool for NetWare. In addition, there is a set of add-on utilities including File and Print services for NetWare (FPNW) and Directory Service Manager for NetWare (DSMN).

NWLink

NetWare uses Internetwork Packet Exchange/Sequenced Packet Exchange (IPX/SPX) as its primary network protocol. Microsoft developed NWLink IPX/SPX Compatible Transport to provide computers running Windows NT the ability to communicate with NetWare servers and clients. NWLink is a native 32-bit Windows NT implementation of IPX/SPX and supports application servers in a NetWare environment. NWLink is included with both Windows NT Server and Windows NT Workstation.

All computers running NWLink or IPX can communicate because they are running a common protocol. Two networking application programming interfaces (APIs) are supported on Windows NT running NWLink to allow these communications:

- Windows Sockets. This interface supports existing NetWare applications written to comply with the NetWare IPX/SPX Sockets interface.

- NetBIOS. This interface supports sending and receiving Novell NetBIOS packets between a computer running NetWare and Novell NetBIOS, and a computer running Windows NT and NWLink NetBIOS.

By itself, NWLink does not provide access to NetWare file and print resources. To allow a computer running Windows NT to access services on NetWare networks, and to provide NetWare clients with the ability to use services on Windows NT Servers, Microsoft has developed several tools for NetWare interoperability.

GSNW

GSNW allow computers running Windows NT Server, and using NWLink as a transport protocol, to access files and printers on NetWare servers. In addition, you can use GSNW to create gateways to NetWare resources. Creating a gateway allows computers running only Microsoft client software to access NetWare resources through the gateway. Any Microsoft network client, such as Windows NT Workstation, Windows 95, or Windows NT Server can access NetWare services through the Windows NT Server running GSNW. Using GSNW, a computer running Windows NT Server connects to a NetWare file server's directory and then shares it, just as if the directory were on the Windows NT Server. Microsoft network clients can then access the directory on the NetWare server by connecting to the share created on the Windows NT Server.

GSNW is designed to provide Windows clients with occasional access to a Net-Ware network. GSNW is not designed to allow a computer running Windows NT Server to be a user-intensive, high-performance gateway.

GSNW can also serve as a migration path. For example, use GSNW to permit gradual migration from NetWare to Windows NT.

FPNW

GSNW provide computers running Windows NT with the ability to connect to NetWare servers for file, print, and application resources. To integrate NetWare clients into a Windows NT Network and also allow them to access resources on computers running Windows NT Server, Microsoft provides FPNW.

FPNW is not included with Windows NT. It is a Windows NT add-on utility that allows a computer running Windows NT Server to function as a NetWare 3.12-compatible file and print server. The server appears just like any other NetWare server to the NetWare clients, and the client can access volumes, files, and printers at the server. No changes or additions to the NetWare client software are necessary, making integration with a Windows NT Server environment more cost-effective. You can add FPNW to an existing application server to maximize usage of hardware resources.

DSMN

DSMN extends Windows NT Server Directory Service features to NetWare servers. With DSMN, you can centrally manage mixed Windows NT and NetWare 2.x, 3.x, and 4.x (in bindery emulation mode) environments with Windows NT Directory Services.

DSMN is not included with Windows NT. It is a Windows NT add-on utility that allows a single network logon for NetWare clients by synchronizing accounts across all NetWare servers. Clients need only remember one account name and password to gain access to file, print, and application resources on the network.

Use DSMN to accomplish the following tasks:

- Specify which NetWare user and group accounts to manage centrally from Windows NT Server. The specified accounts are copied to the domain's directory database on the primary domain controller (PDC). These NetWare accounts become Windows NT Server accounts and must comply with the account policy of the Windows NT Server domain.

- Merge account names from multiple NetWare servers into one account name. If a client has accounts on two NetWare servers and these accounts have different user names, it is possible to merge the accounts' names when adding them to the domain. For example, DavidS and DavidSm could become DavidS.

- Specify which Windows NT Server domain accounts (user and group) to copy back to NetWare servers. This ensures that changes made to domain accounts are synchronized with the NetWare server.

Migration Tool for NetWare

The Windows NT Server Migration Tool for NetWare, included with Windows NT Server, allows you to easily transfer user and group accounts, volumes, folders, and files from a NetWare server to a computer running Windows NT Server. If the server you are migrating to runs FPNW, you can also migrate users' logon scripts.

The Migration Tool for NetWare provides a computer running Windows NT with the capability to perform the following functions:

- Preserve appropriate user account information, including NetWare-specific information such as logon and station restrictions.

- Preserve logon scripts with the user account. Windows NT Server supports NetWare logon script commands.

- Control how user and group names are transferred.

- Set passwords for transferred accounts.

- Control how account restrictions and administrative rights are transferred.

- Create a volume for NetWare users.

- Select the directories and files to transfer.

- Select a destination for transferred directories and files.

- Preserve effective rights on directories and files.

Integrating with NetWare

In this exercise you will answer questions about NT Services for NetWare.

1. With NWLink installed, you can map a drive to a NetWare file share.

   True _____

   False _____

2. Two Windows NT servers with only NWLink installed as a protocol can share each others resources.

   True _____

   False _____

3. GSNW is designed to provide several Microsoft Networking clients high-performance access to a NetWare server's file and print services.

   True _____

   False _____

4. GSNW comes with Windows NT Server.

   True _____

   False _____

5. What special feature of NetWare 4.x needs to be configured for DSMN to access a NetWare 4.x directory?

_____

_____

Lesson Summary

The following information summarizes the key points in this lesson:

- GSNW allow computers running Windows NT Server and NWLink to both directly access files and printers at NetWare servers, and create gateways to NetWare resources for Windows clients.

- FPNW allow NetWare clients to access file, print, and application resources on computers running Windows NT Server.

- DSMN extend Windows NT Server directory service features to NetWare servers. DSMN copies NetWare user and group account information to Windows NT Servers and then incrementally propagates any account changes back to NetWare servers.

- The Migration Tool for NetWare, included with Windows NT Server, allows the transfer of user and group accounts, volumes, folders, and files from a NetWare server to a computer running Windows NT Server.

Lesson 7: Managing Remote Access Servers

Windows NT Remote Access Service (RAS) connects remote or mobile workers to corporate networks. Windows NT RAS is a dial-up networking product. This lesson explains the basic operation of Windows NT RAS, and the implementation of Windows NT Server RAS in a Windows NT Server network.

After this lesson, you will be able to:

- Describe the purpose of RAS and dial-up networking.
- Explain the WAN support included in RAS.
- Identify the remote access protocols that are included in RAS.
- Describe the Point-to-Point Tunneling Protocol (PPTP).
- Explain the security features included with RAS.

Estimated lesson time: 20 minutes

RAS

RAS allows remote users to work on the following systems as if they were connected directly to the network: Windows NT, Windows for Workgroups, MS-DOS version 3.1 or later (with RAS version 1.1a), and MS OS/2 version 3.1 (with RAS version 1.1).

Users run the RAS graphical phonebook on a remote computer and then initiate a connection to the RAS server using a local modem, X.25, or Integrated Services Digital Network (ISDN) card. The RAS server, running on a Windows NT Server computer, authenticates the users, and services the sessions until terminated by the user or network administrator. All services typically available to a local area network (LAN)-connected user (including file- and print-sharing, database access and messaging) can be enabled by means of the RAS connection.

RAS Protocols

Protocols supported by RAS can be examined according to their functions—those protocols that transmit data over LANs and those that transmit data over wide area networks (WANs). Windows NT supports LAN protocols such as Transmission Control Protocol/Internet Protocol (TCP/IP), Internet Packet Exchange/

Sequenced Packet Exchange (IPX/SPX), NWLink, and NetBEUI. Windows NT also supports remote access protocols such as Point-to-Point Protocol (PPP), Serial Line Internet Protocol (SLIP), and the Microsoft RAS protocol.

The Microsoft RAS protocol is a proprietary remote access protocol supporting the NetBIOS standard. This protocol is supported in all previous versions of RAS and is used on Windows NT 3.1, Windows for Workgroups, MS-DOS, and LAN Manager clients. A RAS client dialing in to an older version of Windows (for example, Windows NT 3.1 or Windows for Workgroups) must use the NetBEUI protocol. The RAS server then acts as a "gateway" for the remote client, providing access to servers that use the NetBEUI, TCP/IP, or IPX protocols.

LAN Protocols

Windows NT RAS supports NetBEUI, TCP/IP, and IPX. Thus, you can integrate Windows NT RAS into existing Microsoft, UNIX, or NetWare networks using the PPP remote access standard. Windows NT RAS clients can also connect to existing SLIP-based remote access servers (primarily UNIX servers).

When you install and configure RAS, any protocols already i nstalled on the computer (such as NetBEUI, TCP/IP, and IPX) are automatically enabled for RAS.

Remote Access Protocols

RAS connections can be established through SLIP or PPP.

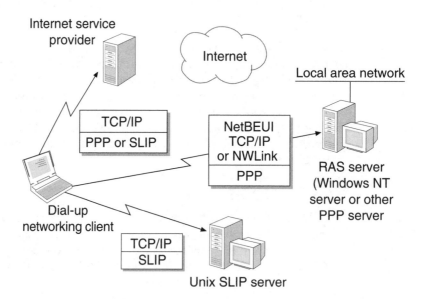

SLIP

SLIP is an industry standard that addresses TCP/IP connections made over serial lines. SLIP was first developed in 1984 to support TCP/IP networking over low-speed serial interfaces. It is supported by Windows NT dial-up networking and gives Windows NT clients easier access to Internet services.

SLIP has several limitations when compared to the newer PPP. SLIP servers cannot use Dynamic Host Configuration Protocol/Windows Internet Naming Service (DHCP/WINS). SLIP connections typically rely on text-based logon sessions and usually require a scripting system to automate the logon process. Although SLIP supports TCP/IP, it does not support IPX/SPX or NetBEUI. In addition, unlike PPP, SLIP transmits authentication passwords as clear text, thereby making the system less secure. Windows NT RAS server does not have a SLIP server component, so it cannot be used as a SLIP server.

PPP

PPP was designed as an enhancement to the original SLIP specification. PPP is a set of industry standard framing and authentication protocols that allow RAS clients and servers to interoperate in a multivendor network. It provides a standard method of sending network data over a point-to-point link. PPP supports several protocols, including AppleTalk, DECnet, Open Systems Interconnection (OSI), NetBEUI, TCP/IP, and IPX. Windows NT supports NetBEUI, TCP/IP, and IPX.

Windows NT Protocol Support Over PPP

PPP support allows computers running Windows NT to dial in to remote networks through any server that complies with the PPP standard. PPP compliance also allows a computer running Windows NT Server to receive calls from, and provide access to, other vendors' remote access software.

Supporting TCP/IP makes Windows NT "Internet ready," and allows remote clients to access the Internet through WinSock applications.

RAS Setup automatically binds to NetBEUI, TCP/IP, and IPX if they are already installed on the computer when RAS is installed. After RAS is installed, each protocol can be configured separately for use with RAS.

PPP Multilink Protocol (MP)

The PPP MP provides the means to increase data transmission rates. MP accomplishes this by combining multiple physical links into a logical bundle to increase bandwidth. Based on the Internet Engineering Task Force (IETF) standard RFC 1717, RAS using PPP MP allows you to easily combine analog modem paths,

Integrated Services Digital Network (ISDN) paths, and even mixed analog and digital communications links on both client and server computers. For example, a client with two 28.8-Kbps modems and two phone lines can use MP to establish a single 57.6-Kbps connection to an MP server with two 28.8-Kbps modems and phone lines. This will speed up access to the Internet or to the intranet, and cut down on the amount of time spent remotely connected, thus reducing remote access cost.

Both the dial-up networking client and the RAS server need to have MP enabled for this protocol to be used.

PPTP

PPTP is a technology that supports multiprotocol virtual private networks (VPNs). This allows you to remotely access your corporate network securely across the Internet. Using PPTP, you can establish a connection to the Internet and then establish a connection to the RAS server on the Internet using PPTP.

Using PPTP to connect to a remote network offers computers running Windows NT the following advantages:

- Lower transmission costs. If you have local access through an Internet Service Provider (ISP), access to the remote network will be less expensive than a long-distance telephone call or using an 800 number.

- Lower hardware costs. If PPTP is used, a RAS server needs only a connection to the Internet. It is not necessary for the RAS server to have multiple modems, ISDN, or X.25 cards.

- Lower administrative overhead. With PPTP in Windows NT 4.0, you manage and secure your network at the RAS server. You need to manage only the user accounts and RAS dial-in permissions.

- Security. PPTP provides security through data encryption. A PPTP connection over the Internet is encrypted and works with the NetBEUI, TCP/IP, and IPX protocols. Data sent by means of a PPTP tunnel consists of encapsulated PPP packets. If dial-up networking is configured to use data encryption, the data sent by means of PPTP is encrypted when sent.

RAS Security Features

Windows NT RAS incorporates a number of security measures to validate remote client access to a network.

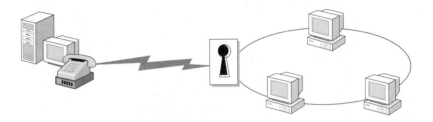

Integrated Domain Security

Windows NT Server provides for enterprise-wide security using a trusted domain, single-network logon model. This eliminates the need for duplicate user accounts across a multiple-server network. The single-network logon model extends to RAS users. The RAS server uses the same user account database as the computer running Windows NT. This allows easier administration because clients can log on with the same user accounts they use at the office. This feature ensures that clients have the same privileges and permissions they ordinarily have while in the office.

To connect to a RAS server, clients must have a valid Windows NT user account as well as the RAS dial-in permission. Clients must first be authenticated by RAS before they can log on to Windows NT.

Encrypted Authentication and Logon Process

By default, all authentication and logon information is encrypted when transmitted over RAS. However, it is possible to allow any authentication method, including clear text. In addition, it is possible to configure RAS and dial-up networking so that all data that passes between a client and server is encrypted.

Auditing

With auditing enabled, RAS generates audit information on all remote connections, including processes such as authentication and logging on.

Intermediary Security Hosts

It is possible to add another level of security to a RAS configuration by connecting a third-party intermediary security host between the RAS client or clients and the RAS server or servers. When an intermediary security host is used, clients must type a password or code to get past the security device before a connection is established with the RAS server.

Callback Security

The RAS server can be configured to provide callbacks as a means of increasing security. When callback security is used, the server receives the call from the client computer, disconnects the connection, and then calls the client back either at a preset telephone number or at a number that was provided during the initial call. This allows another level of security by guaranteeing that the connection to the local network was made from a trusted site, such as a branch office.

PPTP Filtering

When using PPTP, the RAS server must have a direct connection to the Internet and a company's corporate network. This could pose a security risk because the corporate network could be accessed through the RAS server. Use PPTP filtering to help ensure security on a corporate network. When PPTP filtering is enabled, all protocols other than PPTP will be disabled on the selected network adapter card.

Installing RAS

Whether you install RAS during Windows NT installation or later through the Network program in Control Panel, RAS requires the following information for installation:

- The model of modem that will be used.
- The type of communication port to use for the RAS connection.
- Whether this computer will be used to dial in, dial out, or both.
- The protocols to be used.
- Any modem settings such as baud or Kbps rate.
- Security settings including callback.

Configuring a RAS Server

Configuring a RAS server differs from configuring dial-up networking clients. While dial-up networking clients are configured primarily to dial in to remote networks, RAS servers are configured to provide access to network services for these clients. RAS server configuration involves configuring communication ports, network protocols (such as NetBEUI, TCP/IP, and IPX), and encryption settings.

The first step in configuring a RAS server is to specify the hardware that RAS will use, including the type of modem and the port to which the modem will be connected. In the following illustration, the modem is a Hayes Optima 288 V.34, and it is connected to COM1.

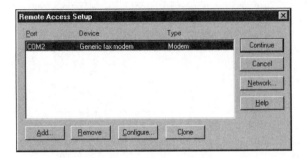

The drivers and ports used by RAS servers are configured through the **Remote Access Setup** dialog box. To access this dialog box, start the Network program in Control Panel. Click the **Services** tab and select the **Remote Access Service**. Then click the **Properties** button. The **Remote Access Setup** dialog box appears. The following table lists the configuration options available through this dialog box.

Option	Use This Option To
Add	Make a port available to RAS and install a modem or X.25 PAD.
Remove	Make a port unavailable to RAS.
Configure	Change the RAS settings for the port, such as the attached device or the intended usage (dialing out only, receiving calls only, or both).
Clone	Copy the same modem setup from one port to another.
Network	Configure network protocol, Multilink, and encryption settings.

RAS Server Port Configuration Options

Click the **Configure** button in the **Remote Access Service** dialog box to configure the RAS server ports. The following illustration shows a possible configuration.

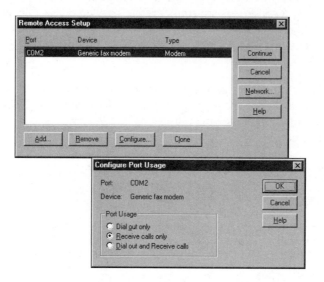

The following table explains the options listed in the **Configure Port Usage** dialog box.

Option	Use This Option To Enable
Dial out only	Dial-up networking clients to use that port to initiate calls.
Receive calls only	RAS servers to receive calls from dial-up networking clients on that port.
Dial out and Receive calls	RAS servers to use that port for either dial-up networking client or server functions.

Port configuration options affect only the specified port. For example, if the server's COM1 port is configure d to receive calls and the COM2 port is configured to dial out and receive calls, a remote client could call in on either COM port, but a local user could only use COM2 for outbound RAS calls.

Once you select the appropriate Port Usage option, click **OK** and the **Remote Access Setup** dialog box reappears.

Configuring Protocols on the Server

Click the **Network** button in the **Remote Access Setup** dialog box, and the **Network Configuration** dialog box appears. In the following illustration, one of the dial-out options has been selected and all three protocols are being used.

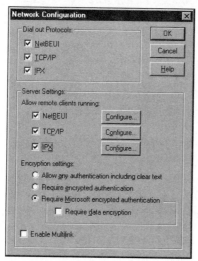

Use the **Network Configuration** dialog box to select and configure the LAN protocols. Network protocol configuration applies to RAS operations on all RAS-enabled ports. The following table describes the protocol configuration options available through the **Network Configuration** dialog box.

Option	Use This Option To
Dial out Protocols	Select the dial-out protocols.
Server Settings	Select and configure the protocols the RAS server can use for servicing remote clients.
Encryption settings	Select an authentication level ranging from clear text for down level clients to Microsoft Encrypted Authentication for Windows NT and Windows 95 clients.
	If **Require Microsoft encrypted authentication** is selected, **Require data encryption** can also be selected.
Enable Multilink	Enable the dial-up networking PPP Multilink Protocol. To use Multilink, both the client and the server must have Multilink enabled.

Event Viewer

The Event Viewer is used to view the system log, which contains events for all Windows NT internal services and drivers. Event Viewer is useful in diagnosing RAS problems, because many RAS events are logged in the system log. For example, if the Windows NT dial-up networking client fails to connect, or if the RAS server fails to start, you should check the system log.

Troubleshooting RAS Connections

Outlined below are some troubleshooting tactics that can be used if problems arise.

Problems with PPP Connections

If the user is having problems being authenticated over PPP, a Ppp.log file can be created to provide debugging information to troubleshoot the problem. The Ppp.log file is stored in the *systemroot*\System32\Ras folder. It is enabled by changing the following registry parameter to a value of 1:

\HKEY_LOCAL_MACHINE\SYSTEM\CurrentControlSet\Services\Rasman\ PPP**Logging**

Authentication Problems

If a dial-up networking client is having problems being authenticated over RAS, try to change the authentication settings for that client. Try the lowest authentication option on each side, and if successful, start increasing the authentication options to determine the highest level of authentication that can be used between the two systems.

Dial-Up Networking Monitor

The dial-up networking monitor, accessed through the Dial-Up Monitor program in Control Panel, shows the status of a session that is in progress. It shows the duration of the call, the amount of data that is being transmitted and received, and the number of errors. In addition, it can show which lines are being used for Multilink sessions.

Multilink and Callback

If a client uses a Multilink-enabled phonebook entry to call a server and that server is configured to call the user back, when the callback is made, it will be to one of the Multilink devices. This is because the RAS Admin utility allows only one number to be stored for callback purposes for each user account. Therefore, the RAS server calls only one of the devices and Multilink functionality is lost.

If the link between the dial-up networking client and the RAS server is made using ISDN with two channels that have the same telephone number, then Multilink will work with callback.

AutoDial Occurs During Logon

During the logon process, when Windows NT Explorer initializes, any persistent network connections or desktop shortcuts that reference network locations will cause AutoDial to attempt a connection. The only way to avoid this is to disable AutoDial or remove the persistent connections and shortcuts.

Configuring RAS

In this exercise you will answer questions about RAS.

1. Other than an analogue modem, what other communication mediums does RAS support?

2. Of the two Remote Access Protocols supported by Windows NT, PPP and SLIP, which is the easiest to use?

3. Of the two Remote Access Protocols, PPP and SLIP, which supports all the protocols shipped with Windows NT Server?

4. Is it possible to combine the bandwidth provided by multiple modems into a single connection? If so, how?

5. Is it possible to provide an encryption session over the Internet? If so, how?

6. Once RAS is installed and configured on the RAS server, do all Windows NT domain users have dial-in access by default?

_____

_____

7. How can you provide additional dial-in security by forcing users to initiate a call from a predefined phone number?

_____

_____

8. How can PPTP be used to increase network security?

_____

_____

Lesson Summary

The following information summarizes the key points in this chapter:

- RAS permits users who are not physically connected to the network to have network access through modems and telephone lines. The RAS server acts as a gateway between the remote client and the network. Any Microsoft dial-up networking client can connect to any Microsoft RAS server.

- RAS can establish connections using standard telephone lines, X.25, and ISDN.

- RAS supports the SLIP and PPP protocols for WAN connections.

- An additional protocol, PPTP, allows secure remote access to corporate networks across the Internet. A connection to the Internet is established first, then a connection to the RAS server using PPTP is established.

- RAS provides several security features, including integrated domain security, encrypted logon, auditing, intermediary security hosts, and callback security.

C H A P T E R   5

Server Monitoring and Optimization

About This Chapter

This chapter introduces the procedures and guidelines for analyzing and optimizing Windows NT Server performance. It emphasizes the importance of collecting and analyzing server usage data for the purposes of optimizing the current configuration and predicting future requirements.

Before You Begin

To complete the lessons in this chapter, you must have:

- The knowledge and skills covered in Chapter 2, "Installation and Configuration."

- The knowledge and skills covered in Chapter 3, "Managing Enterprise Resources."

- The knowledge and skills covered in Chapter 4, "Connectivity."

- Completed the exercises in Chapters 1–4.

Lesson 1: Server Analysis and Optimization Basics

Server analysis and optimization involves knowing what actions to take to improve system performance in response to system demands. This lesson provides an overview of server analysis and optimization in the context of Windows NT 4.0.

After this lesson, you will be able to:

- Define server analysis and optimization.
- Identify the major resources to monitor when performing server analysis and optimization.
- List the Windows NT utilities used for server analysis and optimization.
- Use Performance Monitor for server analysis.
- Identify Performance Monitor views.
- List techniques used when performing server analysis and optimization.
- Identify the Windows NT six-step procedure for performing server analysis and optimization.

Estimated lesson time: 40 minutes

Server Analysis and Optimization

The term server analysis and optimization can mean different things to different people. Limit the scope to Windows NT Server, and those ideas can differ even more. Server analysis and optimization is knowing what actions to take to improve system performance in response to demands on the system. The following graphic illustrates server analysis and optimization and describe its benefits.

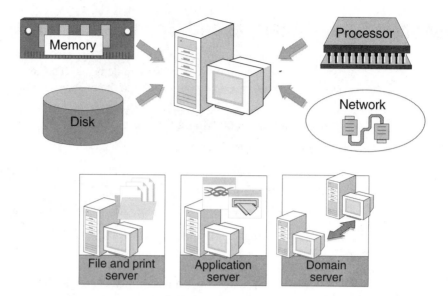

Server analysis and optimization begins with thoughtful and organized record keeping. This is done for the purposes of analyzing resource use to determine the future demands on the system. Server analysis involves looking for the overuse of any hardware resource that causes a decrease in system performance. It is also looking for the residual effect of bottlenecks: other hardware resources that are underused.

Server analysis and optimization involves:

- Creating a baseline of current use.
- Monitoring the use over a period of time.
- Analyzing data to find and resolve abnormalities in the system use.
- Determining expected response times for specific numbers of users and system use.
- Determining how the system should be used.
- Determining when to upgrade the system, or when to add additional system resources.

A properly implemented server analysis and optimization strategy includes the tools and techniques to accomplish the monitoring and analysis of a system.

Windows NT Server Resources to Monitor

A number of resources need to be monitored when analyzing server performance. These resources often have the most impact on the system, and should be monitored when implementing a server analysis strategy.

Server analysis and optimization begins by determining the ceiling throughput (for example interactions per second) of each system resource as it is installed on the system and the network. Determining the throughput during installation establishes the allowable throughput for each resource as it is used.

A number of system resources need to be monitored when implementing a server analysis and optimization strategy. The following resources often have the most impact on server performance:

- Memory
- Processor
- Disk subsystem
- Network subsystem

When monitoring system resources, it is important to not only monitor each resource individually, but also to monitor the system as a whole. By monitoring the entire system, it is easier to detect problems that are a result of resource combinations. The use of one system resource can affect the performance of another, thus masking the usage and performance of the second resource. For example, when the disk subsystem is extremely busy, it is very common for it to fail to perform to the expected level. This failure to perform may result from a system that does not have enough random access memory (RAM). The lack of adequate RAM may then result in excess paging, which lowers the disk subsystem throughput in response to system and user requests. Monitoring all four system resources provides a much clearer look at the effects that resource combinations have on each other.

Memory

Memory has an effect on server analysis and optimization. Consider two main types of memory when you analyze server performance: RAM and cache. Simply put, the more of each the better. Also, consider other factors, such as the size and location of the paging file.

For example, it is generally recommended to move the paging file from the system partition to another position for performance. However, this eliminates the Crashdump utility. The Crashdump utility is a tool used to troubleshoot a system memory dump that is saved to disk if the system crashes.

Processor

The processor has an effect on server analysis and optimization. The type of system processor, as well as the number of processors, affects the overall performance of the system. For example, a Digital Alpha AXP processor provides better performance than an Intel 80486.

Windows NT Server supports symmetric multiprocessing so that if a system has multiple applications running concurrently, or applications that are multithreaded, the overall processor power is shared.

Disk Subsystem

The disk subsystem has an effect on server analysis and optimization. Several factors affect disk subsystem performance, and each of these factors should be taken into consideration during analysis and optimization.

Type and Number of Controllers

The controller type and the number of controllers affect the overall system responsiveness when responding to information requests being read from or written to disk drives. Installing multiple disk controllers can result in higher throughput. Note the throughput of the following controllers:

- IDE controllers have a throughput of about 2.5 MB per second.
- Standard SCSI controllers have a throughput of about 3 MB per second.
- SCSI-2 controllers have a throughput of about 5 MB per second.
- Fast SCSI-2 controllers have a throughput of about 10 MB per second.
- PCI controller cards can transfer data at up to 40 MB per second.

Busmaster Controllers

Busmaster controllers have an on-board processor that handles all interrupts until data is ready to be passed to the central processing unit (CPU) for processing. The on-board CPU controls much of the data processing that would otherwise be handled by the CPU, thus freeing the CPU cycles for other tasks.

Caching

Caching helps improve disk responsiveness, as data is cached on the controller, and does not require RAM or internal cache.

Controllers that Support RAID

Controllers that support hardware-level RAID (redundant array of inexpensive disks) can offer better performance than software implemented RAID. By implementing striping or striping with parity, disk performance may be improved. In one test, for example, writing a 200-MB file to a stripe set (without parity) was 20 percent faster than writing to a single hard disk drive in the same system. The same result may not occur in all tests, so each system needs to be analyzed independently. Chapter one, lesson two outlined the different RAID levels, as well as its performance and fault-tolerance properties.

Type of Work Being Performed

If the applications are disk-bound (many read and write requests), implementing the fastest disk subsystem provides the best performance. For single processor systems, implementing a Fast SCSI-2 as the minimum controller base is generally recommended.

Type of Drives Implemented

Disk performance is generally measured in disk access time. It is not uncommon to find hard disk drives with access speed in the low teens or lower. Implement drives that complement the rest of the architecture, such as the controller. Choose a manufacturer that supplies the fastest drive available in each of its systems.

Network Subsystem

The network subsystem has an effect on server analysis and optimization. Overall network performance and capacity may be affected by a number of factors. Consider each factor in its unique environment to determine whether or not it has an impact on network capacity and server performance.

Network Adapter Type

Implement a high bandwidth card (such as a 32-bit bus mastering card), trying to avoid programmed input/output (PIO) adapters, as they use the CPU to move data from the network adapter to RAM. Note the example transfer speeds of the following adapters:

- 8-bit network adapters transfer up to 400 kilobytes per second (KBps).

- 16-bit adapters transfer up to 800 KBps.

- 32-bit adapters transfer up to 1.2 megabytes per second (MBps).

Multiple Network Adapters

Installing multiple network adapters is beneficial in a server environment because doing so allows the server to process network requests over multiple adapters simultaneously. If your network uses multiple protocols, consider placing each protocol on a different adapter. It is common to have all server-based traffic on a single adapter, for example, while performing host access using Systems Network Architecture (SNA) on a different adapter.

Number of Users

Consider not only the number of users concurrently accessing a server, but also the number of inactive connections, because it requires processing time on the server to monitor each connection.

Routers, Bridges, and Other Physical Network Components

Routers, bridges, and other physical network components affect performance of the network, as do data communications facilities.

Protocols in Use

Most protocols give similar performance, so consider the amount of traffic generated to perform a given function. Reducing the number of protocols installed can increasing performance.

Additional Network Services in Use

Each service adds memory and processor overhead on the system. These services may include the following:

- Services for Macintosh.
- Remote access server (RAS).
- Dynamic Host Configuration Protocol (DHCP).
- Windows Internet Naming Service (WINS).

Applications in Use

Each application adds memory and processor overhead on the system. These applications may include the following:

- Internet Services.
- Messaging applications.
- SQL Server.

- Systems Management Server.

- SNA Server.

Directory Services (Domain Model and Structure)

The following may affect network capacity and performance:

- Number of users: consider not only the number of users and objects in the domain, but the number of simultaneous log on requests validated by the domain controller or controllers.

- Number of Backup Domain Controllers (BDCs): the more domain controllers in a domain, the more domain account synchronization traffic is generated to assure all controllers are synchronized.

- Proximity of BDCs to Primary Domain Controller (PDC) using wide area network (WAN) links: domain account synchronization can use a large percentage of WAN bandwidth. Consider changing the **ReplicationGovernor** parameter to "schedule" the amount of bandwidth that the account synchronization process uses.

Tools for Server Analysis and Optimization

Tools or utilities must be used for capturing data to analyze system resource consumption and usage. Any tool that allows viewing of server usage can help determine resource operation. Listed below are Windows NT tools that you can use to gather data for analysis and optimization. Data gathered using these and other tools is analyzed using the tool itself, or exported to another application, such as Excel. Other retail tools are also available.

Server Manager

Server Manager allows you to perform basic analysis of a server, such as viewing the number of current user connections to a server, the amount of idle time on the connection, and the share names in use. It can also display use of other servers on the network so that analysis can take place from a centralized location.

Performance Monitor

Performance Monitor is a Windows NT 4.0 administrative tool for monitoring the performance of Windows NT Workstations and Servers. It uses a series of counters to track data, such as the number of processes waiting for disk time, the number of network packets transmitted per second, and the percentage of processor utilization. You can view data in real time, log it for future study, use it in charts and reports, and set alerts to warn when a threshold value is exceeded.

Windows NT Diagnostics

You can use the integrated Windows NT Diagnostics application to perform some basic performance analysis tasks. It displays the current configuration of the computer, including processor, memory, disk, and network information.

Task Manager

Task Manager is a tool that allows the viewing, starting, and stopping of applications and processes. It has basic performance-monitoring capabilities for viewing memory and CPU utilization.

Network Monitor

This utility captures and views network traffic moving to and from the computer where Network Monitor is being run. Traffic monitored includes the number of broadcasts, size of packets, and network statistics. After capturing network traffic, view and analyze the detail of the conversation captured for problem resolution or traffic pattern planning.

Response Probe

Response Probe is a utility for applying controlled stress of a specific resource on a system and observing its response. This is done for the purposes of determining maximum throughput and performance characteristics before analyzing capacity in a production environment.

Note Performance Monitor and Response Probe are documented in Chapter 11, "Performance Monitoring Tools," in the *Windows NT Workstation Resource Kit*.

Using Performance Monitor for Server Analysis

Performance Monitor provides a broad view of computer performance. In some cases, it may fully identify a problem. More often, it is used to indicate which specialized tool, such as a profiler, a working set monitor, or a network analyzer, to use next.

This topic identifies the options that are available in Performance Monitor for analyzing server performance, and the objects and counters that may be selected for gathering specific data.

Performance Monitor Options

The following graphic illustrates some of the server analysis options Performance Monitor provides.

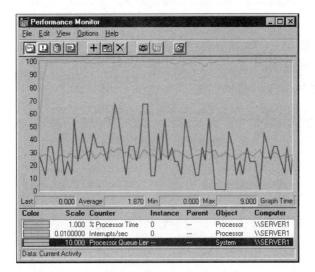

Performance Monitor allows:

- Viewing data from multiple computers simultaneously.

- Seeing how changes that are made affect the computer.

- Changing charts of current activity while viewing them.

- Exporting Performance Monitor data to spreadsheets or database programs, or using it as raw input for Microsoft Visual Basic and C programs.

- Triggering a program or procedure, or sending notices when a threshold is exceeded.

- Logging data about various objects from different computers over time. These log files are used to record typical resource use, monitor a problem, or help in capacity planning.

- Combining selected sections of several log files into a long-term archive.

- Reporting on current activity or trends over time.

- Saving different combinations of counter and option settings for quick starts and changes.

Note Computer initialization startup activities and network traffic can interfere with testing. Wait until the computer settles before testing. Also, disconnect the computer from the network if network activity is not being tested. Network drivers may respond to network events even if they are not directed to the testing computer.

Objects in Performance Monitor

You can measure the behavior of objects in your computer by using Performance Monitor.

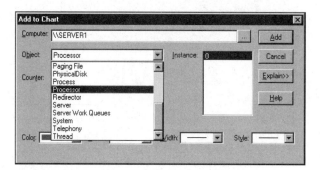

Performance Monitor measures the behavior of computer objects. The objects represent threads and processes, sections of shared memory, and physical devices. Performance Monitor collects data on activity, demand, and space used by the objects. Some objects, known as core objects, always appear in Performance Monitor; others appear only if the service or process is installing.

The table below lists the Windows NT Performance Monitor core objects along with a brief description of each.

Object Name	Description
Cache	An area of physical memory that holds recently used data.
LogicalDisk	Disk partitions and other logical views of disk space.
Memory	RAM used to store code and data.
Objects	Certain system software objects.
Paging File	File used to back up virtual memory allocations.
PhysicalDisk	Hardware disk unit (spindle or RAID device).
Process	Software object that represents a running program.
Processor	Hardware unit that executes program instructions.
Redirector	File system that diverts file requests to network servers.
System	Counters that apply to all system hardware and software.
Thread	The part of a process that uses the processor.

Some objects have multiple instances. Each instance of an object represents a component of the system. For example, a computer can have multiple disk drives. Each disk drive is an instance of the Physical Disk (computer) object.

When the computer being monitored has more than one component of the same object type, Performance Monitor displays multiple instances of the object in the **Instance** box of the **Add to Chart** (or to **View**, **Log**, or **Report**) dialog box. When appropriate, it also displays the _Total instance, which represents a sum of the values for all instances of the object. For example, if a computer has multiple physical disks, there are multiple instances of the PhysicalDisk object in the **Add to Chart** dialog box. The _Total would be an accumulation of all the individual instances.

Some objects are parts of other objects or are dependent upon other objects. The instances of these related objects are shown in the Instances box in the following format:

Parent object = => Child object

where the child object is part of or is dependent upon the parent object. This makes it easier to identify the object.

Performance Monitor was designed to cause minimal impact on the operating system. Be aware, however, that setting high sample rates can have a negative impact on the performance of the computer.

Note Only active instances appear in the Instances box. A process must be started before it is seen in Performance Monitor. If logged data is being charted, only processes that were active when logging began appear in the Instances box.

Counters in Performance Monitor

Performance Monitor counters collect, average, and display data.

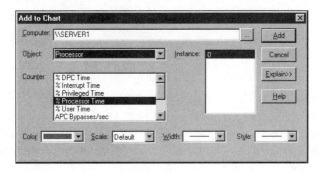

Performance Monitor can collect, average, and display data from internal counters by using the Windows NT registry and the Performance Library DLLs. A counter defines the type of data that is available for a particular type of object.

Performance Monitor collects data on various aspects of hardware and software performance, such as use, demand, and available space. A Performance Monitor counter is activated by adding it to a chart or report or by adding an object to a log.

As previously identified, there are objects for physical components such as Processors, Physical Disks, and Memory and there are other objects, such as Process and Paging files. Each object has a set of counters defined for it. Counters in an object record the activity level of the object. Windows NT Server uses the following typographical convention to name a counter of a particular object:

object: counter

For example, the % Processor Time counter of the Process object would appear as:

Process: % Processor Time

to distinguish it from Processor: % Processor Time or Thread: % Processor Time.

Note When a counter is selected in any view, Performance Monitor collects data for all counters of that object, but displays only the counter selected. This creates minimal overhead, because most overhead in Performance Monitor results from what is displayed on the screen or written to the hard disk.

There are three types of counters:

- Instantaneous counters display the most recent measurement.

  For example, Process: Thread Count displays the number of threads found in the most recent measurement.

- Averaging counters measure a value over time and display the average of the last two measurements. When these counters are started, there is a wait for the second measurement to be taken before any values are displayed.

  For example, Memory: Pages/sec, shows the average number of memory pages found in the last two reads.

- Difference counters subtract the last measurement from the previous one and display the difference if it is positive. If it is negative, they display a zero.

  Performance Monitor does not include any difference counters in its basic set, but they may be included in other applications that use Performance Monitor, and they can also be written. For information about writing performance counters, see the *Win32 Software Development Kit*.

Some hardware and applications designed for Windows NT come with their own counters. Many of these extensible counters are installed automatically with the product, but some are installed separately. In addition, there are a few specialized counters on the Windows NT Resource Kit 4.0 compact disc that can be installed. See the product documentation and Performance Monitor Help for detailed instructions on adding extensible counters.

Tip Click the Explain button in the Add To dialog box to display the definition for each counter. The Explain button works only when current activity is monitored, not logs.

Performance Monitor Views

There are four ways to view data using Performance Monitor: chart, report, alert, and log.

The four views operate independently and concurrently, but only one can be viewed at a time. Each view gets data independently from the target computers, so looking at a counter in all four views requires four times the overhead as looking at the same counter in just one view. Luckily, this overhead is small, so concurrent use of views is not a problem. Use the **View** menu to specify a view in Performance Monitor.

Chart

A chart displays the value of the counter over time. Many counters may be charted at one time.

Report

A report shows the value of the counter. A report of all the counters in Performance Monitor can be created.

Alert

In this view, alerts are set on a counter. This causes an event to be displayed when the counter attains a specified value. Many alerts can be monitored at one time.

Log

In the Log view, the counters are recorded on disk for future analysis. Log files are fed back into Performance Monitor to create charts, reports, or alerts.

Performance Monitor Chart View

The Chart view is especially useful in these instances.

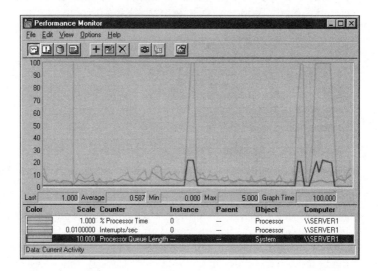

Customized charts that monitor the current performance of selected counters and instances are useful when:

- Investigating why a computer or application is slow or inefficient.

- Continuously monitoring systems to find intermittent performance problems.

- Discovering why capacity needs to be increased.

Different graphs require different settings. Creating charts to reflect these settings requires selecting the computer to be monitored and adding the appropriate objects, counters, and instances. These selections can be saved under a file name for viewing whenever an update on their performance is needed.

To enhance the readability of graphs, vary the scale of the displayed information and the color, width, and style of the line for each counter. You can also modify these properties after a selection is added.

The scale of any displayed value can be changed so that it is displayed in a chart or so that it can be compared with another value. To make very large or small values noticeable, change the vertical maximum on the chart.

In addition, you can use **Chart Options**, to customize charts and to change the method used for updating the chart values.

Note Selecting a counter and then pressing the CTRL+H keys will highlight that counter on the chart.

Performance Monitor Report View

The Report view allows you to display constantly changing counter and instance values for selected objects.

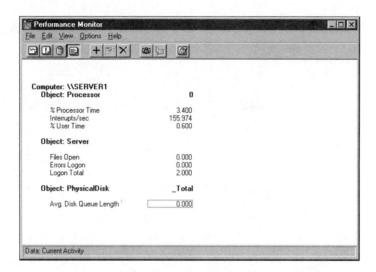

The Report view displays constantly changing counter and instance values for added objects. Values appear in columns for each instance. Report intervals are adjusted, snapshots printed, and data reported or displayed. Reports of averaged counters show the average value during the Time Window interval. Reports of instantaneous counters show the value at the end of the Time Window interval.

Creating reports using current activity can help gain a better understanding of object behavior. The Report view allows:

- Creating a report on all the counters for a given object and then watching them change under various loads.

- Creating reports to reflect the same information that is charting or to monitor other specific situations. These selections can then be saved under a file name and reused when an update on the same information is needed.

After selections are added to a report, the selections, listed by computer and object, appear in the report area, and Performance Monitor displays the changing values of the selections in the report.

Performance Monitor Alert View

The Alert view allows you to continue working while Performance Monitor tracks events and notifies you as requested.

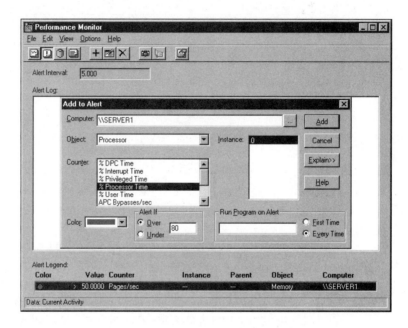

The Alert view allows a person to continue work while Performance Monitor tracks events and notifies the person if requested. Use the Alert view to create an alert log that monitors the current performance of selected counters and instances for objects.

With the alert log, several counters can be measured at the same time. When a counter exceeds a given value, the date and time of the event are recorded in the Alert view. One thousand events are recorded, after which the oldest event is discarded when a new one is added. An event can also generate a network alert. When an event occurs, a specified program can be run every time or just the first time that it occurs.

Alert logs can be created to warn of problems in different situations. These selections can be saved under a file name and reused to see if the problem has been fixed.

An alert condition applies to the value of the counter over the time interval specified. The default time interval is 5 seconds. If an alert is set on Memory: Pages/sec > 50 using the default time interval, the average paging rate for a 5-second period has to exceed 50 per second before the alert is triggered.

Note Alerts cannot be set on two conditions of the same counter for the same instance. For example, an alert cannot be set to be triggered when Processor: %Processor Time on a single processor exceeds 90% and another to be triggered when it falls below 30%. Also, an alert cannot be set on more than one instance of an object with the same name. For example, if two processes are running with the same name, an alert can only be set for the first instance of the process. Both instances will appear in the Instances box, but only data collected from the first instance will trigger the alert.

Performance Monitor Log View

Logging allows you to record information on current activity for later viewing.

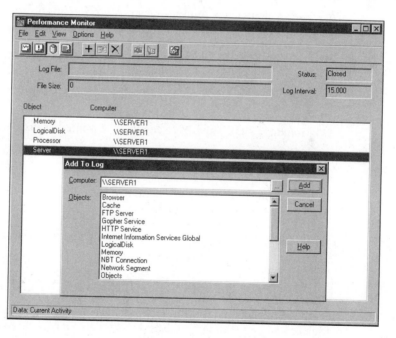

Data can also be collected from multiple systems into a single log file. Log files contain detailed data for detecting performance problems or other detailed analysis. For server analysis and forecasting future resources allocation, it allows the viewing of trends over a long period, and appending or relogging files. Log file data is charted, reported, or exported to compare files or examine patterns.

Log view has a display area for listing objects and their corresponding computers. All counters and instances are logged for a selected object.

When logging is started, a log symbol with the changing total file size appears on the right side of the status bar.

Log files become more usable when bookmarks are added at various points while logging. With bookmarks, major points of interest can be highlighted, or the circumstances under which the file was created can be described. These locations are easily returned to when working with the log file. The **Bookmark** option becomes available when logging is started.

Note Opening a log that is collecting data will stop the log and clear all counter settings. Performance Monitor does not allow peeking at the log from Chart or Report view because the views share the same data source. To peek at a running log, start a second copy of Performance Monitor, and set Data From to the running log.

No matter which view you use—Chart, Alert, Report, or Log—standard built-in features make Performance Monitor more flexible. Performance Monitor allows:

- Using the Update Interval to determine how often performance is measured. There is a tradeoff between the precision of the data and Performance Monitor overhead.

- Using the PRINT SCREEN key to save a bitmap image of the Performance Monitor screen. The image can then be printed or inserted into a document.

- Clearing the Performance Monitor window, deleting a counter, or deleting the full screen.

- Exporting the data in a tab-delimited (.tsv) or comma-delimited (.csv) text file to a spreadsheet or database program.

For specific instructions on these topics, use Performance Monitor Help.

Techniques for Server Analysis and Optimization

Incorporating techniques with server analysis and optimization tools can improve efficiency while yielding more valid and reliable data. The following are some analysis and optimization techniques.

Monitoring Multiple Servers

Monitoring multiple servers is a common need for keeping records of performance on computer networks. One of the common themes of Microsoft network administration tools is the ability to administer multiple network systems from a centralized location.

The best technique is to log the performance data of the server. If Performance Monitoring Service is not being used, log from multiple servers into a single log file.

Typically, detection of decreased performance is performed on all servers on a routine basis. Take the information gathered for bottleneck detection and use it later for server optimization. Log at least all four of the major server resources. To determine the cost of logging the data from multiple servers, log the Network Segment object from one server on each segment.

➤ **To determine the cost of logging multiple server data**

1. Switch Performance Monitor to Log view, configure the objects, and set logging to manual update mode.

2. Click the **Update Counter Data** button a few times. Note the file size.

3. Click the button again and note the new size.

The difference is the cost of logging this data on that system. On a typical system, this is under 7 KB.

When monitoring an application server, collect some additional objects such as processes or even threads. The application itself might provide some extended object counters for Performance Monitor. If so, look at these too.

Another way to watch many systems is to use the Alert view. Alert messages can be sent anywhere on the network just by adding a special name to the system used. At the least, set an alert on the % Free Space on the file server logical drives.

The following are two common recommendations that will improve the performance or analysis of servers:

- Use a Windows NT Server (non-domain controller) or Windows NT Workstation to perform domain administration rather than a domain controller. The member server does not have all the overhead associated with that of a domain controller, and accomplishes the administrative task more quickly than the domain controller can.

- Use Performance Monitor on a Windows NT Server (non-domain controller) or Windows NT Workstation to monitor servers. Note that if Performance Monitor is running on the server that is to be analyzed, then the processor, disk, and memory in that server are affected by the local Performance Monitor. If monitoring is performed over the network, only the network subsystem is affected.

Note Twenty-five is the maximum number of servers that can be concurrently monitored.

Archiving and Storing Performance Data

After data has been gathered, it is important to store that data for future analysis, such as identifying resource trends, or assisting in resolving a problem at a later time.

Trend Analysis

This is accomplished by viewing data over time. The purpose is to identify normal use of the system, and areas of use that are unusual. The data may indicate a system bottleneck, or a need to increase or expand the resource.

Monitoring Desktop Computers

Use Systems Management Server (SMS) to monitor desktop computers. SMS can generate hardware and software inventory of the computers that can be used to determine if the computer is functioning properly. SMS also includes options to remotely control and diagnose client computers. These features give the network administrator greater control and analysis of the network components from a single location.

A Windows NT Approach to Server Analysis and Optimization

The following graphic describes the plan you should use when performing server analysis and optimization. Before starting server analysis and optimization, have a strategy, or procedure to ensure all goals are accomplished.

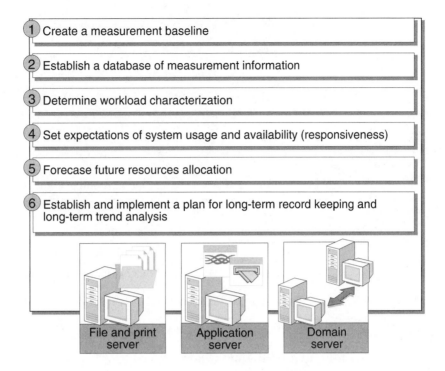

1. Create a measurement baseline

2. Establish a database of measurement information

3. Determine workload characterization

4. Set expectations of system usage and availability (responsiveness)

5. Forecase future resources allocation

6. Establish and implement a plan for long-term record keeping and long-term trend analysis

File and print server   Application server   Domain server

Implementing Server Analysis and Optimization Basics

In this exercise you will answer some question about NT 4.0 Server analysis and optimization.

1. You have just installed a Windows NT Server-based computer, and need to determine its expected usage in different user environments. How can server analysis and optimization assist with this task?

2. You decide that server analysis and optimization will help with your efforts to analyze a computer running Windows NT Server. What steps are you going to perform to accomplish your analysis?

3. What are the four major server resources you should analyze?

_____

_____

4. In your efforts to analyze the computer running Windows NT Server, what Windows NT tools can you use to assist with server analysis and optimization?

_____

_____

5. In your efforts to analyze the computer running Windows NT Server, what techniques can you use when you perform server analysis and optimization?

_____

_____

6. What are the three server environments that you can analyze?

_____

_____

Creating a Real-Time Chart

In this exercise, you will set up a real-time chart and generate activity.

➤ **To enable disk counters**

1. Log on as Administrator, and in the **Password** box, type **password**

2. Click **Start**, point to **Programs**, and then click **Command Prompt**.

3. At the command prompt, type **diskperf -y** and then press ENTER.

4. This step is necessary to enable monitoring of disk counters.

5. Shut down and restart your computer.

➤ **To set up the chart**

1. Log on as Administrator, and in the **Password** box, type **password**

2. Click **Start**, point to **Programs**, point to **Administrative Tools (Common)**, and then click **Performance Monitor**.

3. On the **View** menu, click **Chart**.

4. On the **Edit** menu, click **Add To Chart**.

5. The **Add to Chart** dialog box appears.

6. Using the information provided in the following table, click the following counters that become available for the **Memory**, **Physical Disk**, and **Processor** Objects. Click **Add** after each counter that you add.

Object	Counter	Instance	Description
Memory	Cache bytes	Not applicable	Memory allocated as file cache
Memory	Pages/Sec	Not applicable	Number of pages read from or written to disk to resolve memory references to pages that were not in memory at the time of reference
Physical Disk	%Disk Time	0	Percentage of time physical disk is busy
Physical Disk	Avg. Disk Bytes/Read	0	Average number of bytes transferred from disk
Physical Disk	Avg. Disk Bytes/Write	0	Average number of bytes transferred to disk
Processor	%Privileged Time	0	Percentage of processor time spent in Privilege Mode
Processor	%Processor Time	0	Percentage of time processor
Processor	%User Time	0	Percentage of processor time spent in User Mode

7. Click **Done**.

8. The graph appears, displaying the real-time activities of the memory, physical disk and processor objects.

➤ **To generate chart activity**

1. With Performance Monitor still running, click **Start**, point to **Programs**, point to **Accessories**, and then click **Calculator**.

2. Begin doing calculations.

3. This will generate CPU cycles.

4. Close the Calculator.

5. Return to the Performance Monitor Chart.

6. Select the **%Processor Time** counter. Notice the **%Processor Time** average.

Note To highlight a specific counter on the chart, select a counter, and then press CTRL+H.

---

7. Minimize the Chart window.

8. Load and minimize both Windows NT Explorer and the Disk Administrator.

9. Return to the Performance Monitor Chart.

10. Notice the activity, such as spikes, on the chart.

11. Close Windows NT Explorer and Disk Administrator.

Logging Processor Activity

In this exercise, you will log information and then display the information in a chart.

➤ **To log information**

1. On the **View** menu in Performance Monitor, click **Log**.

2. On the **Edit** menu, click **Add To Log**.

   The **Add To Log** dialog box appears.

3. In the **Objects** dialog box, hold down the CTRL key while you click **Memory**, **Physical Disk**, and **Processor**, and then click **Add**.

4. Click **Done**.

5. On the **Options** menu, click **Log**.

   The **Log Options** dialog box appears.

6. In the **File Name** box type **lab1.log**

7. Under **Update Time**, click **Periodic Update**.

8. In the **Interval** box, click **1**, and then click **Start Log**.

   The Performance Monitor window appears, showing information on the log you are creating. Remember that when a log starts, all the counters for the selected object automatically begin recording data.

9. Create processor activity by starting applications or moving the mouse.

10. Collect at least 1 megabyte (MB) of data. Check the **File Size** box in the Performance Monitor window to determine when your file reaches 1 MB.

11. On the **Options** menu, click **Log**.

    The **Log Options** dialog box appears.

12. Click **Stop Log**.

➤ **To display logged information**

1. On the **View** menu, click **Chart**.

2. On the **Options** menu, click **Data From**.

    The **Data From** dialog box appears.

3. In the **Data From** dialog box, click the button with the ellipsis (...) on it.

    The **Open Input Log File** dialog box appears.

4. Click the **Lab1.log**, and then click **Open**.

    The **Data From** dialog box appears, indicating data values will be displayed from your log file.

5. Click **OK**.

6. On the **Edit** menu, click **Add To Chart**.

7. Using the information provided in the following table, click the following counters that become available for the **Memory**, **Physical Disk**, and **Processor** Objects. Click **Add** after each counter that you add.

Object	Counter	Instance
Memory	Available bytes	Not applicable
Memory	Pages/Sec	Not applicable
Physical Disk	%Disk Time	0
Physical Disk	Avg. Disk Bytes/Read	0
Physical Disk	Avg. Disk Bytes/Write	0
Processor	%Privileged Time	0
Processor	%Processor Time	0
Processor	%User Time	0

8. Click **Done**.

    The chart displays the information collected in your log.

Working with the Data

In this exercise, you will alter how much of the data you view, and you will generate a report from collected data.

➤ **To determine how much data is displayed**

1. Refer to the **Average field** on your chart. What is the average **%Processor Time**?

   In the following steps you will use just a portion of the chart. You will choose a small portion that has large spikes in the chart.

2. On the **Edit** menu, click **Time Window**.

   The **Input Log File Timeframe** dialog box appears. (You can click the menu bar and move the dialog box to the bottom of the screen for better viewing of the chart.)

3. Adjust the sliding window to see only part of the graph that has large spikes for any of the counters, and then click **OK**.

4. What is the **Average %Processor Time** for this part of the graph?

5. How accurate do you think this representation of the processor's use is?

6. Adjust the time window to see the entire graph.

➤ **To create a report**

1. On the **View** menu, click **Report**.

2. On the **Edit** menu, click **Add to Report**.

   The **Add to Report** dialog box appears.

3. Using the information provided in the following table, click the following counters that become available for the **Memory**, **Physical Disk**, and **Processor** Objects. Click **Add** after each counter that you add.

Object	Counter	Instance
Memory	Available bytes	Not applicable
Memory	Pages/Sec	Not applicable
Physical Disk	%Disk Time	0
Physical Disk	Avg. Disk Bytes/Read	0

(continued)

Object	Counter	Instance
Physical Disk	Avg. Disk Bytes/Write	0
Processor	%Privileged Time	0
Processor	%Processor Time	0
Processor	%User Time	0

4. Click **Done**.

The report displays the information collected in your log.

Generating Alerts

In this exercise you will generate alerts from the collected data.

➤ **To generate an alert**

1. On the **View** menu, click **Alert**.

2. On the **Edit** menu, click **Add to Alert**.

   The **Add to Alert** dialog box appears.

3. In the **Object** list, click **Memory**, and in the **Counter** box, click **% Committed Bytes in Use**.

4. In the **Alert If** box, click **Over** and type **50** in the box, and then click **Add**.

5. In the **Object** list, click **Physical Disk**, and in the **Counter** box, select **% Disk Time**.

6. In the **Alert If** box, click **Over** and type **20** in the box, and then click **Add**.

7. In the **Object** list, select **Processor**, and in the **Counter** box, select **% Processor Time**.

8. In the **Alert If** box, click **Over** and type **20** in the box, and then click **Add**.

9. Click **Done**.

   If no alerts appear in the Alert Log. Double-click the three counters at the bottom of the window and lower the value until alerts appear in the list.

10. Exit Performance Monitor.

Lesson Summary

The following information summarizes the key points in this lesson:

- Server analysis and optimization involves creating a baseline of current use, monitoring use over time, and analyzing data to find and resolve abnormalities in the system use.

- Server analysis and optimization also includes determining expected response times for specific numbers of users and system use, determining how the system should be used, and determining when to upgrade the system or when to add additional system resources.

- Resources to monitor on a Windows NT server include memory, processor, disk, and network utilization.

- Performance Monitor and Network Monitor utilities are used to monitor server resources.

Lesson 2: Implementing a Measurement Baseline

This lesson emphasizes the importance of implementing a measurement baseline of information for use in analyzing performance data. Because a baseline must be established prior to analyzing system performance, this lesson focuses on creating a measurement baseline and establishing a database of measurement information, the first two steps of server analysis and optimization. The lesson also identifies a process of collecting and using system data, and introduces tools that can be used to create a database. Performance Monitor is used in this lesson to collect data and create a measurement baseline.

After this lesson, you will be able to:

- Define a measurement baseline and the resources to be measured.
- Use Performance Monitor to create a measurement baseline.
- Establish a database of measurement information.

Estimated lesson time: 30 minutes

Collecting System Data

To determine if a resource is being overused, under used, or is at maximum capacity and performance, first identify what is normal for the environment. Every environment is unique, with different factors affecting how resources are used or consumed. Collecting and saving data from normal access periods helps to determine if the demands on a resource in the future are at expected (normal) levels, below normal expectations, or far above the normal level. To do this, routinely perform the same steps to collect the same data again, comparing it against the baseline data. This continual collection of data is used then to create the database of measurement activity.

Once the current use of a resource is determined, it is possible to use that data to choose a possible course of action. These actions may include:

- Making no adjustments, as the current resource activity is as expected.
- Reallocating users, applications, or services to a less heavily-used server.
- Increasing the ability of users to access the resource, either by adding resource units (for example, hard disk drives or memory), or by adding network servers for access.
- Making a change to the physical structure of the network, with the intent of increasing response time to the user.

Automating System Data Collection

Automatic collection of server analysis data is essential to control the amount of data collected and to facilitate its analysis. When collecting initial and subsequent data, start by determining whether to centralize the monitoring of computers.

Centralized monitoring permits the data from multiple computers to be stored in a single log file, but increases network traffic during production hours. Decentralized monitoring creates more disk traffic on each monitored computer. Decentralization allows the transfer of data generating network traffic to be scheduled to off-hours. Generally, centralized monitoring is useful for relatively a small numbers of servers (25 or fewer).

To reduce the volume of data, collect server analysis and optimization data only during periods of peak activity. Most businesses have a period of peak activity during mid-morning and again during mid-afternoon. Use the Windows NT **at** command to start the Performance Monitor service before each period of expected peak activity, and to stop data collection when activity is expected to slow down. The Schedule service must be started for the **at** command to function. As shown in the following example, the **at** command can operate remotely:

```
at \\computername 9:30 /date:M,T,W,Th,F "monitor START"
at \\computername 11:00 /date:M,T,W,Th,F "monitor STOP"
```

Using the **at** command will start and stop the service. However, to specify the objects to monitor, you will first need to create a .pmw file specifying the objects and interval for logging by the Performance Monitor service.

Creating a Measurement Baseline

Creating a measurement baseline begins by determining the resources you want to measure and locating and using the best tool to get that measurement. The first step involves creating a measurement baseline.

A measurement baseline is a collection of data that indicates how individual system resources, a collection of system resources, or the system as a whole, is being used. This information is compared with later activity to help determine system usage and system response to that usage.

As a rule, monitor all four of the major server resources no matter which Windows NT Server environment (file and print server, application server, and domain server) is the focus. Although the implications in each server environment are different, include memory, processor, disk, and network objects in the baseline regardless of the environment.

Some measurement tools are capable of analyzing the captured data and storing it in the format of the native tool. If a tool cannot provide or is not providing what is needed for analysis, export the data to another application. This new application could be a database application, such as Access or SQL Server, or a spreadsheet application such as Excel.

Once the particular set of data is originally captured, regularly capture it and place it in the database. This provides the ability to analyze trends over time.

Listed below are general Performance Monitor objects that may be used to monitor the four server analysis and optimization resources.

Resources	Objects To Include
Memory	Memory (include Cache in the Application Server environment)
Processor	Processor, System, Server Work Queues
Disk subsystem	PhysicalDisk, LogicalDisk
Network subsystem	Server, Network Segment, Network Interface
Optional objects	Application-specific objects, such as SQL Server, WINS Server, Browser, and RAS

Using Performance Monitor to Create a Measurement Baseline

Performance Monitor is a tool that is included with Windows NT. It is designed to be used as a system data collection and analysis tool.

As previously discussed, Performance Monitor performs data collection and analysis. It can assist with server analysis and optimization in the following two ways:

- Creating a measurement baseline.
- Isolating and gathering data to be placed into a database.

Performance Monitor uses objects and counters to associate statistical information with monitored components. The important features of Performance Monitor for server analysis and optimization are logging, re-logging, and appending log files.

Prior to logging, first select a set of objects to log. For server analysis, it is generally recommended to log the following:

- System.
- Processor.
- Memory.

- Logical disk.
- Physical disk (if using RAID).
- Server.
- Cache.
- Network adapter.
- Network segment activity on at least one server in the segment.

If you are monitoring RAID disks, be sure to start **diskperf** with the **-ye** option.

When relogging, increase the Log Option and update Time Interval to reduce the amount of data saved. If the original log file is recorded at 60 seconds, and the new file is recorded at 600 second intervals (which is fine for most server analysis uses), the new file will be about one-tenth the size of the original log file. To increase the Log Option and update Time Interval, on the **Options** menu, click **Data From**.

Consider appending log files to a master log file to create a single log archive. When relogging, use the name of the archive log file. The new data will be appended at the end. The format of an archive log file is identical to a normal log file. Bookmarks are automatically inserted to mark the start of each appended log to ease browsing of the archive log file.

Take measurements over a week or more to get a complete measurement baseline. As previously mentioned, concentrate on the periods of peak activity—the baseline will indicate these periods.

Using Performance Monitor for Automating Data Collection

The Performance Monitor Service utilities provided in the Windows NT Resource Kit can be used to automate monitoring. It creates log files in the same format that Performance Monitor does. To do this, use Performance Monitor to specify the data to be collected. Set the update **Time Interval** option to the desired frequency for data collection. Name the log file and save the settings in a Performance Monitor Workspace settings file. Configure the Performance Monitor Service to start automatically when the systems boots.

Note Performance Monitor log files can be quite large in size. Make sure adequate disk resources are available for storage of the log file or files. Identify the data that will help in server optimization. Spend time analyzing this data. This can help prevent overloading the system, or prevent you from being overwhelmed by the amount of data. Be sure to create this database on a computer that is not being monitored. If the database is on the same computer, it affects the data being measured.

Establishing a Database of Measurement Information

The purpose behind establishing a database of measurement information is to analyze past performance and measure trends over time.

After determining the resources you want to measure, the second step is to establish a database of measurement information. This step involves collecting information over a period of time and adding that information to a database for the purposes of analyzing past performance and measuring trends over time.

Information in a database is measurable, manageable, and accessible for analysis. Database utilities greatly complement the data collection utilities. Data collection utilities gather large amounts of information; use the database utilities to organize the information into manageable and meaningful subsets. Once data has been collected from all four major resources and added to the database, use the database utility to analyze and pinpoint specific areas of interest or concern, such as the disk subsystem.

Creating a Database Using Different Applications

To create a database of measurement information for a Windows NT Server system, numerous applications may be used, such as:

- Performance Monitor.
- Excel.
- SQL Server.
- Access.
- Microsoft FoxPro.

As mentioned earlier, Performance Monitor is an integrated tool for collecting measurement data for a Windows NT system. The data is collected and saved in log files. These log files, representing data that is collected over time, are displayed as charts or reports within Performance Monitor, or can be exported to other applications.

Excel can be used to import the data from Performance Monitor log files. The data can then be manipulated and analyzed to identify trends and system bottlenecks. You can use the Excel macro language or Visual Basic to automate the data analysis process.

Microsoft database applications, such as Access, FoxPro and SQL Server can be used to import and store large amounts of management data for further analysis using complex searches and queries. Once the data from Performance Monitor is imported into a database application, numerous methods of analysis are available.

Although the actual applications and methods that are used vary, what is crucial is that data is collected over time, and is saved for later analysis.

Implementing a Measurement Baseline

In this exercise you will answer some questions about creating a measurement baseline.

1. Why is it important to collect system data?

    _____

    _____

2. You want to perform server analysis and optimization on a pilot computer running Windows NT Server, and need to create a baseline using Windows NT tools. How would you accomplish this?

    _____

    _____

3. You want to ensure that when you create the baseline you include all the data necessary to perform a proper server analysis, but you don't want to capture too much data. What are the common objects for Performance Monitor that should be included in a baseline?

    _____

    _____

4. You have collected baseline data, and found it to be too much data to store. You realize the necessity of keeping data for analysis, but can't afford the hard disk space that the baseline data requires. How can you keep the data available on the server, but reduce the required disk space requirements?

    _____

    _____

5. When analyzing the baseline data, you notice that all your disk counters are 0. Does that mean that the disk drive is not being used at all?

    _____

    _____

6. During the following week you want to capture data to create your database of measurement information. However, you will be out of the office during this time. No one else in the office is trained to do this task. How can you have the data collected and stored while you are gone?

_____

_____

Creating Performance Monitor Log Files

In this exercise, you will use Windows NT Performance Monitor to create a log file for your computer.

➤ **To create the log file**

1. Log on as Administrator, and in the **Password** box, type **password**

2. Start Performance Monitor, and on the **View** menu, click **Log**.

3. On the **Edit** menu, click **Add to Log**.

4. In the **Objects** box, select all of the listed items by holding down the SHIFT key while you click the mouse; click **Add**, and then click **Done**.

5. On the **Options** menu, click **Log**.

   The **Log Options** dialog box appears.

6. In the **File Name** box, type **lab2.log** in the **Interval (seconds)** list, click **1**, and then click **Start Log**.

   The log file will begin logging statistics, and the file size will grow.

7. When the log has run for two minutes, on the **Options** menu, click **Log**, and then click **Stop Log**.

   You have just created a measurement baseline. Your computer was in a fairly static, low usage state. We will use this baseline to compare the computer under varying loads.

In the following procedure, you will use Performance Monitor to load the log file to use for data analysis.

➤ **To open the data file**

1. On the **Options** menu in Performance Monitor, click **Data From**.

    The **Data From** dialog box appears, prompting for the source of data to display within Performance Monitor.

2. Click **Log File**, and then click the button with the ellipsis (...) on it.

    The **Open Input Log File** dialog box appears.

3. Click **Lab2**, and then click **Open**.

    The **Data From** dialog box appears, displaying C:\ Lab2.log as the source of data to display within Performance Monitor.

4. Click **OK** to return to Performance Monitor.

    Notice that Data: C:\Lab2.log appears on the status bar of the Performance Monitor window.

Viewing and Relogging the Data

In this exercise, you will take the existing log file and create five log files from it. These log files will serve as your database.

In the following procedure, you will view all the objects that have been captured in the initial log file.

➤ **To view logged data**

1. On the **View** menu, click **Chart**.

2. On the **Edit** menu, click **Add To Chart**.

    The **Add To Chart** dialog box appears.

3. Click the arrow next to the **Object** list to view the objects contained in the log file.

    This includes more data than necessary for analysis of the four major check-points. This extra data requires more disk space than necessary.

4. When you're done viewing the items in the **Object** list, click **Cancel** to close it.

5. To close the **Add to Chart** dialog box, click **Cancel**.

    A blank Performance Monitor chart appears.

In the following procedure, you will create a new log file that contains only data relevant to the four major checkpoints. This will serve as our measurement base.

➤ **To create a new log file**

1. On the **View** menu, click **Log**.

   An empty Performance Monitor log appears. Notice that the status bar still displays C:\ Lab2.log as the source of data.

2. On the **Edit** menu, click **Add To Log**.

   The **Add To Log** dialog box appears.

3. In the **Objects** box, click each of the following objects, and then click **Add** to add them to the log:

   - IP.

   - Memory.

   - Network segment.

   - PhysicalDisk.

   - Process.

   - Processor.

   - Server.

   - System.

   - TCP.

   - UDP.

4. Click **Done**.

   Notice that the appropriate objects have been added to the log.

5. On the **Options** menu, click **Log**.

   The **Log Options** dialog box appears.

6. Complete the **Log Options** dialog box using the following information

In This Box	Type or Select This Option
File Name	Baseline.log
Interval (seconds)	1

7. Click **Relog File** to create a new log file with the data of interest.

   The Performance Monitor log window appears. Notice that the value in the **File Size** box is considerably smaller than the original file, and that the window contains just the data of interest.

In the following procedure, you will create four new log files that contain data specific to each of the four major checkpoints. These will serve as our database of measurement information.

➤ **To create additional log files**

1. On the **File** menu, click **New Log Settings**.

   This will clear the existing objects from the log settings.

2. On the **View** menu, click **Log**.

3. On the **Edit** menu, click **Add to Log**.

4. In the **Objects** box, click **Memory**, and then click **Add**.

5. On the **Options** menu, click **Log**.

6. Complete the **Log Options** dialog box using the following information.

In This Box	Type or Select This Option
File Name	Memory.log
Interval (seconds)	1

7. Click **Relog File** to create a new log file with the data of interest.

8. Create three additional log files using the following information. Make sure to set the **Periodic Update Interval** to 1.

Object or Objects	File Name
Processor, system	Processor.log
PhysicalDisk	Disk.log
IP, Network segment, TCP, UDP, Server	Network.log

9. To exit Performance Monitor, on the **File** menu, click **Exit**.

Lesson Summary

This following information summarizes the key points in this lesson:

- Automatic collection of server analysis data is essential to control the amount of data collected and to facilitate its analysis.

- To reduce the volume of data, collect server analysis and optimization data only during periods of peak activity.

- Performance Monitor is an effective tool in establishing a measurement baseline.

Lesson 3: Performance Analysis, Forecasting, and Record Keeping

Once the measurement baseline has been implemented, system performance analysis and future resources allocation forecasting can begin. This lesson looks at the different Windows NT Server environments on which to determine workload performance, set expectations of system usage and availability, forecast future resources allocation, and establish and implement a plan for long-term record keeping.

After this lesson, you will be able to:

- Define performance analysis.
- Identify the various server environments.
- Determine workload characterization.
- Set expectations of system usage and availability.
- Forecast future resources allocation.
- Establish a plan for long-term record keeping.

Estimated lesson time: 25 minutes

Performance Analysis

Performance analysis focuses on determining workload characterization, setting expectations of system use and availability (responsiveness), forecasting future resource allocation, and establishing and implementing a long-term record keeping and long-term trend analysis.

Performance Analysis accomplishes many tasks such as:

- Determining what is normal for the system, and how to deal with abnormalities.
- Setting expectations of how the system or resource should respond, given a specific set of conditions.
- Helping plan for system or resource upgrades and additions.
- Facilitating better input into system budgeting requirements.

By properly analyzing and optimizing Windows NT Server, the overall system will perform in a satisfactory manner, and users are likely to be satisfied with server performance.

Windows NT Server Environments

Before analysis and optimization on a Windows NT Server can begin, determine the type of environment being analyzed. Windows NT Server environments generally fit into one of three categories: file and print server, application server, and domain server. Each of these involves different monitoring considerations and considerations on how to set expectations when performing server analysis and optimization. Chapter 2, lesson 2 defines the server roles in greater detail.

File and Print Server

A file and print server is usually accessed by users for data retrieval and document storage, and occasionally for loading application software over the network.

Application Server

An application server is accessed by users in a client/server environment. The server runs an applications engine that users access using a front-end application.

Domain Server

A domain server is a server that generates data transfer between itself and other servers. A primary domain controller (PDC), for example, synchronizes the accounts database with backup domain controllers (BDCs), or a Windows Internet Naming Service (WINS) Server replicates its database with its replication partner. Domain servers also validate user logon requests.

Determining Workload Characterization

Before expectations can be set for a system, it is necessary to know what is being requested of the system. This process is called workload characterization. A workload unit is a list of service requests made on the system, or made on a specific resource on the system. Examples of workload units are the number of disk access attempts per second, the number of bytes transferred per second, or the process of receiving data from a server (the client sending a request over the network to the server, the server responding over the network to the client).

Determining workload characterization requires understanding what is happening in a specific environment. In a file and print server environment, the area of most concern is disk I/O or the number of users accessing a server, whereas in an application server, the area of most concern is how much memory an application is using. That is not to say that memory usage is not important on a file and print server; rather, concentrate on the device that has the best chance of becoming a system bottleneck.

In a Windows NT Server environment, the two most common workload characteristics are the number of users the system can support, and the expected response time for a specific transaction or task (such as copying a file from the server) given a certain number of users on a specific set of hardware.

Determine what is important to each system by the type of work being performed. This is essential to proper server analysis and optimization.

System Bottlenecks

The data collected for a system sometimes indicates that a problem exists, as indicated in the graphic below.

- Restrict work flow

- Over consumption of a specific resource

- One resolved bottleneck may cause another

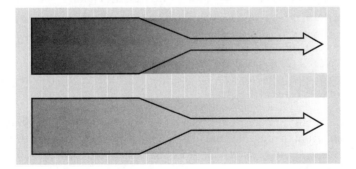

During the process of determining workload characterization, it is possible to encounter a resource that is not performing properly. The response to file access requests, for example, may be much too long for the number of users accessing the server. In this case, a symptom of a bottleneck has been detected.

A bottleneck is the part of the system that is currently restricting work flow. Generally, it is the over-consumption of a specific resource. It may be that the disk controller or drive is extremely slow accessing data, or that the processor is running at 100 percent utilization, or that too many active processes need access to random access memory (RAM). Whatever is causing system responsiveness to suffer is the bottleneck.

It is very common that once one bottleneck has been identified and solved, another bottleneck appears. This new bottleneck was either unnoticed because of the severity of the previous bottleneck, or the new bottleneck was caused by solving the initial bottleneck. If the new bottleneck was caused by solving the initial bottleneck, the new bottleneck may have created more demand on another resource, causing it to become the restriction to work flow. Bottleneck detection is the process of isolating the hardware components that restrict the flow of your work.

System bottlenecks generally appear within the four major server analysis and optimization resources: memory, processor, the disk subsystem, and the network subsystem. Within a Windows NT environment, use Performance Monitor to monitor current activity to determine if any system bottlenecks are present.

Note After successfully identifying and resolving system bottlenecks, be sure to repeat steps one and two of the "Windows NT Server Approach to Server Analysis and Optimization." Do this before analyzing for capacity performance and expected system use.

Using Performance Monitor to Chart Bottlenecks

Performance Monitor collects data about objects (system resources) and counters (attributes, or statistical information that is gathered on an object). This information helps to isolate and identify bottlenecks.

Recall that when adding objects to a log, all counters for the selected objects are collected automatically.

To identify statistical information for each of the individual attributes, use the data from the log file, and view it in a chart or report format. Viewing the information this way allows the selection of individual counters for each of the captured objects.

Finding Memory Bottlenecks

The best thing you can do to improve server performance is to add more memory.
The following graphic illustrates how Performance Monitor is used to find
memory bottlenecks.

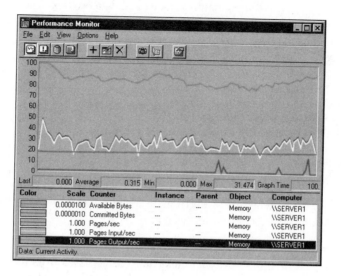

The most common resource bottleneck within Windows NT Server is memory—
specifically RAM. Typically, if only one thing is done to improve performance in
a server, it should be the addition of memory.

Paged and Non-Paged RAM

RAM in Windows NT is divided into two categories: paged and non-paged.
Paged RAM is virtual memory, where all applications believe they have a full
range of memory addresses available. Windows NT does this by giving each application a private memory range called a virtual memory space and by mapping
that virtual memory to physical memory.

Non-paged RAM cannot use this configuration. Data placed into non-paged RAM
must remain in memory and cannot be written to, or retrieved from disk. For
example, data structures used by interrupt routines or those that prevent multiprocessor conflicts within the operating system use non-paged RAM.

Virtual Memory System

The virtual memory system in Windows NT 4.0 combines physical memory, the file system cache, and disk space into an information storage and retrieval system. The system stores program code and data on disk until it is needed, and then moves it into physical memory. Code and data no longer in active use is written back to disk. However, when a computer does not have enough memory, code and data must be written to and retrieved from the disk more frequently—a slow, resource-intensive process that can become a system bottleneck.

Hard Page Faults

The best indicator of a memory bottleneck is a sustained, high rate of hard page faults. Hard page faults occur when the data a program needs is not found in its working set (the physical memory visible to the program) or elsewhere in physical memory, and must be retrieved from disk. Sustained hard page fault rates—over five per second—are a clear indicator of a memory bottleneck.

Use the following list of Performance Monitor memory counters to determine if RAM is a bottleneck in the system:

- Pages/sec: this is the number of requested pages that were not immediately available in RAM, and thus had to be accessed from the disk, or had to be written to the disk to make room in RAM for other pages. Generally, if this value has extended periods with the number of pages per second over five, memory may be a bottleneck in the system.

- Available Bytes: This indicates the amount of available physical memory. It will normally be low, as the Windows NT Disk Cache Manager uses extra memory for caching, and then returns it when requests for memory occur. However, if this value is consistently below 4 MB on a server, it is an indication that excessive paging is occurring.

- Committed Bytes: this indicates the amount of virtual memory that has been committed to either physical RAM for storage, or to pagefile space. If the amount of committed bytes is larger than the amount of physical memory, it may indicate that more RAM is required.

- Pool Nonpaged Bytes: this indicates the amount of RAM in the Non-paged pool system memory area where space is acquired by operating system components as they accomplish their tasks. If the Pool Nonpaged Bytes value has a steady increase without a corresponding increase in activity on the server, it may indicate that a process that is running has a memory leak, and it should be monitored closely.

Counter	Acceptable Average Range	Desire High or Low Value	Action
Pages/sec	0–20	Low	Find process that is causing paging. Add RAM.
Available Bytes	Minimum of 4 MB	High	Find process using RAM. Add RAM.
Committed Bytes	Less than physical RAM	Low	Find process using RAM. Add RAM.
Pool Non-paged Bytes	Remain steady, no increase	Not applicable applicable	Check for memory leak in application.

Finding Processor Bottlenecks

The following graphic is an example of how Performance Monitor can be used to find processor bottlenecks.

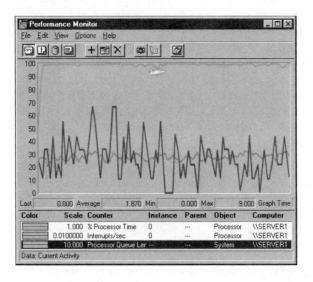

Just about everything that occurs on a server involves the central processing unit (CPU). The processor on an application server is generally busier than the processor on a file and print server. As a result, the processor activity, and what is considered normal, are different between the two types of servers.

Two of the most common causes of CPU bottlenecks are CPU-bound applications and drivers, and excessive interrupts that are generated by inadequate disk or network subsystem components.

Monitor the following Performance Monitor processor counters to help determine if the processor is a bottleneck:

- % Processor Time: this measures the amount of time the processor is busy. When a processor is consistently running over 75 percent processor usage, the processor has become a system bottleneck. Analyze processor usage to determine what is causing the processor activity. This is accomplished by monitoring individual processes. If the system has multiple processors, then monitor the counter "System: % Total Processor Time."

- % Privileged Time: this measures the time the processor spends performing operating system services.

- % User Time: this measures the time the processor spends performing user services, such as running a word processor.

- Interrupts/sec: this is the number of interrupts the processor is servicing from applications or from hardware devices. Windows NT Server can handle thousands of interrupts per second. However, if the number of interrupts consistently exceeds 1,000 on a 80486/66-based system, or 3,500 on a Pentium 90 PCI bus system, a hardware error or interrupt conflict with devices may be occurring. For example, if a conflict occurs between a hard disk controller and a network adapter card, monitor the disk controller and network adapter card to see if excessive requests are being generated. This is done by monitoring the queue lengths for the physical disk and network interface. Generally, if the queue length is greater than two requests, check for slow disk drives or network adapters that could be causing the queue length backlog.

- System: Processor Queue Length: this is the number of requests the processor has in its queue. It indicates the number of threads that are ready to be executed, and are waiting for processor time. Generally, a processor queue length that is consistently higher than two may indicate congestion. Further analysis of the individual processes making requests on the processor is required to determine what is causing the congestion.

- Server Work Queues: Queue Length: this is the number of requests in the queue for the selected processor. A consistent queue of over two indicates processor congestion.

Counter	Acceptable Average Range	Desire High or Low Value	Action
% Processor Time	Less than 75%	Low	Find the process using excessive processor time. Upgrade or add another processor.
% Privileged Time	Less than 75%	Low	Find the process using excessive processor time. Upgrade or add another processor.
% User Time	Less than 75%	Low	Find the process using excessive processor time. Upgrade or add another processor.
Interrupts/sec	Depends on processor	Low	Find the controller card generating interrupts.
System: Processor Queue Length	Less than two	Low	Upgrade or add additional processor.
Server Work Queues: Queue Length	Less than two	Low	Find the process using excessive processor time. Upgrade or add another processor.

Another tool that can be used for finding memory bottlenecks is the Windows NT Task Manager. One of the capabilities that Task Manager provides is an analysis of the amount of memory used.

If it is determined that the processor is a system bottleneck, a number of actions can be performed to improve performance. These include the following:

- Add a faster processor if the system is a file and print server.

- Add multiple processors for application servers, especially if the application is multithreaded.

- Off-load processing to another system in the network (either users, applications, or services).

Finding Disk Bottlenecks

The disk subsystem can be the most important aspect of I/O performance. The following graphic is an example of how Performance Monitor can be used to find disk bottlenecks.

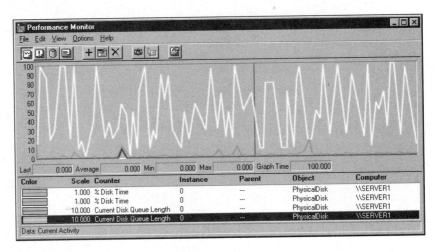

Disks store programs and the data that programs process. While waiting for a computer to respond, it is frequently the disk that is the bottleneck. In this case, the disk subsystem can be the most important aspect of I/O performance, but problems can be hidden by other factors such as the lack of memory.

Performance Monitor disk counters are available with either the LogicalDisk and PhysicalDisk objects. LogicalDisk monitors logical partitions of physical drives. It is useful to determine which partition is causing the disk activity, possibly indicating the application or service that is generating the requests. PhysicalDisk monitors individual hard disk drives, and is useful for monitoring disk drives as a whole.

Performance Monitor disk counters, however, are not enabled by default, and must be enabled manually.

▶ **To activate disk performance statistics on the local computer**

1. Start a command prompt, and type **diskperf -y**

2. Restart the computer.

➤ **To activate disk performance on a remote computer called Server1**

1. Start a command prompt, and type **diskperf -y \\server1**

2. Restart the remote computer.

If using a redundant array of inexpensive disks (RAID) implementation, start **diskperf** with the **-ye** parameter to get enhanced counters.

When analyzing disk subsystem performance and capacity, monitor the following Performance Monitor disk subsystem counters for bottlenecks:

- % Disk Time: this indicates the amount of time that the disk drive is busy servicing read and write requests. If this is consistently close to 100 percent, the disk is being used very heavily. Monitoring of individual processes will help determine which process or processes are making the majority of the disk requests.

- Disk Queue Length: this indicates the number of pending disk I/O requests for the disk drive. If this value is consistently over two, it indicates congestion.

- Avg. Disk Bytes/Transfer: the average number of bytes transferred to or from the disk during write or read operations. The larger the transfer size, the more efficient the system is running.

- Disk Bytes/sec: this is the rate bytes are transferred to or from the disk during write or read operations. The higher the average, the more efficient the system is running.

Counter	Acceptable Average Range	Desire High or Low Value	Action
% Disk Time	Under 50%	Low	Monitor to see if paging is occurring. Upgrade disk subsystem.
Disk Queue Length	0–2	Low	Upgrade disk subsystem.
Avg. Disk Bytes/Transfer	Depends on subsystem	High	Upgrade disk subsystem.
Disk Bytes/sec	Depends on subsystem	High	Upgrade disk subsystem.

If you determine that the disk subsystem is a system bottleneck, a number of solutions are possible. These solutions include the following:

- Add a faster controller, such as Fast SCSI-2, or an on-board caching controller.

- Add more disk drives in a RAID environment. This spreads the data across multiple physical disks and improves performance, especially during reads.

- Offload processing to another system in the network (either users, applications, or services).

Finding Network Bottlenecks

Some of the commonly monitored counters can be used to form an overall picture of how the network is being used. The following graphic is an example of how Performance Monitor can be used to find network bottlenecks.

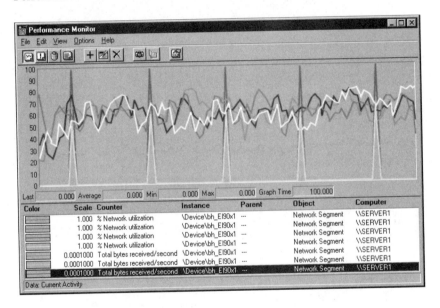

Network bottlenecks are one of the more difficult areas to monitor due to the complexity of most of networks today. While monitoring the network, a number of different objects and counters can be monitored, such as server, redirector, network segment, and protocols. Determining which ones to monitor depends upon the environment. Below are commonly monitored counters. Use them to form an overall picture of how the network is being used and to help in attempts to uncover bottlenecks.

- Server: Bytes Total/sec: this is the number of bytes the server has sent and received over the network. It indicates how busy the server is for transmission and reception of data.

- Server: Logon/sec: this is the number of logon attempts for local authentication, over-the-network authentication, and service accounts in the last second. This counter is beneficial on a domain controller to determine the amount of logon validation occurring.

- Server: Logon Total: this is the number of logon attempts for local authentication, over-the-network authentication, and service accounts since the computer was last started. This counter is beneficial on a domain controller to determine the amount of logon validation occurring.

- Network Segment: % Network utilization: this is the percentage of the network bandwidth in use for the local network segment. This can be used to monitor the effect of different network operations on the network, such as user logon validation, or domain account synchronization.

Note The Network Segment counters are added when the Network Monitor Agent is added through Network Services in Control Panel. When Performance Monitor is actively monitoring Network Segment counters, it places the adapter card into promiscuous mode. While in promiscuous mode, the network adapter card accepts and processes all network traffic, not just traffic destined for itself. This should only be done occasionally, and not left for extended periods, as the processing of all network traffic will affect the performance of the system running the Network Monitor Agent software.

- Network Interface: Bytes Sent/sec: this is the number of bytes sent using this network adapter card.

- Network Interface: Bytes Total/sec: this is the number of bytes sent and received using this network adapter card.

Note The Network Interface counters are added to a TCP/IP host when the SNMP Service is added. These may be added using the Network services in Control Panel.

Counter	Acceptable Average Range	Desire High or Low Value	Action
Bytes Total/sec	Function of number of NICs and protocols used	High	Further analysis to determine cause of problem. Add another adapter.
Logon/sec	Not applicable	High	If logon validation is not completed, add additional domain controllers.
Logons Total	Not applicable	High	If logon validation is not completed, add additional domain controllers.
Network Segment: % Network Use	Generally lower than 30%, though switched networks can achieve higher use	Low	Segment the network. Limit the protocols in use.
Network Interface: Bytes Sent/sec	Function of NIC and protocol or protocols	High	Upgrade network adapter/ physical network.
Network Interface: Bytes Total/sec	Function of NIC and protocol or protocols	High	Upgrade network adapter/ physical network.

By viewing the above counters, it is possible to view the amount of activity on the server for logon requests and data access. If by monitoring these or other counters, the network subsystem is determined to be a bottleneck, numerous actions can help alleviate the bottleneck. These actions include the following:

- Improve the hardware of the server by adding an additional network adapter, upgrading to a better performing adapter, or upgrading to better performing routers and bridges.

- Add more servers to the network, thereby distributing the processing load.

- Check and improve the physical layer components, such as routers.

- Segment the network to isolate traffic to appropriate segments.

Monitoring Network Protocols

To fully understand how to find network bottlenecks, it is also important to monitor the effect that network protocols have on the network itself.

In addition to objects and counters, it is also important to monitor how network protocols affect the network; protocols affect the number of broadcast datagrams being generated, and the number of retransmissions occurring. By monitoring appropriate counters for the protocols in the environment, a clear picture of the use of the network bandwidth in the protocol is determined.

NetBEUI and NWLink

Both NetBEUI and NWLink have similar counters. The following are three common counters for monitoring:

- Bytes Total/sec: this is the total number of bytes sent in frames (data packets) and datagrams (such as broadcasts and acknowledgments).

- Datagrams/sec: this is the number of non-guaranteed datagrams (broadcasts and acknowledgments) sent and received on the network.

- Frames/sec: this is the number of data packets that have been sent and received on the network.

Counter	Acceptable Average Range	Desire High or Low Value	Action
Bytes Total/sec	Function of number of NICs and activity	High	Upgrade NIC. Add additional NIC.
Datagrams/sec	Function of activity	High	Monitor process to determine if causing excessive datagrams.
Frames/sec	Function of activity	High	Reduce broadcast traffic.

TCP/IP

Transmission Control Protocol/Internet Protocol (TCP/IP) counters are added to a system when the TCP/IP protocol has been installed, and the Simple Network Management Protocol (SNMP) Service has been installed. The SNMP Service contains the following objects and counters for TCP/IP related protocols:

- TCP Segments/sec: the number of TCP segments (frames) that are sent and received over the network.

- TCP Segments Re-translated/sec: the number of frames (segments) that are re-translated on the network.

- UDP Datagrams/sec: the number of UDP datagrams (such as broadcasts) that are sent and received.

- Network Interface: Output Queue Length: the length of the output packet queue (in packets). Generally, a queue longer than two indicates congestion, and analysis of the network structure to determine the cause is necessary.

Counter	Acceptable Average Range	Desire High or Low Value	Action
TCP Segments/sec	Function of activity	High	Reduce broadcast traffic. Segment network.
TCP Segments Re-translated	Not applicable	Low	Upgrade physical hardware. Segment network.
UDP Datagrams/sec	Function of activity	Low	Reduce broadcasts.
Network Interface: Output Queue Length	Less than two	Low	Upgrade NIC. Add additional NIC. Verify physical network components.

Setting Expectations of System Usage and Availability

Now that transactions have been defined and any system bottlenecks have been identified and resolved, the next step is to set expectations of system usage and availability. This allows the MIS/network analyst to estimate what the response time should be on a given server (when they are running a specific set of services and applications) with a certain number of users accessing the server concurrently.

When performing server analysis and optimization, consider analyzing the business plan of the organization. It is essential to know the business case and requirements for the system and network before starting to perform server analysis and optimization. When a customer says she wants a two-second response time, for example, she needs to be educated that the Windows NT Server can only affect a small percentage of that time, and it is the application and hardware that will affect the remainder of the time.

By specifying the limits on the system, and making everyone, especially management, aware of the limits and expectations, it is unlikely that any system responsiveness surprises will occur if everything is running within the ranges specified. If something does arise, use Performance Monitor or some other data monitoring application to collect and analyze the data to determine if system limits have been exceeded, or if bottlenecks have developed.

Forecasting Future Resources Allocation

Different applications supply the collection and analysis capabilities to help with forecasting resource allocation. These are the same applications used for creating a database of measurement data. The following graphic describes the types of applications that can be used to help forecast resource allocation.

Formula to identify the need for another Microsoft Windows NT server		
Data	Number of work units on server.................	A
	Capture work unit time..............................	B
	Multiply A by B...	C
Measurement	Project the number of work units of I/O (C) in future......................	D
Expectations	Customer's expectations	E

Result	If D is greater than or equal to E.............	**No change**
Result	If D is less than E....................................	**Further analysis required**

Good analysis of data over a period of time helps you to determine trends, to observe usage patterns, to detect bottlenecks, and to help plan for future upgrades and purchases.

Different methods can be used to forecast future resource requirements of a Windows NT system. Most data collection and monitoring tools, such as Performance Monitor, have the ability to perform some level of analysis with the data that is captured. Database applications, such as Access, Fox Pro, and SQL Server have the ability to import data from measurement tools, and then further query and analyze that data.

Any application capable of importing data and performing analysis on that data is useful when performing server analysis and optimization. Excel can be used to import and analyze database management information. An Excel macro can take the data to be analyzed, and given certain criteria, generate a list of recommendations.

The following formula can help identify whether another Windows NT Server is needed.

➤ **To identify whether another server is needed**

1. Define the number of work units on the server—for example, client requests.

2. Capture the data that is relevant to the workload unit. For example, data that would indicate how long it takes to transfer x bytes of data from server to client.

3. Multiply that number by the number of clients making similar requests.

4. Graph the number of work units of I/O over a specific period of time as a measure of how much can be finished in that period of time. Project the expected growth in work unit I/O in the graph.

If the answer to number four meets the expectations of the customer, then the system should be able to accommodate the requirement, and no change is required.

If the answer to number four does not meet the expectations of the amount of work units performed, this is an indication that further analysis or tuning needs to be completed. The results from further investigation may indicate the need to install another server.

Note It is recommended to first test a pilot system in a controlled environment to determine "best case" values. Then, test in a production environment to determine how the existing environment affects the results of the pilot system.

Always plan server optimization on current requirements, such as what resources the applications currently require, the expected growth, and then forecast from those requirements. It is recommended that you double the best guess to come closer to actual implementation requirements.

The charting capabilities of Excel can compile the data, graph the current use trends, and graph the expected trends, given specific business conditions identified in the business plan (expected number of users to be added, and so on). Variances should be graphed to show possible deviations from the expected performance and capacity numbers.

Establishing a Plan for Long-Term Record Keeping

As in all areas of computer analysis, documentation is essential. This is especially true with server analysis and optimization. Consistent and accurate record keeping will help identify trends as they are happening. Be sure to include baseline data, current activity data, and any other supporting data. This information can keep the organization's management informed of changes in the environment. It helps to build a case for budgeting requests, and to assist with problem identification and resolution.

Creating Management Reports

Once data has been added to the database and analyzed, an organization's management may request that reports be generated. Incorporate the following information into the management reports:

- Current usage patterns and trends from past data.

- A comparison of actual resource usage to resource usage expectations.

- Potential resource needs and budget considerations.

- An illustrated representation of current activity, with maximum and minimum values, along with predictions of expected activity over a specified time period.

The trend analysis these reports provide can also be used for preventative maintenance information. Use this information to identify where adjustments in the current environment are needed, and thereby avoid potential system bottlenecks that may render the system unusable.

In order to properly perform trend analysis, it is necessary to keep an extensive database of information for analysis of past trends and history.

Analyzing Performance Bottlenecks

In this exercise you will answer some questions about determining performance bottlenecks on a Windows NT server in the enterprise.

1. You are analyzing the baseline data collected, and notice that the PhysicalDisk: % Disk Time value is over 90 percent. What should you do to determine why this occurs?

_____

_____

2. If you are not sure if an application is multi-threaded, how can you use Performance Monitor to determine this?

_____

_____

3. You are running TCP/IP as your network protocol, and you want to analyze network use. You attempt to gather as much data as you can on TCP/IP and its use of the network, but you do not find many counters available. You also want to find out how busy the network is, but you cannot seem to find a counter that will accomplish this. What can you do?

_____

_____

4. You have identified and resolved all system bottlenecks, and you now want to generate new data for analysis. Should this collection be done on a pilot or a production system?

_____

_____

5. You need to determine how many users can log on simultaneously to a domain controller and what effect that has on the system. How would you go about arriving at a conclusion?

_____

_____

6. Your company's management team wants to know what the results of the server analysis and optimization has been on the pilot computer running Windows NT Server. You decided to generate a report for them. What should you include?

_____

_____

Lesson Summary

The following information summarizes the key points in this lesson:

- Performance analysis involves determining workload characterization, setting expectations of system use, forecasting resource allocation, and establishing long-term record keeping trend analysis.

- Bottlenecks restrict work flow. The processor, memory, disk, and network subsystems are all potential bottlenecks. In order to solve bottlenecks, it is important to set system usage expectations and to be able to forecast future resource requirements.

- Workload characterization is the set of resources and services that is requested of the system.

- Long term documentation and record keeping of server resources and workload requirements can be used to forecast trends in the enterprise and plan for the future.

Lesson 4: Analyzing File and Print Server Performance

This lesson identifies specific implications of determining workload characterization and the process for analyzing system performance in the file and print server environment. It also identifies specific techniques for forecasting future resource allocation in the file and print server environment.

After this lesson, you will be able to:

- Perform analysis in the file and print server environment.
- Identify resource implications in the file and print server environment.
- Monitor IIS in the file and print server environment.
- Identify forecasting considerations in the file and print server environment.
- Calculate the number of users a file and print server can support.

Estimated lesson time: 20 minutes

Analysis in the File and Print Server Environment

A file and print server is usually accessed by users for data retrieval and document storage, and is occasionally used for loading application software over the network. Analysis of a file and print server focuses on the number of users accessing the server concurrently, and the amount of resource requirements that they are demanding. Numerous workload units are important when monitoring a file and print server.

The following is a list of common workload units for a file and print server and the respective Performance Monitor counter.

Workload Unit	Performance Monitor Counter
Concurrent user sessions	Server: Server Sessions
The number of files open	Server: Files Open
Average transaction size	PhysicalDisk: Avg. Disk Bytes/Transfer
Amount of disk activity	PhysicalDisk: % Disk Time
Type of disk activity	PhysicalDisk: % Disk Read Time
	PhysicalDisk: % Disk Write Time
Network use	Network Segment: % Network Utilization

Sometimes additional resources are being consumed, such as server memory. If that is the case, add additional counters, such as memory counters, to the analysis to receive detailed information on the resource that is being accessed.

Resource Implications in the File and Print Server Environment

The following graphic illustrates some of the resource implications in the file and print server environment.

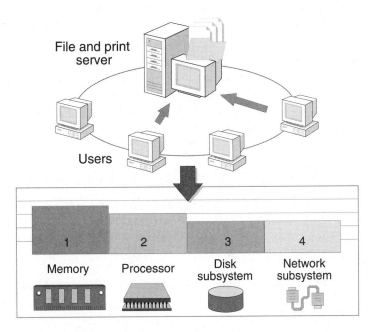

Memory and processor use has the greatest impact on file and print servers. The disk and network subsystems are important, though memory and processor have the greatest potential for being overused on a file and print server.

When monitoring a file and print server, be prepared to see numerous user connections; but many of those connections may be inactive. Consider adjusting the auto-disconnect setting for each file and print server environment.

Memory Implications

Memory is used for caching of opened files in a file and print server environment. Having enough random access memory (RAM) to allow for sufficient caching helps to improve performance when files are opened and continually accessed from the server.

Processor Implications

The processor is used for each network connection on the network; this means that all network connection traffic involves the processor. Having bus mastering network adapters and disk controllers helps to alleviate processing from the central processing unit (CPU), allowing more time for responding to data requests.

Disk Subsystem Implications

The disk subsystem is the primary server resource that users access. It will have a large effect on the overall perception of system performance, and ultimately, its capacity. The fastest and most efficient disk subsystem will provide the best overall performance improvement.

Network Subsystem Implications

A number of factors will affect the network subsystem. It will not matter how fast the disk subsystem is, how many processors are available, or how much RAM is installed in the server; if the network adapter card in the server is too slow, it cannot effectively perform transfers of data from physical network medium to RAM.

Monitoring IIS in a File and Print Server Environment

Having Internet Information Server (IIS) requests fulfilled from the cache (that is, from cache hits) is the best way to optimize for maximum performance. The following graphic is an example of how to monitor the IIS cache in a file and print server environment.

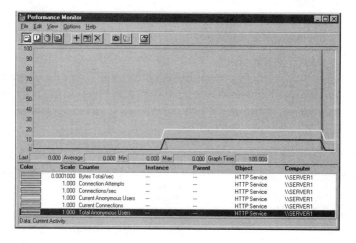

IIS version 2.0 is included with Windows NT Server 4.0. Having IIS fulfill requests from the cache is the best way to optimize IIS for maximum performance. Cache is one of the most important performance issues with IIS. IIS maintains its own cache, separate from the one maintained by the Windows NT operating system.

The IIS cache allocates a portion of physical memory to store objects for future requests. Use the Registry Editor to share the cache for all IIS services installed on the server. However, be aware that if cache size is increased beyond the amount of available physical memory, the performance of other processes may decrease.

To adjust the size of the IIS cache, add the following registry key:

```
\HKEY_LOCAL_MACHINE
\System\CurrentControlSet\Services\InetInfo\Parameters\MemoryCacheSize
```

The range is from 0 bytes to 4 gigabytes (GB). A value of 0 disables IIS caching and severely affects the performance of IIS.

The following are recommended Internet Information Server Global counters to use when monitoring IIS cache usage:

- Cache Flushes.
- Cache Hits %.
- Cache Misses.
- Cache Size.
- Cache Used.
- Cached File Handles.
- Directory Listings.
- Objects.

The following are recommended Gopher Service Performance Monitor counters to use when monitoring cache usage:

- Bytes Sent per second.
- Bytes Total per second.
- Current Anonymous Users.
- Current Connections.
- Current Non-Anonymous Users.
- Directory Listings Sent.

- Files Sent.

- Logon Attempts.

- Maximum Anonymous Users.

- Maximum Connections.

- Maximum Non-Anonymous Users.

- Searches Sent.

- Total Anonymous Users.

Forecasting in a File and Print Server Environment

The following table lists some considerations and recommendations for forecasting in a file and print server environment. These are only general guidelines, each environment may differ in expectations and results.

Considerations	Recommendations
The number of users a specific server can support.	This is somewhat dependent upon the hardware of the server, and more dependent upon the type of transactions the clients perform on the server.
	Monitor the number of user sessions, and the effect each session has on the four major system resources using the counters.
	The most common areas for potential bottlenecks are disk usage and network performance.
If users access the server to retrieve and update individual data files.	Consider the disk and network subsystems. Monitor disk and network objects to determine if any areas are being exposed as a bottleneck.
If the users access the server for data files and also to load their applications.	Add server memory to the list of objects to monitor. When opening files off the server, Windows NT attempts to cache the open files, which may cause a memory bottleneck.

Calculating the Number of Users
That a File and Print Server Can Support

The following graphic shows you how you can calculate the number of users that a file and print server can support.

Formula to calculate the number of users a server can support
Data Monitor a single user making normal transactions on the server. Time it takes to complete a single transaction .... A [   ] Number of expected and desired simultaneous requests ..... B [   ] Multipy A by B .... C [   ]

Result	General capacity requirement..	C
Result	If C does not meet expectations and requirements	Further analysis required

> ### ➤ To calculate the number of users that a particular server can support

1. Test a single user making "normal" transactions on the server. Whether this transaction involves retrieving a word-processing document, a spreadsheet, or some other action, monitor the transaction using the appropriate counters relative to file and print servers.

2. Monitor the time it takes to complete a single "normal" transaction.

3. Monitor the resources utilized and multiply those by the number of users.

This produces a general capacity requirement. Once the amount of time it will take to accomplish the workload unit is determined, the result is compared to the desired number of workload units. If the results are not as expected, then:

- Analyze the system to determine the bottleneck. For a file and print server, start by monitoring memory.

- Calculate the amount of network traffic memory generates, as well as disk activity. The network subsystem can only accommodate x amount of data (10 MB for Ethernet, 4 or 16 MB for Token Ring, and so on). You can then determine projected use and whether it will exceed the network capacity.

If memory and the network subsystem seem to be able to handle the required load, then monitor the disk subsystem and processor utilization. If something is not functioning within given ranges, then either an improvement in the appropriate resource is required, or adding another server to distribute the load is necessary to satisfy the required number of workload units in the production environment.

Analyzing File and Print Performance

In this exercise you will answer some questions about performance analysis in the File and Print server environment.

1. What is your main focus when analyzing a file and print server?

    _____

    _____

2. You are analyzing the memory on your computer running Windows NT Server that is running as a file and print server, and you notice that the amount of available RAM is much too low (only about 10 MB), as your computer has 32 MB of RAM. What could be the cause of this?

    _____

    _____

3. What is the best way to optimize IIS for maximum performance?

    _____

    _____

4. You have analyzed your file and print server, and have determined that the disk subsystem is hitting its performance capacity. What can you do to improve performance without distributing users to another system?

    _____

    _____

Lesson Summary

The following information summarizes the key points in this lesson:

- File and print server analysis focuses on the number of users accessing the server concurrently, and the amount of resource requirements they demand.

- Memory and processor use has the greatest impact on file and print servers.

- IIS requests should be fulfilled from the cache to achieve maximum performance.

- Some considerations when forecasting in a file and print server environment include the number of users a specific server can support, and how they use the server.

- Calculating the number of users a file and print server can support involves measuring how a single user transaction effects server performance, and then multiplying that metric times the number of expected simultaneous requests.

Lesson 5: Analyzing Application Server Performance

This lesson analyzes system performance in the application server environment and discusses how to apply these concepts and processes in the application server environment. This environment can be more complicated to analyze when compared to the file and print server environment because the applications that a server runs, and how users utilize the applications, can vary depending on the enterprise.

After this lesson, you will be able to:

- Perform analysis in the application server environment.
- Identify resource implications in the application server environment.
- Identify forecasting considerations in an application server environment.
- Calculate the number of users an application server can support.

Estimated lesson time: 20 minutes

Analysis in the Application Server Environment

The analysis of an application server largely focuses on workload units. An application server is accessed differently than a file and print server. Where a file and print server is traditionally accessed with fewer numbers of requests (with each request averaging a fairly large size), an application server is usually accessed with smaller, more frequent requests from the client computer. In addition, the application server has the overhead of actually running an application using memory and processor resources.

The following table lists common workload units for an application server and the respective Performance Monitor counters for each workload unit.

Workload Unit	Performance Monitor Counter
Concurrent user sessions	Server: Server Sessions
Processor usage	Processor: % Processor Time
Average disk transaction size	PhysicalDisk: Avg. Disk Bytes/Transfer
Amount of disk activity	PhysicalDisk: % Disk Time
Network use	Network Segment: % Network Utilization

(continued)

Workload Unit	Performance Monitor Counter
Average network transaction size	Will vary for protocol, such as NetBEUI: Frame Bytes/sec
Available memory	Memory: Available Bytes
Amount of paging	Memory: Pages/sec
Usage of cache	Cache: Copy Read Hits %

Also, some applications may provide Performance Monitor counters that give detailed application statistics. For example, Exchange Server provides performance monitor counters and predefined charts. Additionally, SQL Server offers numerous objects and counters specific to its operation, such as SQL Server: I/O Transactions/sec and Cache Hit Ratio. Be sure to include any application-specific counters in the analysis of an applications server.

Resource Implications in the Application Server Environment

The following graphic illustrates some of the resource implications in the application server environment.

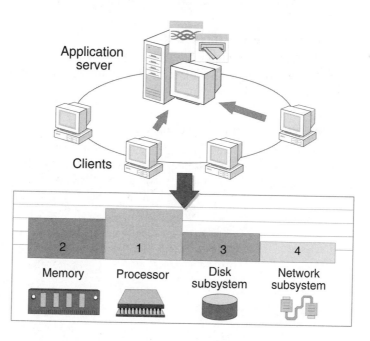

When monitoring application servers, such as in a SQL Server client/server environment, more processor and memory use occurs than in the file and print server environment. Disk and network resources are also used consistently in this environment.

Memory Implications

Memory is used for the server portion of the client/server application. Make sure to add sufficient random access memory (RAM) to support operating system and application needs. The RAM required depends upon the particular system hardware and software configuration and needs.

Processor Implications

Applications run on the server side of the client/server, and as a result, the processor is used to run the threads of the application. If a large number of users access this application from client components, upgrading or adding an additional processor may improve performance. If an application is processor-bound, use the most powerful processor available.

Computers that are capable of symmetric multiprocessing allow use of multiple, though less powerful, processors instead of a single more powerful processor. Also, a mid-range processor may be used if fewer applications are used. Remember, when the processor becomes the bottleneck, additional processors can be added.

Disk Subsystem Implications

Client/server applications typically access large amounts of data, and therefore the demands on the disk subsystem are significant. Consider the disk controller and type of drive investments carefully.

Network Subsystem Implications

Client/server applications transfer many requests over the network for data access. These requests are often queries or commands that do not involve transferring large data files over the network, as in a file and print server environment. It is very important to get the data in and out of the server as quickly as possible.

Forecasting in an Application Server Environment

The following graphic examines disk-bound application server considerations.

If	Then
Applications are disk-bound and disk subsystem is the bottleneck	● For reads, implement hardware RAID or controller caching ● For writes, implement hardware RAID
Applications are memory-intensive and memory is the bottleneck	● Add additional RAM ● Offload applications or services to other servers
Applications are network-intensive and network is the bottleneck	● Upgrade the network components ● Add addtional netowrk adapter cards ● Subnet the network
Application is multithreaded or there are multiple applications	● Add multiple processors
Application is single threaded or there is a single application	● Upgrade the processor

There are several considerations you should think about when forecasting in an application server environment.

If Applications Are Disk-Bound

If the applications are disk-bound, that is, they generate a large amount of data, and make a large number of requests on the disk, monitor the disk subsystem use.

If the disk subsystem is identified as the bottleneck and the application is predominantly reading from the disk subsystem, then a hardware redundant array of inexpensive disks (RAID) implementation and disk or controller caching will provide performance improvement. If multiple drives are necessary, the addition of another controller can improve performance.

If the disk subsystem is identified as the bottleneck and the application is mainly writing to the disk, then a hardware RAID implementation will improve performance. If the application and data is critical, and fault tolerance is important, such as in a SQL Server environment, then a RAID 5 implementation is recommended.

With RAID 5 implementations, the performance gain is less noticeable due to the process of writing parity information to achieve fault tolerance. If fault tolerance is not important, as in the case of loading application software from the server, then a RAID 0 implementation is beneficial to improve performance as data is spread over multiple physical hard disks.

If Applications Are Memory-Intensive

If the applications are memory intensive, then monitor the memory counters as discussed earlier.

If memory is determined to be the bottleneck, add additional RAM or increase internal cache. One common problem is having too small of a secondary cache. The processor uses the secondary cache to provide read-ahead access to RAM. If RAM has been added, but the secondary cache size has not increased, this situation can result in lower cache usage, as the secondary cache must attempt to provide caching for a larger memory space. General recommendations for secondary cache sizes are 256 kilobytes (KB) for 16–32 megabytes (MB) of RAM, and 512 KB for systems above 32 MB of RAM.

Additionally, if memory is determined to be the bottleneck, you can offload other applications or services to other servers. Moving an entire application, such as SQL Server, to another server distributes the load on the current computer, and spreads requests between servers. Some applications, such as Systems Management Server, allow specific components to be moved to "helper" servers to provide a more balanced usage of system hardware resources. It may also be possible to move system services, such as Remote Access Service (RAS), to another computer to offload processing requirements from a single computer.

If Applications Are Network-Intensive

If the applications generate a high volume of network traffic, monitor the network subsystem use. To do this, use Performance Monitor objects and counters, such as Network Segment: % Network Utilization, or a network traffic analyzer. Network Monitor can be used to view overall network statistics, and to view network traffic as well as individual packets. If the network subsystem is determined to be the bottleneck, then:

- Upgrade the network subsystem, including network adapter cards, to better performing models. Upgrading to 32-bit network adapter cards is very beneficial to the server performance.

- Add additional network adapter cards to distribute the load.

- Isolate traffic to specific segments by subnetting the network.

- Upgrade the network components, such as cabling and bridges, to higher performance components.

If Applications Are CPU-Bound

If the applications are central processing unit (CPU)-bound, monitor the processor usage. If the processor is determined to be the bottleneck and the application is multi-threaded, or multiple applications and services are run simultaneously, then consider adding multiple processors in a symmetric multiprocessing computer.

If the processor is determined to be the bottleneck and the application is single-threaded, or very few other applications and services are running, then consider upgrading the processor in a single processor computer.

Calculating the Number of Users an Application Server Can Support

The following graphic explains how to calculate the number of users that an application server can support.

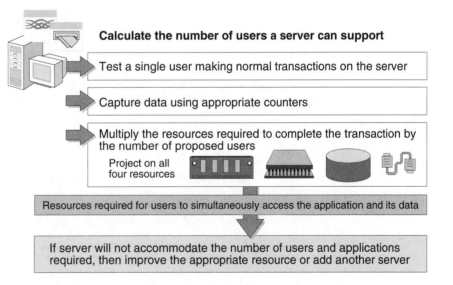

Calculate the number of users a server can support

Test a single user making normal transactions on the server

Capture data using appropriate counters

Multiply the resources required to complete the transaction by the number of proposed users

Project on all four resources

Resources required for users to simultaneously access the application and its data

If server will not accommodate the number of users and applications required, then improve the appropriate resource or add another server

A question that system analysts are often asked is: how many users can a specific server support? The answer to this question depends on many factors including the hardware configuration of the server, the type of applications the server is running, and what server resources these applications require.

➤ **To calculate the number of users that a particular server can support**

1. Test a single user making "normal" transactions on the server using the predominant, front-end application against the engine of the server.

2. Capture data using the appropriate counters relative to application servers. Be sure to use any application-specific counters that are available, such as those added by SQL Server, in the analysis.

3. Multiply the resources required to complete the transaction by the number of proposed users. This will provide an idea of how much resource utilization it will require for all users to simultaneously access the application and its data.

Note Because application servers predominantly use all resources, it is necessary to project on all four resources: memory, processor, disk, and network.

If the analysis indicates that the existing server will not be able to accommodate the number of users and applications required, then either an improvement in the appropriate resource is required, or the addition of another server to distribute the load is necessary.

Some server applications provide their own performance analysis tools. For Exchange, the Loadsim application will simulate a very specific Exchange environment and allow you to run varying number of users against an Exchange server in that environment. When Loadsim is used in conjunction with Performance Monitor, you can chart how your server will perform with increasing numbers of users. This way, resources can added before performance is affected in the production environment.

Analyzing Application Server Performance

In this exercise you will answer questions about analyzing application server performance.

1. How many users can an application server support?

   _____

   _____

2. You are analyzing the processor on your computer running Windows NT Server that is running as an application server, and you notice that the processor is very busy (over 90 percent of the time). What may be the cause of this?

   _____

   _____

3. Your analysis of the application server determined that you needed to add additional RAM to your server (now at 32 MB). The system is not responding as well to requests as it did before the memory upgrade. What may be the problem?

_____

_____

Lesson Summary

The following information summarizes the key points in this lesson:

- An application server is usually accessed with smaller, more frequent requests than a file and print server.

- Memory and processor are typically the more frequently utilized resources on an application server. Not only does the server need to fulfill client requests, but it also needs to run the applications to meet those requests.

- When forecasting in an application server environment, take into account that the number of users will probably increase, resulting in an application that must change to meet the increased demand.

- To calculate the number of users an application server can support, test a single user making normal transactions on the server, capture the data using the appropriate counters, and then multiply the resources required to complete the transaction by the number of proposed users.

Lesson 6: Analyzing Domain Server Performance

Analyzing domain server performance is important because domain servers play a vital role in the enterprise. Windows clients depend on the domain controllers for network logon authentication, browsing, and other network services. In this lesson, you will learn how to analyze system performance in the domain server environment.

After this lesson, you will be able to:

- Perform analysis in the domain server environment.
- Identify resource implications in the domain server environment.
- Identify forecasting considerations in a domain server environment.
- Calculate the number of users a domain server can support.
- Identify solutions to possible server optimization problems.

Estimated lesson time: 20 minutes

Analysis in the Domain Server Environment

A domain server is a server that generates data transfer between itself and other servers, generally without the initiation of the data transfer occurring as the result of a user request. For example, a primary domain controller (PDC) synchronizes the accounts database with backup domain controllers (BDCs); likewise, a Windows Internet Naming Service (WINS) Server replicates its database with its replication partner. Domain servers also validate user logon requests.

The analysis of a domain server largely focuses on different workload units, as the access of a domain server is different from a file and print server or an application server. A domain server, such as a domain controller, is accessed infrequently by users, but it generates activity that is not the direct result of user interaction, such as the synchronization of the domain accounts database.

The following table lists common workload units for a domain server and the respective Performance Monitor counter for each workload unit.

Workload Unit	Performance Monitor Counter
Concurrent logons	Server: Logon/sec
Invalid logon requests (Windows NT client computers only)	Server: Error Logon
Total logon attempts since system startup	Server: Logon Total
Memory use	Memory: Available Bytes Memory: Committed Bytes
Network use	Network Segment: % Network Utilization
NetBIOS name service registrations	WINS Server: Total Number of Registrations/sec
NetBIOS name queries	WINS Server: Queries/sec

Resource Implications in the Domain Server Environment

The following graphic examines domain server environment resource implications.

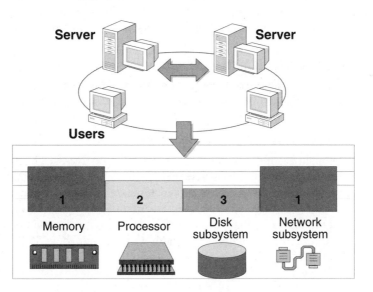

A domain server environment involves communication between servers that are not initiated by client activity, such as domain controllers synchronizing the domain accounts database. When monitoring a domain server environment, system resources are used by the operating system, and they need to be accounted for before planning for user access. Windows NT Server services such as Net Logon, WINS, and the Directory Replicator can all transfer data between servers on the network without a user initiating the transfer. Properly determining the amount of data transferred by the operating system is crucial to determining resource availability for users.

Memory Implications

Each of the domain server transfers will consume some memory. Monitor memory counters to determine the affect that data transfers have on memory. Each service requires additional random access memory (RAM). For domain controllers, it is recommended to have 2.5 times the amount of RAM as the size of the Security Accounts Manager (SAM) database.

Processor Implications

All data transfers use processor cycles: this includes domain accounts database synchronization, WINS database replication, and data replication. During data transfer, fewer processor cycles are available for network access demands from users. Installing an additional processor helps in these environments.

Disk Subsystem Implications

Disk subsystem use is the same as a file and print server, although during internal data transfer times, disk responsiveness for users is affected.

Network Subsystem Implications

Domain account synchronization will take, on average, 1 KB per change if multiple changes are propagated, and as much as 4 KB for a single change. If large numbers of changes are to be synchronized, the synchronization can consume large percentages of wide area network (WAN) links. The default amount of network bandwidth that Windows NT uses for account synchronization is set to 100 percent of available bandwidth. For example, on a 56 KB point-to-point circuit, it could take about 24 hours to replicate a 30,000 user SAM. Perform as few full synchronizations of the domain accounts database as possible—instead perform partial synchronizations.

Forecasting in a Domain Server Environment

The following graphic illustrates server-to-server forecasting considerations in the domain server environment.

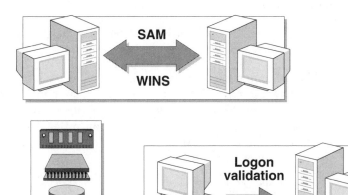

When forecasting in a domain server environment, the analysis process is slightly different than a typical file and print server analysis because more activity is created that is not the result of direct user interaction. The following is a list of common activities that will affect system resources without user intervention:

- Domain account synchronization.

- WINS database replication.

- Internet Protocol (IP) address leases and renewals by means of Dynamic Host Control Protocol (DHCP).

- Browser updates.

- Systems Management Server verification and updates on logon servers.

The first two items in the previous bulleted list, domain account synchronization and WINS database replication, can cause a significant impact on system performance. The others, although they generate some activity, have significantly less impact on performance.

Two of the most common requests concerning domain server environments are how many users can simultaneously log on, and how many domain controllers are required given a specific number of users. Simultaneous logons are hardware independent. One domain controller is suggested for every 2000 users to perform logon validation.

The following is a strategy to use when analyzing the affects of Windows NT Server communications:

- Monitor during the domain account synchronization process to determine the affect synchronization has on memory, processor, disk, and network resources. Using Server Manager, synchronization can be forced, either with a specific server (initiating the request from a BDC) to view the effect of a single synchronization, or from the PDC to view the effect of synchronizing with all domain controllers.

- Monitor during the WINS server replication process. Using WINS Manager, the administrator can initiate the replication process manually when little other activity is occurring on the server. This helps to isolate the effect on the server during the replication process.

- Monitor the effect on the network and server when a single client attempts to log on and be validated. Determining the effects that a single user has on the network is easily projected into the effect on the server or servers, should all users attempt to log on at the same time.

Calculating the Number of Users a Domain Server Can Support

The following graphic lists the recommendations for identifying the number of users in a domain environment.

Recommendations for the number of domain users and hardware size						
Number of users	SAM (MB)	CPU	RAM (MB)	Pagefile (MB)	Registry size limit (MB)	Paged pool size (MB)
5,000	5	486DX/33	16	32	default	default
1,000	10	486DX/66	32	64	default	default
15,000	15	Pentium, MIPS, ALPHA	48	96	default	default
20,000	20	Pentium, MIPS, ALPHA	64	128	30	75
30,000	30	Pentium, MIPS, ALPHA	96	192	50	100
40,000	40	Pentium, MIPS, ALPHA	128	256	75	128

The recommendation for the number of users in a domain is dependent on the following:

- The maximum number of objects in the SAM is 40,000. The makeup of users, groups, and computer accounts does not matter, although:

  - Each user takes 1 KB of disk space.

  - Each local or global group takes 512 bytes and 50 bytes per member.

  - Each computer account takes 0.5 KB of disk space.

- The maximum size of the directory database is 40 MB. The SAM is the largest of the three items that make up the directory database. The SAM is also a part of the registry, and the total registry is limited to 108 MB.

Note The processor type is relatively unimportant in relation to the number of users supported on a domain controller. Processor type is more important when considering client authentication, and when domain controllers are used for more than one purpose. For large domain operations, do not use the domain controller for anything other than normal domain controller activities, such as validating user logon requests and maintaining the user accounts database.

Proposing Solutions

When determining the expected response time, given a specific set of transactions, it is possible to encounter a situation where the numbers do not agree with the anticipated outcome. The current response time, for example, may be much slower than expected given a certain system environment. In this case, if everything seems to be okay and no problems exist in the system, the following number of responses may be possible in the situation:

- Adjust the expectations to be more in line with what is currently being experienced.

- Reallocate resources (applications, services, or users) to other systems currently in the network.

- Expand the current resource that is over-consumed (acting as the system bottleneck).

- Purchase additional systems and then distribute the access load.

- Verify configuration settings.

The appropriate response to a particular situation varies with each scenario. Proper analysis, not only of the system in question, but also in conjunction with the current business plan, helps to dictate the appropriate solution to the problem.

Configuration Settings

If, after monitoring Windows NT server, the server is not responding as expected, verify the configuration setting.

To configure the server service for a particular type of server, use the Server option under Services in the Network program in Control Panel.

- For an application server, click **Maximize Throughput for Network Applications**.

- For a file and print server, click **Maximize Throughput for File Sharing**.

- For a domain server, click **Maximize Throughput for Network Applications.**

Following are the options, and a description of each of the options, on the **Server** menu:

Option	Description
Minimize Memory Used	For use with up to 10 simultaneous connections from client computers. This option is useful for a server that has a user running desktop applications locally.
Balance	For use with up to 64 simultaneous connections.
Maximize Throughput for File Sharing	For use with large number of clients in a file and print server environment.
Maximize Throughput for Network Applications	For use in an application server environment.

Analyzing Domain Server Performance

In this exercise you will answer questions about analyzing domain controller performance.

1. In a domain server environment, what activities will affect system resources without user intervention?

_____

_____

2. Why should you monitor during the domain account synchronization process?

_____

_____

3. Why would you want to monitor the effect on the network and server when a single client attempts to log on and be validated?

_____

_____

Lesson Summary

The following information summarizes the key points in this lesson:

- A domain server is a server that generates data transfer between itself and other server.

- When forecasting in a domain server environment, the analysis process is slightly different than typical server analysis because more activity is created that is not the result of direct user interaction.

C H A P T E R   6

Network Monitoring and Optimization

About This Chapter

The network is a critical component to the performance and functionality of Windows NT Server in the enterprise. Although a Windows NT Server may have ample resources, and the client may be perfectly tuned, a slow and unreliable network can make the client/server system seem sluggish and unimpressive to the user. This chapter looks at ways of recognizing and avoiding this situation through network analysis and optimization with Windows NT Server.

Before You Begin

To complete the lessons in this chapter, you must have:

- The knowledge and skills covered in Chapter 2, "Installation and Configuration."

- The knowledge and skills covered in Chapter 3, "Managing Enterprise Resources."

- The knowledge and skills covered in Chapter 4, "Connectivity."

- The knowledge and skills covered in Chapter 5, "Server Monitoring and Optimization."

Lesson 1: Network Analysis and Optimization Basics

Windows NT Server provides services that support specific user network requirements. Some of these services are automatically installed with Windows NT Server, while others can be added optionally. All network services impact the capacity of a network. This lesson defines the elements of network traffic and describes the tools necessary to analyze network traffic on a Windows NT Server network.

After this lesson, you will be able to:

- Describe a process for network traffic analysis.
- List the various types of network traffic to be analyzed.
- Use Microsoft Network Monitor to capture, view, and save data.

Estimated lesson time: 20 minutes

In a corporate computing environment, end-users expect their network experiences to be fast and reliable, while MIS managers expect corporate servers to be efficient and quickly adaptable to the changing software and user needs. Administrators typically need to optimize their existing network or predict the effect of changes on a growing network.

Analyzing Network Traffic

Before optimization or capacity planning can be accomplished, the administrator must know what network traffic is being generated. Analysis involves determining the effect each Windows NT Server service has on the network. This is done with a network traffic analyzer on the existing corporate network for optimization purposes, or on an isolated network for prediction purposes.

Optimizing an Existing Network

There are two methods for optimizing a network. The first method provides more available bandwidth to the user by reducing the amount of network traffic generated by specific services. The second method provides users with better response time, generally by proper implementation of network services, which may increase network traffic. A properly optimized network will be a compromise between available bandwidth to the user and increased service response time.

Predicting Needs for a Growing Network

Capacity planning is predicting what will happen if one or more factors increases with all the others remaining constant. As a network grows, or different services are added, an administrator should predict the effect and work to stabilize performance during changes.

Windows NT Server Network Services

Windows NT Server provides various network services to support specific requirements of users on the network. Some of these services are automatically installed with Windows NT Server, while others can be added optionally. All network services impact the capacity of a network.

The following table lists the Windows NT Server services that are most commonly utilized and can generate a significant amount of network traffic.

Service	Description
Net Logon	Used to perform user account logon validation and synchronization of the user accounts in the domain. Also supports the establishment and maintenance of trust relationships.
Computer Browser	Provides browsing capabilities that allow users to find resources on the network without having to remember connection syntax and locations.
Dynamic Host Configuration Protocol (DHCP)	Provides automated administration of Transmission Control Protocol/Internet Protocol (TCP/IP) addresses and other configuration parameters to DHCP clients.
Windows Internet Naming Service (WINS)	Provides a centralized location to resolve computer names for browsing and resource access.
Directory Replicator	Provides automated duplication of directories among multiple Windows NT–based computers.
Domain Name System (DNS)	Provides for name resolution of TCP/IP host names into IP addresses.
Internet Explorer	Provides access to World Wide Web (WWW) locations for viewing and downloading files.
Workstation	Provides network access to files, applications, and printers throughout the network.
Server	Allows network clients access to shared resources. Receives and processes workstation requests.

Characterizing Services

A Windows NT Server service can be characterized by answering three important questions:

1. What kind of traffic is generated?
2. How often is this traffic generated?
3. What is the relative impact on the network?

➤ To characterize a service

Use the following guidelines to characterize a service.

1. Use an isolated network. This prevents other traffic from interfering with or skewing the results. The best way to capture network traffic related to a specific network function is to stop all network traffic that is not related to that function. This clears the network for analysis of the traffic of interest.

2. Use a network capturing and analysis tool, such as Network Monitor.

3. Capture the appropriate traffic by initiating the network traffic relative to the service to be characterized. For example, if analyzing logon validation traffic, force the traffic to occur by logging off and logging on at a client computer. Capture the traffic that is generated by logging on to the client.

4. Identify each frame in the capture, ensuring that it is part of the traffic generated by the service and not from another function.

By performing these steps, a guide, or baseline, of how the service operates can be created. Repeating these steps additional times may be necessary to ensure the validity of the data. Make sure that the service or computers are returned to the same state as the initial test to provide for consistent test results.

Network Frame TypesTraffic captured by a network traffic analysis tool is displayed in segments called frames. A frame represents the addressing and protocol information, as well as the data that is transferred from one host to another on the network.

There are three different types of frames: broadcast, multicast, and directed (unicast).

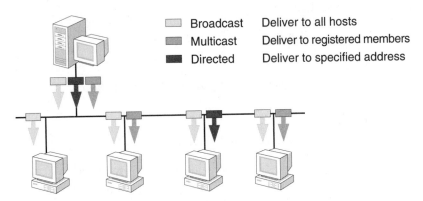

Broadcast frames are delivered to all hosts on the network. They may actually be destined for one specific host, but due to protocol or addressing reasons, they are sent to all hosts.

Broadcasts are sent with the unique destination address of FFFFFFFFFFFF. No host can be configured with this address. All hosts on the network accept this frame, and process it up through its protocol stack until it determines whether to complete processing of the frame or discard it, as it is not meant for the local computer.

Multicast frames are delivered to a portion of the hosts on the network. Similar to broadcast frames, they are not delivered to a specific destination media access control (MAC) address, but to a selected subset of the hosts on the network. Each host has to register the multicast address in order to become a member of that multicast subset. NetBEUI, and some TCP/IP applications make use of multicasts.

Directed frames are the most common type of frames. These frames have a destination address for a specific host on the network. All other hosts that receive this frame discard it because it does not contain the host's hardware address.

Each of the different protocols that ship with Windows NT 4.0 may differ in their implementation of broadcasts. For example, while TCP/IP and NWLink initiate broadcasts, NetBEUI sends multicasts instead of broadcasts.

Examining Network Frames

The following graphic illustrates network frames.

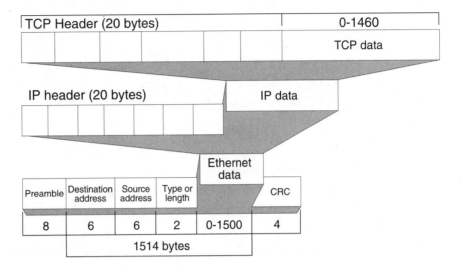

Frames—whether broadcast, multicast, or directed—are broken up into different pieces that can be analyzed separately. Each of these pieces contain data that may be valuable during the analysis phase. For example, by examining the destination address, it can be determined if the frame was a broadcast frame, indicating all hosts had to receive and process this frame, or a directed frame sent to a specific host. By analyzing frames, the network administrator can determine the exact cause of the frame, which helps determine if the service generating these types of frames can be optimized.

The portions of an Ethernet 802.3 frame are listed in the following table.

Frame Field	Description
Preamble	Signals the receiving transceiver that data is coming. Eight bytes in length. This is not seen in a trace.
Destination address	Specifies the target hardware media access control address that should process this frame. Six bytes in length.
Source address	Specifies the source hardware media access control address that last sent this frame. Six bytes in length.

(continued)

continued

Frame Field	Description
Type or length	Specifies the protocol that originated the frame, or the amount of data in the frame. Two bytes in length.
Data	The data portion of the frame. May contain actual data, or be used for further protocol headers and descriptions. Up to 1500 bytes in length.
Cyclic Redundancy Check (CRC)	Used as a checksum on the overall frame contents to determine if data was delivered intact. Four bytes in length. This is not seen in a trace.

Frame Encapsulation

Often, the data portion of the frame may actually contain protocol-specific information, in addition to data. For example, for a TCP-based frame, the data field is segmented into:

- An IP datagram, which includes an IP header of 20 bytes, and IP data.

- A TCP-based frame, (included in the IP data) which consists of a TCP header of 20 bytes, and TCP data.

The TCP data would include any actual data that was being transmitted from the source host to the destination host. Network traffic analysis often requires looking at the different headers, as well as data fields, to determine the reason this frame was generated. The following is part of a frame captured by Network Monitor.

```
ETHERNET: ETYPE = 0x0800 : Protocol = IP: DOD Internet Protocol
ETHERNET: Destination address : 02608C8D95F8
ETHERNET: Source address : 02608C8D5B7B
ETHERNET: Frame Length : 60 (0x003C)
ETHERNET: Ethernet Type : 0x0800 (IP: DOD Internet Protocol)
IP: Total Length = 44 (0x2C)
IP: Fragment Offset = 0 (0x0) bytes
   IP: Time to Live = 32 (0x20)
   IP: Protocol = TCP - Transmission Control
   IP: CheckSum = 0x3B4F
   IP: Source Address = 131.107.2.211
   IP: Destination Address = 131.107.2.212
   IP: Data: Number of data bytes remaining = 24 (0x0018)
 TCP: ....S., len:   4, seq:    17357, ack:       0, win: 8192, src: 1025
dst: 139 (NBT Session)
   TCP: Source Port = 0x0401
   TCP: Destination Port = NETBIOS Session Service
   TCP: Sequence Number = 17357 (0x43CD)
   TCP: Acknowledgment Number = 0 (0x0)
TCP: Flags = 0x02 :.....S.
TCP: Window = 8192 (0x2000)
   TCP: CheckSum = 0x2350
TCP: Option Value = 1460 (0x5B4)
```

Comparing Network Protocols

The type of network traffic a specific function generates is somewhat dependent upon the protocol used. Some protocols base much of their traffic on broadcasts (NWLink), while others use more directed frames, such as Transmission Control Protocol/Internet Protocol (TCP/IP), which can have an impact on a wide area network (WAN). The impact is dependent upon whether broadcasts are being forwarded by the routers throughout the enterprise. If the broadcasts are not being forwarded some functions will operate on the local network, but not have complete functionality throughout the entire enterprise. If the broadcast traffic is being sent throughout the enterprise, complete functionality is available but at the cost of increased traffic on the WAN.

TCP/IP was designed to solve the disadvantages of protocols such as NetBEUI. IP delivers directed datagrams over a routed network environment while using minimum bandwidth, keeping broadcasts to a minimum. Microsoft recommends TCP/IP as the protocol of choice.

The following table compares TCP/IP and NWLink IPX/SPX (Internetwork Packet Exchange/Sequenced Packet Exchange) during four common network operations. The test data was generated on two 80486 computers, one with a 33-MHz processor, and the other with a 25-MHz processor. The client computer has 16 MB of RAM, while the server computer has 32 MB of RAM.

Network Function	TCP/IP	NWLink IPX/SPX (802.2)
Primary domain controller (PDC) start up	81 frames, 11,765 bytes, and 56.6 seconds.	148 frames, 22,410 bytes, and 86.6 seconds.
Windows 95 client start up	58 frames, 8729 bytes, and 22.2 seconds.	32 frames, 5904 bytes, and 15.0 seconds.
User logon validation	41 frames, 6715 bytes, and 2.5 seconds.	28 frames, 5488 bytes, and 2.3 seconds.
Transfer of a 2-MB file	1870 frames, 2,186,572 bytes, and 12.5 seconds.	1873 frames, 2,225,630 bytes, and 11.3 seconds.

Microsoft Network Monitor

A network packet analyzer is a tool that captures, filters, and analyzes network traffic. Data captured by a network packet analyzer can be saved for later analysis, or analyzed immediately after capture. Network packet analyzers can be a combination of specialized hardware and software, or simply software-based.

Network Monitor is a software-based traffic analysis tool. It allows a user to:

- Capture frames directly from the network.
- Display and filter captured frames, immediately after capture or at a later time.
- Edit captured frames and transmit them on to the network.
- Capture frames from a remote computer.

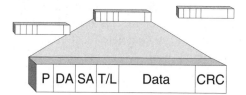

There are two versions of Network Monitor. The basic version is shipped with Windows NT 4.0, and the full version is shipped with Systems Management Server. The table below outlines the differences between these two versions of Network Monitor.

Function	Network Monitor (Simple)	Network Monitor (Full)
Local capturing	To and from the computer running Network Monitor only	All devices on the entire subnet
	Remote capturing	Not available
		Yes
Determining top user of network bandwidth	Not available	Yes
Determining which protocol consumed the most bandwidth	Not available	Yes
Determining which devices are routers	Not available	Yes
Resolving a device name into a media access control address	Not available	Yes
Editing and retransmitting network traffic	Not available	Yes

Installing Network Monitor

Network Monitor is included with Windows NT Server 4.0 (simple version) and with Microsoft Systems Management Server (full version). The full version of

Network Monitor can be installed on Windows for Workgroups, Windows 95, Windows NT Workstation, or Windows NT Server.

Software Installation

Network Monitor consists of two components: the Network Monitor application and the Network Monitor Agent.

Network Monitor Application

The Network Monitor application displays network statistics, captures and displays data, and allows the saving of captured data.

To install the simple version included with Windows NT Server, open Control Panel, Network. Click the **Services** tab. Click **Add**, and then select **Network Monitor Tools and Agent**.

To install the full version of Network Monitor, run **Setup.exe** from the Nmext\ Disk1 directory of the Systems Management Server 1.2 compact disc.

Network Monitor Agent

The Network Monitor Agent allows a computer to capture all network traffic, as well as provide the Network Segment object for Performance Monitor. This object allows the generation of basic network utilization information for computer and network analysis. The Network Monitor Agent must be installed on any computer that is to capture network traffic.

The Network Monitor Agent also has the ability to capture network traffic on a remote subnet. This is useful when analysis is required on a subnet remote to the network administrator. The client computer running the Network Monitor Agent captures and buffers network traffic locally. When the Network Monitor application attempts to display the traffic, it is sent over the network to the computer running the Network Monitor application for display and analysis. There are Network Monitor Agents for both Windows 95 and Windows NT.

Hardware Requirements

Network Monitor requires no special hardware other than a supported network adapter card. Windows NT 4.0 supports a newer version of the network device interface specification (NDIS). This new version, NDIS 4.0, allows a new capturing mode called "local only." This mode provides for capturing network frames without requiring the capturing computer to be placed into promiscuous mode, as did previous implementations of NDIS.

Note Promiscuous mode means the network adapter accepts all frames on the network cable, regardless of the destination address. Promiscuous mode is very taxing on the central processing unit (CPU) of the Network Monitor Agent computer. By not requiring entering into promiscuous mode, performance gains should be realized.

There is a list of Network Monitor tested and supported network adapters in the Windows NT 4.0 Hardware Compatibility List (HCL).

The Network Monitor Interface

The Network Monitor interface is typical of a network sniffer—real-time statistics are displayed as activity is captured on the network.

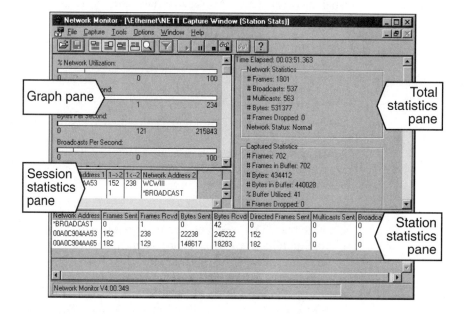

The first window to appear in Network Monitor is the Capture window. This window displays the basic Network Monitor interface. Menus and toolbar buttons are available to control the use of Network Monitor.

The Capture window provides different types of statistical data that is useful in analyzing overall network performance. The Capture window is divided into the four major areas listed in the following table.

Pane	Description
Graph	Displays the current activity as a set of bar charts indicating the % of Network Utilization, the Frames Per Second, Bytes Per Second, Broadcasts Per Second, and Multicasts Per Second during the capture process.
Session Statistics	Displays the summary of the conversations between two hosts, and which host is initiating broadcasts and multicasts.
Total Statistics	Displays statistics for the traffic detected on the network as a whole, the statistics for the frames captured, per second utilization statistics, and network adapter card statistics.
Station Statistics	Displays a summary of the total number of frames initiated by a host, the number of frames and bytes sent and received, and the number of broadcast and multicast frames initiated.

Capturing Data with Network Monitor

As data is being captured, information appears in each of the four sections of the Capture window. This includes current network statistics as well as statistics for the captured data

To capture network traffic, use one of the following three methods:

- From the **Capture** menu, click **Start**.
- Click the **Start Capture** button on the toolbar.
- Press the F10 function key.

To stop the capture, use one of the following three methods:

- From the **Capture** menu, click **Stop**.
- Click the **Stop Capture** button on the toolbar.
- Press the F11 function key.

A common method for controlling the amount of data that is captured is to set a capture filter. A capture filter describes which frames are to be captured, buffered, displayed, and saved. Before any frame can be buffered, it must pass through the filter. Filters are commonly configured either for specific types of traffic (protocols), such as IP, IPX, VINES, and so on, or on source or destination addresses. These addresses can be media access control (hardware) addresses, or protocol addresses (IP or IPX).

Once data has been captured, it can be analyzed immediately or saved to a capture file (.cap) for later analysis.

Displaying Data with Network Monitor

Network Monitor would not be useful if you were not able to easily view the captured data in a way that made viewing cryptic packet data more easily understood.

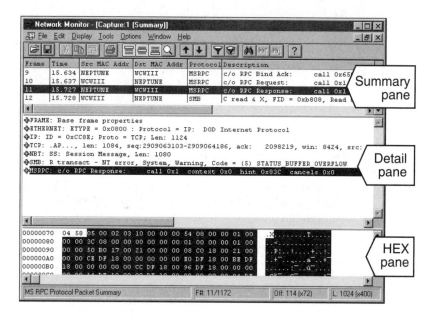

Data analysis with Network Monitor starts with viewing the data that has been captured. Data can be viewed through one of the following methods:

- From the **Capture** menu, click **Display Captured Data**.
- Press F12.
- Choose the **Display Captured Data** toolbar button.

Filtering Data

When viewing captured data, the Capture Summary window displays a summary of all frames captured. A display filter can be set to filter frames of interest, such as those from a particular host, or those using a particular protocol. Display filters can be configured for a specific protocol, such as browser, for a specific media access control or protocol address, or for a unique property of a frame, such as a specific source or destination port. Display filters are configured similarly to configuring capture filters.

Displaying Frames

The Network Monitor Capture Summary window contains three panes.

Summary Pane (Top)

This pane lists all frames that are included in the current view of the captured data. When a frame is highlighted in the Summary pane, Network Monitor displays the frame's contents in the Detail and Hex panes. Colors can be added to highlight specific frames.

You can sort (by clicking the mouse), move, and resize the nine columns in the Summary pane. These columns are:

- Frame: all frames captured during one capture session are numbered in the order of capture time. The frame number appears in this column.

- Time: this column displays the frame's capture time relative to the beginning of the capture process. It can be configured to display the time of day when the frame was captured, or time elapsed since the previous frame capture.

- Src MAC Addr (Source MAC Address): displays the hardware address of the computer that sent the frame.

- Dst MAC Addr (Destination MAC Address): displays the hardware address of the target computer.

- Protocol: the protocol used to transmit the frame.

- Description: a summary of the frame's contents. The summary information can show the first protocol used in that frame, the last protocol used in that frame, or an automatic selection.

- Src Other Addr (Source Other Address): an additional identifying address for the originator of the frame, other than the media access control address. This might be an IP or IPX address.

- Dst Other Addr (Destination Other Address): same as Src Other Addr, except it gives the destination of the frame instead of the source of the frame.

- Type Other Addr (Type Other Address): specifies which type of address is displayed in the previous two columns. For example, if the Src and Dst Other Addr fields are displaying IP or IPX addresses.

Detail Pane (Middle)

This pane displays protocol information for the frame currently highlighted in the Summary pane. When a frame contains several protocol layers, the Detail pane displays the outermost level first.

When selecting a protocol in the Detail pane, the associated hexadecimal strings for the current frame are highlighted (in the same color as that used for the protocol) in the Hex pane. If a protocol has a "+" beside it, more information can be displayed in the Detail pane by clicking the "+", double-clicking the protocol or by highlighting the protocol, and then pressing ENTER. When the protocol information is expanded, a line of data appears for each property associated with that frame.

Hexadecimal Pane (Bottom)

This pane displays in hexadecimal format the content of the selected frame. When information is highlighted in the Detail pane, the corresponding hexadecimal data appears highlighted in the Hex pane. This is often where analysis may center, especially when attempting to determine the appropriate application programming interface (API) call used in a transaction.

Installing Network Monitor

In this exercise, you install Network Monitor on your Windows NT Server-based computer.

➤ **To install Network Monitor**

In this procedure, you install the Network Monitor application that comes with Windows NT Server 4.0.

Note Complete this exercise logged on to your Windows NT Server-based computer as Administrator, and in the **Password** box, type **password**.

---

1. Right click the **Network Neighborhood**, then click **Properties**.

   The Network window.

2. Click **Services**, then click **Add**.

   The Select Network Services windows appears.

3. Select the **Network Monitor Tools and Agent**, then click **OK**.

   A Windows NT Setup window appears.

4. Enter the path to the Windows NT CD ROM installation directory (D:\i386)

   Files are copied to the local computer.

5. When all files are copied, click **Close.**

6. When prompted, Restart your computer.

Capturing Data with Network Monitor

In this exercise, you use Network Monitor to capture and display network traffic.

Note You will only be able to do this exercise if your computer is attached to a network.

► **To start Network Monitor**

In this procedure, you start the Network Monitor application.

1. Click the **Start** menu, and then point to **Programs**.

   A submenu appears.

2. Point to **Administrative Tools**, and then click **Network Monitor**.

   The **Network Monitor** window appears.

► **To capture network data**

In this procedure, you start the data capture process.

1. On the **Capture** menu, click **Start**.

   Network Monitor allocates buffer space for network data and begins capturing frames.

   Tip You can also start the capture by pressing F10, or by choosing the **Start Capture** toolbar button. It looks similar to the Play button of a CD-ROM drive.

2. Minimize Network Monitor, and then proceed to the next procedure to generate network traffic.

► **To generate network traffic**

In this procedure, you generate network traffic by creating a browsing the network.

1. Start **Network Neighborhood**, and then browse your and other domains.

   Lists of resources will appear.

2. Open a share on another computer.

   A list of files on the other computer will appear. This process will generate network traffic.

3. Close all windows related to **Network Neighborhood**.

➤ **To stop the network data capture**

In this procedure, you stop the data capture process.

1. Switch back to **Network Monitor**.

2. On the **Capture** menu, click **Stop**.

   Network Monitor stops capturing frames.

   Tip You can also stop the capture by pressing F11, or by choosing the **Stop Capture** toolbar button. It looks similar to the Stop button of a CD-ROM drive.

➤ **To view network data statistics**

In this procedure, you view the statistics of the current capture session.

1. In the **Session Statistics** pane, place the cursor anywhere in the **1→2** column, and then click the right mouse button.

   A new menu appears, displaying an option of **Sort Column**.

2. Click **Sort Column**.

   Network Monitor sorts the number of frames sent in descending order. The first address in this list shows the source of the most network frames.

➤ **To view computer names**

In this procedure, you view the names that are converted to media access control addresses.

1. On the **Capture** menu, click **Find All Names**.

   Network Monitor attempts to associate media access control addresses with computer names.

   When complete, a **Find All Names** message appears, indicating how many names it could associate.

2. Click **OK**.

   Some of the media access control addresses should have been resolved into computer names.

3. On the **Capture** menu, click **Addresses**.

   The **Address Database** dialog box appears displaying all the names in the database. Some of these names should have been resolved by the **Find All Names** option.

Viewing Data with Network Monitor

In this exercise, you use Network Monitor to view captured network frames.

➤ **To view captured data**

1. On the **Capture** menu, click **Display Captured Data**.

   The **Network Monitor Capture Summary** window appears, displaying the summary record of all frames captured.

Note You can also view the captured data by pressing F12, or by choosing the **Display Captured Data** toolbar button. It looks like a pair of glasses.

➤ **To highlight captured data**

In this procedure, you change the color of all frames that are Browser-based. This is useful when viewing frames for a particular protocol.

1. On the **Display** menu, click **Colors**.

   The **Protocol Colors** dialog box appears.

2. Under **Name**, click **BROWSER**.

   An X appears next to BROWSER.

3. Under **Colors**, set **Foreground** to the color red, and then click **OK**.

   The **Network Monitor Capture Summary** window appears, displaying all Browser frames in red.

➤ **To filter captured data**

In this procedure, you create a display filter to view only the frames that use Remote Procedure Calls (RPCs) to the Server service.

1. On the **Display** menu, click **Filter**.

   The **Display Filter** dialog box appears.

2. Double-click **Protocol==Any**.

   The **Expression** dialog box appears.

3. Click **Disable All**.

   All protocols move under **Disabled Protocols**.

4. In the **Disabled Protocols** list, click **R_SRVSVC**, and then click **Enable**.

   R_SRVSVC moves under **Enabled Protocols**.

5. Click **OK** to return to the **Display Filter** dialog box.

6. Click **OK**.

The **Network Monitor Capture Summary** window appears, displaying all frames that are R_SRVSVC-based. These frames are RPC calls that have been parsed down to the Server service.

➤ **To view frame details**

In this procedure, you view the details of a frame in the data captured and filtered by Network Monitor. Remember that you have created a display filter to only show R_SRVSVC frames.

1. Under the **Description** label, find a frame labeled **RPC Client call srvsvc: NetrShareEnum(..)**.

   This frame is a NetShareEnum request, which requests a list of shared re-sources. The next frame should be a **RPC Server response srvsvc: NetrShareEnum(..)**. This is the server's response to the client's request.

2. Double-click the frame labeled **RPC Server response srvsvc: NetrShareEnum(..)**.

   Three separate windows are displayed. The top window displays the frame summary; the middle window displays the selected frame details; and the bottom window displays the selected frame details in hexadecimal notation.

3. In the Detail (middle) window, select **FRAME** with a plus sign (+) preced-ing it. The plus sign indicates that the protocol can be expanded by double-clicking it. Expand the FRAME details.

Note To expand or collapse details, either click the "+"or "-", or double-click the field label.

The Frame properties expand to show more detail. Notice the size of the frame is listed as **Total frame length**. This field is important when analyzing data to see how large frames are.

4. Double-click **FRAME** with a minus sign (-) preceding it. The properties of the FRAME field are closed, and the minus sign changes back to a plus sign (+).

5. Double-click **ETHERNET**.

   The Ethernet properties expand to show more detail. Notice the **Destination address** of the target computer. This field is important when analyzing data to see if frames are directed, multicast, or broadcast.

   Notice the **Ethernet Type** is designated as 0x0800 (IP). This field designates the protocol used to transmit the frame.

6. Double-click **ETHERNET** to collapse its properties, and then double-click **IP** to expand its properties.

The IP properties expand to show more detail. The properties of interest are **Protocol**, which designates the higher layer TCP/IP protocol to receive the frame (in this case TCP), and the **Source Address** and **Destination Address**. These addresses are the IP addresses of the host that originated the frame, and the eventual target of the frame.

7. Double-click **IP** to collapse its properties, and then double-click **TCP** to expand its properties.

The TCP properties expand to show more detail. The properties of interest are **Source Port**, which designates the end point (service) of the frame (in this case NetBIOS Session Service); the **Sequence Number** and **Acknowledgment Number**, which are used to provide guaranteed delivery service; and **Flags**, which can designate special properties about the frame. In this frame, the flags set are **A**, for Acknowledgment field significant, and **P** for Push function.

8. Double-click **TCP** to collapse its properties, and then double-click **NBT** to expand its properties.

The NBT properties expand to show more detail. In this frame, there isn't much of interest, because it is a session message (transferring data from an earlier session request). Generally, the property of interest is **Destination Name** (or in some frames, it is labeled **Called Name**), which designates the target host's NetBIOS name that should receive this frame.

9. Double-click **NBT** to collapse its properties, and then double-click **SMB** to expand its properties.

The SMB properties expand to show more detail. The properties of interest are **SMB Status**, which designates the success or failure of the command (in this case success), and the **Command**. In this case, the command is **R transact**, which implies a response to a command. Expanding **SMB: Command = R transact**, and then selecting **Pipe function** reveals that the command was a named pipe command.

10. Double-click **SMB** to collapse its properties, and then double-click **MSRPC** to expand its properties.

The MSPRC properties expand to show more detail. The property of interest is **Operation Number**, which designates the command or API call requested. There is no Operation Number in this frame. It is listed in the previous frame (the RPC Client call srvsvc: NetShareEnum).

11. Double-click **MSRPC** to collapse its properties, and then double-click **R_SRVSVC** to expand its properties.

   The R_SRVSVC properties expand to show more detail. This is the actual API call to request a list of shared resources at the destination computer.

12. Expand each R_SRVSVC property with a "+" until you have expanded R_SRVSVC: LPSHARE_Info_1. Scroll down the properties to see a list of all shared resources on the server.

13. In the Hex window (bottom), use the scroll bar to scroll down in the data.

   Notice the data in the frame. You should be able to see the shared resources on the server. This was the same data as returned when browsing the server using Network Neighborhood.

▶ **To view frame statistics**

In this procedure, you view the capture statistics from the data captured by Network Monitor.

1. Double-click any frame in the **Summary** pane (top window).

   Notice the display returns to a single window, with the **Detail** and **Hex** panes closed.

2. On the **Display** menu, click **Disable Filter**.

   Notice all frames are displayed again.

3. Click the last frame in the capture.

   Notice the Time is **0.000**, the addresses are **000000000000**, the Protocol is **STATS**, and the Description is **Number of Frames Captured = .**

4. Double-click to expand this frame.

5. In the **Detail** pane, double-click **STATS**.

   Notice that all the captured statistics are available. Generally, of interest are **Elapsed Time**, **Total Frames Filtered While Capturing**, and **Total Bytes Filtered While Capturing**.

▶ **To save the capture**

In this procedure, you save the captured data. This makes it available for later analysis.

1. On the **File** menu, click **Save As**.

   A **Save Data As** dialog box appears allowing the naming of the file.

2. In the **File Name** box, type **browsing.cap** and then click **OK**.

3. On the **File** menu, click **Close**.

   The **Network Monitor Capture** window appears, still displaying the statistics from the last capture.

Lesson Summary

The following information summarizes the key points in this lesson:

- All Windows NT Server services impact the capacity of a network.

- Windows NT Server services are impacted by the kind of network traffic generated, how often network traffic is generated, and its relative impact on the network.

- Network Monitor is a network packet analyzer that captures, filters, and analyzes network traffic.

Lesson 2: Analyzing Client Initialization Traffic

Client initialization traffic is generated when a user logs on to a client computer. The client's network services are initialized and registered with the appropriate servers only during initialization. This lesson discusses the traffic generated when a client computer starts up.

After this lesson, you will be able to:

- List the tasks that contribute to client initialization traffic.
- Analyze DHCP traffic.
- Analyze WINS client traffic.
- Analyze traffic associated with establishing a file session.
- Analyze logon validation traffic.

Estimated lesson time: 30 minutes

Client Initialization Analysis

Client initialization traffic is generated when a client computer first starts. The following graphic categorizes client initialization traffic.

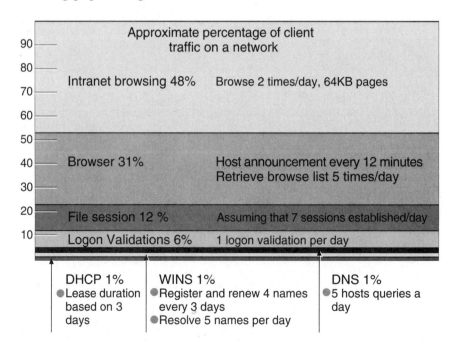

The following table lists the types of client initialization traffic that will be analyzed.

Traffic Type	Description
DHCP	Traffic generated during IP address acquisition, renewal, and release.
WINS	Traffic generated during NetBIOS name registration, resolution, renewal, and release.
File session	Traffic generated when two computers set up a session.
Logon validation	Traffic generated by a user logging on to the network and being validated by a domain controller.

Note The traffic numbers in the graphic represent the percentage of each task's traffic out of a total of 100 percent of the traffic initiated by the client during an eight hour day. These numbers are greatly influenced by the assumptions listed in the graphic. If users log on five times each day, or only once every two weeks, then the other traffic adjusts accordingly.

Analysis of each of these traffic types will be covered in this lesson. Capture and analysis of these network tasks can tell a network administrator how much of the network traffic is generated by client initialization services, and if any of it can be controlled or reduced.

Optimization techniques for each task follow the analysis section.

Analyzing DHCP Traffic

In order for users to join a network using Transmission Control Protocol/Internet Protocol (TCP/IP), their computers must be configured with proper TCP/IP addresses. The following graphic provides an overview of Dynamic Host Configuration Protocol (DHCP) client-to-server traffic.

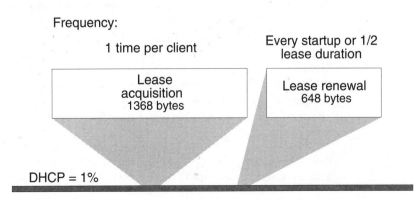

In an IP network environment, before a host (computer, router, printer, and so on) can access the network and communicate with other hosts, it must have a properly configured IP address and subnet mask. These values can be configured manually by the network administrator, or can be assigned automatically using dynamic host configuration protocol (DHCP).

The two phases of DHCP that will be analyzed in this section are:

- IP address lease acquisition to provide the initial address to a host.
- IP address lease renewal to renew the given address.

Relative Impact on the Network

DHCP traffic does not generate a significant use of network bandwidth during normal periods of usage. As such, it is an easy service to characterize. Capture and analysis of DHCP traffic will tell a network administrator if DHCP traffic is taking an excess amount of network bandwidth, possibly due to an extremely small lease duration, or due to a router forwarding DHCP messages from other subnets.

IP Address Lease Acquisition

When a DHCP client starts up, it needs to get an address. The following graphic illustrates some details of an IP address lease acquisition traffic.

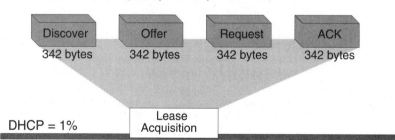

When a new DHCP client initializes, its first step is to acquire an IP address using DHCP. This process results in a conversation between the DHCP client and server consisting of four frames. Each frame is 342 bytes in size (older Microsoft clients used 590 byte DHCP frames) depending upon configuration options contained in the frame. This could include options such as router, Windows Internet Naming Service (WINS) server and Domain Name System (DNS) server address(es), and domain name.

These four frames take about one-quarter of a second and 1368 bytes of network traffic to complete. This traffic occurs one time for each client on the network.

Frames	Description
DHCP Discover	The first frame is the client computer's broadcast to locate a DHCP server. The client has no knowledge of any DHCP servers, so it must initiate a broadcast in order to find one.
DHCP Offer	Once a DHCP server has received the Discover frame, and determined that it can accommodate the client's request, it responds by identifying the IP address the client can lease.
DHCP Request	The client computer will select an offer and respond back to the DHCP server indicating it is accepting the offer.
DHCP ACK	Once a DHCP server has received the client's Request, it acknowledges the lease, providing the lease life, and any optional TCP/IP parameters.

Following are ways to identify DHCP frames, and characteristics of each portion of the frame that impacts network traffic. All four DHCP frames have the same basic characteristics.

```
1  7.081 WIN95      *BROADCAST   DHCP   Discover
2  7.156 DHCP_WINS  *BROADCAST   DHCP   Offer
3  7.159 WIN95      *BROADCAST   DHCP   Request
4  7.269 DHCP_WINS  *BROADCAST   DHCP   ACK
```

Ethernet Header

Following is a portion of the Ethernet header. Notice the Destination address is all Fs, indicating a media access control layer broadcast. Each of the four frames in the lease acquisition phase use broadcast frames. All hosts must accept these frames and process them as far as they can (in this case, until they determine they do not have the designated destination User Datagram Protocol (UDP) Port).

```
ETHERNET: ETYPE = 0x0800 : Protocol = IP: DOD Internet Protocol
  + ETHERNET: Destination address : FFFFFFFFFFFF
  + ETHERNET: Source address : 02608C43A151
  ETHERNET: Frame Length : 342 (0x0156)
  ETHERNET: Ethernet Type : 0x0800 (IP: DOD Internet Protocol)
  ETHERNET: Ethernet Data: Number of data bytes remaining = 328
(0x0148)
```

IP Header

Below is a portion of the IP header. Notice the Source Address is 0.0.0.0, indicating the client does not yet have an IP address. The Destination Address is 255.255.255.255, indicating a network broadcast. This means that if network routers support forwarding of DHCP messages, all four of these frames would be forwarded to other subnets.

```
IP: ID = 0x0; Proto = UDP; Len: 328
IP: Header Length = 20 (0x14)
IP: Total Length = 328 (0x148)
IP: Protocol = UDP - User Datagram
   IP: CheckSum = 0x99A6
   IP: Source Address = 0.0.0.0
   IP: Destination Address = 255.255.255.255
   IP: Data: Number of data bytes remaining = 308 (0x0134)
```

UDP Header

Below is a portion of the UDP header. Notice the Source Port is 68 (BOOTP Client), while the Destination Port is 67 (BOOTP Server). Network routers would need to support these ports in order to forward the DHCP Discover message. If the routers do not forward these ports, either a separate DHCP relay agent is required or DHCP servers are required on each subnet that contains DHCP clients.

```
UDP: IP Multicast: Src Port: BOOTP Client, (68); Dst Port: BOOTP Server
(67); Length = 308 (0x134)
   UDP: Source Port = BOOTP Client
   UDP: Destination Port = BOOTP Server
   UDP: Total length = 308 (0x134) bytes
   UDP: CheckSum = 0xF596
   UDP: Data: Number of data bytes remaining = 300 (0x012C)
```

DHCP Header

The final portion of the frame is the DHCP header. Each of the four frames have the same basic properties. The Client identifier is the hardware address of the requesting client. In later frames, a Server identifier is added to designate the destination DHCP server for the frame.

```
DHCP: Discover        (xid=05DE05DE)
DHCP: Transaction ID  (xid) = 98436574 (0x5DE05DE)
DHCP: Client IP Address (ciaddr) = 0.0.0.0
 DHCP: Your  IP Address (yiaddr) = 0.0.0.0
 DHCP: Server IP Address (siaddr) = 0.0.0.0
 DHCP: Relay IP Address (giaddr) = 0.0.0.0
 DHCP: Client Ethernet Address (chaddr) = 02608C43A151
 DHCP: Server Host Name (sname) = <Blank>
 DHCP: Boot File Name  (file)  = <Blank>
 DHCP: Magic Cookie = [OK]
 DHCP: Option Field    (options)
  DHCP: DHCP Message Type  = DHCP Discover
  DHCP: Client-identifier  = (Type: 1) 02 60 8c 43 a1 51
   DHCP: Host Name         = Win95
```

IP Address Lease Renewal

With every restart of the client, and periodically, it is necessary to renew the IP address acquired from DHCP. The following graphic illustrates DHCP address renewal traffic.

Frequency: Every startup or every 1/2 lease duration

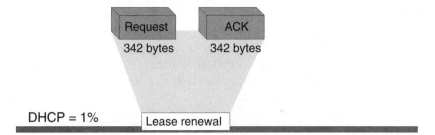

A DHCP client renews its IP address lease before it expires. When a client renews an IP address using DHCP, the conversation is a simple one consisting of the last two frames of the IP address lease phase. Renewal of a DHCP lease occurs two different ways:

- At startup, the client computer requests a renewal of its current IP address with a DHCP Request frame and, if successful, the DHCP server responds with a DHCP ACK frame. The client uses broadcast frames for this process.

- At one-half of the lease duration period, which is a configurable length, clients also renew their IP addresses. At this time, the client issues a DHCP Request frame directly to its DHCP server, and the server will respond with a DHCP ACK, if the address is still valid for the client.

```
1   18.717 WIN95      DHCP_WINS   DHCP    Request
2   18.801 DHCP_WINS  WIN95       DHCP    ACK
```

The DHCP Request and ACK frames for a periodic renewal are directed, not broadcast as they are during address acquisition. This is because the client has renewed the address from the server at startup, so it knows the server's address.

These two frames total 684 bytes in size, and only take 100 milliseconds to complete. The DHCP client will retry its renewal attempt twice, and if unsuccessful, will try again at the next renewal period. If the client is unable to renew its address, and its lease expires, it will attempt to acquire a new address using the entire four frame process as if it were a new DHCP client.

Optimizing DHCP Traffic

Controlling the traffic generated by DHCP can offer small benefits when reducing network traffic. The following graphic illustrates the methods used to control the network traffic generated by DHCP.

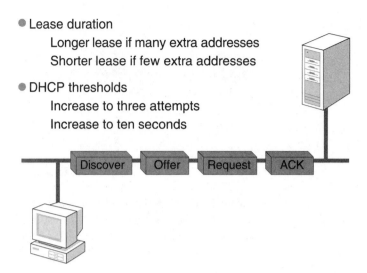

- Lease duration
    Longer lease if many extra addresses
    Shorter lease if few extra addresses
- DHCP thresholds
    Increase to three attempts
    Increase to ten seconds

The implementation of DHCP does not significantly increase the amount of network traffic. The entire process of acquiring an IP address lease through DHCP takes less than one second (approximately 300 milliseconds) on a clear network.

DHCP conversations generally occur in the following instances:

- A DHCP client initializes for the first time (all four frames).

- An automatic renewal, which is only done every one-half lease life (three days by default, or every 36 hours), takes two packets (DHCP Request and DHCP ACK), and approximately 200 milliseconds.

- When a client is moved to a new subnet (DHCP Request, DHCP ACK, and then the four frames as if this were a new client).

- When a DHCP client replaces its network adapter card (all four frames).

- Whenever a client manually refreshes or releases its address with IPCONFIG.

- Whenever a client restarts (DHCP Request and DHCP ACK as broadcast traffic).

This should not have a significant affect on network traffic, even if multiple DHCP clients are acquiring or renewing addresses simultaneously.

Lease Duration

To reduce the amount of traffic generated by DHCP, it is possible to adjust the lease duration for IP address leases. This is done using DHCP Manager, and adjusting the **Lease Duration** in the **Scope Properties** dialog box. Increasing the lease life from the default of three days to, for example 30 days, would certainly reduce the frequency of renewals by the DHCP clients on the network. It is recommended to use short lease lives when the number of clients that will use DHCP to acquire IP addresses is close to the number of IP addresses that can be assigned through DHCP. If the number of DHCP available IP addresses is much larger than the number of DHCP hosts, then longer lease periods make more sense.

DHCP Thresholds

If an internetwork consists of routers that support BOOTP-relay agents and Request for Comments (RFC) 1542, these routers can relay the DHCP Discover messages to other subnets which contain DHCP servers. Most newer router software supports configuring the number of retries that must occur before the router forwards the local request to other subnets. This retry is usually implemented as the number of seconds the request has been outstanding (implemented in the Seconds field). If the local DHCP server is busy, and does not answer the request immediately, configuring this parameter to 10 would allow for two requests from the client that would stay on the local subnet, and then upon the third request, it would be forwarded to other subnets in an attempt to find a DHCP server.

Most DHCP Relay agent software allows for the configuration of IP addresses of DHCP servers that are known throughout the enterprise. In this case, the relay agent can forward the DHCP requests to the appropriate subnets, and not send to subnets that do not contain DHCP servers.

Analyzing DHCP Address Lease Traffic

In this exercise, you will analyze network traffic resulting from the initialization of a Windows 95-based computer, including acquiring an IP address.

You will view capture files that are located on the course CD.

➤ **To load a saved capture file**

Note Complete this exercise from the Network Monitor Capture window.

1. Start **Network Monitor**. If you do not have a network, a message will appear stating you have no network. Click **OK**.

2. On the **File** menu, click **Open**.

   The **Open File** dialog box appears.

3. Open Bootw95.cap.

   The Network Monitor Capture Summary window appears displaying the data from the saved file.

➤ **To analyze DHCP Discover traffic**

In this procedure, you analyze the network traffic generated during IP address acquisition using DHCP. Frames 1 through 4 of this capture file represent the IP address lease process using DHCP. Frame 1 is the DHCP Discover message.

1. Frame 1 is the client's request to find a DHCP server that can lease it an IP address. Double-click frame number 1 to open the Detail and Hex panes. Use these window panes to answer the following questions.

2. In the Detail pane, click the plus sign (+) next to **Frame** to expand the Frame properties. How many bytes are in the frame?

   _____

   _____

3. Click the minus sign (-) to collapse the Frame properties, and then display the Ethernet properties.

4. What is the Destination address?

   _____

   _____

5. Why is this address used?

   _____

   _____

6. Click the minus sign (-) to collapse the Ethernet properties, and then click the plus sign (+) to display the IP properties.

7. What is the **Source Address**?

   _____

   _____

8. Why is this address used?

_____

_____

9. What is the Destination Address?

_____

_____

10. Why is this address used?

_____

_____

11. Collapse the IP properties, and then display the UDP properties.

12. What is the **Destination Port** name and number?

_____

_____

The significance of using BOOTP ports is that in order to forward these requests to another DHCP server on a different subnet, the router would need to support forwarding of BOOTP messages.

13. Collapse the UDP properties, and then display the DHCP properties.

Notice that all IP addresses are blank because the client does not currently have an address and does not know the address of the server.

➤ **To analyze DHCP Offer traffic**

In this procedure, analyze frame 2, which is the DHCP Offer message.

1. In the Summary pane (top), select frame number 2. This is the DHCP server's response to the client's DHCP Discover message.

2. How large is this frame?

_____

_____

Hint: check **Frame: Total frame length**.

3. Did the server respond directly to the client?

_____

_____

Hint: check **Ethernet: Destination Address**.

4. What IP address did the server reply to?

_____

_____

Hint: check **IP: Destination Address**.

5. Why is this address used?

_____

_____

6. What IP address is the server offering to the client?

_____

_____

Hint: check **DHCP: Your IP Address**.

➤ **To analyze DHCP Request traffic**

In this procedure, you analyze frame 3, which is the DHCP Request message.

1. Frame 3 is the client's request of the offered IP address. Is the destination for this reply to the specific server?

_____

_____

Hint : check **Ethernet: Destination Address** as well as **IP: Destination Address**.

2. Why was this method used, when the client knows the server's address?

_____

_____

3. How does a DHCP server know that the client is accepting its offer if the Request message is broadcast to all DHCP servers?

_____

_____

Hint: check **DHCP: Option Field Server Identifier**.

4. What IP address was accepted by the client?

_____

_____

Hint: check **DHCP: Option Field Requested Address**.

➤ **To analyze DHCP ACK traffic**

In this procedure, you analyze frame 4, which is the DHCP ACK message.

1. Frame 4 is the DHCP server's acknowledgment of the IP address lease. How many hosts received this reply?

_____

_____

Hint: check **Ethernet: Destination Address** as well as **IP: Destination Address**.

2. How long is the lease that was accepted?

_____

_____

Hint: check **DHCP: Option Field IP Address Lease Time**.

3. When will be the next time DHCP traffic is generated by this client?

_____

_____

Hint: check **DHCP: Option Field Renewal Time Value (T1)**.

4. How long did it take to acquire the IP address?

_____

_____

Analyzing DHCP Address Renewal Traffic

In this exercise, you analyze DHCP IP address lease renewal traffic.

➤ **To analyze DHCP address renewal traffic**

In this procedure, you analyze the network traffic generated during IP address renewal using DHCP.

1. Open Bootntw.cap.

2. Frame 1 is the client's request to renew its IP address. How many hosts received this request?

_____

_____

Hint: check **Ethernet** and **IP Destination Addresses**.

3. What IP address was requested by the client?

_____

_____

Hint: check **DHCP: Option Field Requested Address**.

4. Frame 2 is the server's response to the renewal request. When will be the next time DHCP traffic is generated by this client?

_____

_____

Hint: check **DHCP: Option Field Renewal Time Value (T1)**.

5. How long did it take to renew the IP address?

_____

_____

6. How much total traffic was generated by the renewal?

_____

_____

Hint: add the **Frame Total frame length** of frames 1 and 2.

Analyzing WINS Client Traffic

The next step TCP/IP clients must take is to register their NetBIOS names. The following graphic illustrates an overview of the network traffic generated by the implementation of WINS.

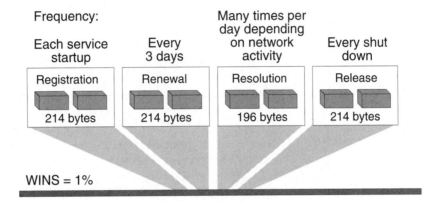

Once a computer has initialized its IP address, the next thing it does is register NetBIOS names. Most access of network resources involves using computer names. Networked computers register their computer name as a NetBIOS name for network access. These names then need to be converted to IP addresses to be provided in the IP portion of a frame. NetBIOS names are registered, resolved, renewed, and released using either b-node broadcasts or using a NetBIOS Name Server, such as WINS. The benefit to using a name server, such as WINS, is that traffic is directed, not broadcast. Broadcast traffic is very costly, because each host must process the frame until it determines it is not able to accommodate the request. With WINS, all hosts—except the WINS server—will discard the frame as soon as they determine the destination media access control (MAC) address is not their own. All NetBIOS over TCP/IP name service functions use UDP Port 137.

Relative Impact on Network

WINS client-related traffic does affect the available network bandwidth, although it does not significantly impact it. Even so, it is important to understand the traffic and to plan for it. If the network is saturated, it is possible to reduce the frequency of WINS traffic, thus freeing bandwidth for other services.

Name Registration and Renewal

NetBIOS names need to be registered for every service or application that supports NetBIOS. The following graphic illustrates name registration and renewal traffic.

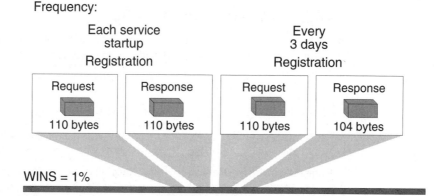

NetBIOS names need to be registered for every service or application that supports NetBIOS. Examples include Workstation and Server services, Network Monitor as an application, and special names to indicate roles on the network, such as primary domain controller (PDC) or backup domain controller (BDC). The actual number of names depends on the specific network services and applications the client computer initializes. Typically, a client would initialize three or four names.

Each name registered generates a total of 214 bytes of network traffic, and takes generally well under 100 milliseconds to complete. Frames sent are as follows:

- A NetBIOS name registration request is directed to the WINS server for each name needed. Each name registration request requires a frame of 110 bytes in size.

```
8  10.135 WIN95     DHCP_WINS   NBT NS: Registration req. for
WIN95    <03>
```

- The WINS server responds with a success or failure message. The response message is 104 bytes in size. If the name is unique a success message is returned to the requesting computer. If the name is not unique, the WINS server will query the registered owner of the name to determine if it is still an active name. If it is, a failure is returned to the requesting client indicating the name is already in use.

```
9  10.185 DHCP_WINS  WIN95      NBT NS: Registration (Node
Status) resp. for WIN95      <03>, Success
```

Name Renewal

When a name is successfully registered with the WINS server, it responds with a success message which includes a time to live (TTL). The TTL indicates when the client will be required to renew the name. Renewing a name registers it again for another TTL period. The TTL determines the amount of traffic that is generated through WINS for name renewals.

The default configuration for the WINS server establishes a renewal interval of 144 hours, or six days, so the server assigns a TTL of 518,400 seconds. As a result, this pattern will be repeated every three days, as WINS clients renew their names every one-half TTL.

The following table presents commonly registered names by a Microsoft client computer.

Name Registered	Description
Computername <00>	Registered by the Workstation service of the client.
Computername <03>	Registered by the Messenger service. This allows the host to receive messages, such as *net send computername*.
Username <03>	Registered by the Messenger service. This allows the user to receive messages, such as *net send username*.
Computername	Registered by the Server service. It appear as *computername* <20>, depending on the utility used to view the names registered. This allows the host to receive connection requests from other hosts.
Workgroup or domainname <00>	Registered as a Group NetBIOS Name, as opposed to a Unique NetBIOS Name, as was the computername. This registers the computer as a member of the domain or workgroup.
Workgroup or domainname <1E>	Registered as a Group NetBIOS Name and is used for browser elections.
Domainname <1B>	Registers the local computer as the domain master browser for the domain. This is registered as a Unique NetBIOS Name.
Domainname <1C>	Registers the local computer as a domain controller for the domain. This is registered as a Group NetBIOS Name.
Workgroup or domainname <1D>	Registers the local client as the local subnet's master browser for the workgroup or domain. This is registered as a Unique NetBIOS Name.

Name Resolution

The next type of traffic produced is name resolution, which happens every time the client accesses a computer name or NetBIOS application. The following graphic illustrates name resolution traffic.

Frequency: Every name access attempt

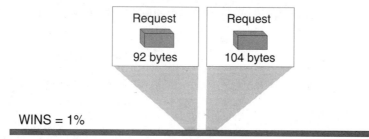

For TCP/IP networks, name resolution converts a computer or host name into an IP address for IP layer communications. The process of resolving NetBIOS names into IP addresses is called NetBIOS name resolution. WINS acts as a NetBIOS name server to provide this resolution of registered names into IP addresses.

Name resolution traffic occurs very frequently on the network. For example, during logon validation, resource browsing, server connections and print job notifications, names must be resolved and name resolution traffic occurs.

Name resolution is normally a two frame conversation, requiring 196 bytes of traffic.

- To resolve a NetBIOS name, the client sends a Name Query Request to the WINS server. This request contains the name to be resolved, as well as a flag indicating it is a query. This occurs for every access attempt of a computer, unless the name and address is present in the NetBIOS name cache. Resolved names reside in the cache for 10 minutes by default.

  ```
  25  24.548 WIN95   DHCP_WINS   NBT NS: Query req. for BDC3
  ```

- If the name queried is registered in the WINS database, the WINS server responds with a Name Query Response frame. It includes a flag to indicate a response to the query, and the IP address of the registered owner of the name.

  ```
  26  24.551 DHCP_WINS  WIN95    NBT NS: Query (Node Status)
  resp. for BDC3, Success
  ```

If the name is not registered with WINS, the WINS server will respond with a "Requested name does not exit" message. The client will then resort to b-node broadcasts in an attempt to resolve the name, assuming the target host is not a WINS client.

Name Release

Finally, when a service stops or a client shuts down, the registered names are released. The following graphic illustrates name release traffic.

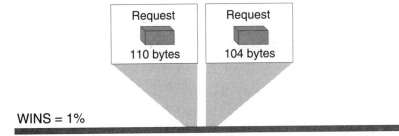

Frequency: Every service shutdown

Once a name has been registered by a computer, the name is owned by that host until it releases the name. When a host stops a service, or shuts down, it releases the name. Releasing a name makes it available for another computer to register. The actual release process includes:

- A release request sent to the WINS server (the same 110 bytes as a registration).

  ```
  1  7.883  WIN95   DHCP_WINS  NBT NS: Release req. for USER3
  <03>
  ```

- A success frame returned by the WINS server (104 bytes). This message designates the successful release of the name by assigning a TTL of 0.

  ```
  2  7.936  DHCP_WINS WIN95    NBT NS: Release (Node Status)
  resp. for USER3     <03>, Success
  ```

There will be two frames (one request and one response) for each name that the client computer has registered.

Optimizing WINS Client-to-Server Traffic

WINS traffic can be optimized through configuration of the Renewal Interval. The following graphic illustrates WINS client-to-server optimization techniques.

- Disable unnecessary services

- Increase NetBIOS name cache

- Implement LMHOSTS

- Adjust renewal rate

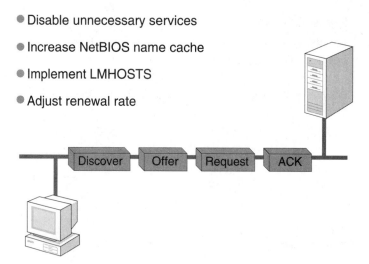

Every NetBIOS name that is registered with a WINS server takes:

- Two frames for registration at client startup.
- Two frames for renewal (every three days by default).
- Two frames for name resolution every attempt to access it by another computer.
- Two frames to release the name when the service or client stops.

There are several techniques for reducing this traffic.

Disable Unnecessary Services

WINS registration and renewal traffic can be lessened by disabling unnecessary network services. Each service that supports NetBIOS must register itself with WINS. If that service is never used, registration time and traffic is wasted, as well as the accompanying renewal traffic. For example, if a computer is not providing NetDDE functions, disable that service. The server service can also be disabled if the client is not providing any network resources.

Increase the NetBIOS Name Cache

After a NetBIOS name has been resolved, it is a placed in an internal NetBIOS name cache. The cache is checked before initiating a request to the WINS server whenever name resolution occurs.

By default, entries stay in the cache for 10 minutes (600,000 milliseconds). Increasing this to a large value will reduce WINS queries for frequently used servers.

To allow entries to remain in the local cache for a longer duration adjust the HKEY_LOCAL_MACHINE\SYSTEM\CurrentControlSet\Services\NetBT\ Parameters\CacheTimeout to a higher value. This would require fewer resolution attempts for frequently used names.

Implement LMHOSTS   *disable it will ↑ speed in access*

Another method of reducing WINS name resolution traffic is to use the LMHOSTS file. LMHOSTS provides resolution of NetBIOS names to IP addresses using a static American Standard Code for Information Interchange (ASCII) text file. The disadvantage of the LMHOSTS file is that it is not dynamic like the WINS server. This means if a new server is brought online, it would need to be manually added to the LMHOSTS file.

Pre-loading an entry from the LMHOSTS file into the NetBIOS name cache would prevent any network traffic from occurring during resolution of that name, as it would be permanently entered into the NetBIOS name cache. This can be beneficial for a commonly accessed server, or set of servers.

Note There is a method that allows the sharing of a centralized LMHOSTS file. This will produce network traffic at startup to find the file, and search for preloaded entries, as well as network traffic during name query attempts.

Adjust the Renewal Rate

While it is possible to adjust the renewal rate (or TTL) of registered names using WINS Manager, it is not recommended. WINS renewal does not generate a large amount of traffic, so the default of six days is adequate. If there is justification to change the TTL, adjust the renewal interval in WINS Manager. The TTL indicates the amount of time the name is reserved for the client's IP address. The Microsoft implementation of WINS configures the client computers to automatically renew their registered names every one-half of the TTL. With default configuration, this would occur every 72 hours. Thus, if a WINS client registered six names (for various network services) at startup, it would renew these same six names every 72 hours.

Analyzing WINS Name Registration Traffic

In this exercise, you analyze name registration traffic from a Windows 95 client startup.

➤ **To analyze WINS name registration traffic**

In this procedure, you analyze the network traffic generated during WINS name registration.

1. If it is not already open, open Bootw95.cap.

2. What is the first name to be registered by the client?

    _____

    _____

    Hint: check **NBT: Question Name** in frame 8.

3. What service is the name registered for?

    _____

    _____

    Hint: refer to Lesson 2, "Analyzing and Optimizing Client Initialization Traffic."

4. Was the name successfully registered?

    _____

    _____

    Hint: check the NBT header of frame number 9.

5. How much traffic was generated by registering this name?

    _____

    _____

6. Was the registration process directed or broadcast?

    _____

    _____

    Hint: check **Ethernet** and **IP Destination Addresses** of frames 8 and 9.

7. How many names were attempted to be registered by the Windows 95 client?

_____

_____

8. How much name registration traffic was generated by the Windows 95 client?

_____

_____

9. When will the next WINS name registration traffic occur on this client?

_____

_____

Hint: check **NBT: Time To Live** in any of the Success response messages from the WINS server to the client.

➤ To analyze name registration conflict traffic

In this procedure, you analyze the network traffic generated during a conflict during WINS name registration.

1. If it is not already open, open Bootntw.cap.

2. In frame 77, the client attempts to register User1 <03>. What kind of response was returned?

_____

_____

Hint: Check the NBT header of frame 78.

3. What did the WINS server do next?

_____

_____

Hint: check frame 81.

4. Was the name still active at the other computer?

_____

_____

Hint: check frame 82.

5. What response did the WINS server then return to the requesting client (NTW1)?

_____

_____

Analyzing WINS Name Resolution Traffic

In this exercise, you will analyze name resolution traffic using WINS.

➤ **To analyze name resolution traffic**

In this procedure, you will analyze the network traffic generated during WINS name resolution.

1. If it is not already open, open Bootntw.cap.

2. Frame 10 is the first name query request. Was this request broadcast or directed?

_____

_____

3. How large was the request?

_____

_____

4. What name is being queried for in frame 10?

_____

_____

Hint: check **NBT: Question Name**.

5. How many domain controllers were registered in DOMAIN0?

_____

_____

Hint: check the NBT response in frame 11.

6. How long did it take to resolve the query to DOMAIN0 <1C>?

_____

_____

7. How much total traffic was generated by the resolution request?

_____

_____

8. What name is being queried for in frame 24?

_____

_____

9. How long did it take for the WINS server to respond to the request?

_____

_____

10. How much traffic was generated by this resolving this name?

_____

_____

Analyzing File Session Traffic

Most network function require sessions to be established. The following graphic illustrates an overview of the network traffic generated by connecting to network resources.

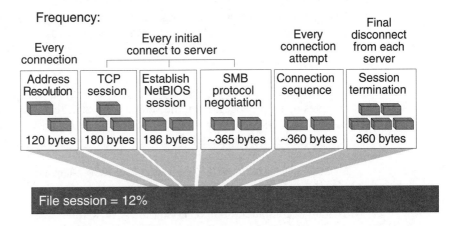

With the exception of name resolution traffic (DHCP, WINS, or DNS), communications between computers requires the establishment of a session.

Relative Impact on the Network

The amount of traffic necessary to establish a file session with a server is not large, only about 11 frames and 1300 bytes. If a user connects to multiple resources on a single server, only one session is established. Each connection would generate the traffic necessary to establish the connection, but not the session. If each user establishes multiple sessions per day, this can impact network traffic. Most file session traffic occurs after session establishment when the files are accessed on the server.

File session traffic is relatively light, and there is little that can be done to optimize it. The more significant amount of traffic is typically generated after a connection is made. However, this same set of frames is used during several types of communications. It is helpful to recognize the session traffic as part of the analysis of other types of traffic.

Establishing a Connection

There are six steps that take place to establish a file session. These same steps will be referred to as part of other types of traffic.

The first step a client performs when establishing a file session with a server is to resolve, or map, the destination computer's name into an IP address. This process is called NetBIOS name resolution, and was discussed in the previous topic.

Media Access Control (MAC) Address Resolution

Once a client has resolved the target NetBIOS name into an IP address, it must then resolve, or map, the IP address into a media access control, or hardware, address. This process is called address resolution, and utilizes the Address Resolution Protocol (ARP).

The address resolution process is a simple one, consisting of a single request of 60 bytes being broadcast from the source computer, requesting the target computer, identified by IP address, to respond with its media access control address. This request is called an ARP Request.

```
5  2.446  WIN95    *BROADCAST  ARP_RARP ARP: Request, Target IP:
131.107.2.210
```

The target computer, upon receiving the ARP Request and identifying its IP address, responds with an ARP Reply, which includes its media access control address. This reply is also 60 bytes in size.

```
6  2.447  PDC3   WIN95     ARP_RARP ARP: Reply, Target IP:
131.107.2.217 Target Hdwr Addr: 02608C43A1
```

These two frames generate a total of 120 bytes of network traffic, and generally will be repeated every time the two computers need to communicate, as the address mapping is only cached for a maximum of 10 minutes.

TCP Session Establishment

Once a client has resolved the target IP address into a media access control address, it can proceed to establish a TCP session. Two hosts must have a TCP session established before any TCP-based communications can take place. TCP offers guaranteed delivery service, which is what file sessions require, thus the need for a TCP session. This process is sometimes called a TCP three-way handshake.

```
7   2.448   WIN95   PDC3    TCP .S, seq: 514312-514315, ack: 0
8   2.449   PDC3    WIN95   TCP .A..S., seq: 73377571-73377574, ack:
514313
9   2.450   WIN95   PDC3    TCP .A, seq: 514313-514313, ack: 73377572
```

These three frames generate a total of 180 bytes of traffic. This sequence only needs to be done once per client and server. Multiple file connections can be established over one TCP session.

NetBIOS Session Establishment

Once a client has established a TCP session, it can proceed with the establishment of a NetBIOS session. Two hosts must have a NetBIOS session established before any further communications can take place. The destination server must validate that it can accept another NetBIOS session, and that the requested name is correct.

```
10  2.450   WIN95   PDC3    NBT SS: Session Request, Dest: PDC3    ,
Source: WIN95
11  2.452   PDC3    WIN95   NBT SS: Positive Session Response
```

These two frames generate a total of 186 bytes of traffic. This sequence only needs to be done once per client and server. Multiple file connections can be established over one NetBIOS session.

SMB Protocol Negotiation

Now that the required TCP session has been established, and the NetBIOS session request has been accepted, the two computers must now negotiate their server message block (SMB) protocols. In this procedure, the client sends a list of all the SMB protocols, called dialects, that it understands to the server.

```
12  2.454   WIN95   PDC3    SMB C negotiate, Dialect = NT LM 0.12
```

The server, upon receiving the list, selects the highest common SMB level understood by the client and the server, and responds to the client indicating the dialect
with which they will communicate. SMB dialects dictate features such as long file
name support, UNI code support, and so on. Each version of client, whether it is
Windows for Workgroups, Windows 95, or Windows NT, support different levels
of SMB dialects.

```
13   2.457   PDC3    WIN95      SMB R negotiate, Dialect # = 5
```

These two frames generate a total of 339 to 379 bytes of traffic, depending upon
the level of SMBs understood. This sequence only needs to be done once per
client and server. Multiple file connections can be established over one set of
negotiated SMB protocols.

Connecting and Disconnecting

Once a session has been established, the actual connection can be made. Data is
then transferred and the connection is broken. The following graphic illustrates
the traffic generated in connecting and disconnecting a shared resource.

Frequency:

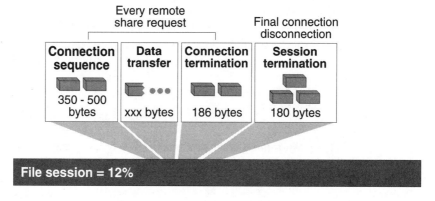

Once the TCP and NetBIOS sessions have been established, and the SMB protocol has been negotiated, the actual connection to the shared network directory can
occur. At this point files are accessed and copied across the network, and finally
the session is terminated.

Connection Sequence

The client sends an SMB session setup and tree connect request to the server,
indicating the share name it desires connection to as well as the user name and
password of the user requesting the connection.

```
14  2.470  WIN95   PDC3    SMB C session setup & X, Username = USER3,
and C tree connect & X
```

The server, upon receiving the request, validates the user name and password, and if able to accept another tree connect to this resource, responds with a success message.

```
15  2.531  PDC3   WIN95    SMB R session setup & X, and R tree connect
& X, Type = A:
```

These two frames generate a varying amount of traffic, depending upon user name, target server name and share name, as well as SMB command options requested by the client. For example, a standard request from a Windows 95 client is around 360 bytes, whereas a Windows NT Workstation connect request can be over 500 bytes.

The entire process of establishing a TCP session, NetBIOS session, SMB protocol negotiation, and a tree connection took 11 frames and about 100 milliseconds from a Windows 95-based client to the Windows NT Server 4.0-based computer in a test environment.

Data Transfer

Once the connection has been established, the vast majority of the network traffic will be generated, as files are accessed from the server and copied or updated by the client.

Analyzing the traffic generated during data transfer can be accomplished by determining an average file size on the server, determining how often files are accessed, and analyzing the efficiency of the installed protocol in transferring the data files. For example, using TCP/IP to transfer a 2-MB file generated 1870 frames, using 2,186,572 bytes in the test environment.

Session Termination

When the user has completed the access of files on the remote directory, the connection can be terminated. Disconnecting a remote drive is a simple process of requesting the disconnection, and the server responding with a success message. Unlike the connection request (where the client designated the server and share name to connect to), for a disconnect request, the client specifies the tree ID (TID) of the remote drive to be disconnected. The TID was assigned by the server in the response to the connection request.

```
34  12.929 WIN95   PDC3    SMB C tree disconnect
35  12.931 PDC3   WIN95    SMB R tree disconnect
```

These two frames, totaling 186 bytes, would be repeated for each disconnection request.

When the last file connection to a server is disconnected, the client and server will then terminate the TCP session. This process involves the client requesting the server to close the session, the server requesting the client to close its session, and a final acknowledgment by the client.

```
36   12.935 WIN95   PDC3    TCP.A...F, seq: 515373-515373, ack: 73379497
37   12.937 PDC3    WIN95   TCP.A...F, seq: 73379497-73379497, ack:
515374
38   12.938 WIN95   PDC3    TCP.A...., seq: 515374-515374, ack: 73379498
```

These three frames generate 180 bytes of network traffic. At this point, if the client wants to connect to another shared resource on the server, the entire process begins again.

Optimizing File Session Traffic

There is limited ability to control file session traffic. The following graphic illustrates the methods used to control the network traffic generated by user file sessions.

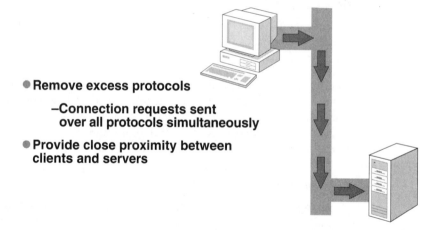

● **Remove excess protocols**

  –**Connection requests sent over all protocols simultaneously**

● **Provide close proximity between clients and servers**

The bulk of file session traffic happens after a session is established. However, session establishment traffic is repeated any time one computer needs to establish a session with another computer. There are at least two methods that can help limit the amount of traffic.

Remove Excess Protocols

The best way to optimize file session traffic is to remove any excess protocols, as connection requests are sent over all protocols simultaneously. Removing protocols not needed will reduce the number of frames on the network.

Provide Close Proximity Between Clients and Servers

Ensuring that commonly accessed servers are in close proximity to the users that most often access them can reduce the network traffic throughout the enterprise. If a single group of users on one subnet generate the most activity to a specific server, move that server to the users' subnet if possible. This will eliminate the traffic generated during file session activity from using valuable network bandwidth on other subnets.

Analyzing Net Use File Session Traffic

In this exercise, you analyze traffic resulting from a **net use** command and from transferring a file.

➤ **To analyze file session connection traffic**

In this procedure, you analyze the network traffic generated by a **net use** command from a Windows 95 client to a Windows NT 4.0 Server.

1. Open W95xfer.cap.

2. What is occurring in frames 1 and 2?

   _____

   _____

3. How much traffic is generated to resolve the IP address into a hardware address?

   _____

   _____

4. How long did it take to resolve the IP address into a hardware address?

   _____

   _____

5. Were the frames directed or broadcast?

   _____

   _____

6. What is occurring in frames 3 and 4?

   _____

   _____

7. What is occurring in frames 5 and 6?

   _____

   _____

8. How much traffic was generated to establish the TCP session in frames 7 through 9?

   _____

   _____

9. Frames 10 and 11 perform NetBIOS session establishment. Was **Instructor** able to accept another NetBIOS session?

   _____

   _____

   Hint: check **NBT: Packet Type** in frame 11.

10. How much traffic was generated during NetBIOS session establishment?

   _____

   _____

11. Frames 12 and 13 are negotiating server message block (SMB) protocols. How many SMB dialects did the client computer understand in frame 12?

   _____

   _____

   Hint: check **SMB: Command Dialect Strings Understood**.

12. What SMB dialect was negotiated between the client and the server?

   _____

   _____

   Hint: check **SMB: Command Protocol Index** of frame 13.

13. Frames 14 and 15 were a result of a network connection. What user was making the connection request?

   _____

   _____

   Hint: check **SMB: Command Account name** in frame 14.

14. What network resource did the client request a connection to?

_____

_____

Hint: check **SMB: Command File Name** in frame 14.

15. What Tree ID was assigned to the connection?

_____

_____

Hint: check **SMB: Header Tree ID** in frame 15.

16. How long did it take from the start of the TCP session to successful completion of the connection request?

_____

_____

➤ **To analyze file session transfer traffic**

In this procedure, you analyze the network traffic generated by the transfer of a file over the network.

1. In frame 17, what SMB command is being carried out?

_____

_____

Hint: check **SMB: Command Transact2 function**.

2. With what file system was the remote drive formatted?

_____

_____

Hint: check **SMB: Command Transaction Data Native FS** in frame 18.

3. What file is being transferred?

_____

_____

4. How large was the file?

_____

_____

Hint: check **SMB: Command File size** in frames 20 or 24.

5. In what frame was the file transferred?

_____

_____

6. How large was the frame that transferred the file?

_____

_____

7. What are the first 40 characters of the file?

_____

_____

Hint: click **NBT: SS Data** in frame 28, and then view the hexadecimal data.

8. From the time the first request regarding the file was issued, how long did it take to copy the file?

_____

_____

➤ **To analyze file session disconnection traffic**

In this procedure, you analyze the network traffic generated by a network disconnection. Frames 34 through 40 were a result of disconnecting the session that was established in frames 7 through 16.

1. In frame 36, what network resource is being disconnected?

_____

_____

Hint: check the TID in frame 36.

2. How long did it take to disconnect the network resource and close the TCP session?

_____

_____

3. How much traffic was generated to disconnect the session?

_____

_____

Analyzing Browsing File Session Traffic

In this exercise, you analyze file session traffic generated from using Network Neighborhood to connect a network resource.

➤ **To analyze file session connection traffic**

In this procedure, you analyze the network traffic generated by a network connection from a Windows 95-based client to a Windows NT 4.0-based server using Network Neighborhood.

1. Open W95netn.cap.

2. Frames 1 through 23 retrieve the browse list from the backup browser BACKUP. How many servers are in the browse list?

   _____

   _____

   Hint: check the SMB hexadecimal data in frame 17.

3. How large was the frame that provided the browse list? How much of the total frame was devoted to the SMB data?

   _____

   _____

4. Frames 24 through 44 retrieve the list of shared resources on the computer Instructor. How many shared resources were returned in the frame?

   _____

   _____

   Hint: check the SMB hexadecimal data in frame 38.

5. How large was the frame that provided the browse list of shared resources? How much of the total frame was devoted to the SMB data?

   _____

   _____

6. What share name is used to retrieve the list of shared resources?

   _____

   _____

   Hint: check **SMB: Command File name** in frame 35.

7. Frames 45 through 51 prepare for the file connection by establishing the prerequisite sessions. Frames 52 and 53 establish the connection to the shared resource. What user account is listed for the connection request?

_____

_____

8. What shared resource was connected?

_____

_____

Hint: check **SMB: Command File name** in frame 52.

9. What file system was resident on the connected drive?

_____

_____

Hint: check **SMB: Command Native FS** in frame 53.

10. Frames 54 through 72 are used to determine all files and directories to be displayed in the drive listing upon connection. What files and directories would have been displayed as a result of the connection?

_____

_____

Hint: check the Hex panes of the server response frames.

11. How large were the three response frames that transferred the list of available files and directories?

_____

_____

Analyzing Logon Validation Traffic

Once the computer has an IP address and NetBIOS names have been registered, the user can log on. The following graphic illustrates an overview of the network traffic generated by logon validation.

Frequency:

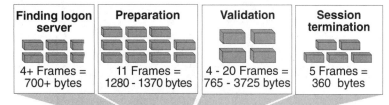

Finding logon server	Preparation	Validation	Session termination
4+ Frames = 700+ bytes	11 Frames = 1280 - 1370 bytes	4 - 20 Frames = 765 - 3725 bytes	5 Frames = 360 bytes

Logon validation = 6%

One of the first user functions a network needs to provide is logon validation. The user requests validation by entering a user name and password in a logon dialog box. One domain controller, in a set of domain controllers for the domain (either primary or backup), will validate the request. In this role, these servers are called logon servers.

The first thing the client needs to do is find a logon server. Once the logon server has been located, a conversation takes place to validate the logon request, check the system time, and possibly run logon scripts, user profiles, and so on.

Relative Impact on the Network

The main question is how many logon servers are required to adequately support user logons. The minimum amount of traffic generated when a client logs on is 3105 bytes, sent in 24 frames. A network administrator should determine how much actual traffic is generated per client during logon validation. This would include logon scripts and other network tasks that are run at logon.

Likewise, an administrator should consider when logon validation traffic takes place. That is, do 1000 users log on at 8:05 A.M. every morning, or do users log on randomly throughout the day or week?

In addition, the administrator needs to find out if users at a remote site will be logging on to this domain.

Finding a Logon Server

The first thing a client must do is locate a logon server. The following graphic illustrates the traffic generated in finding a logon server.

Frequency:

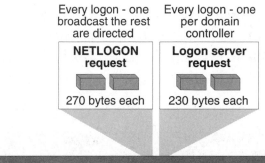

The first step in the logon process is finding a domain controller to validate the user account. This is accomplished using one of the following two methods:

- Broadcasting a request to the NETLOGON mailslot.

- Querying WINS for all registered domain controllers in the domain and then requesting validation using directed frames.

Broadcasting to NETLOGON

This method is used by Windows 95 and Windows NT–based client computers. At a minimum, two frames are required to find a server using the NETLOGON mailslot.

- A request is broadcast at the physical layer (Ethernet), and a subnet broadcast at the IP level. UDP Port 138 (NetBIOS Datagram Service) is used to service the request. The destination NetBIOS name is the domain name being logged into, with a <00> in the 16th position.

    For example, if attempting to find a logon server in the domain DOMAIN3, the request would be sent to "DOMAIN3 <00>" with spaces added through 15 characters, then <00>. This frame will be about 260 bytes for Windows 95, and about 300 for Windows NT, depending upon computer name.

    21 24.525 WIN95 *BROADCAST **NETLOGON LM1.0/2.0 LOGON Request from client**

- Each logon server registered in the domain running the NetLogon service will respond to the client, indicating it can accommodate the logon request. This is done through a directed reply to the requesting computer name using the mailslot \Mailslot\Temp\Netlogon.

```
22  24.537 BDC3    WIN95    NETLOGON LM2.0 Response to LOGON
Request
23  24.538 PDC3    WIN95    NETLOGON LM2.0 Response to LOGON
Request
```

Included in this frame is the Source IP Address and computer name of the logon server. This frame will be about 230 bytes for Windows 95, and about 270 for Windows NT, again depending upon computer name. There will be as many frames as there are responding domain controllers.

Using WINS

If the client computer is configured as an h-node WINS client, it will communicate with a WINS server to find a logon server, as follows:

- Send a query to the WINS server for the domain name, appended with a <1C> as the 16th character. This is a standard query to WINS of 92 bytes.

```
10  12.153 NTW1      DHCP_WINS    NBT NS: Query req. for
DOMAIN3    <1C>
```

- In response to the query, the WINS server returns a frame that includes the IP address of all registered domain controllers in the WINS database for that domain. This frame will vary in size, depending upon the number of domain controllers registered in the domain. For two domain controllers, a response is 116 bytes.

Note The WINS query for <1C> returns the first 25 domain controllers to register the name. Any domain controllers after 25 are not listed in the response, though locally registered servers (as opposed to those discovered through database replication), are given priority in the response message. This is to provide a list of domain controllers that are in close proximity to the client. The first entry is always the PDC.

```
11  12.157 DHCP_WINS  NTW1      NBT NS: Query (Node Status)
resp. for DOMAIN3    <1C>, Success
```

- The client sends a directed message to each server listed in the WINS response asking if it can validate the logon request. The client sends each request, and ignores any responses until after it has completed sending the requests to each server.

```
15. 12.162 NTW1    PDC3   NETLOGON SAM LOGON request from
client
19  12.167 NTW1    BDC3   NETLOGON SAM LOGON request from
client
```

- Each server then responds to the validation request as discussed for the NETLOGON broadcast and response.

Validating the Logon Request

Once a logon server has been located, the client begins a conversation to become validated. The following graphic illustrates the traffic generated in validating the logon request.

Frequency:

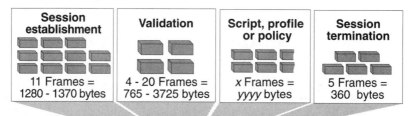

Session establishment	Validation	Script, profile or policy	Session termination
11 Frames = 1280 - 1370 bytes	4 - 20 Frames = 765 - 3725 bytes	x Frames = $yyyy$ bytes	5 Frames = 360 bytes

Logon validation = 6%

During the next part of the logon validation process, the client computer takes the first server response to its request, whether from the NETLOGON broadcast or through the directed NETLOGON requests, and initiates the following traffic between itself and the logon server.

Session Establishment

- The client resolves the NetBIOS name of the selected logon server, either by querying WINS, or by broadcast.

- A TCP session is established with the logon server using the TCP three-way handshake process.

- A NetBIOS session is established with the logon server.

- SMB protocol negotiation occurs.

- SMB tree connection to *logonserver*\IPC$ is established.

This process generates 11 frames, and approximately 1280 bytes of traffic for Windows 95, and 1370 bytes of traffic for Windows NT.

Windows 95 Validation

At process completion, the Windows 95 client initiates a conversation with the logon server using remote application programming interface (API) calls to validate the logon.

- The first API called is NetWkstaUserLogon, which requests logon validation. The server responds with a success or failure message.

```
39  24.621 WIN95    BDC3    SMB C transact, Remote API
40  24.713 BDC3     WIN95   SMB R transact, Remote API
(response to frame 39)
```

- The second API called is NetRemoteTOD. This API retrieves the server's time information to determine the time zone offset for proper calculation of file date and time stamping. The server responds with the correct time as kept at the domain controller.

```
41  24.722 WIN95    BDC3    SMB C transact, Remote API
42  24.726 BDC3     WIN95   SMB R transact, Remote API
(response to frame 41)
```

This set of two API calls and responses totals four frames, and approximately 765 bytes.

Windows NT Validation

When a user at a Windows NT–based computer requests validation, there are three unique steps for validating a logon request:

- The first step in the validation process is to retrieve a list of trusted domains that can be accessed in the **Logon Information** dialog box. This process generates about 12 frames and about 2000 bytes of traffic. This process will occur unless a user logs on, logs off, and then logs back on again within a five minute time period.

- The next step in the process is the establishment of a secure channel between the Windows NT–based computer and the validating domain controller. This process, which occurs at Windows NT initialization, generates eight frames and about 1400 bytes of traffic. This process validates that the Windows NT–based computer is a member of the appropriate domain.

- The final step is the validation request itself. For Windows NT, it is a single API call and response. These two frames generate around 900 bytes of traffic, depending upon name lengths (user, computer, and domain). If the named pipes open to Net Logon has been closed, and additional four frames and 700 bytes of traffic would be generated to create the named pipes session. This would normally occur in the first step of this process, and not need to be done here.

```
68  15.975 NTW1    BDC3   R_LOGON  RPC Client call
logon:NetrLogonSamLogon(..)
69  16.019 BDC3    NTW1   R_LOGON  RPC Server response
logon:NetrLogonSamLogon(..)
```

After the specific user account has been validated, logon scripts, user profiles, or system policies may be executed. This would result in additional network traffic.

For example, a user logging on to the domain from a Windows 95-based client computer would generate an additional 35 frames. These 35 frames show the client computer establishing a session with the PDC, connecting to the NET-LOGON share, and searching for a system policy. This process will add another few seconds to the logon process of the client, as well as the frames required to perform the transfer if the policy file, logon script, or user profile is available.

Session Termination

Finally, the connection to IPC$ is disconnected, and the NetBIOS and TCP sessions are terminated. This takes another five frames and approximately 360 bytes of traffic total.

Optimizing Logon Validation Traffic

The key factor in optimizing logon validation is in providing the proper number of domain controllers. The following graphic illustrates how to determine the proper number of domain controllers.

- Determining the number of domain controllers
- Increasing simultaneous logon validations
- Determining domain controller placement
- Determining hardware requirements

Number of users	SAM	CPU	RAM	Pagefile	Registry size limit	Paged pool size
3,000	5 MB	486DX/33	16 MB	32 MB	Default	Default
7,500	10 MB	486DX/66	32 MB	64 MB		
10,000	15 MB	Pentium or RISC-based	48 MB	96 MB		
15,000	22.5 MB		64 MB	128 MB	30 (MB)	75 (MB)
20,000	30 MB		96 MB	192 MB	50 (MB)	100 (MB)
30,000	45 MB		128 MB	256 MB	75 (MB)	128 (MB)

In order for the network to effectively provide logon validation services to users, the domain needs to contain the proper number of domain controllers.

Determining the Number of Domain Controllers

A conservative recommendation is to have one domain controller available for every 2000 user accounts. This should provide enough domain controllers to handle normal logon validation requests. To ensure that there are enough domain controllers to service user's logon needs, Performance Monitor counters are available to monitor logon requests. These counters are described in the following table.

Object/Counter	Description
Server:Logon/sec	Monitors the number of logon requests per second. These include both successful and unsuccessful attempts for interactive, network, and service account logon requests.
Server:Logon Total	Monitors the total number of interactive, network, and service account logon requests, both successful and unsuccessful attempts since the server was last started.

Increase Simultaneous Logon Validations

By default, domain controllers have their Server service configured for **Maximize Throughput for File Sharing**. While this is the proper setting for a file and print server, it does not provide the best performance for a domain controller that needs to validate logon requests. Instead, configure the Server service of all domain controllers for **Maximize Throughput for Network Applications**. By properly configuring this option, most domain controllers can triple their number of simultaneous logons, from about 6–7 per second, to around 20.

Determining Domain Controller Placement

Generally, the closer in proximity the domain controller is to the client requesting validation, the quicker the validation can be processed. In a remote site, the administrator has to balance the cost of logging on over the wide area network (WAN) to a central domain controller, against the cost of placing a backup domain controller (BDC) at the remote site. The disadvantage to placing domain controllers at each remote site are the cost of WAN traffic during directory services synchronization, and the possibility of having an out-of-date directory services database due to the WAN being down, preventing updates from occurring.

Determining Hardware Requirements

The hardware requirements for domain controllers are determined by the number of accounts in the directory services database. On Windows NT Server, this database is referred to as the security accounts manager (SAM). To determine the size of the SAM, view the file SAM in the following directory location: *SystemRoot*\System32\Config.

The following recommendations should be followed when planning for and optimizing domain controllers:

- The recommended amount of random access memory (RAM) for a domain controller is roughly 2.5 times the size of the SAM.

- The maximum recommended size of the SAM is 40 MB.

- The maximum number of objects in the SAM is 40,000.

  - Each user takes 1 KB of disk space.

  - Each global group takes 512 bytes of disk space, plus 12 bytes per member.

  - Each local group takes 512 bytes of disk space, plus 36 bytes per member.

  - Each computer account takes 512 bytes of disk space.

The following table contains the recommended configurations for domain controllers given a specific number of domain users. This table assumes that each user has a Windows NT–based computer.

Number of Users	SAM	CPU	RAM	Page File	Registry Size Limit	Paged Pool Size
3000	5 MB	486DX/33	16 MB	32 MB	Default	Default
7500	10 MB	486DX/66	32 MB	64 MB	Default	Default
10,000	15 MB	Pentium or RISC-based	48 MB	96 MB	Default	Default
15,000	22.5 MB	Pentium or RISC-based	64 MB	128 MB	30 MB	75 MB
20,000	30 MB	Pentium or RISC-based	96 MB	192 MB	50 MB	100 MB
30,000	45 MB	Pentium or RISC-based	128 MB	256 MB	75 MB	128 MB

Note The processor type is relatively unimportant in relationship to the number of users supported on a domain controller. Processor type is more important when considering client authentication, and when domain controllers are used for more than one purpose. For large domain operations, do not use the domain controller for anything other than normal domain controller activities, such as validating user logon requests and maintaining the user accounts database.

Analyzing Logon Validation Traffic

In this exercise, you analyze logon validation traffic by looking at data from Windows 95 and Windows NT Workstation client computers performing logon validation.

➤ **To analyze Windows 95 logon validation traffic**

In this procedure, you analyze the network traffic generated during user logon validation from a Windows 95-based client computer.

1. If it is not already open, open Bootw95.cap.

2. Frames 19 through 42 perform logon validation for the user. Frame 19 is the first frame that specifically deals with logon validation. What is occurring in frame 19?

   _____

   _____

3. Is this request directed or broadcast?

   _____

   _____

   Hint: check **Ethernet: Destination Address**.

4. Is this frame a network-wide or subnet broadcast?

   _____

   _____

   Hint: check **IP: Destination Address**, and compare it to **IP: Destination Address** of the DHCP Discover message in frame 1.

5. How large is the frame?

   _____

   _____

6. What is the Destination NetBIOS name of the frame?

_____

_____

Hint: check **NBT: Destination Name**.

7. What was the user account that was requesting validation?

_____

_____

Hint: check the NETLOGON frame properties.

8. What logon server responded to the client's request for logon validation first?

_____

_____

Hint: look for **NETLOGON LM2.0 Response to LOGON request**.

9. Once a server is found, the appropriate sessions must be established in order to request validation. What logon server did the client use for logon validation?

_____

_____

Hint: check the server to which the first NetBIOS session is established.

10. Frames 38 through 42 complete the logon validation process. Frame 38 is the first application programming interface (API) in the logon validation process. Logon validation is being requested for what user account?

_____

_____

Hint: view the hexadecimal data while selecting **SMB: Data** in frame 38.

11. How long did it take for the logon validation process to be completed from session establishment to the validation request completion?

_____

_____

12. What is occurring in frames 43 and 44?

_____

_____

13. What is occurring in frames 45 and 46?

14. Frames 51 through 60 occur after logon validation. These 10 frames generated an additional 994 bytes of data. Why did the client computer generate this extra traffic?

   Hint: check frames 51 through 53.

15. Was this file found? Hint: check frames 54 and 56.

➤ **To analyze Windows NT Workstation logon validation traffic**

In this procedure, you analyze the network traffic generated during user logon validation from a Windows NT Workstation-based client computer.

1. If it is not already open, open Bootntw.cap.

2. Frame 10 is the first frame that specifically deals with logon validation. What is occurring in frame 10?

3. What is the Destination NetBIOS name of the frame?

   Hint: check **NBT: Question Name**.

4. How many domain controllers were reported in response to the query?

   Hint: check the NBT frame properties of frame 11.

5. After the client received the list of domain controllers, how did it use the list of domain controllers?

_____

_____

Hint: check frames 15, 16, and 22.

6. Were these requests directed or broadcast?

_____

_____

7. What is the purpose of frame 12?

_____

_____

8. Is this request directed or broadcast?

_____

_____

Hint: check **Ethernet: Destination Address**.

9. What is the destination NetBIOS name of the frame?

_____

_____

Hint: check the NBT frame properties.

10. What was the user account that was requesting validation?

_____

_____

Hint: check the NETLOGON frame properties.

11. Why was this name used?

_____

_____

12. What logon server responded to the client's request for logon validation first?

_____

_____

Hint: look for **NETLOGON SAM Response to SAM LOGON request**.

13. What logon server did the client use for logon validation?

_____

_____

Hint: check the server the first NetBIOS session is established to.

14. Frames 26 through 34 prepare the client for logon validation by establishing the required sessions (session traffic is analyzed in another lab). Frames 35 through 46 prepare the list of domains to be displayed in the **Logon Information** dialog box. Were there any trusted domains the user could log onto?

_____

_____

15. Frames 47 through 55 verify that the Windows NT Workstation is a member of the domain, and has the proper credentials. In frame 53, what were the account and computer names?

_____

_____

16. Frames 66 through 67 perform logon validation. In frame 66, what were the domain, user, and computer names supplied as part of the logon validation?

_____

_____

Hint: expand **R_LOGON, PNETLOGON_LEVEL,** and **PNETLOGON _INTERACTIVE_INFO,** and then select each **USHORT** field. Find the answer in the Hex pane.

17. Frame 67 is the logon server's response to the validation request. How many bytes of data was returned?

_____

_____

Hint: check the total frame size, and check **MSRPC: Stub data** and look in the lower right corner for L:.

18. After validation occurred, what two files did the Windows NT 4.0 Workstation attempt to find?

_____

_____

19. Were either of these two files on the server?

_____

_____

Lesson Summary

The following summarizes the key points in this lesson:

- Client initialization traffic is the first traffic to appear on a network.

- The types of client initialization traffic that were analyzed in this lesson include DHCP, WINS, File session, and logon validation.

- Use network packet analysis to determine traffic due to DHCP, WINS, File Session, and Logon validations, and optimize as appropriate.

Lesson 3: Analyzing and Optimizing Client to Server Traffic

Client-to-server traffic is generated by a client computer communicating with a server computer. Types of client-to-server traffic that are beneficial to analyze include browser, Domain Name System (DNS), and intranet browsing. This lesson examines the traffic generated by a client computer when communicating with a server computer, and discusses ways to reduce unnecessary network traffic.

After this lesson, you will be able to:

- List the tasks that contribute to client-to-server traffic.
- Analyze client browser traffic.
- Analyze domain name system traffic.
- Analyze intranet browsing traffic.

Estimated lesson time: 30 minutes

Client-to-Server Analysis

Client-to-server traffic is generated by a client computer communicating with a server. The following graphic categorizes client-to-server traffic.

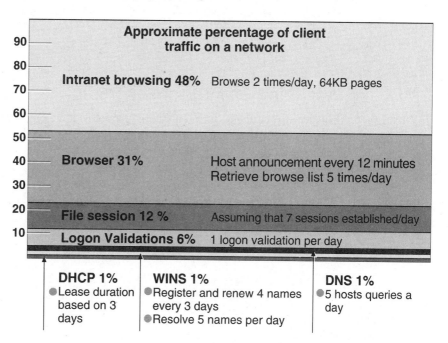

Note The traffic numbers in the graphic represent the percentage of each task's traffic out of a total of 100 percent of the traffic initiated by the client.

Types of client-to-server traffic that are beneficial to analyze include those listed in the following table.

Traffic Type	Description
Browser	Traffic generated by a client when registering itself as a possible provider of network resources, retrieving a list of backup browsers, a list of servers on the network, and a list of resources on a server.
Domain Name System (DNS)	Traffic generated by TCP/IP hosts during TCP/IP host name resolution. Usually generated by TCP/IP utilities such as Ping and Telnet, or applications such as Internet Explorer.
Intranet browsing	Traffic generated by the Internet Explorer browser application to download pages from a Web site.

Analysis of each of these traffic types will be covered in this lesson. Capture and analysis of these network tasks can tell a network administrator how much of the network traffic is generated by client-related services, and if any of it can be controlled or reduced.

Analyzing Client Browser Traffic

To allow users to easily find network resources, the Computer Browser service must be implemented. The following graphic provides a description and overview of the network traffic generated by client browsing.

Frequency:

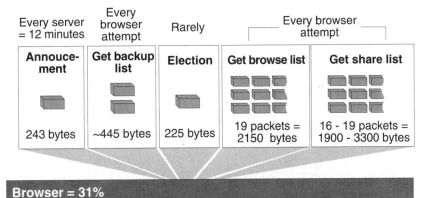

Every server = 12 minutes	Every browser attempt	Rarely	Every browser attempt	
Annouce- ment	**Get backup list**	**Election**	**Get browse list**	**Get share list**
243 bytes	~445 bytes	225 bytes	19 packets = 2150 bytes	16 - 19 packets = 1900 - 3300 bytes

Browser = 31%

After users have successfully logged on to the network, network resource access is generally the next step. To assist users in the process of locating network resources, Microsoft networking implements a network service called the Browser. The client browsing process is as follows:

1. Servers are added to the browse list by issuing announcements to the master browser.

2. The master browser shares the list of servers (as well as domains) with the backup browsers.

3. A client computer retrieves a list of backup browser computers from the master browser.

4. The client computer contacts a backup browser to retrieve a list of servers.

5. The client contacts the server to retrieve a list of shared resources on the server.

Each of these steps produces network traffic. Because a lot of the automatic browser traffic is broadcast-based, browsing a subnet is a simple process. However, most routers are not configured to forward browser broadcasts, and as such, browsing servers on remote subnets is not as simple. Fortunately, it is possible to browse network resources throughout the enterprise, and still not forward the browser broadcasts, by implementing Windows Internet Name Service (WINS).

Relative Impact on the Network

The process of browsing can have a relatively large impact on the network traffic that a client generates. To some extent, browsing happens automatically. Other aspects of browsing, such as the retrieval of a browse list, is initiated by the user.

The portion of the browsing process that uses Browser frames is based almost entirely on broadcast packets, the majority of which are very similar. These properties include:

- Frame sizes that are generally between 200 and 300 bytes in size.

- Media access control layer broadcasts and Internet Protocol (IP) layer subnet broadcasts using User Datagram Protocol (UDP) Port 138 (NetBIOS Datagram Service).

  Every computer that has server capabilities announces itself to the master browser. The following graphic illustrates host announcement traffic.

Frequency:

Each server = 12 minutes

Announcement

~243 bytes

Browser = 31%

A computer that can provide resources on the network will announce itself every 12 minutes, though during initialization the frequency is much higher to ensure the addition into the browse list. This announcement is generally 243 bytes in size.

```
18   17.292  WIN95     *BROADCAST    BROWSER Host Announcement [0x01]
WIN95
```

This announcement happens regardless of whether or not the computer actually has any shared resources. Starting the server, or a file sharing component, causes this announcement to occur initially. It is then repeated every 12 minutes while the server component is running.

Retrieving a Browse List

The majority of client browsing traffic occurs when a client needs to browse the network. The following graphic illustrates the traffic generated in retrieving a browse list.

Frequency:

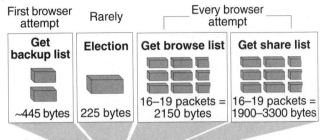

After the server has been added to the browse list, the user can browse its list of shared resources. To do this, the client needs to retrieve a list of available resources. This process involves finding the local master browser to retrieve a list of backup browsers, contacting a backup browser, connecting to and retrieving the browse list.

Get Backup List and Election

Two frames are sent to retrieve a list of backup browsers. If necessary, an election frame is sent, as follows:

- To find the local master browser, the client sends a "Get Backup List Request" to the domain name with a <1D> appended as the 16th character. This request is about 215 bytes in size.

```
89  51.140  NTW1        *BROADCAST      BROWSER Get Backup
List Request [0x09]
```

- The local master browser responds with a "Get Backup List Response." This response lists the available backup browsers. This frame will vary in size. A list of two servers might be 230 bytes, with each new server requiring an additional 27 bytes, plus space for the server comment.

```
91  51.143  PDC3       NTW1            BROWSER Get Backup
List Response [0x0a] 2 Servers
```

- If the local master browser does not respond to the "Get Backup List Request," the client sends an Election frame of 225 bytes. This forces a browser election.

```
73   22.134  BDC3      *BROADCAST    BROWSER Election
[0x08] [Force]
```

Get Browse List

Once the client receives a list of backup browsers, it connects to one of the listed backup browsers, and retrieves the browse list. This entire process can take up to 19 frames and just over 2150 bytes.

Get Share List

Finally, the client selects a server to which it will connect. For a Windows NT client computer, the process of selecting a server and retrieving its list of shared resources generated 19 frames and about 2000 bytes for a list of nine share names. The amount of traffic generated at this point will vary depending upon which domain is being browsed, how many entries are in the browse list, and how many shared resources are available on the target server.

Optimizing Client Browser Traffic

The key methods of optimization are to reduce the size of the browse list or reduce the number of backup browsers. The following graphic illustrates the methods used to control the network traffic generated by client browsing.

- **Disable unnecessary server components**
- **Control potential browers**
- **Eliminate protocols**

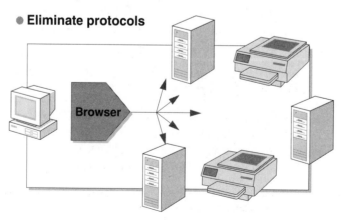

To provide for efficient resource location throughout the enterprise, the Computer Browser service is implemented. This network resource browsing comes at the expense of increased network traffic.

Disabling Unnecessary Server Components

One method of reducing client-related browsing traffic is to disable the server component on computers that are not required to provide shared resources on the network. If a computer rarely, if ever, shares network resources, consider disabling its server component. This will remove the announcements, and reduce the size of the browse list that must be maintained and transferred upon request.

Every server requires 27 bytes in the browse list, plus additional space for the comment, if assigned. Consider limiting or reducing the size of computer comments.

Controlling the Number of Potential Browsers

The number of backup browsers in a network are automatically determined by the browsing software. When another backup browser is needed, a potential browser is notified by the master browser that it should become a backup browser. Potential browsers are configured as follows:

- If a particular Windows NT–based computer should never become a browser server, set the HKEY_LOCAL_MACHINE\SYSTEM\CurrentControlSet\Services\Browser\Parameters\MaintainServerList value to No.

- For Windows 95-based clients, use the Network icon in Control Panel to configure the "File And Printer Sharing Properties" Browse Master parameter to Disabled.

- For Windows for Workgroups, add MaintainServerList to the [network] section of System.ini, and configure it to No.

This will reduce the registration, renewal and release of the <1E> NetBIOS names with WINS or b-node broadcasts.

Eliminating Unnecessary Network Protocols

The browsing system is protocol dependent, meaning that browsing occurs on a protocol-by-protocol basis. If a network uses three protocols, all browser announcements and elections will be repeated three times, one for each protocol. Reducing the number of protocols, if possible, will have a large impact on reducing browser related network traffic.

Analyzing Client Browser Announcements

In this exercise, you analyze client browser announcements from Windows NT Workstation and Windows 95 client startups.

➤ **To analyze Windows NT Workstation browser announcements**

In this procedure, you analyze the network traffic generated during a Windows NT Workstation client's use of browsing.

1. If it is not already open, open Bootntw.cap with Network Monitor.

2. Frame 60 is the Windows NT Workstation client's first browser announcement. What type of client services were announced?

_____

_____

Hint: check **BROWSER: Server Type Summary**.

3. What functions does this imply the client has?

_____

_____

4. How large was the announcement?

_____

_____

5. Was the announcement directed or broadcast?

_____

_____

6. When should we expect to see the next announcement from this computer?

_____

_____

Hint: check **BROWSER: Announcement Interval**.

7. Frame 65 is the next announcement from the computer. How long was it between the first and second announcements?

_____

_____

8. Why didn't the computer wait four minutes before sending the second Host announcement?

_____

_____

Hint: expand **BROWSER: Server Type Summary** in frame 65.

➤ **To analyze Windows 95 browser announcements**

In this procedure, you analyze the network traffic generated during a Windows 95 client's use of browsing.

1. If it is not already open, open Bootw95.cap.

2. Frame 18 is the Windows 95 client's browser announcement. What type of client services were announced?

_____

_____

Hint: check **BROWSER: Server Type Summary**.

3. What functions does this imply the client has?

_____

_____

4. How large was the announcement?

_____

_____

5. Was the announcement directed or broadcast?

_____

_____

Analyzing Client Browser Traffic

In this exercise, you analyze client browser activity.

➤ **To analyze retrieving a local browse list**

In this procedure, you analyze the network traffic generated during a Windows 95 client's retrieval of the browse list.

1. Open W95brows.cap.

2. Normally, the client's first step in browsing a server is to find a backup browser. This does not occur here because the client had just started up, and already had cached a list of backup browsers. What backup browser computer did the client select to retrieve its browse list from?

_____

_____

Hint: check for a WINS query followed by session traffic.

3. Frames 10 and 11 transfer the browse list to the client. How many servers were in the browse list?

_____

_____

Hint: select **SMB: Data** in frame 11, and view the data in the Hex pane.

4. How large was the response that included the list of servers?

_____

_____

5. From the session request to retrieve a list of backup browsers to the completion of the session to retrieve the browse list, how much time expired?

_____

_____

➤ **To analyze the retrieval of a list of shared resources**

In this procedure, you analyze the network traffic generated during a Windows 95 client's retrieval of the list of shared resources from a server. Frames 18 through 41 retrieve a list of resources available on the computer Backup.

1. Frames 18 through 32 prepare for the retrieval of the list of shared resources by querying WINS and establishing the appropriate sessions with the target server. Frames 33 and 35 request and retrieve the browse list. How much traffic was generated by this retrieval?

_____

_____

2. How many shared resources were sent to the client?

_____

_____

Hint: view the SMB hexadecimal data in frame 35.

3. How long did it take to retrieve the list of resources from the initial WINS query through the return of the browse list?

_____

_____

➤ **To analyze the retrieval of a remote browse list**

In this procedure, you analyze the network traffic generated during a Windows 95 client's retrieval of the browse list from a server in a different domain using Network Neighborhood. Frames 43 through 59 connect to a local backup browser and retrieve the list of available domains.

1. The actual transfer of domain occurs in frames 52 and 53. How many domains were registered?

_____

_____

2. How large was the frame returning the list of domains?

_____

_____

3. How long did it take to retrieve the list of domains from session establishment through session termination?

_____

_____

4. What is occurring in frames 60 through 67?

_____

_____

5. What domain is the client attempting to browse? Where did you find the answer?

_____

_____

6. How many backup browsers were in the response?

_____

_____

7. Frames 68 through 80 establish the required sessions with the selected back-up browser in order to retrieve the list of servers in the domain. Frames 81 and 82 retrieve the list of servers in the selected domain. Frames 83 through 88 terminate the sessions. What backup browser was selected to retrieve the list of servers in the domain?

_____

_____

Hint: check for session traffic before the API calls to retrieve the browse list.

8. How many servers were registered in the domain?

_____

_____

9. Frames 89 through 107 retrieve the list of shared resources for a server in Domain3. What server was browsed?

_____

_____

10. What shared resources should have been displayed in Network Neighborhood?

_____

_____

11. How large was the frame that returned the shared resources?

_____

_____

12. How long did the entire process take to retrieve the list of shared resources for Domain3?

_____

_____

➤ **To analyze retrieving a local browse list**

In this procedure, you analyze the network traffic generated during a Windows NT Workstation client's retrieval of the browse list.

1. Open Ntwbrows.cap.

2. What is occurring in frames 1 through 14?

   _____

   _____

3. Why are there two Get Backup List Request frames (frames 1 and 13)?

   _____

   _____

4. How did the client know to send directly to Instructor?

   _____

   _____

5. Frames 15 through 30 retrieve the list of servers in the local domain from a backup browser. Which backup browser was selected?

   _____

   _____

   Hint: check for session traffic before the API to return the browse list.

6. Frames 31 through 45 prepare for share list retrieval by establishing the necessary sessions with the selected server. What service is used to retrieve the list of shared resources when the negotiated SMB protocol is NT LM 0.12?

   _____

   _____

   Hint: check frame 42.

7. Frames 46 and 47 retrieve the list of shared resources. Notice that NT-to-NT APIs are fully parsed, unlike the Windows 95 request. What is the name of the API to retrieve the list of shared resources from a server?

   _____

   _____

8. How may shared resources were returned to the client?

_____

_____

Analyzing DNS Traffic

The traffic generated by client DNS lookups is very simple to analyze. The following graphic illustrates an overview of the network traffic generated by DNS.

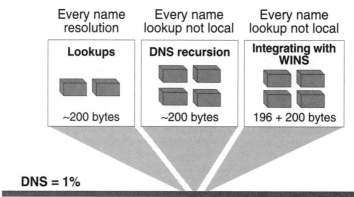

Frequency:

Every name resolution	Every name lookup not local	Every name lookup not local
Lookups	**DNS recursion**	**Integrating with WINS**
~200 bytes	~200 bytes	196 + 200 bytes

DNS = 1%

When users want to access a computer using standard Windows networking commands and utilities, such as Network Neighborhood, or the **net** command, the NetBIOS name of the target computer must be resolved into an IP address. This is often accomplished by WINS. When users want to access a computer using Transmission Control Protocol/Internet Protocol (TCP/IP) utilities, such as Internet Explorer or Ping, the IP host name of the target computer must be resolved into an IP address. This process, called host name resolution, can be accomplished using the DNS.

Relative Impact on the Network

DNS traffic generated from a client computer consists of a query request and response. As such, there is not a lot of traffic for a single request. The impact that client-based DNS traffic has on the network is a result of how often names need to be resolved. That is, the number of query requests that are issued determines the impact that client DNS queries have on network traffic.

Another factor that impacts the traffic on the network is the need for DNS servers to perform recursive lookups. DNS servers have the ability of passing a query request to another DNS server, or to a WINS server, when it cannot resolve the name. Thus, a single query request from a client computer might actually generate more than the simple query and response frame.

DNS Lookups

A DNS lookup conversation consists of a request and response. The following graphic illustrates the DNS lookup traffic.

Frequency:

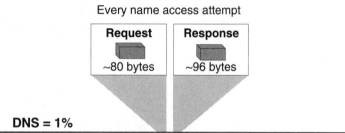

Client Request

When an IP client needs to resolve a TCP/IP host name into an IP address, it sends a DNS query to its DNS server. This request is a frame of varying size, depending upon the length of the host name to be resolved. Host names can be up to 256 characters.

A request to resolve "instructor.test.com" results in a frame of 79 bytes. The request is a directed request to the DNS server. DNS uses UDP Port 53 as its standard port. In the DNS portion of the frame, the client specifies the host name to be resolved. This traffic is repeated for each resolution attempt.

```
1   4.803   WIN95     BACKUP      DNS 0x1:Std Qry for
instructor.test.com.
```

Server Response

When the DNS server receives the request, it determines if it has an entry for the requested name. If it does, it issues a response frame that includes the IP address of the host name in question. This is a directed response to the requesting client computer. In the response frame, the server adds a DNS Answer section that includes the name that was queried, as well as the IP address.

```
2   4.804  BACKUP    WIN95        DNS 0x1:Std Qry Resp. for
instructor.test.com.
```

The query response varies in size, depending upon the length of the host name to be resolved. If the name does not exist, the server will either return a "Name does not exist" message to the requesting client, or pass the request onto another DNS server if recursion is configured.

DNS Recursive Lookups

A recursive name lookup occurs when the queried DNS server does not have a mapping for the requested name, and passes the request to another server to process. The following graphic illustrates the traffic generated by DNS recursive name lookups.

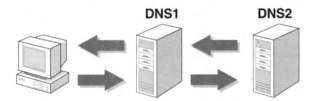

If the client's configured DNS server does not contain a listing for the requested name, it forwards the request to another DNS server for resolution. This forwarding of requests is called recursion, and must be configured by the administrator.

The process starts with a standard DNS lookup request by a client.

```
1   2.686  NTW1     BDC3       DNS 0x1:Std Qry for
instructor.Test.com. of type Host Addr on class I
```

When the first DNS server does not contain the requested mapping, it forwards the request to the recursive partner. The frame size remains the same, because the only change is the destination addresses.

```
2   2.688  BDC3     BACKUP    DNS 0xC:Std Qry for
instructor.Test.com. of type Host Addr on class I
```

If the second DNS server has the requested entry, it responds directly to the first DNS server. The first DNS server will then respond to the client as if it resolved the name without requiring a recursive transmission.

```
3   2.690   BACKUP    BDC3      DNS 0xC:Std Qry Resp. for
instructor.Test.com. of type Host Addr


4   2.693   BDC3      NTW1      DNS 0x1:Std Qry Resp. for
instructor.Test.com. of type Host Addr
```

DNS and WINS Integration

It is possible to configure a DNS server to query a WINS server for a name if it is not contained in the DNS system. This allows for the DNS system to use its static entries, and still provide the benefit of WINS and its dynamic registrations.

```
1   4.684   NTW1      BDC3        DNS 0x1:Std Qry for win95.Test.com.
of type Host Addr on class INET


4   4.688   BDC3      BACKUP      DNS 0x10:Std Qry for
win95.Test.com. of type Host Addr on class INET


7   4.691   BACKUP    DHCP_WINS   DNS 0x8004:Std Qry for
FHEJEODJDFCACACACACACACACACACAAA. of type Unkn


8B  4.694   DHCP_WINS  BACKUP     DNS 0x8004:Std Qry Resp. for
FHEJEODJDFCACACACACACACACACACAAA.


9B  4.695   BACKUP    BDC3        DNS 0x10:Std Qry Resp. for
win95.Test.com. of type Host Addr on class


10  4.698   BDC3      NTW1        DNS 0x1:Std Qry Resp. for
win95.Test.com. of type Host Addr on class
```

Frames 8 and 9 are WINS name query messages from a DNS server to the WINS server. Those two frames use the standard NetBIOS Name Service port (UDP 137), rather than the standard UDP port for DNS, which is 53. Notice that the response messages are always returned to the requester, not the original client. The originally queried DNS server is the server that returns the IP address to the client.

Optimizing DNS Traffic

The main opportunity for optimization is to reduce the need for recursion. The following graphic illustrates the methods used to optimize DNS traffic.

Reduce recursion

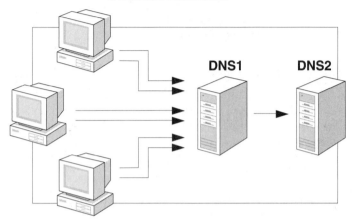

A simple address lookup takes only two directed frames. Optimization efforts should be focused on reducing recursion traffic that may result if a client's DNS server does not have the requested address. There are three methods for reducing recursion traffic:

- Do not configure recursion. Of course, this limits the functionality of DNS by not being able to provide all requested names, or it requires the addition of all host names to each DNS server, which is an administrative burden.

- Ensure that the DNS server that will most likely resolve most of the names for a particular client is designated as its DNS server. This reduces the chance of a recursive lookup and its associated traffic.

- Increase the time to live (TTL) of cached entries. When one DNS server sends a name lookup request to another DNS server, the original DNS server, upon receiving the address, will cache that address for a period of time, which is the TTL of the record. By default, the TTL of a cached resolved name is 60 minutes. The default for a NetBIOS name resolved by a recursive lookup using WINS is 10 minutes. These TTLs are configurable using DNS Manager.

➤ **To configure the TTL for all records of a zone**

1. Start **DNS Manager**, and then select the zone you want.

2. From the **DNS** menu, click **Properties**.

3. In the **Zone Properties** dialog box, click the **SOA Record** tab.

4. In the **Minimum Default TTL** box, select or type the desired TTL.

5. Click **OK**.

This configures the default TTL for all records in the zone. It is also possible to configure the TTL of individual records, so that the most commonly accessed records can be cached for a longer time.

➤ **To configure the TTL for an individual record**

1. Start **DNS Manager**, and then from the **Options** menu, click **Preferences**.

2. In the **Preferences** dialog box, click **Expose TTL**.

3. Click **OK**.

Now, whenever you create or edit a record, the **TTL** box is displayed in the **Properties** dialog box for the record. Configure it as desired on a record-by-record basis.

➤ **To configure the TTL for WINS records**

1. Start **DNS Manager**, and then select the zone you want.

2. From the **DNS** menu, click **Properties**.

3. In the **Zone Properties** dialog box, click the **WINS Lookup** tab.

4. Click **Advanced**, and then in the **Cache Timeout Value** box, type or select the desired value.

5. Click **OK**.

By increasing the TTL of resolved names, the amount of network traffic can be reduced by eliminating the need to recursively query a second attempt for a recently resolved name.

Analyzing DNS Lookup Traffic

In this exercise, you analyze DNS name lookups, including recursive queries and the integration of DNS and WINS.

➤ **To analyze DNS name lookup traffic**

In this procedure, you analyze the network traffic generated by a DNS name lookup request. This results from a Windows NT Workstation client computer issuing a **ping** command.

1. Open Dnsquery.cap.

2. What is occurring in frames 1 and 2?

   _____

   _____

3. What is occurring in frames 3 and 4?

   _____

   _____

4. What name is being queried?

   _____

   _____

5. What is the destination port name and number for the DNS query?

   _____

   _____

6. How much traffic was generated by the DNS lookup request and response?

   _____

   _____

7. Did the query request also specify that recursive queries are allowed?

   _____

   _____

   Hint: check **DNS: DNS Flags** in frame 3.

8. Was the destination DNS server a domain authority server?

_____

_____

Hint: check **DNS: DNS Flags** in frame 4.

9. How long did it take to resolve the name?

_____

_____

The remaining eight frames are the completion of the **ping** command.

In this procedure, you analyze the network traffic generated to process a recursive name lookup.

➤ **To analyze DNS name lookup recursion traffic**

1. Open Dnsrecr.cap.

2. What is occurring in frames 1 and 2?

_____

_____

3. What is occurring in frame 3?

_____

_____

4. What name is being queried?

_____

_____

5. Did the query request also specify that recursive queries are allowed?

_____

_____

Hint: check **DNS: DNS Flags** in frame 3.

6. What is occurring in frames 4 and 5?

_____

_____

7. What is occurring in frames 6 and 7?

_____

_____

8. Frame 7 is the recursive lookup request. Where was the answer sent?

_____

_____

9. What is occurring in frame 8?

_____

_____

10. What was the IP address of instructor.test.com?

_____

_____

11. How much traffic was generated by the initial query and recursive query requests?

_____

_____

12. How long did it take to resolve the name for the client?

_____

_____

The remaining eight frames are the completion of the **ping** command.

➤ **To analyze DNS and WINS integration traffic**

In this procedure, you analyze the network traffic generated by a DNS name lookup request that caused a recursive name lookup to WINS to occur.

1. Open Dnswins.cap.

2. What name is being queried for in frame 1?

_____

_____

3. What is occurring in frame 2?

_____

_____

4. What is occurring in frame 5?

_____

_____

5. Was this a DNS or NetBIOS query?

_____

_____

Hint: check **UDP: Destination Port** in frame 5.

6. How large was frame 5?

_____

_____

7. What are the first nine bytes of the name queried for in frame 5?

_____

_____

8. Select **DNS: Question Name** in frame 5 of **Dnswins.cap**.

   Notice the highlighted data in the Hex pane. It is the hexadecimal representation of the queried name.

9. If it is not already open, open W95brows.cap.

10. Select **NBT: Question Name** in frame 89 of **W95brows.cap**.

11. What name is being queried for?

_____

_____

12. Viewing the Hex pane, what are the first nine bytes of the name queried for in frame 89?

_____

_____

13. Compare the first 9 bytes of the names queried for in the two files. Are there any differences?

   _____

   _____

14. What name does this imply is being queried for in frame 5 of Dnswins.cap?

   _____

   _____

15. What is occurring in frame 7 of Dnswins.cap?

   _____

   _____

16. What is occurring in frame 8?

   _____

   _____

17. What was the IP address of pdc3.test.com?

   _____

   _____

18. How much traffic was generated by the initial query and recursive query requests?

   _____

   _____

19. How long did it take to resolve the name for the client?

   _____

   _____

The remaining ten frames are the completion of the **ping** command, including address resolution.

Analyzing Intranet Browsing Traffic

Intranet browsing can generate extremely large amounts of network traffic. The following graphic illustrates an overview of the network traffic generated by intranet browsing.

Frequency:

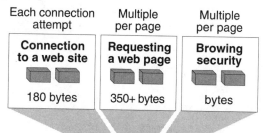

More and more, users are going to Web sites to retrieve static information rather than establishing file connections. One appeal of this process is the graphical interface and the ability to browse information in a quick and easy manner. Another benefit to using Web sites is the ability to share information with users outside the corporate network.

Relative Impact on the Network

Intranet browsing can generate a very large percentage of the network traffic that is initiated by a client computer. The process of finding and connecting to a Web site creates a very small amount of traffic, but the amount of information that is downloaded, which often includes graphics, can be quite large.

Connecting to a Web Site

Connecting to a Web site is a simple process. The first step in the intranet browsing process is resolution of the Web server's name. This can be done through a standard DNS name lookup, or any other method of resolving the name.

TCP Session Established for Every Page

Once the name has been resolved, the client will establish a TCP session with the Web server using TCP Port 80.

```
3    3.869    NTW1        PDC3        TCP....S., len:    4, seq: 419469026-
419469029, ack:         0

4    3.870    PDC3        NTW1        TCP.A..S., len:    4, seq:1535104872-
1535104875, ack: 419469027

5    3.871    NTW1        PDC3        TCP.A...., len:    0, seq: 419469027-
419469027, ack:1535104873
```

Requesting a Web Page

Once the client has connected to the Web server, it can start making requests for information. The client requests pages (files) from the Web server using Hypertext Transfer Protocol (HTTP) commands. The HTTP command that requests a page is GET. In the HTTP section of the frame, the requested file to be downloaded is specified. Initially, this file will be the requested page. After downloading the page, there may be images or graphics that need to be downloaded to the client. These will be requested in additional HTTP GET messages.

```
6    3.881    NTW1        PDC3        HTTP GET Request (from client using
port 1076)
```

This frame varies in size depending on the length of the host name and the file to be downloaded. The frame is 350 bytes for a 14 character host name and 20 character path and file name.

When the Web server receives the request and determines that the requested file is available, it responds with the appropriate number of HTTP response frames needed to transfer the file to the client. If the file is larger than 1238 bytes, there will be at least two response frames from the server to the client to transfer the file. Subsequent frames carry 1450 bytes of data, because most of the HTTP header information is not included.

```
8    3.899    PDC3        NTW1        HTTP Response (to client using port
1076)

9    3.901    PDC3        NTW1        HTTP Response (to client using port
1076)

10   3.906    NTW1        PDC3        TCP.A...., len:    0, seq: 419469327-
419469327, ack:1535107793
```

```
11   3.910   PDC3      NTW1       HTTP Response (to client using port
1076)
```

```
12   3.913   NTW1      PDC3       TCP.A...., len:    0, seq: 419469327-
419469327, ack:1535109146
```

There could be many TCP sessions and HTTP GET commands issued for a single page if graphics have been added to the page. Normally, a new TCP session (and TCP Port) is used to transfer each requested file.

For example, to download /samples/default.htm (from a Microsoft Internet Information Server 2.0 installation) generated 76 frames (including the DNS lookup and response) and 48,539 bytes of traffic. This request consisted of the following files:

- /samples/default.htm–4051 bytes

- /samples/images/backgrnd.gif–10,282 bytes

- /samples/images/h_logo.gif–5081 bytes

- /samples/images/space.gif–844 bytes

- /samples/images/docs.gif–2893 bytes

- /samples/images/tools.gif–2513 bytes

- /samples/images/space2.gif–824 bytes

- /samples/images/h_samp.gif–6060 bytes

- /samples/images/h_browse.gif–3037 bytes

- /samples/images/powered.gif–2758 bytes

These 10 files totaled 38,343 bytes in size. The other 10,200 bytes were used by the DNS lookup and response, the ten HTTP GET commands, the required TCP sessions, and TCP acknowledgments.

Intranet Browsing Security

The default configuration of Internet Information Server 2.0 is to allow anonymous connections. This means that there is no validation of user accounts and passwords before allowing access to the site. While this makes the use of the site easy, it does not provide any level of security. Security can be enabled on most Web servers, including Internet Information Server. This security provides for basic encoding of user account information, or encryption of the user account information using Windows NT security techniques.

Windows NT Challenge/Response Security

If Windows NT Challenge/Response security is enabled on the Web server, each initial request to download a file, after establishing a TCP session, is responded to with an access denied HTTP frame. In this frame, the Status Code is set to Unauthorized, the Reason is set to Access Denied, and the WWW-Authenticate field is set to NTLM (Windows NT Challenge/Response security). Finally, the session is terminated.

```
4   17.518  NTW1        PDC3      HTTP GET Request (from client using port
1108)


6   17.525  PDC3        NTW1      HTTP Response (to client using port
1108)


7   17.532  PDC3        NTW1      TCP.A...F, len:    0, seq:1546747507-
1546747507, ack: 431111858


8   17.533  NTW1        PDC3      TCP.A...., len:    0, seq: 431111858-
431111858, ack:1546747508
```

The client then establishes a new TCP session with the server, and sends its unencoded information to the server. The server then responds with the appropriate encryption key to use.

```
13   17.781  NTW1       PDC3      HTTP GET Request (from client using
port 1109)


15   17.791  PDC3       NTW1      HTTP Response (to client using port
1109)
```

The client finally sends its encrypted authentication information (using the supplied key) to the server. The server then processes the request, and transfers the requested file to the client.

```
16   17.820  NTW1       PDC3      HTTP GET Request (from client using
port 1109)


17   17.873  PDC3       NTW1      HTTP Response (to client using port
1109)


18   17.876  PDC3       NTW1      HTTP Response (to client using port
1109)


19   17.878  PDC3       NTW1      HTTP Response (to client using port
1109)
```

Without security, downloading the /samples/default.htm page took 74 frames and 48,375 (excluding the two DNS frames). With Windows NT Challenge/Response security enabled, the same page took 115 frames and generated 56,145 bytes of traffic to download.

Optimizing Intranet Browsing Traffic

The most effective optimization of intranet browsing traffic is during the creation of Web pages because the majority of Web traffic is caused by the size of the files being copied across the network.

Because intranet browsing can generate very significant amounts of network traffic, anything that can be done to reduce the traffic generated can be beneficial in the overall scheme of network usage.

- Keep Web site pages small. As a general rule, it is good Hypertext Markup Language (HTML) design to limit scrolling of pages. Keeping them small will assist in the downloading of a single page, but make sure necessary information is available on other pages that can be loaded.

- Limit the size of graphics or .Avi files used. Each file must be downloaded to the client computer. The larger the files (especially graphics), the more network traffic generated to download the file. Reuse common graphics throughout the intranet.

- Increase the client's local cache. When browsing an intranet, pages are downloaded to the client, and placed in a directory called the cache. When the designated amount of disk space for the cache is used, and more files are required, the cache must be emptied (deleted). Thus, a previously loaded file must be copied over the network again, instead of loading it from the local hard disk cache.

- Consider whether security is a big concern at your site. With security enabled, additional authentication traffic is required for each session that is established. Allowing anonymous connections will prevent the authentication traffic from occurring on the network.

Analyzing Intranet Browsing Traffic

In this exercise, you analyze intranet browsing traffic.

► **To analyze intranet browsing traffic**

In this procedure, you analyze the network traffic generated by a Windows NT Workstation client using Internet Explorer to browse a Microsoft Internet Information Server computer.

1. Open Ieconnect.cap.

2. What is occurring in frames 1 and 2?

_____

_____

3. After resolving the host name, the client then establishes a TCP session with the Web server in frames 3 through 5. In frame 6, the client makes a request to retrieve a page from the server. What is the destination TCP port?

_____

_____

Hint: check **TCP: Destination Port** for the name, and the TCP header for the port number.

4. What was the HTTP command issued by the client to the server?

_____

_____

Hint: check the lower third of the Summary window for frame 6.

5. What page was requested by the client?

_____

_____

Hint: check the lower third of the Summary window for frame 6.

6. How large was the request frame? How much data was required for the HTTP header and data?

_____

_____

Hint: check **FRAME: Total frame length** and **TCP: Data: Number of bytes remaining** in frame 6.

7. Frames 9 and 10 retrieve the page from the Web server. How large was the page?

_____

_____

Hint: check the lower third of the Summary window for frames 9 and 10.

8. From the beginning of the TCP session, how long did it take to retrieve the page?

_____

_____

➤ **To analyze downloading a Web page with graphics**

In this procedure, you analyze the network traffic generated to process accessing a Web page from a Web server that includes graphics.

1. Open Ieopen.cap.

   In this capture, host name resolution has already occurred.

2. What page was requested in frame 1?

_____

_____

   Hint: check the lower third of the Summary window for frame 1.

3. How much larger was this request than the request to retrieve the default page?

_____

_____

4. Why the difference in the frame sizes to retrieve the two pages?

_____

_____

5. How large was open.htm?

_____

_____

6. How long did it take to retrieve the page?

_____

_____

7. Frame 4 requests an object for the loaded page. What object was requested?

_____

_____

8. Was the object transferred to the client?

9. How long did the server search for the object?

10. Frames 5 through 9 request an object for the loaded page. What object was requested?

11. Was the object transferred to the client?

12. How large was the file?

13. How long did it take to retrieve the page?

14. Frames 10 through 14 request an object for the loaded page. What object was requested?

15. Was the object transferred to the client?

16. How long did it take to retrieve the page?

Lesson Summary

The following information summarizes the key points in this lesson:

- Client-to-server traffic is generated by a client computer communicating with a server computer.

- Browser traffic is generated by a client when registering itself as a possible provider of network resources, retrieving a list of backup browsers, retrieving a list of servers on the network, and retrieving a list of resources on the server.

- DNS traffic is generated by TCP/IP hosts during TCP/IP host name resolution.

- Intranet browsing is traffic generated by the Internet Explorer browser application downloading pages from a web site.

Lesson 4: Analyzing Server to Server Traffic

Most enterprises have multiple servers to support the network activities of users. In order for these servers to properly support users, they must communicate with each other and synchronize data in a timely manner. This lesson presents an analysis of the server-to-server network traffic generated by the different Windows NT services, and how they affect overall network performance.

After this lesson, you will be able to:

- List the services that contribute to server-to-server traffic.
- Analyze account synchronization traffic.
- Analyze trust relationship traffic.
- Analyze server browser traffic.
- Analyze WINS replication traffic.
- Analyze directory replication traffic.
- Analyze DNS server-to-server traffic.

Estimated lesson time: 30 minutes

Server-to-Server Analysis

In analyzing server-to-server traffic, directory services, trust relationships, the browser, WINS, directory replication, and DNS will be considered. The graphic below illustrates an overview of server-to-server traffic.

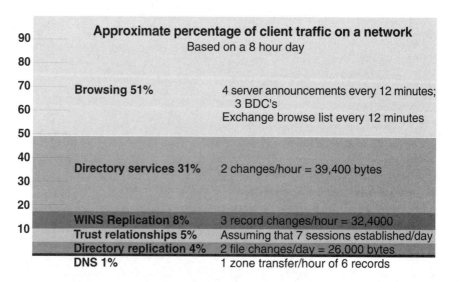

Server-to-server traffic is traffic generated between server computers carrying out network maintenance tasks. The following table lists the types of server-to-server traffic that is beneficial to analyze.

Traffic Type	Description
Account synchronization	Traffic generated by synchronization of the user accounts databases between the PDC and BDCs.
Trust relationships	Traffic generated during the establishment of a trust relationship, as well as the importing of trusted accounts. Also includes traffic generated by pass-through authentication.
Server browser traffic	Traffic generated by server announcements, master browser elections, and browse list exchanges between browser servers.
WINS replication	Traffic generated by the replication of WINS server database records to another WINS server.
Directory replication	Traffic generated during the automatic duplication of a directory structure among computers.
DNS server	Traffic generated due to DNS server zone replication.

Analyzing Account Synchronization Traffic

The user accounts databases are synchronized with every BDC on a regular basis. The following graphic illustrates an overview of the traffic generated during account database synchronization.

Frequency:

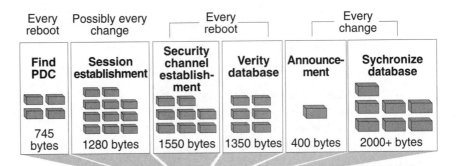

In a Windows NT Server network, user logon validation requests are processed by either the primary domain controller (PDC) or a backup domain controller (BDC). Changes to the user accounts database are made only at the PDC. To ensure that each BDC properly validates each user logon request, it is important that each BDC has an exact copy of the user accounts databases maintained on the PDC.

User Accounts Database Synchronization

User accounts database synchronization occurs on three databases maintained by the system: the security accounts manager (SAM) Accounts database, the SAM Built-in database, and the local security authority (LSA) database. Contents of these databases are listed in the following table.

Database	Description
SAM Accounts database (0)	Contains the user and group accounts that the administrator creates. Also includes all built-in global groups and computer accounts added to the domain, such as domain controllers and Windows NT Workstation-based computers.
SAM Built-in database (1)	Contains the built-in local group accounts, such as Administrators, Users, and Guests.
LSA database (2)	Contains the LSA Secrets that are used for trust relationships and domain controller computer account passwords. Also included in the LSA database are the account policy settings configured by the administrator.

Relative Impact on the Network

Synchronization of the user accounts databases occurs:

- When a BDC is installed or restarted into the domain.

- When forced by the administrator using Server Manager.

- Automatically by domain controllers, depending on Registry configuration.

User accounts database synchronization can generate large amounts of network traffic if many updates are made to the accounts database. The frequency and amount of traffic generated depends on configuration of the Net Logon service, which is responsible for carrying out synchronization.

Finding the PDC

When a BDC initializes, it needs to verify, and possibly update its user accounts database. The first step in this process is to find the PDC. The following graphic illustrates the network traffic generated while finding the PDC.

Frequency: Every reboot

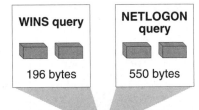

Discovery of the name of the PDC takes four frames, and about 745 bytes of traffic. The process of finding the PDC only occurs at BDC startup. Once the PDC is found, the entry is cached for later use. Frames are as follows:

- The BDC uses a standard Windows Internet Naming Service (WINS) query, sending a request for *Domainname* <1B>. This name is only registered by the PDC. The total for the two frames is 196 bytes.

- The BDC then sends a "Query for Primary DC" message to the IP address returned by WINS for the *Domainname* <1B> query. This is done to determine the name of the PDC. This message is sent as a second class mailslot to \Mailslot\Net\Netlogon. This frame is approximately 270 bytes, depending upon the BDC's name.

```
19    17.771   BDC3         PDC3      NETLOGON  Query for
Primary DC
```

- The PDC then responds to the BDC with a "Response to Primary Query" frame. The PDC's name is listed in the Primary DC Name field, as well as the domain name. This frame is approximately 275 bytes, depending upon the PDC's name.

```
20    17.777   PDC3         BDC3      NETLOGON  Response to
Primary Query
```

Establishing a Session and Secure Channel

Once the BDC has found the PDC, it will establish a session with the PDC and establish a secure channel for transferring account information. The following graphic illustrates the traffic generated in establishing a session and a secure channel to the PDC.

Frequency:

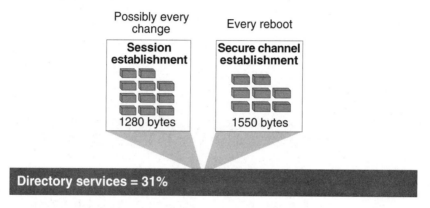

Establishing a Session

This traffic consists of the same frames discussed previously in file session traffic, including possible name resolution, address resolution, Transmission Control Protocol (TCP) session, NetBIOS session, server message block (SMB) protocol negotiation, and a connection to IPC$. This will be about nine frames and 1,200 bytes of traffic.

Establishing a Secure Channel

The final step in preparing to verify the database is to establish a secure channel with the PDC. This traffic only occurs during system startup. The secure channel is not broken until one of the two domain controllers is shut down. This allows the establishment of new sessions to be created (because they can time out), followed by immediate verification and update without requiring the secure channel establishment again.

This takes eight frames totaling 1550 bytes. These eight frames accomplish the following tasks:

- Create a named pipe open request to Net Logon, allowing application programming interface (API) calls to be issued to the Net Logon service.

```
33   18.000  BDC3      PDC3        SMB        C NT create & X,
File = \NETLOGON

34   18.012  PDC3      BDC3        SMB        R NT create & X,
FID = 0x280c
```

- Create a remote procedure call (RPC) connection between the two domain controllers. This is done using RPC bind and RPC bind acknowledgment frames.

```
35   18.017  BDC3      PDC3        MSRPC      c/o RPC Bind:
UUID 12345678-1234-ABCD-EF00-01234567CFFB

36   18.026  PDC3      BDC3        MSRPC      c/o RPC Bind Ack:
call 0x0  assoc grp 0x10EE9  xmit 0x1630
```

- Establish a secure channel by verifying the credentials of the BDC.

  First, the BDC issues a NetrServerReqChallenge to request verification that the account name of the BDC exists at the PDC.

```
37   18.037  BDC3      PDC3        R_LOGON    RPC Client call
logon:NetrServerReqChallenge(..)

38   18.048  PDC3      BDC3        R_LOGON    RPC Server
response logon:NetrServerReqChallenge(..)
```

  Then the BDC verifies its account password at the PDC with a NetrServerAuthenticate2 call.

```
39   18.062  BDC3      PDC3        R_LOGON    RPC Client call
logon:NetrServerAuthenticate2(..)

40   18.134  PDC3      BDC3        R_LOGON    RPC Server
response logon:NetrServerAuthenticate2(..)
```

Once the required sessions and secure channel have been established, database verification can proceed.

Verifying the Database

The BDC can verify its database and synchronize, if necessary. The following graphic illustrates the traffic generated during database verification.

Frequency: Every reboot

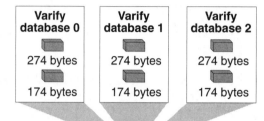

After a secure channel has been established, the BDC can begin to verify its user accounts database as follows:

- Three "RPC Client call" frames are issued. These three frames are NetrDatabaseDeltas (Operation Number 0x7) calls and are used to tell the PDC the serial number, or version ID, of each of the databases at the BDC. They are also used to request updates to the directory services database.

- For each "RPC Client call," there is an "RPC Server response" frame with the requested data, sent from the PDC.

```
43   18.529  BDC3        PDC3       R_LOGON    RPC Client call
logon:NetrDatabaseDeltas(..)

44   18.544  PDC3        BDC3       R_LOGON    RPC Server
response logon:NetrDatabaseDeltas(..)

45   18.560  BDC3        PDC3       R_LOGON    RPC Client call
logon:NetrDatabaseDeltas(..)

46   18.575  PDC3        BDC3       R_LOGON    RPC Server
response logon:NetrDatabaseDeltas(..)

47   18.619  BDC3        PDC3       R_LOGON    RPC Client call
logon:NetrDatabaseDeltas(..)

48   18.635  PDC3        BDC3       R_LOGON    RPC Server
response logon:NetrDatabaseDeltas(..)
```

These six frames total approximately 1344 bytes, depending upon computer names, if no accounts are synchronized. If there are any updated accounts to be synchronized, this will add additional bytes of traffic, and possibly additional frames.

Periodic Updates of the Database

The user accounts database is also updated periodically as changes are made to the PDC's database. The periodic update process involves:

- The PDC announces a change to the SAM
- The BDC connects to IPC$ of the PDC
- The BDC establishes a secure channel to the PDC
- The BDC requests synchronization of the account database
- The BDC uses SMB or RPC calls to transfer the updated data

By default, the PDC verifies its databases every five minutes, looking for changes to any of the three databases. When a change is noticed, it sends a message to all BDCs that need the notification, indicating that an update has been made to one of the databases. The PDC maintains a table of each BDC, and the version ID of each of their databases. If a BDC has an up-to-date database, it is not notified of the update.

Note By default, Windows NT Server 4.0 sends the announcement to a maximum of 10 BDCs at one time. If there are more than 10 BDCs, additional announcements are sent after one of the first 10 BDCs has completed synchronization. This repeats until all BDCs have been synchronized.

PDC Announcement

When the PDC detects a change to one of its databases, it notifies each BDC that needs to be updated with an "Announce Change to UAS or SAM" message to the NETLOGON mailslot.

```
1    15.062  PDC3      BDC3       NETLOGON  Announce Change to UAS or
SAM
```

The frame is directed to the NetBIOS name of the BDC. The NETLOGON portion of the frame identifies this as an operation code of "Announce Change to UAS or SAM" and includes:

- The serial number.

- Encrypted date and time.

- Pulse and Random parameter values.

- The Primary DC Name and Domain Name values.

- The version ID's, or serial numbers, for each of the three databases, as well as the Domain SID (Security Identifier).

Periodic Update

When the BDC receives the update announcement from the PDC, it checks to verify the version numbers referenced in the announcement message. If the announced version ID's are later than the version ID's of the local databases, the BDC requests the updated data. This is done in the following sequence:

- The BDC connects to IPC$ of the PDC. This is only necessary if the connection had timed out from the verification phase at restart, or from the last update. If this is necessary, it may take up to 11 frames and 1280 bytes to establish the required sessions and connection to IPC$. The TCP session will time out after 10 minutes of inactivity.

- The BDC establishes a secure channel to the PDC. This should only be necessary if the secure channel that was established during the initialization phase was broken.

- The BDC uses Net Logon Service to verify the account database. A named pipe open request is made for Net Logon, as well as an RPC session. This generates 719 bytes and four frames.

```
2    15.841   BDC3      PDC3      SMB C NT create & X, File =
\NETLOGON

3    15.855   PDC3      BDC3      SMB R NT create & X, FID =
0xc007

4    15.860   BDC3      PDC3      MSRPC c/o RPC Bind:

5    15.871   PDC3      BDC3      MSRPC c/o RPC Bind Ack:
```

The updated data is transferred using SMB or RPC calls (depending on the size of the update). This will be initiated with an "RPC Client call" issuing the NetrDatabaseDeltas API. The response may require multiple frames, depending upon how much data is returned.

```
6    15.875  BDC3        PDC3        R_LOGON   RPC Client call
logon:NetrDatabaseDeltas(..)

7    15.981  PDC3        BDC3        R_LOGON   RPC Server
response logon:NetrDatabaseDeltas(..)

8    15.986  BDC3        PDC3        SMB C read & X, FID =
0xc007, Read 0x1d8 at 0x00000000

9    15.990  PDC3        BDC3        SMB R read & X, Read 0x1d8
```

This entire process could take as few as 10 frames, and about one second to complete (for the addition of two users). These 12 frames totaled 3259 bytes of data in a test environment with full information for two user accounts, including full name, comment, and group membership. Two frames, one 1138 bytes and the other 590, transferred the two user accounts.

Complete Update

Starting with Windows NT 3.5*x*, most synchronization events are partial updates. This means that the entire database is not delivered to the BDC, rather, only updated records are transferred. However, occasionally it is possible for complete, or full, synchronization to occur. This generally happens if:

- A new BDC is installed.
- The change log file fills, and starts wrapping (over-writing changes).
- An error occurs during a partial synchronization attempt.
- The administrator at the BDC issues a **net accounts /sync** command.

When a full synchronization event occurs, much more data is transferred between the PDC and the BDC than is probably necessary, but to ensure the integrity of the databases, the full data transfer occurs.

▶ **To force a synchronization event**

To force a BDC to synchronize its databases with the PDC, complete the following steps.

1. From Server Manager, click the BDC.

2. From the **Computer** menu, click **Synchronize With PDC**.

3. Click **Yes** when prompted for confirmation to synchronize the controllers.

4. Click **OK** to close the message referencing viewing the Event Log to verify the success of the update.

Analyzing BDC Initialization Traffic

In this exercise, you analyze traffic generated from a BDC initialization, including finding the PDC, establishing a secure channel, and verifying its directory services databases.

➤ **To analyze traffic related to finding the PDC**

In this procedure, you analyze the network traffic generated to find the PDC. Frames 1 through 16 contain general DHCP address renewal, WINS registration, and browser announcement frames. Frames 17 through 24 deal with finding the PDC.

1. Open Bootbdc.cap.

2. What is occurring in frames 17 and 18?

   _____

   _____

3. What is occurring in frames 19 and 20?

   _____

   _____

4. What is occurring in frames 21 and 22?

   _____

   _____

5. How much traffic was generated by the NETLOGON query and response?

   _____

   _____

This traffic should be generated only during initialization of the BDC.

➤ To analyze secure channel establishment traffic

In this procedure, you analyze the network traffic generated to establish a secure channel. Frames 23 through 33 prepare the servers for secure channel establishment by creating the required sessions. Frames 34 through 42 complete the establishment of the secure channel.

1. What service is used to establish a secure channel?

   _____

   _____

   Hint: view **SMB: Command File name** in frame 34.

2. Frames 36 and 37 establish the named pipes session for communications between the domain controllers. How much traffic was generated during the named pipes session creation?

   _____

   _____

3. Frames 38 through 41 establish the secure channel for communications between the domain controllers. How much traffic was generated during the secure channel establishment?

   _____

   _____

4. What server is requesting a secure channel?

   _____

   _____

   Hint: check **R_LOGON: ComputerName** in frame 38.

5. What account is being authenticated as part of the secure channel establishment?

   _____

   _____

   Hint: check **R_LOGON: AccountName** in frame 40.

This traffic should be generated only during initialization of the BDC.

➤ **To analyze database verification traffic**

In this procedure, you analyze the network traffic generated during database verification of the directory services database. Frames 44 and 45, and 53 through 56 verify the version of the directory services databases.

1. How much traffic was generated during the verification of the three databases?

_____

_____

2. Were any updated records transferred during database verification?

_____

_____

Hint: check the R_LOGON hexadecimal data for each of the response frames.

Analyzing Directory Services Database Synchronization Traffic

In this exercise, you analyze traffic generated a BDC synchronizing its directory services database with the PDC.

➤ **To analyze directory services synchronization traffic**

In this procedure, you analyze the network traffic generated during directory services database synchronization for user addition. Frames 1 through 6 are used to determine the IP and media access control (MAC) addresses of a BDC.

1. Open Addusers.cap.

2. Display the details of frame 7 to answer the following questions.

3. What is the purpose of this frame?

_____

_____

Hint: check **NETLOGON: Opcode**.

4. Is this announcement directed or broadcast?

_____

_____

5. If there was only one announcement, and it was sent directly to the BDC, how many BDCs do you think are in this domain?

_____

_____

6. Who was the announcement sent to?

_____

_____

Hint: check **NBT: Destination Name**.

7. How large was the announcement?

_____

_____

After the announcement, the BDC prepares for synchronization by establishing the necessary sessions. This occurs in frames 8 through 18.

8. How much traffic was generated by the named pipe establishment in frames 19 and 20?

_____

_____

9. What user accounts were added to the database?

_____

_____

Hint: check the data in the Hex pane of frames 22 and 24.

10. How large was each frame that transferred a user account?

_____

_____

11. How long did it take from the PDC announcement until the new user accounts were transferred to the BDC and acknowledged?

_____

_____

➤ **To analyze traffic related to subsequent account synchronization**

In this procedure, you analyze the network traffic generated during directory services database synchronization. This traffic is a result of a user account modification.

1. Open Chnguser.cap.

2. Why did this synchronization event generate less traffic than the one in Addusers.cap?

_____

_____

Hint: determine the difference between the two traffic patterns.

3. What user account was modified in the database?

_____

_____

4. Was the entire account synchronized with the BDC, or just the changed data (in this case, the user account description)?

_____

_____

5. How large was the frame that transferred the user account?

_____

_____

6. How long did it take from the PDC announcement until the new user account was transferred to the BDC and acknowledged?

_____

_____

Analyzing Trust Relationship Traffic

Trust relationships produce three types of traffic: establishing the trust, importing accounts, and pass-through authentication. The following graphic illustrates an overview of the traffic generated by trust relationships.

Frequency:

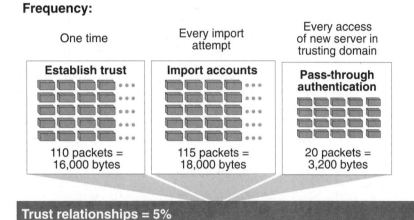

| | One time | Every import attempt | Every access of new server in trusting domain |

| Establish trust | Import accounts | Pass-through authentication |
| 110 packets = 16,000 bytes | 115 packets = 18,000 bytes | 20 packets = 3,200 bytes |

Trust relationships = 5%

In an environment where there is centralized administration and individual control of distributed resources, establishing a master accounts domain with multiple resource domains is a good solution. Trust relationships are a necessary component of this solution as they allow user accounts from the accounts domain to have access to resources in the resource domains.

Establishing a Trust

To establish a trust, one domain must permit a second domain to trust it. Then the second domain adds the first domain as a trusted domain. Once this is accomplished, the administrator of a trusting domain can assign permissions for local resources to accounts that reside in the trusted domain.

Whenever a user in the trusted domain attempts to access resources in a trusting domain, the trusting domain passes account authentication on to the trusted domain.

Relative Impact on the Network

There are three areas that generate network traffic:

- The process of establishing a trust relationship generates about 110 frames and 16,000 bytes of network traffic. This process is only performed one time per trust relationship established.

- Using trusted accounts also generates a lot of traffic. This traffic occurs whenever the trusting domain's administrator needs to assign permissions to a trusted account for a local resource, or add a trusted account to a local group.

- Pass-through authentication is the most frequent type of trust relationship traffic. There are two different types of pass-through authentication: when a user in a trusted domain attempts to access a resource in a trusting domain, and when a user at a Windows NT Workstation computer attempts to log on using a trusted account, and the computer is a member of a trusting domain.

Establishing a Trust

The process of establishing a trust relationship is only done once per set of domains. Establishing a trust relationship is a two-step process.

Permitting the Trust

In step one, the trusted domain permits another domain to trust it. The only network traffic that is generated during the permitting portion of the trust is if there are BDCs in the trusted domain. If there are, then the PDC will announce a change to the SAM. The trusting domain name is added as a hidden account in the SAM Accounts database, and synchronization occurs on this database.

Adding a Trusted Domain

The second part in the process of establishing a trust relationship occurs when the trusting domain adds the first domain as a trusted domain. This sequence of traffic is generated for each set of domains that establish a trust relationship, only one time per set, in each direction of the trust. The trusting PDC:

- Determines the name and address of the trusted PDC using normal WINS and NETLOGON queries. This takes up to 10 frames and generates almost 1200 bytes of traffic.

- Establishes TCP and NetBIOS sessions with the PDC of the trusted domain, as well as negotiates SMB protocols. This is standard file session traffic. This takes seven frames, and generates about 745 bytes of traffic.

- Attempts to connect to IPC$ of the trusted PDC using the trusting domain's account as a normal user. This process fails because the account is not allowed to perform normal file session connections. This is done to validate that the account has been created in the trusted domain. These two frames generate about 400 bytes of traffic, depending upon account (domain) names.

```
18  9.711 INSTRUCTOR  PDC3   SMB  C session setup & X,
Username = DOMAIN0$, and C tree connect & X

19  9.751 PDC3            INSTRUCTOR   SMB  R session setup & X
- NT error, System, Error, Code = (408)
```

- Terminates the session with the PDC of the trusted domain, using three frames and 180 bytes.

- Retrieves a list of backup browsers and servers in the trusted domain using normal browse list retrieval techniques. This can generate around 15 frames and about 2400 bytes.

- Connects to a domain controller in the trusted domain and performing various calls to the LSA of the trusted domain controller. These calls retrieve the domain name of the trusted domain. There is a total of 55 frames and about 8,300 bytes of traffic.

Once the appropriate information has been retrieved from the trusted domain controller, the trusting PDC updates its LSA database. If there are BDCs in the trusting domain, this update needs to be synchronized with all of the BDCs.

Finally, the trusting domain controller will query WINS for all domain controllers of the trusted domain, and attempt to log in to the trusted domain, this time specifying its account as a special type of account "Interdomain Trust User Account." If the logon is successful, the trust relationship has been successfully established. This process, along with the appropriate session teardown frames, generates around 17 frames and about 2300 bytes of traffic.

```
97   11.318  INSTRUCTOR    *BROADCAST    NETLOGON SAM LOGON request
from client

98   11.321  INSTRUCTOR    PDC3          NETLOGON SAM LOGON request
from client

101  11.334  PDC3          INSTRUCTOR    NETLOGON SAM Response to SAM
LOGON request
```

Maintaining a Trust Relationship

There is very little maintenance traffic that is generated as a result of establishing a trust. Each time the trusting PDC is restarted, it must verify the trust relationship. This process generates the same traffic as is generated at the end of the trust establishment phase. The trusting domain controller queries WINS for a list of domain controllers in the trusted domain, and then attempts to log in to the domain using the Interdomain Trust User Account. If successful, the trust has been verified and the password assigned to the trust relationship is changed immediately and then every seven days thereafter.

Importing Trusted Accounts

After a trust relationship has been established, the network administrator at the trusting domain may decide to either add an account from the trusted domain to a local group, or grant the trusted account access to a specific resource on a trusting server. The following traffic is generated by the trusting domain controller:

- Connects to IPC$ of a trusted domain controller, queries LSA, and terminates the sessions. This can generate around 60 frames and 9000 bytes of network traffic. The establishment of TCP and NetBIOS sessions may be required, if they have timed out due to inactivity.

- Connects to IPC$ of a trusted domain controller and queries SAM for a list of trusted accounts. This process generates varying amounts of traffic, depending upon the number of trusted accounts available. For a listing of 12 trusted accounts, it took 53 frames and 9500 bytes. The 12 trusted accounts were returned in only two frames. The first frame returned the list of trusted global groups, while the second request returned the list of trusted user accounts.

This traffic pattern will be repeated every time the list of trusted accounts is requested by a trusting domain member.

Additional traffic will be generated each time the members of a local group, of which a trusted account is a member, are displayed. This traffic would also occur if displaying access permissions for a resource to which a trusted account was assigned access. The trusting domain needs to enumerate the SID of the trusted account into a name that can be displayed in the administrative utility. This process can generate around 45 frames and 7,000 bytes of data. Of these frames, it only required two frames to look up a SID, and return the appropriate account name.

Pass-Through Authentication

The most common source of traffic from a trust relationship is caused whenever a user needs to access resources in another domain. The following graphic illustrates the traffic generated during pass-through authentication.

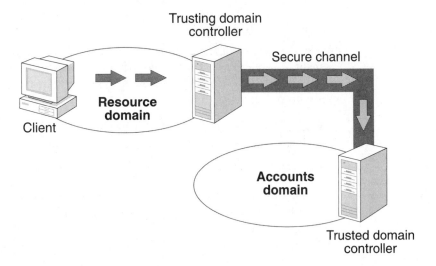

When a user in a trusted domain attempts to access a resource in a trusting domain, its account must be validated. The trusting domain is not able to do this, and in order to validate the account, a process called pass-through authentication takes place.

Another form of pass-through authentication occurs when a Windows NT–based computer is a member of one domain, and the user account that is attempting to log on is a member of a different domain. The validation of the account is handled by pass-through authentication.

Pass-through authentication will be the most common source of traffic related to trust relationships.

Making a Remote Resource Request

The network traffic generated by a user accessing a resource in a remote Windows NT Server domain is as follows:

- Request a browse list from a backup browser in the remote domain.

- Establish TCP and NetBIOS sessions with the target server in the remote domain, as well as negotiate SMB protocols.

At this point, the client attempts to connect to the requested share name at the target computer. The connection request contains the user name, computer name, and domain name. The target computer is not able to validate the logon request, and pass-through authentication occurs. All traffic to this point is normal file session traffic, that might include name and address resolution.

Validating the User Account

When a request to validate a user account that is in a trusted domain occurs, the domain controller in the trusting domain must contact a domain controller in the trusted domain. The traffic generated by the trusting domain controller to complete this process is as follows:

- Establish TCP and NetBIOS sessions with the domain controller in the trusted domain, as well as negotiate SMB protocols.

- Create a null session to IPC$ of the trusted domain controller.

The domain controller of the trusting domain then establishes a named pipe session with the domain controller of the trusted domain, and sends three API calls to the server using RPC. These API's are directed to Net Logon service of the target server, and include:

- NetrServerReqChallenge

- NetrServerAuthenticate2

- NetrLogonSamLogon

The first two APIs (and responses) serve to establish a secure channel between the two domain controllers, and were documented in the section on synchronizing the directory services database earlier in this module. These two APIs, and responses, may not be necessary if the secure channel has already been established between the two domains, which happens during the initial pass-through validation attempt. The third API requests logon validation, and provides the user name, computer name, and domain name of the logon request from the client computer.

```
30   2.541   INSTRUCTOR      PDC3        R_LOGON RPC Client call
logon:NetrLogonSamLogon(..)

31   2.593   PDC3            INSTRUCTOR  R_LOGON RPC Server response
logon:NetrLogonSamLogon(..)
```

These two frames can generate around 950 bytes of traffic, depending upon account names.

The entire process of validating the user account using pass-through authentication requires between 3200 and 4000 bytes of traffic, 20 frames, and 200 milliseconds to complete. A later pass-through validation attempt took only two frames, 942 bytes and 13 milliseconds with the secure channel already established.

Windows NT Accounts and Pass-Through Authentication

The other category of pass-through authentication occurs when a user account in a trusted domain attempts to log on to a Windows NT-based computer that is a member of a trusting domain. In this case, the process is basically the same as a resource access generated pass-through authentication, with the following modifications:

- The request that initiates pass-through authentication is not due to a connection request, but a NetrLogonSamLogon request, which includes the user, domain, and computer account names. This frame is around 420 bytes in size, depending upon names used.

```
20   9.010   NTW1          INSTRUCTOR     R_LOGON RPC Client
call logon:NetrLogonSamLogon(..)
```

- The pass-through authentication request from the trusting domain controller is a NetrLogonSamLogon request to the trusted domain controller. This request will be the same size as the initial client's request.

```
27   9.128   INSTRUCTOR    PDC3           R_LOGON RPC Client
call logon:NetrLogonSamLogon(..)
```

- The trusted domain controller responds with a NetrLogonSamLogon response message, which is then passed back to the initiating client by its local domain controller. This response will be larger than the request, as validation information is returned. It can be around 500 bytes in size.

```
29   9.296   PDC3          INSTRUCTOR     R_LOGON RPC Server
response logon:NetrLogonSamLogon(..)

30   9.300   INSTRUCTOR    NTW1           R_LOGON RPC Server
response logon:NetrLogonSamLogon(..)
```

The secure channel (and all required sessions) are still necessary, and if not established, will be done before the request can be passed along. This traffic will be repeated each new time a trusted account is requesting logon validation at a client computer that is a member of a different domain.

Optimizing Trust Relationship Traffic

Generally, you won't optimize trust relationship traffic. The graphic below illustrates the optimization techniques for trust relationships.

- **Reduce the number of trusts**

- **Use group accounts rather than individual accounts**

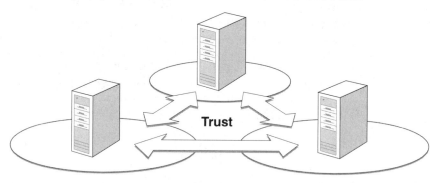

Although trust relationships do not produce a high percentage of traffic, there are two areas that can help reduce trust-related traffic.

Reduce the Number of Trusts

The obvious means of reducing trust relationship traffic is to reduce the number of trusts. This means giving up the benefits of the master domain/resource domain model. However, it may be worth reviewing existing or planned resource domains to ensure that each one is appropriate and necessary.

Verify that each one-way trust is appropriate. For example, in an environment where two domains trust each other, are both trusts really required? If not, break the non-essential trust.

There is very little maintenance traffic related to trust relationships. Once the trust has been established, most of the traffic is generated by importing and verifying trusted accounts, and pass-through authentication.

Use Group Accounts

One way to reduce the traffic associated with the verification of trusted accounts is to:

- At the trusted domain, add the appropriate users to a global group.

- At the trusting domain, add the trusted global group to a local group or local resource.

By adding a set of users from a global group, as opposed to adding the users individually to a local group or resource, the traffic required to verify the SIDs and associate names with the SIDs can be reduced. In a simple test, the lookup of a single SID for a global group took 552 bytes, whereas the same lookup for SIDs for two trusted user accounts took 636 bytes. While this is not that much extra traffic, it was only for two users. Often, many users from a trusted domain are allowed access to a resource in a trusting domain. By using a global group, the traffic required to look up those accounts can be reduced, which could be substantial over a period of time.

Analyzing Trusted Account Traffic

In this exercise, you analyze network traffic generated when importing a trusted account and the verification of an imported account.

➤ To analyze trusted account traffic

In this procedure, you analyze the network traffic generated during the importing of a trusted account. Frames 1 through 62 are establishing sessions and verifying the trust relationship. Frames 63 through 77 are preparing for importing the list of trusted accounts by establishing the necessary sessions. Frames 78 through 96 are used to retrieve the list of trusted accounts.

1. Open Import.cap.

2. How many frames did it take to establish the session with the LSA at the trusted domain controller, and display the trusted accounts?

_____

_____

3. What type of accounts were transferred in response to frame number 90?

_____

_____

Hint: view the hexadecimal data for frame 91.

4. What type of accounts were transferred in response to frame 92?

_____

_____

Hint: view the hexadecimal data for frame 93.

5. How many accounts would have been displayed in User Manager for Domains?

_____

_____

Hint: view the hexadecimal data for frames 91 and 93.

6. How much network traffic was generated to display the list of trusted accounts? Only include the request messages and data frames.

_____

_____

7. How long did the entire process of displaying the list of trusted accounts take?

_____

_____

This traffic pattern would occur each time the trusted domain is selected in any **List names from** box.

➤ To analyze trusted account verification traffic

In this procedure, you analyze the network traffic generated during the verification of a trusted account SID in an attempt to retrieve the account name. This traffic was a result of using User Manager for Domains to view a local group. This local group contained a member that was a trusted account. Frames 1 through 29 are establishing sessions and verifying the trust relationship. Frames 30 through 46 are retrieving the name of the trusted account. This entire set of frames produced about 7500 bytes of network traffic.

1. Open Getname.cap.

2. What frame requested the translation of the account name?

   _____

   _____

   Hint: look for the description of **R_LSARPC** frames.

3. What account was translated in response to this request?

   _____

   _____

4. How large was the response frame?

   _____

   _____

5. How long did it take to resolve the SID into the account name to be displayed?

   _____

   _____

This traffic pattern would occur every time a trusted account was to be displayed in any of the administrative applications.

Analyzing Pass-Through Authentication Traffic

In this exercise, you analyze network traffic generated during pass-through authentication.

➤ **To analyze pass-through authentication traffic**

In this procedure, you analyze the network traffic generated during pass-through authentication due to a trusted user accessing a resource in a trusting domain. Frames 1 through 21 show the Windows 95-based client retrieving the browse list of local servers from its backup browser.

1. Open Passthru.cap.

2. Frames 22 through 38 retrieve the list of available domains. How many domains were available?

   _____

   _____

3. What is the purpose of frame number 39?

_____

_____

Hint: check **BROWSER: Command**.

4. For what domain was the request made?

_____

_____

Hint: check **NBT: Destination Name**.

5. Was the request directed or broadcast?

_____

_____

6. How many backup browsers were there in Domain3?

_____

_____

Hint: check **BROWSER: Backup Servers** in frame 46.

7. Frames 47 through 67 establish a session with a backup browser in Domain3 and retrieve a list of servers in the trusting domain. Why is pass-through authentication not used in the session connection to \\PDC3\IPC$?

_____

_____

Hint: check **SMB: Command Account name** in frame 58.

8. Frames 68 through 113 retrieve the list of shared resources from a specific server in the trusting domain. Pass-through authentication is required in this sequence. In what frame is the first indication of pass-through authentication?

_____

_____

9. Why is pass-through authentication required now, and not back in frame 58?

_____

_____

Hint: check **SMB: Command Account name** in frame 77.

10. What is the user name and domain name that is being pass-through authenticated?

_____

_____

Hint: view the server message block (SMB) data for frame 77.

11. What is occurring in frames 91 through 99?

_____

_____

12. How long did it take to validate the account using pass-through authentication?

_____

_____

13. How many total frames were generated in performing pass-through authentication?

_____

_____

14. How long did it take, from the initial request of the client in frame 77 to the confirmation from the server in frame 102, to perform pass-through authentication?

_____

_____

15. Frames 114 through 139 establish a connection to a resource in the trusting domain. In this sequence, there is another request for pass-through authentication. Why does this occur?

_____

_____

16. How long did it take to validate the account using pass-through authentication this time?

_____

_____

17. How much network traffic was generated to perform pass-through authentication?

_____

_____

18. Why did it only take two frames to pass-through authenticate this account?

_____

_____

➤ **To analyze Windows NT Workstation
logon pass-through authentication traffic**

In this procedure, you analyze the network traffic generated during pass-through authentication as a result of a user logging in to an accounts domain from a Windows NT Workstation with its computer account in a resource domain. Frames 1 through 9 show the Windows NT Workstation-based client initializing DHCP and WINS.

1. Open Ntwpta.cap.

2. What is occurring in frames 10 and 11?

_____

_____

3. How many domain controllers were registered in the domain?

_____

_____

Hint: check **NBT: Owner IP Address** records.

4. What account is requesting validation?

_____

_____

Hint: check **NETLOGON: Unicode User Name** in frames 12, 15, 18, or 19.

5. Does pass-through authentication occur with this logon request?

_____

_____

6. How much traffic was generated to validate this logon request?

_____

_____

7. In Frames 22 through 46, the Windows NT Workstation connects to the validating domain controller, and queries for a list of trusted domains. Are there any trusted domains to be displayed in the **Logon Information** dialog box?

_____

_____

Hint: check **R_LSARPC: PWSTR Buffer** in frame 40.

8. Frames 47 through 55 create the secure channel with the validating domain controller. Frames 56 through 65 are continuing the registration of names with WINS, and performing browser functions. Notice the time delay (just over 10 seconds) between frames 65 and 66. What is occurring in frame 66?

_____

_____

Hint: check the Hex pane details of frame 66.

9. Frames 67 through 87 are a result of frame 66. What is occurring in this set of frames?

_____

_____

Hint: check frames 86 and 87.

10. How long did it take, from initial request by client to response to client, to complete the pass-through authentication?

_____

_____

11. How much traffic was generated by the logon request and response?

_____

_____

This traffic pattern occurs each time a user logs on to the accounts domain from a computer in a resource domain.

The rest of the traffic was TCP acknowledgments, and the client connecting the PDC of its validating domain to query for Ntconfig.pol.

Analyzing Server Browser Traffic

Most of the traffic generated by browsing is due to server-related browsing. The following graphic illustrates an overview of the traffic generated by server browser processes.

Frequency:

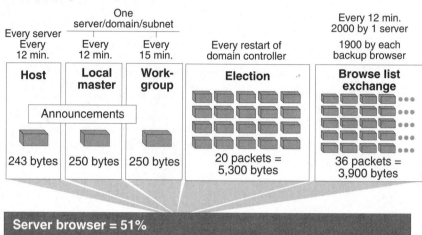

In order to effectively locate network resources, browsing is implemented by default on a Windows NT Server network.

In addition to the client-to-server browser traffic, there are several additional types of browser traffic generated between servers that account for many frames on the network.

The basics of the server browsing process are:

- Upon startup, the PDC of a domain assumes the role of domain master browser of the domain.

- Upon startup, each BDC of the domain becomes either a backup browser or a local master browser, depending on whether there is already a master browser for that domain on that subnet.

- Every 15 minutes, each master browser (on each subnet) announces itself to the master browsers of other domains on the local subnet.

- Every 12 minutes, each domain master browser contacts WINS for a listing of all domains (<1B> names).

- Every 12 minutes, each master browser contacts the domain master browser to update the browse lists.

- Every 12 minutes, each backup browser contacts its local master browser to retrieve an updated browse list.

Types of Server Browser Traffic

All computers with server components, that is, the ability to share network resources, announce themselves to the master browser in their local domain. Servers that operate in any capacity as a potential browser, backup browser, or master browser become involved in several other communications as well:

- Browser elections occur whenever the master browser cannot be located on the local subnet and whenever a domain controller initializes.

- Master browsers in different domains communicate with each other so that servers and resources can be accessed throughout the network.

- Backup browsers receive updated browse lists from the local master browser.

Relative Impact on the Network

Browsing certainly produces a large share of the server-to-server traffic on the network. Optimizing browser traffic may mean reducing the traffic to allow the user more bandwidth, or it may mean increasing the traffic to provide for more up-to-date browse lists to the user when requested.

Browser Announcements and Elections

Host announcements provide notification to the master browser of server availability. Elections are initiated from time to time to make sure that there is always a master browser available.

Announcements

All hosts that have a server component, such as Windows for Workgroups, Windows 95, and Windows NT Workstation-based computers, announce themselves every 12 minutes to the local master browser. This allows the host to be included in the browse list for the domain. This announcement includes any browser capabilities. Each announcement will be around 243 bytes, depending upon capabilities.

```
14   17.474  BDC3      *BROADCAST    BROWSER  Host Announcement [0x01]
```

Elections

If the computer making the announcement has the potential to become the master browser, it determines if it should be the master browser or not. To do this, it first must determine who the master browser is. This is done by issuing an Announcement Request frame. This frame is a subnet broadcast, and is about 220 bytes in size, depending upon the computer name of the requesting computer.

```
57   21.713  BDC3      *BROADCAST     BROWSER Announcement Request
[0x02]
```

If there is a local master browser, it responds to this request with a broadcast response, called a Local Master Announcement. This is the same size as its host announcement.

```
58   21.718  PDC3      *BROADCAST     BROWSER Local Master Announcement
[0x0f] PDC3
```

If there is no master browser, or if the requesting computer thinks it could be the master browser, as indicated by its capabilities as announced in its last host announcement, it forces an election. An election frame is generally around 225 bytes in size.

```
73   22.134  BDC3      *BROADCAST     BROWSER Election [0x08] [Force]
```

All potential browsers, as well as current backup and master browsers, can respond to the election. A host will only respond if it has a higher election criteria than that of the initiator. The browser software on each type of computer (Windows for Workgroups, Windows 95, and Windows NT) waits a specific period of time before responding. This wait period allows for the host with the highest probability of winning (Windows NT, then Windows 95, and finally Windows for Workgroups) to respond first. The election response is around 230 bytes in size.

```
75   22.236  PDC3      *BROADCAST     BROWSER Election [0x08] PDC3
```

After initiating its initial response, the computer will wait a period of time before sending its election response to see if any other computer responds with a higher election criteria.

```
83   23.237  PDC3      *BROADCAST     BROWSER Election [0x08] PDC3

84   24.239  PDC3      *BROADCAST     BROWSER Election [0x08] PDC3

85   25.241  PDC3      *BROADCAST     BROWSER Election [0x08] PDC3
```

After four election responses, the host with the highest criteria wins the election, and initiates a Local Master Announcement to let all browser computers know that it is the master browser.

```
86   26.244  PDC3      *BROADCAST    BROWSER Local Master Announcement
[0x0f] PDC3
```

Establishing Backup Browsers

The master browser will determine if a potential browser should become a backup browser. By default, all BDCs (no matter how many) are backup browsers. If there are not enough for the number of computers on the local subnet, the master browser will request a potential browser to become a backup browser.

Server Browse List Updates

In a routed Transmission Control Protocol/Internet Protocol (TCP/IP) environment, a domain master browser is elected for each domain. There is one domain master browser for each domain throughout the entire enterprise. If available, the domain master browser is the PDC. One of the roles of the domain master browser is to accumulate a list of other domains that exist in the enterprise. This is accomplished in two ways:

- Every 15 minutes, each master browser (one on each subnet that the domain has members on) announces itself to other master browsers. This is done with a Workgroup Announcement frame. This frame is about 250 bytes in size, and is directed to the special NetBIOS name of <01><02>__ MSBROWSE__<02><01>. This name is registered by each master browser. Upon receiving a Workgroup Announcement, a master browser checks its local list of domains. If the Workgroup Announcement is for a new domain, it is added to the list. This list is then exchanged with the domain master browser at 12-minute intervals.

```
1    191.830 INSTRUCTOR    *BROADCAST   BROWSER Workgroup
Announcement [0x0c] DOMAIN0
```

- Every 12 minutes, each domain master browser contacts its WINS server, and queries for all registered domain names. These domains are then added to the master browse list, and exchanged with master browsers at the 12-minute interval. The entire process of retrieving a list of domains from WINS takes 22 frames and generates just over 2100 bytes of traffic for 4 domains. The list of domain was requested and returned in the following two frames:

```
20   312.525 INSTRUCTOR    DHCP_WINS   R_WINSIF  RPC
Client call winsif:R_WinsGetBrowserNames(..)

21   312.531 DHCP_WINS     INSTRUCTOR  R_WINSIF  RPC
Server response winsif:R_WinsGetBrowserNames(..)
```

Now that the domain master browser has a list of domains, it must get this list out to each subnet. A master browser for each domain is elected on each subnet. All master browsers for a single domain retrieve a browse list from the domain's domain master browser every 12 minutes. This includes not only the local computers for the local domain, but also other domains that have been announced on each subnet.

Using two servers in a local domain and one remote domain, it took about 79 frames and 12,000 bytes of traffic for a local master browser to:

- Establish required sessions.

- Determine the computer name of the domain master browser.

- Retrieve the master browse list from the domain master browser.

- Send the local browse list to the domain maser browser.

When the local master browser has received an updated browse list from the domain master browser, it can then provide that list to the backup browsers. Backup browsers retrieve updated browse lists from the local master browser every 12 minutes. The process of a backup browser retrieving a browse list from the master browser is exactly the same as how a client retrieves a browse list from the backup browser, including the TCP and NetBIOS sessions, SMB protocol negotiation, and a connection to IPC$. Two API calls and appropriate responses return the list of local servers and available domains. This generates about 14 frames and just over 2000 bytes of traffic for a list of four domains and four servers.

```
10    84.501   BACKUP       INSTRUCTOR    SMB C transact, Remote API

11    84.509   INSTRUCTOR   BACKUP        SMB R transact

12    84.515   BACKUP       INSTRUCTOR    SMB C transact, Remote API

13    84.519   INSTRUCTOR   BACKUP        SMB R transact
```

The client computers can now retrieve the browse list from the backup browsers when needed.

Optimizing Server Browser Traffic

Three ways to optimized server browser traffic are to reduce the number of protocols in use, reduce the browser entries, and adjust browser parameters. The following graphic illustrates the methods used to control the network traffic generated by browsing.

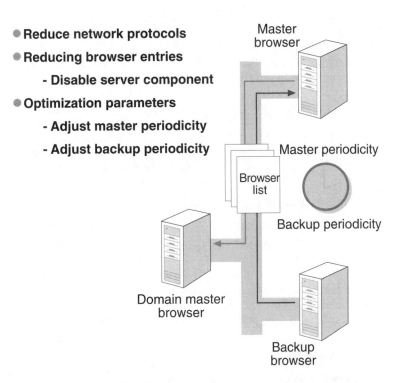

- ● **Reduce network protocols**
- ● **Reducing browser entries**
    - **- Disable server component**
- ● **Optimization parameters**
    - **- Adjust master periodicity**
    - **- Adjust backup periodicity**

Most of the traffic generated by browsing is initiated automatically by the appropriate browsing computers. These are the domain master browser, the master browsers, and the backup browsers. There are three general methods to reduce traffic: reduce the network protocols used, reduce the number of browser entries, or increase the amount of time between browser updates.

Reduce Network Protocols

The browsing process operates separately on each installed and bound protocol. So, if TCP/IP, NWLink IPX/SPX, and NetBEUI are all active on the network, each set of browser traffic, elections, host announcements, workgroup announcements, and so on occur on each protocol independently. This triples the amount of network traffic related to browsing with the only product being a browse list for three independent protocols. If possible, eliminating one or two of these protocols will greatly reduce the traffic generated for browsing.

Reduce Browser Entries

Disable the server component on computers that do not require sharing of resources. This will reduce the size of the browse lists, and therefore the traffic passing between browser servers. Each type of client, whether Windows for Workgroups, Windows 95, or Windows NT, has a method for disabling the server service. Each entry in the browse list is 27 bytes, plus space for the server comment, if any. Consider reducing server comments.

Optimization Parameters

Two parameters can be configured to control the amount of network traffic generated by the browser. Browsing parameters are found in the Registry under HKEY_LOCAL_MACHINE\SYSTEM\CurrentControlSet\Services\Browser\Parameters.

MasterPeriodicity

MasterPeriodicity specifies how frequently a master browser contacts the domain master browser. The default is 720 seconds (12 minutes), with a minimum of 300 seconds (five minutes), and a maximum value of 0x418937 (4,294,967 seconds). This parameter is added as a REG_DWORD, and can be changed dynamically without restarting the computer. This parameter should be added on the master browsers. This parameter does affect WAN traffic, as each subnet that a domain has a member on has a master browser for the domain on that subnet.

BackupPeriodicity

BackupPeriodicity specifies how frequently a backup browser contacts the master browser. Adding this parameter as a REG_DWORD requires restarting your computer. The default value for BackupPeriodicity is 720 seconds. Configuring it to 1800 (30 minutes) will reduce the frequency of browse list updates. This parameter does not affect the WAN, because backup browsers always communicate with a local master browser, never with a remote one.

Analyzing Server Browser Traffic

In this exercise, you analyze server browser activity. The capture files show periodic browser updates and WINS queries related to browsing.

➤ **To analyze server browse list update traffic**

In this procedure, you analyze server browse list update traffic. The computer Backup is a BDC. All domain controllers are automatically browser computers. After Backup has found the master browser, it needs to retrieve the current browse list. This occurs in frames 58 through 70.

1. If it is not already open, open Bootbdc.cap.

2. What is being transferred in frame 68?

_____

_____

Hint: view the hexadecimal data.

3. How many servers are in the list?

_____

_____

4. How large was the response?

_____

_____

5. Was the response directed or broadcast?

_____

_____

6. What is being transferred in frame 70?

_____

_____

Hint: view the hexadecimal data.

7. How many domains are in the browse list?

_____

_____

8. How large was this response?

_____

_____

➤ **To analyze periodic browse list update traffic**

In this procedure, you analyze periodic browse list update traffic. Frames 1 through 22 show a domain master browser retrieving a list of registered domains using WINS. Frames 23 through 40 show a backup browser retrieving a current browse list from its master browser. Every twelve minutes, each backup browser retrieves the current browse list from the master browser.

1. Open Serverbrw.cap.

2. What is being transferred in frame 18?

   _____

   _____

   Hint: check **R_WINSIF: LPBYTE pName**.

3. Select **R_WINSIF: LPBYTE pName = Domain0**, and then view the Hex pane to answer the following question. What name is registered in WINS?

   _____

   _____

4. How large was the response?

   _____

   _____

   This traffic pattern would be repeated every 12 minutes on the subnet with the domain master browser.

5. Frames 23 through 35 prepare for the browse list query by establishing the required sessions. What is being transferred in frame 37?

   _____

   _____

   Hint: view the hexadecimal data.

6. How many servers are in the list?

   _____

   _____

7. How large was the response?

   _____

   _____

8. How much smaller is this response than in the Bootbdc.cap file?

   _____

   _____

9. What is being transferred in frame 39?

   _____

   _____

10. How many domains are in the browse list?

_____

_____

11. How large was this response?

_____

_____

This traffic pattern would be repeated every 12 minutes by default, by every backup browser on each subnet.

Analyzing WINS Replication Traffic

In large networks, there may be multiple WINS servers that need to share databases. The following graphic illustrates an overview of the network traffic generated by the implementation of WINS replication partners.

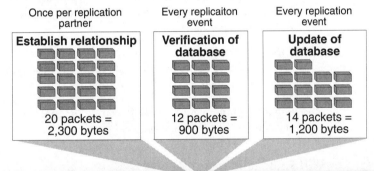

In many large organizations, it is likely that one WINS server will not be sufficient to offer the required level of fault tolerance and performance. Even though a single WINS server can support 10,000 WINS clients, it is recommended to have a backup server. WINS supports the ability of having multiple WINS servers for clients to register and query, while allowing these servers to replicate, or share, their databases with each other. The benefit of this database sharing is that eventually each WINS server will know about all of the other WINS clients that have registered with its WINS partners. This offers faster name resolution for clients.

Relative Impact on the Network

There are three distinct portions to the WINS replication process. First, the replication relationship must be established. After this, before any replication can take place, the database version numbers must be verified. Finally, records can be replicated from one database to another. The amount of traffic generated during replication is dependent upon the size of the records in the WINS database, how many records have been updated, and the frequency of the replication.

WINS Record Sizes

Each entry into the WINS database will vary in size, depending upon the type of entry being added.

- The amount of data stored for a normal (unique) client computer with a single network adapter card is between 40 and 280 bytes, depending on if the client has configured a scope ID (which can be up to 240 characters). A client without a configured scope ID would require 40 bytes in the database for each name registered.

- If the client is multi-homed (having multiple network adapters configured for TCP/IP), the amount of data stored will vary depending upon the number of IP addresses configured for the computer. It will range from 40 bytes up to 280 bytes per host.

- If the name registered is an Internet group name, such as *Domainname* <1C>, it can be up to 480 bytes if it contains it maximum number of registered hosts (which is 25).

Knowing an average record size will help in determining how much traffic will be generated during WINS replication events.

WINS Replication

WINS replication Chapter 4 lesson 2 discussed WINS servers and how they can be configured to replicate databases. Here we look at the traffic generated by this replication.

Establish the Relationship

When configuring a replication partner, the first step in the process is to add the other WINS server as a replication partner. This can be accomplished by using WINS Manager. When adding another WINS server as a replication partner, the following sequence of events occurs:

- The local WINS server establishes a TCP/IP session with the destination WINS server over TCP port 135. This session is a normal TCP three-way handshake, requiring three packets totaling 180 bytes.

- An RPC connection is then established, and the WINS database is initialized. These four frames generate 656 bytes of traffic.

```
48   11.533  DHCP_WINS      Router      MSRPC c/o RPC Bind:
UUID  E1AF8308-5D1F-11C9-91A4-08002B14A0FA

49   11.534  Router         DHCP_WINS  MSRPC c/o RPC Bind
Ack:     call 0x0  assoc grp 0x11793  xmit 0x16D0  r

50   11.541  DHCP_WINS      Router      MSRPC c/o RPC
Request:     call 0x1  opnum 0x3  context 0x0  hint 0x84

51   11.542  Router         DHCP_WINS  MSRPC c/o RPC
Response:    call 0x1  context 0x0  hint 0x80  cancels 0
```

- New TCP session and RPC connections are initialized, and RPC calls are used to validate credentials of the requesting WINS server, as well as getting the name of the remote WINS server. The validation, request, and response frames generate 580 bytes of network traffic.

```
61   11.577  DHCP_WINS      Router      TCP.AP..., len:
198, seq:   4259723-4259920, ack:   1455872

62   11.578  DHCP_WINS      Router      R_WINSIF  RPC Client
call  winsif:R_WinsGetNameAndAdd(..)

63   11.578  Router         DHCP_WINS  TCP.A...., len:
0, seq:   1455872-1455872, ack:   4259985

64   11.585  Router         DHCP_WINS  R_WINSIF  RPC Server
response  winsif:R_WinsGetNameAndAdd(..)
```

- Finally, a new TCP session is established (using TCP Port 42) to verify the partner relationship and request the initial replication.

The entire process of adding a replication partner utilizes approximately 20 frames, totaling about 2000 bytes. In each of these frames, the first 54 bytes are normal Ethernet, IP, and TCP packet headers, with the remaining bytes containing the appropriate WINS RPC call.

If configured to do so, the initial database replication will occur at this point. By default, replication can only occur between configured partners, where both servers have added each other as replication partners. Generally, the first server will be unsuccessful in performing replication, as the second WINS server has not yet added the first server as a replication partner.

The number of records to be transferred may be different with every replication event. With a sample database of 17 records, the total transfer took under two seconds and 14 total frames, including session establishment frames. One data frame contained all 17 names to be added to the partner's database. This frame was 910 bytes in size, with the final 856 bytes representing the actual records.

```
74   14.158  Router          DHCP_WINS      TCP.AP..., len: 856, seq:
1458445-1459300, ack:    4262288
```

Verify the Database

Once the relationship has been established, replication can occur at predefined intervals, or after a specific number of records have been updated. When the relationship is triggered, verification of the relationship and the databases is required. This is a simple process that generates about 12 frames and 900 bytes of traffic using a standard TCP session, two requests and responses, and TCP session termination frames.

Update the Database

Once the replication partner relationship has been configured and verified, data can be transferred. This transfer will involve sending records between the WINS servers. This transfer uses TCP Port 42.

A later update of the database, involving only one record, took less than one second and used 14 frames. The one data record was contained in one frame, devoting 72 bytes for the one record.

```
9   30.473  Router          DHCP_WINS      TCP.AP..., len: 72, seq:
3446968-3447039, ack:    6250858
```

Analyzing WINS Replication Traffic

In this exercise, you analyze WINS replication traffic.

➤ **To analyze WINS replication traffic**

In this procedure, you analyze the network traffic generated during an update to the WINS database during replication. This process generated 28 frames and 2290 bytes of traffic. Frames 1 through 16 represent the replication of the updated database.

1. Open Winsupdt.cap.

2. How long did it take to transfer the new data records?

   _____

   _____

3. What frame contained the records transferred? How large was the frame?

   _____

   _____

4. How many records were transferred?

   _____

   _____

5. What was the average record size?

   _____

   _____

6. Was any of the traffic generated during this transfer of data broadcast?

   _____

   _____

Frames 17 through 28 were used to verify the database version IDs of the remote WINS server. These 12 frames generated 896 of the 2290 bytes.

Analyzing Directory Replication Traffic

The Directory Replicator service can be used to guarantee that user logon scripts are available at each logon server, as well as copying other files configured for replication. The following graphic illustrates an overview of the network traffic generated by the Directory Replicator service.

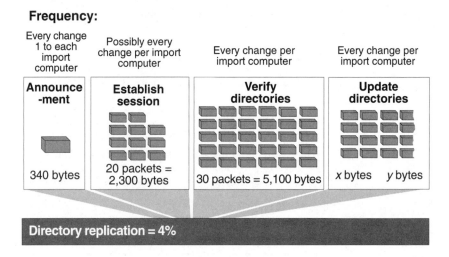

Frequency:

Every change 1 to each import computer	Possibly every change per import computer	Every change per import computer	Every change per import computer
Announce -ment	**Establish session**	**Verify directories**	**Update directories**
340 bytes	20 packets = 2,300 bytes	30 packets = 5,100 bytes	x bytes y bytes

Directory replication = 4%

The Directory Replicator service for Windows NT Server allows automatic replication, or duplication, of a directory tree between multiple computers, without the intervention of a network administrator. It is most commonly used for replicating user logon scripts from the PDC of a domain to BDCs, ensuring that no matter which domain controller a user is validated by, the user can run its logon script.

Relative Impact on the Network

Replication of logon scripts should be fairly simple and infrequent, as they generally are not extremely large in size, often less than 4 KB in size, and don't change frequently. But, if the Directory Replication service needs to replicate other files, logon scripts can be larger in size, and change more frequently, thus requiring more network traffic for replication.

Replicating Directories

Directory replication begins when the export server detects a change to the export directories. The following graphic illustrates the network traffic generated in copying directories to logon services.

Frequency:

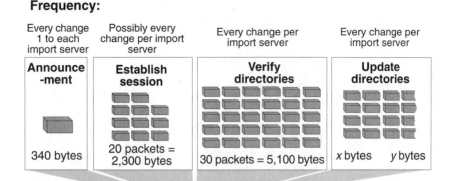

Every change 1 to each import server	Possibly every change per import server	Every change per import server	Every change per import server
Announce -ment	**Establish session**	**Verify directories**	**Update directories**
340 bytes	20 packets = 2,300 bytes	30 packets = 5,100 bytes	*x* bytes *y* bytes

Directory replication = 4%

Pulses

Every so often, the export server notifies the import computers that it is running as an export server, and indicates the first level directories in its export tree. This message serves as a notice to the import computer that it may need to synchronize if the export server has changes, or simply a pulse if no changes are detected. By default, this message is generated to each domain or server in the export server's export list every five minutes.

The directory replication process occurs as the export server detects changes in its export tree (by default the REPL$ share name). The frames are as follows:

- The export server notifies everyone in its export list that there have been changes made to the export tree. This is a broadcast announcement. The size depends on the number of subdirectories and files to be copied, but is generally in the 330 byte range. This announcement uses UDP Port 138 (NetBIOS Datagram Service).

```
1   49.765  PDC3      *BROADCAST    SMB C transact, File =
\MAILSLOT\NET\REPL_CLI
```

- The import computer(s) then make an SMB connection to the export server's REPL$ share. It will take about nine frames and 1286 bytes to establish the session.

- The import computer then queries the export server with a NetrRemoteTOD call. This is due to the fact that the directory replication process does not complete if the two servers' clocks are not within 10 minutes of each other. The request and response frames generate 390 bytes of traffic.

```
21   94.936  BDC3       PDC3        R_SRVSVC  RPC Client call
srvsvc:NetrRemoteTOD(..)

22   94.942  PDC3       BDC3        R_SRVSVC  RPC Server
response srvsvc:NetrRemoteTOD(..)
```

- Next, the import computer creates a file open to \Winreg and named pipe session to verify the export server's Registry parameters for replication. This is to determine if it needs to replicate all files, just the changed files, if it has to wait for a specific time before replicating files, and so on. These 18 frames generate about 3500 bytes of traffic.

```
26   95.499  BDC3       PDC3        SMB C NT create & X, File =
\winreg

27   95.512  PDC3       BDC3        SMB R NT create & X, FID =
0x809

28   95.516  BDC3       PDC3        MSRPC c/o RPC Bind:
UUID 338CD001-2244-31F1-AAAA-900038001003

29   95.526  PDC3       BDC3        MSRPC c/o RPC Bind Ack:
call 0x1  assoc grp 0xFB47  xmit 0x1630
```

- The import computer will then verify the directory using a total of 30 frames and generated just over 5000 bytes of data to verify an export tree and Registry parameters.

- If this is the initial replication event to transfer these files to the import computer, the server simply queries to find all files in the export tree.

```
44   95.610  BDC3       PDC3        SMB C check path, File =
\Scripts

45   95.614  PDC3       BDC3        SMB R check path

46   95.618  BDC3       PDC3        SMB C transact2 Findfirst,
File = \Scripts\*

47   95.625  PDC3       BDC3        SMB R transact2 Open
(response)
```

- If an update of files is required, this connection is used to copy the updated files from the export server to the import computer. The number of frames will vary depending on the amount of data that needs to be replicated between the two computers.

The entire process of replicating two files totaling 1.5 KB generated 160 frames and almost 26,000 bytes of data.

Optimizing Directory Replication Traffic

The Directory Replicator service on Windows NT Server provides the ability to automatically duplicate a source tree to multiple other computers. This process can involve a number of frames, depending on the amount of data to be replicated. By default the export server checks every five minutes for data to be replicated. This frequency interval can be configured in the Registry. This process generates very little network activity unless data on the export server has changed.

A sample directory containing 16 files and 426,000 bytes of data took 1425 frames and approximately 42 seconds to replicate, whereas deleting one file from that same export list took only 251 frames and 48 seconds to verify and update. Additionally, every five minutes (default configuration) the export server will notify each import computer or domain with a list of its first level directories.

Directory Structure

The best way to reduce the amount of traffic generated by the Directory Replicator service is to use a flat, shallow directory structure. Having very large, or deep, and frequently changing top-level replicated directories is very taxing on the Directory Replicator service. The Directory Replicator service checks and then copies an entire top-level directory if any file in that directory has changed. Because some file is likely to change in large directories, the Directory Replicator is constantly rechecking and recopying these directories. It would generate far less traffic if multiple, shallower top-level directories were used in place of a smaller number of deep directory structures. This would put as many of the files as possible in directories where changes are very infrequent.

Using Server Manager to Control Replication

It can be beneficial to prevent the directory replicator service from exporting specific directories during certain periods of the day. To prevent the export server from replicating directories during heavy network usage times, a lock can be added to the export server. This can be done using Server Manager, or the Server option in Control Panel.

➤ **To prevent the export server from replicating directories**

1. From the **Server Properties** dialog box, choose **Replication**.

2. In the **Directory Replication** dialog box, under **Export Directories**, choose **Manage**.

3. Select the directory, and then choose **Add Lock**.

This can be used to help limit the traffic to times when there is less user generated network traffic.

Also in the **Directory Replication** dialog box is the **Wait Until Stabilized** option for each exported directory. When the **Wait Until Stabilized** option is selected, it causes the import computer to recopy the entire subtree whenever any file in that subtree changes. With this option disabled, the import computer will check the time/date/name/attributes/size of each file individually, and copy only those files which have changed.

Registry Parameters

Controlling the amount of data transferred in a replication process often involves updating the Registry with new values. Directory replication entries are found in the Registry under HKEY_LOCAL_MACHINE\SYSTEM\CurrentControlSet \Services\Replicator\Parameters. The two most common parameters to modify to control the Directory Replicator service are Interval and Pulse.

- The Interval parameter determines how often the originating server (called the export server) checks for updates to its specified directory structure, and sends notifications to its target computers (called import computers) to retrieve the new data. The default value for Interval is five minutes. This can be increased to 60 minutes or more (on the export server) to reduce the frequency of replication. Of course, this will also increase the replication delay for each individual change.

- The Pulse parameter acts as a counter to control how often an import computer contacts an export server. If an import computer fails to hear from the export server after <Pulse> * <Interval> minutes, it will contact the export server for an update. The default value of Interval is five minutes (as described above), while the default value of Pulse is two minutes. These parameters mean that if the import computer has not heard from the export server after 10 minutes, it will initiate communications with the export server. Increasing the Pulse parameter will increase the time intervals for the import computer to contact the export server, allowing more time for the export server to contact the import computer.

Analyzing Directory Replication Traffic

In this exercise, you analyze the network traffic generated related to directory replication activity.

➤ **To analyze directory replication traffic**

In this procedure, you analyze the network traffic generated by directory replication of files.

1. Open Repladd.cap.

2. What is the first step of directory replication?

   _____

   _____

   Hint: check **SMB: File name** and the hexadecimal server message block (SMB) data.

3. How large was the announcement?

   _____

   _____

4. Was the announcement directed to the import server?

   _____

   _____

5. What was the destination NetBIOS name?

   _____

   _____

6. Would this announcement have been routed? Why or why not?

   _____

   _____

7. What directory was included in the announcement?

   _____

   _____

   Hint: view the hexadecimal data in the SMB portion of the announcement.

8. Frames 2 through 14 prepare the import server for replication by establishing the required sessions to the export server. What user account is the Directory Replicator service using? Hint: check **SMB: Command Account name** in frame 9.

   _____

   _____

9. Frames 15 through 41 verify the clocks are in synchronization between the two servers, and prepare for replication. This generated 27 frames and almost 5000 bytes of traffic. What information is requested in frame 30?

_____

_____

Hint: view the hexadecimal data.

10. Frames 42 through 145 replicate the new files to the import server. What files were found on the export server?

_____

_____

Hint: view the hexadecimal data or **SMB: Transaction parameters** of frame 45.

11. How many frames did it take to replicate each file?

_____

_____

12. From the time the import server started replicating files, how long did it take to replicate all the files in the export tree?

_____

_____

13. How long did it take from the announcement to the completion of the entire directory replication process?

➤ **To analyze directory replication traffic for removal of files**

In this procedure, you analyze the network traffic generated by Directory Replicator removal of files. Frame 1 announces a change to the export tree. Frames 6 through 30 prepare for replication.

1. Open Repldel.cap.

2. Frames 31 through 36 check for the files to be replicated. What files were found on the export server?

_____

_____

Hint: compare the hexadecimal data of frame 34 with the hexadecimal data of frame 45 in Repladd.cap.

3. Frames 37 through 70 complete the replication process. What files were replicated to the import server?

_____

_____

4. From the time the import server started verifying files (frame 31), how long did it take to complete the processing of the SCRIPTS directory (frame 62)?

_____

_____

5. How long did it take to complete the entire replication process?

_____

_____

Analyzing DNS Server Traffic

DNS server traffic generally comes from two sources: recursive lookups and replication of zone information. The following graphic illustrates an overview of the network traffic generated by DNS servers.

Frequency:

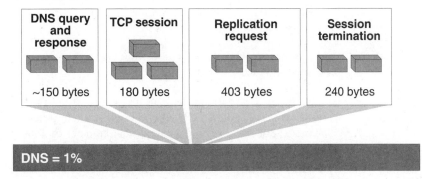

In larger organizations, a single Domain Name System (DNS) name server may not be sufficient to provide name resolution services for the clients. In this environment, it may be necessary to implement primary and secondary servers for a zone. A zone is a database file that contains records for a particular domain.

DNS server-to-server traffic is comprised of zone transfers. This traffic does not occur by default, but must be configured by the administrator. A primary name server is the server that maintains the database file for a particular zone. A secondary zone server does not maintain the database, but receives a copy of the database from the primary name server for the zone. This is very similar to the relationship between a PDC and a BDC for a Windows NT domain.

Relative Impact on the Network

The replication of zone information produces network traffic. When a secondary name server starts up, it contacts its primary name server and initiates replication of the zone. This is called a zone transfer.

DNS Replication Traffic

The process of the secondary name server updating its database from the primary name server is referred to as a zone transfer. The first step in the process is to query the configured primary server to verify that it is active as the primary server, and then retrieve the parameters for zone database replication. This frame is a small DNS query for SOA (Start of Authority) for the domain. It ranges in size, depending upon the domain name requested. A domain name of Test2.com generated a query of 69 bytes.

```
1    19.652  BACKUP     BDC3      DNS 0x4000:Std Qry for Test2.com. of
type SOA on class INET addr.
```

The primary server then responds with its configuration parameters for the zone, including database version number and intervals for replication of data. This response is about 60 bytes larger than the request.

```
2    19.655  BDC3       BACKUP    DNS 0x4000:Std Qry Resp. for
Test2.com. of type SOA on class INET
```

The secondary server then establishes a TCP session to Port 53 of the primary server. This is a standard TCP session establishment process of three frames. Once this is done, the secondary requests a transfer of zone information by designating the **Question Type** field as **Request for zone transfer**. The request varies in size, depending upon the domain name in use. The request for Test2.com was 85 bytes in size.

```
6    19.712  BACKUP     BDC3      DNS 0x0:Std Qry for Test2.com. of type
Req. for zn Xfer on class INET
```

The primary server then responds with the zone information. There is no concept of updated records, so all records are transferred. The number of bytes, and frames, will vary depending upon the number of records and the size of each record. A sample six record transfer, with all six records having small names of 15 characters or less, resulted in one frame totaling 318 bytes.

```
7   19.724  BDC3      BACKUP    DNS 0x0:Std Qry Resp. for Test2.com.
of type SOA on class INET addr.
```

After the transfer, the TCP session is disconnected. This is a standard four-frame TCP session termination sequence.

Once the initial transfer has been completed, the secondary server will contact the primary server to determine if the zone needs to be transferred again. This is done with the initial DNS lookup for SOA, and comparing the version number of the zone file. By default, this occurs every 60 minutes.

A DNS record averages about 26 bytes (compressed). Multiply the number of records in the zone file by 25 to estimate the traffic that will be generated in a zone transfer.

Optimizing DNS Server Traffic

DNS server-to-server traffic consists of zone replication. It is possible to control the replication of the zone between the primary and secondary name servers. To do so, access the **SOA Record** tab from the **Zone Properties** dialog box in **DNS Manager**. The values in the following table can be configured.

Parameter	Description
Refresh Interval	Designates the amount of time the secondary name server will wait before querying the primary name server to see if the database file has changed, and initiate a zone transfer. The default value is 60 minutes.
Retry Interval	Designates the amount of time the secondary name server will wait before attempting to initiate a zone transfer upon failure. The default value is 10 minutes.
Expire Time	Designates the amount of time that the secondary name server will continue to respond to name queries even though it cannot connect to the primary name server for an update.
	The most important parameter is the refresh interval. The smaller it is, the more frequent zone transfers will be. This provides a more up-to-date zone file at the secondary name server, at the expense of increased network traffic.

Analyzing DNS Server Zone Transfer Traffic

In this exercise, you analyze DNS zone transfer activity.

➤ **To analyze DNS periodic zone transfer traffic**

In this procedure, you analyze the network traffic generated by a periodic replication of a zone database during a zone transfer.

1. Open Dnsupdt.cap.

2. Frame 1 is the primary server notifying the secondary server of a change to its zone database. Frame 2 is the secondary responding to the announcement. How much traffic was generated by the announcement and response?

   _____

   _____

3. Frames 3 and 4 are the secondary server's query on the zone, and the primary's response. How much traffic was generated by the query and response?

   _____

   _____

4. What was the version number of the database as returned by the primary in response to the secondary server's request?

   _____

   _____

5. How many records were transferred in this zone transfer?

   _____

   _____

6. How many new records were added to the database?

   _____

   _____

7. How large was the response that transferred the zone database? How much was devoted to DNS?

   _____

   _____

8. Was the entire database transferred, or just the two updated records?

_____

_____

Lesson Summary

The following information summarizes the key points in this lesson

- The services that contribute to server-to-server traffic are directory services, trust relationships, the browser, WINS, directory replication, and DNS.

- Analyzing account synchronization traffic includes BDCs finding the PDC, establishing a session and secure channel, verifying the database, and updates of the database.

- Analyzing trust relationship traffic includes establishing a trust, importing trusted accounts, and authentication.

- Analyzing server browser traffic includes browser announcements and elections, and browse list updates.

- Analyzing WINS replication traffic includes establishing the replication relationship, verifying the database, and updating the database.

- Analyzing Directory replication traffic includes announcements, directory replication session establishment, directory verification, and directory update.

- Analyzing DNS server to server traffic includes DNS query and response, establishing a TCP session, replication of the database, and termination of the session.

Lesson 5: Predicting Network Traffic

Changes or additions are often planned for the network. Predicting traffic patterns for changes requires a different process than analyzing and optimizing an existing network. This lessons explains how to predict network traffic.

After this lesson, you will be able to:

- List the guidelines for predicting network traffic.

- Predict network traffic for a given scenario.

Estimated lesson time: 20 minutes

Guidelines for Predicting Network Traffic

Once a Windows NT Server network has been properly optimized, an administrator is in a position to more accurately predict the effect a new server, service, or additional clients will have on the overall traffic on the network. To properly predict the effect a change will have on network traffic, follow these guidelines:

- Carefully identify and analyze the traffic associated with each specific function to properly project the amount of traffic each service will generate.

- Identify the service to be implemented on the network.

- Determine the variables associated with implementing the service. For example, if analyzing the affect of implementing dynamic host configuration protocol (DHCP), determine how many DHCP servers will be installed, how many DHCP clients will be used, and how long the lease duration is.

- Speculate the following:

  - The traffic that one client or server would generate.

  - The impact of implementing the service using a given number of clients or servers.

  - The frequency of that traffic.

- Recognize that predicting network traffic is not an exact science, but a process to help understand and plan for network traffic. In most cases, adding a service will increase network traffic, but the benefit of implementing the service generally outweighs the additional traffic it generates.

In actual practice, variances will be discovered, and should be expected. It should always be assumed that any calculations for prediction will be off by some percentage. Add additional traffic to your calculation to more closely approximate the actual result.

Summary of Windows NT Network Traffic

Before attempting to predict network traffic, it is necessary to understand the network traffic generated by each service or network function. The following graphic provides a summary of Windows NT Server network traffic.

- **Client–generated network traffic**
    - **–DHCP, WINS, file session logon validation**
    - **–Browsing, DNS intranet browsing**
- **Server–generated network traffic**
    - **–User accounts database synchronization**
    - **–Trust relationships and pass-through authentication**
    - **–Browsing**
    - **–Directory, WINS, and DNS zone replication**

The following table contains a summary of the network traffic patterns. Use this summary when predicting the impact of implementing network services.

Service	Traffic	Frequency
DHCP	Acquire IP address–4 frames and 1368 bytes.	Once per client.
	Renew IP address lease: 2 frames and 684 bytes.	Every startup and at one-half lease life.
Windows Internet Naming Service (WINS) client-to-server	Registration–2 frames and 214 bytes.	Once per service or application at startup.
	Renewal–2 frames and 214 bytes.	Once per service or application every one-half time to live (TTL).
	Resolution–2 frames and 196 bytes.	Varying frequencies.

(continued)

continued

Service	Traffic	Frequency
File sessions	Address resolution–2 frames and 120 bytes.	At each attempt to communicate with another TCP/IP host (when aged from ARP cache).
	TCP session–3 frames and 180 bytes.	Once per first connection to each target TCP host.
	NetBIOS session–2 frames and 186 bytes.	Once per first NetBIOS connection to a target computer.
	SMB protocol negotiation– 2 frames and approximately 350 bytes.	Once per first server message block (SMB) connection to a target computer.
	Connection sequence– 2 frames and approximately 350 bytes.	Once per network resource access.
	Session disconnection– 5 frames and 360 bytes.	Once per final connection to TCP host disconnection.
Logon validation	Session establishment– 15 frames and 2000 bytes.	Once per user logon.
	Validation sequence– 4 frames and 760 bytes (Windows 95).	Once per user logon.
	Validation–20 frames and 3700 bytes for Windows NT computers.	Once per user logon.
	Session breakdown–5 frames and 360 bytes.	Once per user logon.
	Scripts, policies, profiles– varying amount of traffic.	Optional–once per user logon.
Browser	Host Announcement– 1 frame and 243 bytes.	Once per "server" computer every announcement period (12 minutes at steady state).
	Local Master Announcement–1 frame and 250 bytes.	After each Announcement Request or Election and every 12 minutes.

Service	Traffic	Frequency
	Workgroup Announcement–1 frame and 250 bytes.	Once per each master browser every announcement period (15 minutes at steady state).
	Elections–many frames and 225 bytes each.	After each computer capable of becoming the master browser initializes.
	Finding a backup browser–2 frames and approximately 450 bytes.	Once per browsing computer at initial browse attempt.
	Retrieving a browse list–20 frames and 2150 bytes.	Every browse attempt by client, and every 12 minutes for each backup browser.
	Retrieving a list of shared resources–16 frames and 1900 bytes for Windows 95. 19 frames and 3300 bytes for Windows NT-based computers.	Every browse list by client.
	Retrieve list of domains.	Every 12 minutes by each domain master browser.
DNS	Name lookups–two frames and ~180 bytes (depending upon name length). Traffic is multiplied if recursion is required.	Each DNS name lookup request by client. Recursion traffic may not be required if name is still cached at queried DNS server.
	Zone replication–TCP session of three frames and 180 bytes. One frame to request transfer (~85 bytes). One or more frames to transfer the zone records, depending upon size and number of records. TCP session termination–four frames and 240 bytes.	At addition of secondary server to the zone, and periodically (every 60 minutes by default).

(continued)

continued

Service	Traffic	Frequency
Intranet browsing	Downloading a page–TCP session of three frames and 180 bytes.	Once per file requested (page, graphic, AVI, and so on).
	GET command–one frame ~350 bytes depending upon host name and file structure.	Required at each load attempt.
	Multiple frames of up to 1514 bytes to download file.	Required if new or updated file.
User accounts database synchronization	Finding the PDC–4 frames and approximately 745 bytes.	Once per BDC startup.
	Establish session–11 frames and 1280 bytes.	Every synchronization event.
	Establish secure channel– 8 frames and 1550 bytes.	Once per BDC startup.
	Verify the databases–6 frames and 1350 bytes.	Once per BDC startup.
	PDC Update notice– 1 frame and approximately 400 bytes.	Every synchronization event.
	Synchronization of the database–two frames and ~1400 bytes for one user modification.	Every synchronization event.
Establishing a trust relationship	Approximately 110 frames and 16,000 bytes of traffic.	Once per each trust relationship created.
Importing trusted accounts	Approximately 115 frames and 18,600 bytes of traffic for 12 trusted accounts.	Each attempt to import a trusted account into a trusting domain.
Verification of trusted accounts	Approximately 45 frames and 7000 bytes of traffic for a single account (Global Group).	Every attempt to view a resource (or group) that contains a trusted account.

Service	Traffic	Frequency
Pass-through authentication	20 frames and approximately 3700 bytes of traffic.	Once for the first attempt to access a resource on a trusting computer, or logon to a trusted domain from a trusting computer.
Directory replication	Announcement–1 frame and approximately 340 bytes.	Once per importing domain or server for every update of the export tree.
	Establish session–9 frames and approximately 1300 bytes.	Once from each import computer every update event.
	Verify directory–30 frames and approximately 5100 bytes.	Once from each import computer every update event.
	Update directory–various amounts of network traffic.	Once from each import computer every update event.
WINS replication	Establish relationship– 20 frames and 2300 bytes.	Once per replication relationship.
	Database verification–12 frames and approximately 900 bytes.	Once per update request to each replication partner.
	Database update–approximately 14 frames and approximately 2100 bytes (varies with number of updates).	Once per update request to each replication partner.

Traffic Prediction Scenarios

Network traffic prediction is covered for a variety of scenarios. Use the following scenarios as examples when you are making changes to your own network:

- Adding a specific service.

- Adding a single server.

- Adding a single domain local area network (LAN).

- Adding a multiple domain LAN.

- Making changes in a wide area network (WAN) environment.

Predicting Network Traffic for a Specific Service

Predicting the effect of a single service is as simple as plugging in the numbers from the service analysis. The following graphic allows you to practice predicting network traffic for a specific service.

- **IP address acquisition**

    - **–Traffic generated by one client/server = 4 frames and 1,368 bytes**

    - **–Total traffic = 400 frames and 136,800 bytes**

    - **–Frequency = once per client**

- **IP address renewal**

    - **–Traffic enerated by one client/server = 2 frames and 684 bytes**

    - **–Total traffic = 200 frames and 68,400 bytes**

    - **–Frequency = every restart, or every 3.5 days**

A company has decided to implement DHCP to centrally manage the use of Internet Protocol (IP) addresses. The company has 100 clients that can use DHCP to acquire addresses. It will start with one DHCP server, and a lease life of seven days. To determine how much traffic this will generate, consider the following information:

- DHCP lease acquisition traffic:

    - One client and one server: four frames and 1368 bytes.

    - Total network traffic to acquire IP address for 100 clients: 400 frames and 136,800 bytes of traffic. Even if all clients were simultaneously attempting to acquire addresses, this would still only be 10 percent (1,094,400 bits) of a 10-MB Ethernet cable.

    - Frequency: once per client.

- DHCP lease renewal traffic:

    - One client: two frames and 684 bytes.

    - Total network traffic to renew IP address for 100 clients: 200 frames and 68,400 bytes of traffic. Even if all clients were simultaneously attempting to renew their address, this would still only be five percent (547,200 bits) of a 10 MB Ethernet cable.

    - Frequency: every client startup process. If client is not restarted, every 3.5 days per client, assuming the lease duration is set to seven days.

By increasing the lease duration from the default of three days to seven days, the renewal traffic has been reduced by one-half. However, this only affects clients that are left online for at least four days. The disadvantage of doing this is that it will take longer for the inactive address leases to become available again.

Predicting Single Server Network Traffic

If a server is being added, you will need to consider all of the services it is running. The following graphic allows you to practice predicting network traffic when adding a single server.

- **Startup traffic initiated**
    - **–One time traffic = 88 frames and 15,000 bytes**
    - **–Renewable traffic = 15 frames and 2,200 bytes**
    - **–Frequency = every 3 to 3.5 days**
- **Incoming session traffic**
    - **–11 frames and 1,280 bytes per client**
    - **–Total incoming traffic = 1,100 frames and 128,000 bytes**
- **Various traffic per session**
- **Session teardown - 5 frames and 360 bytes per client**

The company has decided to add a new server that will function as a file and print server for 100 clients. The server will function as a DHCP and Windows Internet Name Service (WINS) client. To determine how much traffic this will generate, consider the following information:

- Traffic initiated by the server at startup:
    - DHCP address renewal: 2 frames and 684 bytes every restart and every 3.5 days.
    - WINS registrations include 6 names (Workstation, Server, Messenger, Domain member, Browser Elections, and User name). Each name takes 2 frames and 214 bytes to register. Total registration traffic is 12 frames and 1284 bytes.
    - WINS renewal traffic: 12 frames and 1284 bytes every three days.
    - Browser announcements traffic: 1 frame and 245 bytes every 12 minutes.
    - Total renewable network traffic to boot server: 15 frames and approximately 2200 bytes.

- Extra startup related traffic: 88 frames and approximately 15,000 characters (logon validation and domain membership verification).

- Frequency: every restart.

■ Traffic initiated by a client destined to the server:

- Traffic per client session establishment: 11 frames and 1280 bytes.

- Total file session establishment traffic: 1100 frames and approximately 128,000 bytes.

- Frequency: once per day per client.

■ Traffic initiated by clients to disconnect a session:

- Traffic per client session disconnection: 5 frames and 360 bytes.

- Total file session disconnection traffic: 500 frames and approximately 36,000 bytes.

- Frequency: once per day per client.

Additional traffic will be generated by clients after a session with the server has been established. This traffic will be a result of files being accessed by the client computers. Characterization of this traffic would be on a file-by-file basis. Determine an average file size on the server and then determine the frequency of remote file accesses to the server. This will provide an estimate of traffic generated by a client accessing the files on the server.

Predicting Single Domain LAN Traffic

When a domain is added you need to consider the number of servers that are coming online as well as the number of clients and their associated traffic. The following graphic allows you to practice predicting network traffic when adding a single domain LAN.

● **Startup traffic**

    –PDC startup = 88 frames and 12,800 bytes

    –BDC startup = 78 frames and 11,600 bytes

● **User accounts database synchronization traffic**

    –PDC announcement = 1 frame and 400 bytes per BDC

    –Synchronization traffic = 18 frames and 4,730 bytes for two changes

    –Frequency = possibly every five minutes

    –Browse list updates

A company has decided to add a new domain that will have a primary domain controller (PDC) and three backup domain controllers (BDCs). To determine how much traffic this will generate, consider the following information:

- Traffic initiated during startup of the four domain controllers:

  - Starting a PDC generates 88 frames and 12,800 bytes of traffic.

  - WINS names registered: 7 names totaling 14 frames and 1498 bytes.

  - Browser announcements: 2 frames (Local Master and Workgroup) total 500 bytes (frequency every 12–15 minutes).

  - Starting a BDC generates 78 frames and 11,600 bytes of traffic.

  - WINS names registered: 6 names totaling 12 frames and 1284 bytes.

  - Browser announcements: 1 frame and 250 bytes (frequency every 12 minutes).

  - Total network traffic to boot one PDC and three BDCs: 322 frames and 47,600 bytes.

  - Frequency: every restart of all four computers.

- Traffic generated during synchronization of the user accounts database, assuming 10 changes per hour:

  - Announcement of change: 1 frame and approximately 400 bytes.

  - Total announcement traffic: 3 frames and approximately 1200 bytes.

  - Frequency: every 10–15 minutes.

  - BDC establishing session with PDC: 11 frames and 1280 bytes.

  - BDC updating its database: 8 frames and 3450 bytes for two account changes.

  - Total synchronization traffic: 18 frames and 4730 bytes per BDC. Three BDCs would require a total of 54 frames and 14,190 bytes of traffic to complete synchronization.

    - Frequency: after every announcement of changes to one of the databases.

- Traffic generated by browser updates of the three backup browsers and the local master browser:

  - Establish session to PDC IPC$ share: 11 frames and 1280 bytes.

  - Retrieve browse list: 4 frames and 780 bytes for 4 servers in one domain.

  - Total (15 frames and 2100 bytes) *3 = 45 frames and 6480 bytes.

  - Frequency: Every 12 minutes.

Additional traffic will be generated by client computers logging on to the network, and by domain controller validation. Remember that it takes approximately 39 frames and 6500 bytes of traffic to validate a logon request for a user logging on at a Windows 95-based client computer. To complete a traffic analysis for this domain, determine the frequency of logons and the use of logon scripts.

Other traffic can be generated by other services on these servers, such as DHCP, WINS, or file session generation by client computers.

Predicting Multiple Domain LAN Traffic

Trust relationships become the major additional impact with multiple domains. The following graphic allows you to practice predicting network traffic for a multiple domain LAN.

- **Trust relationship traffic**

    –**Establish trust = 110 frames and 16,000 bytes**

    –**Import trusted accounts = 115 frames and 18,600 bytes**

    –**Pass-through authentication = 20 frames and 3,700 bytes**
- **Startup traffic**

    –**Booting PDC = 88 frames and 12,800 bytes**

    –**Verifying trust - 6 frames and 1,500 bytes**

A company has decided to add a new resource domain that will trust accounts from the master domain. To determine how much traffic this will generate, consider the following information.

Trust Relationship Traffic

- Traffic related to the trusted domain will be the same as the previous example.
- Traffic generated to establish a trust relationship:
  - Traffic to establish trust relationship: 110 frames and 16,000 bytes.
  - Frequency: once per trust per direction (one-way relationship).
- Traffic generated to importing trusted accounts:
  - Traffic to import trusted accounts: 115 frames and 18,600 bytes for 12 trusted accounts.
  - Frequency: every attempt to import a trusted account.

- Traffic generated while performing pass-through authentication:

    - Pass-through authentication traffic: 20 frames and 3700 bytes.

    - Frequency: every access of new server by a trusted account.

Startup Traffic

- Traffic generated during startup of the trusting domain's PDC:

    - Starting a PDC generates 88 frames and 12,800 bytes of traffic.

    - Traffic to verify trust relationship: 6 frames and 1500 bytes.

    - Frequency: every restart of PDC.

Additional traffic may be generated due to additional functionality the trusting servers are to provide, as well as file session activity.

Predicting WAN Environment Traffic

When services or computers are added in a WAN environment, services that cross the WAN need to be considered. The following graphic allows you to practice predicting network traffic for a WAN environment.

- **Logon validation**

    - **Windows 95 client used 39 frames and 6,538 bytes**

- **Directory services database synchronization**

    - **Update of 2 users used 28 frames and 5,654 bytes**

- **Logon validation vs. database synchronization**

    - **Control the amount of traffic generated during directory services database synchronization**

In larger organizations, a single domain may be implemented over multiple physically distinct locations. One of the most common questions concerning WAN implementation is whether to centralize domain controllers or to place BDCs at remote sites.

Logon Validation

In a WAN environment, it may be important to ensure that user logon validation requests can be accommodated by system resources, regardless of the status of the WAN link. In this case, it is necessary to place a BDC at each remote site to ensure users can log on and receive validation in the event the WAN link fails. A Windows 95 client logon sequence takes 39 frames and generates 6538 bytes of data.

Database Synchronization Over a WAN

If a BDC is located at each remote site, it is important to ensure that the process of synchronizing the directory services account database does not utilize the entire WAN bandwidth. (A periodic update of two users generated 18 frames and 4730 bytes of traffic.) Using the entire WAN for account synchronization would effectively prevent user access to remote resources and applications during synchronization.

There are several ramifications when considering placing BDCs WAN links:

- By default Windows NT 4.0 PDCs only send update notices to 10 BDCs at one time. When one of these controllers has completed its updating, a notice is sent to another BDC. This reduces the load on a WAN, but may delay the time in updating to some BDCs.

- When synchronizing the directory services database, it is possible to effectively utilize the entire WAN bandwidth. Consider modifying the NetLogon ReplicationGovernor Registry parameter.

- If the Net Logon service change log becomes full and starts wrapping, a BDC might force a full synchronization event to occur. This could happen if the WAN link is somewhat unstable, resulting in partially completed synchronization events. Consider increasing the NetLogon ChangeLogSize Registry parameter.

Logon Validation vs. Database Synchronization

Optimizing directory services traffic often involves controlling the amount of traffic generated during directory services database synchronization. This will require determining a balance between providing logon validation for users and WAN bandwidth for user access.

If more WAN traffic will be generated by users frequently logging on to the network, as opposed to synchronizing account changes over the WAN, then it would be beneficial to place BDCs at each end of the WAN segments. However, if logons are infrequent, but account changes are more frequent, requiring users to become logon validated over the WAN would be the best use of the WAN bandwidth. Note that this would be at the expense of slower logons, and there is a possibility of not being validated if the link was unavailable.

In most cases it is recommended to locate BDCs local to the users. This provides faster logon validation services.

Other WAN Traffic Considerations

The following graphic presents other considerations when predicting traffic patterns over a WAN.

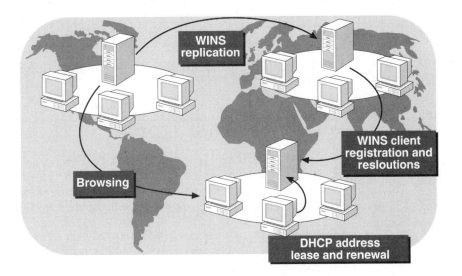

Any traffic patterns can potentially occur over the WAN, thereby causing unforeseen traffic. The most likely sources of WAN traffic will be:

- Browsing: if the domain spans a WAN, each segment will have a separate master browser. Each master browser will contact its domain master browser (PDC) every 12 minutes. This will generate WAN traffic. The amount of traffic generated during this browse list update will be dependent upon the number of entries in the browse list, and other domains in the enterprise. Consider increasing the Browser's MasterPeriodicity Registry parameter.

- WINS replication: if multiple WINS servers are used, WINS database replication will occur. The amount of traffic depends upon the amount of record updates, and the frequency of those updates. Consider increasing the Push/Pull partner configuration settings to control replication traffic.

- WINS client registration and resolutions: this results in smaller amounts of traffic, but more frequent traffic than most other traffic originators. Reduce the number of services started to reduce the number of registrations and renewals.

- DHCP address leases and renewals: this results in smaller amounts of traffic and less frequent requests than other types of traffic originators.

Use the traffic summary numbers presented earlier to determine the affect each traffic pattern might have on the WAN. For example, if 10 client computers started up simultaneously, each having to register five names with a remote WINS server, will that amount of traffic successfully traverse a 56Kbps link? Consider the following:

- Five names at 214 bytes each is 1070 bytes.

- Ten clients registering five names each generates 10,700 bytes of traffic, or 85,600 bits.

- A 56-Kbps link can support 57,344 bits per second.

- 85,600 bits are greater than 57,344 bits.

If these 50 names were to be registered exactly at the same time, then a 56-Kbps link would not be able to handle the traffic. However, it is unlikely that each client would attempt to register their names at the exact same time, so there would be pauses between the attempts, allowing the registration to complete successfully.

Although there are many issues to consider and plan for, a thorough understanding of the issues, the services involved, and the traffic generated by each service will give you the information necessary to make a carefully thought out and designed Windows NT Server network.

Predicting Network Traffic

➤ **To predict network traffic**

1. What process should you use to predict network traffic for a given Windows NT Server service?

   _____

   _____

2. Your site has a 56-Kbps link between two sites. You want to determine how many Windows 95 users can simultaneously log on over the link. How do you determine the number of simultaneous logons over the 56-Kbps link?

   _____

   _____

Lesson Summary

The following information summarizes the key points in this lesson:

- The guidelines for predicting network traffic include carefully identifying and analyzing the traffic associated with each function, identifying services to be implemented on the network, and determining the variables associated with implementing the service.

- You can use traffic prediction scenarios to estimate traffic generated by specific Windows NT services, single Windows NT domains, or WAN environments.

C H A P T E R 7

Troubleshooting Tools and Methods

About This Chapter

This chapter provides strategies for efficiently approaching and solving Windows NT Server problems through the perspective of Windows NT architecture, the registry, and the boot process. It identifies troubleshooting resources available for answering questions and finding information, and introduces some troubleshooting tools available with Windows NT and the *Windows NT Server Resource Kit*.

Before You Begin

To complete the lessons in this chapter, you must have:

- The knowledge and skills covered in Chapter 2, "Installation and Configuration."

- The knowledge and skills covered in Chapter 3, "Managing Enterprise Resources."

- The knowledge and skills covered in Chapter 4, "Connectivity."

- The knowledge and skills covered in Chapter 5, "Server Monitoring and Optimization."

- The knowledge and skills covered in Chapter 6, "Network Monitoring and Optimization."

Lesson 1: Overview of Troubleshooting in the Enterprise

This lesson provides a brief overview of the Windows NT Server troubleshooting environment. It outlines the basic tasks needed to successfully troubleshoot Windows NT Server, lists troubleshooting resources, and formulates a realistic troubleshooting methodology.

After this lesson, you will be able to:

- Identify the tasks involved in troubleshooting Windows NT Server.

- Identify the principal reasons for successful troubleshooting.

- Identify Windows NT Server troubleshooting resources.

- Identify the components of a reliable troubleshooting methodology.

Estimated lesson time: 20 minutes

Troubleshooting Windows NT Server

The goal of troubleshooting is to provide some of the skills and experience needed to identify Windows NT Server problems on mission-critical systems. The most efficient approach is to first consider a problem at an architectural level, and to solve it by analyzing and modifying the Windows NT registry, and the operating system boot process. Expertise in these areas provides both a broad and detailed approach to solving problems within the operating system.

Customers require confidence in an operating system. They expect to implement and maintain mission-critical applications and services within their organizations. They are seeking the skills necessary to successfully isolate and solve problems. As a result, support professionals must have the ability to perform the following tasks:

- Identify and isolate problems using knowledge of the Windows NT Server architecture to recognize related errors, and determine effects rather than causes.

- Navigate the Windows NT Server registry to track driver and service start values and dependencies.

- Track the Windows NT Boot sequence to identify any failure.

- Identify stop screen messages that can be resolved immediately, and those that require the assistance of Microsoft Technical Support using a kernel debugger or the Windows NT Server Crash Dump facility.

Successful Troubleshooting

The following graphic identifies the reasons most commonly given for successful troubleshooting.

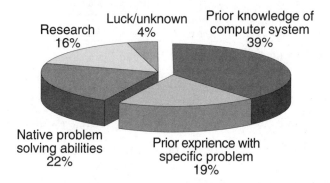

Microsoft conducted a poll of professional troubleshooters to determine the reasons for their success. These professionals attributed over half of the basis for their success to prior knowledge and experience.

It is possible to troubleshoot problems without prior knowledge of the computer system being worked on, or without prior experience with a specific problem; however, the quickest and most effective troubleshooter has experience with the specific operating system and the hardware involved, and has good documentation that describes errors encountered and how to solve them.

Troubleshooting Resources

Knowing where to get help when troubleshooting plays a significant part in successful problem resolution. The following graphic introduces the general troubleshooting resources for Windows NT networks.

There are many troubleshooting resources available.

General Knowledge

Building general knowledge of Windows NT Server includes gaining experience with the product, receiving training, and reading books.

Available training includes:

- Instructor-led classes
- Windows NT self-paced training kits

Recommended reading includes:

- *Inside Windows NT* by Helen Custer—Describes Windows NT architecture
- Windows NT technical documentation—*Microsoft Windows NT Server Concepts and Planning* guide
- *Windows NT Server Resource Kit*

Additional troubleshooting resources include TechNet, Online Services, Microsoft Download Library (MSDL), and Windows NT troubleshooting tools.

TechNet

The Microsoft TechNet compact disc provides information for supporting Microsoft products. The TechNet disc includes the following components:

- A complete set of online Microsoft Resource Kits
- The entire Microsoft Knowledge Base
- TechNet Supplemental (Drivers and Patches) compact disc

Access TechNet on the Worldwide Web at the following location:

http://www.microsoft.com/technet/

Online Services

To gain access to the Microsoft World Wide Web site, use an Internet service provider (ISP), then use Internet Explorer to reach Microsoft Support Online at the following location:

http://www.microsoft.com/support/

The following table shows some of the resources available through this site.

Resource	Description
Frequently Asked Questions	Quick answers to the most common technical questions about Microsoft products.
Software Library	Source of software add-ons, bug fixes, and software updates.
Knowledge Base	Articles about Microsoft products, bug and fix lists, documentation errors, and answers to support questions.
Peer-to-Peer Newsgroups	Daily advice and answers about using Microsoft products.
Microsoft Technical Support	Access to technical support and to Microsoft Service Advantage—a portfolio of support for large organizations.
Tech Chat	Live MSN chat sessions with Microsoft support managers, engineers, and guests.
View Support Options by Product	Alternate navigational views of Microsoft products.

For links that can provide answers to common Windows NT issues, refer to the Windows NT Troubleshooting Guides, a service of Microsoft Support Online, available at:

http://support.microsoft.com/support/

Microsoft Download Library (MSDL)

Microsoft's electronic bulletin board provides support information and products. Access MSDL, through the following telephone number: (425) 936-6735. Note that the modem settings for MSDL are 8 data bits, 1 stop bit, no parity, and no flow control.

Experts

The following technical experts are generally available to provide help with specific problems:

- Solution Providers
- Microsoft Consulting Services
- Contacts from training courses, trade shows, and conferences
- Contacts from professional organizations
- Microsoft Technical Support Specialists

Troubleshooting Tools

Windows NT provides many system tools that can be used for troubleshooting. These tools are found in both the Windows NT Server product and in the *Windows NT Server Resource Kit*.

Troubleshooting Methodology

The following graphic illustrates the basics of troubleshooting.

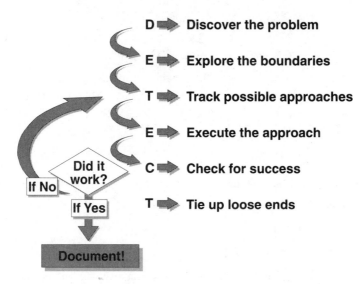

What makes a troubleshooting methodology reliable or unreliable? Unreliable methods are often characterized by haphazard guesswork—by repeatedly trying out solutions without asking enough questions or doing enough research.

The DETECT model was created by Microsoft Technical Support engineers. Based on research in problem-solving, this strategy employs the following six steps.

➤ **To use the DETECT troubleshooting model**

1. Discover the problem—Talk to users at their level and keep in mind that their meaning for terms and procedures may not be as exact as your own. What are the symptoms? What release of software are they running? Is their hardware on the Hardware Compatibility List (HCL)?

2. Explore the boundaries—What has changed since the system last worked correctly? What other software is running when the problem occurs? Is the problem reproducible? Check your problem database and TechNet for similar problems. Is a quick fix available?

3. Track possible approaches—Because you learn the most from your first experience with a problem, using a methodical approach in this phase will help you more in the long run than a trial-and-error approach.

4. Execute an approach—Remember to consider and plan for the downside if this approach does not work. Do you need to back up critical system or application files?

5. Check for success—If the approach was successful, can the problem reappear? If it can, does the user know what to do the next time?

6. Tie up loose ends—After making sure the issue is really closed with the user, reflect on the experience. How would you recommend to approach this kind of problem next time? Document the symptoms, the cause of the problem, and the solution. Include what you did to determine the problem and the solution. Last, share the results with others.

Troubleshooting Windows NT Setup

When troubleshooting Windows NT setup, it is important to make sure that all hardware being used is on the Hardware Compatibility List (HCL).

During the first stage of Setup (referred to as character-based Setup), Windows NT examines your system architecture for foundation level information and drivers. This information includes:

- Central processing unit (CPU) type (x86, MIPS(R), ALPHA, or PPC)
- Motherboard type (PCI, VESA, MCA, EISA, or ISA)
- Hard disk drive controllers
- File systems
- Free space on hard disk drives
- Memory

Windows NT looks for any devices that must be initialized at system startup in order for your computer to run. Windows NT also constructs a "mini" version of Windows NT, which is used to reboot the system into the Graphical User Interface mode (GUI-mode) portion of Setup. Therefore, it is critical that the information Windows NT gathers at this point is accurate.

Windows NT may incorrectly detect controllers and settings if the system is using nonstandard or proprietary bus components or enhancements that do not follow industry standards; these nonstandard enhancements include SMP 1.1, PCI 2.1, special bus drivers, or caching chips for burst-mode transfer. If the information gathered is incorrect, Setup will most likely fail at a later stage. Incorrect detection is often a symptom of a hardware or configuration problem that may also cause the setup to fail.

Disk Format

To access a disk from Windows NT, the drive must be uncompressed or only compressed with NT file system (NTFS) file compression included in Windows NT 3.51 or 4.0. Windows NT is not compatible with Microsoft DoubleSpace, Stacker, or any other compression software or hardware. The root of the Windows NT boot drive cannot be compressed, or an upgrade or installation will fail.

Choosing the Correct Setup Method

There are several methods for installing Windows NT Server. It is important to make sure the method you choose is best for you.

Standard Setup

Installing directly from the compact disc or floppy disks is almost always the best method of setting up your Windows NT system. It offers the best support for alternate Hardware Abstraction Layers (HALs), timing, and third-party drivers. If you have a supported CD-ROM drive, you should choose this setup method.

WINNT or WINNT32 Setup

This method was designed for network installations or for computers with unsupported CD-ROM drives. It builds the boot disks and performs a file copy of the setup directory to the hard disk drive before the setup procedure begins. It is the second best choice.

Installing over a Network

For networks where the Windows NT installation files are kept on a central server, network installations can be accomplished using the WINNT command or by copying the entire I386 directory from the setup compact disc to the hard disk drive and then running WINNT from the local disk drive. This can reduce network traffic and dependency.

Viruses

Windows NT will not install on a system infected by a virus. The troubleshooting guide documents several errors caused by viruses. If your system is infected, please obtain a commercial anti-virus scanner and remove the virus prior to attempting a Windows NT setup. Attempting to remove a virus through other means can render a system unbootable.

More Information

When experiencing problems with Windows NT setup, check with a current version of Microsoft Technet or the Microsoft Knowledge Base for the latest dispatches on problems involving Windows NT setup.

Documenting Problems and Changes

Problem and change management are familiar issues in large mainframe environments, where problems must be resolved quickly, and it is important to ensure that only one major change occurs at a time. Companies are slowly coming to recognize that their personal computer network is also mission-critical, and deserves the same type of attention.

Each problem encountered needs to be tracked and logged. This ever-evolving database of recorded problems and solutions can be used as a system-wide tool to solve future problems. A tracking system can include the following types of information:

- Configuration of the servers and network
- Changes to the hardware, software, and network
- Dates, times, and reasons for all server reboots
- Problems, symptoms, and solutions

Regardless of the methodology that is followed, support professionals must identify problems and implement the most effective solution. Therefore, this book focuses on steps 3 and 4 of the DETECT troubleshooting model—tracking down possible approaches and executing the most effective approach.

Note It is also recommended that you record capacity baselines and performance analysis trends in your tracking system. Good systems management will help prevent problems from occurring.

Troubleshooting in the Enterprise

In this exercise you will answer question about troubleshooting in the enterprise.

1. What are some of the available troubleshooting resources?

   _____

   _____

2. What are the steps in the DETECT troubleshooting model?

   _____

   _____

Lesson Summary

The following information summarizes the key points in this lesson:

- The most efficient approach to troubleshooting in the enterprise is to first consider the problem at an architectural level, and then to solve it by analyzing and modifying the Windows NT registry and the operating system boot process.

- Sources of troubleshooting information include: General Knowledge, TechNet, Online Services, Microsoft Download Library, and Experts.

- A successful troubleshooting model will include discovering the problem, exploring the boundaries of the problem, tracking possible approaches to fixing the problem, executing the approach to fixing the problem, checking for success, and tying up loose ends once the problem is solved.

Lesson 2: Examining Windows NT Architecture

This lesson introduces system architecture as a perspective from which to view performance problems. Knowledge of the architecture provides a broad perspective on the system and an understanding of the interrelationships among the system components. The lesson provides an overview of the architecture and components, and describes strategy and tools for troubleshooting from an architectural perspective.

After this lesson, you will be able to:

- Contrast the major layers in the Windows NT operating system architecture.
- Describe the methods used to troubleshoot problems from an architectural perspective.
- Identify the tools used to troubleshoot problems from an architectural perspective.

Estimated lesson time: 20 minutes

Windows NT Architecture

Understanding Windows NT architecture makes it easier to isolate problems to the failing component. The following graphic provides an overview of the Windows NT architecture.

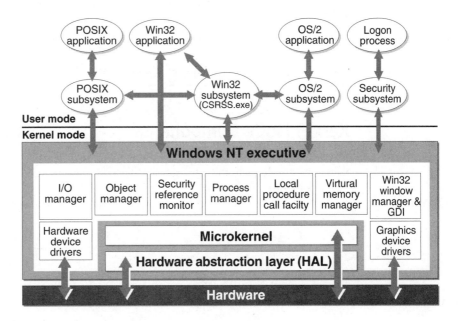

The initial challenges of correcting a system failure are determining where to begin, and then choosing the best approach. Most problem analysis begins with an examination of the system architecture. This gives the broadest outlook, and provides a high-level view that can help isolate the areas in the system that are affected by a failure.

Architecture Layers

The modular components that make up Windows NT Server are organized into layers. These components are the building blocks that make up the system. Troubleshooting at the architectural level is done through these major building-blocks. The layered design results in a very stable base operating system. System enhancements are at the protected subsystem level. New protected subsystems can be added without modification to either the base operating system or to the existing protected subsystems.

Architectural components are dependent upon each other. Problems in lower layer components affect the components in the layers above. Therefore, it is important to identify the component in which the problem began.

There are two major layers in the Windows NT architecture; the user mode and the kernel mode. The layers are described in the following table.

Architecture Layer	Description
Kernel mode	The operating-system code runs in a privileged processor mode known as the kernel, and has access to system data and hardware.
User mode	This layer consists of the Windows NT Environment subsystems and the applications that run in the subsystems. Components here provide the environments in which all user applications run.

Kernel Mode Components

One of the major design goals of Windows NT was to protect the operating system from problems in the applications. The following graphic identifies the kernel mode components.

- **Windows NT executive**   - **Microkernel**

- **Executive services**   - **HAL**

Kernel mode

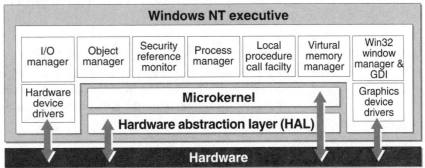

Kernel mode components are in three layers in the Windows NT executive: the executive services, the microkernel, and the hardware abstraction layer (HAL).

Windows NT Executive

The executive provides process structure, interprocess communication, memory management, object management, thread scheduling, interrupt processing, I/O capability, networking and object security. To protect its components from applications and subsystems, the Windows NT executive runs in kernel mode.

Executive Services

The executive services are the interfaces between user-mode protected subsystems and the kernel mode. To improve performance, reduce memory usage, and decrease the complexity of the code in Windows NT, the Window Manager (User) and graphics device interface (GDI) including the graphics device drivers components, are located in kernel address space.

Microkernel

The microkernel is at the heart of the Windows NT executive. It coordinates all I/O functions and synchronizes the activities of the executive services.

Hardware Abstraction Layer (HAL)

The hardware abstraction layer (HAL) hides, or abstracts, hardware differences from higher layers of the operating system. HAL provides a common software abstraction over such devices as clocks, cache and memory controllers, peripheral adapters, symmetric multiprocessing functions, and system buses.

Windows NT Networking Architecture

The Windows NT networking architecture, which is enveloped in the I/O Manager, is also modular in nature. The following graphic introduces the networking architecture layers and emphasizes the need to track an error to its original layer.

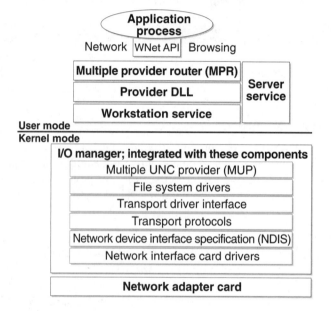

In Windows NT, the networking architecture is built in. It operates on an equal basis with the rest of the NT Executive. The flexible dynamic link library (DLL) and I/O system models that are built into Windows NT allow network software to be added and removed from the operating system.

Like the operating system architecture, the networking architecture is modular, and consists of components in both user mode and kernel mode. Many problems that can be traced through the architecture occur at the networking architecture level.

Knowledge of the Windows NT networking architecture allows visualization of the flow of data from the applications to the network, through the Windows NT networking architecture. By providing both client and server capabilities, a computer running Windows NT Server or Windows NT Workstation can be either a client or server in either a distributed-application environment or a peer-to-peer networking environment. Familiarity with these components provides a basis for understanding the Interprocess Communication (IPC) methods.

The following section examines the networking architecture, and provides background and experiences needed to identify and correct problems that occur at this level.

Kernel Mode Networking Components

Because the I/O system operates in kernel mode, these elements of the networking architecture also operate in kernel mode. The following graphic distinguishes between kernel mode and user mode networking components.

- Network interface card drivers
- Network device interface specification (NDIS) 4.0
- Transport protocols
- Transport driver interface (TDI)
- File system drivers
- Multiple UNC provider (MUP)

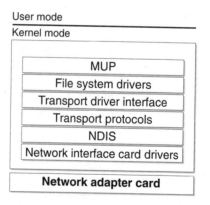

The kernel mode components of the networking architecture are integrated with the I/O system. Here too, the software within each layer is independent of the software in the other layers. These components communicate with user mode processes through networking file system drivers. The kernel mode networking architectural components and their functions are listed in the following table.

Component	Function
Network interface card drivers	These drivers talk directly to the network adapter cards and to the Network Device Interface Specification (NDIS) layer.
Network Device Interface Specification (NDIS) 4.0	NDIS provides a common interface and translator for developers of network adapter card drivers and developers of transport protocols.
Transport Protocols	These protocols define the rules governing communication between two hosts.
Transport Driver Interface (TDI)	All transport drivers use TDI to expose their services to the upper layers of the network architecture. The redirector and the server use TDI to communicate with the transport drivers.
File system drivers	Redirector and server drivers are implemented as file system drivers similar to NTFS or CDFS. An application can make no distinction between accessing files stored on a remote computer and accessing those stored locally on a hard disk. Each networking file system driver has a corresponding user mode process with which it communicates, such as the Workstation and Server services.
Multiple UNC Provider (MUP)	Universal Naming Convention (UNC) names have the format *server name\share name\path\file*. If an application tries to open a file or file-like device (for example, a named pipe) using a UNC name, the MUP determines which network provider (redirector) to communicate with.

Network Interface Card (NIC) Drivers

For each type of network card in a computer, there is a network card driver. The following graphic illustrates an overview of the network interface card drivers.

User mode

Kernel mode

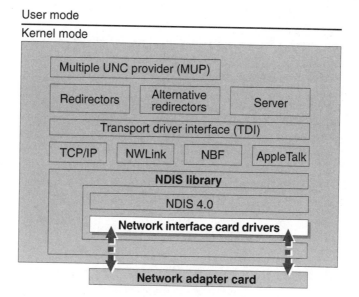

The component at the lowest software level in the networking architecture is the Network Device Interface Specification (NDIS)-compatible network adapter card driver. There is one network interface card (NIC) driver for each type of network adapter card. In order for these drivers to run on Windows NT 4.0, they must comply with the NDIS 4.0 standard.

Typical errors in this level include missing, corrupt, or older network adapter card drivers. Current drivers are available on the World Wide Web and on the Windows NT Server compact disc, in the Drivers directory.

Microsoft tests and certifies all device drivers that are provided on the Windows NT compact disc or that are available from any of the online sources. If an adapter does not appear on the HCL, contact the manufacturer to see if they are writing a Windows NT NDIS 4.0 device driver for the adapter.

Note NDIS 3.0-compatible device drivers will still operate on Windows NT 4.0, but it is recommended that newer NDIS 4.0 compatible drivers be used.

Network Device Interface Specification (NDIS) 4.0

In the past, there was a different network adapter card driver for each network card and each transport protocol. The following graphic illustrates an overview of NDIS.

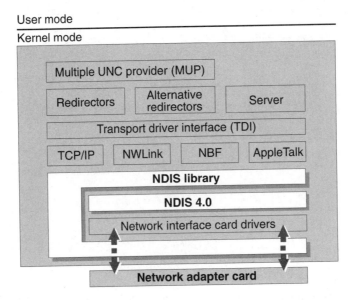

NDIS describes the interface by which NIC drivers communicate with network interface cards, with protocol drivers, and with the operating system.

NDIS allows multiple network adapter cards and multiple protocols to coexist in a single computer. NDIS-compliant network adapter card drivers can communicate with any NDIS-compliant transport protocol through NDIS. Transport Driver Interface (TDI) is the interface to the transports from TDI Clients like the redirector.

The NDIS library is a .sys file that acts like a DLL (also called an export library) containing a set of abstract functions. The main purpose of the NDIS library is to form a wrapper that allows network drivers to send and receive packets on a local area network (LAN) or wide area network (WAN) in an operating system-independent manner. The NDIS library also performs the following functions:

- Acts as an interface between transport driver functions, intermediate driver functions and net card driver functions.

- Submits requests to the operating system.

- Causes a local action that does not need communication with other software functions.

Note Transport protocols are dependent on NDIS. If a protocol issues an error message, use Event Viewer to see if there is a problem in the NDIS layer. Although NDIS version 4.0 continues to support drivers written to the NDIS version 3.0 standard, NDIS version 4.0 drivers can be installed only on Windows NT version 4.0 platforms or, for binary-compatible NIC miniport drivers, on platforms running the corresponding update version of Windows 95.

Transport Protocols

Four transport protocols are NDIS-compliant and are included with Windows NT. The following graphic illustrates an overview of the main transport protocols included in Windows NT.

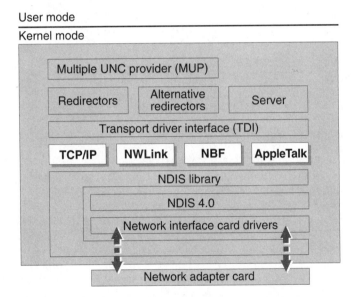

Transport protocols define the rules of communication between two computers. Communication between layers within a computer differs from communication between two computers. The layers within a computer communicate through vertical architectural interfaces. The layers on different computers communicate with their counterparts through transport protocols.

Windows NT transport protocol drivers are written to comply with the TDI at their upper edge, and they make use of the NDIS interface library (the *Ndis.sys* export library) for communicating with NIC drivers at their lower edge. The following table describes the transport protocols.

Transport Protocol	Description
Transmission Control Protocol/ Internet Protocol (TCP/IP)	Provides communication across inter-connected networks made up of computers with diverse hardware architectures.
NWLink	NWLink is an Internetwork Packet Ex-change/Sequence Packet Exchange–com-patible (that is, IPX/SPX-compatible) transport protocol. IPX/SPX is the primary protocol for Novell networks.
NetBIOS Frame (NBF) Protocol	NetBIOS Frame (NBF) protocol provides compatibility with earlier LANs, such as Microsoft LAN Manager and LAN Server.
AppleTalk	Used with Services for Macintosh to host connections from Apple Macintosh clients.

Note TCP/IP, NWLink, and NBF support TDI, Window Sockets, and NetBIOS applications and services.

Troubleshooting Transport Protocols

Several tools and procedures are available to help troubleshoot the transport pro-tocols and related components. The following table describes some of the tools and troubleshooting strategies for each protocol.

Protocol	Troubleshooting Strategy/Tool
TCP/IP	To see that TCP/IP is configured properly, Packet Internet Groper (PING) the Internet Protocol (IP) addresses in the following order: local computer, loopback address, default gateway address on local subnet, default gateway address on remote subnet, and remote node.
	To show configuration status of the IP addresses, DHCP, and Windows Internet Naming Service (WINS), at the com-mand prompt, type the following:
	ipconfig/all
	To trace the active route, at the command prompt, type the following:
	route print

Protocol	Troubleshooting Strategy/Tool
NWLink	To see the Internetwork Packet Exchange (IPX) network number, frame type, and binding configuration, at the command prompt, type the following: **ipxroute config** To view the Service Advertising Protocol (SAP) table, at the command prompt, type the following: **ipxroute servers** To view the routing table, at the command prompt, type the following: **ipxroute table**
NetBIOS Frame (NBF) Protocol	Use Network Monitor to capture a protocol analysis (sniffer) trace.
AppleTalk	Use Network Monitor to capture a protocol analysis (sniffer) trace.

Note For all protocols, the Network Monitor utility is the most effective trouble-shooting tool. To load Network Monitor, use the Network program in Control Panel, and add the Network Monitor Tools and Agent service.

Transport Driver Interface (TDI)

TDI allows transport protocols to be independent of the redirectors and server drivers, just as NDIS allowed them to be independent of the network adapter card drivers. The following graphic illustrates an overview of TDI.

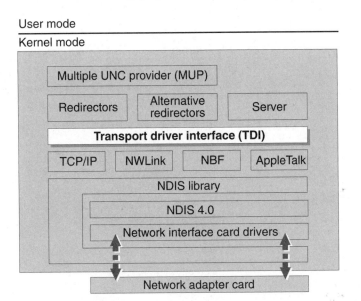

Each of the transport protocols communicates with the redirectors and servers above it using the Transport Driver Interface (TDI) specification.

TDI Features

TDI is a low-level network interface that is exposed at the upper edge of all Windows NT transport drivers. Requiring that all Windows NT transport drivers expose a single common interface (namely, TDI) simplifies the task of developing transport drivers because only the common interface needs to be coded. However, because transport drivers expose only the TDI interface, they can be used only by applications that use TDI. Because TDI is a relatively new network interface, and most existing applications are written to use other existing standard interfaces, such as NetBIOS and Sockets, Windows NT includes emulator modules for two popular existing network interfaces, NetBIOS and Sockets.

Note The redirector and server file system drivers are dependent on the TDI. If one of these file system drivers issues an error message, check Event Viewer to see if there is an underlying problem in the TDI layer or below.

File System Drivers

Both computers running Windows NT Workstation and Windows NT Server can act as either a client or a server, as Windows NT supports peer-to-peer networking. The following graphic illustrates an overview of the redirectors and server drivers.

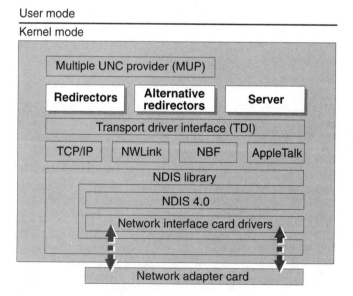

Windows NT supports peer-to-peer networking, in which each computer on the network can act as both a client workstation and a server. The network server and redirector modules are written as Windows NT file system drivers. The most important implication of this design is that the drivers can use all of the security features in Windows NT. Windows NT accomplishes this duality through two kinds of file system drivers—redirectors and servers.

Redirectors

The redirector (RDR) resides above TDI and provides one computer with access to another. The Windows NT operating system redirector allows connection to Windows NT, Windows for Workgroups, LAN Manager, LAN Server, and other servers. The redirector communicates to the transport protocols by means of the TDI interface.

Implementing a redirector as a file system has the following benefits:

- Applications can call a single API (the Windows NT I/O API) to access files on local and remote computers. From the I/O Manager perspective, there is no difference between accessing files stored on a remote computer on the network and accessing those stored locally on a hard disk.

- The redirector runs in kernel mode and can directly call other drivers and other kernel-mode components, such as Cache Manager. This improves the performance of the redirector.

- The redirector can be dynamically loaded and unloaded, like any other file-system driver.

- The redirector can easily coexist with other redirectors. The Windows NT redirector file system driver (Rdr.sys) allows a computer to gain access to resources on other Windows NT computers as if they were local resources. The redirector driver has a companion user mode service called LanmanWorkstation.

Alternative Redirectors

Besides allowing connections to LAN Manager, LAN Server, and Microsoft Network servers, the Windows NT redirector can coexist with redirectors for other networks, such as Novell NetWare and Banyan VINES.

In addition to providing integrated networking, the open design of Windows NT provides transparent access to other networks. For example, a computer running Windows NT Server can concurrently access files stored on Windows NT and NetWare servers.

An example of an alternative redirector on Windows NT Server is Gateway Service for NetWare (GSNW).

GSNW provides computers running Windows NT Server all of the support necessary to connect to NetWare servers, plus the additional capability to re-share the network connections from a NetWare server. The service allows the computers running Windows NT Server to access the NetWare servers as if they were just another client and, in addition, allows the network clients to access files on a NetWare server without having to have a NetWare client redirector on an IPX/SPX protocol stack loaded.

Note For GSNW to work, the transport must include the NWLink protocol.

Server

Windows NT includes a Server service. Like the redirector, the Server service resides above TDI, is implemented as a file system driver, and directly interacts with various other file-system drivers to satisfy I/O requests, such as reading or writing to a file. The Server service supplies the connections requested by client-side redirectors and provides them with access to the resources they request.

Like the Workstation service, the Server service is composed of the following components:

- Srv.sys, a file system driver that handles the interaction with the lower levels and directly interacts with various file system devices to satisfy command requests, such as file read and write.

- A companion user mode service, LanmanServer.

Multiple UNC Provider (MUP)

The MUP is the top layer of the kernel mode network architecture. The following graphic illustrates an overview of the MUP.

User mode

Kernel mode

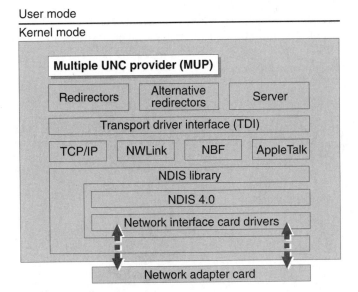

MUP fields I/O requests destined for a file or device that has a universal naming convention (UNC) name. These are names beginning with double backslash characters (\\), indicating that the resource exists on the network. The MUP receives such requests and determines which local redirector recognizes the remote resource.

The MUP is a Windows NT driver (loaded at system boot time) that issues I/O requests to lower-layer drivers.

The MUP driver is activated when an application first attempts to open a remote file or device, specifying a UNC name (instead of a redirected drive letter). When the Win32 subsystem receives such a request, the subsystem appends the UNC name to the string *\DosDevices\UNC* and then calls the Windows NT I/O manager to open the file. This object name is the name of the symbolic link that resolves to *\Device\MUP* a device object that represents the MUP driver.

The MUP driver receives the request and sends an I/O Request packet to each registered redirector. Then it waits for one of them to recognize the resource name and reply. When the redirector recognizes the name, it indicates how much of the name is unique to it. The MUP driver caches this information and thereafter sends requests beginning with that string directly to the Windows NT redirector.

Note If more than one redirector claims a particular resource, the MUP driver uses the configuration registry's list of loaded redirectors to determine which redirector takes precedence. To reorder the list of redirectors, edit the registry database.

Distributed Networking Components (User Mode)

The user mode networking services provide the user interface for networking functionality. The following graphic identifies some networking user mode processes.

- Interprocess communications (IPC)
- Multiple provider router (MPR)
- Provider DLL
- Workstation and server services

```
                    ╭─────────────────╮
                    │   Application    │
                    │     process      │
                    ╰─────────────────╯
          Network │ WNet API │ Browsing
          ┌────────────────────────────┬─────────┐
          │ Multiple provider router (MPR) │        │
          ├────────────────────────────┤ Server  │
          │      Provider DLL          │ service │
          ├────────────────────────────┤         │
          │    Workstation service     │         │
          └────────────────────────────┴─────────┘
    User mode
    Kernel mode
```

The distributed networking components process applications on different computers in a network and on the Internet. In Windows NT, distributed networking components operate in the user mode. The user mode network architectural layer includes services that work in conjunction with kernel mode file system drivers to provide networking connectivity for users and servers. The user mode networking services are described in the following table.

Service	Function
IPC	The connection between the client and server portions of distributed applications must allow data to flow in both directions. There are a number of ways to establish this connection. The Windows NT operating system provides seven different IPC mechanisms.
Multiple provider router (MPR)	DLL that determines which network (and thus which file system) to access when an application uses the Win32 Wnet API for browsing remote file systems.
Provider DLL	Supplies a set of standard functions collectively called the provider interface. This interface allows the MPR to communicate the request to the appropriate Wnet provider software.
Workstation and Server services	A network service (RPC-enabled) that provides a user mode API to manage Windows NT redirectors and Windows NT servers.

IPC

IPC allows developers to create distributed applications. The following graphic illustrates an overview of IPC.

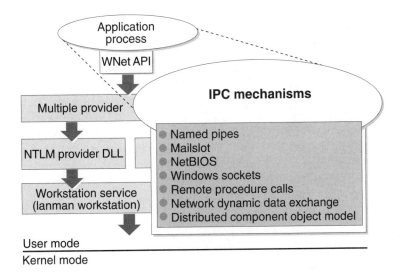

User mode

Kernel mode

Software developers are focusing on a new kind of application, distributed applications. In this level of computing, applications running on the desktop interact with other applications that may reside on remote computers. To accomplish this kind of interaction, an IPC mechanism is necessary. The following table describes the IPC mechanisms.

IPC Mechanism	Description
Named Pipes	A pipe is a part of memory that can be used by one process to pass information to another. A pipe connects two processes, so that the output of one can be used as input to the other.
Mailslots	Mailslots are mechanisms that provide connectionless extensions (datagrams) to connection-oriented services provided by Named Pipes. The server creates a mailslot and can only read from it. The client opens a mailslot and can only write to it.
NetBIOS	Standard programming interface for developing client/server applications.
Windows Sockets	A standard interface to protocols with different address schemes.
Remote Procedure Calls (RPCs)	A message passing facility that allows a distributed application to call services available on various computers in a network.
Network Dynamic Data Exchange (NetDDE)	Enables users to use Dynamic Data Exchange code over a NetBIOS-compatible network.
Distributed Component Object Model (DCOM)	DCOM (or Networked OLE) is a system of software objects designed to be reusable and replaceable. The objects support sets of related functions, such as sorting, random-number generation, and database searches.

MPR

The following graphic illustrates MPR.

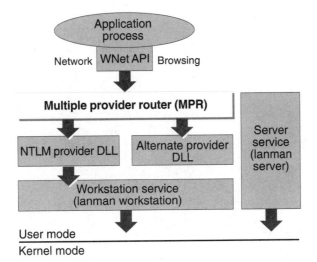

Not all programs use UNC names in their I/O requests. Some applications use the WNet APIs, which are the Win32 network APIs. MPR was created to support these applications.

The MPR is similar to the multiple UNC provider (MUP). The MPR receives WNet commands, determines the appropriate redirector, and passes the command to that redirector. Because different network vendors use different interfaces for communicating with their redirector, there is a series of provider DLLs between the MPR and the redirectors. The provider DLLs expose a standard interface so that the MPR can communicate with them. The DLLs take the request from the MPR and communicate it to their corresponding redirector.

Note The provider DLLs are for connecting resources and browsing the network only. They have nothing to do with the resultant I/O.

Provider DLL

The following graphic illustrates the provider DLL.

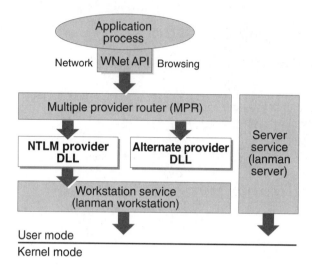

Because different network vendors use different interfaces for communicating with their redirector, each redirector must have a provider DLL. The provider DLLs expose a standard interface so that the MPR can communicate with them. The DLLs take the request from the MPR and communicate it to their corresponding redirector.

The provider DLLs are supplied by the network-redirector vendor and should be installed automatically when the redirector is installed.

NT LAN Manager (NTLM) Provider DLL

This provider DLL is the component that allows a computer running Windows NT Server or Windows NT Workstation to communicate with the network using the Windows NT redirector.

Alternative Provider DLL

For each additional type of network, such as NetWare or VINES, a provider must be installed. These provider DLLs are supplied by the appropriate network vendors.

Workstation and Server Services

Windows NT uses the Workstation and Server services as part of the process to communicate with and receive information from network resources. The following graphic shows how Workstation and Server services function.

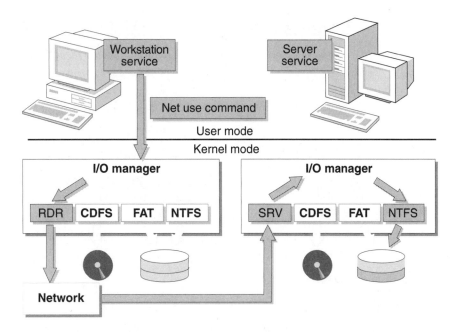

Every computer running Windows NT has both workstation and server components. A user can issue a **net use** command to connect to a remote computer. The request is passed from the application to the redirector (Rdr.sys) through the TDI and the appropriate protocol, down to the NDIS layer and network adapter, and out the network.

On the server side, the request comes from the network, through the network adapter and NDIS layer, through the protocol to the TDI layer, and up to the Server (Srv.sys). The I/O Manager takes the request and passes it to the appropriate file system driver for the requested file. The response to the requesting computer takes the same path back to the requesting client.

The user mode Server service provides the user interface to Srv.sys running in kernel mode. For example, both Server Manager and User Manager for Domains require the Server service To create a shared resource using Windows NT Explorer, the Server service must be running.

Note If connecting to another computer is unsuccessful, try verifying that the Workstation service (Lanman Workstation) has properly started, and that all of its dependent services and drivers have started properly.

Troubleshooting from an Architectural Perspective

In troubleshooting from an architectural perspective, follow this strategy:

- Isolate the problem.
- Check the Hardware Compatibility List.
- Check the hardware configuration.
- Check the Microsoft Knowledge Base.
- Monitor the Event Logs.

Isolate the Problem

When troubleshooting any problem, use a logical approach to isolate the problem. Some questions to ask are:

- What works?
- What doesn't work?
- How are the things that do and don't work related?
- Have the things that don't work ever worked on this computer and network?
- If so, what has changed since they last worked?

Check the Hardware Compatibility List (HCL)

The most common cause of hardware problems is the use of hardware that is not listed on the Hardware Compatibility List (HCL). The HCL included in the Windows NT Workstation Resource Kit lists the hardware components that have been tested and have passed compatibility testing with Windows NT 4.0. It is especially important to refer to the HCL if you plan to use any modems, tape backup units, or Small Computer System Interface (SCSI) adapters. Updates to the Windows NT 4.0 Hardware Compatibility List are at the following World Wide Web location:

http://www.microsoft.com/hwtest/

If the components are on the HCL, check that the connections are secure.

Check the Hardware Configuration

Check the hardware configuration. I/O and interrupt conflicts that went unnoticed under another operating system must be resolved when there is a change to Windows NT. Also, pay close attention to complementary metal-oxide semiconductor (CMOS) configuration parameters when using Windows NT.

If a SCSI device is in use, check its termination. Use active rather than passive terminators whenever possible.

Note Terminators are used to provide the correct impedance at the end of a cable. If the impedance is too high or too low, internal signal reflections can take place. These echoes represent noise on the cable, and can corrupt subsequent signals, which can result in degraded performance or data loss.

Passive terminators are resistors with the appropriate resistance value for the characteristic impedance of the cable. Active terminators are slightly more sophisticated electronics that are better able to maintain the correct impedance necessary to eliminate signal reflection.

Verify that the SCSI cables are not longer than necessary. Acceptable cable lengths vary depending on such factors as whether basic SCSI, SCSI-2, wide SCSI, ultra-wide SCSI, differential SCSI is in use. Consult the hardware documentation for this information.

Check the Microsoft Knowledge Base

The Knowledge Base is a good source of information for hardware problems. The Knowledge Base contains several articles about memory problems, memory parity errors, and SCSI problems, as well as other hardware information. The Knowledge Base appears on the World Wide Web at the following location:

http://www.microsoft.com/support/

Monitor the Event Logs

Careful monitoring of event logs can help predict and identify the sources of system problems. For example, if log warnings show that a disk driver can only read or write to a sector after several retries, the sector will probably go bad eventually. Logs can also confirm problems with application software: if an application crashes, an application event log can provide a record of activity leading up to the event.

The following suggestions will help when using event logs to diagnose problems:

- Archive logs in log format. The binary data associated with an event is discarded if data is archived in text or in comma-delimited format.

- If a hardware component is suspected as the source of system problems, filter the system log to show only those events generated by the component.

- If an event seems related to system problems, search the event log to find other instances of the same event, or to judge the frequency of an error.

Tools for Troubleshooting
from an Architectural Perspective

The following graphic illustrates the Windows NT tools available for trouble-shooting from an architectural perspective.

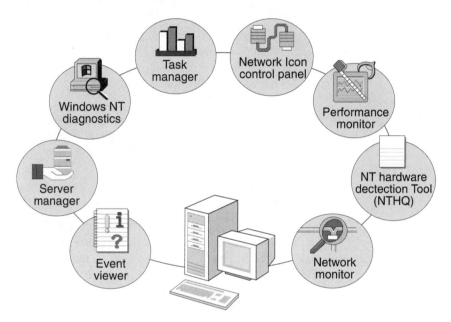

The following table describes tools that can be used to identify and isolate a problem in the Windows NT architecture.

Tool	Description
Event Viewer	Displays events and error messages generated by Windows NT system, services, applications, or user actions. A problem in an architectural layer can cause errors in the layers above.
Server Manager	Verifies that the NetLogon, Workstation, and Server services are running. Because every computer on the network can act as a client or a server, networking problems are often related to inbound or outbound requests.

Tool	Description
Windows NT Diagnostics	Helps examine the status of the network adapter cards, drivers, interrupt request lines (IRQs), network services, and transport protocols. If a processor was recently added, use the Hardware option to see the number of processors that Windows NT recognizes. Information here can be viewed but not modified.
Task Manager	Monitors, stops, and starts active applications and processes.
Network Icon in Control Panel	Use the Network icon in Control Panel to identify the network cards and protocols running on a computer.
Performance Monitor	Use Performance Monitor to measures the computer's efficiency, to identify and troubleshoot possible problems, and to plan for additional hardware needs.
Windows NT Hardware Detection Tool (NTHQ)	Identifies installed hardware and settings for diagnostic purposes.
Network Monitor	Part of Windows NT Server. Use this network traffic and protocol analysis to view the conversation between two hosts on the network. View individual packets to determine the root cause of a problem.

Examining Windows NT Architecture

In this exercise you will answer questions regarding the Windows NT Architecture and methods for troubleshooting its probems.

1. Which strategy should you follow when troubleshooting from an architectural perspective?

   _____

   _____

2. Which Windows NT tools are critical when troubleshooting the architecture? Which role do they play in the troubleshooting process?

   _____

   _____

3. What is the significance of the NDIS library?

_____

_____

4. The active transport protocol is NWLink. What is the most effective means to view configuration information (frame type, network number, binding information)?

_____

_____

5. You are unsuccessful in establishing a session with another computer running Windows NT Server. How would you troubleshoot this problem?

_____

_____

6. Why is RPC a valuable IPC mechanism?

_____

_____

7. You are unsuccessful in running Server Manager. What could be the problem?

_____

_____

Lesson Summary

The following information summarizes the key points in this lesson:

- The two major layers of the Windows NT architecture are User mode and Kernel mode.

- The component at the lowest software level in the networking architecture is the NDIS-compatible network adapter card driver. NDIS 3.0-compatible device drivers will still operate on Windows NT 4.0, but it is recommended that newer NDIS 4.0 compatible drivers be used.

- For all protocols, the Network Monitor utility is the most effective troubleshooting tool.

- The redirector (RDR) provides one computer with access to another.

- The user mode network architectural layer includes services that work in conjunction with the kernel mode file system drivers to provide networking connectivity for users and servers.

Lesson 3: Modifying the System Through the Registry

Efficient troubleshooting requires a high level of familiarity with the registry structure, and an ability to navigate it accurately. This lesson describes the registry structure, and examines specific locations in the registry that are particularly helpful during troubleshooting.

After this lesson, you will be able to:

- Describe how the registry can be used to troubleshoot Windows NT.
- Describe the organizational structure of the registry.
- Examine the registry using the Registry Editor.
- Examine the registry using the registry Help file, command-line Windows NT Diagnostics, and Remote Command utility.
- Identify the main troubleshooting opportunities in **HKEY_LOCAL_MACHINE**.
- Examine **HKEY_LOCAL_MACHINE\HARDWARE**.
- Examine **HKEY_LOCAL_MACHINE\SYSTEM**.

Estimated lesson time: 20 minutes

Registry

The following graphic illustrates the relationship of the registry to Windows NT Server.

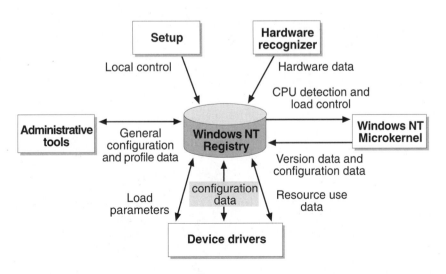

An error message during a system logon attempt shows that a device driver did not load properly. It is important to determine whether the problem is hardware or software. To troubleshoot, consult the registry to see if the hardware is recognized, and to examine driver configuration and load information. Remember that all of the architectural components of the system are centrally controlled through the registry. The registry can reveal the source of the problem, and modification of the registry may provide the solution.

Using the registry to solve the problem requires the following skills:

1. Navigating the registry to find the problem.

2. Using different tools to identify the problem.

3. Making the correct registry modification.

4. Determining which files are affected by the modification.

5. Restoring the registry.

What Is the Registry?

In Windows NT, configuration information is centrally stored in a single database called the registry. The registry replaces the .ini, .sys, and .com configuration files used in Windows graphical environment for MS-DOS and LAN Manager.

Values and entries for all of the system configurations are kept here, including hardware, device drivers, network protocols, and adapter card settings. The registry also holds information about applications and user profiles.

The system is controlled through the registry, which determines what architectural components are integrated into the system, when those components will start, and what they depend upon. The loading of the operating system files is also dependent on registry entries.

Registry Interactions

The following table describes how Windows NT components interact with the registry.

Component	Registry Interaction
Administrative tools	The administrative tools in Windows NT, such as those provided in Control Panel and in the Administrative Tools (Common) folder, can be used to modify configuration data. These administrative tools are helpful for viewing and occasionally making detailed changes to the system configuration. Use Windows NT Diagnostics and the System Policy Editor to view configuration data stored in the registry and to modify certain registry keys.
Setup	When setup programs are run for appl ications or hardware, the Window NT Setup program adds new configuration data to the registry. For example, new information is added when a new Small Computer System Interface (SCSI) adapter is installed, or when the settings for the video display are changed. Setup also reads information from the registry to determine whether prerequisite components have been installed.
Hardware Recognizer	The hardware recognizer runs as part of the Windows NT startup sequence. When a computer running Windows NT starts, the hardware recognizer places in the registry a list of the installed hardware it detects. On computers with Intel processors, hardware detection is done by Ntdetect.com and the Windows NT microkernel.
Windows NT Microkernel	During system startup, the Windows NT microkernel extracts information from the registry. This information includes which device drivers to load and their load order. The Ntoskrnl.exe program also passes information about itself (such as its version number) to the registry.
Device drivers	Device drivers send and receive load parameters and configuration data from the registry. A device driver must report system resources that it uses, such as hardware interrupts and direct memory access (DMA) channels, so that the system can add this information to the registry. Applications and device drivers can read this registry information to provide users with smart installation and configuration programs.

Registry Structure

The registry is structured as a set of five subtrees of keys that contain per-computer and per-user databases. The following graphic illustrates the subtree structure of the registry.

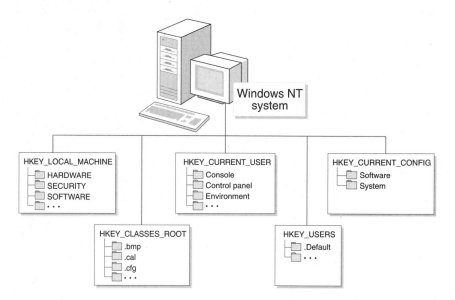

The registry is a database organized in a hierarchical structure, consisting of subtrees and their keys, hives, and value entries.

Subtrees, Keys, and Hives

The registry is structured as a set of five subtrees rooted at the top of the registry hierarchy. A registry subtree contains keys that contain per-computer and per-user databases. Each key can contain value entries and additional subkeys. A hive is a discrete body of keys, subkeys, and values within a subtree. A hive is backed by a single file and a .log file which are in the %SystemRoot%\system32\config\ folder, or the %SystemRoot%\profiles\ folder.

The following table identifies the five subtrees and describes the content of their keys.

Subtree Name	Description
HKEY_LOCAL_MACHINE	Contains information about the local computer, including hardware and operating system data such as bus type, system memory, device drivers, and startup control data. **HKEY_LOCAL_MACHINE** provides the most useful troubleshooting access.
HKEY_CLASSES_ROOT	Contains the data that associates file types (by file name extension) with applications. Also contains configuration data for Component Object Model (COM) and Distributed Component Object Model (DCOM) objects.
HKEY_CURRENT_USER	Contains the user profile for the user who is currently logged on, including environment variables, personal program groups, desktop settings, network connections, printers, and application preferences.
HKEY_USERS	Contains all actively loaded user profiles, including **HKEY_CURRENT_USER** which always refers to a "child" of **HKEY_USERS** and the default profile.
HKEY_CURRENT_CONFIG	Contains data that defines the current hardware profile. This subtree is actually an alias of **HKEY_LOCAL_MACHINE\System\CurrentControlSet\Hardware Profiles\Current** so the contents of the **\Hardware Profiles\Current** subkey appear in **HKEY_CURRENT_CONFIG**.

Note Each subtree name begins with HKEY_ to indicate to software developers that this is a handle that can be used by a program. A handle is a value used to uniquely identify a resource so that a program can access it. When a process opens an object with a write handle, no other process can gain access to the object. This protects the second process from gaining access to an object that is in a changing state.

Most of our attention in this lesson will be in **HKEY_LOCAL_MACHINE**.

A hive is backed by a single file and a .log file, which facilitates recoverability. These files cannot simply be copied in order to back them up when Windows NT is running. This is because the operating system opens them with a write handle that points to the actual file. (The H of **HKEY** is for handle.)

Registry Editor

The Registry Editor is a useful tool for configuring a computer's registry. The following graphic illustrates the configuration options available in the Registry Editor.

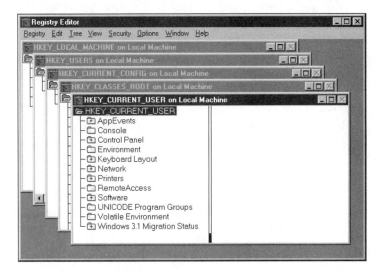

Different tools are available to view and change registry entries. For example, Windows NT Diagnostics provides a graphical display of registry hardware information, and Control Panel contains options to view and change registry information such as drivers and protocols. However, Registry Editor provides more extensive access to the registry.

Using Registry Editor

The Windows NT Setup program installs two versions of Registry Editor: the Windows NT Registry Editor (Regedt32.exe) and the Windows 95 version (Regedit.exe).

The Windows NT Registry Editor is installed in the %SystemRoot%\system32 folder. The Windows 95 version (32-bit) of Registry Editor is installed in the %SystemRoot% folder. The Windows 95 version of Regedit has a search mechanism that searches keys and text.

Some entries can be changed only by using the Windows NT Registry Editor (Regedt32.exe). If entries are changed with the Registry Editor, syntax errors are not recognized, so there is no error warning if an error occurs as a result of a change.

Caution Make sure to back up the registry before making changes using the Registry Editor, and to use Read Only mode when viewing the registry and not making changes. Read Only mode is a built-in safety precaution that does not allow any part of the registry to be accidentally changed or deleted. Activate this option through the Registry Editor Options menu.

In general, if values are changed for any entries in **CurrentControlSet**, the computer must be restarted for the changes to take effect. If Registry Editor is used to change values for entries under **HKEY_CURRENT_USER**, the user may have to log off and log back on for the changes to take effect.

Backing Up the Registry

There are four methods of backing up registry entries:

- Use **Save Registry** under **Backup** in **Administrative Tools (Common)**. This is the recommended method if there is a tape backup. The Windows NT Backup and Restore program can access registry hives while Windows NT is running.

- Use the Regback.exe and Regrest.exe utilities to back up and restore registry hives while Windows NT is running. These utilities are included with the Windows NT Resource Kit.

- On the Registry Editor **Registry** menu, click **Save Key** and complete the **Save Key** dialog box. This procedure saves a single key and everything beneath it in the hierarchy in a specified file name. However, because online restores are not guaranteed, it is recommended that you use Windows NT Backup or Regback.exe to back up the registry.

- Create or update the Emergency Repair disk. However, Rdisk.exe does not back up all of the registry.

Note The Repair Disk program does not update the Default, Sam and Security files if the program is run from Windows NT Explorer or from My Computer. To update all the files, run the Repair Disk program from the command prompt by clicking the **Start** button, clicking **Run**, and typing **rdisk /s** in the **Open** box. Using the **/s** switch forces the Repair Disk program to update all of the registry keys in the %systemroot%\Repair folder.

For more information about the %systemroot%\Repair and %systemroot% \System32\Config folders, and the Emergency Repair Disk, search the Knowledge Base. For information about the Knowledge Base, see the *Windows NT Server Resource Kit*, Chapter 8, "General Troubleshooting."

Gaining Access to a Remote Computer's Registry

Registry Editor contains a troubleshooting option to edit the **HKEY_LOCAL _MACHINE** and **HKEY_USERS** keys of a remote computer. Use this option if there appears to be a problem in the remote computer's registry, such as an incorrectly configured service or device. To gain access to a remote computer's registry, on the Registry Editor **Registry** menu, click **Select Computer**. There is no unique interface for closing the remote registry; close it by clicking **Close** on the **Registry** menu. Because of this, when closing the remote registry, be sure that it is the active one. If the remote registry is left open or if the local registry is inadvertently closed when Registry Editor is quit, the next time Registry Editor is started, the remote registry will appear.

winreg Subkey

Windows NT 4.0 includes the **winreg** subkey, an optional security check to control remote access to the registry. This check determines which users can connect to the registry from another computer. After the user is connected, the access control lists (ACLs) for each registry element govern the user's access to the registry. When a user tries to connect to the registry remotely, Windows NT looks for the **winreg** subkey in one of two ways:

- If **winreg** is in the registry, the ACL for winreg determines which users can connect to the registry remotely. Users must have at least read and write access, including permission to create subkeys and set values, to be permitted to connect to the registry.

- If **winreg** does not appear in the registry, all users can connect to the registry remotely.

After the user is connected to the registry, the ACL for each registry key or subkey determines whether the user can read, edit, add, or delete registry contents.

The winreg subkey must be located in the following registry path:

```
HKEY_LOCAL_MACHINE\SYSTEM
  \CurrentControlSet
    \Control
      \SecurePipeServers
        \winreg
```

Other Tools in the Windows NT Resource Kit

The following graphic identifies the other tools that can be used to interact with the registry.

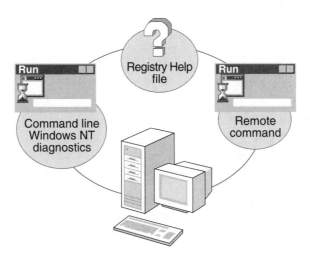

These other tools for the registry are the Registry Help file, the command line version of Windows NT Diagnostics, and Remote Command.

Registry Help File

The registry Help file (Regentry.hlp) provides a database of Windows NT registry entries in the form of a Help file. You can use this Help file while working in Registry Editor to find ranges, minimum-maximum values, and instructions for setting specific values in the registry.

Command Line Windows NT Diagnostics

Windows NT Diagnostics (WinMsdP) is a command-line version of Winmsd.exe. This Windows NT Resource kit utility provides information about system configuration and status. WinMsdP reads the Windows NT registry to gather information about the system. It then dumps this information to a text file named

Msdrpt.txt. The file is saved in the current folder. If a previous file already exists with this name, the new file will be renamed.

The main advantage of WinMsdP is that it can run from the command line without a graphical interface. The standard version of Winmsd.exe (accessible from the **Start** menu by pointing to **Programs**, pointing to **Administrative Tools (Common)**, and then clicking **Windows NT Diagnostics**) can print to a file, but requires user interaction to do so.

WinMsdP can be run from a Remote command prompt such as the one provided by Rcmd.exe or Remote.exe. This allows users to run the utility over the network on remote systems, which is not possible with the standard version of Winmsd.exe.

In addition, by using WinMsdP's command-line parameters, users can create automated batch files. These batch files can be run using the Windows NT At.exe scheduling service. This allows users to gather system information at regular intervals.

Remote Command Service (RCMD)

The Remote Command Service (Rcmd.exe), included in the *Windows NT Server Resource Kit*, provides a secure, robust way to remotely administer and run command-line programs.

RCMD consists of client and server components. The client is a command-line program, Rcmd.exe. The server end, Rcmdsvc.exe, is installed and runs as a service. That is, it can be stopped and started locally or remotely by using the Network icon in Control Panel, or locally with the **net start** and **net stop** commands. As a service, if it is configured for autostart, it will run whenever the system is running, regardless of whether a user is logged on locally.

A command session, or virtual console, is created when a client connects to the server. It is not visible on the desktop, and does not in any way interfere with it. Up to 10 clients can be simultaneously connected to the remote command server on a computer, all operating securely and independently of each other.

Troubleshooting With HKEY_LOCAL_MACHINE

The **HKEY_LOCAL_MACHINE** contains many locations in which vital troubleshooting information can be found. The following graphic illustrates the configuration options available with **HKEY_LOCAL_MACHINE**.

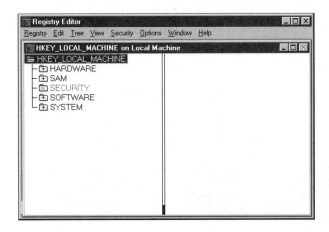

Problems often have their origins in services, device drivers, or startup control data. **HKEY_LOCAL_MACHINE** contains this configuration information, so it is the logical starting point in the registry to begin troubleshooting these kinds of problems.

The following table describes the five subtree keys of **HKEY_LOCAL_MACHINE**.

Subtree Key	Description
HARDWARE	This database describes the physical hardware in the computer, the way device drivers use that hardware, and mappings and related data that link kernel-mode drivers with various user-mode code. All data in this subtree is recreated by Windows NT Detect each time the system is started. Therefore, it is useless to make changes to this data, most of which is stored in binary form. Use Windows NT Diagnostics to view the data.
Security Accounts Manager (SAM)	This contains security information for user and group accounts, and for domains in a computer running Windows NT Server.
SECURITY	This database contains the local security policy, such as specific user rights.
SOFTWARE	This database describes the per-computer software.
SYSTEM	This database controls system startup, device driver loading, Windows NT services, and operating system behavior.

Note The **HARDWARE** and **SYSTEM** subtree keys are the most useful for troubleshooting.

HKEY_LOCAL_MACHINE\HARDWARE

The HKEY_LOCAL_MACHINE\HARDWARE is the location where information about the physical hardware in the computer is stored.

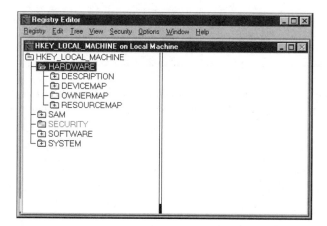

The **HKEY_LOCAL_MACHINE\HARDWARE** key contains the hardware data in the registry that is computed at system startup. This includes information about hardware components on the system board and about the interrupts controlled by specific hardware devices. All information in this key is volatile; the settings are computed each time the system is started and discarded when the system is shut down. The Hardware key contains important sets of data in three subkeys; **Description**, **DeviceMap**, and **ResourceMap**.

Hardware Subkeys

The Hardware subkeys are described in the following table.

Subkey	Description
DESCRIPTION	The **Description** subkey displays information from the hardware database built by the firmware, the Hardware Recognizer (Ntdetect.com), and the Windows NT Executive, which manages the interface between the Kernel and the environment subsystems. On a computer with an Intel processor platform, this database consists of the data found by Ntdetect.com and Ntoskernel.exe. The Hardware Recognizer for Intel-based computers detects the following items: bus/adapter type, video adapter, keyboard, floating-point coprocessor, SCSI adapters, mouse, communication ports, Floppy drives, machine ID, parallel ports. On computers that are not PC-compatible, the manufacturer provides its own Hardware Recognizer. On reduced instruction set computing (RISC)-based computers, this hardware database is a copy of the ARC configuration database in the firmware.
DEVICEMAP	In the **\DeviceMap\Device** subkey, each **Device** contains one or more values to specify the location in the registry for specific driver information. The value for each **Device** subkey describes an actual port name or the path for a **Service** subkey in **HKEY_LOCAL_MACHINE \System\ControlSet\Services,** which contains information about a device driver. That **Service** subkey contains the information that a system administrator may need for troubleshooting and is also the information presented about the device by Windows NT Diagnostics.
OWNERMAP	The **OwnerMap** subkey appears in the registry only when certain types of device buses, such as a Peripheral Component Interconnect (PCI) device bus, are installed on the computer. The OwnerMap subkey contains operating system data to associate drivers of a specified type with devices of the same type on each installed bus.
RESOURCEMAP	Applications and device drivers use this key to read information about the system components, store data directly into the **DeviceMap** subkey, and store data indirectly into the **ResourceMap** subkey. The value for each **Device** subkey describes an actual port name or the path for a **Service** subkey in **HKEY_LOCAL_MACHINE \System\ControlSet\Services.**

Note To view data about a computer's hardware in an easy-to-read format for troubleshooting, run WinMSD, and click the **Devices** button on the **Services** tab.WinMSD extracts the information from the registry and displays it in a more readable format.

HKEY_LOCAL_MACHINE\SYSTEM

The following graphic introduces the location where information about the startup, device driver loading, Windows NT services, and operating system behavior is stored.

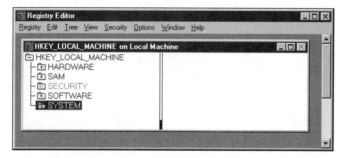

- **Subkeys of HKEY_LOCAL_MACHINE\SYSTEM**
- **\SYSTEM\CurrentControlSet**
- **\SYSTEM\CurrentControlSet\Services**
- **\SYSTEM\CurrentControlSet\Services\<NETWORK Devices>**
- **Finding services and dependencies**

The **HKEY_LOCAL_MACHINE\SYSTEM** key contains information that controls system startup, device driver loading, Windows NT services, and operating system behavior. All startup-related data that must be stored (rather than computed during startup) is saved in the **SYSTEM** key.

This topic examines the contents of **HKEY_LOCAL_MACHINE\SYSTEM** by first looking at all of the subkeys, and then focusing closely on **HKEY_LOCAL _MACHINE\SYSTEM\CurrentControlSet**, the subkey most useful for troubleshooting. The **Services** subkey within **CurrentControlSet** receives particular attention because it shows the Services registry entries. Finally, the topic examines methods for finding services and dependencies in **HKEY_LOCAL _MACHINE\SYSTEM**.

Subkeys of HKEY_LOCAL_MACHINE\SYSTEM

The following graphic identifies the subkeys of **HKEY_LOCAL_MACHINE \SYSTEM**

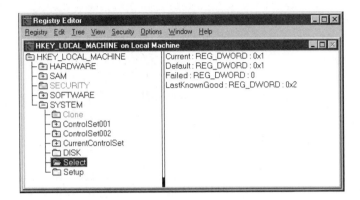

For troubleshooting purposes, the most frequently used subkeys under **HKEY_LOCAL_MACHINE\SYSTEM** are the Control Set subkeys, and the Disk, Setup, and Select subkeys.

System Subkeys

The subkeys of **HKEY_LOCAL_MACHINE\SYSTEM** contain troubleshooting resources. A subkey contains system configuration information, such as which device drivers and services to load and start. There can be many system subkeys in **HKEY_LOCAL_MACHINE\SYSTEM**. The subkeys are described in the following table.

System Subkey	Description
Clone	Copy of **CurrentControlSet** used to initialize computer. Created by kernel initialization process each time the computer is started up. The Clone is not available after user logs on.
ControlSet001	Either a copy of **CurrentControlSet**, or of the LastKnownGood value set to 0x1 (refer to Select description below).
ControlSet002	Either a copy of **CurrentControlSet** or of the LastKnownGood value set to 0x2 (refer to Select description below).
CurrentControlSet	**CurrentControlSet** key is the one used to start the system for the current session.

(continued)

continued

System Subkey	Description
DISK	Contains configuration information about currently defined drive letters, volume sets, stripe sets, stripe sets with parity, and mirror sets, as well as CD-ROM mappings and drive mappings.
Select	Contains information about the control set from which Windows NT booted.
Setup	Contains hardware and software setup information, such as system partition and the source of the Windows NT files.

Note There are at least two control sets, and sometimes more, depending on how often system settings are changed, or whether there are problems with the selected settings. The purpose of multiple control sets is to provide a backup copy if the current control set fails. The control set for the currently selected computer maintains information in the **Select** subkey.

Select Subkey

The Registry subkey **HKEY_LOCAL_MACHINE\SYSTEM\Select** identifies how the control sets are used, and determines which control set is used at startup. This subkey contains the value entries described in the following table.

Value Entry	Description
Current	Identifies the control set from which the **CurrentControlSet** subkey is derived. If this value is 0x1, for example, the subkey producing the **CurrentControlSet** is **ControlSet001**.
Default	Identifies the default control set. If this value is 0x1, for example, the default control set is **ControlSet001**.
Failed	Identifies the control set number of the control set that was last rejected and replaced with a LastKnownGood control set.
LastKnownGood	Identifies the last control set that successfully started the system. If this value is 0x1, for example, the last control set known to be good is **ControlSet001**.

Note Each of the **Select** subkey values contain a REG_DWORD data type, which refers to a specific control set.

HKEY_LOCAL_MACHINE\SYSTEM\CurrentControlSet

The following graphic identifies the contents of **HKEY_LOCAL_MACHINE \SYSTEM\CurrentControlSet.**

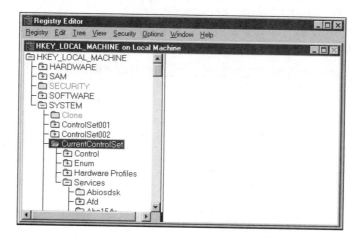

When Windows NT is installed, it creates the Control and Services subkeys for each control set in **HKEY_LOCAL_MACHINE\SYSTEM**. Some information, such as which services are part of which group, and the order in which to load the groups, is the same for all computers running Windows NT. Other information, such as which devices and services to load when the computer starts, is based on the hardware installed on the computer and the network software selected for installation. This information is contained in the **CurrentControlSet**.

The following table describes the contents of **CurrentControlSet**.

Subkey	Description
Control	Contains startup data for Windows NT, including the maximum size of the registry.
Enum	Contains the Plug and Play hardware tree.
Hardware Profile	Enables users to define different configurations for their computers and to select the configuration to use at startup.
Services	Lists all Kernel device drivers, file system drivers, and Win32 service drivers that can be loaded by the boot loader, the I/O Manager, and the Service Control Manager. It also contains subkeys describing which drivers are attached to which hardware devices, as well as the services that are installed on the system.

HKEY_LOCAL_MACHINE\SYSTEM \CurrentControlSet\Services

The following graphic identifies the contents of **HKEY_LOCAL_MACHINE \SYSTEM\CurrentControlSet\Services.**

HKEY_LOCAL_MACHINE\SYSTEM\CurrentControlSet\Services provides services and device driver loading information. These subkeys appear in alphabetical order.

Types of Services

The subkeys under Services include most of the networking components, such as the adapter cards and their drivers, protocol drivers, redirector, server, and so on. The information for a driver under the **Services** key is more easily readable in the Windows NT Diagnostics-Drivers window than in Registry Editor. However, because Windows NT Diagnostics is a view-only tool, changes must be made through an appropriate Control Panel icon or through Registry Editor. When using Registry Editor, make the changes in the **CurrentControlSet**, so that the new values will be used during the next system startup.

Service Values

The value entries displayed in the subkeys are similar to each other. The contents of **HKEY_LOCAL_MACHINE\SYSTEM\Services \Browser** provide a useful example. The following table shows value entries that may provide useful trouble-shooting information from this subkey.

Value	Description
DependOnGroup	At least one service from this group must be loaded before this service is loaded. Look in **SYSTEM \Current-ControlSet\Control\ServiceGroupOrder** to see in what order the driver group loads.
DependOnService	Provides specific services that must be loaded before this service is loaded.
Display Name	A sequence of characters representing human-readable text.
Value	Description
Error Control	Controls whether an error during the startup of this driver will require the system to switch to the LastKnownGood control set. If the value is 0 (Ignore, no error is reported) or 1 (Normal, error reported), startup proceeds. If the value is 2 (Severe) or 3 (Critical), an error is reported and LastKnownGood is used.
ImagePath	Identifies the path and file name of the driver. Use Windows NT Explorer to verify the existence of the named file.
Object Name	Specifies an object name. If Type specifies a Win32 service, this name is the account name that the service will use to log on when the service runs.
Start	The start constant value specifies the starting values for the service. The Start value is ignored for adapters. If Type is a Win32 service value, the Start value must specify an Auto, Demand, or Disabled value.
Type	The type constant value specifies the type of service. For example, when you start Windows NT, the Boot Loader scans the registry for drivers with a Start value of 0 (which indicates that these drivers should be loaded but not initialized before the Kernel) and a Type value of 0x1 (which indicates a Kernel device driver such as a hard disk or other low-level hardware device driver). The drivers are then loaded into memory in the order specified as the List value in CurrentControlSet\Control\Service-GroupOrder.

Start Value

The Start value determines if and when the driver is loaded during system startup. If a service is not starting, first determine when and how it should start. Then look for the services and drivers that should be loaded prior to this driver. The following table describes values for the Start service.

Value	Description
0 (Boot)	Loaded by the Boot Loader (Ntldr) during boot sequence.
1 (System)	Loaded at Kernel initialization during the load sequence.
2 (Auto Load)	Loaded or started automatically at system startup.
3 (Load On Demand)	Driver is manually started by the user or another process. For example, Transmission Control Protocol/ Internet Protocol (TCP/IP) is started by NDIS.
4 (Disabled)	Driver is not to be started under any condition. If a driver is accidentally disabled, reset this value through Server Manager or through the Services icon in Control Panel.

Type Value

The Type service determines the type of driver or service. Knowing the Type value helps to identify where the service fits in the architecture. The following table describes values for the Type service.

Value	Description
1	Kernel device driver.
2	File system driver, which is also a Kernel device driver.
4	Set of arguments for an adapter.
10	A Win32 program that can be started by the Service Controller and that obeys the service control protocol. This type of service runs in a process by itself.
20	A Win32 service that can share a process with other Win32 services.

Note Many of the services that have a Type value of 0x20 are part of Services.exe. For example, if the network protocol is TCP/IP, and is configured to use a Dynamic Host Configuration Protocol (DHCP) server to get IP addresses, these services that have a Type value of 0x20 are in Services.exe. For more information, see *Standard Entries for CurrentControlSet\Services Subkeys* under Overview Topics in Registry Help.

HKEY_LOCAL_MACHINE\SYSTEM\CurrentControlSet\Services\ *Network Devices*

The following graphic illustrates the use of the registry to examine network devices on **HKEY_LOCAL_MACHINE\SYSTEM\...\Parameters**. The **Parameters** subkey can be also checked for network device abnormalities. Find **Parameters** under IEEPR01.

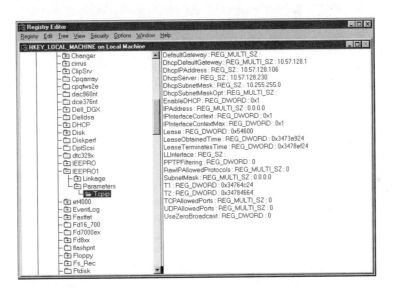

Among the **Services** subkeys, **IEEPRO1** provides an example of additional troubleshooting information related to network devices. The **Parameters** subkeys can be visually checked for abnormalities. Any configurations for the network adapter such as interrupt, I/O address, or transceiver will be located under the Parameters subkey. To ensure TCP/IP is configured correctly, refer to the **Tcpip** subkey under Parameters for the network adapter card. Verify the information by typing **ipconfig /all.**

Some of the values in this example are configurable through the Network icon in Control Panel, such as whether DHCP is enabled.

Parameters can also be added, as well as changed. An example of a parameter you may need to add to **Services\Tcpip\Parameters** is **TcpWindowSize**, to reduce the amount of data in a TCP/IP packet.

Finding Services and Dependencies

The following graphic illustrates a scenario in which a troubleshooter examines services and dependencies. You can use **HKEY_LOCAL_MACHINE \SYSTEM\CurrentControlSet\Services** to identify dependencies and services that can reveal the cause of a problem.

In the **Services** subkey are all kernel device drivers, file system drivers, and Win32 service drivers that can be loaded by the boot loader, the I/O Manager, and the Service Control Manager.

The **Services** subkey also contains subkeys that describe which drivers are attached to which hardware devices, in addition to the services that are installed on the system. This is a resource that allows troubleshooters to explore services and dependencies that may have caused a system problem. A failure of Lanman-Workstation provides an example of how to examine the registry for related services and dependencies.

LanmanWorkstation

For example, the Event Viewer delivers a message that the redirector failed to load. LanmanWorkstation is the redirector. To find related services and dependencies, look in **HKEY_LOCAL_MACHINE\SYSTEM\Current ControlSet \Services\LanmanWorkstation**.

The values that provide service and dependency information most useful for troubleshooting are: DependOnGroup, DependOnService, Error Control, Image Path, Start, and Type.

DependOnGroup

The DependOnGroup values show that LanmanWorkstation depends on TDI in order to load. Did TDI load correctly? To determine this, a troubleshooter can use the TDISHOW utility in the Windows NT Resource Kit.

DependOnService

The DependOnService values show that LanmanWorkstation is not dependent on any other service in order to load.

Note To see a clear example of interdependent services, stop any service using Control Panel. A dialog box automatically shows which additional services will also stop.

Error Control

The Error Control value shows that LanmanWorkstation has a value of 1. This means that there was an error starting LanmanWorkstation. The error was logged in the Event Log, but Windows NT completed startup.

Image Path

The Image Path value shows that Services.exe is the file for LanmanWorkstation, and that it should be in the System32 folder. To verify this, use Windows NT Explorer. If the file is not in the correct location, LanmanWorkstation cannot load.

Start

The Start value shows 4. This means that LanmanWorkstation is disabled. This is the reason that LanmanWorkstation does not start.

Type

The Type value shows 20. This means that LanmanWorkstation is a Win32 service that can share a process with other Win32 services (Services.exe), and should have loaded with the Win32 service.

ServiceGroupOrder Subkey

The device drivers should be loaded and initialized by viewing the registry subkey **HKEY_LOCAL_MACHINE\SYSTEM\CurrentControlSet\Control\ ServiceGroupOrder**. In the example above, DependOnGroup refers to TDI. When the TDI group loads, then LanmanWorkstation will load.

Note Many device drivers are arranged in groups to make startup easier. When device drivers and services are loaded, Windows NT loads the groups in the order defined by ServiceGroupOrder.

Troubleshooting the Registry

1. In Windows NT, what is the registry and its function?

   _____

   _____

2. Define the structure of a registry.

   _____

   _____

3. Which tools are used to view and change registry entries?

   _____

   _____

4. What is one way you could remotely administer the registry?

   _____

   _____

5. In troubleshooting Windows NT, which registry subtree is typically used?

   _____

   _____

6. A hardware component is not active after starting Windows NT. What can you check to determine if it is configured to start automatically?

_____

_____

7. What is the purpose of the ServiceGroupOrder subkey?

_____

_____

8. Which values are the most beneficial when troubleshooting related services and dependency information?

_____

_____

9. You share your computer with another user. Recently, you've noticed that TCP/IP is taking much longer to time out when a remote host has been disconnected from the net. How can you determine if the registry has been changed from standard configuration?

_____

_____

Lesson Summary

The following information summarizes the key points in this lesson:

- The registry can be examined to see if the hardware is recognized, and to examine driver configuration and load information.

- The system is controlled through the registry, which determines what architectural components are integrated into the system.

- The Windows NT Setup program installs two versions of Registry Editor: the Windows NT Registry Editor (Regedt32.exe) and the Windows 95 version (Regedit.exe).

- The registry Help file, command-line Windows NT Diagnostics utility, and the Remote Command utility are resources to help you access the Windows NT configuration and successfully view and modify the registry.

- The Remote Command Service (Rcmd.exe) provides a secure, robust way to remotely administer and run command-line programs.

Lesson 4: Examining the Boot Process

The files used in the operating system boot process are crucial. If one of these files is missing or corrupted, the computer will probably be non-functional, or at the least, be unable to communicate properly with other computers. It is important to know which system components load during the boot process in order to verify that the correct drivers are in place, and to be able to replace any damaged or missing files.

After this lesson you will be able to:

- Identify the phases of a successful Windows NT boot.
- Identify the events of the initial phase of the boot process.
- Identify the events of the boot loader phase of the boot process.
- Identify the events of the kernel phase of the boot process.
- Identify the events of the logon phase of the boot process.
- Identify the contents and switches of Boot.ini.
- Verify which drivers were successfully loaded.
- Replace missing or damaged files.

Estimated lesson time: 20 minutes

Identifying the Steps in a Successful Boot

To be able to identify and isolate file-related problems, you need to examine the files loaded in the boot and load sequence. This lesson describes only the boot process for Intel x86-based computers. Reduced instruction set computing (RISC)-based computers will not be described.

The boot process occurs in four phases. Familiarity with the steps of the boot process in each phase provides a basis for efficient troubleshooting.

The following table gives a brief description of each phase.

Phase	Description
Initial Phase	Performs a self test. Initializes the computer and locates the boot portion of the hard disk. The startup portion of Ntldr (the Loader) is then loaded and initialized from the boot sector.
Boot Loader Phase	Gathers information about the computer's installed hardware and drivers before the kernel loads.
Kernel Phase	Loads and initializes the kernel and device drivers, and loads services.
Logon Phase	The Windows NT boot process is not complete until a user successfully logs on and the Clone control set is copied to the LastKnownGood control set.

Initial Phase

Hardware diagnostics performed during the initial phase are often overlooked in troubleshooting. There are four parts of this phase.

Power On Self Test (POST)

When a computer is turned on or restarted, it goes through a POST routine to determine:

- The amount of real memory.
- Whether the needed hardware components are present.

After the computer POST routine, each adapter card with a BIOS runs its own POST routine. If a hardware failure is detected during the POST, the computer will present on-screen diagnostic procedures.

Initial Startup

The first sector on the hard disk is critical to the startup process. This sector contains the Master Boot Record and the Partition Table.

If the startup disk is a floppy disk, the first sector on the disk is the Partition Boot Sector.

After the POST the system BIOS attempts to locate the startup disk. If there is a floppy disk in drive A, the system BIOS uses drive A as the startup disk. If there is no disk in drive A, the system BIOS then checks the first hard disk that is turned on.

Note Some system BIOS versions enable the user to reconfigure the order in which it checks the floppy disks and hard disks for the startup disk.

Master Boot Record

When the hard disk is the startup disk, the system BIOS reads the Master Boot Record and loads it into memory. The system BIOS then transfers execution to the Master Boot Record. The code in the Master Boot Record scans the Partition Table for the system partition. When the Master Boot Record finds the system partition, it loads sector 0 of the partition into memory, and executes it. Sector 0 on the system partition can be a third-party utility or diagnostic program, or a Partition Boot Sector that contains startup code for an operating system. The Partition Boot Sector code starts the operating system.

If there is no system partition on the first hard disk, the Master Boot Record displays errors such as the following:

- Invalid partition table.
- Error loading operating system.
- Missing operating system.

Note The Master Boot Record is generally operating system-independent. For example, on *x*86-based computers, the same Master Boot Record starts Windows NT, Windows95, MS-DOS, and Windows 3.*x*.

Partition Boot Sector

The Partition Boot Sector is dependent on both the operating system and the file system. On *x*86-based computers, the Windows NT Partition Boot Sector is responsible for the following:

- Finding the boot loader (Ntldr) in the root folder.
- Loading Ntldr into memory.
- Starting execution of Ntldr.

On *x*86-based computers, the system partition must be on the first physical hard disk. The boot partition (the partition containing Windows NT operating system files) can be the same as the system partition, can be on a different partition on the same hard disk, or can even be on a different hard disk.

If the first hard disk does not contain the system partition from which to start the computer, shut down the computer so that the system BIOS can access the correct disk.

If there is a floppy disk in drive A, the system BIOS loads the first sector on the disk into memory. If the floppy disk is bootable, the first sector is the Partition Boot Sector. If the floppy disk is not bootable, errors may appear, such as:

```
Non-System disk or disk error.
Replace and press any key when ready.
```

Note On an *x*86-based computer, the system partition must contain the boot loader and other files that load the operating system. Windows NT Setup designates the partition into which it installs these files as the system partition, but there are situations in which users may want to designate a different partition as the system partition. The Boot Indicator field in the Partition Table indicates whether a partition is the system partition.

Boot Loader Phase

The events of the boot loader phase include: selecting the operating system, detecting hardware, selecting a configuration, and loading the Kernel.

Windows NT Server starts loading with the initial phase, or pre-boot sequence. This sequence initializes the computer and locates the boot portion of the hard disk. The startup portion of Ntldr (the boot loader) is then loaded and initialized from the boot sector. When the initial phase is complete, the boot loader sequence begins.

During the boot loader sequence, Windows NT uses several programs to gather information about the computer's installed hardware and drivers. This occurs before the kernel is loaded. The following table describes the files for these programs.

File	Description
Ntldr	The operating system loader. Ntldr must be in the root directory.
Bootsect.dos	A hidden system file loaded by Ntldr if another operating system such as MS-DOS is selected. Bootsec.dos contains the boot sector that was on the hard disk before Windows NT was installed.
Boot.ini	Boot.ini is the file that builds the Boot Loader Operating System Selection menu.
Ntdetect.com	Ntdetect.com is the file that passes information about the hardware configuration to Ntldr.
Ntoskrnl.exe	The operating system kernel.
Ntbootdd.sys	The device driver used to access devices attached to a SCSI hard disk whose adapter is not using BIOS.
SYSTEM	The registry **HKEY_LOCAL_MACHINE\SYSTEM** hive.

Various device drivers specific to the computer—for example, SCSI drivers, video drivers, and so on are also loaded at this time.

Selecting the Operating System

Ntldr controls the operating system selection process and hardware detection prior to the Windows NT kernel initialization. Ntldr must be in the root folder of the startup disk, and also requires that the following files be located in the root folder:

- Boot.ini
- Ntbootdd.sys (if using the scsi() syntax in the Boot.ini file)
- Bootsect.dos (if dual-booting)
- Ntdetect.com

If the path name in the Boot.ini file for the system partition uses the scsi() syntax, the file Ntbootdd.sys must be in the root folder of the system partition.

When Ntldr starts executing, it clears the screen and displays the boot loader message:

```
OS Loader V4.0
```

Ntldr then performs the following steps:

- Switches the processor to the 32-bit flat memory mode. When *x*86-based computers first start, they run in real mode (that is, they are unable to implement virtual memory). Because Ntldr is a 32-bit program, it must switch the processor to 32-bit flat memory mode before it can perform any other functions.

- Starts the appropriate minifile system. The code to access files on file allocation table (FAT) and NT file system (NTFS) volumes is built into Ntldr. This code enables Ntldr to read, access, and copy files.

- Reads the Boot.ini file, and displays the operating system selections. This screen is called the boot loader screen.

- Allows the user to select an operating system from the boot loader screen.

  - If the user selects an operating system other than Windows NT, Ntldr loads Bootsect.dos and passes control to it. The other operating system then starts up as normal, because Bootsect.dos contains the Partition Boot Sector that was on the primary partition or logical drive before Windows NT was installed.

  - If the user selects a Windows NT version, Ntldr executes Ntdetect.com to gather information about currently installed hardware.

- Ntldr presents the choice of starting the computer in the configuration in use when Windows NT was last shutdown (Default), or in the Last Known Good configuration. This option occurs only if the SPACEBAR is pressed when prompted, or if there is more than one hardware profile.

- As the last part of the boot loader phase, Ntldr loads and starts Ntoskrnl.exe. Ntldr passes the hardware information collected by Ntdetect.com to Ntoskrnl.exe.

Ntldr displays a menu from which to select the operating system to start. If no selection is made, Ntldr loads the operating system specified by the default parameter in the Boot.ini file. Windows NT Setup sets the default entry to the most recently installed copy of Windows NT. To default to an operating system other than the most recently installed version of Windows NT, edit the Boot.ini file to change the default entry.

Detecting Hardware

Ntdetect.com is the hardware detector for *x*86-based computers. Ntdetect.com collects a list of currently installed components and returns this information to Ntldr.

On *x*86-based computers, Ntdetect.com executes after a Windows NT operating system is selected. When Ntdetect.com begins to execute, the following text appears on the screen:

```
NTDETECT V1.0 Checking Hardware . . .
```

Ntdetect.com detects the following components:

- Computer ID
- Bus/Adapter Type
- Video
- Keyboard
- Communication Ports
- Parallel Ports
- Floppy Disks
- Mouse/Pointing Device

Selecting a Configuration

When the version of Windows NT has been selected, and the boot loader has collected hardware information, the following screen appears:

```
OS Loader V4.0
Press SPACEBAR now to invoke Hardware Profile/Last Known Good menu.
```

The boot loader waits a few seconds for the user to press the SPACEBAR. If the SPACEBAR is not pressed, and there is only one hardware profile, the boot loader loads Windows NT by using the Default control set. Otherwise, the following screen appears:

```
Hardware Profile/Configuration Recovery Menu

This menu allows selection of a hardware profile to be used when
Windows NT starts. If the system does not start correctly, switch to a
previous system configuration, which may overcome startup problems.

IMPORTANT: System configuration changes made since the last successful
startup will be discarded.

Original Configuration
<Some other hardware profile>
Use the up and down arrow keys to move the highlight
to the selection you want. Then press ENTER.
```

```
To switch to the Last Known Good Configuration, press 'L'.
To Exit this menu and restart your computer, press F3.

Seconds until highlighted choice will be started automatically: 5
```

The first hardware profile is highlighted. If other hardware profiles have been created, use the DOWN ARROW key to make a selection. For more information about hardware profiles, use the **Find** tab in Windows NT Help, and type the word **profile**

It is possible to select between the Last Known Good Configuration and the Default Configuration. Windows NT automatically uses the Default Configuration if the Last Known Good Configuration is not selected. When the Default Configuration is used, the boot loader uses the registry information that Windows NT saved at the last shutdown.

If the Last Known Good Configuration is selected, the boot loader uses the registry information that it saved at the completion of the last successful startup.

Loading the Kernel

After the hardware configuration is selected, the boot loader loads the Windows NT kernel (Ntoskrnl.exe) and the hardware abstraction layer (Hal.dll) into memory. The boot loader does not initialize these programs yet. Next, the boot loader loads the registry key **HKEY_LOCAL_MACHINE\SYSTEM** from %systemroot%System32\Config\System.

At this point, the boot loader creates the control set it will use to initialize the computer. The value in the **HKEY_LOCAL_MACHINE\SYSTEM\Select** subkey determines which control set in **HKEY_LOCAL_MACHINE\SYSTEM** to use. The loader uses the control set identified by the Default value, unless it is using the Last Known Good Configuration. In this case, the value under LastKnownGood specifies the control set. Based on this selection and the value of the corresponding **Select** subkey, the loader determines which **ControlSet00**x to use. It sets the value of Current in the **Select** subkey to the number of the control set it will use.

At this time, the boot loader scans all of the services in the registry subkey **HKEY_LOCAL_MACHINE\SYSTEM\CurrentControlSet\Services** for device drivers with a Start value of 0x0, which indicates that they should be loaded but not initialized. Device drivers with these values are typically low-level hardware device drivers, such as hard disk device drivers. The Group value for each device driver determines the order in which the boot loader loads them. The registry subkey **HKEY_LOCAL_MACHINE\SYSTEM\CurrentControlSet \Control\ServiceGroupOrder** defines the loading order.

Note On *x*86-based computers, the loading of these device drivers into memory is done using BIOS INT 13 calls in real mode (or by Ntbootdd.sys).

Kernel Phase

The boot loader phase ends when Ntldr passes control to Ntoskrnl.exe. At this point the kernel phase begins. Windows NT initializes in three stages: kernel initialization, loading and initializing device drivers, and loading and initializing services. The process is completed when the user logs on.

Kernel Initialization

The kernel is initializing when the screen turns blue, and text similar to the following appears:

```
Microsoft (R) Windows NT (TM) Version 4.0 (Build 1381)
1 System Processor (16 MB Memory)
```

This means that Ntoskrnl.exe has successfully initialized and that control has passed to it.

The kernel creates the **HKEY_LOCAL_MACHINE\HARDWARE** key by using the information that was passed from the boot loader. This key contains the hardware data that is computed at each system startup. This includes information about hardware components on the system board, and about the interrupts hooked by specific hardware devices.

The kernel creates the Clone control set by making a copy of the control set pointed to by the value of Current. The Clone control set is never modified, because it is intended to be an identical copy of the data used to configure the computer and does not reflect any changes made during the startup process.

Loading and Initializing Device Drivers

The kernel initializes the low-level device drivers that were loaded during the kernel load phase. If an error occurs, the action taken is based on the **HKEY_LOCAL_MACHINE\SYSTEM\CurrentControlSet\Services** *DriverName***ErrorControl** value for the device driver that has a problem.

Ntoskrnl.exe scans the registry, this time for device drivers that have a **HKEY_LOCAL_MACHINE\SYSTEM\CurrentControlSet\Services** *DriverName***Start** value of 0x1. As in the kernel load phase, the Group value for each device driver determines the order in which they are loaded. The registry subkey **HKEY_LOCAL_MACHINE\SYSTEM\CurrentControlSet\Control\ServiceGroupOrder** defines the loading order.

Unlike the kernel load phase, device drivers with a Start value of 0x01 are not loaded by using BIOS or firmware calls, but by using the device drivers loaded during the kernel load phase and just initialized. The device drivers in this second group are initialized as soon as they are loaded. Error processing for the initialization of this group of device drivers is also based on the value of the ErrorControl data item for the device driver.

Loading and Initializing Services

The Session Manager (Smss.exe) starts the higher-order subsystems and services for Windows NT. Information for the Session Manager is in **HKEY_LOCAL _MACHINE\SYSTEM\CurrentControlSet\Control\Session Manager**. Session Manager executes the instructions described below.

BootExecute Data Item

The BootExecute data item contains one or more commands that Session Manager runs before it loads services. The default value for this is Autochk.exe, the Windows NT version of Chkdsk.exe.

```
BootExecute : REG_MULTI_SZ : autocheck autochk*
```

Session Manager can run more than one program. This example shows the item that appears when the Convert utility will be run to convert the x volume from FAT to NTFS on the next system startup:

```
BootExecute : REG_MULTI_SZ : autocheck autochk* autoconv \DosDevices\x:
/FS:ntfs
```

After Session Manager runs the commands, the kernel loads the other registry keys from %systemroot%\System32\Config.

Memory Management Key

Next, the Session Manager creates the paging information required by the Virtual Memory Manager. The configuration information is located in these data items:

```
PagedPoolSize : REG_DWORD 0
NonPagedPoolSize : REG_DWORD 0
PagingFiles : REG_MULTI_SZ : c:\pagefile.sys 32
```

DOSDevices Key

Next, the Session Manager creates symbolic links. These links direct certain classes of commands to the correct component in the file system. The configuration information for these default items is located in the following:

```
PRN : REG_SZ : \DosDevices\LPT1
AUX : REG_SZ : \DosDevices\COM1
NUL : REG_SZ : \Device\Null
UNC : REG_SZ : \Device\Mup
PIPE : REG_SZ : \Device\NamedPipe
MAILSLOT : REG_SZ : \Device\MailSlot
```

Subsystems Key

Because of the messaging architecture of subsystems, the Windows subsystem (Microsoft Win32) must be started. This subsystem controls all I/O and access to the video screen. The process name for this subsystem is CSRSS. The Windows subsystem starts the WinLogon process, which then starts several other vital subsystems.

The configuration information for required subsystems is defined by the value for Required in the registry subkey **HKEY_LOCAL_MACHINE\SYSTEM \CurrentControlSet\Control\Session Manager\SubSystems**.

After all of the hard disk checks are successfully performed, Session Manager sets up the pagefiles defined in **HKEY_LOCAL_MACHINE\SYSTEM \CurrentControlSet\Control\Session Manager\Memory Management**.

The next step of the Session Manager is to load the **SOFTWARE** hive of the registry. Then it loads the required subsystems, as defined in **HKEY_LOCAL_ MACHINE\SYSTEM\CurrentControlSet\Control\Session Manager\ SubSystems\Required**. By default, only the Win32 subsystem is required.

Finally, Smss.exe loads and initializes all drivers with a Start value of 2 in the registry.

Logon Phase

The Windows NT boot process is not considered good until a user successfully logs on. There are three stages in the Logon phase.

Begin Logon

The Windows subsystem automatically starts Winlogon.exe, and Winlogon.exe starts the Local Security Authority subsystem (Lsass.exe). The **Begin Logon** dialog box now appears. This contains the text Press CTRL+ALT+DELETE to log on.

At this time, even though Windows NT may still be initializing network device drivers, the user can log on.

Service Controller

Next, the Service Controller (Screg.exe) executes, which makes a final pass through the registry looking for services that are marked to load automatically. Auto-load services have a Start value of 0x2 in the subkeys **HKEY_LOCAL _MACHINE\SYSTEM\CurrentControlSet\Services\DriverName**. The services that are loaded during this phase are loaded based on their dependencies, because they are loaded in parallel. The dependencies are described in the DependOnGroup and DependOnService entries in the subkey **HKEY_LOCAL _MACHINE\SYSTEM\CurrentControlSet\Services\DriverName**.

Clone Control Set

Windows NT startup is not considered good until a user successfully logs on to the system. After a successful logon attempt, the Clone control set is copied to the LastKnownGood control set.

This is beneficial if a problem was created as a result of a change in the registry, such as a manual parameter update or the addition of a faulty device driver. The user can restart the computer without logging on, and select Last Known Good during the boot sequence. This will load the previously known good control set, bypassing the invalid parameter or conflicting device driver.

Boot.ini File

During installation of Windows NT on an *x*86-based computer, Windows NT Setup puts the Boot.ini file at the root of the system partition. Ntldr uses information in the Boot.ini file to display the screen from which you select the operating system to start.

Examining Boot.ini Contents

On an *x*86-based computer, Windows NT Setup puts the Boot.ini file at the root of the system partition. Boot.ini is a read-only hidden file. Use Windows NT Explorer or My Computer to display hidden files. Below is an example of a Boot.ini file:

```
[boot loader]
timeout=30
default=multi(0)disk(0)rdisk(0)partition(1)\WINNT
[operating systems]
multi(0)disk(0)rdisk(0)partition(1)\WINNT="Windows NT Server Version 4.0"
multi(0)disk(0)rdisk(0)partition(1)\WINNT="Windows NT Server Version 4.0
[VGA mode]" /basevideo /sos
C:\="Windows 95"
```

The Boot.ini file has two sections, boot loader and operating systems.

Boot Loader Section

The boot loader section contains the information shown in the following table.

Parameter	Description
timeout	The number of seconds in which the user may select an operating system from the boot loader screen before Ntldr loads the default operating system. If the value is 0, Ntldr immediately starts the default operating system without displaying the boot loader screen. This value can be set to -1, in which case Ntldr waits for the user to make a selection. The Boot.ini file must be edited to set the value to -1, because it is an illegal value for the System program in Control Panel.
default	The path to the default operating system.

Operating Systems Section

The operating systems section contains the list of available operating systems. Each entry includes the path to the boot partition for the operating system, the string to display in the boot loader screen, and optional parameters.

The Boot.ini file supports the start of multiple versions of Windows NT operating systems, as well as starting other operating system. That operating system can be either Windows 95, MS-DOS, or OS/2.

Boot.ini Switches

Switches can be added to the end of the Windows NT [operating systems] entries in the Boot.ini file. They are not case sensitive.

/basevideo

This switch causes the system to boot using the standard Video Graphics Adapter (VGA) display driver (Vga.sys and Vga.dll) in 640-by-480 resolution. When booting with this switch, the Display program in Control Panel lists the display as "VGA compatible display adapter."

This line contains the **/basevideo** switch, so that if an incorrect display driver is selected the system can still boot using VGA resolution.

/baudrate=*nnnn*

Specifies the baud rate to be used for debugging. If the baud rate is not set, the default baud rate is 9600 if a modem is attached, and 19200 for a null-modem cable. This switch has a secondary effect of forcing the **/DEBUG** switch as well.

/crashdebug

This switch enables the Automatic Recovery and Restart capability that can also be enabled through the System program Control Panel.

/debug

The debugger is loaded when Windows NT starts, and can be activated at any time by a host debugger connected to the computer. This is the mode to use when debugging problems that are regularly reproducible.

/debugport= com*x*

Specifies the com port to use for debugging, where *x* is the selected communications port. Like **/baudrate**, this switch will also force the **/DEBUG** mode.

/nodebug

The **/nodebug** switch specifies that there is no debugging information being monitored. Debugging information is only useful for developers and can slow system performance.

/maxmem:*n*

The **/maxmem** switch specifies the maximum amount of RAM (expressed as *n*) that Windows NT will use.

Use this switch to troubleshoot memory parity errors, mismatched SIMM speeds, and other memory-related problems. To use this switch, the memory must be contiguous. Never specify a value less than 12 for Windows NT Server. This switch does not work on every hardware configuration.

Note Windows NT Server can run with 12 MB of RAM, although it will probably run slowly.

/noserialmice=[COM*x* I COM*x,y,z*]

This switch disables serial mouse detection on the specified COM port or ports. This switch is useful in cases where Windows NT detects a component, such as a modem, attached to a serial port as a mouse during the boot sequence. If this occurs, the component on the serial port will typically be unusable in Windows NT, because the mouse driver was loaded for the port to which the component is attached.

If **/noserialmice** is used without specifying a COM port, serial mouse detection is disabled on ALL serial ports. If **/noserialmice:Com*x*** is specified, serial mouse detection will be disabled on COM*x* only. In the same way, if **/noserialmice:com*x*, *y*, *z*** is specified, serial mouse detection will be disabled on COM ports *x*, *y*, and *z*.

/sos

The **/sos** switch can be added to cause the names of the drivers being loaded during the Windows NT boot to be displayed. By default, the OS Loader screen only echoes progress dots.

Verifying Loaded Drivers

If a Windows NT–based computer does not initialize all services, verify that the required files are loaded. Drivers are loaded during system initialization.

Ntldr attempts to load all drivers with a Start value of 0 during the boot sequence. During the load sequence, the Kernel attempts to initialize those drivers, and then load all drivers with a Start value of 1. The Session Manager (Smss.exe) loads all drivers with a Start value of 2 during its processing. Device drivers with a Start value of 3 are loaded as required as the drivers initialize.

The DRIVERS Resource Kit utility is a command-line utility that verifies that these drivers are successfully loaded. To determine if there are drivers missing, run **Drivers.exe** on a similar computer and compare the results.

To display a list of loaded Kernel mode drivers, run Drivers.exe from the Command Prompt. The following table describes the DRIVERS output. The ModuleName field shows the name of the loaded driver.

Column	Definition
ModuleName	The driver's file name.
Code	The non-paged code in the image.
Data	The initialized static data in the image.
Bss	The uninitialized static data in the image. This data is initialized to 0.
Paged	The size of the data that is paged.
Init	Data not needed after initialization.
LinkDate	The date that the driver was linked.

Note DRIVERS is a command-line utility. It works only on a successfully booted computer. If a computer will not boot, use the Kernel debugger to list the files.

Replacing Damaged or Missing Files

The ability to replace damaged or missing files is a skill that advanced trouble-shooters must have. The following illustrates some of the methods used to replace damaged or missing files.

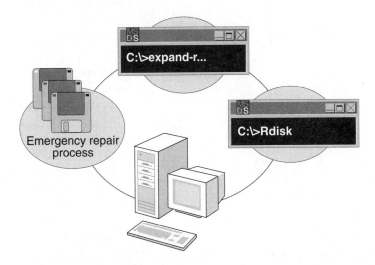

After a missing or corrupt file such as a driver has been identified, there are three ways to replace it, the emergency repair process, **expand -r**, and **rdisk**.

Both the emergency repair process and **expand -r** will install a new version of the file. The emergency repair process can also help identify corrupted or missing files. If the file in question is a registry hive, the Emergency Repair disk can be used to restore the hive.

Tip If a service is behaving unpredictably, a good troubleshooting tactic is to stop and restart the service. If the problem is a missing or corrupted file, then the startup process may recognize the problem and present a meaningful error message, showing the name of the file that is missing or corrupt.

Emergency Repair Process

To begin the Emergency Repair process, with the Windows NT Setup Disk 1 in drive A, start the computer. Insert Disk 2 when prompted. Choose "R" at the Windows NT Setup Welcome Screen. Select the desired repair options and follow the prompts. The following table describes the Emergency Repair process options for helping to isolate and replace damaged files.

Emergency Repair Option	Description
Inspect Registry Files	Prompts for replacement of each registry file. Any changes to the registry hives **SECURITY** and **SAM** are lost, and these files are restored as they were at system installation. Changes to **SOFTWARE** and **SYSTEM** are restored to the last update to the Emergency Repair information.
Inspect Startup Environment	Verifies that Windows NT is an option in the Operating System Select menu. If it is not listed in the Boot.ini file, then the emergency repair process adds a Windows NT option for the next boot attempt.
Verify Windows NT System Files	Identifies and offers to replace files that have been altered from their original state on the Windows NT compact disc. This option also verifies that boot files, such as Ntldr and Ntoskrnl.exe, are present and valid. To find out if one or more service packs must be reinstalled, check Files.lst on each service pack.
Inspect Boot Sector	Verifies that the primary boot sector still references Ntldr, and updates the boot sector if it does not. This is useful if someone uses the MS-DOS Sys.com utility on the hard disk. The Sys.com utility wipes out the Windows NT boot sector and replaces it with an MS-DOS boot sector. Inspecting and repairing the boot sector will restore it to Windows NT, and preserve the ability to dual-boot to MS-DOS.

Expand -r

If the exact file that is missing or damaged is known, use **Expand -r** to retrieve the file from the Windows NT compact disc. Uncompress the file, and store it in the directory where it belongs.

Expand -r is a Windows NT command. But how can it be used if the computer running Windows NT Server is not functioning? If the file belongs on a FAT partition, use another Windows NT-based computer to access and uncompress the file. Then use an MS-DOS boot disk to copy the file to the target directory. If the target directory is on an NTFS partition, install another copy of Windows NT in a different directory or drive, and then use EXPAND -R to replace the file.

Emergency Repair Disk Program (rdisk)

Windows NT automatically creates a REPAIR directory under *SystemRoot* (generally \Winnt). Initially, the contents of the original Emergency Repair Disk are stored in this directory.

Windows NT also includes a utility, **rdisk**, for creating or updating an Emergency Repair Disk, or to update the Emergency Repair information stored in *SystemRoot*\Repair. Use either this disk or the Repair directory during the Emergency Repair process when necessary.

Points to consider when maintaining and using the Emergency Repair Disk are:

- If the **/s** switch was not used before creation of the Emergency Repair Disk, and the Repair process is used to replace the **SAM** and **SECURITY** registry keys, all passwords in the system return to the passwords in effect at the time the **SAM** and **SECURITY** files in %systemroot%\Repair were last updated. If these keys were more recently backed up by using Windows NT Backup, Regback.exe, or Regedt32.exe, more current information can be restored.

- If the Emergency Repair Disk was not updated after Disk Administrator was used to configure volume sets, stripe sets, mirror sets, or stripe sets with parity, it might be difficult or impossible to recover data on these volumes. When any of these volumes is created, Disk Administrator updates the **DISK** subkey in the registry and sets the fault-tolerant bit on the System ID field of the Partition Table for each partition or logical drive in the volume.

- If the boot partition is converted from the FAT file system to the NTFS file system on an *x*86-based computer, be sure to update the Emergency Repair Disk. The NTFS Partition Boot Sector must be on the Emergency Repair Disk, not the FAT Partition Boot Sector.

- Make a copy of the current Emergency Repair Disk.

- Make frequent and consistent backup sets of all important files, including system files. A regular backup routine should include using **rdisk** in order to maintain an up-to-date Emergency Repair disk.

Examining the Boot Process

1. What are the four main phases of the boot process?

   _____

   _____

2. During the Initial Phase, what is the main function of the Master Boot Record?

   _____

   _____

3. Define a brief description of the boot loader phase.

   _____

   _____

4. During the boot process, when is the kernel initialized?

   _____

   _____

5. What is the significance of the **/debug** switch in the Boot.ini file?

   _____

   _____

6. When a user successfully logs in to Windows NT, what event takes place in the registry? Why is this beneficial to the user?

   _____

   _____

7. A scsi driver is suspect for causing scatter gather problems. What is one way to determine the driver date of the currently installed driver?

   _____

   _____

8. When you attempt to boot the computer, it does not respond during kernel initialization. You have attempted to use LastKnownGood, but the computer still fails to respond. What would you do to troubleshoot this problem?

   _____

   _____

9. You had to perform an emergency repair to recover your computer. Now you are unable to log on using your user account. What is the problem?

_____

_____

Lesson Summary

The following information summarizes the key points in this lesson:

- The four phases of a successful Windows NT boot are the Initial Phase, Boot Loader Phase, Kernel Phase, and Logon Phase.

- When the hard disk is the startup disk, the system BIOS reads the Master Boot Record and loads it into memory. The system BIOS then transfers execution to the Master Boot Record. Ntdetect.com collects a list of currently installed components and returns this information to Ntldr.

- On *x86*-based computers, Ntdetect.com executes after a Windows NT operating system is selected.

- The boot.ini file contains the operating system choices that Ntldr displays at startup and the associated boot partition and boot parameters information for each choice.

- The DRIVERS Resource Kit utility (drivers.exe) will display the drivers that have been successfully loaded.

- Both the Emergency Repair process (expand -r) and the Emergency Repair disk utility (rdisk) can be used to replace damaged or missing files.

Lesson 5: Examining Stop Screens

This lesson examines stop screens and some of the tools related to them. Topics include: stop screens, debugging overview, kernel debugger, CrashDump, dump analysis utilities, and Dr. Watson overview.

After this lesson, you will be able to:

- Interpret stop screens.
- Identify debug options.
- Use Kernel Debugger.
- Describe and use CrashDump.
- Describe and use Dump Analysis Utilities.
- Examine Dr. Watson error logs.

Estimated lesson time: 20 minutes

Stop Screens

When Windows NT encounters a fatal error, it displays a stop screen, or "blue screen," with debug information. If system recovery options are enabled, the system will also generate a file containing the debug information.

Even though a stop screen may look intimidating, only a small amount of data on the stop screen is important in determining the cause of the error. When attempting problem detection, analyze the following information on a stop screen:

- At the top of the screen, the error code and parameters.
- In the middle of the screen, the list of modules that have successfully loaded and initialized.
- At the bottom of the screen, the list of modules that are currently on the stack.

This information helps clarify the extent of the problem, the cause of the problem, and ultimately, how to get the system back to an operational state.

Some errors are immediately indicative of the problem, and can be resolved without the intervention of others. Other errors, however, will require Microsoft Technical Support assistance, and may require the setting up of Kernel Debugger for further analysis of the problem.

Stop Screen Sections

The following graphic shows an example stop screen. Each of the numbered areas will be described in the next five sections of the lesson.

```
                                                                    ①
                                                              DSR CTS SND
②  * Stop 0x0000000a (0x0000006c, 0x00000002, 0x00000001, 0x804029cc)
   IRQL_NOT_LESS_OR_EQUAL

   p4-300 irql:1f SYSVER:0xf000030e

   DLL Base DataStmp - Name              DLL Base  DateStmp  - Name
③  0100000 2e53fe55 - ntoskrl.exe        80400000  2e53eba6 - hal.dll
   80010000 2e41884b - Aha154x.sys       80013000  2e4bc29a - SCSIPORT.S

   8001b000 2e4e7b6b - Scsidisk.sys      80220000  2e40660f - Ntfs.sys
   fe420000 2e406607 - floppy.SYS        fe430000  2e406618 - Scsicdrm.S
   fe440000 2e406659 - Fs_Rec.SYS        fe450000  2e40660f - NULL.SYS

   fe460000 2e4065f4 - Beep.SYS          fe470000  2e406634 - Sermouse.S
   fe480000 2e42a4a4 - e8042prt.SYS      fe490000  2e40660d - Mouclass.S
   fe4a0000 2e40660c - Kbdclass.SYS      fe4c0000  2e4065e2 - VIDEOPRT.S

   fe4b0000 2e53d49d - ati.SYS           fe4d0000  2e4065e8 - vga.sys
   fe4e0000 2e406655 - Msfs.SYS          fe4f0000  2e414f30 - Npfs.SYS
   fe510000 2e53f222 - NDIS.SYS          fe500000  2e40719b - elinkii.sy

   fe550000 2e406697 - TDI.SYS           fe530000  2e47c740 - nbf.sys
   fe560000 2e5279d9 - nwlnkipx.sys      fe570000  2e53a89e - nwlnknb.sy
   fe580000 2e494973 - tcpip.sys         fe5a0000  2e5356b8 - afd.sys

   fe5b0000 2e5279d3 - netbt.sys         fe5d0000  2e4167f7 - netbios.sy
   fe5e0000 2e4066b3 - mup.sys           fe5f0000  2e4f9f51 - rdr.sys
④  630000 2e53f24a - srv.sys             fe660000  2ef16062 - nwlnkspx.s

   Address   dword dump Build [1381]                         - Nam
   FF541E4c fe5105df  fe5105df  00000001 ff640128 fe4a8228 000002fe - NDI

   ff541e60 fe501368  fe501368  00000246 00004002 00000000 00000000 - eln
   ff541eb4 fe481509  fe481509  ff6688c8 ff668288 00000000 ff668138 - i80

   ff541ee0 fe481ea8  fe481ea8  fe481078 00000000 ff541f04 8013c58a - i80
   ff541ee4 fe482078  fe482078  00000000 ff541f04 8013c58a ff6688c8 - i80
   ff541ef0 8013c58a  8013c58a  ff6688c8 ff668040 80405900 00000031 - ntc

⑤ 541efc 80405900  80405900  00000031 06060606 06060606 06060606 - hal

   Restart and set the recovery options in the system control panel

   or the /CHRASBUG system start option if this message reapprears,
   contact your system adminstrator or technical support group.
   CRASHDUMP: Initializating miniport driver
```

A Windows NT stop screen contains five major sections. Whenever a stop error occurs, examine these sections for analysis when troubleshooting the problem.

Section 1: Debug Port Status Indicators

These indicators appear if a modem or a null modem cable is connected to the computer and the debug parameter is enabled. The indicator provides serial communication information for the Kernel Debugger. This area shows DSR and CTS. Also, the text SND flashes to show that data is being sent to the COM port.

The following table lists the possible debug port status indicators.

Indicators	Description
MDM	Debugger is using modem controls
CD	Carrier detected
RI	Ring Indicator
DSR	Data Set Ready
CTS	Clear To Send
SND	Byte being sent
RCV	Byte received
FRM	Framing error
OVL	Overflow
PRT	Parity error

Section 2: BugCheck Information

This section contains the error code (or BugCheck code) after the word STOP, up to four developer-defined parameters, and an interpretation of the error. The example shows **0x0000000A** as the error code.

Note The first four lines of the stop screen contain the most critical information about the problem, and should be reported to Microsoft Technical Support.

Under some conditions, only the top line of the stop message is displayed. This can occur if vital services needed for the display have been affected by the fault.

Section 3: Driver Information

This section lists driver information in three columns. The first two columns list the preferred load address (base address in memory) and the link time stamp (date created) for each loaded driver. The third column displays the names of all drivers loaded on the computer at the time the stop message occurred. This information is important because many stop messages contain in their parameter list the address of the instruction that caused the error.

Section 4: Kernel Build Number and Stack Dump

This is the build number of the kernel, Ntoskrnl.exe. (Notice that the sample graphic in this lesson indicates Build 1381.) The presence of service packs and third-party device drivers is not indicated because this is the base build number only.

The stack dump shows the range of addresses that may pertain to the driver that failed. A true stack trace requires Kernel Debugger. Sometimes, the component or driver that caused the error appears in the top few lines of the -Name column of this section. The topmost routines on the stack do not always represent the failing code.

Section 5: Debug Port Information

This section provides confirmation of the communications parameters (COM port and baud rate) used by Kernel Debugger on the target computer, if enabled. It also confirms whether a dump file was created.

Interpreting Stop Screen Content

Understanding the basics of stop screens can assist you in troubleshooting Windows NT. The following graphic provides information on reading stop screens.

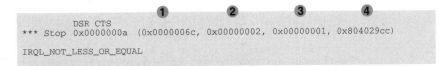

```
          DSR CTS
*** Stop 0x0000000a  (0x0000006c, 0x00000002, 0x00000001, 0x804029cc)

IRQL_NOT_LESS_OR_EQUAL
```

①Address that was referenced improperly

②IRQL that was required to access the memory

③Access permission (write=1, read=0)

④Instruction address that attempted the access

There are many different stop screens, each with accompanying stop codes. The most common stop codes are hardware errors. Other stop codes are caused by corrupted files or file systems. The stop codes are identified on the first line of the stop screen, followed by a parameter list (four hex numbers in parentheses). The stop error, parameters, and modules loaded (below the stop message) often identify the error. For example:

```
*** STOP: 0x0000000a (0x0000006c, 0x00000002, 0x00000001, 0x804029cc)
IRQL_NOT_LESS_OR_EQUAL
```

In this example:

- The first parameter (0x0000006c) identifies the address that was incorrectly referenced.

- The second parameter (0x00000002) identifies the IRQL that was required to access the memory.

- The third parameter (0x00000001) identifies the access as a Write (Read = 0).

- The fourth parameter (0x804029cc) identifies the instruction address that attempted to access the memory referenced in the first parameter.

In this case, the driver that caused the stop screen is identified at the bottom of the screen. The address in the fourth parameter will be within the address ranges of one of the drivers in the list of modules at the bottom of the screen.

Note Each stop screen will have its own unique stop code and accompanying parameters. For information on stop screens, see Microsoft TechNet.

Debugging

System debugging is a means to help search for and eliminate errors by allowing a troubleshooter to step through the program, examine data, and check conditions.

In order to efficiently debug a failed Windows NT-based computer, a trouble-shooter should be familiar with the terminology that will be used both in preparation for debugging, and during the debugging process. Effective debugging also requires a familiarity with the types of debuggers available, and with the options available for debug setup.

Debugging Terminology

To communicate effectively with others, including Microsoft Technical Support, during debugging, you will need to understand and use the following terms.

Symbol File

When code is compiled one of two versions of the executable file can be created: a debug (also known as checked) version, or a non-debug (also known as free) version. The checked version contains extra code that allows a developer to debug problems, but this means a larger and possibly slower executable file. The free version of the executable file is smaller and runs at a normal speed, but cannot be debugged.

Windows NT combines the speed and smaller size of free versions with the debugging capabilities of the checked versions. All executable files, drivers, dynamic-link libraries, and other program files in Windows NT are the free versions. However, each program file has a corresponding symbol file, which contains the debug code that is normally part of the checked file. These symbol files are on the Windows NT Server product compact disc, in the Support\Debug*platform*\Symbols directories, where platform is I386, Alpha, MIPS, or PowerPC. Within the symbols folder there is one sub-folder for each type of file (such as .exe, .dll, and .sys).

Exception

The term exception refers to an event that is unexpected or disrupts the ability of the process to proceed normally. Exceptions can be generated by both hardware and software.

Structured Exception Handling (SEH)

In Windows NT, Structured Exception Handling (SEH) is active. This means that exceptions in software can be trapped to determine if they can be manipulated, or handled so that execution can continue. Software then can be written to handle some of these exceptions without termination. For example:

```
try {
.........CODE.......risky operation
    }
except (filter) determine what error
    {
.........CODE......./ deal with error
    }
        // exception handling logic
```

Stack Trace

A stack is an area of system memory that is used for keeping track of recently acquired data. When an application programming interface (API) or function is called, the arguments to the function and the return address (current location) are pushed onto the stack. When the system halts, the stack is kept intact. The trace is a history of events that occurred in the stack.

Host Computer

The host computer is the computer on which the debugger runs. This computer should run a version of Windows NT that is at least as recent as the one on the target computer.

Target Computer

The target computer is the computer on which the kernel stop error occurs. This computer is the one that needs to be debugged. It can be a computer located within a few feet of the computer on which the debugger runs, or it can be a computer connected by a modem.

Types of Debuggers

In Windows NT, different types of code run in different processor modes. User applications and services run in user mode, and use the services of the operating system and device drivers that run in kernel mode.

Because of the different ways the debugger communicates with the debugger node and the code being debugged, a debugger is needed that knows how to debug in that mode. The following table describes the choice of debuggers for either mode.

Debugger	Mode	Description
NTSD (NT Symbolic Debugger)	User mode	A user mode Debugger that spawns a Console Window for inputting debug commands. A Debug Node is created for the application or service to allow the debugger to control the application execution. Output from the debugger can be sent to the Kernel Debugger port.
CDB	User mode	This debugger is the same as NTSD except that it does not create a separate command window.
KD	Kernel mode	This is a command line based kernel debugger with built-in modem control.
WinDBG	User and kernel mode	A windows based debugger which can be used to debug either kernel or user mode. This tool can be found on the *Windows NT System Developer's Kit*.

Debug Setup

There are three debug setup options; local debugging, remote debugging, and CrashDump.

Local Debugging

Local debugging is on-site debugging using a host computer connected to the target computer by null modem cable.

Remote Debugging

Set up a remote debug session with Microsoft Technical Support by using a Remote Access Service (RAS) server. This process is needed if a memory dump file cannot be generated or if the target computer halts with a stop screen. The connection process involves using a null modem cable to configure both the target computer and the host computer. The host is then networked to a RAS server and the debugging information is sent to Microsoft Technical Support over an asynchronous connection. The debugging information can also be analyzed at the host computer.

CrashDump

CrashDump is a computer memory dump that writes the entire contents of memory to the paging file and marks this file with a special stamp. When the computer is rebooted, Windows NT copies this part of the paging file to Memory.dmp. Set up the target computer to write the contents of its random access memory (RAM) to a memory dump file when a kernel stop error occurs. Use the dump analysis utilities to analyze the memory dump, or send the memory dump file to technical support personnel for their analysis.

Kernel Debugger

There are numerous methods of debugging a Windows NT computer. One method involves using a kernel debugger to perform "live debugging" of a Windows NT computer. Another method involves analyzing a CrashDump file that is a result of a stop screen.

Kernel Debugger displays the files loaded during the boot and load sequences. Combined with the knowledge of the drivers and services to be loaded during the Windows NT boot and load sequences, Kernel Debugger can be used to verify that Windows NT is loading as configured, and can help to identify a missing driver or service. It is recommended that you first run the debugger on the computer when it is fully functional, so that healthy startup sequences can be identified. This makes it easier to recognize any files that might be missing in a troubleshooting situation.

Kernel Debugger Requirements

The following graphic illustrates Kernel Debugger requirements.

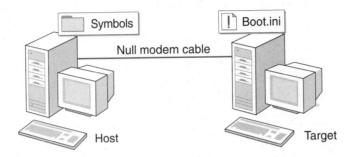

In order to properly use Kernel Debugger to view the kernel mode drivers and services loaded during a Windows NT computer initialization, the following requirements must be met:

- Two Windows NT–based computers: one running Kernel Debugger (host computer), and the other to be debugged (target computer). Both computers should be running the same version of Windows NT.

- A connectivity mechanism between the two computers. For example, they can be connected by a null modem cable or modem connection for remote dial-in.

   Note For more information on setting up a modem connection, see the *Windows NT 4.0 Server Resource Kit.*

- Symbols (code used to debug files) for the target computer must be available on the host computer. These are included on the Windows NT compact disc in the Support\Debug directory.

- Boot.ini modification on the target computer to be debugged must be set to debug mode.

Note If problems occur when attempting to establish a modem session, lower the baud rate on both computers to see if this will allow a connection. For more information on Kernel Debugger, including setup, see the *Windows NT 4.0 Server Resource Kit.*

Kernel Debugger Setup

Kernel Debugger setup involves preparing both the target and host computers. The following graphic illustrates Kernel Debugger setup.

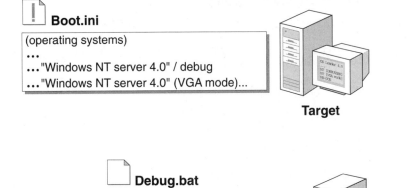

Boot.ini

(operating systems)
...
..."Windows NT server 4.0" / debug
..."Windows NT server 4.0" (VGA mode)...

Target

Debug.bat

nt_debug_port-com1
nt_debug_baud_rate=19200
nt_symbol_path=c:\debug
nt_log_file_open=c:debug.log

Host

Using Kernel Debugger requires a second Windows NT-based computer to run the Kernel Debugger software. Both computers should be running the same version of Windows NT, and must be connected either by a null modem cable for local support or by a modem connection for remote dial-in support.

Remote dial-in support can be configured two ways. In one method, the remote host dials directly into the target host, and the debug information is sent over the modems to the remote host for debugging. This method is not desirable because this connection is somewhat unreliable and difficult to establish.

The preferred method of providing dial-in support is to use RAS. To support RAS, a third computer is required. The third computer uses RAS client software to dial into a RAS server that has a null modem connection to the target computer. These two computers use the Remote.exe utility to provide remote support for Kernel Debugger.

Preparing the Target Computer

To configure the target computer, add the **/debug** switch to the appropriate Windows NT entry in the Boot.ini file, and then select that Windows NT option during the boot sequence. Adding **/debug** enables the debug code and make it available at all times. If the computer has random problems, and the debug code should not always be loaded, use the **/crashdebug** switch instead of **/debug**. This enables the debug code only after a kernel error has occurred.

Preparing the Host Computer

Configuring Kernel Debugger on the host computer requires the following steps:

- Copy the Kernel Debugger files and Windows NT symbols from the Windows NT compact disc to the host computer (the computer that will be running the Kernel Debugger software). The software is found in the \Support\Debug *platform* directory. Copying the entire directory will copy over the debugger application, I386kd.exe (for Intel–based platforms), as well as the required symbol files.

Note The symbols are compressed to run. To expand and install them, run Expndsym.cmd, located in the Support\Debug directory.

- Configure the following environment variables (either manually or in a batch file):

Environment Variable	Description
_NT_DEBUG_PORT	COM port being used for debugging on the local host.
_NT_DEBUG_BAUD_RATE	Initial baud rate for debug port: 9600 for modems, 19,200 for null modem connections.
_NT_SYMBOL_PATH	Path to symbols directory.
_NT_LOG_FILE_OPEN	List name of file to which a log of the debug session will be written. (Optional)

A common problem in configuring the Kernel Debugger occurs if the wrong symbol files are used. A symbol gives the debugger the information it needs to decode errors. To avoid possible errors and misinterpretation of data, use symbols from the same version of Windows NT in which the computer was booted. Also use the correct symbols for the target computer. If any service packs have been installed, it is important to use the symbols from the service packs as well. Always determine the version of Windows NT running on the target computer, as well as any service packs or hot fixes applied to the target computer. Copy the appropriate symbol files to the host computer to enable proper debugging of the target computer.

Note The corresponding symbol file versions of Hal.dll and Ntoskrnl.exe for the target computer are also required. Determine the Hardware Application Layer (HAL) that is being used, as well as whether or not the target computer is a single or multiprocessor computer. Use the proper HAL and kernel symbols, renamed to Hal.dbg, and Ntoskernel.dbg file.

Setting Up Kernel Debugger for Remote Access

Setting up Kernel Debugger for remote access may be necessary when you are out of resources and have exhausted your knowledge. The following graphic provides an overview of how to set up Kernel Debugger for remote access.

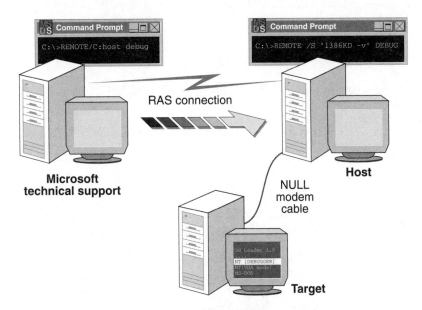

If a stop screen or stop message appears, nobody may be available locally who can help debug the problem. It may be necessary to configure Kernel Debugger to be accessed over a RAS connection. This may be the case when dealing with Microsoft Technical Support.

To support a RAS kernel debugging connection, Windows NT RAS service must be installed and started on a computer on the network. The RAS service can be installed on the host computer running Debugger (using a COM port that is different from the port Kernel Debugger is using with the target computer), or on a separate computer. If security is an issue, set up RAS on the host computer and disable access to the entire network. If RAS is not installed on the host computer, then set up RAS to allow access to the entire network. This will allow a network connection to the host computer.

Both the remote client and the host computer must be running the Remote.exe utility located on the I386\Support\Debug directory on the Windows NT Server compact disc. Run the remote utility on the host computer using the following syntax:

remote /s "i386kd -v" debug

This starts the **remote** utility as a server running I386kd.exe (the Intel version of the debugger), and creates a unique session ID of "debug."

Connect the remote client via RAS. Start **remote** using the following syntax:

remote /c *computername* **debug**

This starts the **remote** utility as a client, and connects to the session "debug" on the computer *computername*.

Note For a complete description of establishing a RAS connection, see the *Windows NT Server Resource Kit*.

Using Kernel Debugger

If you are on an Intel platform, start the debugger on the host computer by running 1386kd.exe. The following graphic illustrates the Kernel Debugger.

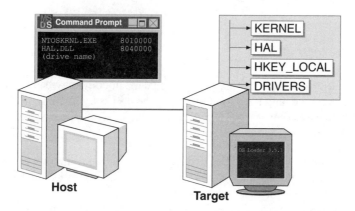

After everything has been configured appropriately, including the connection between the computers, start the debugger on the host computer by running I386kd.exe (for Intel platforms). Restart the target computer and select Windows NT with the **/debug** switch.

When the target computer boots, it will send startup sequence information through the designated COM port. Before the kernel initialization phase, the names of the files being loaded will appear in the **debug** window on the host computer.

Kernel Debugger commands can be used to examine the variables that may be the cause of the stop screen. The following table describes useful commands when using Kernel Debugger.

Command	Description
!reload	Reloads the symbol files if an incompatible symbol file was used. (Also required when the debug computer is connected to the crashed computer.)
!kb	Displays a stack trace from the last frame dumped by **!trap** (See **!trap** below.)
!errlog	The debugger sometimes keeps track of kernel errors logged by the system when a problem occurs. The **!errlog** section contains a dump of this log. In most cases, the error log is empty. If it is not empty, it can sometimes be used to determine the component or process that caused the stop screen.
!process	Lists information on the process currently running on the active processor.
!thread	Lists the thread that is currently running.
!kv	Verbose stack trace used to find the trap frame.
!trap <Trap Frame address)	Dumps the computer state when the trap frame occurred. On *x*86-based platforms, a trap frame is generated whenever there is an interrupt or a system call. This is useful to see the state of the computer when an access fault occurred.
!process 0 0	Lists all processes and their headers.

(continued)

continued

Command	Description
!drivers	Displays the list of drivers currently loaded. Allows the identification of drivers loaded.
	The following information can be determined from executing this command:
	Parameter—Meaning
	Base—The starting address of the device driver code, in hexadecimal. When the code that causes a trap falls between the base address for a driver and the base address for the next driver in the list, then that driver is frequently the cause of the fault. For instance, the base for Ncrc810.sys is 0x80654000. Any address between that and 0x8065a000 belongs to this driver.
	Code Size—The size in kilobytes of the driver code, in both hexadecimal and decimal.
	Data Size—The amount of space in kilobytes allocated to the driver for data, in both hexadecimal and decimal.
	Driver Name—The driver file name.
	Creation Time—The link date of the driver. Do not confuse this with the file date of the driver, which can be set by external utilities. The link date is set by the compiler when a driver or executable file is compiled. It should be close to the file date, but it will not always be the same date.
!vm	Lists the system's virtual memory usage.
.reboot	Restarts the remote computer.
g	Releases the remote computer.

To issue any debugger commands while in Kernel Debugger, first press CTRL+C on the host computer, and then wait for the **kd >** prompt to appear on the host.

CrashDump

CrashDump is a utility that can capture the memory contents at the time of a stop screen. The following graphic illustrates CrashDump.

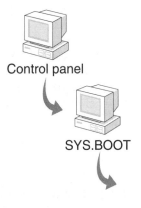

Control panel

SYS.BOOT

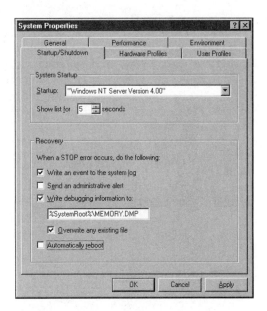

Microsoft Technical Support may not be able to resolve a problem over the phone. In such an event, establish a Kernel Debugger session using RAS. If that is not possible, it may be necessary to create a CrashDump file of the stop screen and stop code.

CrashDump is the preferred method for stop screen debugging because it ensures that a system will be brought back online as quickly as possible. This utility captures the contents of memory when a stop screen occurs and produces a file that can be analyzed to determine the cause of the problem.

After the dump file is created, the file can be referred to Microsoft Technical Support either by sending the file or by preparing a RAS connection for Microsoft Technical Support to dial in and view the file contents remotely. This file can be submitted to Microsoft using the Internet by connecting to ftp.microsoft.com and copying the file to /transfer/incoming/bussys/winnt.

If Recovery is properly configured, the following happens if a stop occurs:

- The system automatically dumps the RAM contents to the pagefile.

- The computer is automatically restarted (if designated in Control Panel).

- The pagefile contents are written to *%SystemRoot%*\Memory.dmp.

Note Writing to Memory.dmp may take time, depending on the size of Pagefile.sys on the computer. It is important to let it complete uninterrupted. The best way to verify completion is to select either "Write An Event To The System Log" or "Send An Administrative Alert" before you begin, and then wait for notification by an event in Event Viewer or by an Administrative alert message.

Dump Analysis Utilities

Three utilities are included on the Windows NT Server 4.0 compact discs for processing memory dump files: **dumpflop**, **dumpchk**, and **dumpexam**. All three utilities are on the compact discs in the Support\Debug*platform* directories, where the *platform* is I386, Alpha, MIPS, or PowerPC.

Of the three utilities, **dumpchk** and **dumpexam** are the most efficient tools available for checking the validity of the dump and dump analysis.

The primary purpose of these utilities is to create text or dump files that can be sent to technical support personnel for analysis.

The Dumpchk Utility

The following graphic illustrates the **dumpchk** utiltiy.

```
C:\debug>dumpchk -q  .u:\******\heaper\memory.dmp
Filename     .    .    .    .    .    .u:\v-red\heaper\memory.dmp
Signature.   .    .    .    .    .    .PAGE

ValidDump.   .    .    .    .    .    .DUMP
MajorVersion .    .    .    .    .    .free system
MinorVersion .    .    .    .    .    .1381
DirectoryTablebase .    .    .    .    .0x00030000
PfnDataBase      .    .    .    .    .0xffbae000

PsLoadedModuleList   .    .    .    .0x80147f30
PsActiveProcessHead  .    .    .    .0x80147e28
MachineImageType .    .    .    .    .i386
NumberProcessors .    .    .    .    .1

BugCheckCode .    .    .    .    .    .0x0000000a
BugCheckParameter1.  .    .    .    .0xe17b7b68
BugCheckParameter2.  .    .    .    .0x00000002
BugCheckParameter3.  .    .    .    .0x00000001
BugCheckParameter4.  .    .    .    .0x00000000

ExceptionCode    .    .    .    .    .0x80000003
ExceptionFlags   .    .    .    .    .0x00000001
ExceptionAddress .    .    .    .    .0x8011cef0

NumberOfRuns .    .    .    .    .    .0x3
NumberOfRuns .    .    .    .    .    .0x1f5d
Run #1
    BasePage .    .    .    .    .    .0x1
    PageCount     .    .    .    .    .0x9d
Run #2
    BasePage .    .    .    .    .    .0x100
    PageCount     .    .    .    .    .0xec0
Run #3
    BasePage .    .    .    .    .    .0x1000
    PageCount     .    .    .    .    .0x1000

* * * * * * * * * * * * *
* * * * * * * * * *--> validating the integrety of the PSloadModuleList
* * * * * * * * * * * * *
* * * * * * * * * *--> performing a quick check <^C to end>
* * * * * * * * * * * * *'
* * * * * * * * * *--> validating all physical addresses
* * * * * * * * * * * * *
* * * * * * * * * *--> validating all virtual addresses
* * * * * * * * * * * * *
* * * * * * * * * *--> This dump file is good!
```

The **Dumpchk** utility performs a validity check on a kernel mode crash dump. The utility validates the dumpfile and assures that it can be read by a debugger. It will be helpful to run **Dumpchk** before sending a dump to Microsoft Technical Support.

The **Dumpchk** utility has the following command-line syntax:

dumpchk [*options*] *CrashDumpFile*

The **Dumpchk** utility displays basic information from the memory dump file and then verifies all the virtual and physical addresses in the file. If any errors are found in the memory dump file, it reports them.

The following table illustrates the most useful **Dumpchk** information.

Category	Value
Major Version	free system
MachineImageType	i386
MinorVersion	1381
NumberProcessors	1
BugCheckCode	0x0000000a
BugCheckParameter1	0xe17b7b68
BugCheckParameter2	0xc0000005
BugCheckParameter3	0x00000000
BugCheckParameter4	0x00000000

The dumpexam Utility

The **dumpexam** utility is a command-line utility that examines a Memory.dmp file. The following graphic provides an overview of **dumpexam**.

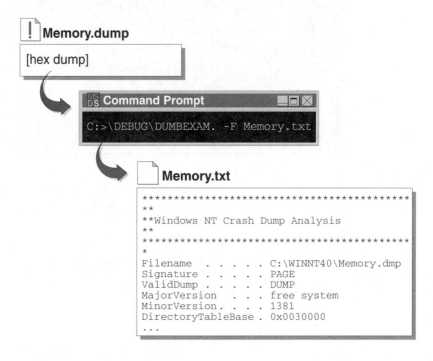

Memory.dump

[hex dump]

Command Prompt

```
C:>\DEBUG\DUMBEXAM. -F Memory.txt
```

Memory.txt

```
*********************************************
**
**Windows NT Crash Dump Analysis
**
*********************************************
*
Filename  . . . . .  C:\WINNT40\Memory.dmp
Signature . . . . .  PAGE
ValidDump . . . . .  DUMP
MajorVersion  . . .  free system
MinorVersion. . . .  1381
DirectoryTableBase .  0x0030000
...
```

After a Memory.dmp file has been generated, Microsoft Technical Support needs to analyze it. This file can be at least the size of the physical RAM in the computer. The size of the file, and the time required to identify the problem can be reduced by using the **dumpexam** utility.

Dumpexam.exe is a Windows NT 4.0 command-line utility that examines a Memory.dmp file, extracts information from the memory dump file, and creates a text file from the information. The file created, Memory.txt, is significantly smaller than Memory.dmp.

Note The dumpexam utility only examines the following bugcheck heuristics:

Stop 0x0000000A - IRQL_NOT_LESS_OR_EQUAL

Stop 0x0000001E - KMODE_EXCEPTION_NOT _HANDLED

If the bugcheck screen does not include a 0x A or 0x 1E, **dumpexam** will not correctly examine the dumpfile.

Three files are required to run **dumpexam**, and they all must be in the same folder. They are in the Support\Debug*platform* directory (where *platform* is I386, ALPHA, MIPS, or PPC) of the Windows NT Server compact disc. The first two files are:

- Dumpexam.exe
- Imagehlp.dll

The third file is dependent on the platform of the computer on which the dump file was generated. For example, Kdextx86.dll is required for an I386 computer.

Dr. Watson Overview

Although Dr. Watson is not directly related to stop screen errors, it is a useful application error debugger built into Windows NT. The following graphic illustrates the Dr. Watson utility.

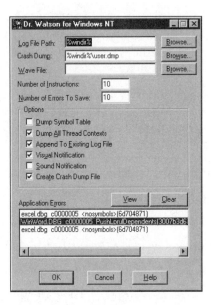

Dr. Watson for Windows NT is an application error debugger. It detects application errors, diagnoses the error, and logs the diagnostic information.

The information obtained and logged by Dr. Watson for a computer running Windows NT is the information needed by technical-support groups to diagnose the application error. The Drwtsn32.log log file is created in the form of an electronic text file. There is also an option of creating a binary crash dump file that can be loaded into the WinDBG for debugging.

If an application error occurs, Dr. Watson for Windows NT will start automatically. To start Dr. Watson when no error occurs, type **drwatson** in the **Run** dialog box.

Analyzing Debugger Results

1. A Stop 0x0000000A appears on the screen after loading a network interface card driver. What information on the screen is the most critical?

_____

_____

2. Which debugger allows you to debug user and kernel mode problems?

_____

_____

3. What are a stack and stack trace?

_____

_____

4. What is a common problem that occurs when debugging? What are the ramifications that can occur if the problem goes unnoticed?

_____

_____

5. When attempting to boot a Windows NT computer, a stop screen message ("Stop 0x0000007B -Inaccessible boot device.") is displayed. What are the first steps you would take to troubleshoot the problem?

_____

_____

6. Your computer generates a stop screen every time you load a video driver. A co-worker has mentioned preparing for a "CrashDump." What is a "CrashDump"?

_____

_____

7. You cannot resolve a stop screen message by yourself, and need to contact Microsoft Technical Support for assistance. You have only a 2400-baud modem. What should you do to prepare for Microsoft Technical Support assistance?

_____

_____

8. Your Windows NT Server–based computer boots fine, but when running an application, a general protection fault occurs. Which application debugger tool could be used to troubleshoot the problem?

_____

_____

9. What are the two user mode services that correspond to the kernel mode file system drivers?

_____

_____

10. Why don't these appear in the Kernel Debug output?

_____

_____

Lesson Summary

The following information summarizes the key points in this lesson:

- When Windows NT encounters a fatal error, it displays a stop screen, or "blue screen," with debug information.

- The first four lines of the stop screen contain the most critical information about the problem, and should be reported to Microsoft Technical Support.

- The stack dump shows the range of addresses that may pertain to the driver that failed.

- System debugging is a way to search for and eliminate errors by allowing a troubleshooter to step through the program, examine data, and check conditions.

- A stack is an area of system memory that is used for keeping track of recently acquired data.

- CrashDump is a computer memory dump that writes the entire contents of memory to the paging file and marks this file with a special stamp.

- The Kernel Debugger enables "live debugging" of a Windows NT computer.

- The Dumpchk and Dumpexam utilities validate and examine crash dump files.

A P P E N D I X

Answer Key

Exercise Answers

Page 16

Chapter 1/Lesson 1
Designing Your Network Using Directory Services

1. Would you recommend a domain model or a workgroup model? Why?

   Domain Model. This allows for simplified administration and advanced file, directory, and share security.

2. How many PDCs are needed? How many BDCs are needed?

   There is only one PDC per domain. Assuming a single domain for this size network, there would only be one PDC. Again, assuming a single domain and this size network, a single BDC would be implemented for redundancy.

3. If two departments within the company want to administer its own user accounts, which domain model would you recommend?

   Complete trust domain model.

4. How many trusts would be required for the two domain model?

   A single two-way trust between domains.

5. If an organization had four domains in a complete trust model, how many trusts would be required?

   4X(4-1)=12

Page 17

Choosing a Domain Model

1. What domain model should you implement? Why?

   Single master domain model. Centralized management with dispersed resources domains for department applications.

2. What domain model will you implement? Why?

   Complete trust model. Domain accounts are spread across domains with trust between domains allowing resource access across domains.

Page 25

Chapter 1/Lesson 2
Choosing a File System

1. Which drive would you put the system partition on? Why?

   The system partition would be put on the 500 MB hard disk drive. This would provide enough disk space on the two remaining drives to house user data.

2. Would you format the system partition as FAT or NTFS? Why?

   The system partition would be formatted as a FAT partition. This would allow access to the FAT partition from MS-DOS if a system file were to become corrupt.

3. How would you format the remaining partitions?

   The remaining partitions would be formatted in NTFS. This would provide file and directory level security as well as increased performance over FAT on these size drives.

Page 32

Chapter 1/Lesson 3
Configuring TCP/IP Parameters

1. When the originating TCP/IP host is sending packets to the receiving TCP/IP host, what TCP/IP configuration parameter does it use to determine if the receiving host is on the local subnet or the remote subnet?

   The subnet mask is used to compare the network of the sending host to the network id of the receiving host. This binary comparison determines if the receiving host is on the local subnet or a remote subnet.

2. When the originating TCP/IP host determines that the destination TCP/IP host is on a remote subnet, what TCP/IP configuration parameter does the originating host send TCP/IP packets to?

   When the sending host determines that the destination host is on a remote subnet, the packets are sent to the default gateway of the sending host. This typically is configured to be the router of that subnet.

3. Other than the TCP/IP address, what other Microsoft TCP/IP parameters are typically sent to the host leasing an address from DHCP?

   DHCP will lease an IP address and also send the subnet mask, default gateway, DNS server address, and WINS server address.

4. What service comes with Windows NT Server to resolve NetBIOS names to IP addresses?

   WINS is a NetBIOS name server used to resolve NetBIOS names to IP addresses.

5. What service comes with Windows NT Server to resolve host names to IP addresses?

   DNS is a host name server used to resolve host names to IP addresses.

6. What protocol is supported by Windows NT Server that facilitates the exchange of routing information between Windows NT Servers and routers?

   RIP facilitates the exchange of IP addresses between routers.

Page 43

Chapter 1/Lesson 4
Calculating the Size of a Directory Services Database

1. What is the size of the directory database in MB?

   SAM size 20 MB for users, 12 MB for computers.

2. Based on the hardware used, what is the largest directory database file size?

   Based on the hardware guidelines, 15 MB is the largest supported SAM.

3. How many master domains should you create?

   Using 15 MB, you will need three master domains.

Page 44

Designing a Directory Service Structure for Nobell Chem

1. How many domains will you need to use?

   One.

2. How many trusts will need to be configured?

   None.

Page 45

Designing the Directory Service Structure for Miller Textiles

1. How many domains will you need to configure?

   26 domains, (Boston[2], Atlanta, Chicago, Portland, 20 branch offices, research site).

2. How many master domains will be configured?

2 (Boston, research site).

3. How many resource domains will need to be configured?

24 (Boston [resource domain], Atlanta, Chicago, Portland, 20 branch offices).

4. How many PDCs will need to be configured?

26 PDCs (Boston[2], Atlanta, Chicago, Portland, 20 branch offices, research site).

5. How many BDCs will need to be configured?

24 BDCs (Boston, Atlanta, Chicago, Portland, 20 branch offices).

6. To which domain will the branch office sites belong?

To their own domain.

7. How many trusts will need to be configured?

26 (Boston [resource domain], Atlanta, Chicago, Portland, 20 branch offices one-way trusts, research site two-way trust).

Page 47

Designing the Directory Service Structure for Terra Firm

1. How many domains will you need to configure?

11 domains (an account domain in Singapore, 10 subsidiaries with 1 domain for each).

2. How many master domains will be configured?

1 (Singapore).

3. How many resource domains will need to be configured?

10 (10 subsidiaries with 1 resource domain for each).

4. How many PDCs will need to be configured?

11 PDCs, 1 for each domain.

5. How many BDCs will need to be configured?

27 BDCs (3 for the accounts domain in Singapore, 10 subsidiaries with 2 each [1 for the accounts domain, 1 for the resource domain]). If the PDC for the resource domain fails, the BDC will do pass-through validation for the Windows NT Workstations in that domain. Malaysia and Australia manufacturing sites (4) with 2 each (1 for the accounts domain, 1 for the resource domain). Malaysia and Australia have line of business application servers; these machines will not validate users. If the BDC for

the accounts domain fails, you do not want the pass-through authentication traffic going back to Singapore because the link is near capacity.

6. To which domain will the branch office sites belong?

   To its own domain.

7. How many trusts will need to be configured?

   10, 1 for each resource domain.

Page 54

Chapter 2/Lesson 2
Resource Requirements

1. What is the minimum amount of RAM recommended for a PDC? (Hint: it has to do the size of the SAM.)

   The recommended minimum amount of RAM for a PDC is 2.5 times the size of the SAM.

2. What resource has the greatest impact on a file and print server's system performance?

   Memory.

3. What resource has the greatest impact on an application file server's system performance?

   Memory.

Page 67

Chapter 2/Lesson 3
Browsing the Network

In this exercise you will answer questions on browsing services and the roles Windows client can play on the network.

1. What are the five browser roles a Windows client can become?

   Domain master browser, master browser, backup browser, potential browser, and non-browser.

2. Is it possible for a Windows for Workgroups client to be the master browser?

   Yes, especially on a network or subnet that does not have any Windows NT clients.

3. When a Windows NT client starts, and it's configured as the preferred master browser, what will it initiate?

   It will initiate a browser election to try and assume the role of master browser.

4. Who will win an election between a preferred master browser and a PDC?

   The PDC will always be the domain master browser, master of all bowsers in the domain.

5. How often do backup browsers communicate with the master browser?

   Every 15 minutes.

6. If a computer is turned off abruptly, and not shut down properly, how long will that computer appear in the browser list?

   51 minutes. Three 12-minute time periods for 36 min, plus the 15 minute interval between the master browser and the backup browser.

7. In a single domain environment that is spread across multiple segments, how many domain master browsers are there? How many master browsers?

   There will only be one domain master browser, the PDC, and each segment will have a master browser.

Page 86

Chapter 3/Lesson 1
Creating User Accounts

1. Can local groups belong to global groups? Why or why not?

   No. Local groups can not belong to global groups. Local groups and accounts are local to the computer and are not part of the domain directory services database; they are not available outside the local computer.

2. Can global groups belong to local groups? Why or why not?

   Yes. This is the recommended way to implement security in the enterprise. Global groups containing domain users can be members of local groups who have permissions on local resources.

3. In a multi-domain environment, what is the most efficient way to minimize the number of groups that users belong to when assigning permissions to resources?

   The number of groups users belong to can be minimized by creating global groups, and making those users members of local groups, rather than assigning domain users to local groups. As users come and go, they only need to be added and deleted from the domain group, not from numerous local groups.

4. Is the Guest account enabled by default on Windows NT Server?

   No. The Guest account is disabled by default.

5. Which group, the local group or the global group, can contain users from multiple domains?

Local groups can contain users from multiple domains.

Page 103

Chapter 3/Lesson 2
Implementing User Policies and Profiles

1. What is the difference between a local and a roaming profile?

A local profile is created and stored on the computer where the user logs on and is only applied at that computer for the user. A roaming profile is stored in a shared folder on a network server and is applied at whichever computer the user logs on from.

2. Describe the purpose of system policy.

To establish a uniform set of rules to maintain computer and user environments across a domain.

3. Who can implement system policy?

An administrator.

4. Name two major functions of System Policy Editor.

Modify default settings for the computer and user policy for the domain.

Create custom settings that apply to individual users, groups of users, or individual computers.

Specify the location from which to download system policy.

5. Name two policies that you might create to secure a computer.

Create a logon banner that is seen by anyone logging on to the computer.

Disable the display of the last user's logon name.

6. If a user logs on to a domain that has system policy, but system policy has not been defined for that user, what happens next?

Windows NT checks to see whether system policy exists for a group that the user is in, and if it does exist, the group settings are merged into HKEY_CURRENT_USER. If a group does not exist, then the default user policy settings are merged into HKEY_CURRENT_USER.

7. Your network has 500 computers running Windows 95 and 400 computers running Windows NT Workstation. The Windows 95 users are complaining that the network is slow when everyone is trying to log on in the morning. What could cause this problem, and how do you resolve it?

   A potential slowdown on the network can occur because, by default, the computers running Windows 95 always search for their policies on the PDC. If load balancing is selected, after the initial logon the Windows 95 client takes its policy from whichever logon server authenticates a user.

Page 115

Chapter 3/Lesson 4
Planning Directory Synchronization

1. What are the two types of synchronization, and how do they differ?

   Full and partial synchronization. Full synchronization takes place when a new BDC comes on line or the change control log of a BDC is being overwritten.

2. What occurs when entries are written into the change control log that over-write previous entries?

   A full synchronization takes place.

3. How does the PDC keep all the BDCs from responding simultaneously for directory updates?

   The PDC sends its change announcements out to individual groups of servers in pulses. This prevents all BDCs from responding simultaneously.

4. How does the ReplicationGovernor keep BDCs from consuming WAN bandwidth?

   The ReplicationGovernor defines the amount and frequency of synchronization data that is transmitted between domain controllers.

5. What impact does changing the ReplicationGovernor have on the change log?

   Changing the ReplicationGovernor can change the amount of time necessary to replicate changes between domain controllers, as well as the number of changes in the change log. It is important to make sure you have enough space in the change log so that the change log does not wrap or begin to overwrite entries that the BDC has not had time to receive.

6. How can replication rates be scheduled for different times of the day?

   The *Microsoft Windows NT Resource Kit* has two command line applications for making registry changes. Regini.exe or Regchg.exe can be used in scheduled batch files to change synchronization times.

Page 131	**Chapter 3/Lesson 5** **Examining Resource Management Scenarios**

Page 132

Scenario 1

1. Did the scenario work?

   No.

2. If the scenario failed, why did it fail?

   Global 2 is a global group in Domain 2, the accounts are in Domain 1. Only accounts in Domain 2 can be members of the Global 2 group.

3. What could the administrator do to make this work?

   The preferred solution would be to assign all accounts to a global group in their domain and assign the global group to a local group in the resource domain. In this case, Andrew, Michelle, and Martin should be assigned to Global 1, Global 1 should be assigned to Local 2, and Local 2 should be granted permissions to the resource.

Page 132

Scenario 2

1. Did the scenario work?

   No.

2. If the scenario failed, why did it fail?

   Global groups cannot be members of other global groups. Global 1 is a global group, and therefore, it cannot be a member of Global 2 global group.

3. What could the administrator do to make this work?

   Andrew, Michelle, and Martin should be assigned to Global 1, and Global 1 should be assigned to Local 2. Local 2 would be given permissions to user the laser printer.

Page 133

Scenario 3

1. Did the scenario work?

   No.

2. If the scenario failed, why did it fail?

   Local groups cannot cross trusts. Local 1 is a local group. It cannot cross the trust between the two domains. The accounts in Domain 1 would not be able to access resources in Domain 2 as long as they were members of a local group in Domain 1.

3. What could the administrator do to make this work?

Andrew, Michelle, and Martin should be assigned to Global 1, and Global 1 should be assigned to Local 2. Global 1 can cross the trust that joins Domain 1 with Domain2. Local 2 would be given permissions to use the laser printer.

Page 134

Scenario 4

1. Did the scenario work?

Yes.

2. If the scenario failed, why did it fail?

Not applicable.

3. What could the administrator do to make this work?

Not applicable.

Page 141

Designing NT Networks

Page 141

Scenario 1

1. How many domains will you need to use?

1.

2. How many trusts will need to be configured?

0.

Page 141

Scenario 2

1. How many trusted domains will you need to configure?

1. (Answers will vary based on design chosen.) This domain will be the accounts domain that will contain all of the user accounts. This solution meets the requirements that users from branch offices will access resources from all four primary sites.

2. How many resource domains will need to be configured?

1. (Answers will vary based on design chosen.) This domain will be the resource domain. Although the sites are working independently now, consolidating the resources into one domain will simplify administration.

3. How many trusts will need to be configured?

1. (Answers will vary based on design chosen.)

Page 142

Scenario 3

1. How many trusted domains will you use?

3. (Answers will vary based on design chosen.) This is for establishing a multiple master domain model containing all the primary sites. This model is chosen because each site will manage their own accounts and resources and also share their resources with the other sites.

2. How many trusting domains will need to be configured?

3. (Answers will vary based on design chosen.) Each of the primary sites will also be set up as trusting domain in the multiple master domain model. Subsites will be members of the regional site domains.

3. How many trusts will need to be configured?

6. (Answers will vary based on design chosen.)

Page 149

Chapter 3/Lesson 6
Managing Files Shares and Permissions

1. Are share permissions as important on an NTFS share as on a FAT share? Why or why not?

Share permissions on a FAT partition are more critical than NTFS because you can assign specific access rights on the share that you can't assign to directories on FAT partitions.

2. You can only compress entire directories at a time; you cannot compress individual files.

True _____

False _____

False. You can compress one file or all files in a directory.

3. When you move a file from one NTFS partition to another NTFS partition, the file inherits the file compression state of the destination directory.

True _____

False _____

True.

4. When you move a file into a directory within an NTFS volume, the file retains its compression state, regardless of the compression settings of the destination directory.

True _____

False _____

True.

5. If a user has Read (RX) permissions and No Access (none) permissions on a file in an NTFS directory, the user will be able to read the file.

True _____

False _____

False.

6. Do file permissions always override directory permissions?

True _____

False _____

Yes. File permission always override directory permissions.

7. Which user can always take ownership of a file regardless of permissions on that file?

Administrator.

Page 162   ## Sharing Printers and Network Resources

1. When sharing a printer on the network, computers can connect to the printer using the share name. Windows NT computers can also connect to the printer by using what name?

The printer name.

2. If you are going to share printers with MS-DOS computers, how many characters can the share name have?

No more than eight characters, optionally followed by a period and one to three characters (with no spaces).

3. When connecting to a network share, what is another method for connecting to the share other than through Network Neighborhood?

You can Map the drive with the *Map Network Drive* command.

4. If you are logged on to Windows NT as user1, is it possible to connect to a share as user2?

Yes ___

No ___

Yes. Use the Connect As option of the Map Network Drive.

Page 165

Chapter 3/Lesson 7
Planning Remote Administration

1. Where are the Remote Administration server tools located?

On the Windows NT Server CD in the Error! Bookmark not defined. folder.

2. What protocol is required to run the Remote Administration server tools?

Remote Procedure Call (RPC). RPC is supported over all the protocols shipped with Windows NT Server.

Page 177

Chapter 4/Lesson 1
Configuring Routable Protocols

1. List two disadvantages of using static TCP/IP addresses and two advantages of using DHCP assigned addresses.

Disadvantages of using static TCP/IP addresses:

- Possibility of misconfiguring address at host.

- Administrative overhead associated with managing static IP addresses and moving hosts around network.

Advantages of using DHCP assigned addresses:

- Minimal user configuration.

- Reduced configuration errors.

- Limited administrative overhead.

- No need to reconfigure DHCP clients that change subnets.

2. From the DHCP Client, how can an administrator find out what IP address the DHCP Client has leased?

From the DHCP client, go to a command prompt, and then use the utility "IPCONFIG" to determine IP address, subnet mask, and default gateway.

At a DHCP Server, how can an administrator find out what IP address a DHCP Client has leased?

At the DHCP Server, use DHCP Manager, select Scope, and then select Active Leases. Finally, select Sort by Name, and then click Properties of the client in question.

3. What does a DHCP Scope consist of? (that is, the four main parameters that must be configured.)

- A range, or pool, of IP addresses that can be leased by DHCP Clients. Each DHCP Server should have a unique range of IP addresses that it can lease to DHCP Clients.

- A valid Subnet Mask for the range of IP addresses.

- Any IP addresses in the range that need to be excluded so they will not be leased to DHCP Clients, such as the IP addresses of the DHCP Servers.

- The duration of the IP address lease, which defaults to three days. The maximum lease duration that can be set to either 'Unlimited' or up to 999 days, 23 hours, and 59 minutes.

- (Optional) A name (maximum of 128 characters) and comment for the DHCP Scope can also be supplied.

4. When an administrator has configured some additional DHCP Options, what is the order of precedence for the various option types (Global, Scope, and Client)?

In order of highest to lowest precedence: Client, Scope, Global.

5. What are the four messages sent between a DHCP Client and a DHCP Server when the DHCP Client is leasing an IP address? What are the four corresponding states that the DHCP Client will be in during this process?

- IP lease request.

- IP lease offers.

- IP lease selection.

- IP lease acknowledgment.

6. Will all routers that can function as an RFC 1542 (BOOTP) relay agent work properly with DHCP?

DHCP clients use the BOOTP protocol to broadcast their lease requests across the network. If the routers on the network are configured to pass BOOTP packets, then DHCP clients can lease addresses from DHCP server across the BOOTP enabled routers.

Page 191

Chapter 4/Lesson 2
Implementing WINS

1. How is WINS used with TCP/IP?

WINS is necessary for use with TCP/IP, resolving NetBIOS names to IP addresses.

2. How does the WINS server learn of the WINS clients' NetBIOS names and IP addresses?

When the WINS client starts, it registers its NetBIOS name and IP address with the WINS server.

3. What are the two major benefits of using WINS on a network?

To reduce NetBIOS name resolution broadcasts and to allow Windows hosts to resolve NetBIOS names across routers.

4. What are some of the drawbacks of using broadcasts to resolve NetBIOS names?

Broadcasts cause additional network traffic and do not typically cross routers.

5. What are some of the drawbacks of using LMHOSTS files to resolve NetBIOS names?

LMHOSTS files are static files that have to be manually changed when a NetBIOS name or IP address changes.

6. What tool is used to view the WINS database?

The WINS Server Manager.

7. What are the two relationships that can be configured between WINS servers for replication?

A Push relationship where changes to the WINS database are replicated based on the number of replications, and a Pull relationship that can be configured based on a replication schedule.

Page 219

Chapter 4/Lesson 6
Integrating with NetWare

1. True or False. With NWLink installed, you can map a dirve to an NetWare file share.

   False. NWLink is the protocol only.

2. True or False. Two Windows NT servers with only NTLink installed as a protocol can share each other's resources.

   True. With NetBIOS over NWLink, full Microsoft network functionality is achieved.

3. True or False. GSNW is designed to provide several Microsoft Networking clients high-performance access to a NetWare server's file and print services.

   False. GSNW is designed to provide Windows clients occasional access to a NetWare network.

4. True or False. GSNW comes with Windows NT Server.

   True.

5. What special feature of NetWare 4.x needs to be configured for DSMN to access a NetWare 4.x directory?

   The NetWare 4.x directory needs to be running Bindery emulation mode.

Page 231

Chapter 4/Lesson 7
Configuring RAS

1. Other than an analog modem, what other communication mediums does RAS support?

   X.25 and ISDN.

2. Of the two Remote Access Protocols supported by Windows NT, PPP and SLIP, which is the easiest to use?

   PPP.

3. Of the two Remote Access Protocols, PPP and SLIP, which supports all the protocols shipped with Windows NT Server?

   PPP.

4. Is it possible to combine the bandwidth provided by multiple modems into a single connection? If so, how?

   Yes. This can be accomplished through PPP Multilink Protocol. Both the client and the server need at least two modems and phone lines, and PPP MP configured correctly.

5. Is it possible to provide an encryption session over the Internet? If so, how?

   With PPTP, or Point-to-Point Tunneling Protocol, an encrypted session between the RAS client and the RAS server can be established.

6. Once RAS is installed and configured on the RAS server, do all Windows NT Domain users have dial-in access by default?

   No. They have to be granted dial-in access through User Manager for Domains.

7. What additional security can you require remote users to adhere to?

   With Callback Security the RAS server will hang up when a call from a user is received, then the server will initiate a call back to that user's pre-defined or provided phone number.

8. How can PPTP filtering be used to increase network security?

   With PPTP Filtering, the RAS server will not allow any packets other than PPTP packets to come from the Internet.

Page 255

Chapter 5/Lesson 1
Implementing Server Analysis and Optimization Basics

1. You have just installed a Windows NT Server-based computer, and need to determine its expected usage in different user environments. How can server analysis and optimization assist with this task?

   Server analysis and optimization provides many benefits, including help in determining the number of users a specific server configuration should support, help in determining the expected response time for a particular user request on the server, help in determining when a resource has reached its maximum capacity for performance, help in determining when it is necessary to either add an additional resource to a system or add another system, and a way of providing management with information that can be used for budgeting purposes.

2. You decide that server analysis and optimization will help with your efforts to analyze a computer running Windows NT Server. What steps are you going to perform to accomplish your analysis?

    Server analysis and optimization generally includes the following steps:

    1. Creating a measurement baseline.

    2. Establishing a database of measurement information.

    3. Determining workload characterization.

    4. Setting expectations of system usage and availability.

    5. Forecasting future resource allocation.

    6. Establishing and implementing a plan for long-term record keeping and long-term trend analysis.

3. What are the four major server resources you should analyze?

    Memory, processor, disk subsystem, and network subsystem.

4. In your efforts to analyze the computer running Windows NT Server, what Windows NT tools can you use to assist with server analysis and optimization?

    Performance Monitor, Network Monitor, Server Manager, Response Probe, and Windows NT Diagnostics.

5. In your efforts to analyze the computer running Windows NT Server, what techniques can you use when you perform server analysis and optimization?

    Monitoring multiple servers, archiving and storing performance data, trend analysis, and monitoring desktop computers.

6. What are the three server environments that you can analyze?

    File and print server environment, application server environment, and the domain server environment.

Page 260

Working with the Data

1. Refer to the **Average field** on your chart. What is the average **%Processor Time**?

    Answers will vary.

4. What is the **Average %Processor Time** for this part of the graph?

Answers will vary.

5. How accurate do you think this representation of the processor's use is?

This value may be accurate for this time-slice, but it may present a very biased viewpoint of your processor's total activity.

You also may get a decrease in accuracy because the system is not collecting as many sample points to compute the processor average.

Page 268

Chapter 5/Lesson 2
Implementing a Measurement Baseline

1. Why is it important to collect system data?

To determine if a resource is being overused, under used, or at maximum capacity and performance, you need to know what is normal for your environment. By collecting and saving data from normal access periods, you can determine if the demands on a resource in the future are at expected (normal) levels, below normal expectations, or far above the normal level.

2. You want to perform server analysis and optimization on a pilot computer running Windows NT Server, and need to create a baseline using Windows NT tools. How would you accomplish this?

The first step would be to ensure the pilot system is not on the corporate network, so you can determine real limits that are not influenced by any corporate network traffic. Then, you would use Performance Monitor to create a log of activity during periods when activity on the system can be simulated to reflect what would be normal for a production server.

3. You want to ensure that when you create the baseline, you include all the data necessary to perform a proper server analysis, but you don't want to capture too much data. What are the common objects for Performance Monitor that should be included in a baseline?

The Performance Monitor objects that are relevant in any environment using Windows NT Server are the following: Memory, Processor, System, Server Work Queues, Physicaldisk, Logicaldisk, Network Segment, Server, and Network Interface.

4. You have collected baseline data, and found it to be too much data to store. You realize the necessity of keeping data for analysis, but can't afford the hard disk space that the baseline data requires. How can you keep the data available on the server, but reduce the required disk space requirements?

If the data needs to be kept, but the size of data reduced, relog the data into a new Performance Monitor log, and either cut out some of the objects collected, or increase the Periodic Update Time Interval value. If this value is increased from 5 seconds to 15 seconds, the new log file is one-third the original size.

5. When analyzing the baseline data, you notice that all your disk counters are 0. Does that mean that the disk drive is not being used at all?

It probably means that the disk performance counters were not enabled. To enable the counters, start a command prompt, carry out the diskperf -y command, and then restart the computer. If monitoring RAID disks, start diskperf with the -ye option.

6. During the following week you want to capture data to create your database of measurement information. However, you will be out of the office during this time. No one else in the office is trained to do this task. How can you have the data collected and stored while you are gone?

You can automate the collection of data using the Windows NT Resource Kit Performance Monitor service and the AT command. You would first create a Performance Monitor Workspace with all the objects that you want collected, and then enable the Performance Monitor service. Use the at command to schedule the starting and stopping of the service at appropriate times.

Page 291

Chapter 5/Lesson 3
Analyzing Performance Bottlenecks

1. You are analyzing the baseline data collected, and notice that the Physical-Disk: % Disk Time value is over 90 percent. What should you do to determine why this occurs?

The first thing to do is to determine whether it is due to reading or writing. This is done by viewing % Disk Read Time and % Disk Write Time. Then, you may want to determine which partition is causing the excess reads or writes by viewing LogicalDisk: % Disk Time for each instance. Next, determine if the disk activity is the result of paging, by viewing Memory: Pages/sec. It could be that lack of memory has caused excess paging to occur, which may result in a disk that is fully utilized.

2. If you are not sure if an application is multithreaded, how can you use Performance Monitor to determine this?

   Select the Thread object, and in the Instance box, find the process for the application. If there are multiple instances listed with the same process name, the application or service is multithreaded, and adding an additional processor should increase performance.

3. You are running TCP/IP as your network protocol, and you want to analyze network use. You attempt to gather as much data as you can on TCP/IP and its use of the network, but you do not find many counters available. You also want to find out how busy the network is, but you cannot seem to find a counter that will accomplish this. What can you do?

   There are a couple of options. One would be to use a network traffic analyzer, such as the Network Monitor, to view the traffic including all TCP/IP traffic. Alternately, you could install the Network Monitor agent that is part of Windows NT to get the percentage of network utilization, and install the Windows NT SNMP Service to get the objects and counters for TCP/IP. This will provide all the counters necessary to analyze TCP/IP and its effect and characteristics on the network.

4. You have identified and resolved all system bottlenecks, and you now want to generate new data for analysis. Should this collection be done on a pilot or a production system?

   You should perform initial server analysis and optimization on a pilot system that is not on the production network. This will allow you to determine ceiling thresholds and capacity for each resource in an artificial environment. Once that is complete, move on to testing the server on the production network, with users performing normal requests of the server. You can then compare the two tests to determine what effect the product environment has on capacity and performance.

5. You need to determine how many users can log on simultaneously to a domain controller and what effect that has on the system. How would you go about arriving at a conclusion?

   You can use the Server: Logon/sec and Logon Total counters to monitor the actual number of users logging on. You should use all the appropriate objects and counters to monitor each of the four major server analysis and optimization resources to determine what effect a user logon and validation has on memory, processor, disk, and network. You can also use Network Monitor to capture the logon procedure. With all this data, you can determine how many users you can simultaneously log on to a single domain controller.

6. Your company's management team wants to know what the results of the server analysis and optimization has been on the pilot computer running Windows NT Server. You decided to generate a report for them. What should you include?

   The report should include the baseline numbers for each resource, the usage trends over the period of time that the report covers, any areas of concern or potential bottlenecks, and any recommendations for improvement of responsiveness, such as additional RAM, more hard disk space, and so on. Graphing the baseline and trend analysis data is very beneficial for a visual analysis of the data.

Page 300

Chapter 5/Lesson 4
Analyzing File and Print Performance

1. What is your main focus when analyzing a file and print server?

   Focus on the number of users accessing the server concurrently and the amount of resource requirements that they are demanding.

2. You are analyzing the memory on your computer running Windows NT Server that is running as a file and print server, and you notice that the amount of available RAM is much too low (only about 10 MB), as your computer has 32 MB of RAM. What could be the cause of this?

   The first thing to verify is what services are running. Each service (and application) will use RAM. If only default, or required, services are running, check the amount of memory that is currently allocated to cache. This is done by viewing Memory: Cache Bytes. If you take the Available Bytes, and add the Cache Bytes, you should come within 12 or so megabytes of your physical RAM. The Windows NT disk cache manager uses available RAM for disk caching to improve performance.

3. What is the best way to optimize IIS for maximum performance?

   Have IIS fulfill requests from the cache.

4. You have analyzed your file and print server, and have determined that the disk subsystem is hitting its performance capacity. What can you do to improve performance without distributing users to another system?

   You can improve the disk controller to a higher performance controller, such as a bus mastering controller, or even implement RAID 0 Striping without Parity, which will improve performance by spreading the requests over multiple hard disks simultaneously.

Page 308

Chapter 5/Lesson 5
Analyzing Application Server Performance

1. How many users can an application server support?

   It depends on many factors, including the server's hardware configuration, the type of applications the server is running, and what server resources these applications require.

2. You are analyzing the processor on your computer running Windows NT Server that is running as an application server, and you notice that the processor is very busy (over 90 percent of the time). What may be the cause of this?

   The first thing to check is whether the processor is busy performing user or system tasks. You can do this by viewing the % Privileged Time and % User Time counters. Use the Process object and select % Processor Time for each object to determine which process is consuming the processor. Once you have determined which process is using the CPU, you may determine to move that process, or another application, to another server. If that is not an option, then if the application is multithreaded, you can add an additional processor in the system. If that is not an option, then upgrade the processor.

3. Your analysis of the application server determined that you needed to add additional RAM to your server (now at 32 MB). The system is not responding as well to requests as it did before the memory upgrade. What may be the problem?

   The problem may occur because the server has a level 2 secondary cache that is too small. It is generally recommended to have 256 KB of secondary cache for a computer with 32 MB of RAM.

Page 316

Chapter 5/Lesson 6
Analyzing Domain Server Performance

1. In a domain server environment, what activities will affect system resources without user intervention?

   Domain account synchronization, WINS database replication, IP address leases and a renewal by means of DHCP, browser updates, and SMS verification and updates on logon servers.

2. Why should you monitor during the domain account synchronization process?

   To determine the effect this has on memory, processor, disk, and network resources.

3. Why would you want to monitor the effect on the network and server when a single client attempts to log on and be validated?

You can use this to easily project the effect on the server or servers, should all users attempt to log on at the same time.

Procedure Answers

Chapter 6/Lesson 2

Page 350   ➤ **To analyze DHCP Discover traffic**

2. In the Detail pane, click the plus sign (+) next to **Frame** to expand the Frame properties. How many bytes are in the frame?

342 bytes, as designated by Total frame length.

4. What is the Destination address?

FFFFFFFFFFFF.

5. Why is this address used?

It is an Ethernet broadcast, because the client does not know the address of the DHCP server. All hosts on the network will process this message.

7. What is the Source Address?

0.0.0.0

8. Why is this address used?

The client does not currently have an IP address, so it uses 0's.

9. What is the Destination Address?

255.255.255.255

10. Why is this address used?

It is a network broadcast, and allows routers that support DHCP forwarding to forward the request to other subnets.

12. What is the **Destination Port** name and number?

The name is BOOTP Server, and the port number is 67.

Page 351

➤ **To analyze DHCP Offer traffic**

2. How large is this frame?

   342 bytes, the same size as the Discover message.

3. Did the server respond directly to the client?

   No, it broadcast a response (all F's).

4. What IP address did the server reply to?

   255.255.255.255

5. Why is this address used?

   The client does not have an address yet, so broadcast traffic is used to reach the client.

6. What IP address is the server offering to the client?

   131.107.2.217

Page 352

➤ **To analyze DHCP Request traffic**

In this procedure, you analyze frame 3, which is the DHCP Request message.

1. Frame 3 is the client's request of the offered IP address. Is the destination for this reply to the specific server?

   No, it is a broadcast request.

2. Why was this method used, when the client knows the server's address?

   By broadcasting the response, the client is telling other DHCP servers that may have offered an address to the client that is has accepted an offer from a different DHCP server.

3. How does a DHCP server know that the client is accepting its offer if the Request message is broadcast to all DHCP servers?

   The Server Identifier in the DHCP Option data lists the IP address of the selected DHCP server.

4. What IP address was accepted by the client?

   131.107.2.217

Page 353

➤ To analyze DHCP ACK traffic

In this procedure, you analyze frame 4, which is the DHCP ACK message.

1. Frame 4 is the DHCP server's acknowledgment of the IP address lease. How many hosts received this reply?

   All hosts, as it is a broadcast response.

2. How long is the lease that was accepted?

   The lease is valid for 7 days.

3. When will be the next time DHCP traffic is generated by this client?

   The renewal time for this address lease is 3 1/2 days. If the client restarts before then, it will renew its address at initialization time. The user can force an address renewal manually with IPCONFIG /RENEW.

4. How long did it take to acquire the IP address?

   Only 185 milliseconds. The Discover message was sent at 9.859 seconds (frame 1), while the ACK was sent at 10.044 (frame 4).

Page 354

Analyzing DHCP Address Renewal Traffic

Page 354

➤ To analyze DHCP address renewal traffic

2. Frame 1 is the client's request to renew its IP address. How many hosts received this request?

   Technically, all hosts received it, but only the DHCP server processed it. All others discarded the frame as they did not have a UDP Port 67 (Bootp Server).

3. What IP address was requested by the client?

   131.107.2.214

4. Frame 2 is the server's response to the renewal request. When will be the next time DHCP traffic is generated by this client?

   The renewal time for this address lease is 3½ days. If the client restarts before then, it will renew at initialization time. The user can force an address renewal manually with IPCONFIG /RENEW.

5. How long did it take to renew the IP address?

   101 milliseconds. Frame 1 was sent at 12.609 and frame 2 was sent at 12.710.

6. How much total traffic was generated by the renewal?

684 bytes of data, and two frames.

Page 362   ## Analyzing WINS Name Registration Traffic

Page 362   ➤ **To analyze WINS name registration traffic**

2. What is the first name to be registered by the client?

WIN95 <03>

3. What service is the name registered for?

It is registered for the Messenger service to receive messages sent to the computer name.

4. Was the name successfully registered?

Yes. The NBT header of frame 9 indicates "Success."

5. How much traffic was generated by registering this name?

214 bytes. Frame 8 (the registration request) was 110 bytes, and frame 9 (the registration response) was 104 bytes.

6. Was the registration process directed or broadcast?

Directed.

7. How many names were attempted to be registered by the Microsoft Windows 95 client?

Six: messenger for computer, workstation name, member of the domain, server name, as a potential browser, and messenger for user.

8. How much name registration traffic was generated by the Windows 95 client?

1284 bytes. Six names at 214 bytes per name.

9. When will the next WINS name registration traffic occur on this client?

The TTL is 518,400 seconds (6 days). Microsoft clients renew at one-half TTL, so the answer is 3 days.

Page 363   ➤ **To analyze name registration conflict traffic**

2. In frame 77, the client attempts to register User1 <03>. What kind of response was returned?

A WACK (Wait Acknowledgment) in frame 78.

3. What did the WINS server do next?

   It queried the registered owner of the name in question to see if the name was still active.

4. Was the name still active at the other computer?

   Yes, the query for User1 <03> was responded to successfully by Win95.

5. What response did the WINS server then return to the requesting client (NTW1)?

   Name Active Error in frame 83.

Page 364   ## Analyzing WINS Name Resolution Traffic

Page 364   ➤ **To analyze name resolution traffic**

2. Frame 10 is the first name query request. Was this request broadcast or directed?

   Directed, as determined by the specific Destination Hardware and IP addresses.

3. How large was the request?

   92 bytes, as determined by the Frame length.

4. What name is being queried for in frame 10?

   DOMAIN0 <1C> in an attempt to find a domain controller for logon validation.

5. How many domain controllers were registered in DOMAIN0?

   Two, 131.107.2.200 and 131.107.2.216

6. How long did it take to resolve the query to DOMAIN0 <1C>?

   3 milliseconds. The request was sent as 18.022 (frame 10), and the response was returned at 18.025 (frame 11).

7. How much total traffic was generated by the resolution request?

   Two frames and 208 bytes of data.

8. What name is being queried for in frame 24?

   The client requesting resolution for INSTRUCTOR.

9. How long did it take for the WINS server to respond to the request?

   3 milliseconds. Frame 24 was sent at 18.059 and the response in frame 25 was sent at 18.062.

10. How much traffic was generated by this resolving this name?

Two frames and 196 bytes of traffic.

Page 371   ## Analyzing net use File Session Traffic

Page 371   ➤ **To analyze file session connection traffic**

2. What is occurring in frames 1 and 2?

Address resolution of the WINS server.

3. How much traffic is generated to resolve the Internet Protocol (IP) address into a hardware address?

Two frames and 120 bytes.

4. How long did it take to resolve the IP address into a hardware address?

Less than 1 millisecond.

5. Were the frames directed or broadcast?

Frame one was broadcast, while frame two was directed.

6. What is occurring in frames 3 and 4?

WINS Name resolution of INSTRUCTOR.

7. What is occurring in frames 5 and 6?

Address resolution of the target server INSTRUCTOR.

8. How much traffic was generated to establish the TCP session in frames 7 through 9?

Three frames and 180 bytes.

9. Frames 10 and 11 perform NetBIOS session establishment. Was Instructor able to accept another NetBIOS session?

Yes, the NBT Packet Type indicates a Positive Session Response.

10. How much traffic was generated during NetBIOS session establishment?

Two frames and 186 bytes.

11. Frames 12 and 13 are negotiating server message block (SMB) protocols. How many SMB dialects did the client computer understand in frame 12?

Six: PC NETWORK PROGRAM 1.0, MICROSOFT NETWORKS 3.0, DOS LM 1.2X002, DOS LANMAN2.1, Windows for Workgroups 3.1a, and NT LM 0.12.

12. What SMB dialect was negotiated between the client and the server?

 # 5 (the sixth protocol, as numbering starts with 0) NT LM 0.12.

13. Frames 14 and 15 were a result of a network connection. What user was making the connection request?

User1.

14. What network resource did the client request a connection to?

\\INSTRUCTOR\PUBLIC

Hint: check SMB: Command File Name in frame 14.

15. What Tree ID was assigned to the connection?

14339 (0x3803 hex)

16. How long did it take from the start of the TCP session to successful completion of the connection request?

36 milliseconds. The TCP session request was at 16.688 seconds (frame 7), and the session setup response was sent at 16.724 (frame 15).

Page 373   ➤ **To analyze file session transfer traffic**

To analyze the network traffic generated by the transfer of a file over the network.

1. In frame 17, what SMB command is being carried out?

Query file system information to determine the file system on the remote drive.

2. With what file system was the remote drive formatted?

FAT.

3. What file is being transferred?

README.TXT

4. How large was the file?

389 bytes.

5. In what frame was the file transferred?

28.

6. How large was the frame that transferred the file?

Frame 28 was 447 bytes in size (the file itself was 389 bytes).

7. What are the first 40 characters of the file?

Contents of \\Instructor\Public include:

8. From the time the first request regarding the file was issued, how long did it take to copy the file?

The initial query on the file was made in frame 17 (at 27.940), and the transfer was acknowledged in frame 33 (at 28.295). That took 355 milliseconds. The actual transfer was completed in frames 27 and 28, the read request and response. These two frames took 25 milliseconds to process.

Page 374

➤ **To analyze file session disconnection traffic**

To analyze the network traffic generated by a network disconnection.

1. In frame 36, what network resource is being disconnected?

\\Instructor\Public. It is found by identifying the Tree ID in the SMB header of the Tree disconnect command. This Tree ID is the same as assigned during the Session Setup response in frame 15.

2. How long did it take to disconnect the network resource and close the TCP session?

8 milliseconds. The tree disconnect request was at 35.040 seconds (frame 36), and the TCP session termination was final at 35.048 (frame 40).

3. How much traffic was generated to disconnect the session?

Five frames and 366 bytes.

Page 375

Analyzing Browsing File Session Traffic

Page 375

➤ **To analyze file session connection traffic**

2. Frames 1 through 23 retrieve the browse list from the backup browser BACKUP. How many servers are in the browse list?

Five: BACKUP, DHCP_WINS, INSTRUCTOR, NTW1, and WIN95.

3. How large was the frame that provided the browse list? How much of the total frame was devoted to the SMB data?

The entire frame was 274 bytes; 160 bytes were used by the SMB data, which included the browse list.

4. Frames 24 through 44 retrieve the list of shared resources on the computer Instructor. How many shared resources were returned in the frame?

Eight: NETLOGON, ADMIN$, IPC$, C$, D$, E$, F$, and PUBLIC.

5. How large was the frame that provided the browse list of shared resources? How much of the total frame was devoted to the SMB data?

The entire frame was 383 bytes and 269 bytes were used by the SMB data which included the list of shared resources.

6. What share name is used to retrieve the list of shared resources?

\\INSTRUCTOR\IPC$

7. Frames 45 through 51 prepare for the file connection by establishing the prerequisite sessions. Frames 52 and 53 establish the connection to the shared resource. What user account is listed for the connection request?

User1.

8. What shared resource was connected?

\\INSTRUCTOR\PUBLIC

9. What file system was resident on the connected drive?

FAT.

10. Frames 54 through 72 are used to determine all files and directories to be displayed in the drive listing upon connection. What files and directories would have been displayed as a result of the connection?

captures, stuff, Kolumz, sql65, nts.40, win95, ntw.40, win95.rk, readme.txt, and netmon.12.

11. How large were the three response frames that transferred the list of available files and directories?

Frame 63 was 542 bytes, frame 65 was 554 bytes, and frame 67 was 578 bytes for a total of 1674 bytes.

Page 385

Analyzing Logon Validation Traffic

Page 385

➤ **To analyze Windows 95 logon validation traffic**

2. Frames 19 through 42 perform logon validation for the user. Frame 19 is the first frame that specifically deals with logon validation. What is occurring in frame 19?

The client is attempting to find a local domain controller.

3. Is this request directed or broadcast?

Broadcast.

4. Is this frame a network-wide or subnet broadcast?

Subnet broadcast, as indicated by 131.107.2.255

5. How large is the frame?

259 bytes.

6. What is the Destination NetBIOS name of the frame?

DOMAIN0 <00>

7. What was the user account that was requesting validation?

User1 at the computer Win95.

8. What logon server responded to the client's request for logon validation first?

The domain controller INSTRUCTOR in frame 22.

9. Once a server is found, the appropriate sessions must be established in order to request validation. What logon server did the client use for logon validation?

The domain controller INSTRUCTOR.

10. Frames 38 through 42 complete the logon validation process. Frame 38 is the first application programming interface (API) in the logon validation process. Logon validation is being requested for what user account?

User1.

11. How long did it take for the logon validation process to be completed from session establishment to the validation request completion?

69 milliseconds to establish and terminate the session. Session establishment was at 31.928 seconds (frame 29) and the user logon request was completed at 31.997 (frame 42).

12. What is occurring in frames 43 and 44?

The client is querying WINS for the IP address for the name DOMAIN0 <1B>.

13. What is occurring in frames 45 and 46?

The client is requesting the computer name for the owner of DOMAIN0 <1B>.

14. Frames 51 through 60 occur after logon validation. These 10 frames generated an additional 994 bytes of data. Why did the client computer generate this extra traffic?

The client is requesting the file CONFIG.POL to be downloaded. This file is the system policy file.

15. Was this file found?

No, it was not present on the server.

Page 387

➤ **To analyze Windows NT Workstation logon validation traffic**

2. Frame 10 is the first frame that specifically deals with logon validation. What is occurring in frame 10?

A WINS query looking for all registered domain controllers.

3. What is the Destination NetBIOS name of the frame?

DOMAIN0 <1C>

4. How many domain controllers were reported in response to the query?

Two, 131.107.2.200 and 131.107.2.216. There are two listings for 131.107.2.200, one for its role as a PDC and one registered as a member of DOMAIN0 <1C>.

5. After the client received the list of domain controllers, how did it use the list of domain controllers?

It then sent NETLOGON requests to each address returned by WINS.

6. Were these requests directed or broadcast?

Directed.

7. What is the purpose of frame 12?

The client is attempting to find a local domain controller.

8. Is this request directed or broadcast?

Broadcast.

9. What is the destination NetBIOS name of the frame?

DOMAIN0 <1C>

10. What was the user account that was requesting validation?

NTW1$ at computer NTW1.

11. Why was this name used?

Because NTW1 is a domain member, it required authentication of its computer account.

12. What logon server responded to the client's request for logon validation first?

The domain controller INSTRUCTOR in frame 17.

13. What logon server did the client use for logon validation?

The domain controller INSTRUCTOR.

14. Frames 26 through 34 prepare the client for logon validation by establishing the required sessions (session traffic is analyzed in another lab). Frames 35 through 46 prepare the list of domains to be displayed in the **Logon Information** dialog box. Were there any trusted domains the user could log onto?

No, the list was empty.

15. Frames 47 through 55 verify that the Windows NT Workstation is a member of the domain, and has the proper credentials. In frame 53, what were the account and computer names?

The account name was NTW1$ and the computer name was NTW1.

16. Frames 66 through 67 perform logon validation. In frame 66, what were the domain, user, and computer names supplied as part of the logon validation?

The domain name is DOMAIN0, the user name is User1 and the computer name is NTW1.

17. Frame 67 is the logon server's response to the validation request. How many bytes of data was returned?

The total frame was 538 bytes, of which 400 were devoted to the R_LOGON section.

18. After validation occurred, what two files did the Windows NT 4.0 Workstation attempt to find?

Default User in frame 71, and ntconfig.pol in frame 74.

19. Were either of these two files on the server?

No, the response to Default User was found in frame 72, and the response to ntconfig.pol was found in frame 75.

Page 398   ## Chapter 6/Lesson 3
Analyzing Client Browser Announcements

Page 398   ➤ **To analyze Windows NT Workstation browser announcements**

2. Frame 60 is the Windows NT Workstation client's first browser announcement. What type of client services were announced?

Workstation, Server, and Windows NT Workstation.

3. What functions does this imply the client has?

This announces the client as a Windows NT Workstation client that can access network resources (Workstation) and may be providing network resources (Server).

4. How large was the announcement?

243 bytes.

5. Was the announcement directed or broadcast?

It was an Ethernet broadcast, as well as an IP subnet broadcast.

6. When should we expect to see the next announcement from this computer?

The Announcement Interval is designated as 4 minutes.

7. Frame 65 is the next announcement from the computer. How long was it between the first and second announcements?

656 milliseconds occurred between frames 60 and 65.

8. Why didn't the computer wait four minutes before sending the second Host announcement?

The computer (NTW1) determined it was a potential browser, so announced that it could become a browser computer.

Page 399   ➤ **To analyze Windows 95 browser announcements**

2. Frame 18 is the Windows 95 client's browser announcement. What type of client services were announced?

Workstation, Server, Windows for Workgroups, and Windows 95 or above.

3. What functions does this imply the client has?

This announces the client as a Windows 95 client that can access network resources (Workstation) and may be providing network resources (Server).

4. How large was the announcement?

260 bytes.

5. Was the announcement directed or broadcast?

It was an Ethernet broadcast, as well as an IP subnet broadcast.

Page 399

Analyzing Client Browser Traffic

Page 399

➤ **To analyze client browser traffic**

2. Normally, the client's first step in browsing a server is to find a backup browser. This does not occur here because the client had just started up, and already had cached a list of backup browsers. What backup browser computer did the client select to retrieve its browse list from?

Instructor was the backup browser selected to display the list of servers in the local domain as frames 1 through 17 indicate.

3. Frames 10 and 11 transfer the browse list to the client. How many servers were in the browse list?

Five: BACKUP, DHCP_WINS, INSTRUCTOR, NTW1, and WIN95.

4. How large was the response that included the list of servers?

274 bytes.

5. From the session request to retrieve a list of backup browsers to the completion of the session to retrieve the browse list, how much time expired?

213 milliseconds. The session request was originated at 6.832 seconds (frame 1), and the browse list transfer was acknowledged at 7.045 (frame 11).

Page 399

➤ **To analyze the retrieval of a list of shared resources**

1. Frames 18 through 32 prepare for the retrieval of the list of shared resources by querying WINS and establishing the appropriate sessions with the target server. Frames 33 and 35 request and retrieve the browse list. How much traffic was generated by this retrieval?

Two frames and 461 bytes.

2. How many shared resources were sent to the client?

Five: NETLOGON, ADMIN$, IPC$, C$, D$.

3. How long did it take to retrieve the list of resources from the initial WINS query through the return of the browse list?

337 milliseconds. The WINS query occurred at 18.007 (frame 18), and the browse list was returned at 18.344 (frame 35).

Page 400 ➤ **To analyze the retrieval of a remote browse list**

1. The actual transfer of domain occurs in frames 52 and 53. How many domains were registered?

Four: Domain0, Domain1, Domain2, and Domain3 as found in frame 53.

2. How large was the frame returning the list of domains?

186 bytes.

3. How long did it take to retrieve the list of domains from session establishment through session termination?

1.7 seconds. The session request was at 31.727 (frame 43), and the session was terminated at 33.432 (frame 59).

4. What is occurring in frames 60 through 67?

The client retrieves a list of backup browsers for the correct domain.

5. What domain is the client attempting to browse? Where did you find the answer?

Domain3 as found in NBT: Destination Name of frame 60.

6. How many backup browsers were in the response?

Two: PDC3 and BDC3 as found in frame 67.

7. Frames 68 through 80 establish the required sessions with the selected backup browser in order to retrieve the list of servers in the domain. Frames 81 and 82 retrieve the list of servers in the selected domain. Frames 83 through 88 terminate the sessions. What backup browser was selected to retrieve the list of servers in the domain?

BDC3.

8. How many servers were registered in the domain?

Two: PDC3 and BDC3, as found in frame 82.

9. Frames 89 through 107 retrieve the list of shared resources for a server in Domain3. What server was browsed?

PDC3, as the session was established with it.

10. What shared resources should have been displayed in Network Neighborhood?

    Netlogon, cdrom, and public. The other shares (Admin$, IPC$, C$, D$, E$, Repl$) were administrative shares, and would not have been displayed in Network Neighborhood.

11. How large was the frame that returned the shared resources?

    391 bytes.

12. How long did the entire process take to retrieve the list of shared resources for Domain3?

    7.262 seconds. Frame 43 (to access list of domains from local backup browser) originated at 31.727, and the retrieval of the list of resources on PDC3 was at 38.989 (frame 101). Included in this trace were a few seconds of delays waiting for user selection (between frames 59–60, and 89–90).

Page 403   ▶ **To analyze retrieving a local browse list**

2. What is occurring in frames 1 through 14?

    The client is attempting to find a backup browser computer.

3. Why are there two Get Backup List Request frames (frames 1 and 13)?

    Frame 1 was a local broadcast looking for a backup browser, while frame 13 was a directed send to Instructor.

4. How did the client know to send directly to Instructor?

    In frame 7, the client queried WINS for DOMAIN0 <1B>, which is the PDC of the domain. Frame 12 was the response, which included the IP address of the owner of Domain0 <1B>. The client knows that the owner of 1B is the domain master browser for the domain.

5. Frames 15 through 30 retrieve the list of servers in the local domain from a backup browser. Which backup browser was selected?

    BACKUP

6. Frames 31 through 45 prepare for share list retrieval by establishing the necessary sessions with the selected server. What service is used to retrieve the list of shared resources when the negotiated SMB protocol is NT LM 0.12?

    The server service, as designated in frame 42 by File = \srvsvc.

7. Frames 46 and 47 retrieve the list of shared resources. Notice that NT-to-NT APIs are fully parsed, unlike the Windows 95 request. What is the name of the API to retrieve the list of shared resources from a server?

    NetrShareEnum

8. How may shared resources were returned to the client?

Eight: NETLOGON, Admin$, IPC$, C$, D$, E$, F$, Public.

Page 410   ## Analyzing DNS Lookup Traffic

Page 410   ### ➤ To analyze DNS name lookup traffic

2. What is occurring in frames 1 and 2?

Address resolution of the DNS server.

3. What is occurring in frames 3 and 4?

DNS query.

4. What name is being queried?

DNS lookup for backup.test.com

5. What is the destination port name and number for the DNS query?

The port name is DNS and the port number is 53.

6. How much traffic was generated by the DNS lookup request and response?

Two frames and 166 bytes.

7. Did the query request also specify that recursive queries are allowed?

Yes, the client did request a recursive query.

8. Was the destination DNS server a domain authority server?

Yes, the Server authority for domain flag was set.

9. How long did it take to resolve the name?

45 milliseconds. The request was sent at 2.114 (frame 3) and the response was received at 2.159 (frame 4).

The remaining eight frames are the completion of the ping command.

Page 411   ### ➤ To analyze DNS name lookup recursion traffic

2. What is occurring in frames 1 and 2?

Address resolution of the DNS server.

3. What is occurring in frame 3?

DNS query.

4. What name is being queried?

DNS lookup for instructor.test.com

5. Did the query request also specify that recursive queries are allowed?

Yes, the Recursive query desired flag was set.

6. What is occurring in frames 4 and 5?

Address resolution of another DNS server.

7. What is occurring in frames 6 and 7?

DNS lookup by BDC3 to Backup (query and response).

8. Frame 7 is the recursive lookup request. Where was the answer sent?

To the intermediate host—in this case, BDC3—because it was the host that made the lookup request to Backup.

9. What is occurring in frame 8?

The DNS server BDC3 is responding to the originating host (NTW1) with the address of the requested host.

10. What was the IP address of instructor.test.com?

131.107.2.200

11. How much traffic was generated by the initial query and recursive query requests?

Four frames and 348 bytes.

12. How long did it take to resolve the name for the client?

8 milliseconds. The request was sent at 1.768 (frame 3) and the response was received at 1.776 (frame 8).

The remaining eight frames are the completion of the ping command.

Page 412   ➤ **To analyze DNS and WINS integration traffic**

2. What name is being queried for in frame 1?

pdc3.test.com

3. What is occurring in frame 2?

A recursive DNS query from BDC3 to Backup.

4. What is occurring in frame 5?

A recursive DNS query from Backup to DHCP_WINS.

5. Was this a DNS or NetBIOS query?

NetBIOS, as designated by the destination port 137 (NetBIOS Name Service).

6. How large was frame 5?

   92 bytes, the exact same size as a WINS query.

7. What are the first nine bytes of the name queried for in frame 5?

   FAEEEDDD (the first byte is a space)

11. What name is being queried for?

    PDC3.

12. Viewing the Hex pane, what are the first nine bytes of the name queried for in frame 89?

    FAEEEDDD (the first byte is a space).

13. Compare the first 9 bytes of the names queried for in the two files. Are there any differences?

    No, the first 9 bytes (which represent PDC3) are the same.

14. What name does this imply is being queried for in frame 5 of Dnswins.cap?

    PDC3.

15. What is occurring in frame 7 of Dnswins.cap?

    Response by the DNS server (Backup) to the requesting DNS server (BDC3).

16. What is occurring in frame 8?

    The DNS server BDC3 is responding to the originating host (NTW1) with the address of the requested host.

17. What was the IP address of pdc3.test.com?

    131.107.2.210

18. How much traffic was generated by the initial query and recursive query requests?

    Six frames and 520 bytes.

19. How long did it take to resolve the name for the client?

    13 milliseconds. The request was sent at 4.127 (frame 1) and the response was received at 4.140 (frame 8).

Page 419

Analyzing Intranet Browsing Traffic

2. What is occurring in frames 1 and 2?

   DNS query for www.test.com

3. After resolving the host name, the client then establishes a TCP session with the Web server in frames 3 through 5. In frame 6, the client makes a request to retrieve a page from the server. What is the destination TCP port?

   The port name is HTTP and the port number is 80.

4. What was the HTTP command issued by the client to the server?

   The command was a GET.

5. What page was requested by the client?

   The requested page was default.htm as designated by / as the Uniform Resource Identifier.

6. How large was the request frame? How much data was required for the HTTP header and data?

   The frame was 329 bytes and 275 were used by HTTP.

7. Frames 9 and 10 retrieve the page from the Web server. How large was the page?

   1480 bytes. Frame 9 returned 1,238 bytes of data, and frame 10 returned 242 bytes.

8. From the beginning of the TCP session, how long did it take to retrieve the page?

   740 milliseconds. The session was started at 9.020 (frame 3) and the acknowledgment was sent at 9.760 (frame 11).

Page 421

➤ **To analyze downloading a Web page with graphics**

2. What page was requested in frame 1?

   open.htm

3. How much larger was this request than the request to retrieve the default page?

   8 bytes. This request was 337 bytes, and the initial request was 329 bytes.

4. Why the difference in the frame sizes to retrieve the two pages?

   The first request was for / (default), and this request was for /open.htm (8 characters longer).

5. How large was open.htm?

   556 bytes.

6. How long did it take to retrieve the page?

   It took 32 milliseconds to retrieve the page, but another 160 milliseconds for the client to acknowledge the receipt of the data.

7. Frame 4 requests an object for the loaded page. What object was requested?

   /WebDocs/media/MOC_WEB.avi

8. Was the object transferred to the client?

   No. Frame 23 indicates the object was not found.

9. How long did the server search for the object?

   244 milliseconds. The request was sent at 3.644 (frame 4) and the response was sent at 3.888 (frame 23).

10. Frames 5 through 9 request an object for the loaded page. What object was requested?

    /WebDocs/graphics/title_black.gif

11. Was the object transferred to the client?

    Yes, frames 16 through 22 transfer the file and acknowledge the transfer.

12. How large was the file?

    6,204 bytes. Frame 16 returned 1,238 bytes of data, frames 17, 19, and 20 each returned 1,460, and frame 21 returned 586 bytes.

13. How long did it take to retrieve the page?

    It only took 127 milliseconds to retrieve the object. The request was sent at 3.759 (frame 9) and the acknowledgment was sent at 3.886 (frame 22).

14. Frames 10 through 14 request an object for the loaded page. What object was requested?

    /WebDocs/graphics/Openimag.gif

15. Was the object transferred to the client?

    Yes, frames 27 through 84 transfer the file and acknowledge the transfer.

16. How long did it take to retrieve the page?

    It only took almost 2 seconds to retrieve the object. The request was sent at 3.805 (frame 13) and the acknowledgment was sent at 5.794 (frame 84). There was a 1.6 second delay between frames 62 and 63.

    This object was 57,422 bytes in size, so it required much more traffic and time to download.

Page 434   **Chapter 6/Lesson 4**
                  Analyzing BDC Initialization Traffic

Page 434   ➤ **To analyze traffic related to finding the BDC**

2. What is occurring in frames 17 and 18?

   The BDC is querying WINS for the owner of DOMAIN0 <1B>.

3. What is occurring in frames 19 and 20?

   The BDC is attempting to resolve the IP address returned by WINS into a hardware address.

4. What is occurring in frames 21 and 22?

   The BDC is querying the PDC for its computer name.

5. How much traffic was generated by the NETLOGON query and response?

   Two frames and 546 bytes.

   This traffic should be generated only during initialization of the BDC.

Page 434   ➤ **To analyze secure channel establishment traffic**

1. What service is used to establish a secure channel?

   NETLOGON

2. Frames 36 and 37 establish the named pipes session for communications between the domain controllers. How much traffic was generated during the named pipes session creation?

   Two frames and 396 bytes.

3. Frames 38 through 41 establish the secure channel for communications between the domain controllers. How much traffic was generated during the secure channel establishment?

   Four frames and 830 bytes.

4. What server is requesting a secure channel?

   BACKUP

5. What account is being authenticated as part of the secure channel establishment?

   BACKUP$. Remember that computer accounts end in $.

   This traffic should be generated only during initialization of the BDC.

Page 436   ➤ **To analyze database verification traffic**

1. How much traffic was generated during the verification of the three databases?

   Six frames and 2,028 bytes.

2. Were any updated records transferred during database verification?

   Yes, User1 was transferred in frame 45.

   This same traffic pattern should be generated only during initialization of the BDC. Periodic updates will not use these same six frames.

Page 436   ## Analyzing Directory Services Database Synchronization Traffic

Page 436   ➤ **To analyze directory services synchronization traffic**

3. What is the purpose of this frame?

   The PDC is announcing it has a change to one of its databases.

4. Is this announcement directed or broadcast?

   Directed.

5. If there was only one announcement, and it was sent directly to the BDC, how many BDCs do you think are in this domain?

   One. There could have been more, but only one needed the update.

6. Who was the announcement sent to?

   BACKUP <00>

7. How large was the announcement?

   392 bytes.

   After the announcement, the BDC prepares for synchronization by establishing the necessary sessions. This occurs in frames 8 through 18.

8. How much traffic was generated by the named pipe establishment in frames 19 and 20?

   Two frames and 396 bytes.

9. What user accounts were added to the database?

   User2 was found in the hexadecimal detail of frame number 22 and User3 and User4 were found in the hexadecimal detail of frame number 24.

10. How large was each frame that transferred a user account?

    Frame number 22 was 1,138 bytes to transfer User2, and frame number 24 was 1,198 bytes to transfer User3 and User4.

11. How long did it take from the PDC announcement until the new user accounts were transferred to the BDC and acknowledged?

Almost 1 second. The announcement was at 38.596 seconds (frame 7), while the acknowledgment was at 39.471 (frame 25).

Page 438   ➤ **To analyze traffic related to subsequent account synchronization**

2. Why did this synchronization event generate less traffic than the one in Addusers.cap?

This synchronization event wasn't required to establish the TCP and NetBIOS sessions, negotiate server message blocks (SMB) protocols, or connect to IPC$. That would indicate these sessions were still active and had not timed out. This can be verified by viewing the Process ID (PID) and the User ID (UID) of the two transfers. They are identical.

3. What user account was modified in the database?

User4 was found in the hexadecimal detail of frame number 9.

4. Was the entire account synchronized with the BDC, or just the changed data (in this case, the user account description)?

The entire account, as viewed in the Hex pane of frame 9.

5. How large was the frame that transferred the user account?

Frame number 9 was 1,014 bytes.

6. How long did it take from the PDC announcement until the new user account was transferred to the BDC and acknowledged?

Just under 1 second (801 milliseconds). The announcement was at 0.280 seconds (frame 1), while the acknowledgment was at 1.081 (frame 10).

Page 447   ## Analyzing Trusted Account Traffic

In this exercise, you analyze network traffic generated when importing a trusted account and the verification of an imported account.

Page 447   ➤ **To analyze trusted account traffic**

2. How many frames did it take to establish the session with the LSA at the trusted domain controller, and display the trusted accounts?

It took 19 frames to open the connection to LSA (frame 78), request and transfer the data, and acknowledge the transfer (frame 96).

3. What type of accounts were transferred in response to frame number 90?

Frame 91 transfers the global groups.

4. What type of accounts were transferred in response to frame 92?

Frame 93 transfers the user accounts.

5. How many accounts would have been displayed in User Manager for Domains?

Nine. Frame 91 transferred 3 global groups and frame 93 transferred 6 user accounts.

6. How much network traffic was generated to display the list of trusted accounts? Only include the request messages and data frames.

Four frames and 2,088 bytes.

7. How long did the entire process of displaying the list of trusted accounts take?

The time it took from frames 1 to 96 was 716 milliseconds.

This traffic pattern would occur each time the trusted domain is selected in any List names from box.

Page 448

➤ **To analyze trusted account verification traffic**

2. What frame requested the translation of the account name?

Frame 40 contained the LsarLookupSids request.

3. What account was translated in response to this request?

Domain Users from Domain0 (frame 41).

4. How large was the response frame?

Frame 41 was 298 bytes in size.

5. How long did it take to resolve the SID into the account name to be displayed?

The entire process, from WINS query to final acknowledgment took only 290 milliseconds.

This traffic pattern would occur every time a trusted account was to be displayed in any of the administrative applications.

Page 449

Analyzing Pass-Through Authentication Traffic

Page 449

➤ **To analyze pass-through authentication traffic**

2. Frames 22 through 38 retrieve the list of available domains. How many domains were available?

Four: Domain0, Domain1, Domain2, and Domain3 as found in frame 32.

3. What is the purpose of frame number 39?

The client is looking on the local subnet for a master browser of the trusting domain in an attempt to retrieve a list of backup browsers for the trusting domain.

4. For what domain was the request made?

DOMAIN3

5. Was the request directed or broadcast?

It was an Ethernet broadcast and an IP subnet broadcast.

6. How many backup browsers were there in Domain3?

Two: PDC3 and BDC3.

7. Frames 47 through 67 establish a session with a backup browser in Domain3 and retrieve a list of servers in the trusting domain. Why is pass-through authentication not used in the session connection to \\PDC3\IPC$?

The connection to IPC$ is established as a null session.

8. Frames 68 through 113 retrieve the list of shared resources from a specific server in the trusting domain. Pass-through authentication is required in this sequence. In what frame is the first indication of pass-through authentication?

Frame number 78, when PDC3 requests name resolution for INSTRUCTOR.

9. Why is pass-through authentication required now, and not back in frame 58?

In frame number 77, the client was attempting to log on using a user account that required validation.

10. What is the user name and domain name that is being pass-through authenticated?

The account name is USER1 and the domain is DOMAIN0.

11. What is occurring in frames 91 through 99?

The trusting domain controller is establishing a secure channel with a trusted domain controller.

12. How long did it take to validate the account using pass-through authentication?

97 milliseconds. The WINS query was issued at 16.687 seconds (frame 78), while the validation response was returned at 16.784 (frame 101).

13. How many total frames were generated in performing pass-through authentication?

24 (frames 78-101), including name resolution, address resolution, session and secure channel establishment.

14. How long did it take, from the initial request of the client in frame 77 to the confirmation from the server in frame 102, to perform pass-through authentication?

174 milliseconds. Frame 77 occurred at 16.630 and frame 102 was at 16.804.

15. Frames 114 through 139 establish a connection to a resource in the trusting domain. In this sequence, there is another request for pass-through authentication. Why does this occur?

In frame number 121, the client is attempting to connect to \\PDC3 \PUBLIC, and the user account needs validation.

16. How long did it take to validate the account using pass-through authentication this time?

Only 10 milliseconds. The request from the trusting domain controller was at 21.819 seconds (frame 122), while the response to the request was at 21.829 (frame 123).

17. How much network traffic was generated to perform pass-through authentication?

Two frames (frames 122 and 123) and 930 bytes.

18. Why did it only take two frames to pass-through authenticate this account?

The sessions established during the first pass-through authentication request was never broken. Only the request and response were required for this attempt.

Page 452   ➤ **To analyze Windows NT Workstation logon pass-through authentication traffic**

2. What is occurring in frames 10 and 11?

WINS query to find registered domain controllers in Domain3.

3. How many domain controllers were registered in the domain?

Two: 131.107.2.210 and 131.107.2.211 (131.107.2.210 was listed twice, once as the PDC, and once as a registered member of the 1C group).

4. What account is requesting validation?

NTW3$.

5. Does pass-through authentication occur with this logon request?

No, the account is a member of Domain3.

6. How much traffic was generated to validate this logon request?

Two frames and 576 bytes (frames 12, 15, 18, or 19 and frames 20 or 21).

7. In Frames 22 through 46, the Windows NT Workstation connects to the validating domain controller, and queries for a list of trusted domains. Are there any trusted domains to be displayed in the **Logon Information** dialog box?

Yes, Domain0 was returned in frame 40.

8. Frames 47 through 55 create the secure channel with the validating domain controller. Frames 56 through 65 are continuing the registration of names with WINS, and performing browser functions. Notice the time delay (just over 10 seconds) between frames 65 and 66. What is occurring in frame 66?

User1 is attempting to log on to Domain0 from the computer NTW3.

9. Frames 67 through 87 are a result of frame 66. What is occurring in this set of frames?

Pass-through authentication occurs between a BDC in the resource domain (BDC3), and a domain controller of the accounts domain (Instructor).

10. How long did it take, from initial request by client to response to client, to complete the pass-through authentication?

138 milliseconds. The request by the client was initiated at 29.214 (frame 66), and the validation response was initiated at 29.352 (frame 89).

11. How much traffic was generated by the logon request and response?

958 bytes for frames 86 and 87.

This traffic pattern occurs each time a user logs on to the accounts domain from a computer in a resource domain.

The rest of the traffic was TCP acknowledgments, and the client connecting the PDC of its validating domain to query for Ntconfig.pol.

Page 460   **Analyzing Server Browser Traffic**

Page 460   ➤ **To analyze server browse list update traffic**

2. What is being transferred in frame 68?

    The list of servers in the local domain.

3. How many servers are in the list?

    Four: BACKUP, DHCP_WINS, INSTRUCTOR, and NTW1.

4. How large was the response?

    230 bytes.

5. Was the response directed or broadcast?

    Directed.

6. What is being transferred in frame 70?

    The list of known domains and domain master browsers.

7. How many domains are in the browse list?

    Four: Domain0, Domain1, Domain2, and Domain3.

8. How large was this response?

    244 bytes.

Page 461   ➤ **To analyze periodic browse list update traffic**

2. What is being transferred in frame 18?

    The list of domains registered.

3. Select **R_WINSIF: LPBYTE pName = Domain0**, and then view the Hex pane to answer the following question. What name is registered in WINS?

    DOMAIN0 <1B>. Notice the 1B in the 16th position of the hex data.

4. How large was the response?

    254 bytes.

    This traffic pattern would be repeated every 12 minutes on the subnet with the domain master browser.

5. Frames 23 through 35 prepare for the browse list query by establishing the required sessions. What is being transferred in frame 37?

    The list of servers in the local domain.

6. How many servers are in the list?

Three: BDC3, NTW3, and PDC3.

7. How large was the response?

203 bytes.

8. How much smaller is this response than in the Bootbdc.cap file?

27 bytes for one additional server (27 bytes are reserved for each computer).

9. What is being transferred in frame 39?

The list of known domains and domain master browsers.

10. How many domains are in the browse list?

Four: DOMAIN0, DOMAIN1, DOMAIN2, and DOMAIN3.

11. How large was this response?

244 bytes.

This traffic pattern would be repeated every 12 minutes by default, by every backup browser on each subnet.

Page 467   ## Analyzing WINS Replication Traffic

Page 467   ➤ **To analyze WINS replication traffic**

2. How long did it take to transfer the new data records?

332 milliseconds. The ARP occurred in frame 1 at 14.125 and the session was terminated at 14.457 in frame 16.

3. What frame contained the records transferred? How large was the frame?

Frame number 10. The frame was 270 bytes.

4. How many records were transferred?

4.

5. What was the average record size?

54 bytes per record. 4 records transferred using a TCP data field of 216 bytes yields 54 bytes per record.

6. Was any of the traffic generated during this transfer of data broadcast?

No, the entire conversation used directed frames. Address resolution in frame 1 used broadcast traffic.

Frames 17 through 28 were used to verify the database version IDs of the remote WINS server. These 12 frames generated 896 of the 2,290 bytes.

Page 472

Analyzing Directory Replication Traffic

Page 474

➤ **To analyze directory replication traffic for removal of files**

2. What is the first step of directory replication?

The export server announcing changes to its export tree.

3. How large was the announcement?

340 bytes.

4. Was the announcement directed to the import server?

No, it was a broadcast.

5. What was the destination NetBIOS name?

Domain0 <00>

6. Would this announcement have been routed? Why or why not?

Most likely no, because it used UDP Port 138 (NetBIOS Datagram Service), which is disabled on most routers.

7. What directory was included in the announcement?

Scripts.

8. Frames 2 through 14 prepare the import server for replication by establishing the required sessions to the export server. What user account is the Directory Replicator service using? Hint: check SMB: Command Account name in frame 9.

Replicate, which was configured as the service account.

9. Frames 15 through 41 verify the clocks are in synchronization between the two servers, and prepare for replication. This generated 27 frames and almost 5,000 bytes of traffic. What information is requested in frame 30?

The Registry information for \System\CurrentControlSet\Services \Replicator\Exports.

10. Frames 42 through 145 replicate the new files to the import server. What files were found on the export server?

1K.txt and 512b.txt.

11. How many frames did it take to replicate each file?

It took 30 frames (frames 62 to 91) to replicate 1K.txt and 30 frames (92 to 121) to replicate 512b.txt.

12. From the time the import server started replicating files, how long did it take to replicate all the files in the export tree?

114 milliseconds. The request for 1K.txt was at 34.524 (frame 62), and 512b.txt was closed at 34.638 (frame 121).

13. How long did it take from the announcement to the completion of the entire directory replication process?

15.3 seconds, but there was a 14 second delay from the announcement to the session request by the import server. The announcement was at 19.541 (frame 1), and the last frame was at 34.872 (frame 156).

Page 473

➤ **To analyze directory replication traffic for removal of files**

2. Frames 31 through 36 check for the files to be replicated. What files were found on the export server?

No files were found.

3. Frames 37 through 70 complete the replication process. What files were replicated to the import server?

None.

4. From the time the import server started verifying files (frame 31), how long did it take to complete the processing of the SCRIPTS directory (frame 62)?

75 milliseconds. The request for SCRIPTS was at 88.065 (frame 31), and SCRIPTS was closed at 88.140 (frame 62).

5. How long did it take to complete the entire replication process?

36.6 seconds, including a 36 second delay from the time of the announcement to the first access by the import server. The announcement was at 51.692 (frame 1) and the final acknowledge was completed at 88.291 (frame 71).

Page 478   ## Analyzing DNS Server Zone Transfer Traffic

Page 478   ➤ **To analyze DNS periodic zone transfer traffic**

2. Frame 1 is the primary server notifying the secondary server of a change to its zone database. Frame 2 is the secondary responding to the announcement. How much traffic was generated by the announcement and response?

   136 bytes.

3. Frames 3 and 4 are the secondary server's query on the zone, and the primary's response. How much traffic was generated by the query and response?

   193 bytes.

4. What was the version number of the database as returned by the primary in response to the secondary server's request?

   7.

5. How many records were transferred in this zone transfer?

   9, as found in the DNS: Answer Entry Count in frame 9.

6. How many new records were added to the database?

   2. The initial transfer contained 7 records, and this transfer was 9 records.

7. How large was the response that transferred the zone database? How much was devoted to DNS?

   376 bytes with 322 bytes for DNS.

8. Was the entire database transferred, or just the two updated records?

   The entire database, not just the updated records.

Page 494   ## Chapter 6/Lesson 5
                  ## Predicting Network Traffic

Page 494   ➤ **To predict network traffic**

1. What process should you use to predict network traffic for a given Windows NT Server service?

   First, characterize the service's traffic patterns. Determine how much traffic is generated by startup of the service, how much by client inter-action, and what the frequency is. Next, determine the number of serv-ers performing the same function. Then, determine the number of

clients interacting with each server. Finally, multiply the amount of traffic generated by each client interaction by the frequency. Add the results together from each server, with the startup traffic.

2. Your site has a 56-Kbps link between two sites. You want to determine how many Windows 95 users can simultaneously log on over the link. How do you determine the number of simultaneous logons over the 56-Kbps link?

A Windows 95 client logon is approximately 6,538 bytes and takes approximately 2.5 seconds. This is 20, 921 bits per seconds (6,538*8/2.5). A 56Kbps line can handle 57,344 bits per second (56*1024). 57,344/ 20,921 = 2.7, so only two simultaneous logons could be handled.

Page 507

Chapter 7/Lesson 1
Troubleshooting in the Enterprise

1. What are some of the available troubleshooting resources?

Technet, Microsoft Web Knowledge Base, Microsoft Download Library, Experts.

2. What are the steps in the DETECT troubleshooting model?

Discover, Explore, Track, Execute, Check for success, Tie up loose ends

Page 509

Chapter 7/Lesson 2
Examining Windows NT Architecture

1. Which strategy should you follow when troubleshooting from an architectural perspective?

Isolate the problem.

Check the Hardware Compatibility List.

Check the hardware configuration.

Check the Microsoft Knowledge Base.

Monitor the Event Logs.

2. Which Windows NT tools are critical when troubleshooting the architecture? Which role do they play in the troubleshooting process?

Event Viewer	**Displays events and error messages generated by Windows NT system, services, applications, or user actions. A problem in an architectural layer can cause errors in the layers above.**
Server Manager	**Verifies that the NetLogon, Workstation, and Server services are running. Because every computer on the network can act as a client or a server, networking problems are often related to inbound or outbound requests.**
Windows NT Diagnostics	**Helps examine the status of the network adapter cards, drivers, interrupt request lines (IRQs), network services, and transport protocols. If a processor was recently added, use the Hardware option to see the number of processors that Windows NT recognizes. Information here can be viewed but not modified.**
Task Manager	**Monitors, stops, and starts active applications and processes.**
Network icon in Control Panel-	**Use the Network icon in Control Panel to identify the network cards and protocols running on a computer.**
Performance Monitor	**Use Performance Monitor to measures the computer's efficiency, identify and troubleshoot possible problems, and to plan for additional hardware needs.**
Windows NT Hardware Detection Tool (NTHQ)	**Identifies installed hardware and settings for diagnostic purposes.**
Network Monitor	**Part of Windows NT Server. Use this network traffic and protocol analysis tool to view the conversation between two hosts on the network. view individual packets to determine the root cause of a problem.**

3. What is the significance of the NDIS library?

The NDIS library is a SYS file that acts like a data link library (DLL, also called an export library) containing a set of abstract functions. The main purpose of the NDIS library is to form a wrapper that allows network drivers to send and receive packets on a LAN or WAN in an operating system-independent manner.

4. The active transport protocol is NWLink. What is the most effective means to view configuration information (frame type, network number, binding information)?

From the Command Prompt type IPXROUTE CONFIG to see the current configuration.

5. You are unsuccessful in establishing a session with another computer running Windows NT Server. How would you troubleshoot this problem?

First, verify that both computers are using the same network protocol (using the Network icon in Control Panel). If they are the same, verify that each can access other computers on the network. You can use Network Monitor to view the traffic generated during the connection attempt.

6. Why is RPC a valuable IPC mechanism?

Allows a distributed application to call services available on various computers in a network without regard to their locations. Remote network operations are handled automatically.

7. You are unsuccessful in running Server Manager. What could the problem be?

The Server service is not started.

Page 558

Chapter 7/Lesson 3
Troubleshooting the Registry

1. In Windows NT, what is the registry and its function?

In Windows NT, configuration information is centrally stored in a single database called the registry. The registry replaces the .ini, .sys, and .com configuration files used in Windows for MS-DOS and Microsoft LAN Manager. Values and entries for all of the system configurations are kept here, including hardware, device drivers, network protocols, and adapter card settings. The registry also holds information about applications and user profiles.

2. Define the structure of a registry.

The registry is structured as a set of five subtrees rooted at the top of the registry hierarchy. A registry subtree contains *keys* that contain per-computer and per-user databases. Each key can contain value entries and additional subkeys. A hiv*e* is a discrete body of keys, subkeys, and values within a subtree.

3. Which tools are used to view and change registry entries?

Different tools are available to view and change registry entries. For example, Windows NT Diagnostics provides a graphical display of registry hardware information, and Control Panel contains options to view and change registry information such as drivers and protocols. Registry Editor provides more extensive access to the registry.

4. What is one way you could remotely administer the registry?

The Remote Command Service (Rcmd.exe), included in the Windows NT Server Resource Kit, provides a secure, robust way to remotely administer and run command-line programs.

5. In troubleshooting Windows NT, which registry subtree is typically used?

HKEY_LOCAL_MACHINE

6. A hardware component is not active after starting Windows NT. What can you check to determine if it is configured to start automatically?

You can use the Devices program in Control Panel to determine if the driver is configured to start automatically. Additionally, you can view HKEY_LOCAL_MACHINE\SYSTEM\CurrentControlSet\Services\ *Service*\Start to determine the driver's start value.

7. What is the purpose of the ServiceGroupOrder subkey?

Many device drivers are arranged in groups to make startup easier. When device drivers and services are being loaded, Windows NT loads the groups in the order defined by ServiceGroupOrder.

8. Which values are the most beneficial when troubleshooting related services and dependency information?

The values that provide service and dependency information most useful for troubleshooting are: DependOnGroup, DependOnService, Error Control, Image Path, Start, and Type.

9. You share your computer with another user. Recently, you've noticed that TCP/IP is taking much longer to time out when a remote host has been disconnected from the net. How can you determine if the registry has been changed from standard configuration?

Access the registry of another computer running Windows NT over the network, and compare the HKEY_LOCAL_MACHINE\SYSTEM\ CurrentControlSet\Services\TCPIP\Parameters registry entries between the two computers.

Page 578

Chapter 7/Lesson 4
Examining the Boot Process

1. What are the four main phases of the boot process?

They are Initial, Boot, Kernel, and Logon.

2. During the Initial Phase, what is the main function of the Master Boot Record?

The code in the Master Boot Record scans the Partition Table for the system partition. When the Master Boot Record finds the system partition, it loads sector 0 of the partition into memory, and executes it.

3. Define a brief description of the boot loader phase.

Gathers information about the computer's installed hardware and drivers before the kernel loads.

4. During the boot process, when is the kernel initialized?

**The kernel is initializing when the screen turns blue, and text similar to the following appears:
Microsoft (R) Windows NT (TM) Version 4.0 (Build 1381) System Processor (16 MB Memory).**

5. What is the significance of the /debug switch in the Boot.ini file?

The debugger is loaded when Windows NT starts, and can be activated at any time by a host debugger connected to the computer. This is the mode to use when debugging problems that are regularly reproducible.

6. When a user successfully logs in to Windows NT, what event takes place in the registry? Why is this beneficial to the user?

After a successful logon attempt, the Clone control set is copied to the LastKnownGood control set. This is beneficial if a problem was created due to a change in the registry, such as a manual parameter update or the addition of a faulty device driver. The user can restart the computer without logging on, and select Last Known Good during the boot sequence. This will load the previously known good control set, bypassing the invalid parameter or conflicting device driver.

7. A scsi driver is suspect for causing scatter gather problems. What is one way to determine the driver date of the currently installed driver?

Use the Windows NT Resource Kit DRIVERS utility to display the list of drivers loaded. If the specific driver is displayed, then check the driver link date.

8. When you attempt to boot the computer, it does not respond during kernel initialization. You have attempted to use LastKnownGood, but the computer still fails to respond. What would you do to troubleshoot this problem?

Restart the computer using Windows NT Server Setup Disk 1, and perform an emergency repair. Select Verify Windows NT System Files, and complete the repair.

9. You had to perform an emergency repair to recover your computer. Now you are unable to log on using your user account. What is the problem?

During the emergency repair process, the SAM and SECURITY hives of the registry were replaced, thus removing all accounts that were added after the system was first installed.

Page 600

Chapter 7/Lesson 5
Analyzing Debugger Results

1. A Stop 0x0000000A appears on the screen after loading a network interface card driver. What information on the screen is the most critical?

The first four lines of the stop screen contain the most critical information about the problem, and should be reported to Microsoft Technical Support.

2. Which debugger allows you to debug user and kernel mode problems?

WinDBG.

3. What are a stack and stack trace?

A stack is an area of system memory that is used for keeping track of recently acquired data. When an API or function is called, the arguments to the function and the return address (current location) are pushed onto the stack. When the system halts, the stack is kept intact. The trace is a history of events that occurred in the stack.

4. What is a common problem that occurs when debugging? What are the ramifications that can occur if the problem goes unnoticed?

A common problem in configuring the Kernel Debugger occurs if the wrong symbol files are used. A symbol gives the debugger the information it needs to decode errors. To avoid possible errors and misinterpretation of data, use symbols from the same version of Windows NT in which the computer was booted. Also use the correct symbols for the target computer. If any service packs have been installed, it is important to use the symbols from the service packs as well. Always determine the version of Windows NT running on the target computer, as well as any service packs or hot fixes applied to the target computer. Copy the appropriate symbol files to the host computer to enable proper debugging of the target computer.

5. When attempting to boot a Windows NT computer, a stop screen message ("Stop 0x0000007B -Inaccessible boot device.") is displayed. What are the first steps you would take to troubleshoot the problem?

First, verify that all hard disks and CD-ROM drives are turned on and properly terminated. Then, restart the computer. If it still fails with the same error, do a virus scan on the disk.

6. Your computer generates a stop screen every time you load a video driver. A co-worker has mentioned preparing for a "CrashDump." What is a "CrashDump"?

CrashDump is the preferred method for stop screen debugging because it ensures that a system will be brought back online as quickly as possible. This utility captures the contents of memory when a stop screen occurs and produces a file that can be analyzed to determine the cause of the problem.

7. You cannot resolve a stop screen message by yourself, and need to contact Microsoft Technical Support for assistance. You have only a 2400-baud modem. What should you do to prepare for Microsoft Technical Support assistance?

First, make sure that Recovery is enabled, and is writing debug information to a file. Reproduce the stop screen, and allow the CrashDump to occur. Run the dumpchk utility to then use Dumpexam.exe to produce a text file from Memory.dmp. This text file will be significantly smaller than the dmp file, making phone transfer much quicker.

8. Your Windows NT Server–based computer boots fine, but when running an application, a general protection fault occurs. Which application debugger tool could be used to troubleshoot the problem?

Dr. Watson for Windows NT. It detects application errors, diagnoses the error, and logs the diagnostic information. The information obtained and logged by Dr. Watson for a computer running Windows NT is the information needed by technical-support groups to diagnose the application error. The Drwtsn32.log log file is created in the form of an electronic text file. There is also an option of creating a binary crash dump file that can be loaded into the WinDBG for debugging.

9. What are the two user mode services that correspond to the kernel mode file system drivers?

LanmanWorkstation and LanmanServer.

10. Why don't these appear in the Kernel Debug output?

They are user mode applications, not kernel mode processes.

Glossary

A

access control entry (ACE) An entry in an access control list (ACL). Each access control entry defines the protection or auditing to be applied to a file or other object for a specific user or group of users. *See also* access control list (ACL).

access control list (ACL) The part of a security descriptor that enumerates both the protections to accessing and the auditing of that accessing that are applied to an object. The owner of an object has discretionary access control of the object and can change the object's ACL to allow or disallow others access to the object. Access control lists are ordered lists of access control entries (ACEs). There are two types of ACLs: discretionary (DACL) and system (SACL). *See also* access control entry (ACE); discretionary access control list (DACL); system access control list (SACL).

access permission A rule associated with an object (usually a directory, file, or printer) to regulate which users can have access to the object and in what manner. *See also* user rights.

access privileges Permissions set by Macintosh users that allow them to view and make changes to folders on a server. By setting access privileges (called *permissions* when set on the computer running Windows NT Server), you control which Macintosh can use folders in a volume. Services for Macintosh (SFM) translates access privileges set by Macintosh users to the equivalent Windows NT permissions.

access token (or security token) An object that uniquely identifies a user who has logged on. An access token is attached to all of the user's processes and contains the user's security ID (SID), the SIDs of any groups to which the user belongs, any permissions that the user owns, the default owner of any objects that the user's processes create, and the default access control list (ACL) to be applied to any objects that the user's processes create. *See also* permissions.

access violation An attempt to carry out a memory operation that is not allowed by Windows NT memory management. This can include an invalid operation (such as writing to a read-only buffer); accessing memory beyond the limit of the current program's address space (a "length violation"); accessing a page to which the system forbids access; or accessing a page that is currently resident but dedicated to the use of an Executive component.

account *See* group account; user account.

account lockout A Windows NT Server security feature that locks a user account if a number of failed logon attempts occur within a specified amount of time, based on account policy lockout settings. (Locked accounts cannot log on.)

account policy Controls the way passwords must be used by all user accounts of a domain or of an individual computer. Specifics include minimum password length, how often a user must change his or her password, and how often users can reuse old passwords. Account policy can be set for all user accounts in a domain when administering a domain, and for all user accounts of a single workstation or member server when administering a computer.

ACK Short for acknowledgment. The Transmission Control Protocol (TCP) requires that the recipient of data packets acknowledge successful receipt of data. Such acknowledgments (ACKs) generate additional network traffic, diminishing the rate at which data passes in favor of reliability. To reduce the impact on performance, most hosts send an acknowledgment for every other segment or when a specified time interval has passed.

acknowledgment *See* ACK.

active Refers to the window or icon that you are currently using or that is currently selected. Windows NT always applies the next keystroke or command you choose to the active window. If a window is active, its title bar changes color to differentiate it from other windows. If an icon is active, its label changes color. Windows or icons on the desktop that are not selected are inactive.

ActiveX An umbrella term for Microsoft technologies that enable developers to create interactive content for the World Wide Web.

adapter card *See* network adapter.

address Within Network Monitor, an address refers to a hexadecimal number that identifies a computer uniquely on the network.

address classes Predefined groupings of Internet addresses, with each class defining networks of a certain size. The range of numbers that can be assigned for the first octet in the IP address is based on the address class. Class A networks (values 1–126) are the largest, with over 16 million hosts per network. Class B networks (128–191) have up to 65,534 hosts per network, and Class C networks (192–223) can have up to 254 hosts per network. *See also* octet.

address pairs Refers to the two specific computers between which you want to monitor traffic by using Network Monitor. Up to four specific address pairs can be monitored simultaneously to capture frames from particular computers on your network. *See also* frame.

Address Resolution Protocol (ARP) A network-maintenance protocol in the TCP/IP suite that provides IP address-to-MAC address resolution for IP packets. Not directly related to data transport. *See also* IP address; media access control (MAC); packet; Transmission Control Protocol/Internet Protocol (TCP/IP).

administrative account An account that is a member of the Administrators local group of a computer or domain.

administrative alerts Administrative alerts relate to server and resource use and warn about problems in areas such as security and access, user sessions, server shutdown due to power loss (when UPS is available), directory replication, and printing. When a computer generates an administrative alert, a message is sent to a predefined list of users and computers. *See also* Alerter service; uninterruptible power supply (UPS).

administrator A person responsible for setting up and managing domain controllers or local computers and their user and group accounts, assigning passwords and permissions, and helping users with networking issues. To use administrative tools such as User Manager or User Manager for Domains, an administrator must be logged on as a member of the Administrators local group of the computer or domain, respectively.

Administrator privilege One of three privilege levels you can assign to a Windows NT user account. Every user account has one of the three privilege levels (Administrator, Guest, and User). *See also* administrator; Guest privilege; User privilege.

Advanced RISC Computing (ARC) ARC names are a generic method of identifying devices within the ARC environment. *See also* reduced instruction set computing (RISC).

agent In SNMP, agent information consists of comments about the user, the physical location of the computer, and the types of service to report based on the computer's configuration. *See also* Simple Network Management Protocol (SNMP).

Alerter service Notifies selected users and computers of administrative alerts that occur on a computer. Used by the Server service and other services. Requires the Messenger service. *See also* administrative alerts; Messenger service.

anonymous-level security token The type of security token used when a server impersonates a client. If, when the client calls the server, the client specifies an anonymous impersonation mode, the server cannot access any of the client's identification information, such as its security identifier (SID) or privileges. The server will have to use an anonymous-level security token when representing the client in successive operations. *See also* access token.

Anonymous user A connection for which the request either did not contain a user name and password or whose user name and password were ignored because authentication is not permitted on the server.

API *See* application programming interface.

AppleShare Client software that is shipped with each Macintosh and with Apple Computer server software. With Services for Macintosh, a Macintosh uses its native AppleShare client software to connect to computers running Windows NT Server that have Services for Macintosh.

AppleTalk Apple Computer network architecture and network protocols. A network that has Macintosh clients and a computer running Windows NT Server with Services for Macintosh functions as an AppleTalk network.

AppleTalk Filing Protocol The presentation layer protocol that manages access of remote files in an AppleTalk network.

AppleTalk Phase 2 The extended AppleTalk Internet model designed by Apple Computer. It supports multiple zones within a network and extended addressing capacity.

AppleTalk Protocol The set of network protocols on which AppleTalk network architecture is based. Setting up Services for Macintosh installs its AppleTalk Protocol stack on a computer running Windows NT Server so that Macintosh clients can connect to it.

AppleTalk Transport The layer of AppleTalk Phase 2 protocols that deliver data to its destination on the network.

application A computer program used for a particular kind of work, such as word processing. This term is often used interchangeably with "program."

application log The application log contains specific events logged by applications. Applications developers decide which events to monitor (for example, a database program might record a file error in the application log). Use Event Viewer to view the application log.

application programming interface (API) A set of routines that an application program uses to request and carry out lower-level services performed by another component, such as the computer's operating system or a service running on a network computer. These maintenance chores are performed by the computer's operating system, and an API provides the program with a means of communicating with the system, telling it which system-level task to perform and when.

application window The main window for an application, which contains the application's menu bar and work area. An application window may contain multiple document windows.

ARC *See* Advanced RISC Computing.

archive bit Backup programs use the archive bit to mark the files after backing them up, if a normal or incremental backup is performed. *See also* backup types.

ARP *See* Address Resolution Protocol.

ARP reply packet All ARP-enabled systems on the local IP network detect ARP request packets, and the system that owns the IP address in question replies by sending its physical address to the requester in an ARP reply packet. The physical/IP address is then stored in the ARP cache of the requesting system for subsequent use. *See also* Address Resolution Protocol (ARP); ARP request packet; Internet Protocol (IP); MAC address.

ARP request packet If two systems are to communicate across a TCP/IP network, the system sending the packet must map the IP address of the final destination to the physical address of the final destination. This physical address is also referred to as a MAC address, a unique 48-bit number assigned to the network interface card by the manufacturer. IP acquires this physical address by broadcasting a special inquiry packet (an ARP request packet) containing the IP address of the destination system. *See also* Address Resolution Protocol (ARP); Internet Protocol (IP); MAC address; media access control (MAC).

AS/400 A type of IBM minicomputer.

ASCII file Also called a text file, a text-only file, or an ASCII text file, refers to a file in the universally recognized text format called ASCII (American Standard Code for Information Interchange). An ASCII file contains characters, spaces, punctuation, carriage returns, and sometimes tabs and an end-of-file marker, but it contains no formatting information. This generic format is useful for transferring files between programs that could not otherwise understand each other's documents. *See also* text file.

associate To identify a file name extension as "belonging" to a certain application so that when you open any file with that extension, the application starts automatically.

attributes Information that indicates whether a file is a read-only, hidden, system, or compressed file, and whether the file has been changed since a backup copy of it was made.

A-type resource record A line (record) in a computer's Domain Name System database that maps a computer's domain name (host name) to an IP address in a DNS zone.

auditing Tracking activities of users by recording selected types of events in the security log of a server or a workstation.

audit policy For the servers of a domain or for an individual computer, defines the type of security events that will be logged.

authentication Validation of a user's logon information. When a user logs on to an account on a computer running Windows NT Workstation, the authentication is performed by that workstation. When a user logs on to an account on a Windows NT Server domain, authentication may be performed by any server of that domain. *See also* Basic (clear-text) authentication; challenge/response authentication; server; trust relationship.

B

backup domain controller (BDC) In a Windows NT Server domain, a computer running Windows NT Server that receives a copy of the domain's directory database, which contains all account and security policy information for the domain. The copy is synchronized periodically and automatically with the master copy on the primary domain controller (PDC). BDCs also authenticate user logons and can be promoted to function as PDCs as needed. Multiple BDCs can exist on a domain. *See also* member server; primary domain controller (PDC).

backup set A collection of files from one drive that is backed up during a single backup operation.

backup set catalog At the end of each backup set, Windows NT Backup stores a summary of file or directory information in a backup set catalog. Catalog information includes the number of tapes in a set of tapes as well as the date they were created, and the dates of each file in the catalog. Catalogs are created for each backup set and are stored on the last tape in the set. *See also* backup set.

backup set map At the end of each tape used for backup, a backup set map maintains the exact tape location of the backup set's data and catalog.

backup types:

copy backup Copies all selected files, but does not mark each file as having been backed up. Copying is useful if you want to back up files between normal and incremental backups, because copying will not invalidate these other backup operations.

daily backup Copies all selected files that have been modified the day the daily backup is performed.

differential backup Copies those files created or changed since the last normal (or incremental) backup. It does not mark files as having been backed up.

incremental backup Backs up only those files created or changed since the last normal (or incremental) backup. It marks files as having been backed up.

normal backup Copies all selected files and marks each as having been backed up. Normal backups give you the ability to restore files quickly because files on the last tape are the most current.

bandwidth In communications, the difference between the highest and lowest frequencies in a given range. For example, a telephone line accommodates a bandwidth of 3000 Hz, the difference between the lowest (300 Hz) and highest (3300 Hz) frequencies it can carry. In computer networks, greater bandwidth indicates faster data-transfer capability and is expressed in bits per second (bps). Also known as "throughput."

Basic (clear-text) authentication A method of authentication that encodes user name and password data transmissions. Basic authentication is called "clear text" because the base-64 encoding can be decoded by anyone with a freely available decoding utility. Note that encoding is not the same as encryption. *See also* challenge/response authentication; encryption.

batch program An ASCII file (unformatted text file) that contains one or more Windows NT commands. A batch program's file name has a .cmd or .bat extension. When you type the file name at the command prompt, the commands are processed sequentially.

batch queue facility A program that effects a logon without user input, used for delayed logons.

BDC *See* backup domain controller.

binary A base-2 number system, in which values are expressed as combinations of two digits, 0 and 1.

binary-file transfer A method of transferring binary files from Windows NT HyperTerminal to a remote computer. Binary files consist of ASCII characters plus the extended ASCII character set. These files are not converted or translated during the transfer process. *See also* ASCII file.

binding A process that establishes the communication channel between a protocol driver (such as TCP/IP) and a network adapter. *See also* network adapter; Transmission Control Protocol/Internet Protocol (TCP/IP).

bits per second (bps) A measure of the speed at which a device, such as a modem, can transfer data.

blue screen The screen displayed when Windows NT encounters a serious error.

bookmarks A Windows NT feature that enables you to highlight major points of interest at various points in a Performance Monitor log file and then return to them easily when you work with that log file later on during performance monitoring. Bookmarks are also used in other applications, such as Microsoft Word.

boot loader Defines the information needed for system startup, such as the location for the operating system's files. Windows NT automatically creates the correct configuration and checks this information whenever you start your system.

boot partition The volume, formatted for either an NTFS or FAT file system, that contains the Windows NT operating system and its support files. The boot partition can be (but does not have to be) the same as the system partition. *See also* file allocation table (FAT); partition; Windows NT File System (NTFS).

Bootstrap protocol (BOOTP) A TCP/IP network protocol, defined by RFC 951 and RFC 1542, used to configure systems. DHCP is an extension of BOOTP. *See also* Dynamic Host Configuration Protocol (DHCP).

bps *See* bits per second.

branch A segment of the directory tree, representing a directory (or folder) and any subdirectories (or folders within folders) it contains.

bridge Connects multiple networks, subnets, or rings into one large logical network. A bridge maintains a table of node addresses and, based on this, forwards packets to a specific subnet, reducing traffic on other subnets. In a bridged network, there can be only one path to any destination (otherwise packets would circle the network, causing network storms). A bridge is more sophisticated than a repeater, but not as sophisticated as a router. *See also* packet; repeaters; router; subnet.

broadcast datagram An IP datagram sent to all hosts on the subnet. *See also* datagram; Internet Protocol (IP); subnet.

broadcast message A network message sent from a single computer that is distributed to all other devices on the same segment of the network as the sending computer.

broadcast name resolution A mechanism defined in RFC 1001/1002 that uses broadcasts to resolve names to IP addresses through a process of registration, resolution, and name release. *See also* broadcast datagram; IP address.

brouter Combines elements of the bridge and the router. Usually, a brouter acts as a router for one transport protocol (such as TCP/IP), sending packets of that format along detailed routes to their destinations. The brouter also acts as a bridge for all other types of packets (such as IPX), just passing them on, as long as they are not local to the LAN segment from which they originated. *See also* bridge; packet; router.

browse To view available network resources by looking through lists of folders, files, user accounts, groups, domains, or computers. Browsing allows users on a Windows NT network to see what domains and computers are accessible from their local computer. *See also* Windows NT browser system.

browse list A list kept by the master browser of all of the servers and domains on the network. This list is available to any workstation on the network requesting it. *See also* browse.

browse master *See* master browser; Windows NT browser system.

buffer A reserved portion of memory in which data is temporarily held pending an opportunity to complete its transfer to or from a storage device or another location in memory. Some devices, such as printers or the adapters supporting them, commonly have their own buffers. *See also* memory.

built-in groups Default groups, provided with Windows NT Server and Windows NT Workstation, that have been granted useful collections of rights and built-in abilities. In most cases, a built-in group provides all of the capabilities needed by a particular user. For example, if a domain user account belongs to the built-in Administrators group, logging on with that account gives a user administrative capabilities over the domain and the servers of the domain. To provide a needed set of capabilities to a user account, assign it to the appropriate built-in group. *See also* group; User Manager; User Manager for Domains.

bulk data encryption The encryption of all data sent over a network.

C

cache A special memory subsystem that stores the contents of frequently accessed RAM locations and the addresses where these data items are stored. In Windows NT, for example, user profiles have a locally cached copy of part of the registry.

caching In DNS name resolution, caching refers to a local cache where information about the DNS domain name space is kept. Whenever a resolver request arrives, the local name server checks both its static information and the cache for the name to IP address mapping. *See also* Domain Name System (DNS); IP address; mapping.

Callback Control Protocol (CBCP) A protocol that negotiates callback information with a remote client.

capture The process by which Network Monitor copies frames. (A *frame* is information that has been divided into smaller pieces by the network software prior to transmission.) *See also* frame.

capture buffer A reserved, resizable storage area in memory where Network Monitor copies all frames it detects from the network. When the capture buffer overflows, each new frame replaces the oldest frame in the buffer.

capture filter Functions like a database query to single out a subset of frames to be monitored in Network Monitor. You can filter on the basis of source and destination addresses, protocols, protocol properties, or by specifying a pattern offset. *See also* capture; frame.

capture password Required to be able to capture statistics from the network and to display captured data using Network Monitor.

capture trigger Performs a specified action (such as starting an executable file) when Network Monitor detects a particular set of conditions on the network.

catalog *See* backup set catalog.

CBCP *See* Callback Control Protocol.

CCP *See* Compression Control Protocol.

centralized network administration A centralized view of the entire network from any workstation on the network that provides the ability to track and manage information on users, groups, and resources in a distributed network.

CGI *See* Common Gateway Interface.

Challenge Handshake Authentication Protocol (CHAP) A protocol used by Microsoft RAS to negotiate the most secure form of encrypted authentication supported by both server and client. *See also* encryption.

challenge/response authentication A method of authentication in which a server uses challenge/response algorithms and Windows NT security to control access to resources. *See also* Basic (clear-text) authentication; encryption.

change log An inventory of the most recent changes made to the directory database such as new or changed passwords, new or changed user and group accounts, and any changes to associated group memberships and user rights. Change logs provide fault tolerance, so if your system crashes before a write completes, Windows NT can complete the write the next time you boot. This log holds only a certain number of changes, however, so when a new change is added, the oldest change is deleted. *See also* directory database; fault tolerance.

CHAP *See* Challenge Handshake Authentication Protocol.

check box A small box in a dialog box or property page that can be selected or cleared. Check boxes represent an option that you can turn on or off. When a check box is selected, an X or a check mark appears in the box.

checksum The mathematical computation used to verify the accuracy of data in TCP/IP packets. *See also* packet; Transmission Control Protocol/Internet Protocol (TCP/IP).

choose To pick an item that begins an action in Windows NT. You often click a command on a menu to perform a task, and you click an icon to start an application.

circular dependency A dependency in which an action that appears later in a chain is contingent upon an earlier action. For example, three services (A, B, and C) are linked. A is dependent upon B to start. B is dependent upon C to start. A circular dependency results when C is dependent upon A to start. *See also* dependency.

clear To turn off an option by removing the X or check mark from a check box. To clear a check box, you can click it, or you can select it and then press the SPACEBAR.

clear-text authentication *See* Basic (clear-text) authentication.

clear-text passwords Passwords that are not scrambled, thus making them more susceptible to network sniffers. *See also* network sniffer.

click To press and release a mouse button quickly.

client A computer that accesses shared network resources provided by another computer, called a server. *See also* server; workstation.

client application A Windows NT application that can display and store linked or embedded objects. For distributed applications, the application that imitates a request to a server application. *See also* DCOM Configuration tool; Distributed Component Object Module (DCOM); server application.

Client Service for NetWare Included with Windows NT Workstation, enabling workstations to make direct connections to file and printer resources at NetWare servers running NetWare 2.*x* or later.

Clipboard A temporary storage area in memory, used to transfer information. You can cut or copy information onto the Clipboard and then paste it into another document or application.

close Remove a window or dialog box, or quit an application. To close a window, you can click **Close** on the **Control** menu, or you can click the close button icon in the upper right corner of the dialog box. When you close an application window, you quit the application.

collapse To hide additional directory levels below a selected directory in the directory tree.

color scheme A combination of complementary colors for screen elements.

command A word or phrase, usually found on a menu, that you click to carry out an action. You click a command on a menu or type a command at the Windows NT command prompt. You can also type a command in the **Run** dialog box, which you open by clicking **Run** on the **Start** menu.

command button A button in a dialog box that carries out or cancels the selected action. Two common command buttons are **OK** and **Cancel**. If you click a command button that contains an ellipsis (for example, **Browse...**), another dialog box appears.

Common Gateway Interface (CGI) A standard interface for HTTP server application development. The standard was developed by the National Center for Supercomputing Applications.

common group Common groups appear in the program list on the **Start** menu for all users who log on to the computer. Only Administrators can create or change common groups.

communications settings Settings that specify how information is transferred from your computer to a device (usually a printer or modem).

community names A group of hosts to which a server belongs that is running the SNMP service. The community name is placed in the SNMP packet when the trap is sent. Typically, all hosts belong to Public, which is the standard name for the common community of all hosts. *See also* packet; Simple Network Management Protocol (SNMP); trap.

compact A command-line utility used to compress files on NTFS volumes. To see command line options, type **compact /?** at the command prompt. To access this utility, you can also right-click any file or directory on an NTFS volume in Windows NT Explorer, then click **Properties** to compress or decompress the files.

compound device A device that plays specific media files. For example, to run a compound device such as a MIDI sequencer, you must specify a MIDI file.

Compression Control Protocol (CCP) A protocol that negotiates compression with a remote client.

computer account Each computer running Windows NT Workstation and Windows NT Server that participates in a domain has its own account in the directory database. A computer account is created when the computer is first identified to the domain during network setup at installation time.

Computer Browser service Maintains an up-to-date list of computers, and provides the list to applications when requested. Provides the computer lists displayed in the **Network Neighborhood**, **Select Computer**, and **Select Domain** dialog boxes; and (for Windows NT Server only) in the Server Manager window.

computer name A unique name of up to 15 uppercase characters that identifies a computer to the network. The name cannot be the same as any other computer or domain name in the network.

configure To change the initial setup of a client, a Macintosh-accessible volume, a server, or a network.

connect To assign a drive letter, port, or computer name to a shared resource so that you can use it with Windows NT.

connected user A user accessing a computer or a resource across the network.

connection A software link between a client and a shared resource such as a printer or a shared directory on a server. Connections require a network adapter or modem.

connection-oriented protocol A network protocol with four important characteristics: the path for data packets is established in advance; the resources required for a connection are reserved in advance; a connection's resource reservation is enforced throughout the life of that connection; and when a connection's data transfer is completed, the connection is terminated and the allocated resources are freed.

control codes Codes that specify terminal commands or formatting instructions (such as line-feeds or carriage returns) in a text file. Control codes are usually preceded by a caret (^).

controller *See* backup domain controller (BDC); primary domain controller (PDC).

Control menu *See* window menu.

control set All Windows NT startup-related data that is not computed during startup is saved in a registry key. This startup data is organized into control sets, each of which contains a complete set of parameters for starting up devices and services. The registry always contains at least two control sets, each of which contains information about all of the configurable options for the computer: the current control set and the Last-KnownGood control set. *See also* current control set; LastKnownGood (LKG) control set.

conventional memory Up to the first 640 KB of memory in your computer. MS-DOS uses this memory to run applications.

CRC *See* cyclic redundancy check.

current control set The control set that was used most recently to start the computer and that contains any changes made to the startup information during the current session. *See also* LastKnown-Good (LKG) control set.

current directory The directory that you are currently working in. Also called "current folder."

cyclic redundancy check (CRC) A procedure used on disk drives to ensure that the data written to a sector is read correctly later. This procedure is also used in checking for errors in data transmission.

The procedure is known as a redundancy check because each data transmission includes not only data but extra (redundant) error-checking values. The sending device generates a number based on the data to be transmitted and sends its result along with the data to the receiving device. The receiving device repeats the same calculation after transmission. If both devices obtain the same result, it is assumed that the transmission is error-free.

D

DACL *See* discretionary access control list; *see also* system access control list (SACL).

daemon A networking program that runs in the background.

database query The process of extracting data from a database and presenting it for use.

data carrier In communications, either a specified frequency that can be modulated to convey information or a company that provides telephone and other communications services to consumers.

Data Carrier Detect (DCD) Tracks the presence of a data carrier. *See also* data carrier.

data communications equipment (DCE) An elaborate worldwide network of packet-forwarding nodes that participate in delivering an X.25 packet to its designated address, for example, a modem. *See also* node; packet; X.25.

Data Encryption Standard (DES) A type of encryption (the U.S. government standard) designed to protect against password discovery and playback. Microsoft RAS uses DES encryption when both the client and the server are using RAS.

data fork The part of a Macintosh file that holds most of the file's information. The data fork is the part of the file shared between Macintosh and PC clients.

datagram A packet of data and other delivery information that is routed through a packet-switched network or transmitted on a local area network. *See also* packet.

Data Source Name (DSN) The logical name used by ODBC to refer to the drive and other information required to access data. The name is use by Internet Information Server for a connection to an ODBC data source, such as a SQL Server database. To set this name, use ODBC in the Control Panel.

data stream Windows NT Network Monitor monitors the network data stream, which consists of all information transferred over a network at any given time.

Data Terminal Equipment (DTE) For example, a RAS server or client. *See also* Remote Access Service (RAS).

dbWeb Administrator The graphical user tool for Microsoft dbWeb that allows an administrator to create definition templates referred to as schemas. Schemas control how and what information from a private database is available to visitors who use the Internet to access the public Microsoft dbWeb gateway to the private database. *See also* schemas.

DCD *See* Data Carrier Detect.

DCE *See* data communications equipment.

DCOM *See* Distributed Component Object Model.

DCOM Configuration tool A Windows NT Server utility that can be used to configure 32-bit applications for DCOM communication over the network. *See also* Distributed Component Object Model (DCOM).

DDE *See* dynamic data exchange.

deadlock condition A run-time error condition that occurs when two threads of execution are blocked, each waiting to acquire a resource that the other holds, and both unable to continue running.

decision tree A geographical representation of a filter's logic used by Windows NT Network Monitor. When you include or exclude information from your capture specifications, the decision tree reflects these specifications.

default button In some dialog boxes, the command button that is selected or highlighted when the dialog box is initially displayed. The default button has a bold border, indicating that it will be chosen automatically if you press ENTER. To override a default button, you can click **Cancel** or another command button.

default gateway In TCP/IP, the intermediate network device on the local network that has knowledge of the network IDs of the other networks in the Internet, so it can forward the packets to other gateways until the packet is eventually delivered to a gateway connected to the specified destination. *See also* gateway; network ID; packet.

default network In the Macintosh environment, this refers to the physical network on which a server's processes reside as nodes and on which the server appears to users. A server's default network must be one to which that server is attached. Only servers on AppleTalk Phase 2 internets have default networks.

default owner The person assigned ownership of a folder on the server when the account of the folder or volume's previous owner expires or is deleted. Each server has one default owner; you can specify the owner.

default printer The printer that is used if you choose the **Print** command without first specifying which printer you want to use with an application. You can have only one default printer; it should be the printer you use most often.

default profile *See* system default profile; user default profile.

default user Every user profile begins as a copy of default user, a default user profile stored on each computer running Windows NT Workstation or Windows NT Server.

default zone The zone to which all Macintosh clients on the network are assigned by default.

dependency A situation in which one action must take place before another can happen. For example, if action A does not occur, then action D cannot occur. Some Windows NT drivers have dependencies on other drivers or groups of drivers. For example, driver A will not load unless some driver from the G group loads first. *See also* circular dependency.

dependent service A service that requires support of another service. For example, the Alerter service is dependent on the Messenger service. *See also* Alerter service; Messenger service.

DES *See* Data Encryption Standard.

descendent key All of the subkeys that appear when a key in the registry is expanded. A descendent key is the same thing as a subkey. *See also* key; registry; subkey.

desired zone The zone in which Services for Macintosh appears on the network. *See also* default zone.

desktop The background of your screen, on which windows, icons, and dialog boxes appear.

desktop pattern A design that appears across your desktop. You can create your own pattern or select a pattern provided by Windows NT.

destination directory The directory to which you intend to copy or move one or more files.

destination document The document into which a package or a linked or embedded object is being inserted. For an embedded object, this is sometimes also called the container document. *See also* embedded object; linked object; package.

device Any piece of equipment that can be attached to a network—for example, a computer, a printer, or any other peripheral equipment.

device contention The way Windows NT allocates access to peripheral devices, such as modems or printers, when more than one application is trying to use the same device.

device driver A program that enables a specific piece of hardware (device) to communicate with Windows NT. Although a device may be installed on your system, Windows NT cannot recognize the device until you have installed and configured the appropriate driver. If a device is listed in the Hardware Compatibility List, a driver is usually included with Windows NT. Drivers are installed when you run the Setup program (for a manufacturer's supplied driver) or by using Devices in Control Panel. *See also* Hardware Compatibility List (HCL).

DHCP *See* Dynamic Host Configuration Protocol.

DHCP Relay Agent The component responsible for relaying DHCP and BOOTP broadcast messages between a DHCP server and a client across an IP router. *See also* Bootstrap protocol (BOOTP); Dynamic Host Configuration Protocol (DHCP).

dialog box A window that is displayed to request or supply information. Many dialog boxes have options you must select before Windows NT can carry out a command.

dial-up line A standard dial-up connection such as telephone and ISDN lines.

dial-up networking The client version of Windows NT Remote Access Service (RAS), enabling users to connect to remote networks.

directory Part of a structure for organizing your files on a disk, a directory (also called a folder) is represented by the folder icon in Windows NT, Windows 95, and on Macintosh computers. A directory can contain files and other directories, called subdirectories or folders within folders.

With Services for Macintosh, directories on the computer running Windows NT Server appear to Macintosh users as volumes and folders if they are designated as Macintosh accessible.

See also directory tree; folder.

directory database A database of security information such as user account names and passwords, and the security policy settings. For Windows NT Workstation, the directory database is managed by using User Manager. For a Windows NT Server domain, it is managed by using User Manager for Domains. (Other Windows NT documents may refer to the directory database as the "Security Accounts Manager (SAM) database.") *See also* Windows NT Server Directory Services.

directory replication The copying of a master set of directories from a server (called an export server) to specified servers or workstations (called import computers) in the same or other domains. Replication simplifies the task of maintaining identical sets of directories and files on multiple computers, because only a single master copy of the data must be maintained. Files are replicated when they are added to an exported directory and every time a change is saved to the file. *See also* Directory Replicator service.

Directory Replicator service Replicates directories, and the files in those directories, between computers. *See also* directory replication.

Directory Service Manager for NetWare (DSMN) A component of Windows NT Server. Enables network administrators to add NetWare servers to Windows NT Server domains and to manage a single set of user and group accounts that are valid at multiple servers running either Windows NT Server or NetWare.

directory services *See* Windows NT Server Directory Services.

directory tree A graphical display of a disk's directory hierarchy. The directories and folders on the disk are shown as a branching structure. The top-level directory is the root directory.

disabled user account A user account that does not permit logons. The account appears in the user account list of the User Manager or User Manager for Domains window and can be re-enabled at any time. *See also* user account.

discovery A process by which the Windows NT Net Logon service attempts to locate a domain controller running Windows NT Server in the trusted domain. Once a domain controller has been discovered, it is used for subsequent user account authentication.

discretionary access control Allows the network administrator to allow some users to connect to a resource or perform an action while preventing other users from doing so. *See also* discretionary access control list; system access control list (SACL).

discretionary access control list (DACL) The discretionary ACL is controlled by the owner of an object and specifies the access particular users or groups can have to that object. *See also* system access control list (SACL).

disjoint networks Networks that are not connected to each other.

disk configuration information The Windows NT registry includes the following information on the configuration of your disk(s): assigned drive letters, stripe sets, mirror sets, volume sets, and stripe sets with parity. Disk configuration can be changed by using Disk Administrator. If you choose to create an Emergency Repair Disk, disk configuration information will be stored there, as well as in the registry.

display filter Functions like a database query, allowing you to single out specific types of information. Because a display filter operates on data that has already been captured, it does not affect the contents of the Network Monitor capture buffer. *See also* capture buffer.

display password Required to be able to open previously saved capture (.cap) files in Network Monitor.

Distributed Component Object Model (DCOM) Use the DCOM Configuration tool to integrate client/server applications across multiple computers. DCOM can also be used to integrate robust Web browser applications. *See also* DCOM Configuration tool.

distributed server system In Windows NT, a system in which individual departments or workgroups set up and maintain their own remote access domains.

DLL *See* dynamic-link library.

DNS *See* Domain Name System.

DNS name servers In the DNS client/server model, the servers containing information about a portion of the DNS database, which makes computer names available to client resolvers querying for name resolution across the Internet. *See also* Domain Name System (DNS).

DNS service The service that provides domain name resolution. *See also* DNS name servers.

document A self-contained file created with an application and, if saved on disk, given a unique file name by which it can be retrieved. A document can be a text file, a spreadsheet, or an image file, for example.

document file A file that is associated with an application. When you open a document file, the application starts and loads the file. *See also* associate.

document file icon Represents a file that is associated with an application. When you double-click a document file icon, the application starts and loads the file. *See also* associate.

document icon Located at the left of a document window title bar, the document icon represents the open document. Clicking the document icon opens the window menu. Also known as the control menu box.

domain In Windows NT, a collection of computers, defined by the administrator of a Windows NT Server network, that share a common directory database. A domain provides access to the centralized user accounts and group accounts maintained by the domain administrator. Each domain has a unique name. *See also* directory database; user account; workgroup.

domain controller In a Windows NT Server domain, refers to the computer running Windows NT Server that manages all aspects of user-domain interactions, and uses information in the directory database to authenticate users logging on to domain accounts. One shared directory database is used to store security and user account information for the entire domain. A domain has one primary domain controller (PDC) and one or more backup domain controllers (BDCs). *See also* backup domain controller (BDC); directory database; member server; primary domain controller (PDC).

domain database *See* directory database.

domain model A grouping of one or more domains with administration and communication links between them that are arranged for the purpose of user and resource management.

domain name Part of the Domain Name System (DNS) naming structure, a domain name is the name by which a domain is known to the network. Domain names consist of a sequence of labels separated by periods. *See also* Domain Name System (DNS); fully qualified domain name (FQDN).

domain name space The database structure used by the Domain Name System (DNS). *See also* Domain Name System (DNS).

Domain Name System (DNS) Sometimes referred to as the BIND service in BSD UNIX, DNS offers a static, hierarchical name service for TCP/IP hosts. The network administrator configures the DNS with a list of host names and IP addresses, allowing users of workstations configured to query the DNS to specify remote systems by host names rather than IP addresses. For example, a workstation configured to use DNS name resolution could use the command **ping remotehost** rather than **ping 172.16.16.235** if the mapping for the system named **remotehost** was contained in the DNS database. DNS domains should not be confused with Windows NT networking domains. *See also* IP address; ping.

domain synchronization *See* synchronize.

dots per inch (DPI) The standard used to measure print device resolution. The greater the DPI, the better the resolution.

double-click To rapidly press and release a mouse button twice without moving the mouse. Double-clicking carries out an action, such as starting an application.

down level A term that refers to earlier operating systems, such as Windows for Workgroups or LAN Manager, that can still interoperate with Windows NT Workstation or Windows NT Server.

downloaded fonts Fonts that you send to your printer either before or during the printing of your documents. When you send a font to your printer, it is stored in printer memory until it is needed for printing. *See also* font; font types.

DPI *See* dots per inch.

drag To move an item on the screen by selecting the item and then pressing and holding down the mouse button while moving the mouse. For example, you can move a window to another location on the screen by dragging its title bar.

drive icon An icon in the All Folders column in Windows NT Explorer or the Names Column in My Computer that represents a disk drive on your system. Different icons depict floppy disk drives, hard disk drives, network drives, RAM drives, and CD-ROM drives.

driver *See* device driver.

drop folder In the Macintosh environment this refers to a folder for which you have the Make Changes permission but not the See Files or See Folders permission. You can copy files into a drop folder, but you cannot see what files and subfolders the drop folder contains.

DSDM Acronym for DDE share database manager. *See also* dynamic data exchange (DDE); Network DDE DSDM service.

DSMN *See* Directory Service Manager for NetWare.

DSN *See* Data Source Name.

DSR Acronym for Data Set Ready signal, used in serial communications. A DSR is sent by a modem to the computer to which it is attached to indicate that it is ready to operate. DSRs are hardware signals sent over line 6 in RS-232-C connections.

DTE *See* Data Terminal Equipment.

dual boot A computer that can boot two different operating systems. *See also* multiple boot.

DWORD A data type composed of hexadecimal data with a maximum allotted space of 4 bytes.

dynamic assignment The automatic assignment of TCP/IP properties in a changing network.

dynamic data exchange (DDE) A form of interprocess communication (IPC) implemented in the Microsoft Windows family of operating systems. Two or more programs that support dynamic data exchange (DDE) can exchange information and commands. *See also* interprocess communication (IPC).

Dynamic Host Configuration Protocol (DHCP) A protocol that offers dynamic configuration of IP addresses and related information. DHCP provides safe, reliable, and simple TCP/IP network configuration, prevents address conflicts, and helps conserve the use of IP addresses through centralized management of address allocation. *See also* IP address.

dynamic-link library (DLL) An operating system feature that allows executable routines (generally serving a specific function or set of functions) to be stored separately as files with .dll extensions and to be loaded only when needed by the program that calls them.

dynamic routing Dynamic routing automatically updates the routing tables, reducing administrative overhead (but increasing traffic in large networks). *See also* routing table.

dynamic Web pages Web pages that are derived or assembled only when the client requests them. Dynamic pages are used to deliver very current information, to deliver responses to forms and queries, and to provide a customized page. They are often associated with databases, such as SQL databases. *See also* static Web pages.

E

EISA *See* Extended Industry Standard Architecture.

embedded object Presents information, created in another application, which has been pasted inside your document. Information in the embedded object does not exist in another file outside your document.

EMS *See* Expanded Memory Specification.

encapsulated PostScript (EPS) file A file that prints at the highest possible resolution for your printer. An EPS file may print faster than other graphical representations. Some Windows NT and non-Windows NT graphical applications can import EPS files. *See also* font types; PostScript printer; print processor.

encryption The process of making information indecipherable to protect it from unauthorized viewing or use, especially during transmission or when it is stored on a transportable magnetic medium.

enterprise server Refers to the server to which multiple primary domain controllers (PDCs) in a large organization will replicate. *See also* primary domain controller (PDC).

environment variable A string consisting of environment information, such as a drive, path, or file name, associated with a symbolic name that can be used by Windows NT. To define environment variables, use System in Control Panel or use the **Set** command from the Windows NT command prompt.

EPS *See* encapsulated PostScript file.

error logging The process by which errors that cannot readily be corrected by the majority of end users are written to a file instead of being displayed on the screen. System administrators, support technicians, and users can use this log file to monitor the condition of the hardware in a computer running Windows NT to tune the configuration of the computer for better performance, and to debug problems as they occur.

event Any significant occurrence in the system or an application that requires users to be notified, or an entry to be added to a log.

Event Log service Records events in the system, security, and application logs. The Event Log service is located in Event Viewer.

exception A synchronous error condition resulting from the execution of a particular computer instruction. Exceptions can be either hardware-detected errors, such as division by zero, or software-detected errors, such as a guard-page violation.

Executive The Executive is the part of the Windows NT operating system that runs in kernel mode. *Kernel mode* is a privileged processor mode in which a thread has access to system memory and to hardware. (In contrast, *user mode* is a nonprivileged processor mode in which a thread can only access system resources by calling system services.) The Windows NT Executive provides process structure, thread scheduling, interprocess communication, memory management, object management, object security, interrupt processing, I/O capabilities, and networking. *See also* Hardware Abstraction Layer (HAL); Kernel.

Executive messages Two types of character-mode messages occur when the Windows NT Kernel detects an inconsistent condition from which it cannot recover: STOP messages and hardware-malfunction messages.

Character-mode STOP messages are always displayed on a full character-mode screen rather than in a Windows-mode message box. They are also uniquely identified by a hexadecimal number and a symbolic string.

Character-mode hardware-malfunction messages are caused by a hardware condition detected by the processor.

The Executive displays a Windows-mode STATUS message box when it detects conditions within a process (generally, an application) that you should know about.

expand To show hidden directory levels in the directory tree. With My Computer or Windows NT Explorer, directories that can expand have plus-sign icons which you click to expand.

expanded memory A type of memory, up to 8 megabytes, that can be added to an 8086 or 8088 computer, or to an 80286, 80386, 80486, or Pentium computer. The use of expanded memory is defined by the Expanded Memory Specification (EMS). Note: Windows NT requires an 80486 or higher computer.

Expanded Memory Specification (EMS)
Describes a technique for adding memory to IBM PC systems. EMS bypasses the limits on the maximum amount of usable memory in a computer system by supporting memory boards containing a number of 16K banks of RAM that can be enabled or disabled by software. *See also* memory.

Explorer *See* Windows NT Explorer.

export path In directory replication, a path from which subdirectories, and the files in those subdirectories, are automatically exported from an export server. *See also* directory replication.

export server In directory replication, a server from which a master set of directories is exported to specified servers or workstations (called import computers) in the same or other domains. *See also* directory replication.

Extended Industry Standard Architecture (EISA)
A 32-bit bus standard introduced in 1988 by a consortium of nine computer industry companies. EISA maintains compatibility with the earlier Industry Standard Architecture (ISA) but provides for additional features.

extended memory Memory beyond one megabyte in 80286, 80386, 80486, and Pentium computers. Note: Windows NT requires an 80486 or higher computer.

extended partition Created from free space on a hard disk, an extended partition can be subpartitioned into zero or more logical drives. Only one of the four partitions allowed per physical disk can be an extended partition, and no primary partition needs to be present to create an extended partition. *See also* free space; logical drive; primary partition.

extensible counters Performance Monitor counters that are not installed with Windows NT. Extensible counters typically are installed independently. Extensible counters should be monitored to make certain that they are working properly.

extension A file name extension usually indicates the type of file or directory, or the type of application associated with a file. In MS-DOS, this includes a period and up to three characters at the end of a file name. Windows NT supports long file names, up to the file name limit of 255 characters.

extension-type association The association of an MS-DOS file name extension with a Macintosh file type and file creator. Extension-type associations allow users of the PC and Macintosh versions of the same application to share the same data files on the server. Services for Macintosh has many predefined extension-type associations. *See also* name mapping.

external command A command that is stored in its own file and loaded from disk when you use the command.

F

family set A collection of related tapes containing several backup sets. *See also* backup set.

FAT *See* file allocation table.

fault tolerance Ensures data integrity when hardware failures occur. In Windows NT, fault tolerance is provided by the Ftdisk.sys driver. In Disk Administrator, fault tolerance is provided using mirror sets, stripe sets with parity, and volume sets. *See also* mirror set; stripe sets with parity; volume set.

FCB *See* file control block.

Fiber Distributed Data Interface (FDDI) A type of network media designed to be used with fiber-optic cabling. *See also* LocalTalk; Token Ring.

file A collection of information that has been given a name and is stored on a disk. This information can be a document or an application.

file allocation table (FAT) A table or list maintained by some operating systems to keep track of the status of various segments of disk space used for file storage. Also referred to as the FAT file system.

File and Print Services for NetWare (FPNW) A Windows NT Server component that enables a computer running Windows NT Server to provide file and print services directly to NetWare-compatible client computers.

file control block (FCB) A small block of memory temporarily assigned by a computer's operating system to hold information about a file that has been opened for use. An FCB typically contains such information as the file's identification, its location on disk, and a pointer that marks the user's current (or last) position in the file.

file creator A four-character sequence that tells the Macintosh Finder the name of the application that created a file. With Services for Macintosh, you can create extension-type associations that map PC file name extensions with Macintosh file creators and file types. These associations allow both PC and Macintosh users to share the same data files on the server. *See also* extension-type association.

file fork One of two subfiles of a Macintosh file. When Macintosh files are stored on a computer running Windows NT Server, each fork is stored as a separate file. Each fork can be independently opened by a Macintosh user.

file name The name of a file. MS-DOS supports the 8.3 naming convention of up to eight characters followed by a period and a three-character extension. Windows NT supports the FAT and NTFS file systems with file names up to 255 characters. Because MS-DOS cannot recognize long file names, Windows NT Server automatically translates long names of files and folders to 8.3 names for MS-DOS users. *See also* long name; name mapping; short name.

file name extension The characters that follow the period in a file name, following the FAT naming conventions. Filename extensions can have as many as three characters and are often used to identify the type of file and the application used to create the file (for example, spreadsheet files created by Microsoft Excel have the extension .xls). With Services for Macintosh, you can create extension-type associations that map PC file name extensions with Macintosh file creators and types.

File Replication service A Windows NT service that allows specified file(s) to be replicated to remote systems, ensuring that copies on each system are kept in synchronization. The system that maintains the master copy is called the exporter, and the systems that receive updates are known as importers.

File Server for Macintosh service A Services for Macintosh service that enables Macintosh clients and PC clients to share files. Also called MacFile.

file sharing The ability for a computer running Windows NT to share parts (or all) of its local file system(s) with remote computers. An administrator creates share points by using the file sharing command in My Computer or Windows NT Explorer or by using the **net share** command from the command prompt.

file system In an operating system, the overall structure in which files are named, stored, and organized. NTFS and FAT are types of file systems.

File Transfer Protocol (FTP) A service supporting file transfers between local and remote systems that support this protocol. FTP supports several commands that allow bidirectional transfer of binary and ASCII files between systems. The FTP Server service is part of the Internet Information Server. The FTP client is installed with TCP/IP connectivity utilities.

file type In the Macintosh environment, this refers to a four-character sequence that identifies the type of a Macintosh file. The file type and file creator are used by the Macintosh Finder to determine the appropriate desktop icon for that file.

find tab Displays the words you can use to search for related topics. Use this tab to look for topics related to a particular word. It is located in the Help button bar near the top of the Help window.

firewall A system or combination of systems that enforces a boundary between two or more networks and keeps intruders out of private networks. Firewalls serve as virtual barriers to passing packets from one network to another.

flat name space A naming system in which computer names are created from a short sequence of characters without any additional structure superimposed.

floppy disk A disk that can be inserted in and removed from a disk drive. Floppies are most commonly available in a 3.5- or 5.25-inch format.

flow control An exchange of signals, over specific wires, in which each device signals its readiness to send or receive data.

folder A grouping of files or other folders, graphically represented by a folder icon, in both the Windows NT and Macintosh environments. A folder is analogous to a PC's file system directory, and many folders are, in fact, directories. A folder may contain other folders as well as file objects. *See also* directory.

font A graphic design applied to a collection of numbers, symbols, and characters. A font describes a certain typeface along with other qualities such as size, spacing, and pitch. *See also* font set; font types.

font set A collection of font sizes for one font, customized for a particular display and printer. Font sets determine what text looks like on the screen and when printed. *See also* font.

font types:
  device fonts Reside in the hardware of your print device. They can be built into the print device itself or can be provided by a font cartridge or font card.

downloadable soft fonts Fonts that are stored on disk and downloaded as needed to the print device.

plotter fonts A font created by a series of dots connected by lines. Plotter fonts can be scaled to any size and are most often printed on plotters. Some dot-matrix printers also support plotter fonts.

PostScript fonts Fonts that are defined in terms of the PostScript page-description language rules from Adobe Systems. When a document displayed in a screen font is sent to a PostScript printer, the printer uses the Post-Script version if the font exists. If the font doesn't exist but a version is installed on the computer, that font is downloaded. If there is no PostScript font installed in either the printer or the computer, the bitmapped font is translated into PostScript and the printer prints text using the bitmapped font.

raster fonts Fonts that are stored as bitmaps. If a print device does not support raster fonts, it will not print them. Raster fonts cannot be scaled or rotated.

screen fonts Windows NT fonts that can be translated for output to the print device. Most screen fonts (including TrueType fonts) can be printed as well.

TrueType fonts Device-independent fonts that can be reproduced on all print devices. True-Type fonts are stored as outlines and can be scaled and rotated.

vector fonts Fonts that are useful on devices such as pen plotters that cannot reproduce bitmaps. They can be scaled to any size or aspect ratio. (*See also* plotter fonts, earlier in this entry.)

fork *See* data fork; file fork; resource fork.

FPNW *See* File and Print Services for NetWare.

FQDN *See* fully qualified domain name.

frame In synchronous communication, a package of information transmitted as a single unit from one device to another. *See also* capture.

Frame Relay A synchronous High-level Data Link Control (HDLC) protocol–based network that sends data in HDLC packets. *See also* High-level Data Link Control (HDLC).

framing rules Are established between a remote computer and the server, allowing continued communication (frame transfer) to occur. *See also* frame.

free space Free space is an unused and unformatted portion of a hard disk that can be partitioned or subpartitioned. Free space within an extended partition is available for the creation of logical drives. Free space that is not within an extended partition is available for the creation of a partition, with a maximum of four partitions allowed per disk. *See also* extended partition; logical drive; primary partition.

FTP *See* File Transfer Protocol.

full name A user's complete name, usually consisting of the last name, first name, and middle initial. The full name is information that can be maintained by User Manager and User Manager for Domains as part of the information identifying and defining a user account. *See also* user account.

full-screen application A non–Windows NT application that is displayed in the entire screen, rather than a window, when running in the Windows NT environment.

full synchronization Occurs when a copy of the entire database directory is sent to a backup domain controller (BDC). Full synchronization is performed automatically when changes have been deleted from the change log before replication takes place, and when a new BDC is added to a domain. *See also* backup domain controller (BDC); directory database.

fully qualified domain name (FQDN) Part of the TCP/IP naming convention known as the Domain Name System, DNS computer names consist of two parts: host names with their domain names appended to them. For example, a host with host name **corp001** and DNS domain name **trey-research.com** has an FQDN of **corp001.trey-research.com**. (DNS domains should not be confused with Windows NT networking domains.) *See also* Domain Name System (DNS).

G

gateway Describes a system connected to multiple physical TCP/IP networks, capable of routing or delivering IP packets between them. A gateway translates between different transport protocols or data formats (for example IPX and IP) and is generally added to a network primarily for its translation ability. Also referred to as an IP router. *See also* IP address; IP router.

Gateway Service for NetWare Included with Windows NT Server, enables a computer running Windows NT Server to connect to NetWare servers. Creating a gateway enables computers running only Microsoft client software to access NetWare resources through the gateway. *See also* gateway.

General MIDI A MIDI specification controlled by the MIDI Manufacturers Association (MMA). The specification provides guidelines that authors of MIDI files can use to create files that sound the same across a variety of different synthesizers.

global account For Windows NT Server, a normal user account in a user's domain. Most user accounts are global accounts. If there are multiple domains in the network, it is best if each user in the network has only one user account in only one domain, and each user's access to other domains is accomplished through the establishment of domain trust relationships. *See also* local account; trust relationship.

global group For Windows NT Server, a group that can be used in its own domain, member servers and workstations of the domain, and trusting domains. In all those places it can be granted rights and permissions and can become a member of local groups. However, it can only contain user accounts from its own domain. Global groups provide a way to create handy sets of users from inside the domain, available for use both in and out of the domain.

Global groups cannot be created or maintained on computers running Windows NT Workstation. However, for Windows NT Workstation computers that participate in a domain, domain global groups can be granted rights and permissions at those workstations, and can become members of local groups at those workstations. *See also* domain; group; local group; trust relationship.

globally unique identifier (GUID) *See* universally unique identifier (UUID).

Gopher A hierarchical system for finding and retrieving information from the Internet or an intranet. Similar to FTP, Gopher uses a menu system and enables links to other servers.

group In User Manager or User Manager for Domains, an account containing other accounts that are called members. The permissions and rights granted to a group are also provided to its members, making groups a convenient way to grant common capabilities to collections of user accounts. For Windows NT Workstation, groups are managed with User Manager. For Windows NT Server, groups are managed with User Manager for Domains. *See also* built-in groups; global group; local group; user account.

group account A collection of user accounts. Giving a user account membership in a group gives that user all of the rights and permissions granted to the group. *See also* local account; user account.

group category One of three categories of users to which you can assign Macintosh permissions for a folder. The permissions assigned to the group category are available to the group associated with the folder.

group memberships The groups to which a user account belongs. Permissions and rights granted to a group are also provided to its members. In most cases, the actions a user can perform in Windows NT are determined by the group memberships of the user account the user is logged on to. *See also* group.

group name A unique name identifying a local group or a global group to Windows NT. A group's name cannot be identical to any other group name or user name of its own domain or computer. *See also* global group; local group.

guest Users of Services for Macintosh who do not have a user account or who do not provide a password are logged on as a guest, using a user account with guest privileges. When a Macintosh user assigns permissions to everyone, those permissions are given to the group's guests and users.

guest account On computers running Windows NT Workstation or Windows NT Server, a built-in account used for logons by people who do not have a user account on the computer or domain or in any of the domains trusted by the computer's domain.

Guest privilege One of three privilege levels that you can assign to a Windows NT user account. The guest account used for Macintosh guest logons must have the Guest privilege. *See also* Administrator privilege; user account; User privilege.

GUID Acronym for globally unique identifier. *See* universally unique identifier (UUID).

H

HAL *See* Hardware Abstraction Layer.

handle A handle is a value used to uniquely identify a resource so that a program can access it.

In the registry, each of the first-level key names begins with HKEY_ to indicate to software developers that this is a handle that can be read by a program.

handshaking Refers to flow control in serial communication, which defines a method for the print device to tell Windows NT that its buffer is full. *See also* buffer.

Hardware Abstraction Layer (HAL) A thin layer of software provided by the hardware manufacturer that hides, or abstracts, hardware differences from higher layers of the operating system.

Through the filter provided by the HAL, different types of hardware all look alike to the rest of the operating system. This allows Windows NT to be portable from one hardware platform to another. The HAL also provides routines that allow a single device driver to support the same device on all platforms.

The HAL works closely with the Kernel.

See also Executive; Kernel.

Hardware Compatibility List (HCL) The Windows NT Hardware Compatibility List lists the devices supported by Windows NT. The latest version of the HCL can be downloaded from the Microsoft Web page (microsoft.com) on the Internet.

HCL *See* Hardware Compatibility List.

HDLC *See* High-level Data Link Control.

heterogeneous environment An internetwork with servers and workstations running different operating systems, such as Windows NT, Macintosh, or Novell NetWare, using a mix of different transport protocols.

hexadecimal A base-16 number system that consists of the digits 0 through 9 and the uppercase and lowercase letters A (equivalent to decimal 10) through F (equivalent to decimal 15).

High-level Data Link Control (HDLC) A protocol that governs information transfer. Under the HDLC protocol, messages are transmitted in units called frames, each of which can contain a variable amount of data but which must be organized in a particular way.

high memory area (HMA) The first 64 KB of extended memory (often referred to as HMA). *See also* memory.

High-Performance File System (HPFS) The file system designed for the OS/2 version 1.2 operating system.

hive A section of the registry that appears as a file on your hard disk. The registry subtree is divided into hives (named for their resemblance to the cellular structure of a beehive). A hive is a discrete body of keys, subkeys, and values that is rooted at the top of the registry hierarchy. A hive is backed by a single file and a .log file, which are in the *systemroot*\System32\Config or the *systemroot*\Profiles*user_name* folder. By default, most hive files (Default, SAM, Security, and System) are stored in the *systemroot* \System32\Config folder.

The *systemroot*\Profiles folder contains the user profile for each user of the computer. Because a hive is a file, it can be moved from one system to another but can only be edited by using a Registry Editor.

HMA *See* high memory area.

h-node A NetBIOS implementation that uses the p-node protocol first, then the b-node protocol if the name service is unavailable. For registration, it uses the b-node protocol, then the p-node protocol. *See also* NetBIOS; p-node; registration.

home directory A directory that is accessible to the user and contains files and programs for that user. A home directory can be assigned to an individual user or can be shared by many users.

home page The initial page of information for a collection of pages. The starting point for a Web site or section of a Web site is often referred to as the home page. Individuals also post pages that are called home pages.

hop Refers to the next router. In IP routing, packets are always forwarded one router at a time. Packets often hop from router to router before reaching their destination. *See also* IP address; packet; router.

host Any device that is attached to the network and uses TCP/IP. *See also* Transmission Control Protocol/Internet Protocol (TCP/IP).

host group A set of zero or more hosts identified by a single IP destination address. *See also* host; IP address.

host ID The portion of the IP address that identifies a computer within a particular network ID. *See also* IP address; network ID.

host name The name of a device on a network. For a device on a Windows or Windows NT network, this can be the same as the computer name, but it may not be. The host name must be in the host table or be known by a DNS server for that host to be found by another computer attempting to communicate with it. *See also* Domain Name System (DNS); host table.

HOSTS file A local text file in the same format as the 4.3 Berkeley Software Distribution (BSD) UNIX \etc\hosts file. This file maps host names to IP addresses. In Windows NT, this file is stored in the *\systemroot*\System32\Drivers\Etc directory. *See also* IP address.

host table The HOSTS and LMHOSTS files, which contain mappings of known IP addresses mapped to host names.

HPFS *See* High-Performance File System.

HTML *See* Hypertext Markup Language.

HTTP *See* Hypertext Transport Protocol.

HTTP keep-alives An optimizing feature of the HTTP service. HTTP keep-alives maintain a connection even after the initial connection request is completed. This keeps the connection active and available for subsequent requests. HTTP keep-alives were implemented to avoid the substantial cost of establishing and terminating connections. Both the client and the server must support keep-alives. Keep-alives are supported by Internet Information Server version 1.0 and later and by Microsoft Internet Explorer version 2.0 and later. *See also* TCP/IP keep-alives.

hue The position of a color along the color spectrum. For example, green is between yellow and blue. To set this attribute, use Desktop in Control Panel.

hyperlink A way of jumping to another place on the Internet. Hyperlinks usually appear in a different format from regular text. You initiate the jump by clicking the link.

Hypertext Markup Language (HTML) A simple markup language used to create hypertext documents that are portable from one platform to another. HTML files are simple ASCII text files with codes embedded (indicated by markup tags) to indicate formatting and hypertext links. HTML is used for formatting documents on the World Wide Web.

Hypertext Transport Protocol (HTTP) The underlying protocol by which WWW clients and servers communicate. HTTP is an application-level protocol for distributed, collaborative, hypermedia information systems. It is a generic, stateless, object-oriented protocol. A feature of HTTP is the typing and negotiation of data representation, allowing systems to be built independently of the data being transferred.

I

ICMP *See* Internet Control Message Protocol.

icon A graphical representation of an element in Windows NT, such as a disk drive, directory, group, application, or document. Click the icon to enlarge an application icon to a window when you want to use the application. Within applications, there are also toolbar icons for commands such as cut, copy, and paste.

IDC *See* Internet Database Connector.

IDE *See* integrated device electronics.

IETF *See* Internet Engineering Task Force.

IGMP *See* Internet Group Management Protocol.

IIS *See* Internet Information Server.

IIS object cache An area of virtual memory that the IIS process uses to store frequently used objects, such as open file handles and directory listings. The IIS object cache is part of the working set of the IIS process, Inetinfo.exe, and it can be paged to disk.

IMC *See* Internet Mail Connector.

impersonation Impersonation occurs when Windows NT Server allows one process to take on the security attributes of another.

import To create a package by inserting an existing file into Object Packager. When you import a file, the icon of the application you used to create the file appears in the Appearance window, and the name of the file appears in the Contents window. *See also* package.

import computers In directory replication, the servers or workstations that receive copies of the master set of directories from an export server. *See also* directory replication; export server.

import path In directory replication, the path to which imported subdirectories, and the files in those subdirectories, will be stored on an import computer. *See also* directory replication; import computers.

Inetinfo A process containing the FTP, Gopher, and HTTP services. This process is about 400 KB in size. In addition to the FTP, Gopher, and HTTP services, this process contains the shared thread pool, cache, logging, and SNMP services of Internet Information Server.

input/output activity (I/O) Read or write actions that your computer performs. Your computer performs a "read" when you type information on your keyboard or you select and choose items by using your mouse. Also, when you open a file, your computer reads the disk on which the file is located to find and open it.

Your computer performs a "write" whenever it stores, sends, prints, or displays information. For example, your computer performs a write when it stores information on a disk, displays information on your screen, or sends information through a modem or to a printer. *See also* I/O addresses.

input/output control (IOCTL) An IOCTL command enables a program to communicate directly with a device driver. This is done, for example, by sending a string of control information recognized by the driver. None of the information passed from the program to the device driver is sent to the device itself (in other words, the control string sent to a printer driver is not displayed on the printer).

insertion point The place where text will be inserted when you type. The insertion point usually appears as a flashing vertical bar in an application's window or in a dialog box.

integrated device electronics (IDE) A type of disk-drive interface in which the controller electronics reside on the drive itself, eliminating the need for a separate adapter card.

Integrated Services Digital Network (ISDN)
A type of telephone line used to enhance WAN speeds, ISDN lines can transmit at speeds of 64 or 128 kilobits per second, as opposed to standard telephone lines, which typically transmit at only 9600 bits per second (bps). An ISDN line must be installed by the telephone company at both the server site and the remote site. *See also* bits per second (bps).

interactive logon A network logon from a computer keyboard, when the user types information in the **Logon Information** dialog box displayed by the computer's operating system. *See also* remote logon.

intermediary devices Microsoft RAS supports various kinds of intermediary devices (security hosts and switches) between the remote access client and the remote access server. These devices include a modem-pool switch or security host. *See also* Remote Access Service (RAS).

internal command Commands that are stored in the file Cmd.exe and that reside in memory at all times.

internet In Windows NT, a collection of two or more private networks, or private inter-enterprise TCP/IP networks.

In Macintosh terminology, refers to two or more physical networks connected by routers, which maintain a map of the physical networks on the internet and forward data received from one physical network to other physical networks. Network users in an internet can share information and network devices. You can use an internet with Services for Macintosh by connecting two or more AppleTalk networks to a computer running Windows NT Server.

Internet The global network of networks. *See also* World Wide Web (WWW).

Internet Assigned Numbers Authority (IANA) The central coordinator for the assignment of unique parameter values for Internet protocols. IANA is chartered by the Internet Society (ISOC) and the Federal Network Council (FNC) to act as the clearinghouse to assign and coordinate the use of numerous Internet protocol parameters. Contact IANA at http://www.iana.org/iana/.

Internet Assistant Several Internet Assistant add-on software components are available for Microsoft Office products. Each Internet Assistant adds functionality that is relevant to creating content for the Internet. For example, Internet Assistant for Microsoft Word enables Word to create HTML documents from within Microsoft Word.

Internet Control Message Protocol (ICMP)
A maintenance protocol in the TCP/IP suite, required in every TCP/IP implementation, that allows two nodes on an IP network to share IP status and error information. ICMP is used by the ping utility to determine the readability of a remote system. *See also* ping; Transmission Control Protocol/Internet Protocol (TCP/IP).

Internet Database Connector (IDC) Provides access to databases for Internet Information Server by using ODBC. The Internet Database Connector is contained in Httpodbc.dll, which is an Internet Server API DLL.

Internet Engineering Task Force (IETF) A consortium that introduces procedures for new technology on the Internet. IETF specifications are released in documents called Requests for Comments (RFCs). *See also* Requests for Comments (RFCs).

Internet Group Management Protocol (IGMP)
A protocol used by workgroup software products and supported by Microsoft TCP/IP.

Internet group name A name known by a DNS server that includes a list of the specific addresses of systems that have registered the name. *See also* Domain Name System (DNS).

Internet Information Server (IIS) A network file and application server that supports multiple protocols. Primarily, Internet Information Server transmits information in Hypertext Markup Language (HTML) pages by using the Hypertext Transport Protocol (HTTP).

Internet Mail Connector (IMC) The Internet Mail Connector is a component of Microsoft Exchange Server that runs as a Windows NT Server service. You can use the Internet Mail Connector to exchange information with other systems that use the Simple Mail Transfer Protocol (SMTP).

Internet Network Information Center (InterNIC) The coordinator for DNS registration. To register domain names and obtain IP addresses, contact InterNIC at http://internic.net.

Internet Protocol (IP) The messenger protocol of TCP/IP, responsible for addressing and sending TCP packets over the network. IP provides a best-effort, connectionless delivery system that does not guarantee that packets arrive at their destination or that they are received in the sequence in which they were sent. *See also* packet; Transmission Control Protocol (TCP); Transmission Control Protocol/Internet Protocol (TCP/IP).

Internet Protocol Control Protocol (IPCP) Specified by RFC 1332. Responsible for configuring, enabling, and disabling the IP protocol modules on both ends of the point-to-point (PPP) link. *See also* Point-to-Point Protocol (PPP); Requests for Comments (RFCs).

Internet Relay Chat (IRC) A protocol that enables two or more people, each in remote locations, who are connected to an IRC server to hold real-time conversations. IRC is defined in RFC 1459.

Internet router A device that connects networks and directs network information to other networks, usually choosing the most efficient route through other routers. *See also* router.

Internet Server Application Programming Interface (ISAPI) An API for developing extensions to the Microsoft Internet Information Server and other HTTP servers that support ISAPI. *See also* application programming interface (API).

Internet service provider (ISP) A company or educational institution that enables remote users to access the Internet by providing dial-up connections or installing leased lines.

internetworks Networks that connect local area networks (LANs) together.

interprocess communication (IPC) The ability, provided by a multitasking operating system, of one task or process to exchange data with another. Common IPC methods include pipes, semaphores, shared memory, queues, signals, and mailboxes. *See also* named pipe; queue.

interrupt An asynchronous operating system condition that disrupts normal execution and transfers control to an interrupt handler. Interrupts can be issued by both software and hardware devices requiring service from the processor. When software issues an interrupt, it calls an interrupt service routine (ISR). When hardware issues an interrupt, it signals an interrupt request (IRQ) line.

interrupt moderation A Windows NT performance optimizing feature that diverts interrupts from the network adapters when the rate of interrupts is very high. The system accumulates the interrupts in a buffer for later processing. Standard interrupt processing is resumed when the interrupt rate returns to normal.

interrupt request line (IRQ) A hardware line over which devices can send signals to get the attention of the processor when the device is ready to accept or send information. Typically, each device connected to the computer uses a separate IRQ.

intranet A TCP/IP network that uses Internet technology. May be connected to the Internet. *See also* Internet; Transmission Control Protocol/Internet Protocol (TCP/IP).

I/O addresses Locations within the input/output address space of your computer, used by a device such as a printer or modem. *See* also input/output activity (I/O).

IOCTL *See* input/output control.

IP *See* Internet Protocol.

IP address Used to identify a node on a network and to specify routing information. Each node on the network must be assigned a unique IP address, which is made up of the *network ID*, plus a unique *host ID* assigned by the network administrator. This address is typically represented in dotted-decimal notation, with the decimal value of each octet separated by a period (for example, 138.57.7.27).

In Windows NT, the IP address can be configured statically on the client or configured dynamically through DHCP. *See also* Dynamic Host Configuration Protocol (DHCP); node; octet.

IPC *See* interprocess communication.

IPCP *See* Internet Protocol Control Protocol.

IP datagrams The basic Internet Protocol (IP) information unit. *See also* datagram; Internet Protocol (IP).

IP router A system connected to multiple physical TCP/IP networks that can route or deliver IP packets between the networks. *See also* packet; routing; Transmission Control Protocol/Internet Protocol (TCP/IP).

IPX *See* IPX/SPX.

IPX/SPX Acronym for Internetwork Packet Exchange/Sequenced Packet Exchange, which is a set of transport protocols used in Novell NetWare networks. Windows NT implements IPX through NWLink.

IRC *See* Internet Relay Chat.

IRQ *See* interrupt request line.

ISAPI *See* Internet Server Application Programming Interface.

ISDN *See* Integrated Services Digital Network.

ISDN interface card Similar in function to a modem, an ISDN card is hardware that enables a computer to connect to other computers and networks on an Integrated Services Digital Network.

ISO Abbreviation for the International Standards Organization, an international association of member countries, each of which is represented by its leading standard-setting organization—for example ANSI (American National Standards Institute) for the United States. The ISO works to establish global standards for communications and information exchange.

ISP *See* Internet service provider.

iteration One of the three key concepts in DNS name resolution. A local name server keeps the burden of processing on itself and passes only iterative resolution requests to other name servers. An iterative resolution request tells the name server that the requester expects the best answer the name server can provide without help from others. If the name server has the requested data, it returns it, otherwise it returns pointers to name servers that are more likely to have the answer. *See also* Domain Name System (DNS).

In programming, iteration is the art of executing one or more statements or instructions repeatedly.

J

jump Text, graphics, or parts of graphics that provide links to other Help topics or to more information about the current topic. The pointer changes shape whenever it is over a jump. If you click a jump that is linked to another topic, that topic appears in the Help window. If you click a jump that is linked to more information, the information appears in a pop-up window on top of the main Help window.

K

keep-alives *See* HTTP keep-alives; TCP/IP keep-alives.

Kermit Protocol for transferring binary files that is somewhat slower than XModem/CRC. However, Kermit allows you to transmit and receive either seven or eight data bits per character. *See also* XModem/CRC.

Kernel The Windows NT Kernel is the part of the Windows NT Executive that manages the processor. It performs thread scheduling and dispatching, interrupt and exception handling, and multiprocessor synchronization. The Kernel synchronizes activities among Executive-level subcomponents, such as I/O Manager and Process Manager. It also provides primitive objects to the Windows NT Executive, which uses them to create User-mode objects. The Kernel works closely with the Hardware Abstraction Layer (HAL). *See also* Executive; Hardware Abstraction Layer (HAL).

Kernel debugger The Windows NT Kernel debugger (KD) is a 32-bit application that is used to debug the Kernel and device drivers, and to log the events leading up to a Windows NT Executive STOP, STATUS, or hardware-malfunction message.

The Kernel debugger runs on another Windows NT host computer that is connected to your Windows NT target computer. The two computers send debugging (troubleshooting) information back and forth through a communications port that must be running at the same baud rate on each computer.

Kernel driver A driver that accesses hardware. *See also* device driver.

key A folder that appears in the left pane of a Registry Editor window. A key can contain subkeys and value entries. For example: Environment is a key of HKEY_CURRENT_USER. *See also* subkey.

keyboard buffer A temporary storage area in memory that keeps track of keys you typed, even if the computer did not immediately respond to the keys when you typed them.

key map A mapping assignment that translates key values on synthesizers that do not conform to General MIDI standards. Key maps ensure that the appropriate percussion instrument is played or the appropriate octave for a melodic instrument is played when a MIDI file is played. *See also* Musical Instrument Digital Interface (MIDI).

kiosk A computer, connected to the Internet, made available to users in a commonly accessible location.

L

LAN *See* local area network.

LastKnownGood (LKG) control set The most recent control set that correctly started the system and resulted in a successful startup. The control set is saved as the LKG control set when you have a successful logon. *See also* current control set.

lease In Windows NT, the network administrator controls how long IP addresses are assigned by specifying lease durations that specify how long a computer can use an assigned IP address before having to renew the lease with the DHCP server. *See also* Dynamic Host Configuration Protocol (DHCP); IP address.

leased line A high-capacity line (most often a telephone line) dedicated to network connections.

license group License groups show a relationship (also known as a mapping) between users and computers. A license group comprises a single descriptive name for the group, a specified number of Per-Seat licenses assigned to the group, and a specific list of users who are members of the group.

line printer daemon (LPD) A line printer daemon (LPD) service on the print server receives documents from line printer remote (LPR) utilities running on client systems.

linked object A representation or placeholder for an object that is inserted into a destination document. The object still exists in the source file and, when it is changed, the linked object is updated to reflect these changes.

list box In a dialog box, a type of box that lists available choices—for example, a list of all files in a directory. If all of the choices do not fit in the list box, there is a scroll bar.

LMHOSTS file A local text file that maps IP addresses to the computer names of Windows NT networking computers outside the local subnet. In Windows NT, this file is stored in the *systemroot* \System32\Drivers\Etc directory. *See also* IP address; subnet.

local account For Windows NT Server, a user account provided in a domain for a user whose global account is not in a trusted domain. Not required where trust relationships exist between domains. *See also* global account; trust relationship; user account.

local area network (LAN) A group of computers and other devices dispersed over a relatively limited area and connected by a communications link that enables any device to interact with any other on the network.

local group For Windows NT Workstation, a group that can be granted permissions and rights only for its own workstation. However, it can contain user accounts from its own computer and (if the workstation participates in a domain) user accounts and global groups both from its own domain and from trusted domains.

For Windows NT Server, a group that can be granted permissions and rights only for the domain controllers of its own domain. However, it can contain user accounts and global groups both from its own domain and from trusted domains.

Local groups provide a way to create handy sets of users from both inside and outside the domain, to be used only at domain controllers of the domain. *See also* global group; group; trust relationship.

local guest logon Takes effect when a user logs on interactively at a computer running Window NT Workstation or at a member server running Windows NT Server, and specifies Guest as the user name in the **Logon Information** dialog box. *See also* interactive logon.

Local Mail Delivery Agent The component of the SMTP server that processes messages that have been received by the SMTP server and downloads the messages to the user's local computer.

local printer A printer that is directly connected to one of the ports on your computer. *See also* port.

LocalTalk The name given by Apple Computer to the Apple networking hardware built into every Macintosh. LocalTalk includes the cables and connector boxes that connect components and network devices that are part of the Apple-Talk network system. LocalTalk was formerly known as the AppleTalk Personal Network.

local user profiles User profiles that are created automatically on the computer at logon the first time a user logs on to a computer running Windows NT Workstation or Windows NT Server.

lock A method used to manage certain features of subdirectory replication by the export server. You can lock a subdirectory to prevent it from being exported to any import computers, or use locks to prevent imports to subdirectories on an import computer. *See also* directory replication; export server; import computers; subtree.

log books Kept by the system administrator to record the backup methods, dates, and contents of each tape in a backup set. *See also* backup set; backup types.

log files Created by Windows NT Backup and contain a record of the date the tapes were created and the names of files and directories successfully backed up and restored. Performance Monitor also creates log files.

logical drive A subpartition of an extended partition on a hard disk. *See also* extended partition.

Logical Unit (LU) A preset unit containing all of the configuration information needed for a user or a program to establish a session with a host or peer computer. *See also* host; peer.

log off To stop using the network and remove your user name from active use until you log on again.

log on To provide a user name and password that identifies you to the network.

logon hours For Windows NT Server, a definition of the days and hours during which a user account can connect to a server. When a user is connected to a server and the logon hours are exceeded, the user will either be disconnected from all server connections or allowed to remain connected but denied any new connections.

logon script A file that can be assigned to user accounts. Typically a batch program, a logon script runs automatically every time the user logs on. It can be used to configure a user's working environment at every logon, and it allows an administrator to affect a user's environment without managing all aspects of it. A logon script can be assigned to one or more user accounts. *See also* batch program.

logon script path When a user logs on, the computer authenticating the logon locates the specified logon script (if one has been assigned to that user account) by following that computer's local logon script path (usually C:\Winnt \System32\Repl\Imports\Scripts). *See also* authentication; logon script.

logon workstations In Windows NT Server, the computers from which a user is allowed to log on.

long name A folder name or file name longer than the 8.3 file name standard (up to eight characters followed by a period and a three-character extension) of the FAT file system. Windows NT Server automatically translates long names of files and folders to 8.3 names for MS-DOS users.

Macintosh users can assign long names to files and folders on the server, and by using Services for Macintosh, you can assign long names to Macintosh-accessible volumes when you create them. *See also* file allocation table (FAT); file name; name mapping; short name.

loopback address The IP address 127.0.0.1, which has been specified by the Internet Engineering Task Force as the IP address to use in conjunction with a loopback driver to route outgoing packets back to the source computer. *See also* loopback driver.

loopback driver A network driver that allows the packets to bypass the network adapter completely and be returned directly to the computer that is performing the test. *See also* loopback address.

LPD *See* line printer daemon.

LPR Acronym for line printer remote. *See also* line printer daemon.

LU *See* Logical Unit.

luminosity The brightness of a color on a scale from black to white on your monitor.

M

MAC *See* media access control.

MAC address A unique 48-bit number assigned to the network adapter by the manufacturer. MAC addresses (which are physical addresses) are used for mapping in TCP/IP network communication. *See also* Address Resolution Protocol (ARP); ARP request packet; media access control (MAC).

MacFile *See* File Server for Macintosh service.

MacFile menu The menu that appears in Windows NT Server when Services for Macintosh is set up. You can create Macintosh-accessible volumes, and set permissions and other options by using commands on this menu.

Macintosh-accessible volume Storage space on the server used for folders and files of Macintosh users. A Macintosh-accessible volume is equivalent to a shared directory for PC users. Each Macintosh-accessible volume on a computer running Windows NT Server will correspond to a directory. Both PC users and Macintosh users can be given access to files located in a directory that is designated as both a shared directory and a Macintosh-accessible volume.

Macintosh-style permissions Directory and volume permissions that are similar to the access privileges used on a Macintosh.

MacPrint *See* Print Server for Macintosh.

Mac volume *See* Macintosh-accessible volume.

Mail Server (MailSrv) The MailSrv utility no longer ships with the *Windows NT Server Resource Kit*.

Make Changes The Macintosh-style permission that gives users the right to make changes to a folder's contents; for example, modifying, renaming, moving, creating, and deleting files. When Services for Macintosh translates access privileges into Windows NT Server permissions, a user who has the Make Changes privilege is given Write and Delete permissions.

Management Information Base (MIB) A set of objects that represent various types of information about a device, used by SNMP to manage devices. Because different network-management services are used for different types of devices or protocols, each service has its own set of objects. The entire set of objects that any service or protocol uses is referred to as its MIB. *See also* Simple Network Management Protocol (SNMP).

mandatory user profile A profile that is downloaded to the user's desktop each time he or she logs on. A mandatory user profile is created by an administrator and assigned to one or more users to create consistent or job-specific user profiles. They cannot be changed by the user and remain the same from one logon session to the next. *See also* roaming user profile; user profile.

mapping In TCP/IP, refers to the relationship between a host or computer name and an IP address, used by DNS and NetBIOS servers on TCP/IP networks.

In Windows NT Explorer, refers to mapping a driver letter to a network drive.

In Windows NT License Manager, refers to the relationship between users and computers in license groups. *See also* Domain Name System (DNS); IP address; license group.

mapping file A file defining exactly which users and groups are to be migrated from NetWare to Windows NT Server, and what new user names and passwords are to be assigned to the migrated users.

Master Boot Record The most important area on a hard disk, the data structure that starts the process of booting the computer.

The Master Boot Record contains the partition table for the disk and a small amount of executable code. On *x*86-based computers, the executable code examines the partition table and identifies the system (or bootable) partition, finds the system partition's starting location on the disk, and loads an image of its Partition Boot Sector into memory. The Master Boot Record then transfers execution to the Partition Boot Sector. *See also* Partition Table.

master browser A kind of network name server which keeps a browse list of all of the servers and domains on the network. Also referred to as browse master. *See also* browse; Windows NT browser system.

master domain In the master domain model, the domain that is trusted by all other domains on the network and acts as the central administrative unit for user and group accounts.

maximize To enlarge a window to its maximum size by using the **Maximize** button (at the right of the title bar) or the **Maximize** command on the window menu.

Maximize button The small button containing a window icon at the right of the title bar. Mouse users can click the **Maximize** button to enlarge a window to its maximum size. Keyboard users can use the **Maximize** command on the window menu.

maximum password age The period of time a password can be used before the system requires the user to change it. *See also* account policy.

MCI *See* Media Control Interface.

media access control (MAC) A layer in the network architecture that deals with network access and collision detection.

media access control (MAC) driver *See* network card driver.

Media Control Interface (MCI) A standard control interface for multimedia devices and files. Using MCI, a multimedia application can control a variety of multimedia devices and files.

member server A computer that runs Windows NT Server but is not a primary domain controller (PDC) or backup domain controller (BDC) of a Windows NT domain. Member servers do not receive copies of the directory database. Also called a stand-alone server. *See also* backup domain controller (BDC); directory database; primary domain controller (PDC).

memory A temporary storage area for information and applications. *See also* expanded memory; extended memory.

menu A list of available commands in an application window. Menu names appear in the menu bar near the top of the window. The window menu, represented by the program icon at the left end of the title bar, is common to all applications for Windows NT. To open a menu, click the menu name.

menu bar The horizontal bar containing the names of all of the application's menus. It appears below the title bar.

Messenger service Sends and receives messages sent by administrators or by the Alerter service. *See also* Alerter service.

MIB *See* Management Information Base.

Microsoft dbWeb A database publishing gateway provided in the *Windows NT Server Resource Kit*. dbWeb can run under Internet Information Server to provide public access to private enterprise ODBC sources as specified by an administrator of the private enterprise.

MIDI *See* Musical Instrument Digital Interface.

MIDI setup Specifies the type of MIDI device you are using, the channel and patch settings needed to play MIDI files, and the port your device is using. *See also* Musical Instrument Digital Interface (MIDI).

Migration Tool for NetWare Included with Windows NT, it enables you to easily transfer user and group accounts, volumes, folders, and files from a NetWare server to a computer running Windows NT Server.

MIME *See* Multipurpose Internet Mail Extensions.

minimize To reduce a window to a button on the taskbar by using the **Minimize** button (at the right of the title bar) or the **Minimize** command on the **Control** menu. *See also* maximize.

Minimize button The small button containing a short line at the right of the title bar. Mouse users can click the **Minimize** button to reduce a window to a button on the taskbar. Keyboard users can use the **Minimize** command on the **Control** menu.

minimum password age The period of time a password must be used before the user can change it. *See also* account policy.

minimum password length The fewest characters a password can contain. *See also* account policy.

mirror set A fully redundant or shadow copy of data. Mirror sets provide an identical twin for a selected disk; all data written to the primary disk is also written to the shadow or mirror disk. This enables you to have instant access to another disk with a redundant copy of the information on a failed disk. Mirror sets provide fault tolerance. *See also* fault tolerance.

m-node A NetBIOS implementation that uses the b-node protocol first, then the p-node protocol if the broadcast fails to resolve a name to an IP address. *See also* IP address; network basic input/output system (NetBIOS); p-node.

modem Short for modulator/demodulator, a communications device that enables a computer to transmit information over a standard telephone line.

MPR *See* MultiProtocol Routing.

MS-DOS-based application An application that is designed to run with MS-DOS, and therefore may not be able to take full advantage of all Windows NT features.

multicast datagram IP multicasting is the transmission of an IP datagram to a host group (a set of zero or more hosts identified by a single IP destination address). An IP datagram sent to one host is called a unicast datagram. An IP datagram sent to all hosts is called a broadcast datagram. *See also* broadcast datagram; host; IP address.

multihomed computer A system that has multiple network adapters, or that has been configured with multiple IP addresses for a single network adapter. *See also* IP address; network adapter.

multihomed system A system with multiple network adapters attached to separate physical networks.

multilink dialing Multilink combines multiple physical links into a logical "bundle." This aggregate link increases your bandwidth. *See also* bandwidth.

multiple boot A computer that runs two or more operating systems. For example, Windows 95, MS-DOS, and Windows NT operating systems can be installed on the same computer. When the computer is started, any one of the operating systems can be selected. Also known as dual boot.

multiport serial adapter A communications device that enables a computer to simultaneously transmit information over standard telephone lines to multiple computers. Similar to multiple modems contained in one device. *See also* modem.

MultiProtocol Routing (MPR) Enables routing over IP and IPX networks by connecting LANs or by connecting LANs to WANs. *See also* IPX/SPX; local area network (LAN); wide area network (WAN).

Multipurpose Internet Mail Extensions (MIME) A standard mechanism for specifying and describing the format of Internet message bodies. MIME enables the exchanging of objects, different character sets, and multimedia in electronic mail on different computer systems. Defined in RFC 1521.

Musical Instrument Digital Interface (MIDI) An interface that enables several devices, instruments, or computers to send and receive messages for the purpose of creating music, sound, or lighting.

N

named pipe An interprocess communication mechanism that allows one process to communicate with another local or remote process.

name mapping Is provided by Windows NT Server and Windows NT Workstation to ensure access by MS-DOS users to NTFS and FAT volumes (which can have share names of up to 255 characters, as opposed to MS-DOS, which is restricted to eight characters followed by a period and a three-character extension). With name mapping, each file or directory with a name that does not conform to the MS-DOS 8.3 standard is automatically given a second name that does. MS-DOS users connecting the file or directory over the network see the name in the 8.3 format; Windows NT Workstation and Windows NT Server users see the long name. *See also* Domain Name System (DNS); long name; Windows Internet Name Service (WINS).

name resolution service TCP/IP internetworks require a name resolution service to convert computer names to IP addresses and IP addresses to computer names. (People use "friendly" names to connect to computers; programs use IP addresses.) *See also* IP address; Transmission Control Protocol/Internet Protocol (TCP/IP).

NDIS *See* network device interface specification.

NDS *See* NetWare Directory Services.

NetBEUI A network protocol usually used in small, department-size local area networks of 1 through 200 clients. It can use Token Ring source routing as its only method of routing. *See also* router; Token Ring.

NetBIOS *See* network basic input/output system.

NetBT Short for NetBIOS over TCP/IP. The session-layer network service that performs name-to-IP address mapping for name resolution. *See also* IP address; name resolution service; network basic input/output system (NetBIOS); Transmission Control Protocol/Internet Protocol (TCP/IP).

Net Logon service For Windows NT Server, performs authentication of domain logons, and keeps the domain's directory database synchronized between the primary domain controller (PDC) and the other backup domain controllers (BDCs) of the domain. *See also* backup domain controller (BDC); directory database; primary domain controller (PDC).

NetWare Directory Services (NDS) A NetWare service that runs on NetWare servers. The service enables the location of resources on the network.

network adapter An expansion card or other device used to connect a computer to a local area network (LAN). Also called a network card; network adapter card; adapter card; network interface card (NIC).

network adapter card *See* network adapter.

network administrator A person responsible for planning, configuring, and managing the day-to-day operation of the network. This person may also be referred to as a system administrator.

network basic input/output system (NetBIOS) An application programming interface (API) that can be used by applications on a local area network. NetBIOS provides applications with a uniform set of commands for requesting the lower-level services required to conduct sessions between nodes on a network and to transmit information back and forth. *See also* application programming interface (API).

network card *See* network adapter.

network card driver A network device driver that works directly with the network card, acting as an intermediary between the card and the protocol driver. With Services for Macintosh, the AppleTalk Protocol stack on the server is implemented as a protocol driver and is bound to one or more network drivers.

Network DDE DSDM service The Network DDE DSDM (DDE share database manager) service manages shared DDE conversations. It is used by the Network DDE service. *See also* dynamic data exchange (DDE).

Network DDE service The Network DDE (dynamic data exchange) service provides a network transport and security for DDE conversations. *See also* dynamic data exchange (DDE).

network device driver Software that coordinates communication between the network adapter and the computer's hardware and other software, controlling the physical function of the network adapters.

network device interface specification (NDIS) In Windows networking, the Microsoft/3Com specification for the interface of network device drivers. All transport drivers call the NDIS interface to access network cards. With Services for Macintosh, the AppleTalk Protocol stack on the server is implemented as an NDIS-compliant protocol and is bound to an NDIS network driver. All network drivers and protocol drivers shipped with Windows NT Workstation and Windows NT Server conform to NDIS.

network directory *See* shared directory.

network driver *See* network device driver.

network driver interface specification *See* network device interface specification (NDIS).

Network File System (NFS) A service for distributed computing systems that provides a distributed file system, eliminating the need for keeping multiple copies of files on separate computers.

network ID The portion of the IP address that identifies a group of computers and devices located on the same logical network.

Network Information Service (NIS) A service for distributed computing systems that provides a distributed database system for common configuration files.

network interface card (NIC) *See* network adapter.

Network News Transfer Protocol (NNTP) The protocol used to distribute network news messages to NNTP servers and to NNTP clients (news readers) on the Internet. NNTP provides for the distribution, inquiry, retrieval, and posting of news articles by using a reliable stream-based transmission of news on the Internet. NNTP is designed so that news articles are stored on a server in a central database, thus enabling a user to select specific items to read. Indexing, cross-referencing, and expiration of aged messages are also provided. Defined in RFC 977.

network number In the Macintosh environment, the network number (also referred to as the network range) is the address or range of addresses assigned to the network, which is used by AppleTalk routers to route information to the appropriate network. Each physical network can have a range of network numbers.

network protocol Software that enables computers to communicate over a network. TCP/IP is a network protocol, used on the Internet. *See also* Transmission Control Protocol/Internet Protocol (TCP/IP).

network range In the Macintosh environment, a range of network numbers (routing addresses) associated with a physical network in Phase 2. Apple manuals sometimes refer to a network range as a cable range. *See also* network number; routing.

network sniffer A hardware and software diagnostic tool that can also be used to decipher passwords, which may result in unauthorized access to network accounts. Clear-text passwords are susceptible to network sniffers.

NFS *See* Network File System.

NIC Acronym for network interface card. *See* network adapter.

NIS *See* Network Information Service.

NNTP *See* Network News Transfer Protocol.

node In the PC environment, a node is any device that is attached to the internetwork and uses TCP/IP. (A node can also be referred to as a host.) In the Macintosh environment, a node is an addressable entity on a network. Each Macintosh client is a node.

nonpaged memory Memory that cannot be paged to disk. *See also* memory; paging file.

non–Windows NT application Refers to an application that is designed to run with Windows 3.*x*, MS-DOS, OS/2, or POSIX, but not specifically with Windows NT, and that may not be able to take full advantage of all Windows NT features (such as memory management). *See also* POSIX.

NT *See* Windows NT Server; Windows NT Workstation.

NT File System *See* Windows NT File System.

NTFS *See* Windows NT File System.

NWLink IPX/SPX Compatible Transport A standard network protocol that supports routing, and can support NetWare client/server applications, where NetWare-aware Sockets-based applications communicate with IPX/SPX Sockets-based applications. *See also* IPX/SPX; Sockets.

O

object Any piece of information, created by using a Windows-based application, that can be linked or embedded into another document. *See also* embedded object; linked object.

object-cache scavenger A component of the IIS process that periodically flushes from the cache objects that have changed or that have not been referenced in its last timed interval. The default time interval for the object-cache scavenger is 30 seconds.

octet In programming, an octet refers to eight bits or one byte. IP addresses, for example, are typically represented in dotted-decimal notation, that is, with the decimal value of each octet of the address separated by a period. *See also* IP address.

ODBC *See* Open Database Connectivity.

offset When specifying a filter in Windows NT Network Monitor based on a pattern match (which limits the capture to only those frames containing a specific pattern of ASCII or hexadecimal data), you must specify where the pattern occurs in the frame. This number of bytes (from the beginning or end of the frame) is known as an offset. *See also* frame; hexadecimal.

OLE A way to transfer and share information between applications. *See also* ActiveX; embedded object; linked object.

one-way trust relationship One domain (the trusting domain) "trusts" the domain controllers in the other domain (the trusted domain) to authenticate user accounts from the trusted domain to use resources in the trusting domain. *See also* trust relationship; user account.

opcode Operation code; a code, usually a number, that specifies an operation to be performed. An opcode is often the first component in a contiguous block of data; it indicates how other data in the block should be interpreted.

open To display the contents of a directory, a document, or a data file in a window.

Open Database Connectivity (ODBC ODBC is an application programming interface that enables applications to access data from a variety of existing data sources.

Open Systems Interconnection (OSI) model TCP/IP protocols map to a four-layered conceptual model consisting of Application, Transport, Internet, and Network Interface. Each layer in this TCP/IP model corresponds to one or more layers of the International Standards Organization (ISO) seven-layer OSI model consisting of Application, Presentation, Session, Transport, Network, Data-link, and Physical. *See also* ISO.

orphan A member of a mirror set or a stripe set with parity that has failed in a severe manner, such as in a loss of power or a complete head crash. When this happens, the fault-tolerance driver determines that it can no longer use the orphaned member and directs all new reads and writes to the remaining members of the fault-tolerance volume. *See also* fault tolerance; mirror set; stripe sets with parity.

orphaned member *See* orphan.

OSI *See* Open Systems Interconnection model.

owner In Windows NT, every file and directory on an NTFS volume has an owner, who controls how permissions are set on the file or directory and who can grant permissions to others.

owner category In the Macintosh environment, this refers to the user category to which you assign permissions for the owner of a folder or a Macintosh volume. *See also* Macintosh-accessible volume.

P

package An icon that represents an embedded or linked object. When you choose the package, the application used to create the object either plays the object (for example, a sound file) or opens and displays the object. *See also* embedded object; linked object.

packet A transmission unit of fixed maximum size that consists of binary information representing both data and a header containing an ID number, source and destination addresses, and error-control data.

packet assembler/disassembler (PAD) A connection used in X.25 networks. X.25 PAD boards can be used in place of modems when provided with a compatible COM driver. *See also* X.25.

packet header The part of a packet that contains an identification number, source and destination addresses, and—sometimes—error-control data. *See also* packet.

PAD *See* packet assembler/disassembler.

page fault In the processor, a page fault occurs when a process refers to a virtual memory page that is not in its working set in main memory.

A *hard page fault* occurs when data that a program needs is not found in its working set (the physical memory visible to the program) or elsewhere in physical memory, and must be retrieved from disk.

A page fault will not cause the page to be fetched from disk if that page is on the standby list, and hence already in main memory, or if it is in use by another process with which the page is shared. In this case, a *soft page fault* occurs.

paging file A special file on a PC hard disk. With virtual memory under Windows NT, some of the program code and other information is kept in RAM while other information is temporarily swapped into virtual memory. When that information is required again, Windows NT pulls it back into RAM and, if necessary, swaps other information to virtual memory. Also called a swap file.

PAP *See* Password Authentication Protocol.

parity Redundant information that is associated with a block of information. In Windows NT Server, stripe sets with parity means that there is one additional parity stripe per row. Therefore, you must use at least three, rather than two, disks to allow for this extra parity information. Parity stripes contain the XOR (the Boolean operation called exclusive OR) of the data in that stripe. Windows NT Server, when regenerating a failed disk, uses the parity information in those stripes in conjunction with the data on the good disks to recreate the data on the failed disk. *See also* fault tolerance; stripe set; stripe sets with parity.

partial synchronization The automatic, timed delivery to all domain BDCs (backup domain controllers) of only those directory database changes that have occurred since the last synchronization. *See also* backup domain controller (BDC); synchronize.

partition A partition is a portion of a physical disk that functions as though it were a physically separate unit. *See also* extended partition; system partition.

Partition Table An area of the Master Boot Record that the computer uses to determine how to access the disk. The Partition Table can contain up to four partitions for each physical disk. *See also* Master Boot Record.

pass-through authentication When the user account must be authenticated, but the computer being used for the logon is not a domain controller in the domain where the user account is defined, nor is it the computer where the user account is defined, the computer passes the logon information through to a domain controller (directly or indirectly) where the user account is defined. *See also* domain controller; user account.

password A security measure used to restrict logons to user accounts and access to computer systems and resources. A password is a unique string of characters that must be provided before a logon or an access is authorized. For Windows NT, a password for a user account can be up to 14 characters, and is case-sensitive. There are four user-defined parameters to be entered in the **Account Policy** dialog box in User Manager or User Manager for Domains: maximum password age, minimum password age, minimum password length, and password uniqueness.

With Services for Macintosh, each Macintosh user must type a user password when accessing the Windows NT Server. You can also assign each Macintosh-accessible volume a volume password if you want, which all users must type to access the volume. *See also* account policy.

Password Authentication Protocol (PAP) A type of authentication that uses clear-text passwords and is the least sophisticated authentication protocol.

password uniqueness The number of new passwords that must be used by a user account before an old password can be reused. *See also* account policy; password.

patch map The part of a channel-map entry that translates instrument sounds, volume settings, and (optionally) key values for a channel.

path A sequence of directory (or folder) names that specifies the location of a directory, file, or folder within the directory tree. Each directory name and file name within the path (except the first) must be preceded by a backslash (\). For example, to specify the path of a file named Readme.wri located in the Windows directory on drive C, you type c:\windows\readme.wri.

PC Any personal computer (such as an IBM PC or compatible) using the MS-DOS, OS/2, Windows, Windows for Workgroups, Windows 95, Windows NT Server, or Windows NT Workstation operating systems.

PCMCIA *See* Personal Computer Memory Card International Association.

peer Any of the devices on a layered communications network that operate on the same protocol level.

Peer Web Services A collection of services that enable the user of a computer running Windows NT Workstation to publish a personal Web site from the desktop. The services include the WWW service, the FTP service, and the Gopher service.

pel Also known as a pixel, which is short for picture element, the smallest graphic unit that can be displayed on the screen.

Perl Practical Extraction and Report Language. A scripting (programming) language that is frequently used for CGI scripts.

permissions Windows NT Server settings you set on a shared resource that determine which users can use the resource and how they can use it. *See also* access permission.

Services for Macintosh automatically translates between permissions and Macintosh access privileges, so that permissions set on a directory (volume) are enforced for Macintosh users, and access privileges set by Macintosh users are enforced for PC users connected to the computer running Windows NT Server.

Personal Computer Memory Card International Association (PCMCIA) A standard for removable peripheral devices (called PC cards) about the size of a credit card, which plug into a special 68-pin connector found most commonly in portable computers. Currently available PCMCIA cards include memory, hard disk, modem, fax, network, and wireless communication devices.

personal group In the **Start** menu on the **Programs** list, a program group you have created that contains program items. Personal groups are stored with your logon information and each time you log on, your personal groups appear. *See also* group.

Physical Unit (PU) A network-addressable unit that provides the services needed to use and manage a particular device, such as a communications link device. A PU is implemented with a combination of hardware, software, and microcode.

PIF *See* program information file.

ping A command used to verify connections to one or more remote hosts. The **ping** utility uses the ICMP echo request and echo reply packets to determine whether a particular IP system on a network is functional. The ping utility is useful for diagnosing IP network or router failures. *See also* Internet Control Message Protocol (ICMP); router.

pipe An interprocess communication mechanism. Writing to and reading from a pipe is much like writing to and reading from a file, except that the two processes are actually using a shared memory segment to communicate data. *See also* named pipe.

pixel *See* pel.

plotter font *See* font types.

p-node A NetBIOS implementation that uses point-to-point communications with a name server to resolve names as IP addresses. *See also* h-node; IP address; network basic input/output system (NetBIOS).

pointer The arrow-shaped cursor on the screen that follows the movement of a mouse (or other pointing device) and indicates which area of the screen will be affected when you press the mouse button. The pointer changes shape during certain tasks.

Point-to-Point Protocol (PPP) A set of industry-standard framing and authentication protocols that is part of Windows NT RAS to ensure interoperability with third-party remote access software. PPP negotiates configuration parameters for multiple layers of the OSI model. *See also* Open Systems Interconnection model (OSI).

Point-to-Point Tunneling Protocol (PPTP) PPTP is a new networking technology that supports multiprotocol virtual private networks (VPNs), enabling remote users to access corporate networks securely across the Internet by dialing into an Internet service provider (ISP) or by connecting directly to the Internet. *See also* virtual private network (VPN).

POP *See* Post Office Protocol.

pop-up menu *See* window menu.

port A location used to pass data in and out of a computing device. This term can refer to an adapter card connecting a server to a network, a serial 232 port, a TCP/IP port, or a printer port.

port ID The method TCP and UDP use to specify which application running on the system is sending or receiving the data. *See also* Transmission Control Protocol (TCP); User Datagram Protocol (UDP).

POSIX Acronym for Portable Operating System Interface, an IEEE (Institute of Electrical and Electronics Engineers, Inc.) standard that defines a set of operating-system services. Programs that adhere to the POSIX standard can be easily ported from one system to another.

Post Office Protocol (POP) The Post Office Protocol version 3 (POP3) is a protocol that permits a workstation to dynamically access a mail drop on a server in a useful fashion. Usually, this means that a POP3 server is used to allow a workstation to retrieve mail that an SMTP server is holding for it. POP3 is specified in RFC 1725.

PostScript printer A printer that uses the Post-Script page description language to create text and graphics on the output medium, such as paper or overhead transparency. Examples of PostScript printers include the Apple Laser-Writer, the NEC LC-890, and the QMS PS-810. *See also* font types.

POTS Acronym for plain-old telephone service. Also an acronym for point of termination station, which refers to where a telephone call terminates.

power conditioning A feature of an uninterruptible power supply (UPS) that removes spikes, surges, sags, and noise from the power supply. *See also* uninterruptible power supply (UPS).

PPP *See* Point-to-Point Protocol.

PPTP *See* Point-to-Point Tunneling Protocol.

predefined key The key represented by a registry window, the name of which appears in the window's title bar. *See also* key; registry.

primary domain controller (PDC) In a Windows NT Server domain, the computer running Windows NT Server that authenticates domain logons and maintains the directory database for a domain. The PDC tracks changes made to accounts of all computers on a domain. It is the only computer to receive these changes directly. A domain has only one PDC. *See also* directory database.

primary group The group with which a Macintosh user usually shares documents stored on a server. You specify a user's primary group in the user's account. When a user creates a folder on the server, the user's primary group is set as the folder's associated group (by default).

primary partition A partition is a portion of a physical disk that can be marked for use by an operating system. There can be up to four primary partitions (or up to three, if there is an extended partition) per physical disk. A primary partition cannot be subpartitioned. *See also* extended partition; partition.

print device Refers to the actual hardware device that produces printed output.

printer Refers to the software interface between the operating system and the print device. The printer defines where the document will go before it reaches the print device (to a local port, to a file, or to a remote print share), when it will go, and various other aspects of the printing process.

printer driver A program that converts graphics commands into a specific printer language, such as PostScript or PCL. *See also* font types.

printer fonts Fonts that are built into your printer. These fonts are usually located in the printer's read-only memory (ROM). *See also* font; font types.

printer permissions Specify the type of access a user or group has to use the printer. The printer permissions are No Access, Print, Manage Documents, and Full Control.

printer window Shows information for one of the printers that you have installed or to which you are connected. For each printer, you can see what documents are waiting to be printed, who owns them, how large they are, and other information.

printing pool Consists of two or more identical print devices associated with one printer.

print processor A PostScript program that understands the format of a document's image file and how to print the file to a specific printer or class of printers. *See also* encapsulated PostScript (EPS) file.

print server Refers to the computer that receives documents from clients.

Print Server for Macintosh A Services for Macintosh service that enables Macintosh clients to send documents to printers attached to a computer running Windows NT; enables PC clients to send documents to printers anywhere on the AppleTalk network; and enables Macintosh users to spool their documents to the computer running Windows NT Server, thus freeing their clients to do other tasks. Also called MacPrint.

print sharing The ability for a computer running Windows NT Workstation or Windows NT Server to share a printer on the network. This is done by using the **Printers** folder or the **net share** command.

print spooler A collection of dynamic-link libraries (DLLs) that receive, process, schedule, and distribute documents.

private volume A Macintosh-accessible volume that is accessible by only one Macintosh user. For a volume to be a private volume, the permissions on its root directory must give the volume's owner all three permissions (Make Changes, See Files, and See Folders), while giving the primary group and everyone categories no permissions at all. When a private volume's owner uses the Chooser to view the volumes available on the server, the private volume is listed; however, no other users can see the private volume when viewing the volumes available on the server. *See also* Macintosh-accessible volume.

privilege level One of three settings (User, Administrator, or Guest) assigned to each user account. The privilege level a user account has determines the actions that the user can perform on the network. *See also* Administrator privilege; Guest privilege; user account; User privilege.

process When a program runs, a Windows NT process is created. A process is an object type which consists of an executable program, a set of virtual memory addresses, and one or more threads.

processor affinity mask A Windows NT bit mask that associates processors with network adapters. All deferred procedure calls (DPCs) originating from the network adapter are handled by its associated processor.

program file A file that starts an application or program. A program file has an .exe, .pif, .com, or .bat file name extension.

program group On the **Start** menu, a collection of applications. Grouping your applications makes them easier to find when you want to start them. *See also* common group; personal group.

program icon Located at the left of the window title bar, the program icon represents the program being run. Clicking the program icon opens the window menu.

program information file (PIF) A PIF provides information to Windows NT about how best to run MS-DOS-based applications. When you start an MS-DOS-based application, Windows NT looks for a PIF to use with the application. PIFs contain such items as the name of the file, a start-up directory, and multitasking options.

program item An application, accessory, or document represented as an icon in the **Start** menu or on the desktop.

promiscuous mode A state of a network card in which it passes on to the networking software all of the frames that it detects on the network, regardless of the frames' destination address. *See also* frame; network adapter.

propagate Copy. For example, NetWare user accounts are propagated to the Windows NT primary domain controller when using Directory Service Manager for NetWare (DSMN).

property In Windows NT Network Monitor, a property refers to a field within a protocol header. A protocol's properties, collectively, indicate the purpose of the protocol.

protocol A set of rules and conventions for sending information over a network. These rules govern the content, format, timing, sequencing, and error control of messages exchanged among network devices.

protocol driver A network device driver that implements a protocol, communicating between Windows NT Server and one or more network adapter card drivers. With Services for Macintosh, the AppleTalk Protocol stack is implemented as an NDIS-protocol driver, and is bound to one or more network adapter card drivers.

protocol parser A dynamic-link library (DLL) that identifies the protocols used to send a frame onto the network. *See also* dynamic-link library (DLL); frame.

protocol properties Refers to the elements of information that define a protocol's purpose. Because the purposes of protocols vary, properties differ from one protocol to another.

protocol stack The implementation of a specific protocol family in a computer or other node on the network.

proxy A computer that listens to name query broadcasts and responds for those names not on the local subnet. The proxy communicates with the name server to resolve names and then caches them for a time period. *See also* caching; Domain Name System (DNS); subnet.

PSTN Acronym for public switched telephone network.

PU *See* Physical Unit.

public key cryptography A method of encrypting data transmissions to and from a server.

pull partner A WINS server that pulls in replicas from its push partner by requesting it and then accepting the pushed replicas. *See also* Windows Internet Name Service (WINS).

push partner A WINS server that sends replicas to its pull partner upon receiving a request from it. *See also* Windows Internet Name Service (WINS).

Q

queue In Windows NT terminology, a queue refers to a group of documents waiting to be printed. (In NetWare and OS/2 environments, queues are the primary software interface between the application and print device; users submit documents to a queue. However, with Windows NT, the printer is that interface—the document is sent to a printer, not a queue.)

quick format Deletes the file allocation table (FAT) and root directory of a disk but does not scan the disk for bad areas. This function is available in Disk Administrator or when checking disks for errors. *See also* file allocation table (FAT); root directory.

R

RAID Acronym for Redundant Array of Inexpensive Disks. A method used to standardize and categorize fault-tolerant disk systems. Six levels gauge various mixes of performance, reliability, and cost. Windows NT includes three of the RAID levels: Level 0, Level 1, and Level 5.

RAM An acronym for random-access memory. RAM can be read from or written to by the computer or other devices. Information stored in RAM is lost when you turn off the computer. *See also* memory.

RAS *See* Remote Access Service.

recursion One of the three key concepts in DNS name resolution. A resolver typically passes a recursive resolution request to its local name server, which tells the name server that the resolver expects a complete answer to the query, not just a pointer to another name server. Recursive resolution effectively puts the workload onto the name server and allows the resolver to be small and simple. *See also* Domain Name System (DNS); iteration.

reduce To minimize a window to an icon by using the **Minimize** button or the **Minimize** command. A minimized application continues running, and you can click the icon on the toolbar to make it the active application.

reduced instruction set computing (RISC) A type of microprocessor design that focuses on rapid and efficient processing of a relatively small set of instructions. RISC architecture limits the number of instructions that are built into the microprocessor, but optimizes each so that it can be carried out very rapidly—usually within a single clock cycle.

refresh To update displayed information with current data.

registration In Windows NT NetBT name resolution, registration is the process used to register a unique name for each computer (node) on the network. A computer typically registers itself when it starts.

registry The Windows NT registry is a hierarchical database that provides a repository for information about a computer's configuration on Windows NT Workstation and about hardware and user accounts on Windows NT Server. It is organized in subtrees and their keys, hives, and value entries. *See also* hive; key; subtree; user account.

registry size limit (RSL) The total amount of space that can be consumed by registry data is restricted by the registry size limit, which is a kind of universal maximum for registry space that prevents an application from filling the paged pool with registry data. *See also* hive; paging file.

Remote Access Service (RAS) A service that provides remote networking for telecommuters, mobile workers, and system administrators who monitor and manage servers at multiple branch offices. Users with RAS on a Windows NT–based computer can dial in to remotely access their networks for services such as file and printer sharing, electronic mail, scheduling, and SQL database access.

remote administration Administration of one computer by an administrator located at another computer and connected to the first computer across the network.

remote logon Occurs when a user is already logged on to a user account and makes a network connection to another computer. *See also* user account.

remote procedure call (RPC) A message-passing facility that allows a distributed application to call services available on various machines in a network. Used during remote administration of computers. *See also* remote administration.

Remote Procedure Call service *See* RPC service.

renew Client computers are periodically required to renew their NetBIOS name registrations with the WINS server. When a client computer first registers with a WINS server, the WINS server returns a message that indicates when the client will need to renew its registration. *See also* network basic input/output system (NetBIOS); Windows Internet Name Service (WINS).

repeaters The most basic LAN connection device, repeaters strengthen the physical transmission signal. A repeater simply takes the electrical signals that reach it and then regenerates them to full strength before passing them on. Repeaters generally extend a single network (rather than link two networks).

replication *See* directory replication.

replicators One of the Windows NT built-in local groups for workstations and member servers, used for directory replication functions. *See also* directory replication.

Requests for Comments (RFCs) The official documents of the IETF (Internet Engineering Task Force) that specify the details for protocols included in the TCP/IP family. *See also* Internet Engineering Task Force (IETF); Transmission Control Protocol/Internet Protocol (TCP/IP).

resolution In Windows NetBT name resolution, resolution is the process used to determine the specific address for a computer name.

resolvers DNS clients that query DNS servers for name resolution on networks. *See also* Domain Name System (DNS).

resource Any part of a computer system or a network, such as a disk drive, printer, or memory, that can be allotted to a program or a process while it is running, or shared over a local area network.

resource domain A trusting domain that establishes a one-way trust relationship with the master (account) domain, enabling users with accounts in the master domain to use resources in all of the other domains. *See also* domain; trust relationship.

resource fork One of two forks that make up each Macintosh file. The resource fork holds Macintosh operating system resources, such as code, menu, font, and icon definitions. Resource forks have no relevance to PCs, so the resource forks of files on the server are never accessed by PC clients. *See also* data fork; file fork.

response In Windows NT RAS, responses are strings expected from the device, which can contain macros.

RFC *See* Requests for Comments.

right *See* permissions; user rights.

RIP *See* routing information protocol.

RISC *See* reduced instruction set computing.

roaming user profile User profile that is enabled when an administrator enters a user profile path into the user account. The first time the user logs off, the local user profile is copied to that location. Thereafter, the server copy of the user profile is downloaded each time the user logs on (if it is more current than the local copy) and is updated each time the user logs off. *See also* user profile.

root directory The top-level directory on a computer, a partition, or Macintosh-accessible volume. *See also* directory tree.

router In the Windows NT environment, a router helps LANs and WANs achieve interoperability and connectivity and can link LANs that have different network topologies (such as Ethernet and Token Ring). Routers match packet headers to a LAN segment and choose the best path for the packet, optimizing network performance.

In the Macintosh environment, routers are necessary for computers on different physical networks to communicate with each other. Routers maintain a map of the physical networks on a Macintosh internet (network) and forward data received from one physical network to other physical networks. Computers running Windows NT Server with Services for Macintosh can act as routers, and you can also use third-party routing hardware on a network with Services for Macintosh. *See also* local area network (LAN); packet; wide area network (WAN).

routing The process of forwarding packets to other routers until the packet is eventually delivered to a router connected to the specified destination. *See also* packet; router.

routing information protocol (RIP) Enables a router to exchange routing information with a neighboring router. *See also* routing.

routing table Controls the routing decisions made by computers running TCP/IP. Routing tables are built automatically by Windows NT based on the IP configuration of your computer. *See also* dynamic routing; routing; static routing; Transmission Control Protocol/Internet Protocol (TCP/IP).

RPC *See* remote procedure call.

RPC Locator service The Remote Procedure Call Locator service allows distributed applications to use the RPC Name service. The RPC Locator service manages the RPC Name service database.

The server side of a distributed application registers its availability with the RPC Locator service. The client side of a distributed application queries the RPC Locator service to find available compatible server applications. *See also* remote procedure call (RPC).

RPC service The Remote Procedure Call service is the RPC subsystem for Microsoft Windows NT. The RPC subsystem includes the endpoint mapper and other miscellaneous RPC services. *See also* remote procedure call (RPC).

RSL *See* registry size limit.

S

SACL *See* system access control list.

SAM Acronym for Security Accounts Manager. *See* directory database; Windows NT Server Directory Services.

SAP In the Windows environment, SAP is an acronym for Service Advertising Protocol, a service that broadcasts shared files, directories, and printers categorized first by domain or workgroup and then by server name.

In the context of routing and IPX, SAP is also an acronym for Service Advertising Protocol, used by servers to advertise their services and addresses on a network. Clients use SAP to determine what network resources are available.

In NetBEUI, SAP is an acronym for Service Access Point, in which each link-layer program identifies itself by registering a unique service access point.

Not to be confused with SAP financial database application software for the mainframe computer.

saturation The purity of a color's hue, moving from gray to the pure color.

scavenging Cleaning up the WINS database. *See also* Windows Internet Name Service (WINS).

Schedule service Supports and is required for use of the **at** command. The **at** command can schedule commands and programs to run on a computer at a specified time and date.

schemas Schemas control how and what information from a private database is available to visitors who use the Internet to access the public Microsoft dbWeb gateway to the private database. *See also* dbWeb Administrator.

Schema Wizard Interactive tool in dbWeb Administrator that leads a user through creation of HTML pages or through implementing an ISAPI application.

screen buffer The size reserved in memory for the command prompt display.

screen dump *See* snapshot.

screen elements The parts that make up a window or dialog box, such as the title bar, the **Minimize** and **Maximize** buttons, the window borders, and the scroll bars.

screen fonts Fonts displayed on your screen. Soft-font manufacturers often provide screen fonts that closely match the soft fonts for your printer. This ensures that your documents look the same on the screen as they do when printed. *See also* font; font types.

screen saver A moving picture or pattern that appears on your screen when you have not used the mouse or the keyboard for a specified period of time. To select a screen saver, either use Display in Control Panel or right-click on the desktop for properties.

scroll To move through text or graphics (up, down, left, or right) in order to see parts of the file that cannot fit on the screen.

scroll arrow An arrow on either end of a scroll bar that you use to scroll through the contents of the window or list box. Click the scroll arrow to scroll one screen at a time, or continue pressing the mouse button while pointing at the scroll arrow to scroll continuously.

scroll bar A bar that appears at the right or bottom edge of a window or list box whose contents are not completely visible. Each scroll bar contains two scroll arrows and a scroll box, which enable you to scroll through the contents of the window or list box.

scroll box In a scroll bar, a small box that shows the position of information currently visible in the window or list box relative to the contents of the entire window.

scroll buffer The area in memory that holds information that does not fit on the screen. You can use the scroll bars to scroll through the information.

SCSI *See* small computer system interface.

Search button *See* find tab.

section header In Windows NT RAS, a section header is a string, comprising up to 32 characters between square brackets, that identifies the specific device to which the section applies.

secure attention sequence A series of keystrokes (CTRL+ALT+DEL) that will always display the Windows NT operating system logon screen.

secure communications channel Created when computers at each end of a connection are satisfied that the computer on the other end has identified itself correctly by using its computer account. *See also* computer account.

Secure Sockets Layer (SSL) A protocol that supplies secure data communication through data encryption and decryption. SSL enables communications privacy over networks by using a combination of public key cryptography and bulk data encryption.

security A means of ensuring that shared files can be accessed only by authorized users.

Security Accounts Manager (SAM) *See* directory database; Windows NT Server Directory Services.

security database *See* directory database.

security host A third-party authentication device that verifies whether a caller from a remote client is authorized to connect to the Remote Access server. This verification supplements security already authorized to connect to the Remote-Access server.

security ID (SID) A unique name that identifies a logged-on user to the security system. Security IDs (SIDs) can identify one user or a group of users.

security identifier *See* security ID (SID).

security log Records security events. This helps track changes to the security system and identify any possible breaches of security. For example, depending on the Audit settings in User Manager or User Manager for Domains, attempts to log on to the local computer might be recorded in the security log. The security log contains both valid and invalid logon attempts as well as events related to resource use (such as creating, opening, or deleting files). *See also* event.

security policies For Windows NT Workstation, the security policies consist of the Account, User Rights, and Audit policies, and are managed by using User Manager.

For a Windows NT Server domain, the security policies consist of the Account, User Rights, Audit, and Trust Relationships policies, and are managed by using User Manager for Domains.

security token *See* access token.

seed router In the Macintosh environment, a seed router initializes and broadcasts routing information about one or more physical networks. This information tells routers where to send each packet of data. A seed router on an AppleTalk network initially defines the network number(s) and zone(s) for a network. Services for Macintosh servers can function as seed routers, and you can also use third-party hardware routers as seed routers. *See also* packet; router.

See Files The Macintosh-style permission that give users the right to open a folder and see the files in the folder. For example, a folder that has See Files and See Folders Macintosh-style permissions is given the Windows NT-style R (Read) permission. *See also* permissions.

See Folders The Macintosh-style permission that gives users the right to open a folder and see the files contained in that folder. *See also* permissions.

select To mark an item so that a subsequent action can be carried out on that item. You usually select an item by clicking it with a mouse or pressing a key. After selecting an item, you choose the action that you want to affect the item.

selection cursor The marking device that shows where you are in a window, menu, or dialog box and what you have selected. The selection cursor can appear as a highlight or as a dotted rectangle around text.

semaphore Generally, semaphores are signaling devices or mechanisms. However, in Windows NT, system semaphores are objects used to synchronize activities on an interprocess level. For example, when two or more processes share a common resource such as a printer, video screen, or memory segment, semaphores are used to control access to those resources so that only one process can alter them at any particular time.

sequence number The identifier with which TCP marks packets before sending them. The sequence numbers allow the receiving system to properly order the packets on the receiving system. *See also* packet; Transmission Control Protocol (TCP).

Serial Line Internet Protocol (SLIP) An older industry standard that is part of Windows NT RAS to ensure interoperability with third-party remote access software.

server In general, refers to a computer that provides shared resources to network users. *See also* member server.

server application A Windows NT application that can create objects for linking or embedding into other documents. For distributed applications, the application that responds to a client application. *See also* client application; DCOM Configuration tool; Distributed Component Object Model (DCOM); embedded object; linked object.

Server Manager In Windows NT Server, an application used to view and administer domains, workgroups, and computers.

server message block (SMB) A file-sharing protocol designed to allow systems to transparently access files that reside on remote systems.

Server service Provides RPC (remote procedure call) support, and file, print, and named pipe sharing. *See also* named pipe; remote procedure call (RPC).

server zone The AppleTalk zone on which a server appears. On a Phase 2 network, a server appears in the default zone of the server's default network. *See also* default network; default zone; desired zone; zone.

service A process that performs a specific system function and often provides an application programming interface (API) for other processes to call. Windows NT services are RPC-enabled, meaning that their API routines can be called from remote computers. *See also* application programming interface (API); remote procedure call (RPC).

Service Access Point (SAP) *See* SAP.

Service Advertising Protocol (SAP) *See* SAP.

Services for Macintosh *See* Windows NT Server Services for Macintosh.

session A link between two network devices, such as a client and a server. A session between a client and server consists of one or more connections from the client to the server.

SFM Acronym for Windows NT Services for Macintosh.

share To make resources, such as directories and printers, available to others.

shared directory A directory that network users can connect to.

shared network directory *See* shared directory.

shared resource Any device, data, or program that is used by more than one other device or program. For Windows NT, shared resources refer to any resource that is made available to network users, such as directories, files, printers, and named pipes. Also refers to a resource on a server that is available to network users. *See also* named pipe.

share name A name that refers to a shared resource on a server. Each shared directory on a server has a share name, used by PC users to refer to the directory. Users of Macintosh use the name of the Macintosh-accessible volume that corresponds to a directory, which may be the same as the share name. *See also* Macintosh-accessible volume.

share permissions Are used to restrict a shared resource's availability over the network to only certain users.

Shiva Password Authentication Protocol (SPAP) A two-way (reversible) encryption mechanism employed by Shiva. Windows NT Workstation, when connecting to a Shiva LAN Rover, uses SPAP, as does a Shiva client connecting to a Windows NT Server. *See also* encryption.

shortcut key A key or key combination, available for some commands, that you can press to carry out a command without first selecting a menu. Shortcut keys are listed to the right of commands on a menu.

short name A valid 8.3 (up to eight characters followed by a period and a three-character extension) MS-DOS or OS/2 file name that the computer running Windows NT Server creates for every Macintosh folder name or file name on the server. PC users refer to files on the server by their short names; Macintosh users refer to them by their long names. *See also* long name; name mapping.

SID *See* security ID.

silent mode During IP routing in silent mode, the computer listens to RIP broadcasts and updates its route table but does not advertise its own routes. *See also* routing; routing information protocol (RIP); routing table.

simple device A device that you use without specifying a related media file. An audio compact-disc player is a simple device.

Simple Mail Transfer Protocol (SMTP) A member of the TCP/IP suite of protocols that governs the exchange of electronic mail between message transfer agents.

Simple Network Management Protocol (SNMP) A protocol used by SNMP consoles and agents to communicate. In Windows NT, the SNMP service is used to get and set status information about a host on a TCP/IP network. *See also* Transmission Control Protocol/Internet Protocol (TCP/IP).

single user logon Windows NT network users can connect to multiple servers, domains, and applications with a single network logon.

SLIP *See* Serial Line Internet Protocol.

small computer system interface (SCSI A standard high-speed parallel interface defined by the American National Standards Institute (ANSI). A SCSI interface is used for connecting microcomputers to peripheral devices such as hard disks and printers, and to other computers and local area networks.

SMB *See* server message block.

SMS *See* Systems Management Server.

SMTP *See* Simple Mail Transfer Protocol.

SNA *See* System Network Architecture.

snapshot A copy of main memory or video memory at a given instant, sent to a printer or hard disk. A graphical image of the video screen can be saved by taking a snapshot of video memory, more commonly called a screen dump.

sniffer *See* network sniffer.

Sniffer files Files saved from Network General Sniffer, a third-party protocol analyzer. *See also* network sniffer.

SNMP *See* Simple Network Management Protocol.

socket A bidirectional pipe for incoming and outgoing data between networked computers. The Windows Sockets API is a networking API used by programmers creating TCP/IP-based sockets applications. *See also* application programming interface (API); named pipe.

Sockets Windows Sockets is a Windows implementation of the widely used UC Berkeley sockets API. Microsoft TCP/IP, NWLink, and AppleTalk protocols use this interface. Sockets interfaces between programs and the transport protocol and works as a bidirectional pipe for incoming and outgoing data. *See also* application programming interface (API); named pipe; socket.

source directory The directory that contains the file or files you intend to copy or move.

source document The document where a linked or embedded object was originally created. *See also* embedded object; linked object.

SPAP *See* Shiva Password Authentication Protocol.

special access permission On NTFS volumes, a custom set of permissions. You can customize permissions on files and directories by selecting the individual components of the standard sets of permissions. *See also* access permission.

split bar Divides Windows NT Explorer into two parts: The directory tree is displayed on the left, and the contents of the current directory are on the right. *See also* directory tree.

spoofing Refers to a case where an Internet user mimics ("spoofs") the source IP address for an Internet server, proxy server, or firewall of a system to which it is trying to gain access.

spooler Software that accepts documents sent by a user to be printed, and then stores those documents and sends them, one by one, to available printer(s). *See also* spooling.

spooling A process on a server in which print documents are stored on a disk until a printing device is ready to process them. A spooler accepts each document from each client, stores it, then sends it to a printing device when it is ready.

SQL Acronym for structured query language, a database programming language used for accessing, querying, and otherwise managing information in a relational database system.

SSL *See* Secure Sockets Layer.

stabilize During subdirectory replication, when a subdirectory is stabilized, the export server waits two minutes after changes before exporting the subdirectory. The waiting period allows time for subsequent changes to take place so that all intended changes are recorded before being replicated. *See also* directory replication; export server; subtree.

stand-alone server *See* member server.

static mapping A method provided on a WINS server to assign a static (unchanging) IP address to a client.

static object Information that has been pasted into a document. Unlike embedded or linked objects, static objects cannot be changed from within the document. The only way you can change a static object is to delete it from the document, change it in the application used to create it, and paste it into the document again. *See also* embedded object; linked object.

static routing Static routing limits you to fixed routing tables, as opposed to dynamically updating the routing tables. *See also* dynamic routing; routing table.

static Web pages Standard Web pages that are created in advance and stored for later delivery to clients. *See also* dynamic Web pages.

status bar A line of information related to the application in the window. Usually located at the bottom of a window. Not all windows have a status bar.

STATUS message A message displayed by the Executive in a Windows-mode message box when the Executive detects a condition within a process that you should know about.

STATUS messages can be divided into three types:

System-information messages. Just read the information in the message box and click **OK**. The Kernel continues running the process or thread.

Warning messages. Some advise you to take an action that will enable the Kernel to keep running the process or thread. Others warn you that, although the process or thread will continue running, the results might be incorrect.

Application-termination messages. These warn you that the Kernel is about to terminate either a process or a thread.

See also Executive messages; STOP message.

STOP message A character-mode message that occurs when the Kernel detects an inconsistent condition from which it cannot recover. Always displayed on a full character-mode screen, uniquely identified by a hexadecimal number and a symbolic string. The content of the symbolic string can suggest, to a trained technician, the part of the Kernel that detected the condition from which there was no recourse but to stop. However, the cause may actually be in another part of the system. *See also* Executive messages; STATUS message.

string A data structure composed of a sequence of characters, usually representing human-readable text.

stripe set Refers to the saving of data across identical partitions on different drives. A stripe set does not provide fault tolerance; however stripe sets with parity do. *See also* fault tolerance; partition; stripe sets with parity.

stripe sets with parity A method of data protection in which data is striped in large blocks across all of the disks in an array. Data redundancy is provided by the parity information. This method provides fault tolerance. *See also* fault tolerance; stripe set.

subdirectory A directory within a directory. Also called a folder within a folder.

subkey A key within a key. Subkeys are analogous to subdirectories in the registry hierarchy. Keys and subkeys are similar to the section heading in .ini files; however subkeys can carry out functions. *See also* key; registry.

subnet A portion of a network, which may be a physically independent network segment, that shares a network address with other portions of the network and is distinguished by a subnet number. A subnet is to a network what a network is to an internet.

subnet mask A 32-bit value that allows the recipient of IP packets to distinguish the network ID portion of the IP address from the host ID. *See also* IP address; packet.

substitution macros Placeholders that are replaced in command strings.

subtree During directory replication, this refers to the export subdirectory and all of its subdirectories. *See also* directory replication.

swap file *See* paging file.

switched circuit *See* dial-up line.

SYN attack SYN (synchronizing character) messages maliciously generated by an intruder in an attempt to block legitimate access to a server by proliferating half-open TCP port connections. Also called SYN flooding.

synchronize To replicate the domain database from the primary domain controller (PDC) to one backup domain controller (BDC) of the domain, or to all of the BDCs of a domain. This is usually performed automatically by the system, but can also be invoked manually by an administrator. *See also* backup domain controller (BDC); domain; primary domain controller (PDC).

syntax The order in which you must type a command and the elements that follow the command. Windows NT commands have up to four elements: command name, parameters, switches, and values.

system access control list (SACL) The system ACL is controlled by the system administrator, and allows system-level security to be associated with an object. SACL APIs can be used only by a process with System Administrator privileges. *See also* discretionary access control list (DACL).

system default profile In Windows NT Server, the user profile that is loaded when Windows NT is running and no user is logged on. When the **Begin Logon** dialog box is visible, the system default profile is loaded. *See also* user default profile, user profile.

system disk A disk that contains the MS-DOS system files necessary to start MS-DOS.

system log The system log contains events logged by the Windows NT components. For example, the failure of a driver or other system component to load during startup is recorded in the system log. Use Event Viewer to view the system log.

System Network Architecture (SNA) System Network Architecture is a communications framework developed by IBM. Microsoft System Network Architecture (SNA) is an optional solution that provides a gateway connection between personal computer LANs or WANs and IBM mainframe and AS/400 hosts. *See also* AS/400; gateway.

system partition The volume that has the hardware-specific files needed to load Windows NT. *See also* partition.

system policy A policy, created by using the System Policy Editor, to control user work environments and actions, and to enforce system configuration for Windows 95. System policy can be implemented for specific users, groups, computers, or for all users. System policy for users overwrites settings in the current user area of the registry, and system policy for computers overwrites the current local machine area of the registry. *See also* registry.

systemroot The name of the directory that contains Windows NT files. The name of this directory is specified when Windows NT is installed.

Systems Management Server Part of the Windows NT BackOffice suite. Systems Management Server includes desktop management and software distribution that significantly automates the task of upgrading software on client computers.

T

T1 or T3 connection Standard measurement of network bandwidth.

tag file A configuration file that contains information about a corresponding file on a Gopher server or links to other servers. This information is sent to clients in response to a Gopher request.

tape set A tape set (sometimes referred to as a tape family) in Windows NT Backup is a sequence of tapes in which each tape is a continuation of the backup on the previous tape. *See also* backup set; backup types.

TAPI *See* Telephony API.

Task list A window that shows all running applications and their status. View the Task list in the **Applications** tab in Task Manager.

Task Manager Task Manager enables you to start, end, or run applications, end processes (an application, application component, or system process), and view CPU and memory use data. Task Manager gives you a simple, quick view of how each process (application or service) is using CPU and memory resources. (Note: In previous versions of Windows NT, Task List handled some of these functions.)

To run Task Manager, right-click the toolbar and then click Task Manager.

TCP *See* Transmission Control Protocol.

TCP/IP *See* Transmission Control Protocol/ Internet Protocol.

TCP/IP keep-alives An optimizing feature of the TCP/IP service. TCP/IP periodically broadcasts messages to determine whether an idle connection is still active. *See also* HTTP keep-alives.

TDI *See* transport driver interface.

Telephony API (TAPI) An API used by programs to make data/fax/voice calls, including Hyper-Terminal, Dial-up Networking, Phone Dialer, and other Win32 communications applications written for Windows NT.

Telnet (VTP) A terminal emulation protocol for logging on to remote computers. Once referred to as Virtual Terminal Protocol (VTP). Defined in RFC 854, among others.

template accounts Accounts that are not actually used by real users but serve as a basis for the real accounts (for administrative purposes).

terminate-and-stay-resident program (TSR) A program running under MS-DOS that remains loaded in memory even when it is not running so that it can be quickly invoked for a specific task performed while any other application is operating.

text box In a dialog box, a box in which you type information needed to carry out a command. The text box may be blank or may contain text when the dialog box opens.

text file A file containing text characters (letters, numbers, and symbols) but no formatting information. A text file can be a "plain" ASCII file that most computers can read. Text file can also refer to a word-processing file. *See also* ASCII file.

text-file transfer A method for transferring files from HyperTerminal to a remote computer. With this method, files are transferred as ASCII files with minimal formatting characters, such as linefeeds and carriage returns. All font-formatting information is removed. *See also* ASCII file.

text-only An ASCII file that contains no formatting. *See also* ASCII file.

TFTP *See* Trivial File Transfer Protocol.

thread Threads are objects within processes that run program instructions. They allow concurrent operations within a process and enable one process to run different parts of its program on different processors simultaneously.

throughput *See* bandwidth.

time-out If a device is not performing a task, the amount of time the computer should wait before detecting it as an error.

time slice The amount of processor time allocated to an application, usually measured in milliseconds.

title bar The horizontal bar (at the top of a window) that contains the title of the window or dialog box. On many windows, the title bar also contains the program icon and the **Maximize**, **Minimize**, and **Close** buttons.

Token Ring A type of network media that connects clients in a closed ring and uses token passing to enable clients to use the network. *See also* Fiber Distributed Data Interface (FDDI); LocalTalk.

toolbar A series of icons or shortcut buttons providing quick access to commands. Usually located directly below the menu bar. Not all windows have a toolbar.

topic Information in the Help window. A Help topic usually begins with a title and contains information about a particular task, command, or dialog box.

transforms Rules the administrator creates to add, remove, and modify domain names appended to inbound and outbound messages.

Transmission Control Protocol (TCP) A connection-based Internet protocol responsible for breaking data into packets, which the IP protocol sends over the network. This protocol provides a reliable, sequenced communication stream for network communication. *See also* Internet Protocol (IP); packet.

Transmission Control Protocol/Internet Protocol (TCP/IP) A set of networking protocols that provide communications across interconnected networks made up of computers with diverse hardware architectures and various operating systems. TCP/IP includes standards for how computers communicate and conventions for connecting networks and routing traffic.

transport driver interface (TDI) In Windows networking, the common interface for network components that communicate at the Session layer.

trap In SNMP, a discrete block of data that indicates that the request failed authentication. The SNMP service can send a trap when it receives a request for information that does not contain the correct community name and that does not match an accepted host name for the service. Trap destinations are the names or IP addresses of hosts to which the SNMP service is to send traps with community names. *See also* IP address; Simple Network Management Protocol (SNMP).

trigger A set of conditions that, when met, initiate an action. For example, before using Network Monitor to capture data from the network, you can set a trigger to stop the capture or to execute a program or command file.

Trivial File Transfer Protocol (TFTP) A file transfer protocol that transfers files to and from a remote computer running the TFTP service. TFTP was designed with less functions than FTP. Defined in RFC 1350, among others. *See also* File Transfer Protocol (FTP).

Trojan horse A program that masquerades as another common program in an attempt to receive information. An example of a Trojan horse is a program that masquerades as a system logon to retrieve user names and password information, which the writers of the Trojan horse can use later to break into the system.

TrueType fonts Fonts that are scalable and sometimes generated as bitmaps or soft fonts, depending on the capabilities of your printer. TrueType fonts can be sized to any height, and they print exactly as they appear on the screen.

trust *See* trust relationship.

trust relationship A link between domains that enables pass-through authentication, in which a trusting domain honors the logon authentications of a trusted domain. With trust relationships, a user who has only one user account in one domain can potentially access the entire network. User accounts and global groups defined in a trusted domain can be given rights and resource permissions in a trusting domain, even though those accounts do not exist in the trusting domain's directory database. *See also* directory database; global group; pass-through authentication; user account.

trust relationships policy A security policy that determines which domains are trusted and which domains are trusting domains. *See also* trust relationship.

TSR *See* terminate-and-stay-resident program.

two-way trust relationship Each domain trusts user accounts in the other domain to use its resources. Users can log on from computers in either domain to the domain that contains their account. *See also* trust relationship.

type *See* file type.

Type 1 fonts Scalable fonts designed to work with PostScript devices. *See also* font; font types; PostScript printer.

U

UAM *See* user authentication module.

UDP *See* User Datagram Protocol.

unavailable An unavailable button or command is displayed in light gray instead of black, and it cannot be clicked.

UNC name *See* universal naming convention name.

unicast datagram An IP datagram sent to one host. *See also* broadcast datagram; Internet Protocol (IP); multicast datagram.

Unicode A fixed-width, 16-bit character-encoding standard capable of representing the letters and characters of virtually all of the world's languages. Unicode was developed by a consortium of U.S. computer companies.

Uniform Resource Locator (URL) A naming convention that uniquely identifies the location of a computer, directory, or file on the Internet. The URL also specifies the appropriate Internet protocol, such as HTTP, FTP, IRC, or Gopher.

uninterruptible power supply (UPS) A battery-operated power supply connected to a computer to keep the system running during a power failure.

universally unique identifier (UUID) A unique identification string associated with the remote procedure call interface. Also known as a globally unique identifier (GUID).

universal naming convention (UNC) name A full Windows NT name of a resource on a network. It conforms to the *server_name**share_name* syntax, where *server_name* is the server's name and *share_name* is the name of the shared resource. UNC names of directories or files can also include the directory path under the share name, with the following syntax: *server_name* *share_name**directory**file_name*.

UPS *See* uninterruptible power supply.

UPS service Manages an uninterruptible power supply connected to a computer. *See also* uninterruptible power supply (UPS).

URL *See* Uniform Resource Locator.

user account Consists of all of the information that defines a user to Windows NT. This includes such things as the user name and password required for the user to log on, the groups in which the user account has membership, and the rights and permissions the user has for using the system and accessing its resources. For Windows NT Workstation, user accounts are managed with User Manager. For Windows NT Server, user accounts are managed with User Manager for Domains. *See also* group.

user account database *See* directory database.

user authentication module Software component that prompts clients for their user names and passwords. *See also* clear-text passwords.

User Datagram Protocol (UDP) A TCP complement that offers a connectionless datagram service that guarantees neither delivery nor correct sequencing of delivered packets (much like IP). *See also* datagram; Internet Protocol (IP); packet.

user default profile In Windows NT Server, the user profile that is loaded by a server when a user's assigned profile cannot be accessed for any reason; when a user without an assigned profile logs on to the computer for the first time; or when a user logs on to the Guest account. *See also* system default profile; user profile.

User Manager A Windows NT Workstation tool used to manage the security for a workstation. User Manager administers user accounts, groups, and security policies.

User Manager for Domains A Windows NT Server tool used to manage security for a domain or an individual computer. User Manager for Domains administers user accounts, groups, and security policies.

user name A unique name identifying a user account to Windows NT. An account's user name cannot be identical to any other group name or user name of its own domain or workgroup. *See also* user account.

user password The password stored in each user's account. Each user generally has a unique user password and must type that password when logging on or accessing a server. *See also* password; volume password.

User privilege One of three privilege levels you can assign to a Windows NT user account. Every user account has one of the three privilege levels (Administrator, Guest, and User). Accounts with User privilege are regular users of the network; most accounts on your network probably have User privilege. *See also* Administrator privilege; Guest privilege; user account.

user profile Configuration information that can be retained on a user-by-user basis, and is saved in user profiles. This information includes all of the per-user settings of the Windows NT environment, such as the desktop arrangement, personal program groups and the program items in those groups, screen colors, screen savers, network connections, printer connections, mouse settings, window size and position. When a user logs on, the user's profile is loaded and the user's Windows NT environment is configured according to that profile. *See also* personal group; program item.

user rights Define a user's access to a computer or domain and the actions that a user can perform on the computer or domain. User rights permit actions such as logging onto a computer or network, adding or deleting users in a workstation or domain, and so forth.

user rights policy Manages the assignment of rights to groups and user accounts. *See also* user account; user rights.

users In the Macintosh environment, a special group that contains all users who have user permissions on the server. When a Macintosh user assigns permissions to everyone, those permissions are given to the groups users and guests. *See also* guest.

UUENCODE (UNIX-to-UNIX Encode) A utility that converts a binary file (such as a word-processing file or a program) to text so that it can be transmitted over a network. UUDECODE (UNIX-to-UNIX Decode) is the utility used to convert the file back to its original state.

UUID *See* universally unique identifier.